# Lecture Notes in Computer Science 69

Edited by G. Goos, J. Hartmanis

T0230328

**Springer**
*Berlin*
*Heidelberg*
*New York*
*Barcelona*
*Hong Kong*
*London*
*Milan*
*Paris*
*Tokyo*

Carol Peters (Ed.)

# Cross-Language Information Retrieval and Evaluation

Workshop of the Cross-Language Evaluation Forum, CLEF 2000
Lisbon, Portugal, September 21-22, 2000
Revised Papers

Springer

Series Editors

Gerhard Goos, Karlsruhe University, Germany
Juris Hartmanis, Cornell University, NY, USA
Jan van Leeuwen, Utrecht University, The Netherlands

Volume Editor

Carol Peters
Istituto di Elaborazione della Informazione
Consiglio Nazionale delle Ricerche
Area della Ricerca CNR
Via Moruzzi, 1, 56124 Pisa, Italy
E-mail: carol@iei.pi.cnr.it


Cataloging-in-Publication Data applied for

Die Deutsche Bibliothek - CIP-Einheitsaufnahme

Cross language information retrieval and evaluation : revised papers /
Workshop of the Cross Language Evaluation Forum, CLEF 2000, Lisbon,
Portugal, September 21 - 22, 2000. Carol Peters (ed.). - Berlin ; Heidelberg ;
New York ; Barcelona ; Hong Kong ; London ; Milan ; Paris ; Singapore ;
Tokyo : Springer, 2001
   (Lecture notes in computer science ; Vol. 2069)
   ISBN 3-540-42446-6




CR Subject Classification (1998): H.3, I.2

ISSN 0302-9743
ISBN 3-540-42446-6 Springer-Verlag Berlin Heidelberg New York

Springer-Verlag Berlin Heidelberg New York
a member of BertelsmannSpringer Science+Business Media GmbH

http://www.springer.de

© Springer-Verlag Berlin Heidelberg 2001

Typesetting: Camera-ready by author, data conversion by Boller Mediendesign
Printed on acid-free paper      SPIN: 10781690      06/3142      5 4 3 2 1 0

# Preface

The first evaluation campaign of the Cross-Language Evaluation Forum (CLEF) for European languages was held from January to September 2000. The campaign culminated in a two-day workshop in Lisbon, Portugal, 21–22 September, immediately following the fourth European Conference on Digital Libraries (ECDL 2000). The first day of the workshop was open to anyone interested in the area of Cross-Language Information Retrieval (CLIR) and addressed the topic of CLIR system evaluation. The goal was to identify the actual contribution of evaluation to system development and to determine what could be done in the future to stimulate progress. The second day was restricted to participants in the CLEF 2000 evaluation campaign and to their experiments. This volume constitutes the proceedings of the workshop and provides a record of the campaign.

CLEF is currently an activity of the DELOS Network of Excellence for Digital Libraries, funded by the EC Information Society Technologies to further research in digital library technologies. The activity is organized in collaboration with the US National Institute of Standards and Technology (NIST). The support of DELOS and NIST in the running of the evaluation campaign is gratefully acknowledged.

I should also like to thank the other members of the Workshop Steering Committee for their assistance in the organization of this event.

April 2001                                                                                       Carol Peters

## CLEF 2000 Workshop Steering Committee

Martin Braschler, Eurospider, Switzerland
Julio Gonzalo Arroyo, UNED, Madrid, Spain
Donna Harman, NIST, USA
Michael Hess, University of Zurich, Switzerland
Michael Kluck, IZ Sozialwissenschaften, Bonn, Germany
Carol Peters, IEI-CNR, Pisa, Italy
Peter Schäuble, Eurospider, Switzerland

# Table of Contents

# Introduction

Carol Peters

Istituto di Elaborazione della Informazione, CNR
Area della Ricerca di San Cataldo, 56124 Pisa, Italy
carol@iei.pi.cnr.it

The objective of the Cross-Language Evaluation Forum (CLEF) is to develop and maintain an infrastructure for the testing and evaluation of information retrieval systems operating on European languages, in both monolingual and cross-language contexts, and to create test-suites of reusable data that can be employed by system developers for benchmarking purposes. The first CLEF evaluation campaign started in early 2000 and ended with a workshop in Lisbon, Portugal, 22-23 September 2000.

This volume constitutes the proceedings of the workshop and also provides a record of the results of the campaign. It consists of two parts and an appendix. The first part reflects the presentations and discussions on the topic of evaluation for cross-language information retrieval systems during the first day of the workshop, whereas the second contains papers from the individual participating groups reporting their experiments and analysing their results. The appendix presents the evaluation techniques and measures used to derive the results and provides the run statistics. The aim of this Introduction is to present the main issues discussed at the workshop and also to provide the reader with the necessary background to the experiments through a description of the tasks set for CLEF 2000. In conclusion, our plans for future CLEF campaigns are outlined.

## 1 Evaluation for CLIR Systems

The first two papers in Part I of the proceedings describe the organization of cross-language evaluation campaigns for text retrieval systems. CLEF is a continuation and expansion of the cross-language system evaluation activity for European languages begun in 1997 with the track for Cross-Language Information Retrieval (CLIR) in the Text REtrieval Conference (TREC) series. The paper by Harman et al. gives details on how the activity was organized, the various issues that had to be addressed, and the results obtained. The difficulties experienced during the first year, in which the track was coordinated centrally at NIST (US National Institute for Standards and Technology) led to the setting up of a distributed coordination in four countries (USA, Germany, Italy and Switzerland) with native speakers being responsible for the preparation of topics (structured statements of possible information needs) and relevance judgments (assessment of the relevance of the ranked lists of results submitted by participating systems). A natural consequence of this distributed coordination was the

C. Peters (Ed.): CLEF 2000, LNCS 2069, pp. 1-6, 2001.
© Springer-Verlag Berlin Heidelberg 2001

decision, in 1999, to transfer the activity to Europe and set it up independently as CLEF. The infrastructure and methodology adopted in CLEF is based on the experience of the CLIR tracks at TREC.

The second paper by Kando presents the NTCIR Workshops, a series of evaluation workshops for text retrieval systems operating on Asian languages. The 2000-2001 campaign conducted by NTCIR included cross-language system evaluation for Japanese-English and Chinese-English. Although both CLEF and NTCIR have a common basis in TREC there are interesting differences between the methodology adopted by the two campaigns. In particular, NTCIR employs multigrade relevance judgments rather than the binary system used by CLEF and inherited from TREC. Kando motivates this decision and discusses the effects.

The CLEF campaign provides participants with the possibility to test their systems on both general-purpose texts (newspapers and newswires) and domain-specific collections. The third paper by Kluck and Gey examines the domain-specific task, begun in TREC and continued in CLEF, and describes the particular document collection used: the GIRT database for social sciences.

The rest of the papers in the first part of this volume focus on some of the main issues that were discussed during the first day of the workshop. These included the problem of resources, the transition from the evaluation of cross-language text retrieval systems to systems running on other media, the need to consider the user perspective rather than concentrating attention solely on system performance, and the importance of being able to evaluate single system components rather than focusing on overall performance. A further point for discussion was the addition of new languages to the multilingual document collection.

The problem of resources has always been seen as crucial in cross-language system development. In order to be able to match queries against documents, some kind of lexical resource is needed to provide the transfer mechanism, e.g. bilingual or multilingual dictionaries, thesauri, or corpora. In order to be able to process a number of different languages, suitable language processing tools are needed, e.g. language-specific tokenizers, stemmers, morphologies, etc.. It is generally held that the quality of the resource used considerably affects system performance. This question was discussed at length during the workshop. The paper by Gonzalo presents a survey on the different language resources used by the CLEF 2000 participants. Many of the resources listed were developed by the participants themselves, thus showing that an evaluation exercise of this type is not only evaluating systems but also the resources used by the systems. The need for more pooling and sharing of resources between groups in order to optimize effort emerges clearly from this survey. Gonzalo concludes with some interesting proposals for the introduction of additional tasks, aimed at measuring the effect of the resources used on overall system performance, in a future campaign.

The papers by Oard and by Jones both discuss CLIR from the user perspective. Oard focuses on the document selection question: how the users of a CLIR system can correctly identify the - for them - most useful documents from a ranked list of results when they cannot read the language of the target collection. He advocates the advantages of an interactive CLIR evaluation and makes a proposal as to how an evaluation of this type could be included in CLEF. Jones also supports the extension of evaluation exercises in order to assess the usefulness of techniques that can assist the user with relevance judgment and information extraction. In this respect, he mentions the importance of document summarization – already included in the NTCIR evaluation programme. In addition, Jones talks about work in cross-language multimedia information retrieval and suggests directions for future research. He asserts that specifically-developed standard test collections are needed to advance research in this area.

In the final paper in Part I, Gey lists several areas in which research could lead to improvement in cross-language information retrieval including resource enrichment, the use of pivot languages and phonetic transliteration. In particular, he discusses the need for post-evaluation failure analysis and shows how this could provide important feedback resulting in improved system design and performance. CLEF provides the research community with the necessary infrastructure for studies of this type.

# 2    The CLEF 2000 Experiments

There were several reasons behind the decision to coordinate the cross-language system evaluation activity for European languages independently and to move it to Europe. One was the desire to extend the number of languages covered, another was the intention to offer a wider range of retrieval tasks to better meet the needs of the multilingual information retrieval research community.

As can be seen from the descriptions of the experiments in Part II of this volume, CLEF 2000 included four separate evaluation tracks:

- multilingual information retrieval
- bilingual information retrieval
- monolingual (non-English) information retrieval
- cross-language domain-specific information retrieval

The main task – inherited from TREC - required searching a multilingual document collection, consisting of national newspapers in four languages (English, French, German and Italian) of the same time period, in order to retrieve relevant documents. Forty topics were developed on the basis of the contents of the multilingual collection – ten topics for each collection - and complete topic sets were produced in all four languages. Topics are structured statements of hypothetical user needs. Each topic consisted of three fields: a brief title statement; a one-sentence description; a more complex narrative specifying the relevance assessment criteria. Queries are constructed using one of more of these fields. Additional topic sets were then created for Dutch, Finnish, Spanish and Swedish, in each case translating from the original. The main requirement was that, for each language, the topic set should be as linguistically representative as possible, i.e. using the terms that would naturally be expected to represent the set of topic concepts in the given language. The methodology followed was that described in the paper by Harman et al..

A bilingual system evaluation task was also offered, consisting of querying the English newspaper collection using any topic language (except English). Many newcomers to cross-language system evaluation prefer to begin with the simpler bilingual task before moving on to tackle the additional issues involved in truly multilingual retrieval.

One of the aims of the CLEF activity is to encourage the development of tools to manipulate and process languages other than English. Different languages present different problems. Methods that may be efficient for certain language typologies may not be so effective for others. Issues that have to be catered for include word order, morphology, diacritic characters, language variants. For this reason, CLEF 2000 included a track for French, German and Italian monolingual information retrieval.

The cross-language domain-specific task has been offered since TREC-7. The rationale of this subtask is to test retrieval on another type of document collection, serving a different kind of information need. The implications are discussed in the paper by Kluck and Gey in the first part of this volume.

The papers in Part II describe the various experiments by the participating groups with these four tasks. Both traditional and innovative approaches to CLIR were experimented, and different query expansion techniques were tried. All kinds of source to target transfer mechanisms were employed, including both query and document translation. Commercial and in-house resources were used and included machine translation, dictionary and corpus-based methods. The strategies used varied from traditional IR to a considerable employment of natural language processing techniques. Different groups focused on different aspects of the overall problem, ranging from the development of language-independent tools such as stemmers to much work on language-specific features like morphology and compounding. Many groups compared different techniques in different runs in order to evaluate the effect of a given technique on performance. Overall, CLEF 2000 offered a very good picture of current issues and approaches in CLIR.

The first paper in this part by Martin Braschler provides an overview and analysis of all the results, listing the most relevant achievements and comparing them with those of previous years in the CLIR track at TREC. As one of the main objectives of CLEF is to produce evaluation test-suites that can be used by the CLIR research community, Braschler also provides an analysis of the test collection resulting from the CLEF 2000 campaign, demonstrating its validity for future system testing, tuning and development activities. The appendix presents the evaluation results for each group, run by run.

# 3    CLEF in the Future

The CLEF 2001 campaign is now under way. The main tasks are similar to those of the first campaign. There are, however, some extensions and additions. In particular the multilingual corpus has been considerably enlarged and Spanish (news agency) and Dutch (national newspaper) collections for 1994 have been added. The multilingual task in CLEF 2001 involves querying collections in five languages (English, French, German, Italian and Spanish) and there will be two bilingual tracks: searching either the English or the Dutch collections. Spanish and Dutch have also been included in the monolingual track. There will be seven official topic languages, including Japanese. Additional topics will be provided in a number of other European languages, including Finnish, Swedish and Russian, and also in Chinese and Thai.

CLEF 2000 concentrated on the traditional metrics of recall and precision – however these have limitations in what they tell us about the usefulness of a retrieval system to the user. CLEF 2001 will thus also include an experimental track designed to test interactive CLIR systems and to establish baselines against which future research progress can be measured. The introduction of this track is a direct result of discussions which began in the workshop with the presentations by Oard and by Jones, and of the proposal by Oard reported in Part I of this volume.

Two main issues must be considered when planning future CLEF campaigns: the addition of more languages, and the inclusion of new tasks.

The extension of language coverage, discussed considerably at the workshop, depends on two factors: the demand from potential participants and the existence of sufficient resources to handle the requirements of new language collections. It was decided that Spanish and Dutch met these criteria for CLEF 2001. CLEF 2002 and 2003 will be mainly funded by a contract from the European Commission (IST-2000-31002) but it is probable that, in the future, it will be necessary to seek support from national funding agencies as well if more languages are to be included. The aim will be to cover not only the major European languages but also some representative samples of minority languages, including members from each major group: e.g. Germanic, Romance, Slavic, and Ugro-Finnic languages. Furthermore, building on the experience of CLEF 2001, we intend to continue to provide topics in Asian languages.

CLEF 2000 concentrated on cross-language text retrieval and on measuring overall system performance. However, in the future, we hope to include tracks to evaluate CLIR systems working on media other than text. We are now beginning to examine the feasibility of organizing a spoken CLIR track in which systems would have to process and match spoken queries in more than one language against a spoken document collection. Another important innovation would be to devise methods that enable the assessment of single system components, as suggested in the paper by Gonzalo.

CLIR system development is still very much in the experimental stage and involves expertise from both the natural language processing and the information retrieval fields. The CLEF 2000 Workshop provided an ideal opportunity for a number of key players, with very different backgrounds, to come together and exchange ideas and compare results on the basis of a common experience: participation in the CLEF evaluation campaign. CLEF is very much a collaborative effort between organizers and participants with the same common goal: the improvement of CLIR system performance. The discussions at the workshop have had considerable impact on the organization of the 2001 campaign. The success of future campaigns will depend on the continuation and strengthening of this collaboration.

More information on the organization of the current CLEF campaign and instructions on how to contact us can be found at: http://www.clef-campaign.org/.

# Acknowledgements

To a large extent, CLEF depends on voluntary work. I should like to acknowledge the generous collaboration of a number of people and organizations. First of all, I wish to thank the other members of the CLEF Coordinating Group for all their efforts aimed at making both the campaign and the workshop a great success:

Martin Braschler, Eurospider, Switzerland

Julio Gonzalo Arroyo, UNED, Madrid, Spain

Donna Harman, NIST, USA

Michael Hess, University of Zurich, Switzerland

Michael Kluck, IZ Sozialwissenschaften, Bonn, Germany

Peter Schäuble, Eurospider, Switzerland

Felisa Verdejo Maillo, UNED, Madrid, Spain

Ellen Voorhees, NIST, USA

Christa Womser-Hacker, University of Hildesheim, Germany

I must also express my gratitude to the ECDL 2000 Conference organisers for their assistance in the local organisation of the CLEF Workshop, and in particular Caroline Hagège and Nuno Mamede, (Local Coordinators) and Eulália Carvalho, and José Luis Borbinha (ECDL Chair).

It is not easy to set up an infrastructure that meets the needs of a large number of languages. I should like to thank the following organisations who voluntarily engaged translators to provide topic sets in Dutch, Finnish and Swedish, working on the basis of the set of source topics:

- the DRUID project for the Dutch topics;
- the Department of Information Studies, University of Tampere, Finland, engaged the UTA Language Centre for the Finnish topics;
- SICS Human Computer Interaction and Language Engineering Laboratory for the Swedish topics.

The support of all the data providers and copyright holders is also gratefully acknowledged, and in particular:

- The Los Angeles Times, for the English data collection;
- Le Monde S.A. and ELDA: European Language Resources Distribution Agency, for the French data.
- Frankfurter Rundschau, Druck und Verlagshaus Frankfurt am Main; Der Spiegel, Spiegel Verlag, Hamburg, for the German newspaper collections.
- InformationsZentrum Sozialwissenschaften, Bonn, for the GIRT database.
- Hypersystems Srl, Torino and La Stampa, for the Italian data.
- Schweizerische Depeschenagentur (SDA) and Associated Press (AP) for the newswire data of the training collection.

Without their help, this evaluation activity would be impossible.

Last, but not least, I thank Julio Gonzalo for his help and encouragement in the preparation of this volume.

# CLIR Evaluation at TREC

Donna Harman[1], Martin Braschler[2], Michael Hess[3], Michael Kluck[4],
Carol Peters[5], Peter Schäuble[2], and Páraic Sheridan[6]

[1] National Institute of Standards and Technology, Gaithersburg, Md, SA.
donna.harman@nist.gov
[2] Eurospider Information Technology AG, Zürich, Switzerland
braschler@eurospider.com schauble@eurospider.com
[3] Dept. of Computer Science, niversity of Zurich, Switzerland
hess@ifi.unizh.ch
[4] InformationsZentrum Sozialwissenschaften IZ , Bonn, Germany
mkl@bonn.iz-soz.de
[5] Istituto di Elaborazione della Informazione - CNR, Pisa, Italy
carol@iei.pi.cnr.it
[6] MNIS-Te twise Labs, Syracuse, N.Y. SA.
paraic@textwise.com

**Abstract.** Starting in 1997, the National Institute of Standards and
Technology conducted 3 years of evaluation of cross-language information
retrieval systems in the Te t REtrieval Conference TREC . Twenty-
two participating systems used topics test questions in one language to
retrieve documents written in English, French, German, and Italian. A
large-scale multilingual test collection has been built and a new technique
for building such a collection in a distributed manner was devised.

## 1 Introduction

The increasing globalization of information has led to an heightened interest in
retrieving information that is in languages users are unable search effectively.
Often these users can adequately read retrieved documents in non-native languages, or can use existing gisting systems to get a good idea of the relevance of
the returned documents, but are not able to create appropriate search questions.
Ideally they would like to search in their native language, but have the ability
to retrieve documents in a *cross-language* mode.

The desire to build better cross-language retrieval systems resulted in a workshop on this subject at the Nineteenth Annual International ACM-SIGIR Conference on Research and Development in Information Retrieval in 1996. Whereas
many of the participants at this conference were concerned with the lack of sufficient parallel text to form a basis for research, one of the papers presented at
that workshop provided the hope of avoiding the use of parallel corpora by the
use of *comparable* corpora.

This paper, by Páraic Sheridan, Jean Paul Ballerini and Peter Schäuble of
the Swiss Federal Institute of Technology ETH , 1 , used stories from the Swiss

C. Peters (Ed.): CLEF 2000, LNCS 2069, pp. 7–23, 2001.
© Springer-Verlag Berlin Heidelberg 2001

news agency Schweizerische Depeschen Agentur SDA that were taken from the same time period. These newswire stories are not translations but are produced independently in each language French, German and Italian in the various parts of Switzerland. Whereas the stories do not overlap perfectly, there is in fact a high overlap of stories e.g. international events which are of interest in all parts of Switzerland. The paper detailed the use of this collection of stories to produce a test collection that enabled the evaluation of a series of cross-language retrieval experiments 2 .

In 1997 it was decided to include cross-language information retrieval CLIR system evaluation as one of the tracks at the Sixth Text REtrieval Conference TREC held at the National Institute of Standards and Technology NIST 3 http://trec.nist.gov. The aim was to provide researchers with an infrastructure for evaluation that would enable them to test their systems and compare the results achieved using different cross-language strategies. This track was done in cooperation with the Swiss Federal Institute of Technology, who not only obtained permission for TREC to use the SDA data, but also provided considerable guidance and leadership to the track.

The main goals of the CLIR track in TREC were:

1. to create the infrastructure for testing cross-language information retrieval technology through the creation of a large-scale multilingual test collection and a common evaluation setting
2. to investigate effective evaluation procedures in a multilingual context and
3. to provide a forum for the exchange of research ideas.

There were CLIR tracks for European languages in TREC-6, TREC-7, and TREC-8. The TREC proceedings for each year available on-line at http://trec.nist.gov, contain overviews of the track, plus papers from all groups participating in the CLIR track that year. The rest of this paper summarizes the CLIR work done in those three years, with those summaries derived from the various track overviews 4 , 5 , 6 . To conserve space, the numerous individual papers are not included in the references but can be found in the section for the cross-language track in the appropriate TREC proceedings. A table listing all participants for a given TREC is given in each result section to faciliate the location of the individual papers. Note that there are additional publications from these groups including further results and analyses, and the references in the track overviews should be checked to obtain these.

## 2 TREC- CLIR Track Task Description

The TREC-6 Cross-Language Information Retrieval CLIR track required the retrieval of either English, German or French documents that are relevant to topics written in a different language. Participating groups could choose any cross-language combination, for example English topics against German documents or French topics against English documents. In order have a baseline retrieval performance measurement for each group, the results of a monolingual retrieval experimental run in the document language were also to be submitted. For instance, if a cross-language experiment was run with English topics retrieving German documents, then the result of an equivalent experiment where German topics retrieve German documents must also have been submitted. These results would be considered comparable since the topics are assumed to be proper translations across the languages.

The different document collections used for each language are outlined in Table 1. The Associated Press collection consists of newswire stories in English, while the French SDA collection is a similar collection of newswire stories from the Swiss news agency  Schweizerische Depeschen Agentur . The German document collection has two parts. The first part is composed of further newswire stories from the Swiss SDA while the second part consists of newspaper articles from a Swiss newspaper, the  Neue Zuercher Zeitung' NZZ . The Italian data is included in this table for completeness although it was not used in TREC-6.

The newswire collections in English, French and German were chosen to overlap in timeframe  1988 to 1990  for two reasons. First, since a single set of topics had to be formulated to cover all three document languages, having the same timeframe for newswire stories increased the likelihood of finding a greater number of relevant documents in all languages. The second reason for the overlapping timeframe was to allow groups who use corpus-based approaches for cross-language retrieval to investigate what useful corpus information they could extract from the document collections being used. One of the resources provided to CLIR track participants was a list of 83,698 news documents in the French and German SDA collections which were likely to be comparable based on an alignment of stories using news descriptors assigned manually by the SDA reporters, the dates of the stories, and common cognates in the texts of the stories.

| Document Collections | | | |
|---|---|---|---|
| Doc. Language | Source | No. Documents | Size |
| English | AP news, 1988-1990 | 242,918 | 760MB |
| German | SDA news, 1988-1990 | 185,099 | 330MB |
| | NZZ articles, 1994 | 66,741 | 200MB |
| French | SDA news, 1988-1990 | 141,656 | 250MB |
| Italian | SDA news, 1989-1990 | 62,359 | 90MB |

**Table 1.** Document Collections used in the CLIR track.

The 25 test topic descriptions were provided by NIST in English, French and German, using translations of topics originally written mostly in English  see Figure 1 for an example topic, including all its translations . Participating groups who wished to test other topic languages were permitted to create translations of the topics in their own language and use these in their tests, as long as the translated topics were made publicly available to the rest of the track participants. The final topic set therefore also had translations of the 25 topics in Spanish, provided by the University of Massachusetts, and Dutch, provided by TNO in the Netherlands.

```
<num> Number: CL9
<E-title> Effects of logging

<E-desc> Description:
What effects has logging had on desertification?

<E-narr> Narrative:
Documents with specific mention of local government's or international
agencies' efforts to stop deforestation are relevant. Also relevant
are documents containing information on desertification and its
side effects such as climate change, soil depletion, flooding, and
hurricanes caused by excessive logging.

<num> Number: CL9
<F-title> Les effets de la déforestation

<F-desc> Description:
Quels sont les effets de la déforestation sur la désertification?

<F-narr> Narrative:
Tous les documents qui donnent des analyses spécifiques sur les mesures
des gouverments locaux ou des agences internationales pour frêner
la déforestation sont pertinants. Les articles qui contiennent des
renseignements sur la désertification et ses effets secondaires comme
les changements de climat, l'épuisement de la terre, les inondations et
les ouragans sont également applicables.

<num> Number: CL9
<G-title> Auswirkungen von Abholzung

<G-desc> Description:
Welche Auswirkungen hat das Abholzen auf die Ausbreitung der Wüste?

<G-narr> Narrative:
Alle Artikel über Bemühungen von Regierungen ebenso wie von
internationalen Agenturen die Wüstenausbreitung zu bremsen, sind
wesentlich. Ebenso relevant sind Artikel über Ausbreitung der Wüsten
und ihre Mitwirkungen, wie zum Beispiel Klimawechsel, Verarmung der
Erde und Orkane die auf übermässige Abholzung zurückzuführen sind.
```

**Fig. 1.** Sample CLIR topic statement from TREC-6, showing all languages.

Although not strictly within the definition of the cross-language task, participation by groups who wanted to run mono-lingual retrieval experiments in either French or German using the CLIR data was also permitted. Since the CLIR track was run for the first time in TREC-6, this was intended to encourage new IR groups working with either German or French to participate. The participation of these groups also helped to ensure that there would be a sufficient number of different system submissions to provide the pool of results needed for relevance judgements.

The evaluation of CLIR track results was based on the standard TREC evaluation measures used in the ad hoc task. Participating groups were free to use different topic fields  lengths  and to submit either automatic or manual experiments according to the definitions used for the main TREC ad hoc task.

## TREC-  Results

A total of thirteen groups, representing six different countries, participated in the TREC-6 CLIR track  Table 2 . Participating groups were encouraged to run as many experiments as possible, both with different kinds of approaches to CLIR and with different language combinations. An overview of the submitted runs is given in Table  3 and shows that the main topic languages were used equally, each used in 29 experiments, whereas English was somewhat more popular than German or French as the choice for the document language to be retrieved. This is in part because the groups who used the query translations in Spanish and Dutch only evaluated those queries against English documents. A total of 95 result sets were submitted for evaluation in the CLIR track.

| TREC-6 Participants | |
|---|---|
| **Participant** | **Country** |
| CEA Saclay  no online paper | France |
| Cornell  SabIR Research Inc. | SA |
| Dublin City  niversity | Ireland |
| Duke  niversity  niversity of Colorado  Microsoft Research | SA |
| IRIT  SIG | France |
| New Me ico State  niversity | SA |
| Swiss Federal Institute of Technology  ETH | Switzerland |
| TwentyOne TNO  -Twente DFKI Xero  -Tuebingen | Netherlands |
| niversity of California, Berkeley | SA |
| niversity of Maryland, College Park | SA |
| niversity of Massachusetts, Amherst | SA |
| niversite of Montreal  Laboratoire CLIPS, IMAG | Canada |
| Xero  Research Centre Europe | France |

**Table 2.** Organizations participating in the TREC-6 CLIR track

**Language Combinations**

| Doc. Language | Query Language | | | | | Total |
|---|---|---|---|---|---|---|
| | English | German | French | Spanish | Dutch | |
| English | 7 | 15 | 10 | 2 | 6 | 40 |
| German | 12 | 10 | 4 | - | - | 26 |
| French | 10 | 4 | 15 | - | - | 29 |
| Total | 29 | 29 | 29 | 2 | 6 | 95 |

**Table 3.** Overview of submissions to CLIR track.

An important contribution to the track was made by a collaboration between the University of Maryland and the LOGOS corporation, who provided a machine translation of German documents into English. Only the German SDA documents were prepared and translated in time for the submission deadline. This MT output was provided to all participants as a resource, and was used to support experiments run at ETH, Duke University, Cornell University, the University of California at Berkeley, and the University of Maryland.

Cross-language retrieval using dictionary resources was the approach taken in experiments submitted by groups at New Mexico State University, University of Massachusetts, the Commissariat a l'Energie Atomique of France, the Xerox Research Centre Europe, and TNO in the Netherlands. Machine readable dictionaries were obtained from various sources, including the Internet, for different combinations of languages, and used in different ways by the various groups.

The corpus-based approach to CLIR was evaluated by ETH, using similarity thesauri, and the collaborative group of Duke University, the University of Colorado, and Bellcore, who used latent semantic indexing  LSI . An innovative approach for cross-language retrieval between English and French was tested at Cornell University. This approach was based on the assumption that there are many similar-looking words  near cognates  between English and French and that, with some simple matching rules, relevant documents could be found without a full translation of queries or documents.

An overview of results for each participating group is presented in Figure 2. This figure represents the results based on only 21 of the 25 test topics, but the results from all 25 are not significantly different. The figure shows results for each group and each document language for which experiments were submitted. The y axis represents the average precision achieved for the *best* experiment submitted by each group and each document language. Cross-language experiments are denoted by, for example,   to French , whereas the corresponding monolingual experiments are denoted,  French . For example, the figure shows that the best experiment submitted by Cornell University performing cross-language retrieval of French documents achieved average precision of 0.2.

Note that the presentation of results in Figure 2 does not distinguish between fully automatic cross-language retrieval, and those groups who included some interactive aspect and user involvement in their experiments. The groups at Xerox, Berkeley and Dublin City University submitted experiments which involved manual interaction. Also some groups participated only in a monolingual capacity: Dublin City University, University of Montreal, and IRIT France.

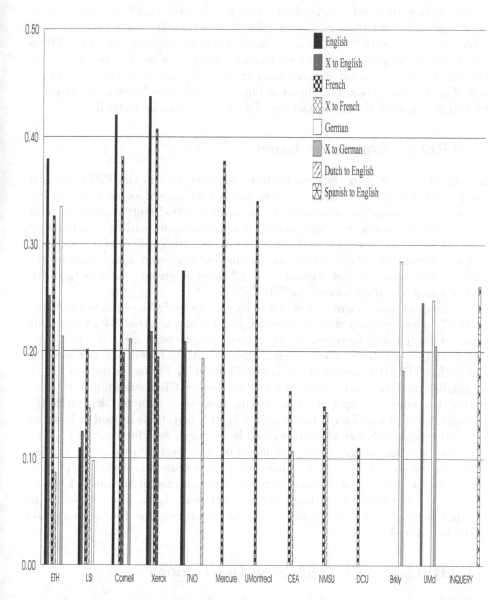

**Fig. 2.** CLIR Track Results  Average Precision, best run

Although Figure 2 does not provide a sound basis for between-group comparisons, some general comments can be made on the overall results. Comparing cross-language results to the corresponding monolingual experiments, it seems that cross-language retrieval is performing in a range of roughly 50  to 75  of the equivalent monolingual case. This is consistent with previous evaluations of cross-language retrieval. Many different approaches to cross-language retrieval were tried and evaluated, and groups using each of the different approaches have achieved good results. For example, the corpus based method used by ETH to perform cross-language retrieval for German documents worked as well as the machine translation based methods used by the University of Maryland and Cornell. The dictionary based method used by Xerox for cross-language retrieval to French did about the same as the use of cognate overlap by Cornell.

## TREC- Evaluation Issues

In general the testing paradigm and test collection used in the TREC-6 CLIR track worked well, but there were two issues that caused concern. First, the many possible language pairs used by the various participants made it difficult to compare across systems, and presented a somewhat unrealistic evaluation in that many situations require retrieval of documents irregardless of the language of those documents. This would suggest that an improved task would be the retrieval of a ranked list of documents in all three languages, i.e. a merged list, and this task was implemented in TREC-7.

The second issue was more difficult to solve. The TREC-6 topics were created at NIST by two persons who were native English speakers but who had strong skills in French and German. Because these people were new to TREC and NIST staff was unable to provide much guidance due to lack of knowledge skills, the TREC-6 CLIR topics are more simplistic than TREC topics normally done in English, and this may have allowed the simpler CLIR techniques to work better than would be expected. Additionally there were some problems with the translations produced for the topics at NIST, and corrections needed to be made by native speakers before the topics could be released. As a final problem, NIST assessors working in non-native languages tend to be much slower in making relevance judgments, and this became considerably worse when working in three languages. Only 13 out of 25 topics were evaluated in time for any analysis before TREC, with the rest not finished until several months later. This problem with non-native speakers led to forming collaborative partnerships for the evaluation effort in TREC-7.

## TREC- CLIR Track Task Description

In TREC-7, the task was changed slightly and participants were asked to retrieve documents from a multilingual pool. They were able to chose the topic language, and then had to find relevant documents in the pool regardless of the languages the texts were formulated in. As a side effect, this meant that most groups had to solve the additional task of merging results from various bilingual runs. The languages present in the pool were English, German, French and Italian, with Italian being a new language introduced for TREC-7. There were 28 topics distributed, each topic being translated into four languages. To allow for participation of groups that did not have the resources to work in all four languages, a secondary evaluation was provided that permitted such groups to send in runs using English topics to retrieve documents from a subset of the pool just containing texts in English and French. There were no monolingual runs as part of the cross-language track in TREC-7.

The TREC-7 task description also defined a subtask GIRT , working with a second data collection containing documents from a structured data base in the field of social science. Unfortunately, the introduction of this data was probably premature, since no groups were able to work with this data in TREC-7. The data was used again in TREC-8 see task description in TREC-8 for more information on this data .

The document collection for the main task contained the same documents used in TREC-6, with an extension to Italian texts from SDA see Table 1 . Note that Italian texts were only available for 1989 and 1990, and therefore the Italian SDA collection is considerably smaller than the SDA for French or the English AP texts.

There were significant changes in the way the topics were created for TREC-7 because of the problems in TREC-6. Four different sites, each located in an area where one of the topic languages is natively spoken, worked on both topic creation and relevance judgments.

The four sites were:

- English: NIST, Gaithersburg, MD, USA  Ellen Voorhees
- French: EPFL Lausanne, Switzerland  Afzal Ballim
- German: IZ Sozialwissenschaften, Germany  Jürgen Krause, Michael Kluck
- Italian: CNR, Pisa, Italy  Carol Peters .

Seven topics were chosen from each site to be included in the topic set. The 21 topics from the other sites were then translated, and this ultimately led to a collection of 28 topics, each available in all four languages. Relevance judgments were made at all four sites for all 28 topics, with each site examining only the pool of documents in their native language.

## TREC-  Results

A total of nine groups from five different countries submitted results for the TREC-7 CLIR track  Table 4 . The participants submitted 27 runs, 17 for the main task, and 10 for the secondary English to French  English evaluation. Five groups  Berkeley, Eurospider, IBM, Twenty-One and Maryland  tackled the main task. English was, not surprisingly, the most popular topic language, with German coming in a strong second. Every language was used by at least one group.

| **TREC-7 Participants** | |
|---|---|
| **Participant** | **Country** |
| CEA  Commissariat a Energie Atomique | France |
| Eurospider Information Technology AG | Switzerland |
| IBM T.J. Watson Research Center | SA |
| Los Alamos National Laboratory | SA |
| Te  tWise LLC | SA |
| Twenty-One   niversity of Twente  TNO-TPD | Netherlands |
| niversity of California, Berkeley | SA |
| niversity of Maryland, College Park | SA |
| niversite of Montreal  Laboratoire CLIPS, IMAG | Canada |

**Table 4.** Organizations participating in the TREC-7 CLIR track

Figure 3 shows a comparison of runs for the main task. Shown are the best automatic runs against the full document pool for each of the five groups that worked on the main task. As can be seen, most participants performed in a fairly narrow band. This is interesting given the very different approaches of the individual participants: IBM used translation models automatically trained on parallel and comparable corpora, Twenty-One used sophisticated dictionary lookup and a  boolean- avoured  weighting scheme, Eurospider employed corpus-based techniques, using similarity thesauri and pseudo-relevance feedback on aligned documents and the Berkeley and Maryland groups used off-the-shelf machine translation systems.

A particularly interesting aspect of TREC-7 CLIR track was how participants approached the merging problem. Again, many interesting methods were used. Among the solutions proposed were: Twenty-One compared averages of similarity values of individual runs, Eurospider used document alignments to map runs to comparable score ranges through linear regression and IBM used modeling of system-wide probabilities of relevance. But it was also possible to avoid the merging problem, for example, the Berkeley group expanded the topics to all languages and then ran them against an index containing documents from all languages, therefore directly retrieving a multilingual result list.

## TREC-  Evaluation Issues

One of the distinguishing features of the TREC-7 CLIR track was that the topic development and relevance assessments were done in a distributed manner. Based on the experiences of TREC-6, this was a critical necessity, but it is important to understand the possible impact of this decision on the results.

Topic development is clearly subjective, and depends on the creator's own particular background. Additionally for CLIR it must be presumed that both the language and cultural background also impact the choice and phrasing of topics. A close examination of the topics in TREC-7 would probably permit an

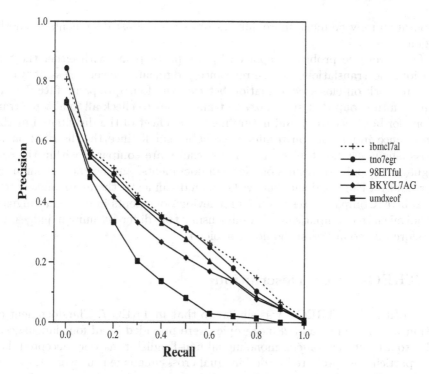

**Fig. 3.** Results of the main TREC-7 CLIR evaluation, X to EGFI

astute observer to group them fairly accurately according to source language and creation site. This should not be considered negative nor should it affect the validity of the results. However, it causes some problems both in the translation of the topics and in their assessment.

Topic translation raises the typical problems involved in any translation: a total understanding of the source is necessary in order to achieve a perfect rendering of the target. But this is complicated in CLIR by the need to find an acceptable balance between precision with respect to the source and naturalness with respect to the target language. Ideally the translations should re ect how a native-speaker would phrase a search for that topic in their language and culture.

Accurate assessment of relevance for retrieved documents for a given topic implies a good understanding of the topic. The fact that the CLIR track used a distributed scenario for building topics and making relevance judgments meant that relevance judgments were usually not done by the creators of the topics. In addition to general problems of judgment consistency when this occurs, there is also the in uence of the multilingual multicultural characteristics of the task. The way a particular topic is discussed in one language will not necessarily be reproduced in the documents in other languages. Therefore a topic which did not appear to raise problems of interpretation in the language used for its preparation may be much more difficult to assess against documents in another language.

There were no problems reported by the participants with either the topic creation, the translations, or the relevance judgments. Nevertheless, it was decided to work on closer coordination between the four groups in TREC-8, and to get a fifth group that specializes in translations to check all final topic translations for both accuracy and naturalness. The effect of the distributed method of relevance judgments on results is probably small since the distribution was across languages, not topics. As long as results are compared within the same language, i.e. pairs of results on German documents, and not across languages, i.e. results on English documents vs German documents, there are unlikely to be issues here. Comparing results from retrieving documents in different languages is equivalent to comparison of results using two different human judges, and therefore this comparison should be avoided.

## TREC- Task Description

The CLIR task in TREC-8 was similar to that in TREC-7. The document collection was the same, and 28 new topics were provided in all four languages. In order to attract newcomers, monolingual non-English runs were accepted however, participants preferred to do bilingual cross-language runs when they could not do the full task.

The TREC-8 task description also included the vertical domain subtask, containing documents from a structured database in the field of social science the GIRT collection . This collection comes with English titles for most documents, and a matching bilingual thesaurus. The University of California at Berkeley conducted some very extensive experiments with this collection.

The topic creation and relevance assessment sites for TREC-8 were:

- English: NIST, Gaithersburg, MD, USA  Ellen Voorhees
- French: University of Zurich, Switzerland  Michael Hess
- German: IZ Sozialwissenschaften, Germany  Jürgen Krause, Michael Kluck
- Italian: CNR, Pisa, Italy  Carol Peters .

At each site, an initial 10 topics were formulated. At a topic selection meeting, the seven topics from each site that were felt to be best suited for the multilingual retrieval setting were selected. Each site then translated the 21 topics formulated by the others into the local language. This ultimately led to a pool of 28 topics, each available in all four languages. It was decided that roughly one third of the topics should address national regional, European and international issues, respectively. To ensure that topics were not too broad or too narrow and were easily interpretable against all document collections, monolingual test searches were conducted. As a final check on the translations, Prof. Christa Womser-Hacker from the University of Hildesheim volunteered her students to review all topic translations.

# TREC-  Results

A total of twelve groups from six different countries submitted results for the TREC-8 CLIR track  Table 5 . Eight participants tackled the full task  up from five in TREC-7 , submitting 27 runs  up from 17 . The remainder of the participants either submitted runs using a subset of languages, or concentrated on the GIRT subtask only. English was the dominant topic language, although each language was used by at least one group as the topic language.

| TREC-8 Participants | |
|---|---|
| **Participant** | **Country** |
| Claritech | SA |
| Eurospider Information Technology AG | Switzerland |
| IBM T.J. Watson Research Center | SA |
| IRIT  SIG | France |
| John Hopkins   niversity, APL | SA |
| MNIS-Te tWise Labs | SA |
| New Me ico State   niversity | SA |
| Sharp Laboratories of Europe Ltd | England |
| Twenty-One   niversity of Twente  TNO-TPD | Netherlands |
|   niversity of California, Berkeley | SA |
|   niversity of Maryland, College Park | SA |
|   niversite of Montreal  Laboratoire CLIPS, IMAG | Canada |

**Table 5.** Organizations participating in the TREC-8 CLIR track

Figure 4 shows a comparison of runs for the main task. The graph shows the best runs against the full document pool for each of the eight groups. Because of the diversity of the experiments conducted, the figures are best compared on the basis of the specific features of the individual runs, details of which can be found in the track papers. For example, New Mexico State runs use manually translated queries, which are the result of a monolingual user interactively picking good terms. This is clearly an experiment that is very different from the runs of some other groups that are essentially doing  ad hoc  style cross-language retrieval, using no manual intervention whatever.

Approaches employed in TREC-8 by individual groups include:

– experiments on pseudo relevance feedback by Claritech
– similarity thesaurus based translation by Eurospider
– statistical machine translation by IBM
– combinations of n-grams and words by John Hopkins University
– use of conceptual interlingua by MNIS-Textwise
– query translation using bilingual dictionaries by Twenty-One
– evaluation of the Pirkola measure by University of Maryland

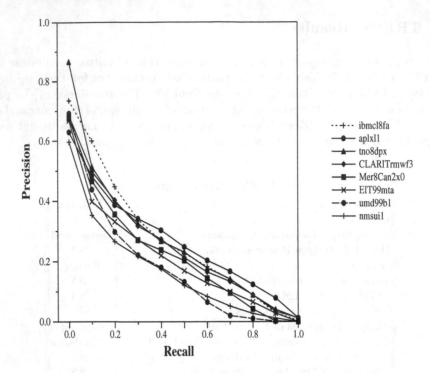

**Fig. 4.** Results of the main TREC-8 CLIR evaluation, X to EGFI

- transaction models derived from parallel text by University of Montreal
- use of an online machine translation system by IRIT

Merging remained an important issue for most participants. The University of Maryland tried to circumvent the problem by using an unified index in some of their runs, but the other groups working on the main task all had to rely on merging of some sort to combine their individual, bilingual cross-language runs. Some of the approaches this year include: merging based on probabilities that were calculated using log Rank by various groups including IBM, merging using linear regression on document alignments by Eurospider, linear combinations of scores by John Hopkins, and of course, straight, score-based merging.

Two groups submitted runs for the GIRT subtask. The University of California at Berkeley participated exclusively in the subtask only, and did some very comprehensive experiments using both the English titles of the documents and the English German thesaurus supplied with the collection. These runs show some of the interesting properties of GIRT. It is also possible to do ad hoc style runs on GIRT, ignoring controlled vocabulary, English titles and the thesaurus. This approach was taken by Eurospider.

# 10   TREC- Evaluation Issues and Summary

It was generally felt that the final check on the translation quality and the elimination of topics that were likely to have problems in interpretation across languages improved the process of distributed evaluation. Two issues remain however that warrant further discussion. These issues are not unique to TREC-8, although they appear to have grown worse over the three years of CLIR in TREC.

First, there is the issue of the size of the pools in the various languages. Relevance judgments in TREC are done using a pooling method, i.e. the top-ranked documents from each submitted run are put into a  pool , removing duplicates, and this pool is judged by humans. There have been studies done both on the completeness of these pools and on the consistency of relevance judgments across assessors 7 , 8 , with the results showing that the pooling method produces stable results for the 50-topic TREC  English  ad hoc task.

But these conclusions are based on having enough topics to allow a stable average across assessors, enough documents in the pools to assure most relevant documents have been found, and enough participating groups to contribute different sets of documents to the pool. Voorhees showed that the use of 25 topics is a minimum to insure stability across assessors, and therefore the averages for the CLIR results can be considered stable for comparison.

The small size of the pools, particularly in German and Italian, may imply that the collections cannot be viewed as complete. For TREC-6, where mostly monolingual runs were judged, there was a per-topic average of 350 documents judged in English and in German  500 in French . But the merged runs judged for TRECs 7 and 8 produced far fewer documents for German and Italian in the pools  160 German 100 Italian judged for TREC-7 146 German  155 Italian for TREC-8 , and it is likely that additional relevant documents exist for these languages in the collection. This does not make the use of these collections invalid, but does require caution in their use when it is probable that many new Italian or German documents will be retrieved. For further analysis on this point see 9 , and 6 .

The second issue involves the problem of cross-language resources. Looking at TREC-8 for example, two main points stand out with respect to the main task: first, 21 out of 27 submitted runs used English as the topic language, and second, at least half of all groups used the Systran machine translation system in some form for parts of their experiments. While English was also the most popular choice for TREC-7, the percentage of runs that used non-English topics was substantially higher  7 out of 17 .

Part of the reason for the heavy use of English as the topic language is that 75  of the TREC-8 participants are from English speaking countries. But an additional factor is the lack of resources that do not use English as the source language, e.g. dictionaries for German to Italian. One reason for the choice of Systran by so many groups also lies in a lack of resources: using Systran allowed the groups to do something with certain language pairs that they would otherwise not have been able to include in their experiments. Because Systran offers mainly combinations of English with other languages, this in uenced the domination of English as topic language.

Both of these reasons contributed to the decision to move the European cross-language task to Europe in 2000 within the new CLEF evaluation. It was generally felt that more Europeans would join such an activity and that these groups would bring with them increased knowledge of non-English resources.

The three years of European cross-language evaluation done at NIST not only achieved the initial goals, but laid the foundation for continued CLIR evaluation in Europe and now starting in Asia. The first large-scale test collection for cross-language retrieval was built and will continue to be distributed for test purposes. Twenty-two groups have taken part in the evaluations, cumulatively reporting over 100 experiments on diverse methods of cross-language retrieval. And finally, a new technique has been devised to produce the necessary topics and relevance judgments for the test collections in a distributed manner such that the collection properly re ects its multilingual and multicultural origins.

## Acknowledgements

We thank the Neue Zürcher Zeitung  NZZ , the Schweizerische Depeschenagentur  SDA  and the Asssociated Press  AP  for making their data available to the TREC community. We would also like to express our gratitude to everyone involved in topic creation and relevance assessment at NIST, the IZ Sozialwissenschaften, CNR-Pisa, EPFL, the University of Zurich and the University of Hildesheim.

## References

1. Sheridan, P. and Ballerini, J. P. and and Schäuble P.  Building a Large Multilingual Test Collection from Comparable News Documents. In  Grefenstette, G.  ed.   Cross-Language Information Retrieval. Kluwer Academic Publishers, Boston  1998  chapter 11.
2. Sheridan, P. and Ballerini, J. P.  E periments in Multilingual Information Retrieval using the SPIDER System. In  Proceedings of the 19th ACM SIGIR Conference on Research and Development in Information Retrieval, Zurich, Switzerland,  1996 , 58 65.
3. Voorhees, E. and Harman, D.  1998   Overview of the  Si th  Te t  REtrieval Conference  TREC-6 . In  Proceedings of the  Si th  Te t  REtrieval Conference  TREC-6 . NIST  Special  Publication  500-240  1998 , 1-24. Also at http://trec.nist.gov/pubs.html
4. Schäuble, P. and Sheridan P.  1998   Cross-Language Information Retrieval  CLIR  Track Overview. In  Proceedings of the  Si th  Te t  REtrieval Conference  TREC-6 . NIST  Special  Publication  500-240  1998 , 31-44. Also at http://trec.nist.gov/pubs.html
5. Braschler, M., Krause, J., Peters C., and Schäuble P.  Cross-Language Information Retrieval  CLIR  Track Overview. In  Proceedings of the Seventh  Te t  REtrieval Conference  TREC-7 . NIST Special Publication 500-242  1999 , 25-32. Also at http://trec.nist.gov/pubs.html

6. Braschler, M., Peters C., and Schäuble P.  Cross-Language Information Retrieval  CLIR  Track Overview. In  Proceedings of the Eighth Te t REtrieval
Conference  TREC-8 . NIST Special Publication 500-246  2000 , 25-34. Also at
http://trec.nist.gov/pubs.html
7. Voorhees, Ellen M.  Variations in Relevance Judgments and the Measurement of Retrieval E ectiveness. In  Proceedings of the 21st ACM SIGIR Conference on Research
and Development in Information Retrieval, Melbourne, Australia  1998 , 315-323.
8. Zobel, Justin  How Reliable are the Results of Large-Scale Information Retrieval
E periments  In  Proceedings of the 21st ACM SIGIR Conference on Research and
Development in Information Retrieval, Melbourne, Australia  1998 , 307-314.
9. Voorhees, E.M., and Harman, D.K.  Overview of the Eighth Te t REtrieval
Conference  TREC-8 . In  Proceedings of the Eighth Te t REtrieval Conference  TREC-8 . NIST Special Publication 500-246  2000 , 1-24. Also at
http://trec.nist.gov/pubs.html

# NTCIR Workshop : Japanese- and Chinese-English Cross-Lingual Information Retrieval and Multi-grade Relevance Judgments

Noriko Kando

National Institute of Informatics (NII)
Tokyo 101-8430, Japan
kando@nii.ac.jp

**Abstract.** This paper introduces the NTCIR Workshops, a series of evaluation workshops designed to enhance research in Japanese and Asian language text retrieval, cross-lingual information retrieval, and related text processing techniques such as summarization, extraction, etc. by providing large-scale test collections and a forum of researchers. Twenty-eight groups from six countries participated in the first workshop and forty-six groups from eight countries have registered for the second. The test collections used in the Workshops are basically TREC-type collections but they contain several unique characteristics including multi-grade relevance judgments. Finally some thoughts on future directions are suggested.

## 1 Introduction

The purposes of the NTCIR Workshop [1] are the following:

1. to encourage research in information retrieval (IR), cross-lingual information retrieval (CLIR) and related text processing technology including term recognition, information extraction and summarization by providing large-scale reusable test collections and a common evaluation setting that allows cross-system comparisons
2. to provide a forum for research groups interested in comparing results and exchanging ideas or opinions in an informal atmosphere
3. to investigate methods for constructing test collections or data sets usable for experiments and methods for laboratory-type testing of IR and related technology

For the first NTCIR Workshop, the process started with the distribution of the training data set on 1st November 1998, and ended with the workshop meeting which was held on 30th August - 1st September 1999 in Tokyo, Japan [2]. The participation in the workshop was limited to the active participants, i.e. the members of the research groups that submitted the results of the tasks. Many interesting papers with various approaches were presented and the meeting ended in enthusiasm. The third day of the Workshop was organised as the NTCIR/IREX Joint Workshop. The IREX Workshop [3], another evaluation workshop for IR and information extraction (named entities) using Japanese newspaper articles, was held consecutively. IREX and

C. Peters (Ed.): CLEF 2000, LNCS 2069, pp. 24-35, 2001.

NTCIR worked together to organise the second NTCIR Workshop. The research group in National Taiwan University has proposed the Chinese IR Task and is organising it at the NTCIR Workshop 2. The process of the NTCIR Workshop 2 started in June 2000 and will be ended with the meeting on 7-9th March 2001 [4].

From the beginning of the NTCIR project, we have focused on two directions of investigation, *i.e.,* (1) traditional IR system testing and (2) challenging issues. For the former, we have placed emphasis on IR with Japanese or other Asian languages and CLIR. Indexing texts written in Japanese or other East Asian languages like Chinese is quite different from indexing texts in English, French or other European languages since there is no explicit boundary (i.e. no space) between words in a sentence. CLIR is critical in the Internet environment, especially between languages with completely different origins and structure like English and Japanese. Moreover in scientific texts or everyday-life documents like Web documents, foreign language terms often appear in Japanese texts both in their original spelling and in transliterated forms. To overcome the word mismatch that may be caused by such expression variance, cross-linguistic strategies are needed for even monolingual retrieval Japanese documents of the type described in [5].

For the challenging issues, we have been interested in (2a) document genres (or types), and (2b) intersection of natural language processing (NLP) and IR. Each document genre has own user group and way of usage, and the criteria determining "successful search" may vary accordingly though traditional IR research has looked at the generalised system which can handle any kind of documents. For example, Web document retrieval has different characteristics from those of newspaper or patent retrieval both with respect to the nature of the document itself and the way of usage. We have investigated appropriate evaluation methods for each genre.

In IR with Asian Languages, NLP can play important roles such as identifying word boundaries and so on. Moreover, NLP techniques help to make the "information" in the retrieved documents more usable for users, for example, by pinpointing the answer passages in the retrieved documents, extracting information, summarization, supporting the comparison of multiple documents and so on. The importance of such technology to make retrieved information immediately exploitable by the user is increasing in the Internet environment in which novice end users have to face huge amount of heterogeneous information resources. Therefore both IREX and NTCIR included both IR task and NLP-related tasks from the beginning.

In the next section, we outline the Workshops. Section 3 describes the test collections used and Section 4 discusses some thoughts on future directions.

## 2 Overview of the NTCIR Workshop

This section introduces the tasks, procedures and evaluation results of the first NTCIR. We then discuss the characteristic aspects of CLIR with scientific documents, which was a task at the first NTCIR Workshop.

## 2.1 Tasks

Each participant has conducted one or more of the following tasks at each workshop.

*NTCIR Workshop 1*
– *Ad Hoc Information Retrieval Task:* to investigate the retrieval performance of systems that search a static set of documents using new search topics.
– *Cross-Lingual Information Retrieval Task:* an ad hoc task in which the documents are in English and the topics are in Japanese.
– *Automatic Term Recognition and Role Analysis Task:* (1) to extract terms from titles and abstracts of documents, and (2) to identify the terms representing the "object", "method", and "main operation" of the main topic of each document.

The test collection NTCIR-1 was used in these three tasks. In the Ad Hoc Information Retrieval Task, the document collection containing Japanese, English and Japanese-English paired documents is retrieved by Japanese search topics. In Japan, document collections often naturally consist of such a mixture of Japanese and English. Therefore the Ad Hoc IR Task at the NTCIR Workshop 1 is substantially CLIR though some of the participating groups discarded the English part and did the task as Japanese monolingual IR.

*NTCIR Workshop 2*
– *Chinese IR Task:* including English-Chinese CLIR (E-C) and Chinese monolingual IR (C-C) using the test collection CHIB01, consisting of newspaper articles from five newspapers in Taiwan R.O.C.
– *Japanese-English IR Task:* using the test collection of NTCIR-1 and -2, including monolingual retrieval of Japanese and English (J-J, E-E) and CLIR of Japanese and English (J-E, E-J, J-JE, E-JE).
– *Text Summarization Challenge:* text summarization of Japanese newspaper articles of various kinds. The NTCIR-2 Summ collection and TAO Summ Collection are used.

The new challenging task is called "Challenge". Each task or challenge has been proposed and organised by different research groups in a rather independent way while keeping good contacts and discussion with the NTCIR Project organising group headed by the author. How to evaluate and what should be evaluated as a new Challenge" has been thoroughly discussed through a discussion group.

## 2.2 Participants

**NTCIR Workshop 1.** Below is the list of active participating groups that submitted task results. Thirty-one groups, including participants from six countries, enrolled to participate in the first NTCIR Workshop. Of these groups, twenty-eight groups enrolled in IR tasks (23 in the Ad Hoc Task and 16 in the Cross-Lingual Task), and nine in the Term Recognition task. Twenty-eight groups from six countries submitted results. Two groups worked without any Japanese language expertise.

Communications Research Laboratory (MPT), Fuji Xerox, Fujitsu Laboratories, Hitachi, JUSTSYSTEM, Kanagawa Univ. (2), KAIST/KORTERM, Manchester Metropolitan Univ., Matsushita Electric Industrial, NACSIS, National Taiwan

Univ., NEC (2 groups), NTT, RMIT & CSIRO, Tokyo Univ. of Technology, Toshiba, Toyohashi Univ. of Technology, Univ. of California Berkeley, Univ. of Lib. and Inf. Science (Tsukuba, Japan), Univ. of Maryland, Univ. of Tokushima, Univ. of Tokyo, Univ. of Tsukuba, Yokohama National Univ., Waseda Univ.

**NTCIR Workshop 2.** Forty-six groups from eight countries registered for the second NTCIR Workshop. Among them, 16 registered for Chinese IR, 30 for Japanese-English IR tasks, and 15 for Text Summarization.

ATT Labs & Duke Univ., Chinese Univ. of Hong Kong, Communications Research Laboratory -MPT, Fuji Xerox, Fujitsu Laboratories (2), Gifu Univ., Hitachi Co., HongKong Polytechnic, IoS, Johns Hopkins Univ., JR Res. Labs, JUSTSYSTEM, Kanagawa University, KAIST/KORTERM, Matsushita Electric Industrial, Nat. TsinHua Univ., Univ. of Osaka, NII (3), Univ. of Tokyo (2), NEC, New Mexico Univ., NTT & NAIST, OASIS, Queen College-City University of New York, Ricoh Co., Surugadai Univ., Toshiba/Cambridge/Microsoft, Trans EZ, Toyohashi Univ. of Technology (2), Univ. of California Berkeley, Univ. of Electro-Communication (2), Univ. of Exeter, Univ. of Lib. and Inf. Science (Tsukuba, Japan), Univ. of Maryland, Univ. of Montreal , Yokohama National Univ. (2), Waseda Univ.

## 2.3 Procedures and Evaluation

**NTCIR Workshop 1:**
- *November 1, 1998:* distribution of the training data (document data, 30 ad hoc topics, 21 cross-lingual topics and their relevance assessments)
- *February 8, 1999:* distribution of the test data (the 53 new test topics)
- *March 4, 1999:* submission of results
- *June 12, 1999:* distribution of evaluation results
- *August 30-September 1, 1999:* Workshop meeting

**NTCIR Workshop 2:**
- *June, 2000:* distribution of the training data
- *August 10, 2000:* distribution of the test data for the Japanese IR task (new documents and 49 J/E topics)
- *August 30, 2000:* distribution of the test data for the Chinese IR task (new documents and 50 C/E topics)
- *September 8, 2000:* dry run in the Summarization task
- *September 18, 2000:* submission of results in the Japanese IR task
- *October 20, 2000:* submission of results in the Chinese IR task
- *November, 2000:* test in the Summarization task
- *January 10, 2001:* distribution of evaluation results
- *March 7-9, 2001:* Workshop meeting at the NII in Tokyo.

A participant could submit the results of more than one run. For IR tasks, both automatic and manual query constructions were allowed. In the case of automatic construction, the participants had to submit at least one set of results of the searches using only <Description> fields of the topics as the mandatory runs. The intention of this is to enhance the cross-system comparison. For optional automatic runs and manual runs, any fields of the topics could be used. In addition, each participant had to complete and submit a system description form describing the detailed features of the system.

Human analysts assessed the relevance of retrieved documents to each topic. The relevance judgments (right answers) for the test topics were delivered to active participants who submitted search results. Based on these assessments, interpolated recall and precision at 11 points, average precision (non-interpolated) over all relevant documents, and precision at 5, 10, 15, 20, 30, and 100 documents were calculated using TREC's evaluation program, which is available from the ftp site of Cornell University.

For the Text Summarization Task, both intrinsic and extrinsic evaluations have been conducted. For the former, emphasis is placed on round-table evaluation and creating a reusable data set. Professional captionists created two kind of summaries as "right answer"; abstract-type summaries which involved the reorganisation of sentences, and extract-type summaries. Each submitted summary was then rated by these professional captionists comparing it with those two "right answers" and the automatically created random summary of the article. The results will serve as reference data for the round-table discussion at the workshop meeting, where all the participants share the experience and can have detailed discussion of the technology. For the extrinsic evaluation, we chose an IR task based evaluation, which is similar to the method used at SUMMAC [6].

## 2.4 Results of the NTCIR Workshop 1 and Discussion

Recall/precision (R/P) graphs of the top Ad Hoc and top Cross-Lingual runs for all runs are shown in *Figs. 1* and *2*. For further details of each approach, please consult the paper for each system in the Workshop Proceedings, which is available online at http://www.nii.ac.jp/ntcir/OnlineProceedings/.

One of the most interesting things found in the IR evaluation is that among the best systems, the two systems of JSCB and BK, which took completely different approaches, both obtained very high scores. JSCB used NLP techniques very well on a vector space model with pseudo relevance feedback and BKJJBIFU focused on the statistical approach of weighting algorithms based on long experience with the expanding probabilistic model using logistic regression and used simple bi-gram segmentation.

Many groups used weighting schemes that have been reported as working well against English documents but have not been tested on Japanese documents. This is probably because of shortness of time in the Workshop schedule. Extension of the experiments on the weighting schemes is confidently expected.

Quasi-paired documents of a native language and English such as the ones included in the NTCIR-1 & 2 collections can be easily found in the real world, for example, on the Web, or in scholarly documents, commercial documents describing a company's products, government documents, and so on. Using these documents to prepare bilingual or multilingual lexical resources that are usable for cross-lingual information access is a practical approach to the problem.

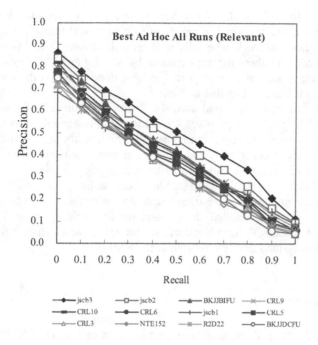

**Fig. 1.** Top Ad Hoc Runs (Level 1)

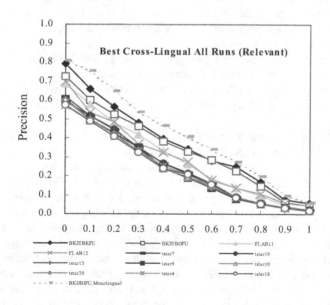

**Fig.2.** Top Cross-Lingual Runs (Level 1)

*Transliteration:* In the NTCIR Workshop 1, one group used transliteration of Katakana (phonetic characters used to represent foreign terms) terms in CLIR, which worked well. It seemed to work especially well on technical terms and is expected to be effective in reducing the problems caused by word mismatch because of the various ways of expression of a concept in Japanese documents, as discussed above. More investigation is expected on this matter.

*Round-table Evaluation:* We conducted the Term Recognition Task as a round-table evaluation. The organiser prepared evaluation results according to a proposed evaluation measure called "most common answer" for each submitted result and these were used as reference data for the round-table discussion. For term recognition, there can be various directions of evaluation criteria according to the purpose of the research and application. A single "gold standard" cannot be meaningful for this task. Instead, we placed emphasis on sharing ideas on "what is the problem in term recognition research", and detailed discussions on the techniques used and their purpose. We then discussed further directions for this investigation based on the common experience gained through the task at the workshop.

# 3 Test Collections

Through the NTCIR Workshops and its ex-partner (now colleague of NTCIR) IREX, the following test collections or data sets usable for laboratory-type testing of IR and related test processing technology were constructed.

- *CHIB-1;* more than 130,000 Chinese articles from 5 Taiwan newspapers of 1998 and 1999. 50 Chinese topics and English translation, 4-grade relevance judgments
- *NTCIR-1;* ca.330,000 Japanese and English documents. 83 Japanese topics, 3-grade relevance judgments. A tagged corpus
- *NTCIR-2;* ca.400,000 Japanese and English documents, 49 Japanese topics and English translation, 4-grade relevance judgments. The Segmented data
- *NTCIR-2 Summ;* ca.100 + ca.2000 (*NTCIR-2 TAO Summ*) manually created summaries of various types of Japanese articles from *Mainichi Newspaper* of 1994, 1995 and 1998.
- *IREX-IR;* ca. 200,000 Japanese newspaper articles from *Mainichi Newspaper* of 1994 and 1995, 30 Japanese topics, 3-grade judgments
- *IREX-NE;* Named entity extraction from Japanese newspaper articles

A sample document record of the NTCIR-1 is shown in *Fig. 3*. The documents are author abstracts of conference papers presented at academic meetings hosted by 65 Japanese academic societies. More than half of them are English-Japanese paired. Documents are plain texts with SGML-like tags. A record may contain document ID, title, a list of author(s), name and date of the conference, abstract, keyword(s) that were assigned by the author(s) of the document, and the name of the host society.

A sample topic record is shown in *Fig. 4*. Topics as defined as statements of "user needs" rather than "queries", which are the strings actually submitted to the system, since we would like to allow both manual and automatic query construction from the topics.

```
<REC>
<ACCN>gakkai-0000011144</ACCN>
<TITL TYPE="kanji">電子·原稿・電子·出版・電子·図書館-「SGML実験誌」の作成実験を通して
</TITL>
<TITE TYPE="alpha">Electronic manuscripts, electronic publishing, and electronic library </TITE>
<AUPK TYPE="kanji">根岸 正光</AUPK>
<AUPE TYPE="alpha">Negishi, Masamitsu</AUPE>
<CONF TYPE="kanji">研究発表会(情報学基礎)</CONF>
<CNFE TYPE="alpha">The Special Interest Group Notes of IPSJ</CNFE>
<CNFD>1991. 11. 19</CNFD>
<ABST TYPE="kanji"><ABST.P>電子出版というキーワードを中心に、文献の執筆、編集、印
刷、流通の過程の電子化について、その現状を整理して今後の動向を検討する。とくに、電子出
版に関する国際規格であるSGML (Standard Generalized Markup Language)に対するわが国での動き
に注目し、学術情報センターにおける「SGML実験誌」およびその全文CD-ROM版の作成実験を
通じて得られた知見を報告する。また電子図書館について、その諸形態を展望する。出版文化に
依拠するこの種の社会システムの場合、技術的な問題というのは、その技術の社会的な受容・浸
透の問題であり、この観点から標準化の重要性を論じる。</ABST.P></ABST>
<ABSE TYPE="alpha"><ABSE.P>Current situation on electronic processing in preparation, editing,
printing, and distribution of documents is summarized and its future trend is discussed, with focus on the
concept: "Electronic publishing: Movements in the country concerning an international standard for
electronic publishing. Standard Generalized Markup Language (SGML) is assumed to be important, and
the results from an experiment at NACSIS to publish an "SGML Experimental Journal" and to make its
full-text CD-ROM version are reported. Various forms of "Electronic Library" are also investigated. The
author puts emphasis on standardization, as technological problems for those social systems based on the
cultural settings of publication of the country, are the problems of acceptance and penetration of the
technology in the society.</ABSE.P></ABSE>
 <KYWD TYPE="kanji">電子出版 // 電子図書館 // 電子原稿 // SGML // 学術情報センター // 全文デ
ータベース</KYWD>
 <KYWE TYPE="alpha">Electronic publishing // Electronic library // Electronic manuscripts // SGML //
NACSIS // Full text databases</KYWE>
<SOCN TYPE="kanji">情報処理学会</SOCN>
<SOCE TYPE="alpha">Information Processing Society of Japan</SOCE>
</REC>`
```

**Fig. 3.** Sample Document Record in the NTCIR-1.

A topic contains SGML-like tags and consists of a title, a description, a detailed narrative, and a list of concepts and field(s). The title is a very short description of the topic and can be used as a very short query that resembles those often submitted by end-users of Internet search engines. Each narrative may contain a detailed explanation of the topic, term definitions, background knowledge, the purpose of the search, criteria for judgment of relevance, and so on.

## 3.1 Relevance Judgments (Right Answers)

The relevance judgments were undertaken by pooling methods. Assessors and topic authors are always the users of the document genre. The relevance judgments were conducted using multi-grades: three grades in the NTCIR-1 and four grades in the NTCIR-2 and CHIB01. We think that multi-grade relevance judgments are more natural or close to the judgments done in the real life. To run TREC's evaluation program to calculate mean average precision, recall-level precision, document level precision, we set two thresholds for the level of relevance.

```
<TOPIC q=0005>
<TITLE>
特徴次元リダクション
</TITLE>
<DESCRIPTION>
クラスタリングにおける特徴次元リダクション
</DESCRIPTION>
<NARRATIVE>
オブジェクトのクラスタリングを行なうとき、オブジェクトを特徴ベクトルで表現することが望
まれる。アプリケーションによっては、オブジェクトの次元は数千、数万となることがある。こ
のような場合、事前に次元を落とすことが必要になる。正解文書は、特徴次元リダクションの方
法について、理論面から、または実験によって、提案、比較などを行なっているもの。画像処理
などの実験の操作の一部として特徴次元リダクションを用いているだけでは要求を満たさない。
</NARRATIVE>
<CONCEPT>
特徴選択, 主成分分析, 情報の粒度, 幾何クラスタリング
</CONCEPT>
<FIELD>
1.電子・情報・制御
</FIELD>
</TOPIC>
```

**Fig. 4.** Sample Topic Record in the NTCIR-1

For NTCIR-1 and 2, the assessors are researchers in each subject domain since they contains scientific documents; two assessors judged the relevance to a topic separately and assigned one of the three or four degrees of relevance. After cross-checking, the primary assessors of the topic, who created the topic, made the final judgment. The TREC's evaluation program was run against two different lists of relevant documents produced by two different thresholds of relevance, *i.e.*, **Level 1** , in which "highly relevant (S)" and "relevant (A)" are rated as "relevant", and **Level 2**, in which S, A and "partially relevant (B)" were rated as "relevant" though the NTCIR-1 does not contain "highly relevant (S)".

Relevance judgments in the CHIB01 were conducted according to the method originally proposed by Lin and her supervisor Kuang-hua Chen, who is one of the organisers of the Chinese IR Task at the NTCIR Workshop 2 [7]. Three different groups of users; information specialists including librarians, subject specialists, and ordinary people conducted judgments separately and assigned to each document one of four different degrees of relevance; very relevant (3), relevant (2), partially relevant (1) and irrelevant (0). Then, three relevance judgments assigned by each assessor were averaged out to between 0 and 1 using the formula below;

(Assessor1 + Assessor2 + Assessor3) / 3 / 3

The so-called *rigid relevance* means the final relevance should be between 0.6667 and 1. This is equivalent to each assessor assigning "relevant (2)" or higher to the document, and corresponds to *Level 1* in NTCIR-2. The so-called *relaxed relevance* means that the final relevance should between 0.3333 and 1.That is to say, it is equivalent to each assessor assigning "partial relevant (1)" or higher to the document, and corresponds to Level 2 in NTCIR-2. The TREC's evaluation program was run against these two levels of relevance.

The reason why three different groups of users were employed as assessors is because the genre of newspaper articles is used by various kinds of users. The idea of averaging out the assessments by different user groups is new compared to the traditional approach of test collection building in which the topic author should be the most qualified assessor. A similar idea was mentioned by Dr Andrei Broder, Vice President for Research and Chief Scientist at Alta Vista, in his invited talk at the TREC-9 Conference held on 13-16th of November 2000. He proposed the need to average out the relevance judgment of 15 to 20 users in the evaluation of Web search engines since the users of the systems are very heterogeneous and systems can not know the user's profile during the search.

*Additional Information:* In NTCIR-1 and 2, relevance judgment files contain not only the relevance of each document in the pool but also contain extracted phrases or passages showing the reason why the analyst assessed the document as "relevant". Situation-oriented relevance judgments were conducted based on the statement of "purpose of search" or "background" in <NARRATIVE> in each topic as well as topic-oriented relevance judgments, which are more common in ordinary IR systems laboratory testing. However, only topic-oriented judgments are used in the formal evaluation of this Workshop.

*Rank-Degree Sensitive Evaluation Metric on Multi-grade Relevance Judgments:* In the NTCIR Workshop 2, we plan to use a metrics which is sensitive to the degree of relevance of the documents and their rank in the ranked list of the retrieved documents. Intuitively, the highly relevant documents are more important for users than partial relevant ones and the documents retrieved in the higher ranks in the ranked list are more important. Therefore the systems producing the search results in which higher relevant documents in higher ranks in the ranked list should be rated as better.

Multi-grade relevance judgments are used in several test collections such as Cystic Fibrosis [8] and OHUMED [9] though specific evaluation metrics for them were not produced for the collection. We are now examining the several rank-degree sensitive metrics proposed so far including, Average Search Length [10], Relative Relevance and Ranked Half-Life [11], and Cumulated Gains [12], and will then choose or propose appropriate measures for our purpose.

## 3.2 Linguistic Analysis

NTCIR-1 contains "Tagged Corpus". This contains detailed hand-tagged part-of-speech (POS) tags for 2,000 Japanese documents selected from NTCIR-1. Spelling errors are also manually collected. Because of the absence of explicit boundaries between words in Japanese sentences, we set three levels of lexical boundaries (i.e., word boundaries, and strong and weak morpheme boundaries). In NTCIR-2, the segmented data of the whole J (Japanese document) Collection is provided. They are segmented into three levels of lexical boundaries using a commercially available morphological analyser called HAPPINESS.

## 3.3 Robustness of the IR System Testing Using NTCIR-1

The test collection NTCIR-1 has been tested from the following aspects so that it can be used as a reliable tool for IR system testing:
(A) exhaustivity of the document pool
(B) inter-analyst consistency and its effect for system evaluation
(C) topic-by-topic evaluation.

The results of these studies have been reported and published on various occasions [13-16]. As a result, in terms of exhaustiveness, pooling the top 100 documents from each run worked well for topics with fewer than 50 relevant documents. For topics with more than 100 relevant documents, although the top 100 pooling covered only 51.9% of the total relevant documents, coverage was higher than 90% if combined with additional interactive searches. Therefore, we decided to use the top 100 pooling and conducted additional interactive searches for topics with more than 50 relevant documents.

We found a strong correlation between the system rankings produced using different relevant judgments and different pooling methods, regardless of the inconsistency of the relevance assessments among analysts and regardless of the different pooling methods [13-15]. A similar analysis has been reported by Voorhees [17]. We concluded that NTCIR-1 is reliable as a tool for system evaluation based on these analyses.

# 4 Future Directions

In the future, we would like to enhance the investigation in the following directions;
1.   Evaluation of CLIR systems including Asian languages
2.   Evaluation of retrieval of new document genres
3.   Evaluation of technology to make retrieved information immediately usable
    One of the problems of CLIR is the availability of resources that can be used for translation [18-19]. Enhancement of creating and sharing the resources is important. In the NTCIR Workshops, some groups automatically constructed a bilingual lexicon from quasi-paired document collection. We ourselves also conducted research on CLIR using automatically generated bilingual keyword clusters based on graph-theory [20]. Such paired documents can be easily found in non-English speaking countries and on the Web. Studying the algorithms to construct such resources and sharing them is one practical way to enrich the applicability of CLIR. International collaboration is needed to construct multilingual test collections and organising evaluation of CLIR since creating topics and relevance judgments are language- and cultural-dependent, and must be done by native speakers. With respect to new genres, we are especially interested in Web documents and multimedia documents. For these document types, the user group, usage, purpose of search, criteria for successful retrieval are quite different than the ones for traditional text retrieval and the investigation of these aspects is challenging.

# Acknowledgments

We thank all the participants for their contributions, the assessors, the task chairs, and the program committee. Special thanks are due to Donna Harman, Ellen Voorhees, Mun Kew Leong, Ross Wilkinson, Sung H. Myaeng, and Stephen Robertson for their extensive advice and continuous support. The hard work of the former and current NTCIR project members should be acknowledged: Kazuko Kuriyama, Keizo Oyama, Toshihiko Nozue, Masaharu Yoshioka, Koji Eguchi, Souichiro Hidaka, Hideyuki Kato, Yuko Miyamoto, and Urara Numata.

# References

[1] NTCIR Project: http://research.nii.ac.jp/ntcir/
[2] NTCIR Workshop 1: Proceedings of the First NTCIR Workshop on Research in Japanese Text Retrieval and Term Recognition, Aug. 30-Sept. 1, 1999, Tokyo, ISBN 4-924600-77-6. (http://research.nii.ac.jp/ntcir/workshop/OnlineProceedings/)
[3] TREC URL: http://trec.nist.gov/
[4] NTCIR Workshop 2: http://research.nii.ac.jp/ntcir-ws2/
[5] Kando, N.: Cross-Linguistic Scholarly Information Transfer and Database Services in Japan. Annual Meeting of the ASIS, Washington DC. 1997
[6] http://www.itl.nist.gov/iaui/894.02/related_projects/ tipster_summac/
[7] Chiang, Yu-ting: *A Study on Design and Implementation for Chinese Information Retrieval Benchmark.* Master Thesis, National Taiwan University, 1999, 184 p.
[8] Shaw, W.M., Jr, et al.: The cystic fibrosis database: Content and research opportunities. Library and Information Science Research, 13, 347-366, 1991.
[9] Hersh, W., et al.: OHSUMED: an Interactive Retrieval Evaluation and New Large Test Collection for Research. Proceedings of ACM-SIGIR'94. p.192-201, 1994.
[10] Losee, R.M.: Text retrieval and filtering: analytic models of performance. Kluwer, 1998
[11] Borlund, P., Ingwersen, P.: Measures of relative relevance and ranked half-life: Performance indicators for interactive IR. Proceedings of ACM-SIGIR 98, p.324-331, 1998.
[12] Jarvelin, K., Kekalainen, J.: IR evaluation methods for retrieving highly relevant documents. Proceedings of ACM-SIGIR 2000, p. 41-48, 2000.
[13] Kando, N. et al.: NTCIR-1: Its Policy and Practice, IPSJ SIG Notes, Vol.99, No.20, pp. 33-40, 1999 [in Japanese].
[14] Kuriyama, K. et al.: Pooling for a Large Scale Test Collection: Analysis of the Search Results for the Pre-test of the NTCIR-1 Workshop, IPSJ SIG Notes, May, 1999 [in Japanese].
[15] Kuriyama, K. et al.: Construction of a Large Scale Test Collection: Analysis of the Training Topics of the NTCIR-1, IPSJ SIG Notes, July 1999 [in Japanese].
[16] Kando, N. et al.: Construction of a Large Scale Test Collection: Analysis of the Test Topics of the NTCIR-1, in Proceedings of IPSJ Annual Meeting [in Japanese]. Sept, 30-Oct.3, 1999.
[17] Voorhees, E.M.: Variations in Relevance Judgments and the Measurement of Retrieval Effectiveness, in Proceedings of the ACM SIGIR '98, pp. 315-323.
[18] Ballesteros, L. et al.: Resolving ambiguity for cross-language retrieval, in Proceedings of the ACM SIGIR '98, pp. 64-71.
[19] Shauble, P. et al.: Cross-language Information Retrieval (CLIR) Track overview, in Proceedings of TREC 6, pp. 25-30, 1998.
[20] Kando, N. et al.: Cross-Lingual Information Retrieval using Automatically Generated Multilingual Keyword Clusters, in Proceedings of the 3rd IRAL, pp. 86-94, 1998.

# Language Resources in Cross-Language Text Retrieval: A CLEF Perspective

Julio Gonzalo

Departamento de Lenguajes y Sistemas Informáticos de la   NED
Ciudad   niversitaria s n, 28040 Madrid, Spain
ulio@lsi.uned.es
http://sensei.lsi.uned.es/NL

**Abstract.** Language resources such as machine dictionaries and le ical
databases, aligned parallel corpora or even complete machine translation systems are essential in Cross-Language Te t Retrieval  CLTR , although not standard tools for the Information Retrieval task in general.
We outline the current use and adequacy for CLTR of such resources,
focusing on the participants and e periments performed in the CLEF
2000 evaluation. Our discussion is based on a survey conducted on the
CLEF participants, as well as the descriptions of their systems that can
be found in the present volume. We also discuss how the usefulness of the
CLEF evaluation campaign could be enhanced by including additional
tasks which would make it possible to distinguish between the e ect on
the results of the resources used by the participating systems, on the one
hand, and the retrieval strategies employed, on the other.

## 1   Introduction

Broadly speaking, traditional Information Retrieval  IR  has paid little attention to the linguistic nature of texts, keeping the task closer to a *string processing* approach rather than a *Natural Language Processing* NLP  one. Tokenization, removal of non-content words and crude stemming are the most
 language-oriented  IR tasks. So far, more sophisticated approaches to indexing and retrieval  e.g. phrase indexing, semantic expansion of queries, etc.  have
generally failed to produce the improvements that would compensate for their
higher computational cost. As a consequence, the role of language resources in
standard text retrieval systems has remained marginal.

The Cross-Language Information Retrieval  CLIR  challenge - in which queries and documents are stated in different languages - is changing this landscape:
the indexing spaces of queries and documents are different, and the relationships
between them cannot be captured without reference to cross-linguality. This
means that Language Engineering becomes an essential part of the retrieval process. As the present volume attests, research activities in CLIR include the development, adaptation and merging of translation resources  the study of methods
to restrict candidate terms in query translation  the use of Machine Translation  MT  systems, in isolation or  more commonly  in combination with other
strategies, etc.

C. Peters (Ed.): CLEF 2000, LNCS 2069, pp. 36–47, 2001.

In this paper, we will study the use of Language Resources by groups participating in CLEF 2000, assuming that this provides a representative snapshot of the research being conducted in CLIR as a whole. We will use  language resources  in its broadest sense to include not only dictionaries and corpora but also Natural Language Processing tools  stemmers, morphological analyzers and compound splitters, MT systems, etc. .

The next section summarizes the language resources, and their current capabilities and shortcomings, used in the first CLEF campaign. In Section 3 we propose possible ways to complement the current CLEF evaluation activity to take into account the balance between the quality of language resources, on one hand, and cross-language retrieval techniques, on the other. The final section brie y extracts some conclusions.

## 2   Language Resources in CLEF 2000

We have collected information about the language resources and tools employed in the first CLEF campaign, using two sources of information: a survey conducted on the CLEF participants, and the papers contained in the present volume.

The survey was sent to all participants in CLEF, and we received 14 responses. The teams were asked to list the resources used  or tested  in their CLTR system, specifying the provider, the availability and the approximate size coverage of the resource. They were also asked a  whether the resources were adapted enriched for the experiment, and how  b  what were the strengths and limitations of the resources employed  and c  their opinion about key issues for future CLTR resources. Finally, we scanned the descriptions of systems contained in the present volume to complete the information obtained in the responses to the survey.

We have organized language resources into three groups: dictionaries  from bilingual word pair lists to lexical knowledge bases , aligned corpora  from the Hansard corpus to data mined from the web  and NLP software  mainly MT systems, stemmers and morphological analyzers . Before discussing in more depth each of these three categories, some general observations can be made:

- More than 40  of the resources listed have been developed by the participants in the CLIR evaluation. This is a strong indication that CLEF is not just evaluating CLIR strategies built on top of standard resources, but also evaluating resources themselves.
- Only 5 out of 34 resources are used by more than one group: a free dictionary  Freedict 5 , a web-mined corpus  WAC 21 , an online MT service  Babelfish 1 , a set of stemmers  Muscat 8  and an automatic morphology system  Automorphology 14 . This is partially explained by the fact that many participants use their own resources, and there are only two cases of effective resource sharing: the web-mined corpus developed by U Montreal RALI  three users including the developers  and the Automorphology system developed by the U. of Chicago  used also by the U. Maryland group  22 .

| Languages | developer/provider | size | teams |
|---|---|---|---|
| EN,GE,FR,IT | IAI | EN 40K, GE 42K<br>FR 33K, IT 28K | IAI |
| EN-GE,FR,IT | IAI | EN/FR 39K, EN/GE 46K,<br>EN/IT 28K | IAI |
| NL-EN | Canadian web company | ? | Syracuse U. |
| NL-EN,GE,FR,IT | www.travlang.com/Ergane | NL 56K, EN 16K, FR 10K<br>GE 14K, IT 4K | CWI,<br>U Montreal/RALI |
| EN-GE | www.quickdic.de | EN 99K, GE 130K | U. Maryland |
| EN-FR | www.freedict.com | EN 20K, FR 35K, | U. Maryland,<br>U. Glasgow |
| EN-IT | www.freedict.com | EN 13K, IT 17K | U. Maryland,<br>U. Glasgow |
| EN-GE | www.freedict.com | 88K | IRIT |
| EN-GE | www.leo.online | 224K | U. Dortmund |
| FI,SW,GE→EN | ? | 100K | U. Tampere |
| GE-EN | ? | ? | Eurospider |
| EN-FR | Termium | 1M per lang. | U. Montreal/RALI |
| GE-FR,IT | Eurospider sim. thesauri | ? | Eurospider |
| GE-EN-SP-NL<br>IT-FR-CZ-ET | EuroWordNet/ELRA | EN 168K, IT 48K,<br>GE 20K, FR 32K | U. Sheffield |
| EN/GE/NL | CELEX/LDC | 51K lemmas | U. Sheffield |
| NL-GE,FR,<br>EN,SP | VLIS/Van Dale | 100K lemmas | TNO/Twente |

**Table 1.** Dictionaries and lexical databases

- The coverage and quality of the resources are very different. In general, the participating teams found that good resources in coverage, consistency, markup reliability, translation precision, richness of contextual information are expensive, and free resources are of poor quality. With a few remarkable exceptions, better resources seem to lead to better results.
- Of all the key issues for the future, the one quoted most often by CLEF participants was simply availability and sharing of lexical resources. This is partially explained by the points mentioned above:
  - many resources used in CLEF are developed by the participants themselves, and it is not clear whether they are accessible to other researchers or not, except for a few cases.
  - a general claim is that good resources especially dictionaries are expensive, and freely available dictionaries are poor.
  - the diversity and minimal overlapping of the resources used by CLEF participants indicate lack of awareness of which resources are available

and what is their cost benefit for CLIR tasks. Hopefully, the CLEF activities should provide an excellent forum to overcome many of these difficulties.

– Two trends seem to be consolidating:
  • The lack of parallel corpora is being overcome, in corpus-based approaches, either by mining the web  U Montreal RALI 18  or by using comparable corpora  Eurospider 12 .
  • The distinction between corpus-based and dictionary-based approaches is becoming less useful to classify CLIR systems, as they tend to merge whatever resources are available. U Montreal RALI, Eurospider, TNO Twente 18 , IRIT 11 systems are examples of this tendency.

## 2.1  i i  a ie

It is easy to imagine the features of an ideal dictionary for CLIR: wide coverage and high quality, extensive information to translate phrasal terms, translation probabilities, domain labels, rich examples of usage to permit contextual disambiguation, domain-specific extensions with coverage of named entities, semantically-related terms, clean markup . . . In general, such properties are listed by CLEF participants as features that are lacking in present resources and desirable features for future CLIR resources.

In practice, 14 different lexical resources were used by the 18 groups participating in CLEF this year  see Table 1 . They are easier to obtain and use than aligned corpora and thus their use is more generalized. The distinctive feature of the dictionaries used in CLEF is their variety:

– Under the term  dictionary  we find a whole range of lexical resources, from simple lists of bilingual word pairs to multilingual semantic databases such as EuroWordNet.
– In most cases, however, the lexical knowledge effectively used by the CLEF systems is quite simple. Definitions, domain labels, examples of usage, semantically related terms, are examples of lexical information that are hardly used by CLEF participants. Information on translation probabilities, on the other hand, is something that the dictionaries did not provide and would have been used by many teams, according to the survey.
– The size of the dictionaries used also covers a wide spectrum: from the 4000 terms in the Italian part of the Ergane dictionary  3  to the 1 million terms per language in the Termium database  9  used by the U Montreal RALI group. Sizes that differ by more than two orders of magnitude
– Some of them  four at least  are freely available in the web  two are obtainable via ELRA  4  European Language Resources Association  or LDC Linguistic Data Consortium  7  one is distributed by a publishing company Van Dale  and at least three have a restricted distribution.

– Only one dictionary is used by more than one group  Freedict in its English-French and English-Italian versions . As has already been pointed out, this is a strong indication that sharing resources  knowledge about resources is not yet a standard practice in the CLIR community.
– As could be expected, the more expensive the resource, the higher its quality and coverage and the better the results, in the opinion of the participants. Freely available dictionaries tend to be the most simple and noisy, and have lower coverage.

Table 1 does not include the GIRT thesaurus, which was provided to all participants in the specific-domain retrieval task. UC Berkeley  13 , for instance, used this social sciences bilingual thesaurus to produce a domain specific translation list  the list was used, together with a generic bilingual dictionary for uncovered words, to produce better results than an MT approach. This is an interesting result that shows that, although thesauri are not considered as lexical resources per se, they can be successfully adapted for translation purposes. The similarity thesaurus included in Table 1 was derived automatically from comparable corpora  see below .

## 2.2   lig e        a

Only 5 aligned corpora were used by CLEF participants, mainly by the JHU  APL group  see Table 2 . Most of them are domain-specific  e.g. the Hansard corpus  6  or the United Nations corpus 16   and not particularly well suited to the CLEF data. Obviously the lack of aligned corpora is a major problem for corpus-based approaches. However, the possibility of mining parallel web pages seems a promising research direction, and the corpora and the mining software developed by U Montreal  RALI  and made freely available to CLEF participants have been used by more groups than any other resource  U Montreal RALI, JHU APL  19 , IRIT, TNO  Twente .

| Resource | Languages | developer/provider | size | teams |
| --- | --- | --- | --- | --- |
| WAC (web corpus) | FR,EN, IT,GE | U. Montreal/RALI | 100MB per lang. | U. Montreal/RALI, JHU/APL, IRIT |
| web corpus | EN/NL | TNO/Twente | 3K pages | TNO/Twente |
| Hansard | EN-FR | LDC | 3M sentence pairs | JHU/APL |
| UN | EN-SP-FR | LDC | 50K EN-SP-FR docs | JHU/APL |
| JOC | EN-FR-SP-IT-GE | ELRA | 10K sentences | JHU/APL |

**Table 2.** Aligned Corpora

| Resource | Languages | developer/provider | teams |
|----------|-----------|-------------------|-------|
| babelfish.altavista.com | EN,FR,GE,IT,SP | Altavista/Systran | U. Dortmund, U. Salamanca, U.C. Berkeley |
| Systran MT system | EN-FR,GE,IT | Systran | JHU/APL |
| L&H Power Translator Pro 7.0 | EN-FR,GE,IT | Lernout & Hauspie | U.C. Berkeley |
| stemmers | EN,GE,FR IT,NL | open.muscat.com | CWI, West Group |
| stemmers (from assoc. dic.) | IT,FR,GE | U.C. Berkeley | U.C. Berkeley |
| ZPRISE stemmers | FR,GE | NIST | U. Glasgow |
| stat. stemmer | FR,GE, IT,EN | U. Chicago, U. Maryland | U. Maryland |
| Spider stemmers | FR,IT,GE | Eurospider | Eurospider |
| Automorphology | EN,GE, IT,FR | U. Chicago | U.Chicago, U. Maryland |
| morph. analyser | FIN,GE, SWE,EN | LINGSOFT | U. Tampere |
| compound splitter | NL | Twente | CWI/Twente |
| MPRO morph. anal. | GE | IAI | IAI |
| stemmers based on morph. anal. | FR,GE | ? | West Group |
| morph. analyser/ POS tagger | IT | ITC-IRST | ITC-IRST |
| grammars | EN,IT, GE,FR | IAI | IAI |

**Table 3.** NLP software

Besides parallel corpora, a German Italian French comparable corpus consisting on Swiss national news wire, provided by SDA  Schweizerische Depeschenagentur  was used to produce a multilingual similarity thesaurus  12 . The performance of this thesaurus and the availability of comparable corpora  much easier to obtain, in theory, than parallel corpora  makes such techniques worth pursuing.

Overall, it becomes clear that corpus-based approaches offer two advantages over dictionaries: a  they make it possible to obtain translation probabilities and contextual information, which are rarely present in dictionaries, and b they would provide translations adapted to the searching domain, if adequate corpora were available. The practical situation, however, is that aligned translation equivalent corpora are not widely available, and are very costly to produce. Mining the web to construct bilingual corpora and using comparable corpora appear to be promising ways to overcome such difficulties, according to CLEF results.

## 2.3          a e

Stemmers, morphological analyzers and MT systems have been widely used by the participants. The list of tools can be seen in Table 3. Some results are worth pointing out:

- The best groups in the German monolingual retrieval task all did some kind of compound analysis, confirming that morphological information  beyond crude stemming  may be crucial for languages with a rich morphology. Variants of the Porter stemmer for languages other than English are, according to CLEF participants, much less reliable than the original English stemmer.
- The best monolingual results for the other languages in the monolingual task, Italian and French, are obtained by two groups that concentrated on monolingual retrieval IRST 10 and West Group 20  and applied extensive lexical knowledge: lexical analysis and part-of-speech tagging in the case of IRST, and lexicon-based stemming in the case of West Group.
- Automatic stemming learned from corpora and association dictionaries appears as a promising alternative to stemmers a la Porter. Three groups  Chicago, UC Berkeley and Maryland  tested such techniques in CLEF 2000.
- MT systems are the only language resources that are not mainly developed by the same groups that participate in the CLEF evaluation. All the MT systems used are commercial systems: the free, online version of Systran software  babelfish , a Systran MT package and a Lernout   Hauspie version of the Power Translator.

## Language Resources in CLIR Evaluation

Systems competing in CLEF and TREC multilingual tracks usually make two kinds of contributions: the creation adaptation combination of language resources, on one hand, and the development of retrieval strategies making use of such resources, on the other hand. A problem of CLEF tasks is that they are designed to measure overall system performance. While the results indicate promising research directions, it is harder to discern which language resources worked better  because they were tested with different retrieval strategies  and it is also unclear what were the best retrieval strategies  as they were tested using different language resources . Of course, the main evaluation task should always be an overall task, because a good resource together with a good retrieval strategy will not guarantee a good overall system  for instance, the resource may not be compatible with the kind of information demanded by the retrieval algorithm . But CLEF could perhaps benefit from additional tracks measuring resources and retrieval strategies in isolation. In the rest of this section, we list some possibilities:

## 3.1  Ta    i  a Fi  e       li g al        e

A frequent approach to CLIR by CLEF participants is to translate the queries and or documents and then perform a monolingual search with an IR system of their own. A wide range of IR systems are used in CLEF, from vector model systems to n-gram language models and database systems. This produces a different monolingual retrieval baseline for each individual group, making it hard to compare the cross-language components of each system.

A possible complementary task would be to ask participants to generate queries and or document translations, and then feed a standard system e.g. the Zprise system provided on demand by NIST to participants  with monolingual runs. A substantial number of participants would probably be able to provide such translations, and the results would shed some additional light on CLEF results with respect to the translation components used.

## 3.2  Ta    i  Fi  e      e

A track in which all participants use the same set of language resources, provided by the CLEF organization, would make it possible to compare retrieval algorithms that participate in the main tracks with different resources. Ideally, CLEF could cooperate with the European Language Resources Association  ELRA  to provide a standard set of resources covering  at least  the languages included in the multilingual track. We see some obvious benefits:

- Such standard resources would enormously facilitate the participation in the multilingual track for groups that need to scale up from systems working on a specific pair of languages.
- A track of this type would highlight promising retrieval strategies that are ranked low simply because they are tested with poor resources.

What kind of resources should be made available  There is no obvious answer, in our opinion, to this question. Fixing a particular type of language resource will restrict the potential number of participating systems, while providing all kinds of resources will again make the comparison of results problematic.

From the experience of CLEF 2000, it seems reasonable to start with a multilingual dictionary covering all languages in the multilingual track, or a set of bilingual dictionaries  translation lists covering a similar functionality. In its catalogue, ELRA offers at least two resources that would fit the requirements for the CLEF 2001 multilingual track  which will include English, Spanish, German, Italian and French : One is a basic multilingual lexicon with 30000 entries per language, covering the five languages in the multilingual track  2 . This dictionary has already been evaluated for CLIR purposes in  17 . The other one is the EuroWordNet lexical database, which offers interconnected wordnets for 8 European languages in a size range  for the five languages in the multilingual task  between 20000 word meanings for German and 168000 for English  23 . EuroWordNet was used in CLEF 2000 by the Sheffield group  15 .

## 3.3  Ta    i   a  a ge   e       e ie

In a real world application, the coverage of query terms by the language resources is essential for the response of a system. Coverage, however, is poorly measured in CLEF for a majority of systems that do query translation: the whole set of queries  summing up title, description and narrative  contain only a couple of thousand term occurrences  including stop words , and the results are quite sensitive to the ability to provide translations for a few critical terms. In addition, many relevant problems in cross-language retrieval systems are under represented in current queries.

As an example, let us consider a system that makes a special effort to provide adequate translations for proper nouns. This tends to be a critical issue in the newspapers domain, where a high percentage of queries include, or even consist of, this type of terms. Figure 1 gives a snapshot of queries to the EFE newswire database that re ects the importance of proper nouns [1]. However, the set of 40 queries in CLEF 2000 only contains three names of people  Pierre Bérégovoy ,  Luc Jouret  and  Joseph di Mambro  with a total of five occurrences, less than 0.1 occurrences per query.

> ...
> Jul 26 08 33 49 2000  (joaquin garrigues walker)
> Jul 26 08 34 34 2000  (descenso and moritz)
> Jul 26 08 34 52 2000  (convencion republicana)
> Jul 26 08 38 32 2000  (baloncesto real-madrid)
> Jul 26 08 38 37 2000  (caricom)
> Jul 26 08 38 41 2000  SHA REZA PAHLEVI
> Jul 26 08 38 43 2000  SHA REZA PAHLEVI
> Jul 26 08 38 45 2000  SHA REZA PAHLEVI
> Jul 26 08 38 54 2000  (noticias internacional )
> Jul 26 08 40 18 2000  (CONCORDE)
> Jul 26 08 40 34 2000  (DOC) AND (CONCORDE)
> Jul 26 08 42 31 2000  (MANUEL FERNANDEZ ALVAREZ)
> ...

**Fig. 1.** A 9 minute snapshot of EFE news archive search service

---

[1] EFE is the provider of Spanish data for the CLEF 2001 campaign

Another example is a system that tries to find variants and translations for named entities in general. In the CLEF 2000 queries, there are approximately 31 terms  excluding geographical names  that can be associated with named entities, such as  Electroweak Theory  or  Deutsche Bundesbahn . This represents only around 0.1  of the total number of terms.

A final example can be the ability of the resources to translate certain acronyms, such as  GATT . There are 5 acronyms in the collection  excluding country names  its coverage may affect the final results, but this variation will not be representative as to how well the resources used cover acronym translation.

It is impractical to think of a substantially larger set of queries for CLEF that is representative of every possible query style or cross-language issue. However, a practical, compromise would be to use a multilingual aligned corpora  such as the UN corpus  with documents containing a summary or a descriptive title. The titles or the summaries could be used as queries to retrieve the corresponding document in a known-item retrieval task. Obviously, such a task is no closer to real world IR than CLEF or TREC ad-hoc queries, but it would produce useful complementary information on the performance consistency of systems on a large query vocabulary, and would probably leave room to test particular issues such as proper noun translation or recognition of named entities.

## Conclusions

The systems participating in CLEF 2000 provide a representative snapshot on language resources for CLIR tasks. From the reported use of such resources in CLEF, together with the results of a survey conducted on the participant groups, some interesting conclusions can be drawn:

- There is a wide variety  in type, coverage and quality  of resources used in CLIR systems, but little reuse or resource sharing. CLEF campaigns could provide a key role in improving availability, dissemination and sharing of resources.
- Corpus-based approaches, which were less popular due to the lack of parallel corpora, are successfully employing web-mined parallel corpora and comparable corpora.
- The distinction between corpus-based and dictionary-based approaches is becoming less useful to classify CLIR systems, as they tend to merge whatever resources are available.
- Richer lexical analysis seems to lead to better monolingual results in languages other than English, although the difference is only significant for German, where decompounding is essential.
- System builders devote a significant part of their efforts to resource building. Indirectly, CLEF campaigns are also evaluating such resources. We have proposed three complementary tasks that would re ect the systems resources duality in CLIR better than a single, overall retrieval task: a  a task with a

fixed monolingual IR system, fed with query translations provided by participants  b  a task with fixed resources provided by CLEF  c  a task with a large set of queries to provide a significant number of cases for relevant CLIR problems  e.g. proper nouns or vocabulary coverage .

## Acknowledgements

I am indebted to Carol Peters and Felisa Verdejo for their valuable comments on earlier versions of this paper, and to Manuel Fuentes for providing the EFE query log.

## References

1   Babel Fish Corporation.        a el sh c m
2   Basic multilingual le icon (MEMODATA).
            icp grenet  r  E        cata te t_ et html   asmulle
3   Ergane multi-lingual dictionary.          tra lang c m Ergane
4   European Language Resources Association.          icp grenet  r  E
5   Freedict dictionaries.         ree ict c m
6   Hansard French/English.         l c upenn e u   atal g   D          html
7   Linguistic Data Consortium (LDC).         l c upenn e u.
8   Omsee - the Open Source Search Engine (formerly Muscat).          msee c m
9   Termium.        termiumplus  ureau elatra ucti n gc ca
10  Nicola Bertoldi and Marcello Federico. Italian te t retrieval for CLEF 2000 at ITC-IRST. In *this   lume.* 2001.
11  Mohand Boughanem and Nawel Nassr. Mercure at CLEF 1. In *this    lume.* 2001.
12  Martin Braschler and Peter Schäuble. E periments with the Eurospider retrieval system for clef 2000. In *this    lume.* 2001.
13  Fredric C. Gey, Hailing Jiang, Vivien Petras, and Aitao Chen. Cross-language retrieval for the CLEF collections - comparing multiple methods of retrieval. In *this   lume.* 2001.
14  John Goldsmith, Derrick Higgins, and Svetlana Soglasnova. Automatic language-specific stemming in information retrieval. In *this    lume.* 2001.
15  Tim Gollins and Mark Sanderson. Sheffield University CLEF 2000. In *this   lume.* 2001.
16  David Gra . Overview of the UN parallel te t corpus.
            l c upenn e u rea me_ les un rea me html 1994.
17  G. Grefenstette. The problem of cross-language information retrieval. In   r ss   anguage In  rmati n   etrie al. Kluwer AP, 1998.
18  Djoerd Hiemstra, Wessel Kraaij, Renée Pohlmann, and Thijs Westerveld. Translation resources, merging strategies and relevance feedback for cross-language information retrieval. In *this    lume.* 2001.
19  Paul McNamee, James Mayfield, and Christine Piatko. A language-independent approach to european te t retrieval. In *this    lume.* 2001.
20  Isabelle Moulinier, J. Andrew McCulloh, and Elizabeth Lund. West Group at CLEF 2000  Non-english monolingual retrieval. In *this    lume.* 2001.
21  Jian-Yun Nie, Michel Simard, and George Foster. Multilingual information retrieval based on parallel te ts from the web. In *this    lume.* 2001.

22  Douglas W. Oard, Gina-Anne Levow, and Clara Cabezas. CLEF e periments at the University of Maryland  statistical stemming and back-o  translation strategies. In *this   lume*. 2001.
23  P. Vossen. *Eur    r  et a multilingual  ata ase  ith le ical semantic net   r s.* Kluwer Academic Publishers, 1998.

# The Domain-Specific Task of CLEF - Specific Evaluation Strategies in Cross-Language Information Retrieval

Michael Kluck[1] and Fredric C. Gey[2]

[1] InformationsZentrum Sozialwissenschaften Bonn
kluck@bonn.iz-soz.de
[2] UC Data Archive & Technical Assistance
University of California, Berkeley, CA 94720 USA
gey@ucdata.berkeley.edu

**Abstract.** This paper describes the domain-specific cross-language information retrieval (CLIR) task of CLEF, why and how it is important and how it di ers from general cross-language retrieval problem associated with the general CLEF collections. The inclusion of a domain-specific document collection and topics has both advantages and disadvantages

## 1   Introduction

For the past decade, the trend in information retrieval test-collection development and evaluation has been toward general, domain-independent text such as newswire information. This trend has been fostered by the needs of intelligence agencies and the non-specific nature of the World Wide Web and its indexing challenges. The documents in these collections  and in the general CLEF collections  contain information of non-specific nature and therefore could potentially be judged by anyone with good general knowledge.

Critics of this strategy believe that the tests are not sufficient to solve the problems of more domain-oriented data collections and topics. Particularly for cross-language information retrieval, we may have a vocabulary disconnect problem since the vocabulary for a specific area may not exist in a Machine Translation  MT  system used to translate queries or documents. Indeed, the vocabulary may have been redefined in a specific domain to mean something quite different from its general meaning. The rationale of the inclusion of domain specific collections into the tests is to test retrieval systems on another type of document collection, serving a different kind of information need. The information provided by these domain specific documents is far more targeted than news stories. Moreover, the documents contain quite specific terminology related to the respective domain. The hypothesis to be tested is whether domain-specific enhancements to information retrieval provide  statistically significant  improvement in performance over general information retrieval approaches.

C. Peters (Ed.): CLEF 2000, LNCS 2069, pp. 4 –56, 2001.
© Springer-Verlag Berlin Heidelberg 2001

Information retrieval has a rich history of test collections, beginning with Cranfield, which arose out of the desire to improve and enhance search of scientific and technical literature. The GIRT collections defined below of the TREC-8 evaluation and of this first CLEF campaign provide an opportunity for IR to return to its roots and to illuminate those particular research problems and specific approaches associated with domain-specific retrieval. Other recent examples of domain specific collections are the OHSUMED collection 10 for the medical domain and the NTCIR collection 12 for science and engineering. The OHSUMED collection has been explored for its potential in query expansion 13, 11 and was utilized in the filtering track of the TREC-9 conference see http: trec.nist.gov . The NTCIR collection is the first major test collection in Japanese and the NTCIR evaluations have provided the first large-scale test of Japanese-English crosss language information retrieval.

## 2    Advantages and Disadvantages of Domain Specific CLIR

A domain-specific language requires appropriate indexing and retrieval systems. Recent results clearly show this difficulty of differentiating between domain-specific in this case: sociological terms and common language terms: words used in sociology are common words that are also in general use, such as community or immigrant 9 . In many cases there exists a clear difference between the scientific meaning and the common meaning. Furthermore, there are often considerable difference between scientific terms when used in different domains, owing to different connotations, theories, political implications, ethical convictions, and so on. This means that it can be more difficult to use automatically generated terms and queries for retrieval. For example, Ballesteros and Croft 1 have noted, for a dictionary-based cross-language query system: queries containing domain-specific terminology which is not found in general dictionaries were shown to suffer an additional loss in performance . In some discipline for instance in biology different terminologies have evolved in quite narrow subfields as Chen at al. 3 have shown for the research dealing with the species of worms and ies and their diverging terminology.

For several domains Haas 9 has carried out in-depth-research and stated: T tests between discipline pairs showed that physics, electrical engineering, and biology had significantly more domain terms in sequences than history, psychology, and sociology ... the domains with more term sequences are those which may be considered the hard sciences, while those with more isolated domain terms tend to be the social sciences and humanities.

Nevertheless, domain specific test collections offer new possibilities for the testing of retrieval systems as they allow the domain specific adjustment of the system design and the test of general solutions for specific areas of usage. Developers of domain specific CLIR systems need to be able to tune their systems to meet the specific needs of a more targeted user group.

The users of domain specific collections are typically interested in the completeness of coverage. They may not be satisfied with finding just some relevant documents from a collection. For these users the situation of too much overlap between the relevant documents within the result sets of the different evaluated systems is much more important and has to be solved.

## Domain Specific Evaluation Procedures

Domain-specificity has consequences not only for the data but also for the topic creation and assessment processes. Separate specific topics have to be created because the data are very different from that found in newspapers or newswires. The GIRT documents treat more long-term societal or scientific problems in an in-depth manner  current problems or popular events  as they are represented in news articles  are dealt with after some time lag. Nevertheless, the TREC CLEF domain-specific task attempted to cover German newswire and newspaper articles as well as the GIRT collection. Thus topics were developed which combined both general and domain specific characteristics. It proved to be challenging to discover topics which would retrieve news stories as well as scientific articles.

The topic developers must be familiar with the specific domain as well as the respective language in which the topic has been created or into which the topic is to be translated. The same is true for the assessors  they must have domain related qualifications and sufficient language skills to develop the relevance judgements.

Therefore each domain specific sub-task needs its own group of topic developers and relevance assessors in all languages used for the sub-task. Finally the systems being tested must be able to adjust general principles for retrieval systems to the domain-specific area.

## The GIRT Domain-Specific Social Science Test Collection

The TREC-7, TREC-8 and CLEF 2000 evaluations have offered a domain specific subtask and collection for CLIR in addition to the generally used collections. The test collection for this domain specific subtask is called GIRT  German Information Retrieval Test database  and comes from the social sciences. It has been used in several German tests of retrieval systems  6, 14, 2  The GIRT collection was made available for research purposes by the InformationsZentrum Sozialwissenschaften  IZ    German Social Sciences Information Centre , Bonn. For pre-test research by the IZ and the University of Konstanz a first version, the GIRT1 collection contained about 13,000 documents. For the TREC7 and TREC8 evaluations, the GIRT2 collection was offered which included GIRT1 supplemented with additional documents and contained about 38,000 documents. In the CLEF2000 campaign the GIRT3 collection was used which included the GIRT2 data and additional sampled documents for a total of about 76,000 documents. Figure 1 presents a sample document from the GIRT3 collection.

```
<DOCNO>19940100925</DOCNO>
<TITLE>Psychisch kranke Mitarbeiter in Betrieben : die Sichtweise der betrieblichen
   Helfer</TITLE>
<TITLE-ENG>Mentally ill employees in companies : the viewpoint of company assistants</TITLE-
   ENG>
<AUTHOR>Schubert, Andreas</AUTHOR>
<PUBLICATION-YEAR>1988</PUBLICATION-YEAR>
<LANGUAGE>DE</LANGUAGE>
<CONTROLLED-TERM>psychische Krankheit,Mitarbeiter,Betrieb,Helfer,soziales
   Netzwerk,Bezugsperson,Integration</CONTROLLED-TERM>
<CLASSIFICATION>Industriesoziologie, Betriebssoziologie, Arbeitssoziologie, industrielle
   Beziehungen,soziale Probleme,Sozialpolitik</CLASSIFICATION>
<TEXT>"Ausgehend von der äußerst problematischen Situation psychisch kranker und
   behinderter Menschen auf dem allgemeinen Arbeitsmarkt wird die besondere Bedeutung
   innerbetrieblicher Hilfen dargestellt. Dazu wird modellhaft die Situation eines Mitarbeiters mit
   'seelischen Problemen' in einem Betrieb skizziert, um somit die potentiellen Bezugspersonen
   und damit ein mögliches innerbetriebliches soziales Netzwerk zu kennzeichnen. Die
   Fragestellung der dargestellten Untersuchung ist, inwieweit die per Gesetz zur Unterstützung
   Behinderter und damit auch psychisch behinderter Mitarbeiter verpflichteten 'betrieblicher
   Helfer', diese Funktion tatsächlich wahrnehmen, d.h. inwieweit das Hilfspotential dieser
   Gruppe sich umsetzt in ein für den Betroffenen erfahrbares innerbetriebliches soziales
   Netzwerk. Dazu werden die Ergebnisse einer schriftlichen Befragung von 144 betrieblichen
   Helfern referiert. Als Fazit der Untersuchung muß von einem relativ geringen Kenntnisstand
   betrieblicher Helfer bzgl. der Auswirkungen psychischer Krankheit ausgegangen werden, von
   negativen Einschätzungen der Leistungs- und Integrationsmöglichkeiten psychisch
   behinderter Mitarbeiter und von einer starken Tendenz dieser Gruppe, die Problematik und
   damit die Betroffenen auszugrenzen oder, bei betriebsinternen Vorfällen, an betriebliche
   Entscheidungsträger wie direkte Vorgesetzte, Personal- und Betriebsleitung 'abzuschieben'.
   Da häufig weder interne noch externe Fachleute hinzugezogen werden, ist der Aufbau eines
   innerbetrieblichen Netzwerkes als sehr schwierig einzuschätzen. Positive Beispiele belegen
   allerdings die Integrationsmöglichkeiten für psychisch Behinderte auch in 'normalen'
   Betrieben." (Autorenreferat)</TEXT>
<TEXT-ENG>"Because of the extremly problematical situation of psychologically disturbed
   people so far as the job market is concerned this paper stresses the importance of help inside
   the concerns. In order to show potential sources of help and thus a possible supportive
   network inside a firm a model case of a worker with 'psychological problems' is sketched.
   This investigation was aimed at discovering how far the legal obligation to assist handicapped
   people inside industrial concerns, and thus also psychologically handicapped workers, is
   actually fulfilled by the 'industrial helpers', i.e. how far the potential help offered by these
```

**Fig. 1.** GIRT Sample document English text truncated

The GIRT data have been collected from two German databases offered commercially by the IZ via traditional information providers  STN International, GBI, DIMDI  and on CD-ROM  WISO III : FORIS  descriptions of social sciences current research projects in the German speaking countries , and SOLIS  references of social sciences literature originated in German speaking countries, containing journal articles, monographs, articles in collections, scientific reports, dissertations . The FORIS database contains about 35,000 documents on current and finished research projects of the last ten years. As projects are living objects the documents are often changed  thus, about 6,000 documents are changed or newly entered each year. SOLIS contains more than 250,000 documents with a yearly addition of about 10,000 documents.

The GIRT3 data contain selected bibliographical information  author, language of the document, publication year , as well as additional information elements describing the content of the documents: controlled indexing terms, free terms, classification texts, and abstracts  TEXT  - all in German  GIRT1 and GIRT2 data contained some other fields . Besides the German information there are English translations of the titles  for 71  of the documents  available. For some documents  about 8    there are also English translations of the abstracts  TEXT-ENG . One exception is the TITLE field where the original title of the document is stored: in some cases the original title has already been English, thus, no English translation has been necessary and the field TITLE-ENG is missing, although the title is in fact English. The information elements of the GIRT collection are quite similar to those of the OHSUMED collection which has been developed by William Hersh  10  for the medical domain, but that test collection is bigger  348,566 documents . The OHSUMED fields are: title, abstract, controlled indexing term  MeSH , author, source, publication type.

Most of the GIRT3 documents have German abstracts  96   of the documents , some have English abstracts  8    . For the 76,128 documents 755,333 controlled terms have been assigned, meaning, on average, each document has nearly 10 indexing terms. Some documents  nearly 9    have free terms assigned which are only given by the indexing staff of the IZ to make proposals for new terms to be included in the thesaurus. The documents have on average two classifications assigned to each of them. The indexing rules allow assignment of one main classification, as well as one or more additional classifications if other  sub- areas are treated in the document. The average number of authors for each document is nearly two. The average document size of the GIRT documents is about 2 KB.

| Field label | Occurrences of field | percent in GIRT3 docs | Avg. of entries per doc |
|---|---|---|---|
| DOC | 76,128 | 100.00 | 1.00 |
| DOCNO | 76,128 | 100.00 | 1.00 |
| LANGUAGE | 76,128 | 100.00 | 1.00 |
| PUBLICATION YEAR | 76,128 | 100.00 | 1.00 |
| TITLE | 76,128 | 100.00 | 1.00 |
| TITLE-ENG | 54,275 | 71.29 | - |
| TEXT | 73,291 | 96.27 | - |
| TEXT-ENG | 6,063 | 7.96 | - |
| CONTROLLED-TERM | 755,333 | - | 9.92 |
| FREE-TERM | 6,588 | - | 0.09 |
| CLASSIFICATION | 169,064 | - | 2.22 |
| AUTHOR | 126,322 | - | 1.66 |

**Table 1.** Statistics of the GIRT3 data collection

The GIRT multilingual thesaurus  German-English , based on the Thesaurus for the Social Sciences  4  provides the vocabulary source for the indexing terms within CLEF  see Figure 2 . A Russian translation of the German thesaurus is also available. The German-English thesaurus has about 10,800 entries, of which 7,150 are descriptors and 3,650 non-descriptors. For each German descriptor

there is an English or Russian equivalent. The German non-descriptors have
been translated into English in nearly every case, but this is not true for the
Russian word list. There are smaller differences to the trilingual German-English-
Russian word list, because it was completed earlier 1996 than the latest version
of the Thesaurus 1999 . Thus, English or Russian indexing terms could be used
for retrieval purposes by matching to the equivalent German terms from the
respective version of the thesaurus.

```
<entry>
  <german>Absatzpolitik</german>
  <related-concept>ABSATZPOLITIK</related-concept>
  <broader-term>Unternehmenspolitik</broader-term>
  <narrower-term>Werbung</narrower-term>
  <narrower-term>Produktgestaltung</narrower-term>
  <narrower-term>Preispolitik</narrower-term>
  <english>sales policy</english>
</entry>
```

**Fig. 2.** GIRT Thesaurus Entry

The first GIRT collection  GIRT1 , which was utilized for the pre-tests, contained a subset of the databases FORIS and SOLIS with about 13,000 documents
which were restricted to the publication years 1987-1996 and to the topical areas
of  sociology of work , women studies  and  migration and ethnical minorities
 with some additional articles without topical restrictions from two German top
journals on sociology being published in this time-span . This topical restriction
was obtained by choosing the appropriate classification codes as search criteria.
The GIRT2 collection - offered in TREC7 and TREC8 - contained a subset of
the databases FORIS and SOLIS, which included the GIRT1 data, followed the
same topical restrictions, but was enlarged to the publication years 1978-1996.
This led to a specific topicality of the data, which had to be considered during
the topic development process and restricted the possibilities of selecting topics. The distribution of descriptors and even of the words within the documents
was also affected by these topical restrictions. The GIRT3 collection - offered in
the CLEF2000 campaign - has been broadened to all documents in this time-
span regardless of their topics. Thus, this collection is an unbiased representative
sample of documents in German social sciences between 1978 and 1996.

## Experiences and Opportunities in TREC CLEF with Domain Specific CLIR

Although specific terminology and vocabularies must be changed for each new
domain, this is more than compensated for by features which can be exploited
in domain-specific cross-language information retrieval. Existing domain-related

```
- <top>
    <num>girt002</num>
    <E-title>Kids and Computer Games</E-title>
    <E-desc>How are computer games used by children?</E-desc>
    <E-narr>Find information on how children use computer games and on the consequences of such
        use.</E-narr>
  </top>
- <top>
    <num>girt002</num>
    <G-title>Kinder und Computerspiele</G-title>
    <G-desc>Was gibt es über die Nutzung von Computerspielen durch Kinder?</G-desc>
    <G-narr>Alle Informationen über die Benutzung und Auswirkung der Nutzung von
        Computerspielen durch Kinder sind von Interesse. Ebenso sind Untersuchungen über die
        Gründe von Gewalt sowie Programme und Maßnahmen gegen Gewalt relevant.</G-narr>
  </top>
```

**Fig. 3.** GIRT Topic 002    Children and computer games

vocabularies or thesauri can be utilized to reduce ambiguity of search and increase precision of the results. For multilingual thesauri an additional benefit accrues from using them as translation tools because the related term pairs of languages are available. Use of the MESH multilingual thesaurus for CLIR was explored by Eichmann Ruiz and Srinivasan 5  for the OHSUMED collection.

Additional aids are given if there exist translated parts of the documents  often the case for scientific literature, where English titles are frequently available for documents in other languages . This can allow a direct search against the translated document parts. The same advantage arises within existing document structures where the use of the specific meaning of different information elements allows a targeted search  i.e. if an author field exists, it possible to distinguish between a person as subject of an article or as the author of it .

Thus far the GIRT collections have received limited attention by groups engaged in cross-language information retrieval. At TREC-8 there were two groups participating and at CLEF three groups participated and one of those submitted only a monolingual entry. The best monolingual entry was submitted by the Xerox European Research Centre, while the cross-language entries came from the Berkeley Group 7  and the Dortmund Group 8 .

## Conclusion

This paper has discussed the domain-specific retrieval task at CLEF. The GIRT collection, oriented toward the social science domain, offers new opportunities in exploring cross-language information retrieval for specialized domains. The specific enhancements available with the GIRT collection are:

- a collection indexed manually to a controlled vocabulary
- bi-lingual titles  German and English  for almost all documents
- a hierarchical thesaurus of the controlled vocabulary
- multilingual translations of the thesaurus  German, English, Russian

The multilingual thesaurus can be utilized as a vocabulary source for query translation and as a starting point for query expansion to enhance cross-language retrieval. Because each document is manually assigned, on average, by ten controlled vocabulary terms, the collection also offers the opportunity for research into multi-class text categorization.

# References

1  Lisa Ballesteros and W. Bruce Croft. Statistical methods for cross-language information retrieval. In Gregory Gre enstette, editor, *r ss anguage In rmati n etrie al*, pages 21 40. Kluwer, 1998.
2  Gisbert Binder, Matthias Stahl, and Lothar Faulborn. Vergleichsuntersuchung MESSENGER - FULCRUM projektbericht available at http //www.bonn.iz-soz.de/publications/series/working-papers/ab18.pdf. In *I r eits ericht r nn*, 2000.
3  Hsinchun Chen, Joanne Martinez, Tobun Ng, and Bruce Schatz. A concept space approach to addressing the vocabulary problem in scientific information retrieval An e periment on the worm community system. In *urnal the merican S ciet r In rmati n Science*, volume 48 (1), pages 17 31, 1997.
4  Hannelore Schott (ed.). *hesaurus r the S cial Sciences l German English l English German E iti n* . InformationsZentrum Sozialwissenschaften Bonn, 2000.
5  David Eichmann, Miguel Ruiz, and Padmini Srinivasan. Cross-language information retrieval with the UMLS metathesaurus. In *W B Croft A Mo at C J van Rijsbergen R Wilkinson and J Zobel, editors, r cee ings the st nnual In ternati nal SIGI n erence n esearch an De el pment in In rmati n etrie al el urne ustralia*, pages 72 80, August 1998.
6  Elisabeth Frisch and Michael Kluck. Pretest zum projekt german inde ing and retrieval testdatabase (GIRT) unter anwendung der retrievalsysteme messenger und freewaissf. In *I r eits ericht r nn*, 1997.
7  Fredric Gey, Hailing Jiang, Vivien Petras, and Aitao Chen. Cross-language retrieval for the CLEF collections - comparing multiple methods of retrieval. In *this lume*.
8  Norbert Govert. Bilingual information retrieval with HyREX and internet translation services. In *this lume*.
9  Stephanie W. Haas. Disciplinary variation in automatic sublanguage term identification. In *urnal merican S ciet r In rmati n Science*, volume 48, pages 67 79, 1997.
10  William Hersh, Chris Buckley, TJ Leone, and David Hickman. OHSUMED An interactive retrieval eavaluation and new large test collection for research. In W. Bruce Croft and C.J. van Rijsbergen, editors, *r cee ings SIGI the Se enteenth nnual Internati nal SIGI n erence n esearch an De el pment in In rmati n etrie al*, pages 192 201, 1994.
11  William Hersh, Susan Price, and Larry Donohoe. Assessing thesaurus-based query e pansion using the umls thesaurus. In *r cee ings the nnual I Fall S mp sium*, pages 344 348, 2000.
12  Noriko Kando, Kazuko Kuriyama, Toshihiko Nozue, Koji Eguchi, Hiroyuki Kato, and Souichiro Hidaka. Overview of IR tasks at the first NTCIR workshop. In Noriko Kando and Toshihiko Nozue, editors, *he First I r sh p n*

   *apanese  e t  etrie al an   erm  ec gniti n*            *apan*, pages 11 22,
   September 1999.

13  Padmini Srinivasan.   uery e pansion and MEDLINE. In *In  rmati n  r cessing*
    *an   anagement*, volume 32(4), pages 431 443, 1996.

14  Christa Womser-Hacker(ed.)  et al.      r e t urs *In  rmati nsmanagement*
    *Durch uhrung einer E aluierungsstu ie   ergleich  er In  rmati n  etrie al*
    *S steme I S D   ES I      S II  e tE ten er   ni ersit      nstan .*
    1998.

# Evaluating Interactive
# Cross-Language Information Retrieval:
# Document Selection

Douglas W. Oard

Human Computer Interaction Laboratory
College of Information Studies and
Institute for Advanced Computer Studies
University of Maryland, College Park, MD 20742, USA
oard@glue.umd.edu.edu,
http://www.glue.umd.edu/~oard/

**Abstract.** The problem of finding documents that are written in a language that the searcher cannot read is perhaps the most challenging application of Cross-Language Information Retrieval (CLIR) technology. The first Cross-Language Evaluation Forum (CLEF) provided an e cellent venue for assessing the performance of automated CLIR techniques, but little is known about how searchers and systems might interact to achieve better cross-language search results than automated systems alone can provide. This paper e plores the question of how interactive approaches to CLIR might be evaluated, suggesting an initial focus on evaluation of interactive document selection. Important evaluation issues are identified, the structure of an interactive CLEF evaluation is proposed, and the key research communities that could be brought together by such an evaluation are introduced.

## 1 Introduction

Cross-language information retrieval  CLIR  has somewhat uncharitably been referred to as  the problem of finding people documents that they cannot read.  Of course, this is not strictly true. For example, multilingual searchers might want to issue a single query to a multilingual collection, or searchers with a limited active vocabulary  but good reading comprehension  in a second language might prefer to issue queries in their most  uent language. In this paper, however, we focus on the most challenging case  when the searcher cannot read the document language at all.

Before focusing on evaluation, it might be useful to say a few words about why anyone might want to find a document that they cannot read. The most straightforward answer, and the one that we will focus on here, is that after finding the document they could somehow obtain a translation that is adequate to support their intended use of the document  e.g., learning from it, summarizing it, or quoting from it . CLIR and translation clearly have a symbiotic

C. Peters (Ed.): CLEF 2000, LNCS 2069, pp. 57–71, 2001.
© Springer-Verlag Berlin Heidelberg 2001

relationship translation makes CLIR more useful, and CLIR makes translation more useful if you never find a document that you cannot read, why would you need translation .

In the research literature, it has become common to implicitly treat CLIR as a task to be accomplished by a machine. Information retrieval is a challenging problem, however, and many applications require better performance than machines alone can provide. In such cases, the only practical approach is to develop systems in which humans and machines interact to achieve better results than a machine can produce alone. A simple example from monolingual retrieval serves to illustrate this point. The top-ranked two documents that result from a Google search for interactive CLIR are about interactive products developed by the Council on Library and Information Resources. But an interactive searcher can easily recognize from the brief summaries that the next few documents in the ranked list use the search terms in the same manner as this paper. In this case, a system that might be judged a failure if used in a fully automatic top-document mode actually turns out to be quite useful when used as the automatic portion of a human-machine system.

The process by which searchers interact with information systems to find documents has been extensively studied for an excellent overview, see 3 . Essentially, there are two key points at which the searcher and the system interact: query formulation and document selection. Query formulation is a complex cognitive process in which searchers apply three kinds of knowledge what they think they want, what they think the information system can do, and what they think the document collection being searched contains to develop a query. The query formulation process is typically iterative, with searchers learning about the collection and the system, and often about what it is that they really wanted to know, by posing queries and examining retrieval results. Ultimately we must study the query formulation process in a cross-language retrieval environment if we are to design systems that effectively support real information seeking behaviors. But the Cross-Language Evaluation Forum CLEF is probably not the right venue for such a study, in part because the open-ended nature of the query formulation process might make it difficult to agree on a sharp focus for quantitative evaluation in the near term.

Evaluation of cross-language document selection seems like a more straightforward initial step. Interactive document selection is essentially a manual detection problem given the documents that are nominated by the system as being of possible interest, the searcher must recognize which documents are truly of interest. Modern information retrieval systems typically present a ranked list that contains summary information for each document e.g., title, date, source and a brief extract and typically also provide on-demand access to the full text of one document at a time. In the cross-language case, we assume that both the summary information and the full text are presented to the searcher in the form of automatically generated translations a process typically referred to as machine translation. [1] Evaluation of document selection seems to be well suited to the CLEF framework because the  ground truth  needed for the evaluation  identifying which documents *should have* been selected  can be determined using the same pooled relevance assessment methodology that is used in the present evaluation of fully automatic systems

Focusing on interactive CLIR would not actually be as a radical departure for CLEF as it might first appear. As Section 2 explains, the principal CLEF evaluation measure  mean average precision  is actually designed to model the automatic component of an interactive search process, at least when used in a monolingual context. Section 3 extends that analysis to include the effect of document selection, concluding that a focused investigation of the cross-language document selection problem is warranted. Sections 4 and 5 then sketch out the broad contours of what an interactive CLEF evaluation with such a focus might look like. Finally, Section 6 addresses the question of whether the necessary research base exists to justify evaluation of interactive CLIR by identifying some key research communities that are well positioned to contribute to the development of this technology.

## 2    Deconstructing Mean Average Precision

Two types of measures are commonly used in evaluations of cross-language information retrieval effectiveness: ranked retrieval measures and set-based retrieval measures. In the translingual topic tracking task of the Topic Detection and Tracking evaluation, a set based measure  detection error cost  is used. But ranked retrieval measures are reported far more commonly, having been adopted for the cross-language retrieval tasks in CLEF, TREC and NTCIR. The `trec_ev`  software used in all three evaluations produces several useful ranked retrieval measures, but comparisons between systems are most often based on the mean uninterpolated average precision  $MAP$  measure. $MAP$ is defined as:

$$MAP \quad E_i \, E_j \; \frac{j}{r \; i,j}$$

where $E_i$  is the sample expectation over a set of queries, $E_j$  is the sample expectation over the documents that are relevant to query $i$, and $r \; i,j$  is the rank of the $j^{th}$ relevant document for query $i$.

The MAP measure has a number of desirable characteristics. For example, improvement in precision at any value of recall or in recall at any value of precision will result in a corresponding improvement in MAP. Since MAP is so widely reported, it is worth taking a moment to consider what process the computation actually models. One way to think of MAP is as a measure of effectiveness for the one-pass interactive retrieval process shown in Figure 1 in which:

---

[1] Note that the subsequent translation step  translation to support the ultimate use of the document  may or may not be accomplished using machine translation, depending on the degree of  uency that is required.

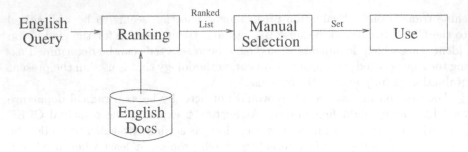

**Fig. 1.** A one-pass monolingual search process.

1. The searcher creates a query in a manner similar to those over which the outer expectation is computed.
2. The system computes a ranked list in a way that seeks to place the topically relevant documents as close to the top of the list as is possible, given the available evidence query terms, document terms, embedded knowledge of language characteristics such as stemming, ... .
3. The searcher starts at the top of the list and examines each document and or summaries of those documents until they are satisfied.
4. The searcher becomes satisfied after finding some number of relevant documents, but we have no *a priori* knowledge of how many relevant documents it will take to satisfy the searcher. Note that here we implicitly assume that every document is either relevant or it is not in other words, we don't account for differences in the perceived degree of relevance , and that relevance assessments are independent i.e., having seen one document does not change the searcher's opinion of the relevance of another relevant document .
5. The searcher's degree of satisfaction is related to the number of documents that they need to examine before finding the desired number of relevant documents.

Although actual interactive search sessions often include activities such as learning and iterative query reformulation that are not modeled by this simple process, it seems reasonable to expect that searchers would prefer systems which perform better by this measure over systems that don't perform as well.

## Modeling the Cross-Language Retrieval Process

One striking feature of the process described above is that we have implicitly assumed that the searcher is able to recognize relevant documents when they see them. Although there will undoubtedly be cases when a searcher either overlooks a relevant document or initially believes a document to be relevant but later decides otherwise, modeling the searcher as a perfect detector is not an unreasonable assumption when the documents are written in a language that the searcher can read. If the documents are written in a language that the searcher can not read, the final three steps above could be modified as illustrated in Figure 2 to:

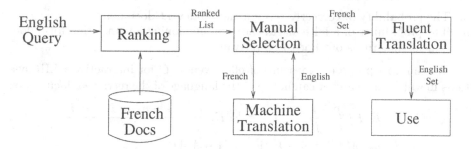

**Fig. 2.** A one-pass cross-language search process for searchers who cannot read French.

**3a.** The searcher starts at the top of the list and examines a   a       a i **all**
           e     a   la i   of each document               a     a   la i     of
those documents  until they are satisfied.
**4.a** The searcher becomes satisfied after identifying a number of      **ibl   el**
   e a       documents that    e  **belie e i**        ie    to assure that they have
found the desired number of relevant documents, but we have no *a priori* knowledge of how many relevant documents it will take to satisfy the searcher. [2]
**5a.** The searcher commissions       e      a   la i            e   ele  e
     e   , and the searcher's degree of satisfaction is related to both the number of documents that they needed to examine and the fraction of the translated documents that actually turn out to be relevant.[3]

Of course, this is only one of many ways in which a cross-language retrieval system might be used.[4] But it does seem to represent at least one way in which a cross-language retrieval system might actually be employed, and it does so in a way that retains a clear relationship to the MAP measure that is already in widespread use. The actual outcome of the process depends on two factors:

– The degree to which the automatically produced translations support the searcher's task of recognizing possibly relevant documents.

---

[2] To retain a comparable form for the formula, it is also necessary to assume that the last document selected by the searcher actually happens to be relevant.

[3] This formulation does not e plicitly recognize that the process may ultimately yield far too many or far too few relevant documents. If too few result, the searcher can proceed further down the list, commissioning more translations. If too many result, the searcher can adopt a more conservative strategy ne t time.

[4] An alternative process would be to begin at the top of the list and commission a uent human translation of one document at a time, only proceeding to another document after e amining the previous one.

– The searcher's propensity to select documents as being possibly relevant in the presence of uncertainty.

We model the combined effect of these factors using two parameters:

$p_r$ The probability of correctly recognizing a relevant document.

$p_f$ The probability of a false alarm i.e., commissioning a translation for a document that turns out not to be relevant .

We can now propose a measure of effectiveness $C$ for interactive CLIR systems in which the searcher can not read the language of the retrieved documents:

$$ C \quad k \cdot E_i \, E_j \, \frac{p_r \cdot j}{r \; i,j} \quad 1 - k \; E_i \, E_j \, \frac{j \quad 1 - p_f \quad r \; i,j \; - j}{r \; i,j} $$
$$ k \cdot p_r \cdot MAP \quad 1 - k \; 1 - p_f \; 1 - MAP $$

where the free parameter $k \in 0,1$ re ects the relative importance to the searcher of limiting the number of examined documents the first term and of limiting the translation of non-relevant documents the second term .[5] The first term re ects a straightforward adjustment to the formula for mean average precision to incorporate $p_r$. In the second term, success is achieved if the document is actually relevant $j$ or if the document is not relevant $r \; i,j \; - j$ and is not selected by the searcher for translation $1 - p_f$ .[6] In practice, we expect one or the other term to dominate this measure. When the machine translation that is already being produced for use in the interface will suffice for the ultimate use of any document, $k \approx 1$, so:

$$ C \approx p_r \cdot MAP $$

By contrast, when human translation is needed to achieve adequate uency for the intended use, we would expect $k \approx 0$, making the second term dominant:

$$ C \approx 1 - p_f \; 1 - MAP $$

In either case, it is clear that maximizing $MAP$ is desirable. When machine translation can adequately support the intended use of the documents, the factor that captures the searcher's contribution to the retrieval process is $p_r$ which should be as large as possible . By contrast, when human translation is necessary, the factor that captures the searcher's contribution is $p_f$ which should be as small as possible . This analysis suggests three possible goals for an evaluation campaign:

$MAP$. This has been the traditional focus of the CLIR evaluations at TREC, NTCIR and CLEF. Improvements in $MAP$ can benefit a broad range of applications, but with 70-85 of monolingual $MAP$ now being routinely reported in the CLIR literature, shifting some of the focus to other factors would be appropriate.

---

[5] The linear combination oversimplifies the situation somewhat, and is best thought of here as a presentation device rather than as an accurate model of value.

[6] For notational simplicity, $p_r$ and $p_f$ have been treated as if they are independent of $i$ and $j$.

$p_r$. A focus on $p_r$ is appropriate when the cost of finding documents dominates the total cost, as would be the case when present fully automatic machine translation technology produces sufficiently uent translations.

$p_f$. A focus on $p_f$ is appropriate when the cost of obtaining a translations that are suitable for the intended use dominates the total cost, as would be the case when substantial human involvement in the translation process is required. Although it may appear that $p_f$   0 could be achieved by simply never commissioning a translation, such a strategy would be counterproductive since no relevant documents would ever be translated. The searcher's goal in this case must therefore be to achieve an *adequate* value for $p_r$ while minimizing $p_f$.

The second and third of these goals seem equally attractive, since both model realistic applications. The next section explores the design of an evaluation framework that would be sufficiently  exible to accommodate either focus.

## Evaluating Document Selection

Although there has not yet been any coordinated effort to evaluate cross-language document selection, we are aware of three reported user study results that have explored aspects of the problem. In one, Oard and Resnik adopted a classification paradigm to evaluate browsing effectiveness in cross-language applications, finding that a simple gloss translation approach allowed users to outperform a Naive Bayes classifier  8 . In the second, Ogden et al., evaluated a language-independent thumbnail representation for the TREC-7 interactive track, finding that the use of thumbnail representations resulted in even better instance recall at 20 documents than was achieved using English document titles  9 . Finally, Oard, et al. described an experiment design at TREC-9 in which documents judged by the searcher as relevant were moved higher in the ranked list and documents judged as not relevant were moved lower  7 . They reported that the results of a small pilot study were inconclusive. All three of these evaluation approaches re ect the effect of $p_r$ and $p_f$ in a single measure, but they each exploit an existing evaluation paradigm that limits the degree of insight that can be obtained. Four questions must be considered if we are to evaluate an interactive component of a cross-language retrieval system in a way that re ects a vision of how that system might actually be used:

- What process do we wish to model
- What independent variable s   causes  do we wish to consider
- What dependent variable s   effects  do we wish to understand
- How should the measure s  of effectiveness be computed

Two processes have been modeled in the Text Retrieval Conference  TREC interactive track evaluations. In TREC-5, -6, -7 and -8, subjects were asked to identify different instances of a topic  e.g., different countries that import Cuban sugar . This represents a shift in focus away from topical relevance and towards what is often called  situational relevance.  In the situational relevance frame-work, the value of a document to a searcher depends in part on whether the searcher has already learned the information contained in that document. In the TREC interactive track, subjects were not rewarded for finding additional documents on the same aspect of a topic. The TREC-9 interactive track mod-eled a related process in which searchers were required to synthesize answers to questions based on the information in multiple documents.

Moving away from topical relevance makes sense in the context of mono-lingual retrieval because the searcher's ability to assess the topical relevance of documents by reading them is already well understood  c.f., 15 . Such is not the case in cross-language applications, where translation quality can have a substantial impact on the searcher's ability to assess the topical relevance. An initial focus on a process based on topical relevance can thus be both informa-tive and economical  since the same relevance judgments used to evaluate fully automatic systems can be used .

The next two questions deal with cause and effect. The complexity of an evaluation is roughly proportional to the product of the cardinality of the inde-pendent variables, so it is desirable to limit the choice of independent variables as much as possible. In the TREC, NTCIR and CLEF evaluations of the fully automatic components of CLIR systems, the independent variable has been the retrieval system design and the dependent variable has been retrieval system effectiveness. Since we are interested in the interactive components of a cross-language retrieval system, it would be natural to hold the fully automatic com-ponents of the retrieval system design constant and vary the user interface design as the independent variable. This could be done by running the automatic com-ponent once and then using the same ranked list with alternate user interface designs. Although it might ultimately be important to also consider other de-pendent variables  e.g., response time , retrieval effectiveness is an appropriate initial focus. After all, it would make little sense to deploy a fast, but ineffective, retrieval system.

The final question, the computation of measure s  of effectiveness, actually includes two subquestions:

- What measure s  would provide the best insight into aspects of effectiveness that would be meaningful to a searcher
- How can any effects that could potentially confound the estimate of the measure s  be minimized

When a single-valued measure can be found that re ects task performance with adequate fidelity, such a measure is typically preferred because the effect of alternative approaches can be easily expressed as the difference in the value of that measure. Mean average precision is such a measure for ranked retrieval systems. Use of a ranked retrieval measure seems inappropriate for interactive evaluations, however, since we have modeled the searcher's goal as *selecting* rather than *ranking*  relevant documents.

One commonly used single-valued measure for set-based retrieval systems is van Rijsbergen's $F$ measure, which is a weighted harmonic mean of recall and precision:

$$F_\alpha = 1 - \frac{1}{\frac{\alpha}{P} + \frac{1-\alpha}{R}}$$

$$\alpha = \frac{1}{\beta^2 + 1}$$

where $P$ is the precision the fraction of the selected documents that are relevant , $R$ is the recall the fraction of the relevant documents that are selected , and $\beta$ is the ratio of relative importance that the searcher ascribes to recall and precision 14 . It is often assumed that $\beta = 1$ which results in the unweighted harmonic mean , but the value for $\beta$ in an interactive CLIR evaluation should be selected based on the desired balance between on $p_r$ and $p_f$ that is appropriate for the process being modeled.

Another possibility would be to adopt an additive utility function similar to that used for set-based retrieval evaluation in the TREC filtering track and the Topic Detection and Tracking TDT evaluation:

$$C_{a,b} = N_r - a \cdot N_f + b \cdot N_m$$

where $N_r$ is the number of relevant documents that are selected by the user, $N_f$ is the number of false alarms non-relevant documents that are incorrectly selected by the user , $N_m$ is the number of misses relevant documents that are incorrectly rejected by the user , and $a$ and $b$ are weights that reflect the costs of misses and and false alarms relative to the value of correctly selecting a relevant document.

Regardless of which measure is chosen, several factors must be considered in any study design:

- A system effect, which is what we seek to measure.
- A topic effect in which some topics may be easier than others. This could result, for example, from the close association of an unambiguous term a proper name, perhaps with one topic, while another might only be found using combinations of terms that each have several possible translations.
- A topic-system interaction, in which the effect of a topic compared to some other topic varies depending on the system. This could result, for example, if one system was unable to translate certain terms that were important to judging the relevance of a particular topic.
- A searcher effect, in which one searcher may make relevance judgments more conservatively than another.
- A searcher-topic interaction, in which the effect of a searcher compared to some other searcher varies depending on the topic. This could result, for example, from a searcher having expert knowledge on one some topic that other searchers must judge based on a less detailed understanding.

- A searcher-system interaction, in which the effect of a searcher compared to some other searcher varies depending on the system. This could result, for example, from one searcher having better language skills, which might be more important when using one system than another.
- A searcher-topic-system interaction.

In the CLEF evaluation for fully automatic CLIR, the topic has been modeled as an additive effect and accommodated by taking the mean of the uninterpolated average precision over a set of  hopefully  representative topics. In the TREC interactive track, the topic and searcher have been modeled as additive effects, and accommodated using a $2 \times 2$ Latin square experiment design. Four searchers were given 20 minutes to search for documents on each of six topics in the TREC-5 and TREC-6 interactive track evaluations  10,11 . Eight searchers were given 15 minutes to search for documents on each of eight topics in the TREC-7 interactive track evaluation  12 . Twelve searchers were given 20 minutes to search for documents on each of six topics in the TREC-8 interactive track evaluation  4 . In each case, the Latin square was replicated as many times as the number of searchers and topics allowed in order to minimize the effect of the multi-factor interactions. Cross-site comparisons proved to be uninformative, and were dropped after TREC-6  11 . The trend towards increasing the number of searchers re ects the difficulty of discerning statistically significant differences with a limited number of searchers and topics  4 . User studies require a substantial investment   each participant in the TREC-8 interactive track was required to obtain the services of twelve human subjects with appropriate qualifications  e.g., no prior experience with either system  for about half a day each and to develop two variants of their interactive retrieval system.

## An Interactive CLIR Track for CLEF

The foregoing discussion suggests that it would be both interesting and practical to explore interactive CLIR at one of the major CLIR evaluations  TREC, CLEF, and or NTCIR . In thinking through what such an evaluation might look like in the context of CLEF, the following points should be considered:

  e i e    e ig . The replicated Latin square design seems like a good choice because there is a wealth of experience to draw upon from TREC. Starting at a small scale, perhaps with four searchers and six topics, would help to minimize barriers to entry, an important factor in any new evaluation. Options could be provided for teams that wished to add additional searchers in groups of 4. Allowing searchers 20 minutes per topic is probably wise, since that has emerged as the standard practice in the TREC interactive track. The topic selection procedure will need to be considered carefully, since results for relatively broad and relatively narrow topics might differ.

  al a i     ea   e. There would be a high payoff to retaining an initial focus on topical relevance, at least for the first evaluation, since documents found by interactive searchers could simply be added to the relevance judgment pools for the main  fully automatic  evaluation. The $F_\beta$ measure might be a good choice, although further analysis would be needed to determine an appropriate value for $\beta$ once the relative importance of $p_r$ and $p_f$ is decided, and other measures should also be explored. The instructions given to the subjects will also be an important factor in minimizing a potential additional effect from misunderstanding the task. Subjects without formal training in relevance assessment sometimes confound the concept of topical relevance  the relationship between topic and document that is the basis for evaluation in CLEF  with the concept of situational relevance  a relationship between a searcher's purpose and a document that captures the searcher's assessment of the suitability of the document for that  possibly unstated purpose . Providing clear instructions and adequate time for training will be essential if relevance assessments are to be obtained from subjects that are comparable to the ground truth relevance judgments produced by the CLEF assessors.

**e    a g  age.** It would be desirable to agree on a common document collection because it is well known that the performance of retrieval systems varies markedly across collections. That may be impractical in a place as linguistically diverse as Europe, however, since the choice of any single document language would make it difficult for teams from countries where that language is widely spoken to find cross-language searchers. For the first interactive cross-language evaluation, it might therefore make more sense to allow the use of documents in whichever language s  would be appropriate for the searchers and for the translation resources that can be obtained.

**e  ie al    e .** Interactive cross-language retrieval evaluations should focus on the interactive components of the system, so to the extent possible the fully automatic components should be held constant. If the participants agree to focus on interactive document selection, the use of a common ranked list with different interfaces would seem to be appropriate. Providing a standard ranked list of documents for each topic would help reduce barriers to entry by making it possible for a team to focus exclusively on user interface issues if that is their desire. Since cross-site comparisons were found to be uninformative in the TREC interactive track, it is probably not necessary to require the use of these standard ranked lists by every team.

Two non-technical factors will also be important to the success of an interactive cross-language retrieval track within a broader evaluation campaign. The first, an obvious one, is that coordinating the track will require some effort. A number of experiment design issues must be decided and communicated, results assembled, reports written, etc. The second, perhaps even more important, is that the track would benefit tremendously from the participation of one or more teams that already have experience in both the TREC interactive track and at least one cross-language retrieval evaluation. Several teams with this sort of experience exist, including Sheffield University in the U.K., the IBM Thomas J. Watson Research Center, New Mexico State University, the University of California at Berkeley and the University of Massachusetts at Amherst in the USA, and the Royal Melbourne Institute of Technology in Australia. With this depth of experience, the critical mass needed to jump start the evaluation process may indeed be available.

## Forming a Research Community

CLEF is an example of what is known as an evaluation-driven research paradigm, in which participants agree on a common problem, a common model of that problem, and a common set of performance measures. Although evaluation-driven research paradigms risk the sort of local optimization that can result from choice of a single perspective, a key strength of the approach is that it can foster rapid progress by bringing together researchers that might not otherwise have occasion to collaborate, to work in a common framework on a common problem. It is thus natural to ask what about the nature of the research community that would potentially participate in an interactive CLIR evaluation. One measure of the interest in the field is that a workshop on this topic at the University of Maryland attracted eighteen participants from nine organizations and included five demonstrations of working prototype systems [1]. Another promising factor is the existance of three complementary literatures that offer potential sources of additional insights into how the cross-language document selection task might be supported: machine translation, abstracting text summarization, and human-computer interaction.

Machine translation has an extensive research heritage, although evaluation of translation quality in a general context has proven to be a difficult problem. Recently, Taylor and White inventoried the tasks that intelligence analysts perform using translated materials and found two discarding irrelevant documents and finding documents of interest that correspond exactly with cross-language document selection [13]. Their ultimate goal is to identify measurable characteristics of translated documents that result in improved task performance. If that line of inquiry proves productive, the results could help to inform the design of the machine translation component of document selection interfaces.

The second complementary literature is actually a pair of literatures, alternately known as abstracting a term most closely aligned with the bibliographic services industry and text summarization a term most closely aligned with research on computational linguistics . Bibliographic services that process documents in many languages often produce abstracts in English, regardless of the document language. Extensive standards already exist for the preparation of abstracts for certain types of documents e.g., Z39.14 for reports of experimental work and descriptive or discursive studies [6], and there may be knowledge in those standards that could easily be brought to bear on the parts of the cross-language document selection interface that involve summarization. There is also some interest in the text summarization community in cross-language text summarization, and progress on that problem might find direct application in CLIR applications. One caveat in both cases is that, as with translation, the quality of a summary can only be evaluated with some purpose in mind. Document selection requires what is known in abstracting as an  indicative abstract.  Research on  informative  or  descriptive  abstracts may not transfer as directly.

Finally, the obvious third complementary literature is human-computer interaction. Several techniques are known for facilitating document selection in monolingual applications. For example, the  keyword in context  technique is commonly used in document summaries provided by Web search engines highlighting query terms and showing them in the context of their surrounding terms. Another example is the  show best passage  feature that some text retrieval systems  e.g., Inquery  provide. Extending ideas like these to work across languages is an obvious starting point. Along the way, new ideas may come to light. For example, Davis and Ogden allowed searchers to drill down during cross-language document selection by clicking on a possibly mistranslated word to see a list of alternative translations  2 .

Drawing these diverse research communities together with the existing CLIR community will be a challenge, but there is good reason to believe that each would find an interactive CLIR evaluation to be an attractive venue. The design of tractable evaluation paradigms has been a key challenge for both machine translation and text summarization, so a well designed evaluation framework would naturally attract interest from those communities. Human-computer interaction research is an enabling technology rather than an end-user application, so that community would likely find the articulation of an important problem that is clearly dependent on user interaction to be of interest. As we have seen in the CLIR and TREC interactive track evaluations, the majority of the participants in any interactive CLIR evaluation will likely self-identify as information retrieval researchers. But experience has shown that the boundaries become fuzzier over time, with significant cross-citation between complementary literatures, as the community adapts to new challenges by integrating new techniques. This community-building effect is perhaps one of the most important legacies of any evaluation campaign.

## Conclusion

Reviewing results from the TREC interactive track, Hersh and Over noted that  users showed little difference across systems, many of which contained features shown to be effective in non-interactive experiments in the past  4 . Pursuing this insight, Hersh et al. found that an 81  relative improvement in mean average precision resulted in only a small  18  and not statistically significant improvement in instance recall  5 . If this were also true of CLIR, perhaps we should stop working on the problem now. The best CLIR systems already report mean average precision values above 75  of that achieved by their monolingual counterparts, so there appears to be little room for further improvement in the fully automated components of the system. But the results achieved by Hersh et al. most likely depend at least in part on the searcher's ability to read the documents that are presented by the retrieval system, and it is easy to imagine

CLIR applications in which that would not be possible without some form of automated translation. If we are to make rational decisions about where to invest our research effort, we must begin to understand CLIR as an interactive process. Beginning with a focus on the cross-language document selection process seems to be appropriate, both for the insight that it can offer and for the tractability of the evaluation.

We somewhat euphemistically refer to our globally interconnected information infrastructure as the World-Wide Web. At present, however, it is far less than that. For someone who only reads English, it is presently the English-Wide Web. A reader of only Chinese sees only the Chinese-Wide Web. We are still faced with two problems that have been with us since the Tower of Babel: how to find the documents that we need, and how to use the documents that we find. The global series of CLIR evaluations TREC, NTCIR and CLEF have started us on the path of answering the first question. It is time to take the second step along that path, and begin to ask how searchers and machines can work together to find documents in languages that the searcher cannot read better than machines can alone.

## Acknowledgments

The author is grateful to the participants in the June 2000 workshop on interactive cross-language retrieval, and especially to Bill Ogden, Gina Levow and Jianqiang Wang, for stimulating discussions on this subject, and to Rebecca Hwa, Paul Over and Bill Hersh for their helpful comments on earlier versions of this paper. This work was supported in part by DARPA contract N6600197C8540 and DARPA cooperative agreement N660010028910.

## References

1. Workshop on interactive searching in foreign-language collections (2000) http //www.clis.umd.edu/conferences/hcil00/
2. Davis, M., Ogden, W. C.   uilt Implementing a large-scale cross-language te t retrieval system. In Proceedings of the 20th International ACM SIGIR Conference on Research and Development in Information Retrieval (1997)
3. Hearst, M. A.  User interfaces and visualization. In Baeza-Yates, R., Ribeiro-Neto, B., Modern Information Retrieval, chapter 10. Addison Wesley, New York (1999) http //www.sims.berkeley.edu/~hearst/irbook/chapters/chap10.html.
4. Hersh, W., Over, P.  TREC-8 interactive track report. In The Eighth Te t REtrieval Conference (TREC-8) (1999) 57 64 http //trec.nist.gov.
5. Hersh, W., Turpin, A., Price, S., Chan, B., Kraemer, D., Sacherek, L., Olson, D. Do batch and user evaluations give the same results? In Proceedings of the 23nd Annual International ACM SIGIR Conference on Research and Development in Information Retrieval (1998) 17 24
6. National Information Standards Organization    Guidelines for Abstracts (ANSI/NISO Z39.14-1997) NISO Press (1997)

7. Oard, D. W., Levow, G.-A., Cabezas, C. I.  TREC-9 e periments at Maryland Interactive CLIR. In The Ninth Te t Retrieval Conference (TREC-9) (2000) To appear. http //trec.nist.gov.
8. Oard, D. W., Resnik, P.  Support for interactive document selection in cross-language information retrieval. Information Processing and Management  5(3) (1999) 363 379
9. Ogden, W., Cowie, J., Davis, M., Ludovik, E., Molina-Salgado, H., Shin, H.  Getting information from documents you cannot read  An interactive cross-language te t retrieval and summarization system.  In Joint ACM DL/SIGIR Workshop on Multilingual Information Discovery and Access (1999) http //www.clis.umd.edu/conferences/midas.html.
10. Over, P.  TREC-5 interactive track report. In The Fifth Te t REtrieval Conference (TREC-5) (1996) 29 56 http //trec.nist.gov.
11. Over, P.  TREC-6 interactive track report. In The Si th Te t REtrieval Conference (TREC-6) (1997) 73 82 http //trec.nist.gov.
12. Over, P.  TREC-7 interactive track report. In The Seventh Te t REtrieval Conference (TREC-7) (1998) 65 71 http //trec.nist.gov.
13. Taylor, K., White, J.  Predicting what MT is good for  User judgments and task performance.  In Third Conference of the Association for Machine Translation in the Americas (1998) 364 373 Lecture Notes in Artificial Intelligence 1529.
14. van Rijsbergen, C. J.  Information Retrieval. Butterworths, London, second edition (1979)
15. Wilbur, W. J.  A comparison of group and individual performance among sub-ject e perts and untrained workers at the document retrieval task  Journal of the American Society for Information Science, 49(6) (1998) 517 529

# New Challenges for Cross-Language Information Retrieval: Multimedia Data and the User Experience

Gareth J.F. Jones

Department of Computer Science, University of E eter, EX4 4PT, U.K.
G. .F. ones@exeter.ac.uk,
http://www.dcs.ex.ac.uk/~gareth

**Abstract.** Evaluation e ercises in Cross-Language Information Retrieval (CLIR) have so far been limited to the location of potentially relevant documents from within electronic te t collections. Although there has been considerable progress in recent years much further research is required in CLIR, and clearly one focus of future research must continue to address fundamental retrieval issues. However, CLIR is now sufficiently mature to broaden the investigation to consider some new challenges. Two interesting further areas of investigation are the user e perience of accessing information from retrieved documents in CLIR, and the e -tension of e isting research to cross-language methods for multimedia retrieval.

## 1 Introduction

The rapid expansion in research into Cross-Language Information Retrieval CLIR in recent years has produced a wide variety of work focusing on retrieval from different language groupings and using varying translation techniques. Formal evaluation exercises in CLIR have so far concentrated exclusively on cross-language and multilingual retrieval for electronic text collections. This work only re ects one aspect of the complete Information Access IA process required for Cross-Language Information Access CLIA . In this paper the complete process of IA is taken to involve a number of processes: user description of information need in the form of a search request, identification of potentially relevant documents by a retrieval engine, relevance judgement by the user of retrieved documents, and subsequent user extraction of information from individual retrieved documents. These issues all become more complicated in cross-language and multilingual environments, where in particular the relevance assessment and information extraction stages have received very little attention. Although there have been a number of individual studies exploring IA techniques for retrieved documents, e.g. 1 2 3 , thus far there have been no common tasks on which IA techniques can be compared and contrasted for either monolingual or multilingual data. In addition, CLIR and other related retrieval technologies are now sufficiently mature to begin exploration of the more challenging task of cross-language retrieval from multimedia data.

C. Peters (Ed.): CLEF 2000, LNCS 2069, pp. 72– 2, 2001.

This paper explores issues in CLIA evaluation in more detail and reviews relevant existing work in multimedia retrieval. Section 2 focuses on CLIA from the user's perspective, Section 3 reviews current research in Multimedia Information Retrieval MIR , Section 4 considers the challenges of Cross-Language Multimedia Information Retrieval CLMIR , and Section 5 gives some concluding thoughts.

## 2 The User in Cross-Language Information Access

The user is actively involved in most stages of the Information Access process. User activities of course include forming search requests, but also the judgement of retrieved document relevance and the extraction of information from individual retrieved documents. Extending evaluation exercises beyond assessing the effectiveness of document retrieval to these other stages of IA is important in order to assess the usefulness of techniques which are designed to assist the user with relevance judgement and information extraction. This section reviews some existing relevant work in these areas.

### 2.1    ele a  e    ge e

For monolingual text retrieval it is typically assumed that the user can rapidly make relevance judgements about retrieved documents by skimming a portion of the document. Users are typically provided with the title and first few sentences of the document to decide its possible relevance to their request. A more sophisticated method of providing summary information for relevance judgement is suggested by query-biased summaries as described in  4 . Another approach suggested for this situation uses a graphical representation of the document contents with respect to the query terms to show the level of matching between a query and an individual document, and the distribution of search terms within the document. There are several examples of graphical representations which can be used in this way including Thumbnail document images  1  and document TileBars  2 . Limited experiments have suggested that users are able to make relevance judgements with some degree of reliability based only on a graphical representation of this form without actually accessing linguistic information within the document.

### 2.2        a g age ele a  e    e   e

Assessment of relevance can be more complicated for cross-language retrieval. Clearly this depends on the users and their level of  uency in the document language. If the users are  uent in the document language, perhaps they don't really need CLIR at all. However, to keep matters simple let's consider here only the situation of the user knowing little or nothing about the document language, e.g. a typical English reader with Chinese documents or a Japanese reader with German documents. In this situation, even selecting a document as potentially relevant is impossible using the document itself in its raw form. Existing work in this area has begun to discuss ideas such as using Machine Translation  MT  techniques for assessing relevance in ranked retrieval lists, e.g. augmenting the summaries which typically appear in these ranked lists with corresponding translations into the request language. If the user finds a document potentially interesting it is retrieved in the usual way and then fully translated to the request language using MT prior to presentation to the user  3 . So far studies have only been suggestive that these methods are useful rather than having been formally evaluated as such. An alternative approach is suggested in  5 and  6  where users were presented with simple gloss translations of returned documents. In gloss translations terms in the documents are replaced by one or more likely translations of the word. It is generally observed that users are able to disambiguate alternative translations to select the contextually correct one. The graphical relevance assessment methods outlined in the previous section can also be applied to CLIR  one example of this approach is given in  1 . At present, there do not appear to have been any comparative evaluations of the relative effectiveness of these various relevance judgement strategies.

## 2.3      a i      e      e ie e        e

Evaluation measures in CLIR have focussed on the traditional metrics of *recall* and *precision*. While obviously useful, these are rather limited instruments in what they tell us generally about the usefulness of a retrieval system to the user, particularly for systems involving cross-language and multimedia retrieval.

As suggested in the last section, after the user has selected a potentially relevant document it can be translated into the request language using an MT system prior to being presented to the user. The automatic translation process is imperfect, stylistic problems will often be introduced, but factual errors may be introduced as well. With respect to translation of informative documents, such as mail messages or news reports, factual accuracy is probably more important than style. For example, if the output of an MT system gets the day or time of a meeting wrong considerable inconvenience could result, regardless of how well the prose might be constructed. A useful CLIA motivated investigation here may be to explore whether the translated version of the document actually contains the data required to satisfy the user's information need. The system may have successfully retrieved a relevant document, and this will show up positively in precision and recall measurements, but a further important question is: can the information in the document which causes it to be relevant be made available to the user in a form that they can understand, e.g. in a different language. Essentially this is looking for a quantitative measure of the reliability of the translation process which could be directly bound into a retrieval task or could be connected to a task exploring the answering of an information need by particular documents. A further evaluation task could be to look at interactive information seeking in CLIR, this would allow exploration of issues such as the possible involvement of the user in the translation process.

We might further want to look at summarisation in CLIR, both for document browsing and accessing facts. Summarisation has so far not been included in the TREC evaluation programme, but this is a topic of increasing importance as recognised in the Japanese NTCIR evaluation programme where it has been included as a formal task in the 2nd NTCIR workshop programme.

Recent TREC tracks have looked at the user's interaction with data and query development in interactive retrieval, and more recently a track looking at Question-Answering has been introduced 7  8 . These are currently only running for monolingual text retrieval, but could potentially be extended to CLIR, both separately and possibly in combination.

## Multimedia Information Retrieval

Existing research in CLIR has focussed almost exclusively on text retrieval. However, documents may originate in various different media, e.g. typed text, spoken data, document images from paper or video data. Research in Multimedia Information Retrieval  MIR  has focussed almost exclusively on monolingual retrieval. However, this work is itself now sufficiently mature to begin exploration into systems capable of effective cross-language retrieval tasks. This section brie y reviews research in spoken document and scanned document retrieval. The following section then considers the extension of this work to cross-language tasks.

### 3.1     e       e     e ie al

Spoken Document Retrieval  SDR  has been an active area of research for around 10 years. The first work was carried out by Rose in the early 1990's  9 . Rose used a fixed-vocabulary word spotter to assign spoken documents to one of ten predefined categories. The first research to address a more standard ad hoc information retrieval task was carried out at ETH Zurich by Glavitsch and Schauble  10 . This research explored the use of a set of predefined subword units for open-vocabulary retrieval of spoken data. Two other early research projects were conducted at Cambridge University. Both of these explored the use of a subword phone lattice and large vocabulary speech recognition for document indexing. One project by James  11  investigated the retrieval of BBC radio news broadcasts and the larger Video Mail Retrieval  VMR  project focussed on the retrieval of video mail messages  12  13 . The first large scale digital video library project to explore SDR was Informedia at Carnegie Mellon University. This ongoing project began by focusing on automated retrieval of broadcast television news  14 .

Figure 1 shows a manual transcription of a spoken message from the VMR1b collection used in the VMR project  12 . This transcription has been constructed carefully to include dis uency markers such as           h  and   o  _ re th ,
as well as  p  se  markers. This punctuation is inserted here by inference from listening to the prosody of the speech, and is added to aid reading of the messages. Inserting these markers automatically as part of a transcription process

```
M524p003  tongue-click  O K,  pause   've finally arranged a time and
a date that everyone on the pro ect can make.  loud-breath   um
 tongue-click  The time is ten o'clock and the date is Wednesday the
twenty fifth.  pause   ah  Monday and Tuesday were out unfortunately,
 loud-breath   ah  if anyone can't make this time and date please can
they let me know as soon as possible  pause  and  'll arrange  pause  the
meeting for another  loud-breath  mutually acceptable time.  loud-breath
The main thing that we're going to be discussing is the upcoming
deadline.
```

**Fig. 1.** Example of a manual VMR message transcription with transcriber inserted punctuation.

```
M524p003    T E K. R. O. F NALL  ARRANGED A T ME AND A L G T OF T E R VAL
 ROD CT AND WON'T LEARN T AT T ME T    T E OF CAND DATE T ERE     ON
WEDNE DA  T E TWENT  F FT  W  LE MANAGER OF T E ROAD AND FOR T E OVERALL
CAR L KE T    T ME  N D RECT CONTROL AND A   OON A   O   BLE AND RANGE
OF A MEET NG FOR A N CLEAR    ORT ON T E MA N T  NG WE NEVER D  C     T E
NEW  T AT K ND OF L NE
```

**Fig. 2.** Example of 20K Large Vocabulary Speech Recogniser VMR message transcription.

would be a very challenging task. Applying the recorded audio file of the example message to the 20K Large Vocabulary Speech Recognition LVR system used in the VMR project produces the transcription shown in Fig. 2. Automated transcription of all messages in VMR1b gave retrieval performance of around 80 of that achieved with the manual text transcription.

SDR has featured as a track at the annual TREC conferences for the last 4 years. This began with a known-item search task in TREC 6 15 and has moved on to progressively more challenging ad hoc tasks in subsequent years 7 8 . The data used in the TREC SDR tasks was broadcast TV and radio news. Techniques have been developed to deliver performance levels for spoken data very similar to near correct manual transcriptions, and it has been decided that the SDR in its current form will not be run at future TRECs.

While it appears that SDR is largely solved for retrieval of English language broadcast news there are a number of challenges which still remain. These include proper investigation and evaluation of SDR for other languages, such as European and Asian languages. While many of the techniques developed for English SDR may well prove effective for other languages, the features of these languages may require enhancement of existing methods or the development of new ones. An important point with respect to spoken data is the availability of suitable speech recognition systems. One of the results of existing SDR studies is the high correlation between speech recognition accuracy and retrieval performance. An important investigation is to explore how to perform the best retrieval for languages where high quality speech recognition resources are not currently available.

Another important issue in SDR is to explore the effectiveness with which information can be extracted from retrieved spoken documents. The linear nature of speech means that accessing information from within individual spoken documents is fundamentally slower and more difficult than from text documents which can be scanned visually very rapidly. For relevance judgement it is time consuming to scan through audio files in order to overview their contents. For this reason most SDR systems make use of some form of graphical visualisation and often display the automatically transcribed document contents in the user interface 13 16 . Although not previously used in SDR, the graphical methods outlined in Sect. 2 might be used to assist relevance judgement here.

Comparing the automatic transcription in Fig. 2 with the manual one shown in Fig. 1, it can be seen that there are many mistakes. Some important factual information is preserved, but other details are completely lost. This illustrates an interesting aspect of speech recognition quality and its evaluation with respect to IA. While it has been shown in various studies that it is possible to achieve good SDR performance, even with a high number of recognition errors in the document transcription, the transcriptions may be ineffective for addressing user information needs. For example, although we have the correct day of the meeting in the automated transcription of example message    p    , we have lost the time. This highlights the importance of making the maximum use of the original data in the IA process and further motivates the use of visualisation in SDR interfaces. In these interfaces as well as reviewing the text transcription, SDR systems typically allow the user to play back the audio file itself, thus limiting the impact of recognition errors on the information extraction process 13 16 .

## 3.2       e      age  e  ie al

While most contemporary documents are available in online electronic form many archives exist only in printed form. This is particularly true of important historical documents, but also many comparatively recent documents even if originally produced electronically are now only available in their final printed form. In order to automatically retrieve items of this type their content must be indexed by scanning and then applying some form of Optical Character Recognition  OCR  process to transcribe the document contents.

Research in document image retrieval has covered a number of topics related to the identification of relevant documents in various application tasks. However, work in actual ad hoc retrieval of documents in response to a user search request has been concentrated on a limited number of studies. The most extensive work has been carried out over a number of years at the University of Nevada, Las Vegas  17  where retrieval effectiveness for a number of different collections, indexing technologies and retrieval methods has been explored. Another study into the effect of recognition errors for document image retrieval focusing on Japanese text is reported in  18 . Document image retrieval was the focus of the Confusion Track run as part of TREC 5  19 . This was a known-item search task and a number of participating groups reported results using a variety of indexing methods. Techniques explored included the use of indexing using n-gram sequences, methods to allow for substitution, deletion or insertion of letters in indexing terms, and attempting to correct OCR errors using dictionary-based methods. The Confusion Track has not been run at subsequent TREC evaluation where the focus has moved to the SDR task. A detailed review of research in document image retrieval is given in 20 .

Assessing the relevance of retrieved documents could be achieved by presentation of the first section of document image to the user. Selected document images can then be shown to the user in their entirety. Navigation within documents might be achieved using some form of graphical representation of the distribution of search terms similar to those developed for SDR interfaces. There is little difference between this scenario for document images and retrieval of typed electronic text, except that the document contents would only be searchable by approximate matching with the output of the OCR system. Occurrences of search terms in the displayed document images could be highlighted to assist with browsing, but again this can only be based on an approximate match, so may be errorful.

## Cross-Language Multimedia Retrieval

There has so far been very little work in the area of Cross-Language Multimedia Information Retrieval  CLMIR . This is a potentially important future research topic as the growth of multilingual and multimedia document collections is likely to lead inevitably to the growth of multilingual multimedia collections. This section brie y reviews existing work in CLMIR and suggests some directions for further research.

There are few examples of published work in Cross-Language Speech Retrieval  CLSR . A study carried out at ETH, Zurich used French language text requests to retrieve spoken German news documents  21 . The requests were translated using a *similarity thesaurus* constructed using a parallel collection of French and German new stories. A more recent study reported in  22  explores the retrieval of English voice-mail messages from the VMR1 collection with French text requests using request translation performed with a dictionary-based method and a standard MT system. Results from these investigations suggest that standard CLIR techniques, such as *pseudo relevance  eedback*  23  are effective for CLSR, and that retrieval performance degradations arising from CLIR and SDR are additive. However, these are both small scale studies and their conclusions need to be verified on much larger collections. A review of existing technologies applicable to CLSR is contained in  24 .

It is not clear how IA should be approached for a CLSR tasks. When the example VMR1b message shown in Fig. 1 is applied to the *Power Translator Pro* MT System the French translation shown in Fig. 3 is produced. For a user with a moderate level of knowledge of French language it can be seen that this translation is generally fairly impressive, clearly indicating the content of the message. Assuming that this translation was not available, a French speaker

M524p003  tongue_click  O K,  pause     'ai arrangé un temps et une
date que tout le monde sur le pro et peut faire finalement.  loud_breath
um   tongue_click  Le temps est dix heures et la date est mercredi
les vingt cinquieme.  pause    ah  lundi et mardi étaient dehors
malheureusement,  loud_breath    ah  si n'importe qui ne peut pas faire
ce temps et la date peut s'il vous plaît ils m'ont laissé savoir des
que possible  pause  et  'arrangerai  pause   la réunion pour un autre
 loud_breath  temps mutuellement acceptable.  loud_breath  La chose
principale que nous allons discuter est la date limite prochaine.

**Fig. 3.** Example of manual VMR message transcription with transcriber inserted punctuation translated into French using *Power Translator Pro.*

M524p003        LE K. R. O. F NALL  A ARRANGÉ  N TEM    ET  NE L M ERE D
 ROD  T D  R VAL ET N'A  RENDRA  A  CE TEM   Q E CE T   E DE CAND DAT
E T MERCRED  LE  V NGT C NQ  EME   ENDANT Q E D RECTE R DE LA RO TE ET
 O R LA VO T RE TOTALE COMME CE TEM    DAN  CONTRÔLE D RECT ET DE  Q E
 O   BLE ET GAMME D' NE RÉ N ON  O R  N    ORT N CLÉA RE   R LA C O E
R NC  ALE NO   NE D  C TON   AMA  LE  NO VELLE  Q   GENRE DE L GNE

**Fig. 4.** Examples of 20K Large Vocabulary Speech Recogniser VMR message transcription translated into French using *Power Translator Pro.*

without any knowledge of English may find the graphical visualisation and gloss translation strategies useful in making relevance judgements for this document. However, they might experience considerable difficulty in extracting information from a relevant document transcription. This latter problem would, of course, be much more significant for most users if the document were originally in Chinese.

Figure 4 shows the output of applying the example LVR transcription shown in Fig. 2 to the *Power Translator Pro* translation system. Once again the translation is a respectable version of the English data input. The primary problem here though is with the information contained in the transcribed English input to the MT system. Thus a key fundamental unresolved research issue is how this incorrectly transcribed information can be accessed across languages by non-specialists in the document language. The user can listen to the soundtrack, or perhaps seek the assistance of a professional translation service, but this does not provide a solution to the problem of rapid automated CLIA for users unfamiliar with the document language.

So far there have not been any reported research results in cross-language retrieval from document images collections. A review of the technologies and possible approaches to this is given in 25 , but research results are not reported. One problem for cross-language document image retrieval relates to the translation of the output of OCR either for retrieval or content access. A feature of OCR systems is that they make errors in the recognition of individual characters within a word. These errors can sometimes be corrected in post processing, but often they cannot. These recognised  words  are not present in standard dictionaries and thus cannot be translated directly, either by an MT system or by simple dictionary lookup. A method of approximate matching with dictionary entries, perhaps involving steps such as part-of-speech matching and word co-occurrence analysis, might prove effective, but there will remain the possibility of translation errors which result from incorrect word recognition.

These translation problems will impact on the accuracy of translations presented to the user for relevance assessment and information extraction. Problems similar to those illustrated for SDR in Fig. 4 may result, but the extent of this problem needs to be explored experimentally.

In conclusion, in order to advance research in CLMIR there is a need for standard test collections, either based on existing monolingual multimedia retrieval collections or developed specifically to support research in CLMIR.

## Concluding Remarks

This paper has suggested some new research tasks in CLIR designed to address some important challenges of cross-language access to linguistic information. Specifically it has looked at topics in assessing the relevance of retrieved documents and extracting information from individual documents, and current research in multimedia retrieval and its extension to a cross-language environment.

## References

1   W. Ogden, J. Cowie, M. Davis, E. Ludovik, H. Molina-Salgado, and H. Shin. Getting Information from Documents you Cannot Read  An Interactive Cross-Language Te t Retrieval and Summarization System. In   r cee ings     the     int     D  SIGI     r sh p  n    ultilingual Disc   er  an     ccess, Berkeley, U.S.A., 1999. ACM.

2   M. A. Hearst. TileBars  Visualisation of Term Distribution Information in Full Te t Information Access. In   r cee ings    the       SIG    I     n erence  n    uman Fact rs in    mputing S stems     I , Denver, CO, 1995. ACM.

3   G. J. F. Jones, N. H. Collier, T. Sakai, K. Sumita, and H. Hirakawa. Cross-Language Information Access  a case study for English and Japanese. In In  r    mati n   r cessing S ciet     apan    int SIG FI an   SIG      r sh p, pages 47 54, Tokyo, 1998. IPSJ.

4   A. Tombros and M. Sanderson. The Advantages of   uery-Biased Summaries in Information Retrieval. In   r cee ings    the     st  nnual Internati nal    SIGI     n erence  n   esearch an  De el pment in In  rmati n   etrie al, pages 2 10, Melbourne, 1998. ACM.

5   D. W. Oard and P. Resnik. Support for Interactive Document Selection in Cross-Language Information Retrieval. In  rmati n  r cessing an    anagement, 35 363 379, 1999.

6   M. W. Davis and W. C. Ogden. Implementing Cross-Language Te t Retrieval Systems for Large-Scale Te t Collections and the World Wide Web. In   r cee ings    the     I     Spring S mp sium  n  r ss  anguage  e t an  Speech    etrie al, pages 9 17, Stanford, U.S.A., 1997. AAAI.

7  D. K. Harman and E. M. Voorhees, editors. *he Se enth   e t   Etrie al   n er ence   E   , Gaithersburg, MD, 1999. NIST.

8  D. K. Harman and E. M. Voorhees, editors. *he Eighth   e t   Etrie al   n erence   E   , Gaithersburg, MD, 2000. NIST.

9  R. C. Rose. Techniques for Information Retrieval from Speech Messages. *inc ln a  rat r   urnal*, 4(1) 45 60, 1991.

10  U. Glavitsch and P. Schäuble. A System for Retrieving Speech Documents. In *r cee ings   the   th  nnual Internati nal   SIGI   n erence  n  esearch an  De el pment in In  rmati n   etrie a*, pages 168 176. ACM, 1992.

11  D. A. James. *he  pplicati n   lassical In rmati n  etrie al  echni ues t Sp  en D  cuments*. PhD thesis, Cambridge University, February 1995.

12  G. J. F. Jones, J. T. Foote, K. Sparck Jones, and S. J. Young. Retrieving Spoken Documents by Combining Multiple Inde  Sources. In  *r cee ings   the   th nnual Internati nal   SIGI   n erence  n  esearch an  De el pment in In rmati n   etrie al*, pages 30 38, Zurich, 1996. ACM.

13  M. G. Brown, J. T. Foote, G. J. F. Jones, K. Sparck Jones, and S. J. Young. Open-Vocabulary Speech Inde ing for Voice and Video Mail Retrieval. In  *r cee ings ultime ia  *, pages 307 316, Boston, 1996. ACM.

14  A. G. Hauptmann and M. J. Witbrock. Informedia  News-on-Demand Multimedia Information Aquistion and Retrieval. In M. T. Maybury, editor, *Intelligent ultime ia In  rmati n   etrie al*, pages 215 239. AAAI/MIT Press, 1997.

15  D. K. Harman and E. M. Voorhees, editors. *he Si th   e t   Etrie al   n erence   E   , Gaithersburg, MD, 1998. NIST.

16  J. Hirschberg, S. Whittaker, D. Hindle, F. Pereira, and A. Singhal. Finding Information in Audio  A New Paradigm for Audio Browsing and Retrieval.  In *r cee ings   the ES  E   r sh p n  ccessing In  rmati n in Sp  en u i *, pages 117 122, Cambridge, U.K., 1999. ESCA.

17  K. Taghva, J. Borsack, and A. Condit. Evaluation of Model-Based Retrieval E ectiveness for OCR Te t. *ransacti ns  n In  rmati n S  stems*, 41(1) 64 93, 1996.

18  K. Marukawa, T. Hu, H. Fujisawa, and Y. Shima.  Document Retrieval Tolerating Character Recognition Errors - Evaluation and Application. *In  rmati n r cessing an  anagement*, 30(8) 1361 1371, 1996.

19  D. K. Harman and E. M. Voorhees, editors. *he Fi th   e t   Etrie al   n erence   E   , Gaithersburg, MD, 1997. NIST.

20  M. Mitra and B. B. Chaudhuri. Information Retrieval from Documents  A Survey. *In  rmati n   etrie al*, 2 141 163, 2000.

21  P. Sheridan, M. Wechsler, and P. Schauble.  Cross-Language Speech Retrieval Establishing a Baseline Performance. In  *r cee ings   the   th  nnual Inter nati nal   SIGI   n erence  n  esearch an  De el pment in In  rmati n etrie al*, Philadelphia, 1997. ACM.

22  G. J. F. Jones.  Applying Machine Translation Resources for Cross-Language Information Access from Spoken Documents. In  *r cee ings  achine ranslati n an  ultilingual  pplicati ns in the  e  illennium*, pages 4  (1 9), E eter, 2000.

23  L. Ballesteros and W. B. Croft. Phrasal Translation and  uery E pansion Techniques for Cross-Language Information Retrieval. In  *r cee ings   the   th  n nual Internati nal   SIGI   n erence  n  esearch an  De el pment in In rmati n   etrie al*, pages 84 91, Philadelphia, 1997. ACM.

24  G. J. F. Jones and D. A. James. A Critical Review of State-Of-The-Art Technolo-
    gies for Cross-Language Speech Retrieval. In *r cee ings    the     I    Spring
    S mp sium  n  r ss  anguage  e t an  Speech  etrie al*, pages pp99 110, Stan-
    ford, 1997. AAAI. AAAI Technical Report SS-97-05.
25  D. W. Oard. Issues in Cross-Language Retrieval from Dcoument Image Collec-
    tions. In *r cee ings    the     S mp sium  n D cument Image   n erstan ing
    echn l g  SDI    *, Annapolis, MD, 1999.

# Research to Improve Cross-Language Retrieval Position Paper for CLEF

Fredric C. Gey

UC Data Archive & Technical Assistance,
University of California
Berkeley, CA 94720 USA
gey@ucdata.berkeley.edu

**Abstract.** Improvement in cross-language information retrieval results can come from a variety of sources   failure analysis, resource enrichment in terms of stemming and parallel and comparable corpora, use of pivot languages, as well as phonetic transliteration and Romanization. Application of these methodologies should contribute to a gradual increase in the ability of search software to cross the language barrier.

## 1   Failure Analysis

In my opinion there has been a dearth of detailed failure analysis in cross-language information retrieval, even among the best-performing methods in comparative evaluations at TREC, CLEF, and NTCIR 7 . Just as a post-mortem can determine causation in mortality, a query-by-query analysis can often shed light on why some approaches succeed and others fail. Among the sets of queries utilized in these evaluations we always find several queries which all participants perform poorly   as measured by the median precision over all runs for that query . When the best performance is significantly better than the median it would be instructive to determine why that method succeeded while others failed. If the best performance is not much better than the median, then something inherently difficult in the topic description presents a research challenge to the CLIR community. Two examples are illustrative, one from TREC and the other from CLEF.

The TREC-7 conference was the first multilingual evaluation where a particular topic language was to be run against multiple language document collections. The collection languages were the same as in CLEF   English, French, German, Italian . Topic 36, whose English title is   Art Thefts   has the French translated equivalent   Les voleurs d'art . The Altavista Babblefish translation of the French results in the phrase   The robbers of art , which grasps the significance, if not the additional precision of the original English. However, when combined with aggressive stemming, the meaning can be quite different. The Berkeley French⟶Multilingual first stemmed the word   voleurs' to the stem   vol', and the translation of this stem to English is   ight' and to German   ug,' significantly different from the original unstemmed translation. In fact our F⟶EFGI

C. Peters (Ed.): CLEF 2000, LNCS 2069, pp. 3–  , 2001.
© Springer-Verlag Berlin Heidelberg 2001

performance for this query was 0.0799 precision versus our E⟶EFGI precision of 0.3830.

For the CLEF evaluation, one query provides a significant example of the challenges facing CLIR, even with a single language such as English. Query 40 about the privatization of the German national railway was one which seems to have presented problems with all participating groups  the median precision over all CLEF multilingual runs was 0.0537 for this query . As an American group, the Berkeley group was challenged by the use of the English spelling  privatisation' which couldn't be recognized by any machine translation softwares. The German version of the topic was not much better   in translation its English equivalent became  de-nationalization' a very uncommon synonym for  privatization,' and one which yielded few relevant documents. By comparison, our German manual reformulation of this query resulted in an average precision of 0.3749 for best CLEF performance for this query.

These examples illustrate that careful post-evaluation analysis might provide the feedback which can be incorporated into design changes and improved system performance.

## 2    Resource Enrichment

### 2.1    e   e  a          l g

The CLEF evaluation seems to be the first one in which significant experiments in multiple language stemming and morphology was used. Some groups developed  poor man  stemmers by taking the corpus word lists and developing stem classes based upon common prefix strings. The Chicago group applied their automatic morphological analyzer to the CLEF collections to generate a custom stemmer for each language's collection 5 , while the Maryland group extended the Chicago approach by developing a four-stage statistical stemming approach 14 . The availability of the Porter stemmers in French, German and Italian  from http: open.muscat.com  also heavily in uenced CLEF entries. The conclusion seems to be that stemming plays an important role in performance improvement for non-English European languages, with results substantially better than for English stemming.

### 2.2    a allel        a a     eb  i i g

Parallel corpora have been recognized as a major resource for CLIR. Several entries in CLEF, in particular the Johns Hopkins APL 11  used aligned parallel corpora in French and English from the Linguistic Data Consortium. More recently emphasis has been given toward mining the WWW for parallel resources. There are many sites, particularly in Europe, which have versions of the same web page in different languages. Tools have been built which extract parallel bilingual corpora from the web  13, 16 . These were applied in CLEF  by the Montreal Group 12  and the Twente TNO group 6

## 2.3    a able    a  lig  e

Comparable corpora are bilingual corpora which can be created through alignment of similar documents on the same topic in different languages. An example might be the foreign edition of a newspaper where stories about the same news item are written independently. Techniques for alignment require relaxation of time position  a story might appear a few days later  and the establishment of the contextual environment of topic. There has been research into the statistical alignment of comparable corpora by Picchi and Peters with Italian and English  15  and Fung with English and Chinese  2  but the techniques have not made their way into general practice. Comparable corpora will only become widely used if tools for their acquisition are created as open-source software and tools for their alignment are refined and also made available.

## 2.4    e g a  i a      e   a  e

A major need is to provide geographic and proper name recognition across languages. Proper names are often not in either machine translation programs or bilingual dictionaries, nor are geographic place names. A particular case in point was the TREC-6 cross language query CL1 about Austrian President Kurt Waldheim's connection with Nazism during WW II   one translation system translated from the German  Waldheim' to English  forest home'.

It has been suggested that more than thirty percent of content bearing words from news services are proper nouns, either personal and business enterprise names or geographic place name references. The availability of electronic gazetteers such as:

- National Imagery and Mapping Agency's country name files:
  http:  164.214.2.59 gns html Cntry_Files.html

- Census Bureau's gazetteer for United States:
  http:  tiger.census.gov

- Arizona State University's list of place name servers
  http:  www.asu.edu lib hayden govdocs maps geogname.htm

- Global Gazeteer of 2880532 cities and towns around the world
  http:  www.calle.com world

give some hope that geographic name recognition could be built into future CLIR systems.

While work has been done on extracting proper nouns in English and some other languages through the Message Understanding Conference series, it is not clear that anyone has mined parallel texts to create specialized bilingual lexicons of proper names.

## Pivot Languages

In multilingual retrieval between queries and documents in   languages, one
seems to be required to possess resources   machine translation, bilingual dictionaries, parallel corpora, etc.   between each pair of languages. Thus      2
resources are needed. This can be approximated with the substitution of transi-
tivity among        resources if a general purpose pivot language is used. Thus to
transfer a query from German to Italian, where machine translation is available from German to English and English to Italian respectively, the query
is translated into English and subsequently into Italian, and English becomes
the pivot language. This method was used by the Berkeley group in TREC-7
 3  and CLEF 4 . The Twente TNO group has utilized Dutch as a pivot language between pairs of language where direct resources were unavailable in both
TREC-8 10  and CLEF 6 . One can easily imagine that excellent transitive machine translation could provide better results than poor direct resources such
as a limited bilingual dictionary. In some cases resources may not even exist
for one language pair   this will be come increasingly common with the increase in the number of languages for which cross-language information search
is desired. For example, a CLIR researcher may be unable to find an electronic
dictionary resource between English and Malagasy  the language of Madagas-
car , but there are French newspapers in this former colony of France where
French is still an official language. Thus, an electronic French-Malagasy dictionary may be more complete and easier to locate than an English-Malagasy
one. Similarly the Russian language may provide key resources to transfer words
from the Pashto  Afgan , Farsi, Tajik, and Uzbek languages  see, for example,
http:  members.tripod.com Groznijat b_lang bl_sourc.html .

## Phonetic Transliteration and Romani ation

One of the most important and neglected areas in cross-language information
retrieval is, in my opinion, the application of transliteration to the retrieval process. The idea of transliteration in CLIR derives from the suggestion by Buckley in the TREC-6 conference that for English-French CLIR  English query
words are treated as potentially mis-spelled French words.  1  In this way English query words can be replaced by French words which are lexicographically
similar and the query can be can proceed monolingually. More generally, we can
often find that many words, particularly in technology areas, have been borrowed
phonetically from English and are pronounced similarly, yet with phonetic cus-
tomization in the borrower language. The problems of automatic recognition of
phonetic transliteration has been studied by Knight and Graehl for the Japanese
katakana alphabet  9  and by Stalls and Knight for Arabic 17 . Another kind of
transliteration is Romanization, wherein an unfamiliar script, such as Cyrillic, is
replaced by its Roman alphabet equivalent. When done by library catalogers, the
transformation is one-to-one, i.e. the original script can be recovered by reverse
transformation. This is not the case for phonetic transliteration where more than

one sound in the source language can project to a single representation in the target language. The figure below comes from the entry for economic policy' in the GIRT special domain retrieval thesaurus of CLEF 8 . The GIRT creators have provided a translation of the thesaurus into Russian which our group

```
- <list>
  - <entry>
      <german>Wirtschaftspolitik</german>
      <russian>экономическая политика</russian>
      <translit>ekonomicheskaia politika</translit>
    </entry>
  </list>
```

**Fig. 1.** German-Russian GiRT Thesaurus with Transliteration

has transliterated into its Roman equivalent using the U.S. Library of Congress specification see http: lcweb.loc.gov rr european lccyr.html . It is clear that either a fuzzy string or phonetic search with English words economic', policy', or politics' would retrieve this entry from the thesaurus or from a collection of Russian documents. Generalized string searches of this type have yet to be incorporated into information retrieval systems.

## Summary and Acknowlegments

This paper has presented a personal view of what developments are needed to improve cross-language information retrieval performance. Two of the most exciting advances in cross-language information retrieval are mining the web for parallel corpora to build bi-lingual lexicons and the application of phonetic transliteration toward search in the absence of translation resources. Comparable corpora development, which has perhaps the greatest potential to advance the field, has yet to achieve its promise in terms of impact, probably because of the lack of generally available processing tools.

I wish to thank Hailing Jiang and Aitao Chen for their support in running a number of experiments and Natalia Perelman for implementing the Russian transliteration of the GIRT thesaurus. Major funding was provided by DARPA Department of Defense Advanced Research Projects Agency under research grant N66001-00-1-8911, Mar 2000-Feb 2003 as part of the DARPA Translingual Information Detection, Extraction, and Summarization Program TIDES .

## References

1  C Buckley, J Walz, M Mitra, and C Cardie. Using clustering and superconcepts within smart Trec-6. In E.M. Voorhees and D. K. Harman, editors, *he Si th*

 e t   Etrie al    n erence    E        IS   Special   u licati n          , pages
107 124, August 1998.

2  Pascal Fung. A statistical view on bilingual le icon e traction  From parallel
corpora to non-parallel corpora. In D Farwell L Gerber E Hovy, editor,   r
cee ing              n erence    achine  ranslati n an  the In  rmati n S up
enns l ania    S    ct  er            , pages 1 16. Springer-Verlag, 1998.

3  F. C. Gey, H. Jiang, and A. Chen. Manual queries and machine tranlation in cross-
language retrieval at trec-7. In E.M. Voorhees and D. K. Harman, editors,   he
Se enth  e t  Etrie al    n erence    E        IS   Special   u licati n         ,
pages 527 540. National Institute of Standards and Technology, July 1999.

4  Fredric Gey, Hailing Jiang, Vivien Petras, and Aitao Chen. Cross-language retrieval for the clef collections - comparing multiple methods of retrieval. In this
lume. Springer, 2000.

5  John Goldsmith, Darrick Higgins, and Svetlana Soglasnova. Automatic language-
specific stemming in information retrieval. In this    lume. Springer, 2000.

6  Djoerd Hiemstra, Wessel Kraaij, Renee Pohlmann, and Thijs Westerveld. Translation resources, merging strategies, and relevance feedback for cross-language
information retrieval. In this    lume. Springer, 2000.

7  Noriko Kando and Toshihiko Nozue, editors.   r cee ings    the First      I
    r sh p  n  apanese  e t  etrie al an    erm   ec gniti n. NACSIS (now Na-
tional Informatics Institute, Tokoyo, 1999.

8  Michael Kluck and Fredric Gey. The domain-specific task of clef - structure
and opportunities for specific evaluation strategies in cross-language information
retrieval. In this    lume. Springer, 2000.

9  K. Knight and J. Graehl. Machine transliteration. In    mputati nal   inguistics
   , 1998.

10  Wessel Kraaij, Renee Pohlmann, and Djoerd Hiemstra. Twenty-one at trec-8  Using language technology for information retrieval. In Ellen Voorhees and D Harman, editors,    r ing    tes   the Eighth  e t  Etrie al    n erence    E    ,
pages 203 217, November 1999.

11  Paul McNamee, James Mayfield, and Christine Piatko. A language-independent
approach to european te t retrieval. In this    lume. Springer, 2000.

12  Jian-Yun Nie, Michel Simard, and George Foster. Multilingual information retrieval based on parallel te ts from the web. In this    lume. Springer, 2000.

13  Jian-Yun Nie, Michel Simard, Pierre Isabelle, and Richard Durand.  Cross-
language information retrieval based on parallel te ts and automatic mining of
parallel te ts from the web. In SIGI        r cee ings    the    n   nnual Inter
nati nal    SIGI    n erence  n  esearch an  De el pment in In  rmati n
etrie al    ugust           er ele        S  , pages 74 81. ACM, 1999.

14  Douglas Oard, Gina-Anne Levow, and Clara Cabezas. Clef e periments at the
university of maryland  Statistical stemming and backo   translation strategies.
In this    lume. Springer, 2000.

15  Eugenio Picchi and Carol Peters. Cross language information retrieval  A system
for comparable corpus querying. In Gregory Gre enstette, editor,   r ss  anguage
In  rmati n   etrie al, pages 81 91. Kluwer, 1998.

16  Phillip Resnick. Mining the web for bilingual te t. In   r cee ings    th  nnual
eeting   the  ss ciati n  r  mputati nal  inguistics          llege  ar
ar lan    une    , 1999.

17  B. Stalls and K. Knight. Translating names and technical terms in arabic te t. In
    r c   the    I G        r sh p  n   mputati nal  ppr aches t  Semitic
anguages       , 1998.

# CLEF 2000 – Overview of Results

Martin Braschler

Eurospider Information Technology AG
Schaffhauserstr. 18
8006 Zürich, Switzerland
braschler@eurospider.ch

**Abstract.** The first CLEF campaign was a big success in attracting increased participation when compared to its predecessor, the TREC8 cross-language track. Both the number of participants and of experiments has grown considerably. This paper presents details of the various subtasks, and attempts to summarize the main results and research directions that were observed. Additionally, the CLEF collection is examined with respect to the completeness of its relevance assessments. The analysis indicates that the CLEF relevance assessments are of comparable quality to those of the well-known and trusted TREC ad-hoc collections.

## 1 Introduction

CLEF 2000 has brought a substantial increase in the number of participating groups compared to its predecessor, the TREC8 cross-language (CLIR) track [1]. This means that the number and diversity of experiments that were submitted has also increased. The following report tries to summarize the main results and main research directions that were observed during the first CLEF campaign.

Multilingual retrieval was the biggest subtask in CLEF, and also received the most attention. Therefore, it will be the main focus of this paper. That the majority of participants tried to tackle this subtask is an encouraging sign. It is evidence that these groups try to adapt their systems to a multitude of languages, instead of focusing on a few obvious pairs. However, the smaller subtasks of bilingual and monolingual retrieval served important purposes as well, both in terms of helping to better understand the characteristics of individual languages, as well as in attracting new groups that have not previously participated in the TREC CLIR track or any other TREC track.

In the following, details with respect to the number of runs for the subtasks and different languages are given. The discussion continues with a summary of some defining characteristics of individual experiments by the participants, and comparisons of the results that were obtained. Finally, the resulting CLEF test collection is investigated for the completeness of its relevance assessments.

C. Peters (Ed.): CLEF 2000, LNCS 2069, pp. 89-101, 2001.
© Springer-Verlag Berlin Heidelberg 2001

## 2    Subtasks

In total, 20 groups from 10 different countries participated in one or more of the subtasks that were offered for CLEF 2000 (see Table 1). Of these, 16 did some form of cross-language experiments (either multilingual, bilingual or both), while the remaining 4 concentrated exclusively on monolingual retrieval. Three groups worked on the GIRT domain-specific subtask. Nine groups participated in more than one subtask, but no group tried all four.

**Table 1.** List of participants

| | |
|---|---|
| CWI (Netherlands) | Univ. Dortmund (Germany) |
| Eurospider (Switzerland) | Univ. Glasgow (UK) |
| IAI (Germany) | Univ. Maryland (USA) |
| IRIT (France) | Univ. Montreal/RALI (Canada) |
| ITC-irst (Italy) | Univ. Salamanca (Spain) |
| Johns Hopkins Univ./APL (USA) | Univ. Sheffield (UK) |
| New Mexico State Univ. (USA) | Univ. Tampere (Finland) |
| Syracuse Univ. (USA) | Univ. of California at Berkeley (USA) |
| TNO/Univ. Twente (Netherlands) | West Group (USA) |
| Univ. Chicago (USA) | Xerox XRCE (France) |

Table 2 compares the number of participants and experiments to those of earlier TREC CLIR tracks.

Please note that in TREC6, only bilingual retrieval was offered, which resulted in a large number of runs combining different pairs of languages [10]. Starting with TREC7, multilingual runs were introduced, which usually consist of multiple runs for the individual languages that are later merged. The number of experiments for TREC6 is therefore not directly comparable to later years.

**Table 2.** Development in the number of participants and experiments

| Year | # Participants | # Experiments |
|---|---|---|
| TREC6 | 13 | (95) |
| TREC7 | 9 | 27 |
| TREC8 | 12 | 45 |
| CLEF | 20 | 95 |

CLEF was clearly a breakthrough in promoting larger participation. While the number of participants stayed more or less constant in the three years that the CLIR track was part of TREC, this number nearly doubled for the first year that CLEF was a stand-alone activity.

A total of 95 individual experiments were submitted, also a substantial increase over the number in the TREC8 CLIR track. A breakdown into the individual subtasks can be found in Table 3.

**Table 3.** Experiments listed by subtask

| Subtask | # Participants | # Runs |
|---|---|---|
| Multilingual | 11 | 28 |
| Bilingual | 10 | 27 |
| Monolingual French | 9 | 10 |
| Monolingual German | 11 | 13 |
| Monolingual Italian | 9 | 10 |
| Domain-specific GIRT | 3 | 7 |

All topic languages were used for experiments, including the translations of the topics into Dutch, Finnish, Spanish and Swedish, which were provided by independent third parties. German and English were the most popular topic languages, with German being used slightly more than English. However, this is partly due to the fact that English was not an eligible topic language for the bilingual and monolingual subtasks. Table 4 shows a summary of the topic languages and their use.

**Table 4.** Experiments listed by topic language

| Language | # Runs |
|---|---|
| English | 26 |
| French | 17 |
| German | 29 |
| Italian | 11 |
| Others | 13 |

A large majority of runs (80 out of 95) used the complete topics, including all fields. Since it is generally agreed that using such lengthy expressions of information needs does not well reflect the realities of some applications such as web searching, it probably would be beneficial if the number of experiments using shorter queries increases in coming years. Similarly, the number of manual experiments was low (6 out of 95). Manual experiments are useful in establishing baselines and in improving the overall quality of relevance assessment pools. Therefore, an increase in the number of these experiments would be welcome; especially since they also tend to focus on interesting aspects of the retrieval process that are not usually covered by batch evaluations.

# 3    Characteristics of Experiments

Table 5 shows a summary of the use of some core elements of multilingual information retrieval in the participants' systems. Most groups that experimented with cross-language retrieval concentrated on query translation, although two groups, University of Maryland and Eurospider, also tried document translation.

There is more variation in the type of translation resources that were employed. A majority of systems used some form of a dictionary for at least one language combination. There is also a sizeable number of participants that experimented with translation resources that were constructed automatically from corpora. Lastly, some groups either used commercial machine translation (MT) systems or manual query reformulations. A lot of groups combined more than one of these types of translation resources, both by using different types for different languages or by using more than one type for individual language pairs.

**Table 5.** Some main characteristics of experiments by individual participants

| | CWI | Eurospider | IAI | IRIT | ITC-irst | Johns Hopkins U/APL | New Mexico SU | Syracuse U | TNO/U Twente | U Chicago | U Dortmund | U Glasgow | U Maryland | U Montreal/RALI | U Salamanca | U Sheffield | U Tampere | UC Berkeley | West Group | Xerox XRCE |
|---|---|---|---|---|---|---|---|---|---|---|---|---|---|---|---|---|---|---|---|---|
| ***Trans. Approach*** | | | | | | | | | | | | | | | | | | | | |
| Query translation | • | • | • | • | | • | • | • | • | | • | • | | • | • | • | • | • | • | • |
| Document trans. | | • | | | | | | | | | | | | • | | | | | | |
| No translation | | | | | | • | | | | • | | | | | | | | | • | • |
| ***Trans. Resources*** | | | | | | | | | | | | | | | | | | | | |
| Dictionary | • | • | • | • | | | | • | • | • | | • | • | • | • | | | • | • | • |
| Corpus-based | | • | | • | | | • | | • | | | • | | • | • | | | | | |
| MT | | • | | | | | • | | | | | • | | | | | | • | | |
| Manual | | | | | | | • | | | | | | | | | | | | • | |
| ***Ling. Processing*** | | | | | | | | | | | | | | | | | | | | |
| Stemming | • | • | • | • | • | | • | | • | • | • | • | • | • | • | • | • | • | • | ? |
| Decompounding | • | • | • | | | | | | • | | | | | | | • | • | | • | |

Considerable effort was invested this year in stemming and decompounding issues. This may be partly due to increased participation by European groups, which exploited their intimate knowledge of the languages in CLEF. Nearly all groups used some form of stemming in their experiments. Some of these stemming methods were elaborate, with detailed morphological analysis and part-of-speech annotation. On the other hand, some approaches were geared specifically towards simplicity or language-independence, with multiple groups relying on statistical approaches to the problem. The German decompounding issue was also addressed by several groups, using methods of varying complexity.

Some additional noteworthy characteristics include:

- A new method for re-cstimating translation probabilities during blind relevance feedback by the TNO/University of Twente group [5].
- Extensive GIRT experiments, including the use of the GIRT thesaurus, by the University of California at Berkeley [3].
- The use of 6-grams as an alternative to stemming/decompounding by Johns Hopkins University/APL [7].
- The use of lexical triangulation, a method to improve the quality of translations involving an intermediary pivot language, by the University of Sheffield [4].

- Mining the web for parallel texts, which can then be used in corpus-based approaches. This was used by University of Montreal/RALI [9] and the TNO/University of Twente group, as well as Johns Hopkins University/APL.
- The combination of both document translation and query translation, by Eurospider [2].
- Interactive experiments by New Mexico State University.

For a detailed discussion of these and more characteristics, please refer to the individual participants' papers in this volume.

# 4    Results

## 4.1    Multilingual

Eleven groups submitted results for the multilingual subtask. Since for many of these groups this subtask was the main focus of their work, they sent multiple different result sets. Figure 1 shows the best experiments of the five top groups in the automatic category for this subtask.

It is interesting to note that all five top groups are previous TREC participants, with one of them going all the way back to TREC1 (Berkeley). These groups outperformed newcomers substantially. This may be an indication that the "veteran" groups benefited from the experience they gained in previous years, whereas the new groups still experienced some "growing pains". It will be interesting to see if the newcomers catch up next year. The two top performing entries both used a combination of translations from multiple sources. The entry from Johns Hopkins University achieved good performance even though avoiding the use of language-specific resources.

## 4.2    Bilingual

The best results for the bilingual subtask come from groups that also participated in the multilingual subtask (see Figure 2). Additionally, University of Tampere and CWI also submitted entries that performed well. Both these entries use compound-splitting for the source language (German and Dutch, respectively), which likely helped to get a better coverage in their dictionary-based approaches.

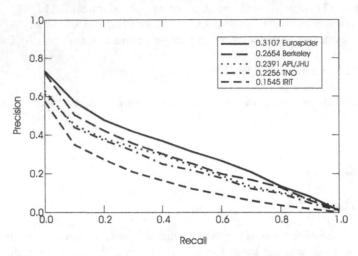

**Fig. 1.** The best entries of the top five performing groups for the multilingual subtask.

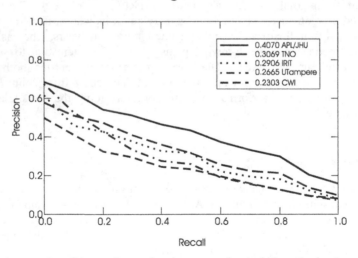

**Fig. 2.** The best entries of the top five performing groups for the bilingual subtask.

### 4.3    Monolingual

Some of the best performing entries in the monolingual subtask came from groups that did not conduct cross-language experiments and instead concentrated on monolingual retrieval. Two such groups are West Group and ITC-irst, which produced the top-performing French and Italian entries, respectively (see Figure 3 and

4). Both groups used elaborate morphological analysis in order to obtain base forms of query words and document terms. However, the performance of the top groups in French and Italian monolingual retrieval is in general very comparable.

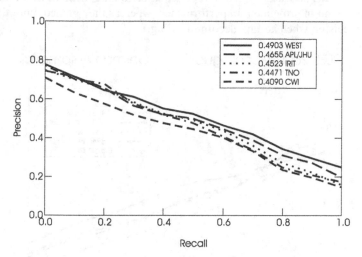

**Fig. 3.** The best entries of the top five performing groups for the French monolingual subtask.

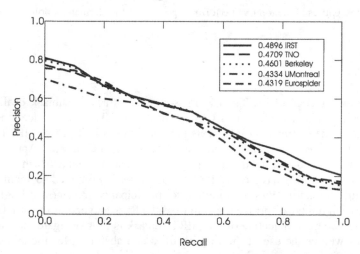

**Fig. 4.** The best entries of the top five performing groups for the Italian monolingual subtask.

In contrast, the differences for German monolingual are substantially larger (see Figure 5). The best run by the top performing group outperforms the best entry by the fifth-placed group by 37% for German, whereas for French and Italian the difference is only 20% and 13%, respectively. One likely explanation for the larger spread is the decompounding issue: the four best performing groups all addressed this peculiarity of the German language either by splitting the compounds (Eurospider, TNO, West Group) or through the use of n-grams (Johns Hopkins). Especially the results by West Group seem to support the notion that decompounding was crucial to obtaining good performance in this subtask [8]. They report that stemming without decompounding gave practically no improvement in performance, whereas they gained more than 25% in average precision when adding decompounding.

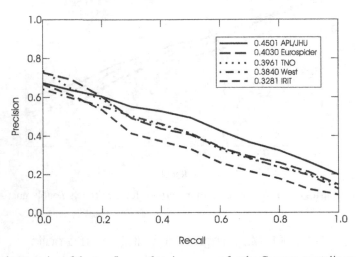

**Fig. 5.** The best entries of the top five performing groups for the German monolingual subtask.

## 4.4   GIRT

Continuing the practice of the TREC8 cross-language track, a subtask dealing with domain-specific data was offered to CLEF participants. The data collection was an extended set of the German "GIRT" texts previously used in TREC-CLIR. The texts come from the domain of social science, and are written in German. Approximately three quarter (71%) of the texts have English titles, and around 8% have English abstracts. The texts also have controlled thesaurus terms assigned to them and the corresponding thesaurus was distributed to participants in German/English and German/Russian bilingual form. No group used the Russian version for official CLEF experiments. The main objective of the GIRT subtask is to investigate the use of this thesaurus, as well as the use of the English titles and abstracts, for monolingual and cross-language information retrieval (see also [6]).

Three groups submitted a total of seven runs. Xerox focused on monolingual experiments, whereas University of California at Berkeley investigated only cross-language retrieval on this collection. University of Dortmund submitted results from both monolingual and cross-language experiments.

While the Dortmund group used machine translation, a range of different translation approaches was used by Berkeley: thesaurus lookup, "entry vocabulary module (EVM)" and machine translation. They used a combination of all three approaches as well, giving them superior performance to any of the single approaches.

## CLEF 2000 Domain-specific Task - GIRT

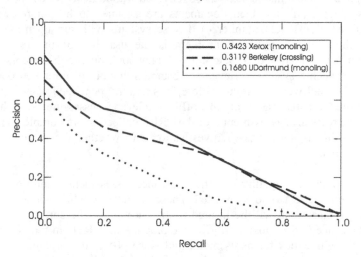

Fig. 6. The best entries of the groups participating in the GIRT domain-specific subtask.

# 5 Completeness of Relevance Assessments

The results reported in this paper rely heavily on the concept of judging the relevance of documents with respect to given topics. The relevance of documents is usually judged by one or more human "assessors", making this a costly undertaking. These "relevance assessments" are then used for the calculation of the recall/precision figures that underlie the graphs and figures presented here and in the appendix of this volume.

It is therefore not surprising that the quality of the relevance assessments is of concern to the participants. Indeed, with evaluation forums such as TREC becoming more and more popular, this issue has been frequently raised in the last few years. Two main concerns can be discerned:

*Concern 1:* The "quality" of the relevance judgments. Of concern is the ability of the persons doing the assessment to sufficiently understand the topics and documents, and the consistency of the judgments (no personal bias, clear interpretation of the judging guidelines, etc.). On the one hand, it has been shown that agreement between assessors, when documents are judged by more than one person, is usually rather low. On the other hand, it has also been repeatedly demonstrated that while this disagreement can change absolute performance figures, the overall ranking of the systems remains stable.

*Concern 2:* The "completeness" of the relevance judgments. Of concern is the use of so-called "pooling methods". The use of human judges for relevance makes it impractical to judge every document in today's large scale test collections. Therefore, only a sample of documents, namely those retrieved with high scores by the evaluated systems, is judged. All unjudged documents are assumed to be not relevant. The assertion is that a sufficient number of diverse systems will turn up most relevant documents this way. A potential problem is the usability of the resulting test collection for the evaluation of a system that did not contribute to this "pool of judged documents". If such a system retrieves a substantial number of unjudged documents that are relevant, but were not found before, it is unfairly penalized when calculating the evaluation measures based on the official relevance assessments. It has been shown that the relevance assessments for the TREC collection are complete enough to make such problems unlikely. An investigation into whether the same is true for CLEF follows below.

In order to study the quality of the relevance assessments, multiple sets of independent judgments would be needed. These are not available, which means that the subsequent discussion will be limited to the question of the completeness of the assessments. Since CLEF closely follows the practices of TREC in the design of the topics and the guidelines for assessment, and since NIST, the organizer of TREC, actively participates in the coordination of CLEF, the quality of the assessments in general can be assumed to be comparable (see [12] for an analysis of the TREC collections).

One way to analyze the completeness of the relevance judgments is by focusing on the "unique relevant documents" [13]. For this purpose, an unique relevant document is defined as a document which was judged relevant with respect to a specific topic, but that would not have been part of the pool of judged documents had a certain group not participated in the evaluation. I.e., only one group retrieved the document with a score high enough to have it included in the judgment pool. This addresses the concern that systems not directly participating in the evaluation are unfairly penalized. By subtracting relevant documents only found by a certain group, and then reevaluating the results for this group, we simulate the scenario that this group was a non-participant. The smaller the change in performance that is observed, the higher is the probability that the relevance assessments are sufficiently complete.

For CLEF, this kind of analysis was run for the experiments that were submitted to the multilingual subtask. A total of twelve sets of relevance assessments were used: the original set, and eleven sets that were built by taking away the relevant documents uniquely found by one specific participant. The results for every multilingual experiment were then recomputed using the set without the group-specific relevant documents. Figure 7 shows the number of unique relevant documents per group participating in CLEF. The key figures obtained after rerunning the evaluations can be found in Table 6 and Figure 8.

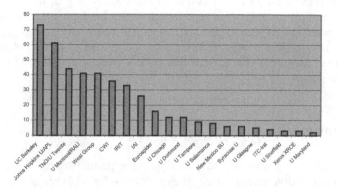

**Fig. 7.** Number of unique relevant documents contributed by each CLEF participant for the multilingual subtask.

**Table 6.** Key figures for investigation into the effect of "unique relevant documents" on the recall and precision measures. Presented are the observed changes in mean average precision.

| Mean absolute diff. | 0.0013 | Mean diff. in percent | 0.80% |
|---|---|---|---|
| Max absolute diff. | 0.0059 | Max diff. in percent | 5.99% |
| Standard deviation | 0.0012 | Standard deviation | 1.15% |

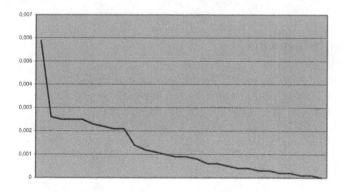

**Fig. 8.** Changes in mean average precision (absolute values) for all multilingual runs submitted to CLEF. The majority of runs experiences a change of less than 0.002.

These numbers were calculated based on the absolute values of the differences. Note that even though relevant documents are removed from the evaluation, mean average precision can actually increase after recalculation due to interpolation effects. The figures reported for TREC in [11] are based on signed numbers, and therefore not directly comparable. For CLEF, calculating these numbers the TREC way, the mean difference is -0.0007, equivalent to a change of -0.57 percent. This compares favorably with an observed mean difference of -0.0019 (-0.78%) for TREC8 ad hoc and -0.0018 (-1.43%) for TREC9 Chinese CLIR. The ranking of the systems is also very stable: the only two systems that switch ranks have an original performance difference of less than 0.1%, a difference that is well below any meaningful statistical significance. The relevance assessments for the CLEF test collection therefore seem to be well suited for evaluating systems that did not directly participate in the original evaluation campaign.

# 6     Conclusions

CLEF 2000 was a big success in attracting more participation. The participating groups submitted a diverse collection of experiments for all languages and subtasks. Some foci seem to have changed slightly from last year at the TREC8 cross-language track; specifically, increased European participation appears to have strengthened the emphasis on language-specific issues, such as stemming and decompounding. Those groups that concentrated on these issues had considerable success in the monolingual subtasks. The best performing cross-language experiments (the multilingual and bilingual subtasks) came from "veteran" TREC participants. It appears that these groups benefited from their experience, and it will be interesting to see if some of the newcomers can catch up in 2001.

An investigation into the completeness of the relevance assessments for the CLEF collection, an important precondition for the usefulness of the test collection in future evaluations, produced encouraging numbers. This makes the collection an attractive choice for a wide range of evaluation purposes outside the official CLEF campaign.

# 7     Acknowledgements

The author would like to thank Ellen Voorhees and Paul Over at NIST for their assistance in calculating and interpreting the numbers needed for the analysis of the relevance assessments. Their help was greatly appreciated.

# References

1. Braschler, M., Peters, C., Schäuble, P.: Cross-Language Information Retrieval (CLIR) Track Overview. In *Proceedings of the Eighth Text Retrieval Conference (TREC8)* (1999)
2. Braschler, M., Schäuble, P.: Experiments with the Eurospider Retrieval System for CLEF 2000. See this volume.
3. Gey, F. C., Jiang, H., Petras, V., Chen, A.: Cross-Language Retrieval for the CLEF Collections – Comparing Multiple Methods of Retrieval. See this volume.
4. Gollins, T., Sanderson M.: Sheffield University: CLEF 2000 Submission – Bilingual Track: German to English. See this volume.
5. Hiemstra, D., Kraaij, W., Pohlmann, R., Westerveld, T.: Translation Resources, merging strategies and relevance feedback for cross-language information retrieval. See this volume.
6. Kluck, M., Gey, F. C.: The Domain-Specific Task of CLEF – Specific Evaluation Strategies in Cross-Language Information Retrieval. See this volume.

7. McNamee, P., Mayfield, J., Piatko, C.: A Language-Independent Approach to European Text Retrieval. See this volume.
8. Moulinier, I., McCulloh, A., Lund, E.: West Group at CLEF2000: Non-English Monolingual Retrieval. See this volume.
9. Nie, J.-Y., Simard, M., Foster, G.: Multilingual Information Retrieval based on Parallel Texts from the Web. See this volume.
10. Schäuble, P. Sheridan, P.: Cross-Language Information Retrieval (CLIR) Track Overview. In *Proceedings of the Sixth Text Retrieval Conference (TREC6)* (1997)
11. Voorhees, E. M., Harman, D.: Overview of the Eighth Text REtrieval Conference (TREC-8). In *Proceedings of the Eighth Text Retrieval Conference (TREC8)* (1999)
12. Voorhees, E. M.: Variations in relevance judgments and the measurement of retrieval effectiveness. Information Processing and Management, 36:697-716 (2000)
13. Zobel, J.: How reliable are the results of large-scale information retrieval experiments? In *Proceedings of the 21$^{st}$ Annual International ACM SIGIR Conference on Research and Development in Information Retrieval* (1998)

# Translation Resources, Merging Strategies, and Relevance Feedback for Cross-Language Information Retrieval

Djoerd Hiemstra[1], Wessel Kraaij[2], Renée Pohlmann[2], and Thijs Westerveld[1]

[1] University of Twente, CTIT, P.O. Bo  217, 7500 AE Enschede, The Netherlands
{hiemstra,westerve}@cs.utwente.nl
[2] TNO-TPD, P.O. Bo  155, 2600 AD Delft, The Netherlands
{kraai ,pohlmann}@tpd.tno.nl

**Abstract.** This paper describes the official runs of the Twenty-One group for the first CLEF workshop. The Twenty-One group participated in the monolingual, bilingual and multilingual tasks. The following new techniques are introduced in this paper. In the bilingual task we e -perimented with di erent methods to estimate translation probabilities. In the multilingual task we e perimented with refinements on raw-score merging techniques and with a new relevance feedback algorithm that re-estimates both the model s translation probabilities and the relevance weights. Finally, we performed preliminary e periments to e ploit the web to generate translation probabilities and bilingual dictionaries, notably for English-Italian and English-Dutch.

## 1 Introduction

Twenty-One is a project funded by the EU Telematics Applications programme, sector Information Engineering. The project subtitle is  Development of a Multimedia Information Transaction and Dissemination Tool . Twenty-One started early 1996 and was completed in June 1999. Because the TREC ad-hoc and cross-language information retrieval  CLIR  tasks fitted our needs to evaluate the system on the aspects of monolingual and cross-language retrieval performance, TNO-TPD and University of Twente participated under the  ag of  Twenty-One  in TREC-6  7  8. Since the cooperation is continued in other projects: Olive and Druid, we have decided to continue our participation in CLEF as  Twenty-One .[1] For all tasks, we used the TNO vector retrieval engine. The engine supports several term weighting schemes. The principal term weighting scheme we used is based on the use of statistical language models for information retrieval as explained below.

---

[1] Information on Twenty-one, Olive and Druid is available at
http://dis.tpd.tno.nl/

C. Peters (Ed.): CLEF 2000, LNCS 2069, pp. 102–115, 2001.
© Springer-Verlag Berlin Heidelberg 2001

## 2  The Approach

All runs were carried out with an information retrieval system based on a simple unigram language model. The basic idea is that documents can be represented by simple statistical language models. Now, if a query is more probable given a language model based on document $^{(1)}$, than given e.g. a language model based on document $^{(2)}$, then we hypothesise that the document $^{(1)}$ is more relevant to the query than document $^{(2)}$. Thus the probability of generating a certain query given a document-based language model can serve as a score to rank documents with respect to relevance.

$$P(\,_1,\,_2,\cdots,\,_n)\ P\qquad P\ \prod_{i=1}^{n}\big(1-\,_i\big)P(\,_i)\ +\ _iP(\,_i)\qquad 1$$

Formula 1 shows the basic idea of this approach to information retrieval, where the document-based language model is interpolated with a background language model to compensate for sparseness. In the formula, $_i$ is a random variable for the query term on position $i$ in the query $1 \leq i \leq$, where is the query length, which sample space is the set $^{(1)},\,^{(2)},\ldots,\,^{(m)}$ of all terms in the collection. The probability measure $P(\,_i)$ defines the probability of drawing a term at random from the collection, $P(\,_i)$ defines the probability of drawing a term at random from the document and $_i$ defines the importance of each query term. The marginal probability of relevance of a document $P$ might be assumed uniformly distributed over the documents in which case it may be ignored in the above formula.

### 2.1    el    a g age    a i   e ie al

Information retrieval models and statistical translation models can be integrated into one unifying model for cross-language information retrieval [2,5]. Let $_i$ be a random variable for the source language query term on position $i$. Each document gets a score defined by the following formula.

$$P(\,_1,\,_2,\cdots,\,_n)\ P$$
$$P\ \prod_{i=1}^{n}\sum_{j=1}^{m}P(\,_i\mid\,_i^{(j)})\Big(\big(1-\,_i\big)P(\,_i^{(j)})\ +\ _iP(\,_i^{(j)})\Big)\qquad 2$$

In the formula, the probability measure $P(\,_i\mid\,_i^{(j)})$ defines the translation probabilities.

### 2.2  T a  la i  i    a  i e

In practice, the statistical translation model will be used as follows. The automatic query formulation process will translate the query $_1,\,_2,\cdots,\,_n$ using a probabilistic dictionary. The probabilistic dictionary is a dictionary that list pairs   ,   together with their probability of occurrence, where   is from the sample space of  $_i$ and  is from the sample space of  $_i$. For each  $_i$ there will be one or more realisations  $_i$ of  $_i$ for which $P$  $_i$  $_i$   $_i$   0, which will be called the possible translations of  $_i$. The possible translations should be grouped for each $i$ to search the document collection, resulting in a structured query.

For instance, suppose the original French query on an English collection is  déchets dangereux , then possible translations of  déchets  might be   waste ,  litter  or  garbage , possible translations of  dangereux  might be   dangerous  or  hazardous  and the structured query can be presented as follows.

$$\text{ste   itter   g r ge ,   ngero s  h   r o s}$$

The product from $i$   1 to   in this case   2 of equation 2 is represented above by using the comma as is done in the representation of a query of length 2 as  $_1$,  $_2$. The sum from $j$   1 to   of equation 2 is represented by displaying only the realisations of  $_i$ for which $P$  $_i$  $_i$   0 and by separating those by   '. So, in practice, translation takes place during automatic query formulation  query translation , resulting in a structured query like the one displayed above that is matched against each document in the collection. Unless stated otherwise, whenever this paper mentions  query terms', it will denote the target language query terms: realisations of  $_i$. Realisations of  $_i$, the source language query terms, will usually be left implicit. The combination of the structured query representation and the translation probabilities will implicitly define the sequence of the source language query terms  $_1$,  $_2$,$\cdots$,  $_n$, but the actual realisation of the sequence is not important to the system.

### 2.3    babili    i  a i

The prior probability of relevance of a document $P$    , the probability of term occurrence in the collection $P$  $_i$  and the probability of term occurrence in the relevant document $P$  $_i$    are defined by the collection that is searched. For the evaluations reported in this paper, the following definitions were used, where $t$  ,    denotes the number of occurrences of the term   in the document  , and $d$    denotes the number of documents in which the term   occurs. Equation 3 is the definition used for the unofficial  document length normalisation  runs reported in section 5.

$$P \qquad \frac{\sum_t t \quad ,}{\sum_{t,} \ t \quad , k} \qquad\qquad 3$$

$$P \ _i \quad _i \qquad \frac{t \quad _i,}{\sum_t t \quad ,} \qquad\qquad 4$$

$$P \ _i \quad _i \qquad \frac{d \quad _i}{\sum_t d} \qquad\qquad 5$$

The translation probabilities $P$  $_i$  $_i$  and the value of  $_i$, however, are unknown. The collection that is searched was not translated, or if it was translated, the translations are not available. Translation probabilities should therefore be estimated from other data, for instance from a parallel corpus. The value of $\lambda_i$ determines the importance of the source language query term. If $\lambda_i$ 1 then the system will assign zero probability to documents that do not contain any of the possible translations of the original query term on position $i$. In this case, a possible translation of the source language term is mandatory in the retrieved documents. If $\lambda_i$ 0 then the possible translations of the original query term on position $i$ will not affect the final ranking. In this case, the source language query term is treated as if it were a stop word. For ad-hoc queries, it is not known which of the original query terms are important and which are not important and a constant value for each $\lambda_i$ is taken. The system's default value is $\lambda_i$ 0.3.

## 2.4    le e a i

Equation 2 is not implemented as is, but instead it is rewritten into a weighting algorithm that assigns zero weight to terms that do not occur in the document. Filling in the definitions of equation 3, 4 and 5 in equation 2 results in the following formula. The probability measure $P_{i\ i}{}^{(j)}$ will be replaced by the translation probability estimates $_i j$.

$$P_{,\ 1,\ 2,\cdots,\ n} \quad \frac{\sum_t t_{,}}{\sum_{t,}\ t_{,k}} \prod_{i\ 1}^{n}\sum_{j\ 1}^{m}\ _i j\ \left(1-\ _i\ \frac{d^{(j)}}{\sum_t d}\right)\ _i\frac{t^{(j)}_{,}}{\sum_t t_{,}}$$

The translation probabilities can be moved into the inner sum. As summing is associative and commutative, it is not necessary to calculate each probability separately before adding them. Instead, respectively the document frequencies and the term frequencies of the disjuncts can be added beforehand, properly multiplied by the translation probabilities. Only $_i$ in the big sum is constant for every addition and can therefore be moved outside the sum, resulting in:

$$P_{,\ 1,\ 2,\cdots,\ n} \quad \frac{\sum_t l_{,}}{\sum_{t,}\ t_{,k}} \prod_{i\ 1}^{n}\ \left(1-\ _i\ \frac{\sum_j^m\ _1\ _i j\ d^{(j)}}{\sum_t d}\right)\ _i\frac{\sum_j^m\ _1\ _i j\ t^{(j)}_{,}}{\sum_t t_{,}}$$

Using simple calculus see e.g. 4 , the probability measure can now be rewritten into a term weighting algorithm that assigns zero weight to non-matching terms, resulting in equation 6. The formula ranks documents in exactly the same order as equation 2.

$$P_{,\ 1,\ 2,\cdots,\ n} \quad \log\sum_t t_{,} \quad \sum_{i\ 1}^{n}\log 1\ \frac{_i\ \sum_j^m\ _1\ _i j\ t^{(j)}_{,}}{1-\ _i\ \sum_j^m\ _1\ _i j\ d^{(j)}}\ \frac{\sum_t d}{\sum_t t_{,}} \qquad 6$$

Equation 6 is the algorithm implemented in the TNO retrieval engine. It contains a weighted sum of respectively the term frequencies and the document frequencies where the weights are determined by the translation probabilities $_i j$. Unweighted summing of frequencies was used before for on-line stemming in 6 in a vector space model retrieval system. Unweighted summing of frequencies is implemented in the Inquery system as the  synonym operator . Grouping possible translations of a source language term by the Inquery synonym operator has shown to be a successful approach to cross-language information retrieval 1,10 .

The model does not require the translation probabilities $_i j$ to sum up to one for each $i$, since they are conditioned on the target language query term and not on the source language query term. Interestingly, for the final ranking it does not matter what the actual sum of the translation probabilities is. Only the relative proportions of the translations define the final ranking of documents. This can be seen by $_i j$ which occurs in the numerator and in the denominator of the big fraction in equation 6.

## 2.5     ele a e Fee ba     e                     a g age e ie al

This paper introduces a new relevance feedback method for cross-language information retrieval. If there were some known relevant documents, then the values of $_i j$ and $_i$ could be re-estimated from that data. The idea is the following. Suppose there are three known relevant English documents to the French query  déchets dangereux . If two out of three documents contain the term  waste and none contain the terms  litter  and  garbage  then this is an indication that  waste  is the correct translation and should be assigned a higher translation probability than  litter  and  garbage . If only one of the three known relevant document contains one or more possible translations of  dangereux  then this is an indication that the original query term  déchets  is more important  possible translations occur in more relevant documents  than the original query term  dangereux  and the value of $_i$ should be higher for  déchets  than for  dangereux .

The actual re-estimation of $_i j$ and $_i$ was done by iteratively applying the EM-algorithm defined by the formulas in equation 7. In the algorithm, $_i j^{(\ )}$ and $_i^{(\ )}$ denote the values on the $p$th iteration and $r$ denotes the number of known relevant documents. The values are initialised with the translation probabilities from the dictionary and with $_i^{(0)}$  0.3. The re-estimation formulas should be used simultaneously for each $p$ until the values do not change significantly anymore.

$$_i j^{(\ 1)}\ \frac{1}{r}\sum_1^r\ \frac{_i j^{(\ )}\ 1-\ _i^{(\ )}\ P\ _i\ ^{(j)}\ \ _i^{(\ )}P\ _i\ ^{(j)}}{\sum_1^m\ _i\ ^{(\ )}\ 1-\ _i^{(\ )}\ P\ _i\ ^{(\ )}\ \ _i^{(\ )}P\ _i\ ^{(\ )}}$$

$$_i^{(\ 1)}\ \frac{1}{r}\sum_1^r\ \frac{_i^{(\ )}\ \sum_1^m\ _i\ ^{(\ )}P\ _i\ ^{(\ )}}{\sum_1^m\ _i\ ^{(\ )}\ 1-\ _i^{(\ )}\ P\ _i\ ^{(\ )}\ \ _i^{(\ )}P\ _i\ ^{(\ )}}$$

7

The re-estimation of $_i j$ and $_i$ was done from  pseudo-relevant' documents. First the top 10 documents were retrieved using the default values of $_i j$ and

$i$ and then the feedback algorithm was used on these documents to find the new values. The actual algorithm implemented was a variation of equation 7 of the form: 1   $r$   1   · default value   $\sum^r$  $_1$ ... to avoid that e.g.  $_i$   1 after re-estimation.

## Translation Resources

As in previous years we applied a dictionary-based query translation approach. The translations were based on the VLIS lexical database of Van Dale publishers 3 . Because VLIS currently lacks translations into Italian, we used two other resources: i  the Systran web based MT engine ii  a probabilistic lexicon based a parallel web corpus. The next section will describe the construction of this new resource in more detail.

### 3.1     a allel    eb        a

We developed three parallel corpora based on web pages in close cooperation with RALI, Université de Montréal. RALI already had developed an English-French parallel corpus of web pages, so it seemed interesting to investigate the feasibility of a full multilingual system based on web derived lexical resources only. We used the PTMiner tool  8  to find web pages which have a high probability to be translations of each other. The mining process consists of the following steps:

1. Query a web search engine for web pages with a hyperlink anchor text   English version  and respective variants.
2.  For each web site  Query a web search engine for all web pages on a particular site.
3.  For each web site  Try to find pairs of path names that match certain patterns, e.g.: / ep rt ent/rese rch/ e  ers/eng ish/ho e.ht      and / ep rt ent/rese rch/ e  ers/it  i n.ht  .
4.  For each pair  download web pages, perform a language check using a probabilistic language classifier, remove pages which are not positively identified as being written in a particular language.

The mining process was run for three language pairs and resulted in three modest size parallel corpora. Table 1 lists sizes of the corpus during intermediate steps. Due to the dynamic nature of the web, a lot of pages that have been indexed, do not exist anymore. Sometimes a site is down for maintenance. Finally a lot of pages are simply place holders for images and are discarded by the language identification step.

These parallel corpora have been used in different ways: i  to refine the estimates of translation probabilities of a dictionary based translation system  corpus based probability estimation ii  to construct simple statistical translation models  8 . The former application will be described in more detail in Section 5.2 the latter in Section 5.3. The translation models for English-Italian and English-German, complemented with an already existing model for English-French formed also the basis for a full corpus based translation multilingual run which is described elsewhere in this volume  7 .

**Table 1.** Intermediate sizes during corpus construction

| language | number of web sites | number of candidate pages | number of candidate pairs | retrieved and cleaned pairs |
|---|---|---|---|---|
| EN-IT | 3,651 | 1,053,649 | 23,447 | 4,768 |
| EN-DE | 3,817 | 1,828,906 | 33,577 | 5,743 |
| EN-NL | 3,004 | 1,170,082 | 24,738 | 2,907 |

## Merging Intermediate Runs

Our strategy to multilingual retrieval is to translate the query into the document languages, perform separate language specific runs and merge the results into a single result file. In previous CLIR evaluations, we compared different merging strategies:

> **bi**  Here the idea is that document scores are not comparable across collections, because we are basically ignorant about the distribution of relevant documents in the retrieved lists, round robin assumes that these distributions are similar across languages.

a        e This type of merging assumes that document scores are comparable across collections.

a    ba e  It has been observed that the relationship between probability of relevance and the log of the rank of a document can be approximated by a linear function, at least for a certain class of IR systems. If a training collection is available, one can estimate the parameters of this relationship by applying regression. Merging can subsequently be based on the estimated probability of relevance. Note that the actual score of a document is only used to rank documents, but that merging is based on the rank, not on the score.

The new CLEF multilingual task is based on a new document collection which makes it hard to compute reliable estimates for the linear parameters  a training set is not available. A second disadvantage of the rank based merging strategy is that the linear function generalises across topics. Unfortunately in the multilingual task, the distribution of relevant documents over the subcollections is quite skewed. All collections have several  differing  topics without relevant documents, so applying a rank based merging strategy would hurt the performance for these topics, because the proportion of retrieved documents in every collection is the same for every topic.

The raw score merging strategy  which proved successful last year  does not need training data and also does not suffer from the equal proportions strategy. Unfortunately, usually scores are not totally compatible across collections. We have tried to identify factors which cause these differences. We have applied two normalisation techniques. First of all we treat term translations as a weighted concept vector  cf. section 2 . That means that we can normalise scores across topics by dividing the score by the query length. This amounts to computing the geometric average of probabilities per query concept. Secondly, we have observed that collection size has a large in uence on the occurence probability estimates $P_i C$ because the probability of rare terms is inversely proportional to the collection size.

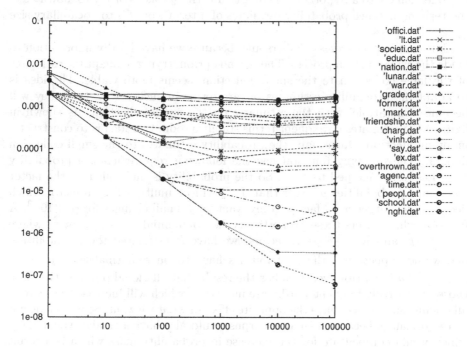

**Fig. 1.** Probability estimates vs collection size

Figure 4 shows the probability estimates of a sample of words of 1 document when we add more documents to the collection. The occurrence probability of common words stabilises fast when the collection size increases. The more rare a word is however, the higher is the degree of overestimation of its occurrence probability. This effect is a consequence of the sparse data problem. In fact, a small collection will never yield correct term occurrence probability estimates.

The collection-size dependency of collection-frequency  or global term frequency  estimates has a direct in uence on the distribution of document scores for a particular query. When the collection is small, the scores will be lower than the scores on a large collection. This is due to the fact that the score we study is based on the maximum likelihood ratio. So the median of the distribution of document scores for a particular topic  set  is inversely related with the collection size. Thus when we use the raw scores of different subcollections as a basis for merging, large collections will be favoured.

We hypothesised that we could improve the merging process, if we could correct the estimates for their dependence on the collection size. Suppose we have just two collections with a different size  and different language : $C_1, C_2$ with vocabulary size  $_1,$ $_2$ and number of tokens  $_1,$ $_2$ respectively, with $_1$      $_2$. Now we could try to either extrapolate the term occurrence probability estimates on collection $C_1$ to a hypothetical collection with  $_2$ tokens or try to  downscale' the term occurrence probability estimates of a term from $C_2$ to vocabulary size  $_1.$

The first option seems cumbersome, because we have hardly information to guide the extrapolation process. The second option, trying to adapt the estimates of the large collection to the small collection, seems more viable. The idea is to adapt the probability estimates of rare terms in such a way, that they will become  compatible' with the estimates on the small collection. As shown in figure 4 the estimates of frequent terms stabilise soon. Our idea is to construct a mapping function which maps the probability estimates to the small collection domain. The mapping function has the following requirements: a probability $1$  $_2$ has to be mapped to $1$  $_1$. So the probability is multiplied by the factor  $_2$ $_1$ and probabilities $p$ larger than $1$  $_2$ will be multiplied by a factor which decreases for larger $p$. In fact we only want very small changes for $p$     $10^{-3}$. A function which meets these properties is the polynomial       $-a$  $^2$ where $p$  and $a$    $\frac{2-\frac{1}{2}}{2}$ . Because we have re-estimated the probabilities, one would expect that the probabilities have to be re-normalised    $p$  $_i$ $p$  $_i$ $\sum$  $^2 p$  $_i$   . However, this has the result that all global probabilities  also those of relatively frequent words  are increased, which will increase the score of all documents, i.e. will have the opposite effect of what we want. So we decide not to re-normalise, because a smaller corpus would also have a smaller vocabulary, which would compensate for the increase in probability mass which is a result of the transformation.

# Results

## 5.1      li g al

We indexed the collections in the 4 languages separately. All documents were lemmatised using the Xelda morphological toolkit from Xerox XRCE and stopped with language specific stoplists. For German, we splitted compounds and added both the full compound and its parts to the index. This strategy is motivated by our experience with a Dutch corpus  Dutch is also a compounding language  9  and tests on the TREC CLIR test collection. Table 2 shows the results of the monolingual runs, runs in bold are judged runs, runs in italic font are unofficial runs  mostly post-hoc . The table also lists the proportion of documents which has been judged. The standard runs include fuzzy lookup of unknown words. The expand option adds close orthographical variants for every query term.

The official runs were done without document length normalisation defined by equation 3.

**Table 2.** Results of the monolingual runs

| run name | | avp | above median | description | j 1000 | j 100 | j 10 |
|---|---|---|---|---|---|---|---|
| tn ut | | 0.3760 | – | standard | 18.64 | 79.05 | 100 |
| **tnoutdd2** | | 0.3961 | 28/37 | e pand | 18.72 | 81.22 | 100 |
| tn ut | l | 0.3968 | – | length normalisation | 18.58 | 78.22 | 97.50 |
| tn ut | | 0.4551 | – | standard | 16.13 | 79.42 | 100 |
| **tnout 2** | | 0.4471 | 18/34 | e pand | 16.21 | 80.88 | 100 |
| tn ut | l | 0.4529 | – | length normalisation | 16.00 | 77.88 | 97.50 |
| tn utii | | 0.4677 | – | standard | 16.59 | 78.92 | 100 |
| **tnoutii2** | | 0.4709 | 18/34 | e pand | 16.67 | 80.33 | 100 |
| tn utii l | | 0.4808 | – | length normalisation | 16.66 | 77.25 | 98 |
| tn utee | i | 0.4200 | – | standard | 17.81 | 71.10 | 100 |
| tn utee | | 0.4169 | – | e pand | 17.84 | 70.75 | 99.75 |
| tn utee | l | 0.4273 | – | length normalisation | 17.82 | 69.30 | 98.00 |

The first thing that strikes us, is that the pool depth is 50, contrary to what has been practice in TREC in which the top 100 documents are judged for relevance. Section 5.4 analyses the CLEF collection further. Length normalisation usually gives a modest improvement in average precision. The expand' option was especially effective for German. The reason is probably that compound parts are not always properly lemmatised by the German morphology. Especially the German run performs well with 28 out of 37 topics above average. This relatively good performance is probably due to the morphology, which includes compound splitting.

## 5.2   ili g al

Table 3 lists the results of the bilingual runs. All runs use Dutch as a query language. The base run of 0.3069 can be improved by several techniques: a higher lambda, document length normalisation or Porter stemming instead of dictionary-based stemming. The latter can be explained by the fact that Porter's algorithm is an aggressive stemmer that also removes most of the derivational affixes. This is usually beneficial to retrieval performance. The experiment with corpus based frequencies yielded disappointing results. We first generated topic translations in a standard fashion based on VLIS. Subsequently we replaced the translation probabilities $P$            by rough corpus based estimates. We simply looked up all English sentences which contained the translation and determined the proportion of the corresponding  aligned  Dutch sentences that contained the original Dutch query word. If the pair was not found, the original probability was left unchanged. Unfortunately a lot of the query terms and translations were not found in the aligned corpus, because they were lemmatised whereas the corpus was not lemmatised. At least this mismatch did hurt the estimates. The procedure resulted in high translation probabilities for words that did not occur in the corpus and low probabilities for words that did occur.

**Table 3.** Results of the bilingual runs

| run name | avp | above median | description |
|---|---|---|---|
| **tnoutne** | 0.3069 | 27/33 | standard |
| *tn utne l* | 0.3278 | - | doclen norm |
| *tn utne p* | 0.3442 | - | 0.7 |
| tnoutne2 | 0.2762 | 25/33 | corpus frequencies |
| *tn utne stem* | 0.3366 | - | Porter stemmer    doclen norm |
| **tnoutne4** | 0.2946 | 20/33 | pseudo relevance feedback (PRF) |
| *tn utne* | 0.3266 | - | PRF bugfi    doclen norm, Porter |
| *tn utne retr* | 0.4695 | - | retrospective relevance feedback |

The pseudo relevance feedback runs were done with the experimental language models retrieval engine at the University of Twente, using an index based on the Porter stemming algorithm. The run tagged with *tnoutne -stem* is the baseline run for this system. The official pseudo relevance feedback run used the top 10 documents retrieved to re-estimate relevance weights and translation probabilities, but turned out to contain a bug. The unofficial fixed run *tnoutne -fi* performs a little bit worse than the baseline. The run *tnoutne -retro* uses the relevant documents to re-estimate the probabilities retrospectively  see e.g.  11  . This run reaches an impressive performance of 0.4695 average precision, much higher even than the best monolingual English run. This indicates that the algorithm might be helpful in an interactive setting where the user's feedback is used to retrieve a new, improved, set of documents. Apparently, the top 10 retrieved contains too much noise to be useful for the re-estimation of the model's parameters.

### 5.3     l ili  g  al

Table 4 shows that our best multilingual run was a run with Dutch as a query language. This is on one hand surprising  because this run is composed of 4 bilingual runs instead of 3 for the EN→X run. But the translation is based on the VLIS lexical database which is built on lexical relations with Dutch as a source language. Thus the translations in the NL→X case are much cleaner than the EN→X case. In the latter case, Dutch serves as a pivot language. On the other hand, the NL→IT translation is quite cumbersome. We first used Xelda to translate the Dutch queries to English stopped and lemmatised files. These files were subsequently translated by Systran.

**Table 4.** Results of the     $\to EN, FR,$    E,    runs

| run name | avp | above median | description |
|----------|-----|--------------|-------------|
| tnoute 1 | 0.2214 | 25/40 | baseline run |
| **tnoute 2** | 0.2165 | 26/40 | merged |
| *tn ute* | 0.2219 | – | fi ed |
| tnoute 3 | 0.1960 | 25/40 | Web based EN-IT le icon |
| tnoutn 1 | 0.2256 | 23/40 | query language is Dutch |

Another interesting point is that the intermediate bilingual run based on the parallel web corpus performed quite well, with an average precision of 0.2750 versus 0.3203 of Systran. The translation of this run is based on a translation model trained on the parallel web corpus. The English topics were simply stopped and translated by the translation model. We took the most probable translation and used that as Italian query. We plan to experiment with a more refined approach where we import the translation probabilities into structured queries.

## 5.4   T e     F   lle i

This section reports on some of the statistics of the CLEF collection and compares it to the TREC cross-language collection. Table 5 lists the size, number of judged documents, number of relevant documents and the judged fraction, which is the part of the collection that is judged per topic.

**Table 5.** CLEF collection statistics, 40 topics  1-40

| collection | total docs. | judged docs. | relevant docs. | no hits in topic | judged fraction |
|------------|-------------|--------------|----------------|------------------|-----------------|
| english | 110,250 | 14,737 | 579 | 2, 6, 8, 23, 25, 27, 35 | 0.0033 |
| french | 44,013 | 8,434 | 528 | 2, 4, 14, 27, 28, 36 | 0.0048 |
| german | 153,694 | 12,283 | 821 | 2, 28, 36 | 0.0020 |
| italian | 58,051 | 8,112 | 338 | 3, 6, 14, 27, 28, 40 | 0.0035 |
| total | 366,008 | 43,566 | 2,266 | | 0.0022 |

Table 6 lists the same information for the TREC collection. The collections are actually quite different. First of all, the CLEF collection is almost half the size of the TREC collection and heavily biased towards German and English documents. Although the CLEF organisation decided to judge only the top 50

**Table** . TREC collection statistics, 56 topics  26-81

| collection | total docs. | judged docs. | relevant docs. | no hits in topic | judged fraction |
|---|---|---|---|---|---|
| english | 242,866 | 18,783 | 2,645 | 26, 46, 59, 63, 66, 75 | 0.0014 |
| french | 141,637 | 11,881 | 1,569 | 76 | 0.0015 |
| german | 185,099 | 8,656 | 1,634 | 26, 60 ,75, 76 | 0.0008 |
| italian | 62,359 | 7,396 | 671 | 26, 44, 51, 60, 63, 75, 80 | 0.0021 |
| total | 631,961 | 46,716 | 6,519 | | 0.0013 |

of documents retrieved and not the top 100 documents retrieved as in TREC, the number of documents judged per topic is only a little lower for the CLEF collection: about 814 documents per topic vs. 834 for TREC. Given the fact that the 56 TREC topics were developed over a period of two years and the CLEF collection has 40 topics already, the organisation actually did more work this year compared to pervious years. Another striking difference is the number of relevant documents per topic, only 57 for CLEF and 116 for TREC. This might actually make the decision to only judge the top 50 of runs not that harmful for the usefulness of the CLEF evaluation results.

## Conclusions

This year's evaluation has confirmed that cross-language retrieval based on structured queries, no matter what the translation resources are, is a powerful technique. Re-estimating model parameters based on pseudo relevant documents does not result in improvement of retrieval performance. However, the relevance weighting algorithm shows an impressive performance gain if the relevant documents are used retrospectively. This indicates that the algorithm might in fact be a valuable tool for processing user feedback in an inter-active setting. Finally, merging based on the collection size re-estimation technique proved not successful. Further analysis is needed to find out why the technique did not work on this collection, as it was quite successful on the TREC-8 collection.

## Acknowledgements

We would like to thank the Druid project for sponsoring the translation of the topic set into Dutch. We thank Xerox XRCE for making the Xelda morphological toolkit available to us. Furthermore we would like to thank Jiang Chen  RALI, Université de Montréal , Jian-Yun Nie  RALI  for help with the PTMiner web mining tools, and Michel Simard  RALI  for helping with the construction of aligned corpora and building translation models.

# References

1. L. Ballesteros and W. B. Croft. Resolving ambiguity for cross-language retrieval. In *r cee ings the st SIGI n erence esearch an De el pment in In rmati n etrie al SIGI* , pages 64 71, 1998.
2. D. Hiemstra and F.M.G. de Jong. Disambiguation strategies for cross-language information retrieval. In *r cee ings the thir Eur pean n erence n esearch an ance echn l g r Digital i raries E D* , pages 274 293, 1999.
3. D. Hiemstra and W. Kraaij. Twenty-One at TREC-7 Ad-hoc and cross-language track. In *r cee ings the se enth e t etrie al n erence E* , NIST Special Publication 500-242, pages 227 238, 1999.
4. D. Hiemstra. A probabilistic justification for using tf.idf term weighting in information retrieval. *Internati nal urnal n Digital i raries*, 3(2) 131 139, 2000.
5. W. Kraaij, R. Pohlmann, and D. Hiemstra. Twenty-one at TREC-8 using language technology for information retrieval. In *r cee ings the eighth e t etrie al n erence E* , NIST Special Publication 500-246, pages 285 300, 2000.
6. W. Kraaij and R. Pohlmann. Viewing stemming as recall enhancement. In H.P. Frei, D. Harman, P. Schäuble, and R. Wilkinson, editors, *r cee ings the th SIGI n erence n esearch an De el pment in In rmati n etrie al SI GI* , pages 40 48, 1996.
7. J.Y. Nie. Using parallel web pages for multilingual information retrieval. In *r cee ings EF* , 2000 (elsewhere in this volume).
8. J.Y. Nie, M. Simard, P. Isabelle, and R. Durand. Cross-language information retrieval based on parallel te ts and automatic mining of parallel te ts in the web. In *SIGI* , pages 74 81, 1999.
9. R. Pohlmann and W. Kraaij. The e ect of syntactic phrase inde ing on retrieval performance for Dutch te ts. In L. Devroye and C. Chrisment, editors, *r cee ings I* , pages 176 187, 1997.
10. A. Pirkola. The e ects of query structure and dictionary setups in dictionary-based cross-language information retrieval. In *st n erence n esearch an De el pment in In rmati n etrie al SIGI* , pages 55 63, 1998.
11. S.E. Robertson and K. Sparck Jones. Relevance weighting of search terms. *urnal the merican S ciet r In rmati n Science*, 27 129 146, 1976.

# Cross-Language Retrieval for the CLEF Collections    Comparing Multiple Methods of Retrieval

Fredric C. Gey[1], Hailing Jiang[2], Vivien Petras[2], and Aitao Chen[2]

[1] UC Data Archive & Technical Assistance,
[2] School of Information Management and Systems
University of California
Berkeley, CA 94720 USA

**Abstract.** For our participation in CLEF, the Berkeley group participated in the monolingual, multilingual and GIRT tasks. To help enrich the CLEF relevance set for future training, we prepared a manual reformulation of the original German queries which achieved e cellent performance, more than 110  better than average of median precision. The GIRT task performed English-German Cross-Language IR by comparing commercial machine translation with thesaurus lookup techniques and query e pansion techniques. Combining all techniques using simple data fusion produced the best results.

## 1 Introduction

Unlike monolingual retrieval where the queries and documents are in the same language and where mechanistic techniques can be applied, Cross-language information retrieval  CLIR  must combine linguistic techniques  phrase discovery, machine translation, bilingual dictionary lookup  with robust monolingual information retrieval. The Berkeley Text Retrieval Research group has been using the technique of logistic regression from the beginning of the TREC series of conferences. Indeed our primary development has been a result of the U.S. TREC conferences and collections which provided the first large-scale test collection for modern information retrieval experimentation. In TREC-2 2  we derived a statistical formula for predicting probability of relevance based upon statistical clues contained within documents, queries and collections as a whole. This formula was used for document retrieval in Chinese 3  and Spanish in TREC-4 through TREC-6. We utilized the identical formula for English queries against German documents in the cross-language track for TREC-6. In TREC-7 the formula was also used for cross-language runs over multiple European languages. During the past year the formula has proven well-suited for Japanese and Japanese-English cross-language information retrieval 7 , even when only trained on English document collections. Our participation in the NTCIR Workshop in Tokyo
  http:  www.rd.nacsis.ac.jp ntcadm workshop work-en.html
led to different techniques for cross-language retrieval, ones which utilized the

C. Peters (Ed.): CLEF 2000, LNCS 2069, pp. 116–12 , 2001.
© Springer-Verlag Berlin Heidelberg 2001

power of human indexing of documents to improve retrieval via bi-lingual lexicon development and a form of text categorization which associated terms in documents with humanly assigned index terms 1 . These techniques were applied to English-German retrieval for the GIRT-1 task and collection in the TREC-8 conference 5

## 2 Logistic Regression for Document Ranking

The document ranking formula used by Berkeley in all of our CLEF retrieval runs was the TREC-2 formula 2 . The ad hoc retrieval results on the TREC test collections have shown that the formula is robust for long queries and manually reformulated queries. Applying the same formula trained on English TREC collections to other languages has performed well, as on the TREC-4 Spanish collections, the TREC-5 Chinese collection 6 and the TREC-6 and TREC-7 European languages French, German, Italian 4, 5 . Thus the algorithm has demonstrated its robustness independent of language as long as appropriate word boundary detection segmentation can be achieved. The logodds of relevance of document to query is given by

$$\log \quad R \quad , \quad \frac{P\ R\ ,}{P\ \overline{R}\ ,} \qquad\qquad 1$$

$$-3.51 \quad \frac{1}{\overline{N}\ 1} \quad .0929 * N \qquad\qquad 2$$

$$37.4 \sum_{i\ 1} \frac{i}{35} \quad 0.330 \sum_{i\ 1} \log \frac{i}{80}$$

$$-0.1937 \sum_{i\ 1} \log \frac{i}{} \qquad\qquad 3$$

where $P\ R\ $ , is the probability of relevance of document with respect to query , $P\ \overline{R}\ $ , is the probability of irrelevance of document with respect to query . Details about the derivation of these formulae may be found in our NTCIR workshop paper 7 . It is to be emphasized that training has taken place exclusively on English documents but the matching has proven robust over seven other languages in monolingual retrieval, including Japanese and Chinese where word boundaries form an additional step in the discovery process.

## Submissions for the CLEF Main Tasks

For CLEF we submitted 8 runs, 4 for the Monolingual non-English task and 4 for the Multilingual task.

The following sections give a description for each run.

For the Monolingual task we submitted

| Run Name | Language | Run type | Priority |
|---|---|---|---|
| BKMOGGM1 | German | Manual | 1 |
| BKMOFFA2 | French | Automatic | 2 |
| BKMOGGA1 | German | Automatic | 3 |
| BKMOIIA3 | Italian | Automatic | 4 |
| For the Multilingual task we submitted | | | |
| BKMUEAA1 | English | Automatic | 1 |
| BKMUGAM1 | German | Manual | 2 |
| BKMUEAA2 | English | Automatic | 3 |
| BKMUGAA3 | German | Automatic | 4 |

**Table 1.** Summary of eight official CLEF runs.

## 3.1     li g al   e ie al    e   F   lle i

**BKMOIIA3** Berkeley Monolingual Italian against Italian Automatic Run 3
The original query topics in Italian were searched against the Italian collection
La Stampa . For indexing this collection, we used a stopword list, the Italian-to-
lower normalizer and the Italian stemmer from association dictionary described
in Section 4.

BKMOFFA2 Berkeley Monolingual French against French Automatic Run
2

The original query topics in French were searched against the French collection Le Monde . For indexing this collection, we used a stopword list, the
French-to-lower normalizer and the French stemmer from association dictionary described in Section 4.

BKMOGGA1 Berkeley Monolingual German against German Automatic
Run 1

The original query topics in German were searched against the German collection Frankfurter Rundschau and Der Spiegel . For indexing the collection,
we used a stopword list that contained also capitalized versions of words and
the German stemmer from association dictionary described in Section 3.4. We
did not use a normalizer for this collection because all nouns in German are
capitalized and hence this clue might be used in retrieval.

4. BKMOGGM1 Berkeley Monolingual German against German Manual
Run 1 The original query topics in German were extended with additional
query terms obtained by searching the German CLEF collection Frankfurter
Rundschau and Der Spiegel with the original German query topics and looking
at the results for these original queries with the help of Aitao Chen's Cross-
language Text Retrieval System Web-interface . The additional query terms were
obtained by either directly looking at the documents or looking at the top ranked
document terms for the original query text. The searcher spent about 10 to
25 minutes per topic or query depending on familiarity with the context and
meaningfulness of the returned documents and top ranked document terms. For
indexing the collection, we used a stopword list that contained also capitalized

versions of words and the German stemmer  from association dictionary  built
by Aitao Chen. We didn't use a normalizer for this collection.

## 3.2      li g al  e       a  e

Our monolingual performance can be found in Table 2. While average of medians
cannot be considered a meaningful statistic from which inference can be made,

| Run ID | BKMOIIA3 | BKMOFFA2 | BKMOGGA1 | BKMOGGM1 |
|---|---|---|---|---|
| Retrieved | 34000 | 34000 | 37000 | 37000 |
| Relevant | 338 | 528 | 821 | 821 |
| Rel. Ret | 315 | 508 | 701 | 785 |
| Precision | | | | |
| at 0.00 | 0.7950 | 0.7167 | 0.6342 | 0.6907 |
| at 0.10 | 0.7617 | 0.6824 | 0.5633 | 0.6584 |
| at 0.20 | 0.6601 | 0.5947 | 0.5173 | 0.6442 |
| at 0.30 | 0.6032 | 0.5195 | 0.3999 | 0.6037 |
| at 0.40 | 0.5756 | 0.4825 | 0.3687 | 0.5624 |
| at 0.50 | 0.5336 | 0.4404 | 0.3181 | 0.5428 |
| at 0.60 | 0.4189 | 0.3627 | 0.2731 | 0.4970 |
| at 0.70 | 0.3098 | 0.2960 | 0.2033 | 0.4580 |
| at 0.80 | 0.2417 | 0.2422 | 0.1704 | 0.4006 |
| at 0.90 | 0.1816 | 0.1936 | 0.1364 | 0.2959 |
| at 1.00 | 0.1533 | 0.1548 | 0.0810 | 0.2059 |
| Brk. Prec. | 0.4601 | 0.4085 | 0.3215 | 0.4968 |
| Med. Prec. | 0.4453 | 0.4359 | 0.3161 | 0.3161 |

**Table 2.** Results of four official CLEF monolingual runs.

we have found it useful to average the medians of all queries as sent by CLEF
organizers. Comparing our overall precision to this average of medians gives
us some fuzzy gauge of whether our performance is better, poorer, or about the
same as the median performance. Thus the bottom two rows of the table present
the Berkeley overall precision over all queries for which performance has been
judged and, below it, the average of the median precision for each query over
all submitted runs. From this we see that Berkeley's automatic runs are about
the same as the overall 'average' while Berkeley's German-German manual run
comes in at overall precision 57 percent better than Average of Median precisions
for German-German monolingual runs. As we shall see in the next section, an
improved German query set had an even greater impact on multilingual retrieval.

Another observation to make is that of the skewedness of relevancy. More
than twice as many relevant documents come from the German collection than
the Italian collection. Thus a better German query set may have an impact on
multilingual retrieval more than a better Italian query set.

### 3.3     l ili g al   e  ie al     e    F   lle  i

Several interesting questions have arisen in recent research on CLIR. First, is CLIR merely a matter of a marriage of convenience between machine translation combined with ordinary monolingual information retrieval In our CLEF work we made use of two widely available machine translation packages, the SYSTRAN system found at the AltaVista site, and the Lernout and Hauspie Power Translator Pro Version 7.0. For the GIRT retrieval we made comparisons to Power Translator. For CLEF multilingual we combined translations and dictionary lookup from multiple sources, having found that different packages made different mistakes on particular topics. Second, what is the role of language specific stemming in improved performance Our experience with the Spanish tracks of TREC have convinced us that some form of stemming will always improve performance. For this particular evaluation we chose to create a stemmer mechanistically from common leading substring analysis of the entire corpus. The impact of the stemmer on performance will be discussed at the end of the official results discussion. Third, is performance improved by creating a multilingual index by pooling all documents together in one index or by creating separate language indexes and doing monolingual retrieval for each language followed by data fusion which combines the individual rankings into a unified ranking independent of language This was one of the major focuses of our experiments at CLEF.

1. BKMUEAA1 Berkeley Multilingual English against all Automatic Run 1

The original query topics in English were translated once with the Systran system

http: babel.altavista.com translate.dyn and with L H Powertranslator. The English topics were translated into French, German, and Italian. The two translated files for each language were pooled and then put together in one query file the English original query topics were multiplied by 2 to gain the same frequency of query terms in the query file . The final topics file contained 2 English original , French, German, and Italian versions one Powertranslator and one Systran for each topic. During the search, we divided the frequency of the search terms by 2 to avoid over-emphasis of equally translated search terms. The collection consisted of all languages. For indexing the English part of this collection, we used a stopword list, the default normalizer and the Porter stemmer. For indexing the French part of this collection, we used a stopword list, the French-to-lower normalizer and the French stemmer from association dictionary in section 3.5 . For indexing the German part of the collection, we used a stopword list that contained also capitalized versions of words and the German stemmer from association dictionary build by Aitao Chen. We didn't use a normalizer for this collection. For indexing the Italian part of this collection, we used a stopword list, the Italian-to-lower normalizer and the Italian stemmer from association dictionary .

| Run ID | BKMUEAA1 | BKMUEAA2 | BKMUGAA2 | BKMUGAM1 |
|---|---|---|---|---|
| Retrieved | 40000 | 40000 | 40000 | 40000 |
| Relevant | 2266 | 2266 | 2266 | 2266 |
| Rel. Ret. | 1434 | 1464 | 1607 | 1838 |
| Precision | | | | |
| at 0.00 | 0.7360 | 0.7460 | 0.7238 | 0.7971 |
| at 0.10 | 0.5181 | 0.5331 | 0.5046 | 0.6534 |
| at 0.20 | 0.4287 | 0.4465 | 0.4229 | 0.5777 |
| at 0.30 | 0.3545 | 0.3762 | 0.3565 | 0.5032 |
| at 0.40 | 0.2859 | 0.2929 | 0.3027 | 0.4373 |
| at 0.50 | 0.2183 | 0.2290 | 0.2523 | 0.3953 |
| at 0.60 | 0.1699 | 0.1846 | 0.1990 | 0.3478 |
| at 0.70 | 0.1231 | 0.1454 | 0.1682 | 0.3080 |
| at 0.80 | 0.1020 | 0.0934 | 0.1295 | 0.2238 |
| at 0.90 | 0.0490 | 0.0480 | 0.0622 | 0.1530 |
| at 1.00 | 0.0136 | 0.0081 | 0.0138 | 0.0474 |
| Brk. Prec. | 0.2502 | 0.2626 | 0.2654 | 0.3903 |
| Med. Prec. | 0.1843 | 0.1843 | 0.1843 | 0.1843 |

**Table 3.** Results of four official CLEF multilingual runs.

2. BKMUEAA2  Berkeley Multilingual English against all Automatic Run 2

The original query topics in English were translated once with Systran and with L H PowerTranslator. The English topics were translated into French, German, and Italian. The 2 translated versions for each language were pooled together in one query file  resulting in 3 topics files, one in German with the Systran and Powertranslator version, one in French with the Systran and Powertranslator version, and one in Italian accordingly . The original English topics file was searched against the English collection  Los Angeles Times . The pooled German topics file was searched against the German collection, the pooled French topics file was searched against the French collection, and the pooled Italian topics file was searched against the Italian collection. The frequency of the search terms was divided by 2 to avoid over-emphasis of equally translated search terms. This resulted in 4 result files with the 1000 top ranked records for each topic. These 4 result files were then pooled together and sorted by weight  rank  for each record and topic. The pooling method is described below. For a description of the collections see BKMOGGM1, BKMOFFA2, BKMOIIA3, BKMUEAA1.

3. BKMUGAA2  Berkeley Multilingual German against all Automatic Run 2

The original query topics in German were translated once with Systran and with Powertranslator. The German topics were translated into English, French, and Italian. The 2 translated versions for each language were pooled together in one query file. The original German topics file was multiplied by 2 to gain the same frequency of query terms in the query file searched. The final topics file contained 2 German  original , English, French, and Italian versions  one Powertranslator and one Systran  for each topic. During the search, we divided the frequency of the search terms by 2 to avoid over-emphasis of equally translated search terms. For a description of the collection see BKMUEAA1.

4. BKMUGAM1  Berkeley Multilingual German against all Manual Run 1

The manually extended German query topics  see description from BKMOGGM1  were now translated with Powertranslator into English, French and Italian. These translations were pooled together with the German originals in one file. This topics file was searched against the whole collection including all 4 languages. For a description of the collection see BKMUEAA1.

## 3.4    e ele      F   l ili g al  e      a e

Our multilingual performance can be found in Table  3.

As contrasted with the average of medians for monolingual, the values in the last row of the table are the same for all columns. Our automatic runs performed almost identically at about 38 percent better than average of medians, while the run BKMUGAM1 at overall precision 0.39 is 112 percent greater than the average of multilingual query medians.

## 3.5    il i g a i   le   e   e        a g age      a i
##       e  ie al

A stemmer for the French collection was created by first translating all the distinct French words found in the French collection into English using SYS-TRAN. The English translations were normalized by reducing verbs to the base form, nouns to the singular form, and adjectives to the positive form. All the French words which have the same English translations after normalization were grouped together to form a class. A member from each class is selected to represent the whole class in indexing. All the words in the same class were replaced by the class representative in indexing.

The German stemmer and Italian stemmer were created similarly.

We submitted four monolingual runs and four multilingual runs. These eight runs were repeated without the French, German, and Italian stemmers. The overall precision for each of the eight runs without stemming are shown in column 3 of table  4. Column 4 shows the overall precision with the French, German, and Italian stemmers. Column 5 shows the improvement in precision which can be attributed to the stemmers.

The overall precision for pooling queries and without stemming  the method we applied two years ago  for the multilingual run using English queries was .2335. With stemming and pooling documents, the overall precision for the same run was .2626, which is 12.46 percent better. This can be considered as additional evidence that adding a stemming capability will result in an improvement in automatic multilingual retrieval.

| RUN ID | TASK | RESULTS (unstemmed) | OFFICIAL RESULTS (stemmed) | Change Change |
|--------|------|---------------------|----------------------------|---------------|
| BKMUEAA1 | multilingual | 0.2335 | 0.2502 | 7.15pct |
| BKMUEAA2 | multilingual | 0.2464 | 0.2626 | 6.57pct |
| BKMUGAA3 | multilingual | 0.2524 | 0.2654 | 5.15pct |
| BKMUGAM1 | multilingual | 0.3749 | 0.3903 | 4.10pct |
| BKMOFFA2 | monolingual | 0.3827 | 0.4085 | 6.74pct |
| BKMOGGA1 | monolingual | 0.3113 | 0.3215 | 3.27pct |
| BKMOGGM1 | monolingual | 0.4481 | 0.4968 | 10.86pct |
| BKMOIIA3 | monolingual | 0.4054 | 0.4601 | 13.49pct |

**Table 4.** Results of Stemming Experiments

## 3.    a a F i       li g al        e      li g

The second idea centers on pooling documents from monolingual retrieval runs. The brain-dead solution would be to simply combine the retrieval results from four monolingual retrieval runs and sort the combined results by the estimated probability of relevance. The problem with the simple combination approach is that when the estimated probability of relevance is biased toward one document collection as the above statistics show for German , the documents from that collection will always appear in the top in the combined list of ranked documents. For our final run, we took a more conservative approach by making sure the top 50 documents from each of the four monolingual list of documents will appear in top 200 in the combined list of documents.

## 3.    Fail e    al i

A query-by-query analysis can be done to identify problems. We have not had time to do this, but one query stands out. Query 40 about the privatization of the German national railway was one which seems to have given everyone problems the median precision over all CLEF runs was 0.0537 for this query . As an American group, we were particularly vexed by the use of the English spelling 'privatisation' which couldn't be recognized by either of our machine translation softwares. The German version of the topic was not much better   in translation its English equivalent became 'de-nationalization' a very uncommon synonym for 'privatization,' and one which yielded few relevant documents. By comparison, our German manual reformulation of this query resulted in an average precision of 0.3749 for best CLEF performance for this query.

## GIRT Retrieval

A special emphasis of our current funding has focussed upon retrieval of specialized domain documents which have been assigned individual classification identifiers by human indexers. These classification identifiers come from what we call  domain ontologies , of which thesauri are a particular case. Since many millions of dollars are expended on developing these classification ontologies and applying them to index documents, it seems only natural to attempt to exploit the resources previously expended to the fullest extent possible to improve retrieval. In some cases such thesauri are developed with identifiers translated  or provided  in multiple languages. This has been done in Europe with the GEMET  General European Multilingual Environmental Thesaurus  effort and with the OECD General Thesaurus  available in English, French, and Spanish . A review of multilingual thesauri can be found in  8 .

The GIRT collection consists of reports and papers  grey literature  in the social science domain. The collection is managed and indexed by the GESIS organization  http:  www.social-science-gesis.de . GIRT is an excellent example of a collection indexed by a multilingual thesaurus, originally German-English, recently translated into Russian. We worked extensively with a previous version of the GIRT collection in our cross-language work for TREC-8  5

## 4.1  T e    T   lle  i

There are 76128 German documents in GIRT subtask collection. Of them, about 54275  72 percent  have English TITLE sections. 5317 documents  7 percent  have also English TEXT sections. Almost all the documents contain manually assigned thesaurus terms. On average, there are about 10 thesaurus terms assigned to each document.

In our experiments, we indexed only the TITLE and TEXT sections in each document  not the E-TITLE or E-TEXT . The CLEF rules specified that indexing any other field would need to be declared a manual run. For our CLEF runs this year we added a German stemmer similar to the Porter stemmer for the German language. Using this stemmer led to a 15 percent increase in average precision when tested using the GIRT-1 collection of TREC-8.

## 4.2    e  T a  la i

In CLIR, essentially either queries or documents or both need to be translated from one language to another. Query translation is almost always selected for practical reasons of efficiency, and because translation errors in documents can propagate without discovery since the maintainers of a text archive rarely read every document.

For the CLEF GIRT task, our focus has been to compare the performance of different translation strategies. We applied the following three methods to translate the English queries to German: Thesaurus lookup, Entry Vocabulary Module  EVM , machine translation  MT . The resulted German queries were run against the GIRT collection.

**T e a**                The GIRT social science Thesaurus is a German-English bilingual thesaurus. Each German item in this thesaurus has a corresponding

English translation. We took the following steps to translate the English query to German by looking up the thesaurus:

a. Create an English-German transfer dictionary from the Social Science Thesaurus. This transfer dictionary contains English items and their corresponding German translations. This  vocabulary discovery  approach was taken by Eichmann, Ruiz and Srinivasan for medical information cross-language retrieval using the UMLS Metathesaurus 9 .

b. Use the part-of-speech tagger LT-POS developed by University of Edinburgh

http:  www.ltg.ed.ac.uk  software  pos  index.html  to tag the English query and identify noun phrases in the English query. One problem with thesaurus lookup is how to match the phrasal items in a thesaurus. We have taken a simple approach to deal with this problem: use POS tagger to identify noun phrases.

For last year's GIRT task at the TREC-8 evaluation, we extracted an English-German transfer dictionary from the GIRT thesaurus and used it to translate the English queries to German. This approach left about 50 percent of English query words untranslated. After examining the untranslated English query words carefully, we found that most of them fell into the following two categories: one category contains general terms that are not likely to occur in a domain-specific thesaurus like GIRT. Examples are  country ,  car ,  foreign ,  industry ,  public , etc. The other category are terms that occur in the thesaurus but in a different format from the original English query words. For example,  bosnia-herzegovina  does not appear in the thesaurus, but  bosnia  and  herzegovina  does.

**F      a     ig      e T  e a**    To deal with the general terms in the first category, a general-purpose dictionry was applied after thesaurus lookup. A fuzzy-matching strategy was used to address the problem for the second category. It counts the letter pairs that two strings have in common and uses Dice's coefficient as a means of accessing the similarity between the two strings. This fuzzy-matching strategy successfully recovered some query terms, for example,

| original query terms | thesaurus terms |
|---|---|
| asylum policy | policy on asylum |
| anti-semitism | antisemitism |
| bosnia-herzegovina | bosnia and herzegovina |
| gypsy | gipsy |
| German Democratic Republic | German Democratic |
| Republic (gdr) | |

Fuzzy matching also found related terms for some query terms which do not appear in the thesaurus at all, for example see the following table.

| original query terms | thesaurus terms |
|---|---|
| nature protection legislation | nature protection |
| violent act | violence |
| bosnia | bosnian |

We tested this combined approach using last year's GIRT-1 data. The results showed about 18 percent increase as measured by average precision compared with simple thesaurus lookup.

**ab la       le**       In the GIRT collection, about 72 percent of the documents have both German titles and English titles. 7 percent have also English text sections. This feature allows us to build a EVM which maps the English words appearing in English Title and text sections to German thesaurus terms. This mapping can then be used to translate the English queries. More details about this work can be found in 5 .

**a  i eT a  la i       T** For comparison, we also applied the Lernout and Hauspie Power Translator product to translate the English queries into German.

**e gi g  e l**   While our CLEF Multilingual strategy focussed on merging monolingual results run independently on different subcollections, one per language, all our GIRT runs were done on a single subcollection, the German text part of GIRT. When analyzing the experimental training results, we noticed that different translation methods retrieved sets of documents that contain different relevant documents. This implies that merging the results from different translation methods may lead to better performance than of any one of the methods. Since we use the same retrieval algorithm and data collection for all the runs, the probability that a document is relevant to a query from different runs are commensurable. So, for each document retrieved, we used the sum of its probability from the different runs as its final probability to create the ranking for the merged results.

## 4.3    e  l  a     al  i

Our GIRT results are summarized in Table  5. The runs can be described as follows: BKGREGA4 used our entry vocabulary method to map from query term to thesaurus term, the top ranked thesaurus term and its translation was used to create the German query. BKGREGA3 used the results of machine translation by the L  H Power Translator software. The run BKGREGA2 used thesaurus lookup of English terms in the query and a general purpose English German dictionary for not found terms as well as the fuzzy matching strategy described above. The final run BKGREGA1 pooled the merged results from the other three runs according to the sum of probabilities of relevance. Note that it performs significantly better than the other three runs, and about 61 percent better than the average of median precisions for the CLEF GIRT. One reason is that different individual runs performed much better on different queries. The three individual methods achieved best precision in eight of the 25 queries and the fusion run achieved best precision for another 4 queries.

| Run ID | BKGREGA1 | BKGREGA2 | BKGREGA3 | BKGREGA4 |
|---|---|---|---|---|
| Retrieved | 23000 | 23000 | 23000 | 23000 |
| Relevant | 1193 | 1193 | 1193 | 1193 |
| Rel. Ret. | 901 | 772 | 563 | 827 |
| at 0.00 | 0.7013 | 0.5459 | 0.6039 | 0.6139 |
| at 0.10 | 0.5610 | 0.4436 | 0.3662 | 0.4482 |
| at 0.20 | 0.4585 | 0.4172 | 0.2881 | 0.3583 |
| at 0.30 | 0.4203 | 0.3576 | 0.2633 | 0.3292 |
| at 0.40 | 0.3774 | 0.3165 | 0.2486 | 0.2465 |
| at 0.50 | 0.3454 | 0.2856 | 0.2266 | 0.2004 |
| at 0.60 | 0.2938 | 0.2548 | 0.1841 | 0.1611 |
| at 0.70 | 0.2025 | 0.1816 | 0.1107 | 0.1477 |
| at 0.80 | 0.1493 | 0.1439 | 0.0663 | 0.1252 |
| at 0.90 | 0.0836 | 0.0829 | 0.0575 | 0.0612 |
| at 1.00 | 0.0046 | 0.0075 | 0.0078 | 0.0003 |
| Brk. Prec. | 0.3119 | 0.2657 | 0.2035 | 0.2299 |
| Med. Prec. | 0.1938 | 0.1938 | 0.1938 | 0.1938 |

**Table 5.** Results of four official GIRT English-German runs.

## Summary and Acknowledgments

Berkeley's participation in CLEF has enabled us to explore refinements in cross-language information retrieval. Specifically we have explored two data fusion methods   for the CLEF multilingual we developed a technique for merging from monolingual, language specific rankings which ensured representation from each constituent language. For the GIRT English-German task, we obtained improved retrieval by fusion of the results of multiple methods of mapping from English queries to German. A new stemming method was developed which maps classes of words to a representative word in both English and the targeted languages of French, German, and Italian. For future research we are creating a Russian version of the GIRT queries to test strategies for Russian-German retrieval via a multilingual thesaurus.

This research was supported in part by the Information and Data Management Program of the National Science Foundation under grant IRI-9630765 from the Information and Data Management program of the Computer and Information Science and Engineering Directorate. Major support was also provided by DARPA  Department of Defense Advanced Research Projects Agency  under research grant N66001-00-1-8911, Mar 2000-Feb 2003 as part of the DARPA Translingual Information Detection, Extraction, and Summarization Program TIDES .

# References

1  F Gey A Chen and H Jiang. Applying te t categorization to vocabulary enhancement for japanese-english cross-language information retrieval. In S. Annandiou, editor,  *he Se enth   achine   ranslati n Summit    r sh p  n        r  r ss language In  rmati n   etrie al  Singap re*, pages 35  40, September 1999.

2  W Cooper A Chen and F Gey. Full te t retrieval based on probabilistic equations with coefficients fitted by logistic regression. In D. K. Harman, editor,  *he Sec n   e t   Etrie al    n erence     E   *, pages 57  66, March 1994.

3  A Chen J He L Xu F Gey and J Meggs. Chinese te t retrieval without using a dictionary. In A. Desai Narasimhalu Nicholas J. Belkin and Peter Willett, editors,  *r cee ings   the   th  nnual Internati nal    SIGI    n erence n   esearch an  De el pment in In  rmati n   etrie al   hila elphia*, pages 42  49, 1997.

4  F. C. Gey and A. Chen. Phrase discovery for english and cross-language retrieval at trec-6. In D. K. Harman and Ellen Voorhees, editors,  *he Si th   e t   Etrie al   n erence    E    IS  Special   u licati n       *, pages 637  647, August 1998.

5  F. C. Gey and H. Jiang. English-german cross-language retrieval for the girt collection  e ploiting a multilingual thesaurus. In Ellen Voorhees, editor,  *he Eighth   e t   Etrie al   n erence    E    ra t n te    pr cee ings*, pages 219  234, November 1999.

6  J. He, L. Xu, , A. Chen, J. Meggs, and F. C. Gey. Berkeley chinese information retrieval at trec-5  Technical report. In D. K. Harman and Ellen Voorhees, editors,  *he Fi th   e t   Etrie al   n erence    E    IS  Special   u licati n       *, pages 191  196, November 1996.

7  A Chen F Gey K Kishida H Jiang and    Liang. Comparing multiple methods for japanese and japanese-english te t retrieval. In N. Kando, editor,  *he First    I    r sh p  n  apanese  e t  etrie al an   erm  ec gniti n       apan*, pages 49  58, September 1999.

8  J. Purat.  *he    rl    ultilingual En ir nmental   hesauri.* www.sims.berkeley.edu/research/metadata/papers/purat98, 1998.

9  D Eichmann M Ruiz and P Srinivasan. Cross-language information retrieval with the umls metathesaurus. In W B Croft A Mo at C J van Rijsbergen R Wilkinson and J Zobel, editors,  *r cee ings   the   st  nnual Internati nal    SIGI    n erence n   esearch an  De el pment in In  rmati n   etrie al   el  urne ustralia*, pages 72  80, August 1998.

# A Language-Independent Approach to European Text Retrieval

Paul McNamee, James Mayfield, and Christine Piatko

Johns Hopkins University Applied Physics Lab
11100 Johns Hopkins Road
Laurel, MD 20723-6099 USA
Paul.McNamee@jhuapl.edu
James.Mayfield@jhuapl.edu
Christine.Piatko@jhuapl.edu

**Abstract.** We present an approach to multilingual information retrieval that does not depend on the existence of specific linguistic resources such as stemmers or thesauri. Using the HAIRCUT system we participated in the monolingual, bilingual, and multilingual tasks of the CLEF-2000 evaluation. Our approach, based on combining the benefits of words and character n-grams, was effective for both language-independent monolingual retrieval as well as for cross-language retrieval using translated queries. After describing our monolingual retrieval approach we compare a translation method using aligned parallel corpora to commercial machine translation software.

## 1 Background

The Hopkins Automated Information Retriever for Combing Unstructured Text (HAIRCUT) is a research retrieval system developed at the Johns Hopkins University Applied Physics Lab (APL). One of the research areas that we want to investigate with HAIRCUT is the relative merit of different tokenization schemes. In particular we use both character n-grams and words as indexing terms. Our experiences in the TREC evaluations have led us to believe that while n-grams and words are comparable in retrieval performance, a combination of both techniques outperforms the use of a single approach [7]. Through the CLEF-2000 evaluation we demonstrate that unsophisticated, language-independent techniques can form a credible approach to multilingual retrieval. We also compare query translation methods based on parallel corpora with automated machine translation.

## 2 Overview

We participated in the monolingual, bilingual, and multilingual tasks. For all three tasks we used the same eight indices, a word and an n-gram (n=6) based index in each of the four languages. Information about each index is provided in Table 1. In all of

C. Peters (Ed.): CLEF 2000, LNCS 2069, pp. 129-139, 2001.
© Springer-Verlag Berlin Heidelberg 2001

our experiments documents were indexed in their native language because we prefer query translation over document translation for reasons of efficiency.

**Table 1.** Index statistics for the CLEF collection

|  | # docs | collection size (MB gzipped) | name | # terms | index size (MB) |
|---|---|---|---|---|---|
| English | 110,282 | 163 | enw | 219,880 | 255 |
|  |  |  | en6 | 2,668,949 | 2102 |
| French | 44,013 | 62 | frw | 235,662 | 96 |
|  |  |  | fr6 | 1,765,656 | 769 |
| German | 153,694 | 153 | gew | 1,035,084 | 295 |
|  |  |  | ge6 | 3,440,316 | 2279 |
| Italian | 58,051 | 78 | itw | 278,631 | 130 |
|  |  |  | it6 | 1,650,037 | 1007 |

We used two methods of translation in the bilingual and multilingual tasks. We used the Systran® translator to convert French and Spanish queries to English for our bilingual experiments and to convert English topics to French, German and Italian in the multilingual task. For the bilingual task we also used a method based on extracting translation equivalents from parallel corpora. Parallel English/French documents were most readily available to us, so we only applied this method when translating French to English.

## 2.1    Index Construction

Documents were processed using only the permitted tags specified in the workshop guidelines. First SGML macros were expanded to their appropriate character in the ISO-8859-1 character set. Then punctuation was eliminated, letters were downcased, and only the first two of a sequence of digits were preserved (e.g., 1920 became 19##). Diacritical marks were preserved. The result is a stream of blank separated words. When using n-grams we construct indexing terms from the same stream of words; the n-grams may span word boundaries but sentence boundaries are noted so that n-grams spanning sentence boundaries are not recorded. Thus n-grams with leading, central, or trailing spaces are formed at word boundaries. We used a combination of unstemmed words and 6-grams with success in the TREC-8 CLIR task [8] and decided to follow the same strategy this year. As can be seen from Table 1, the use of 6-grams as indexing terms increases both the size of the inverted file and the dictionary.

## 2.2    Query Processing

HAIRCUT performs rudimentary preprocessing on queries to remove stop structure, *e.g.,* affixes such as "… would be relevant" or "relevant documents should…." A list of about 1000 such English phrases was translated into French, German, and Italian using both Systran and the FreeTranslation.com translator. Other than this preprocessing, queries are parsed in the same fashion as documents in the collection.

In all of our experiments we used a simple two-state hidden Markov model that captures both document and collection statistics [9]. This model is alternatively described as a linguistically motivated probabilistic model [11] and has been compared to the vector cosine and probabilistic models [4]. After the query is parsed each term is weighted by the query term frequency and an initial retrieval is performed followed by a single round of relevance feedback.

To perform relevance feedback we first retrieve the top 1000 documents. We use the top 20 documents for positive feedback and the bottom 75 documents for negative feedback, however we check to see that no duplicate or neo-duplicate documents are included in these sets. We then select terms for the expanded query based on three factors, a term's initial query term frequency (if any), the cube root of the ($\alpha$=3, $\beta$=2, $\gamma$=2) Rocchio score, and a metric that incorporates an idf component. The top-scoring terms are then used as the revised query. After retrieval using this expanded and reweighted query, we have found a slight improvement by penalizing document scores for documents missing many query terms. We multiply document scores by a penalty factor:

$$PF = 1.0 - \left( \frac{\# \text{ of missing terms}}{\text{total number of terms in query}} \right)^{1.25}$$

We use only about one-fifth of the terms of the expanded query for this penalty function.

|  | # Top Terms | # Penalty terms |
|---|---|---|
| words | 60 | 12 |
| 6-grams | 400 | 75 |

We conducted our work on a 4-node Sun Microsystems Ultra Enterprise 450 server. The workstation had 2 GB of physical memory and access to 50 GB of dedicated hard disk space.

The HAIRCUT system comprises approximately 25,000 lines of Java code.

## 3    Monolingual Experiments

Our approach to monolingual retrieval was to focus on language independent methods. We refrained from using language specific resources such as stoplists, lists of phrases, morphological stemmers, dictionaries, thesauri, decompounders, or semantic lexicons (e.g. Euro WordNet). We emphasize that this decision was made, not from a belief that these resources are ineffective, but because they are not universally available (or affordable) and not available in a standard format. Our processing for each language was identical in every regard and was based on a combination of evidence from word-based and 6-gram based runs. We elected to use all of the topic sections for our queries.

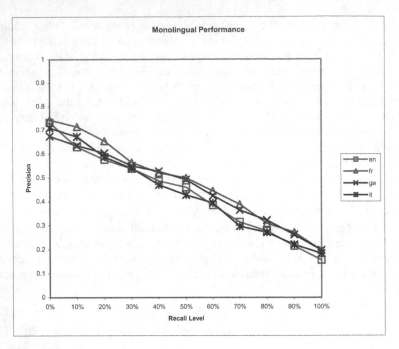

**Fig. 1.** Recall-precision curves for the monolingual task. The English curve is unofficial and is produced from the bilingual relevance judgments.

The retrieval effectiveness of our monolingual runs is fairly similar for each of the four languages as evidenced by Figure 1. We expected to do somewhat worse on the Italian topics since the use of diacritical marks differed between the topic statements and the document collection; consistent with our 'language-independent' approach we did not correct for this. Given the generally high level of performance, both in average precision and recall, and in the number of 'best' and 'above median' topics for the monolingual tasks (see Table 2), we believe that we have demonstrated that language independent techniques can be quite effective.

**Table 2.** Results for monolingual task

|          | avg prec | recall    | # topics | # best | # ≥ median |
|----------|----------|-----------|----------|--------|------------|
| aplmofr  | 0.4655   | 523 / 528 | 34       | 9      | 21         |
| aplmoge  | 0.4501   | 816 / 821 | 37       | 10     | 32         |
| aplmoit  | 0.4187   | 329 / 338 | 34       | 6      | 20         |
| aplmoen  | 0.4193   | 563 / 579 | 33       | (unofficial English run) |

One of our objectives was to compare the performance of the constituent word and n-gram runs that were combined for our official submissions. Figure 2 shows the precision-recall curves for the base and combined runs for each of the four languages. Our experience in the TREC-8 CLIR track [8] led us to believe that n-grams and words are comparable, however each seems to perform slightly better in different

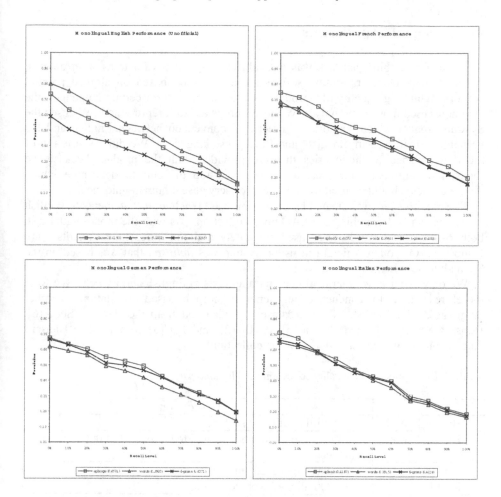

**Fig. 2.** Comparison of retrieval performance using unstemmed words, 6-grams, and a combination of the two approaches for each of the four languages.

languages. In particular, n-grams performed appreciably better on translated German queries, something we attribute to a lack of decompounding in our word-based runs. This trend was continued this year, with 6-grams performing just slightly better in Italian and French, somewhat better in German, but dramatically worse in our unofficial runs of English queries against the bilingual relevance judgments. We are stymied by the disparity between n-grams and words in English and have never seen such a dramatic difference in other test collections. Nonetheless, the general trend seems to indicate that combination of these two schemes has a positive effect as measured by average precision.

Our method of combining two runs is to normalize scores for each topic in a run and then to merge multiple runs by the normalized scores.

## 4     Bilingual Experiments

Our goal for the bilingual task was to evaluate two methods for translating queries, commercial machine translation software and a method based on aligned parallel corpora. While high quality MT products are available only for certain languages, the languages used most commonly in Western Europe are well represented. We used the Systran product which supports bi-directional conversion between English and the French, German, Italian, Spanish, and Portuguese languages. We did not use any of the domain specific dictionaries that are provided with the product because we focused on automatic methods, and it seemed too difficult to determine which dictionary(ies) should be used for a particular query absent human guidance.

The run, *aplbifrc*, was created by converting the French topic statements to English using Systran and searching the LA Times collection. As with the monolingual task both 6-grams and words were used separately and the independent results were combined. Our other official run using Systran was *aplbispa* that was based on the Spanish topic statements.

We only had access to large aligned parallel texts in English and French. We were therefore unable to conduct experiments in corpora-based translation in other languages. Our English / French dataset included text from the Hansard Set-A[6], Hansard Set-C[6], United Nations[6], RALI[12], and JOC[3] corpora. The Hansard data accounts for the vast majority of the collection.

**Table 3.** Description of the parallel collection used for *aplbifrb*

|  | Description |
|---|---|
| Hansard Set-A | 2.9 million aligned sentences |
| Hansard Set-C | aligned documents, converted to ~400,000 aligned sentences |
| United Nations | 25,000 aligned documents |
| RALI | 18,000 aligned web documents |
| JOC | 10,000 aligned sentences |

The process that we used for translating an individual topic is shown in Figure 3. First we perform a pre-translation expansion on a topic by running that topic in its source language on a contemporaneous expansion collection and extracting terms from top ranked documents. Thus for our French to English run we use the Le Monde collection to expand the original topic which is then represented as a weighted list of sixty words. Since the Le Monde collection is contemporaneous with the target LA Times collection it is a terrific resource for pre-translation query expansion. Each of these words is then translated to the target language (English) using the statistics of the aligned parallel collection. We selected a single 'best' translation for each word and the translated word retained the weight assigned during topic expansion. Our method of producing translations is based on a term similarity measure similar to mutual information [2]; we do not use any dimension reduction techniques such as CL-LSI [5]. The quality of our translation methodology is demonstrated for Topic C003 in Table 4. Finally we processed the translated query on the target collection in four ways, using both 6-grams and words and by using and not using relevance feedback.

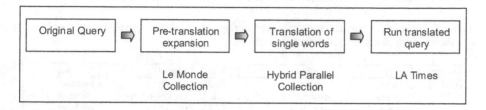

**Fig. 3.** Translation approach for *aplbifrb*, our official French/English bilingual run using aligned parallel corpora.

---

**Official French Query**
<F-title> La drogue en Hollande

<F-desc> Quelle est la politique des Pays-Bas en matière de drogue?

<F-narr> Les documents pertinents exposent la réglementation et les décisions du gouvernement néerlandais concernant la vente et la consommation de drogues douces et dures.

**Official English Query**
<E-title> Drugs in Holland

<E-desc> What is the drugs policy in the Netherlands?

<E-narr> Relevant documents report regulations and decisions made by the Dutch government regarding the sale and consumption of hard and soft drugs.

**Systran translation of French query**
<F-title> Drug in Holland

<F-desc> Which is the policy of the Netherlands as regards drug?

<F-narr> The relevant documents expose the regulation and the decisions of Dutch government concerning the sale and the consumption of soft and hard drugs.

---

**Fig. 4.** Topic C003 in the official French and English versions and as translated by Systran from French to English.

We obtained superior results using translation software instead of our corpora-based translation. The precision-recall graph in Figure 5 shows a clear separation between the Systran-only run (*aplbifrc*) with average precision 0.3358 and the corpora-only run (*aplbifrb*) with average precision of 0.2223. We do not interpret this difference as a condemnation of our approach to corpus-based translation. Instead we agree with Braschler et al. that "MT cannot be the only solution to CLIR [1]."    Both translation systems and corpus-based methods have their weaknesses. A translation system is particularly susceptible to named entities not being found in its dictionary. Perhaps as few as 3 out of the 40 topics in the test set mention obscure names: topics 2, 8, and 12. Topics 2 and 8 have no relevant English documents, so it is difficult to assess whether the corpora-based approach would outperform the use of dictionaries or translation tools on these topics. The run *aplbifra* is simply a combination of *aplbifrb* and *aplbifrc* that we had expected to outperform the individual runs.

**Table 4.** Topic C003. French terms produced during pre-translation expansion and single word translation equivalents derived from parallel texts.

| Weight | French | English | Weight | French | English |
|--------|--------|---------|--------|--------|---------|
| 0.0776 | drogue | drug | 0.0085 | prison | prison |
| 0.0683 | drogues | drugs | 0.0084 | suppression | removal |
| 0.0618 | douces | freshwater | 0.0083 | problème | problem |
| 0.0595 | dures | harsh | 0.0083 | produits | products |
| 0.0510 | consommation | consumer | 0.0082 | pénalisation | penalty |
| 0.0437 | matière | policy | 0.0080 | santé | health |
| 0.0406 | bas | low | 0.0078 | actuellement | now |
| 0.0373 | vente | sales | 0.0078 | consommateurs | consumers |
| 0.0358 | hollande | holland | 0.0078 | sévir | against |
| 0.0333 | néerlandais | netherlands | 0.0077 | réflexion | reflection |
| 0.0174 | cannabis | cannabis | 0.0077 | rapport | report |
| 0.0161 | stupéfiants | narcotic | 0.0077 | professeur | professor |
| 0.0158 | dépénalisation | decriminalization | 0.0077 | personnes | people |
| 0.0150 | usage | use | 0.0077 | souterraine | underground |
| 0.0141 | trafic | traffic | 0.0077 | partisans | supporters |
| 0.0133 | lutte | inflation | 0.0076 | sida | aids |
| 0.0133 | toxicomanie | drug | 0.0076 | débat | debate |
| 0.0124 | légalisation | legalization | 0.0076 | francis | francis |
| 0.0123 | héroïne | heroin | 0.0075 | europe | europe |
| 0.0119 | toxicomanes | drug | 0.0075 | membres | members |
| 0.0117 | usagers | users | 0.0092 | peines | penalties |
| 0.0105 | drogués | drug | 0.0092 | cocaïne | cocaine |
| 0.0104 | répression | repression | 0.0091 | alcool | alcohol |
| 0.0103 | prévention | prevention | 0.0089 | seringues | syringes |
| 0.0098 | loi | act | 0.0089 | risques | risks |
| 0.0098 | substances | substances | 0.0088 | substitution | substitution |
| 0.0098 | trafiquants | traffickers | 0.0087 | distinction | distinction |
| 0.0098 | haschich | hashish | 0.0087 | méthadone | methadone |
| 0.0095 | marijuana | marijuana | 0.0087 | dealers | dealers |
| 0.0094 | problèmes | problems | 0.0086 | soins | care |

There are several reasons why our translation scheme might be prone to error. First of all, the collection is largely based on the Hansard data, which are transcripts of Canadian parliamentary proceedings. The fact that the domain of discourse in the parallel collection is narrow compared to the queries could account for some difficulties. And the English recorded in the Hansard data is formal, spoken, and uses Canadian spellings whereas the English document collection in the tasks is informal, written, and published in the United States. It should be also noted that generating 6-grams from a list of words rather than from prose leaves out any n-grams that span word boundaries; such n-grams might capture phrasal information and be of particular value. Finally we had no opportunity to test our approach prior to submitting our results; we are confident that this technique can be improved.

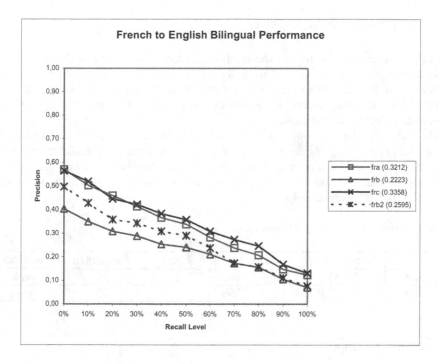

**Fig. 5.** Comparison of *aplbifra* (combination), *aplbifrb* (parallel corpus), and *aplbifrc* (Systran).

With some post-hoc analysis we found one way to improve the quality of our corpus-based runs. We had run the translated queries both with, and without the use of relevance feedback. It appears that the relevance feedback runs perform worse than those without this normally beneficial technique. The dashed curve in Figure 5 labeled 'frb2' is the curve produced when relevance feedback is not used with the corpora-translated query. When not utilizing post-translation relevance feedback we observed an improvement in average precision from 0.2694 to 0.3145. Perhaps the use of both pre-translation and post-translation expansions introduces too much ambiguity about the query.

Below are our results for the bilingual task. There were no relevant English documents for topics 2, 6, 8, 23, 25, 27, and 35, leaving just 33 topics in the task.

**Table 5.** Results for bilingual task

|          | avg prec | % mono | recall (579) | # best | # ≥ median | method |
|----------|----------|--------|--------------|--------|------------|--------|
| aplbifra | 0.3212   | 80.57% | 527          | 6      | 27         | Combine aplbifrb/aplbifrc |
| aplbifrb | 0.2223   | 55.75% | 479          | 4      | 23         | Corpora FR to EN |
| aplbifrc | 0.3358   | 84.23 %| 521          | 7      | 23         | Systran FR to EN |
| aplbispa | 0.2595   | 73.28% | 525          | 5      | 27         | Systran SP to EN |
| aplbige  | 0.4034   | 83.49% | 529          | unofficial run | | Systran GE to EN |
| aplbiit  | 0.3739   | 77.38% | 545          | unofficial run | | Systran IT to EN |

# 5   Multilingual Experiments

We did not focus our efforts on the multilingual task. We selected English as the topic language for the task and used Systran to produce translations in French, German, and Italian. We performed retrieval using 6-grams and words and then performed a multi-way merge using two different approaches, merging normalized scores and merging runs by rank.

The large number of topics with no relevant documents in the collections of various languages suggests that the workshop organizers were successful in selecting challenging queries for merging. It seems clear that more sophisticated methods of multilingual merging are required to avoid a large drop in precision from the monolingual and bilingual tasks.

**Table 6.** Results for official multilingual submissions

|         | avg prec | recall      | # best | # ≥ median | method |
|---------|----------|-------------|--------|------------|--------|
| aplmua  | 0.2391   | 1698 / 2266 | 1      | 30         | rank   |
| aplmub  | 0.1924   | 1353 / 2266 | 3      | 23         | score  |

# 6   Conclusions

The CLEF-2000 workshop has provided an excellent opportunity to explore the practical issues involved in cross-language information retrieval. We approached the monolingual task believing that it is possible to achieve good retrieval performance using language-independent methods. This methodology appears to have been borne out based on the results we obtained using a combination of words and n-grams. For the bilingual task we kept our philosophy of simple methods, but also used a high-powered machine translation product. While our initial experiments using parallel corpora for translation were not as effective as those with machine translated queries, the results were still quite credible and we are confident this technique can be improved further.

# References

1.   M. Braschler, M-Y. Kan, and P. Schauble, 'The SPIDER Retrieval System and the TREC-8 Cross-Language Track.' In E. M. Voorhees and D. K. Harman, eds., Proceedings of the *Eighth Text REtrieval Conference (TREC-8)*. To appear.
2.   K. W. Church and P. Hanks, 'Word Association Norms, Mutual Information, and Lexicography.' In *Computational Linguistics*, 6(1), 22-29, 1990.
3.   European Language Resource Association, http://www.icp.grenet.fr/ELRA/home.html
4.   D. Hiemstra and A. de Vries, 'Relating the new language models of information retrieval to the traditional retrieval models.' CTIT Technical Report TR-CTIT-00-09, May 2000.
5.   T. K. Landauer and M. L. Littman, 'Fully automated cross-language document retrieval using latent semantic indexing.' In the *Proceedings of the Sixth Annual Conference of the UW Centre for the New Oxford English Dictionary and Text Research*. 31-38, 1990.

6.  Linguistic Data Consortium (LDC), http://www.ldc.upenn.edu/
7.  J. Mayfield and P. McNamee, 'Indexing Using Both N-grams and Words.' E. M. Voorhees and D. K. Harman, eds., *Proceedings of the Seventh Text REtrieval Conference (TREC-7)*, NIST Special Publication 500-242, August 1999.
8.  J. Mayfield, P. McNamee, and C. Piatko, 'The JHU/APL HAIRCUT System at TREC-8.' In E. M. Voorhees and D. K. Harman, eds., *Proceedings of the Eighth Text REtrieval Conference (TREC-8)*. To appear.
9.  D. R. H. Miller, T. Leek, and R. M. Schwartz, 'A Hidden Markov Model Information Retrieval System.' In the Proceedings of the 22nd International Conference on Research and Development in Information Retrieval (SIGIR-99), pp. 214-221, August 1999.
10. E. Miller, D. Shen, J. Liu, and C. Nicholas, 'Performance and Scalability of a Large-Scale N-gram Based Information Retrieval System.' In the *Journal of Digital Information*, 1(5), January 2000.
11. J. Ponte and W. B. Croft, 'A Language Modeling Approach to Information Retrieval.' In the Proceedings of the 21st International Conference on Research and Development in Information Retrieval (SIGIR-98), pp. 275-281, August 1998.
12. Recherche Appliquée en Linguistic (RALI), http://www-rali.iro.umontreal.ca/

# Experiments with the Eurospider Retrieval System for CLEF 2000

Martin Braschler[1], Peter Schäuble[1]

[1] Eurospider Information Technology AG
Schaffhauserstr. 18, 8006 Zürich, Switzerland
{braschler|schauble}@eurospider.com

**Abstract.** The experiment setup that was used for Eurospider's CLEF participation is described and a preliminary analysis of the results that were obtained is given. Three runs each were submitted for the multilingual and monolingual tasks. The goal of these experiments was to investigate query translation using different methods, as well as document translation. A main focus was the use of so-called similarity thesauri for query translation. This approach produced promising results, and shows potential for future adaptations.

## 1   Introduction

This paper describes our experiments conducted for CLEF 2000. We will begin by outlining our system setup, including details of the collection and indexing. This is followed by a description of the particular characteristics of the individual experiments, and a preliminary analysis of our results. The paper closes with a discussion of our findings.

Eurospider participated in the multilingual and monolingual retrieval tasks. For multilingual retrieval, we investigated both document and query translation, as well as a combination of the two approaches. For translation, we used similarity thesauri, a bilingual wordlist and a machine translation system. Various combinations of these resources were tested and are discussed in the following.

## 2   Multilingual Retrieval

The goal of the multilingual task in CLEF is to pick a topic language, and use the queries to retrieve documents regardless of their language. I.e., a mixed result list has to be returned, potentially containing documents in all languages. The CLEF test collection consists of newspapers for German (Frankfurter Rundschau, Der Spiegel), French (Le Monde), Italian (La Stampa) and English (LA Times).

C. Peters (Ed.): CLEF 2000, LNCS 2069, pp. 140-148, 2001.
© Springer-Verlag Berlin Heidelberg 2001

We submitted three runs for this task, labeled EITCLEFM1, EITCLEFM2, and EITCLEFM3. They represent increasingly complex experiments. All runs use the German topics and all topic fields. We spent our main effort to produce these multilingual experiments. In contrast, the monolingual runs were base runs for the multilingual work, and were sent in mainly to have a comparison base.

We investigated both query translation (also abbreviated "QT" in the following) and document translation ("DT"). Technologies used for query translation were similarity thesauri ("ST"), a bilingual wordlist ("WL") and a commercially available machine translation ("MT") system. For document translation, the same MT system was used.

Following is a description of these key technologies.

*Similarity Thesaurus:* The similarity thesaurus is an automatically calculated data structure, which is built on suitable training data. It links terms to lists of their statistically most similar counterparts [3]. If multilingual training data is used, the resulting thesaurus is also multilingual. Terms in the source language are then linked to the most similar terms in the target language [4]. Such a thesaurus can be used to produce a "pseudo-translation" of the query by substituting the source language terms with those terms from the thesaurus that are most similar to the query as a whole.

We used training data provided by the Schweizerische Depeschenagentur (SDA, the Swiss national news wire) to build German/French and German/Italian similarity thesauri. A subset of this data was used earlier as part of the TREC6-8 CLIR test collection. All in all, we used a total of 11 years of news reports. While SDA produces German, French and Italian news reports, it is important to note that these stories are not actual translations. They are written by different editorial staff in different places, to serve the interests of the different audiences. Therefore, the SDA training collection is a comparable corpus (as compared to a parallel corpus, which contains actual translations of all items). The ability of the similarity thesaurus calculation process to deal with comparable corpora is a major advantage, since these are usually easier to obtain than the rare parallel corpora.

Unfortunately, we were not able to obtain suitable German/English training data in time to also build a German/English thesaurus. Instead, we opted to use a bilingual German/English wordlist. As will be shown below, this was likely a disadvantage.

*Bilingual wordlist:* Because of the lack of English training data, we used a German/English bilingual wordlist for German/English crosslingual retrieval. We assembled this list from various free sources on the Internet. This means that the wordlist is simplistic in nature (only translation pairs, no additional information such as grammatical properties or word senses) and noisy (i.e. there is a substantial amount of incorrect entries).

*Machine translation system:* For a limited number of language pairs, commercial enduser machine translation products are available nowadays. Since some of these systems are inexpensive and run on standard PC hardware, we decided to try and link such a product with both our translation component and our retrieval software. We therefore used MT to translate the document collection, enabling us to use the translated documents in our retrieval system, and also to translate the queries, combining those with the translation output from the similarity thesaurus.

*Indexing:* We used the standard RotondoSpider retrieval system developed at Eurospider for indexing and retrieval. Additional components were used for query translation and blind feedback.

Indexing of German documents and queries used the Spider German stemmer, which is based on a dictionary coupled with a rule set for decompounding of German nouns.

Indexing of French documents and queries used the Spider French rule-based stemmer. French accents were retained, since we decided that the quality of the data from Le Monde ensured consistent use of accenting.

Indexing of Italian documents and queries used the Spider Italian rule-based stemmer. There was a simple preprocessing that replaced the combination "vowel + quote" with an accented vowel, since the La Stampa texts use this alternative way of representation for accented characters. This simple rule produces some errors if a word was intentionally quoted, but the error rate was considered too small to justify the development of a more sophisticated replacement process.

Indexing of English documents used an adapted version of the Porter rule-based stemmer.

The Spider system was configured to use a straight Lnu.ltn weighting scheme for retrieval, as described in [5].

The ranked lists for the three multilingual runs were obtained as follows:

*EITCLEFM1:* We built one large unified index containing all the German documents plus all the English, French and Italian documents in their German translations as obtained by MT. It is then possible to perform straight monolingual German retrieval on this combined collection. An added benefit is the avoidance of the merging problem that typically arises when results are calculated one language at a time. Since only one search has to be performed on one index, only one ranked list is obtained.

*EITCLEFM2:* Our second submission has a different focus. Instead of document translation, we used only query translation for this experiment. We obtained individual runs for each language pair (German/German, German/French, German/Italian, and German/English). For each pair, we used two different translation strategies (or in the case of German/German, two different retrieval strategies). For retrieval of the French and Italian documents, we translated the German queries both using an appropriate similarity thesaurus and using the MT system. For search on the English collection, we again used the MT system, but additionally used the German/English bilingual wordlist. The two German monolingual runs were a simple, straightforward retrieval run, and a run that was enhanced through blind relevance feedback (for a discussion of blind feedback and some possible enhancements to it, see e.g.[2]). The choice of relevance feedback was to "imitate" the expansion effect of the similarity thesaurus for the other languages. We expanded the query by the twenty statistically best terms from the top 10 initially retrieved documents.

The two runs for each language are merged by adding up the ranks of a document in both individual runs to form a new score. In order to boost documents with high ranks, we used the logarithms of the ranks of the documents in both experiments.

```
new_score = MAX - (log(rank_run_1) + log(rank_run_2));
```

The step resulted in four runs, one per language combination. These were then merged by taking a document each in turn from each run, thus producing the final ranked list (this process is sometimes also referred to as "interleaving").

*EITCLEFM3:* The last multilingual experiment combines elements from both the QT and DT-based runs. To produce the final ranked list, these two runs are merged by setting the score to the sum of the logarithms of the ranks, as described above.

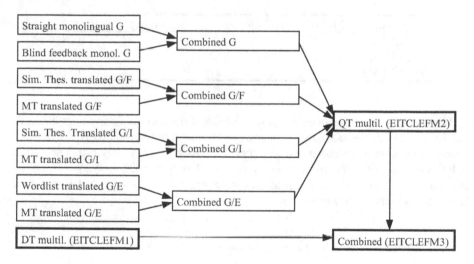

**Fig. 1.** Procedure to obtain the multilingual experiments

# 3  Monolingual Retrieval

We also submitted three runs for the monolingual task named EITCLEFGG, EITCLEFFFF and EITCLEFII (German, French and Italian monolingual, respectively). These runs all use the full topics (all fields). As mentioned earlier, they were produced mainly to serve as baselines for comparison. The main effort was invested into the multilingual experiments.

EITCLEFGG: *This was our German monolingual submission. It is the straight retrieval run that was used to produce the EITCLEFM2 run (see above).*

*EITCLEFFF and EITCLEFII:* These two runs were also obtained through straight monolingual retrieval using the French and Italian queries, respectively.

# 4 Results

Looking at the results, the document translation-based run outperforms the query translation-based run. However, looking at the individual parts that make up the QT-based run, we notice that the translation using the bilingual wordlist performs poorly. It seems likely that the actual difference would be significantly smaller if a good English similarity thesaurus was available.

**Table 1.** Average precision numbers for the multilingual experiments

| Runs against Multilingual Collection | Average Precision |
|---|---|
| EITCLEFM1 | 0.2816 |
| EITCLEFM2 | 0.2500 |
| EITCLEFM3 | 0.3107 |

The combined run produces the best results, and does so on a consistent basis. As shown in table 2, the majority of queries improves, often substantially, in terms of average precision when compared to either the DT-only or QT-only run. The picture is less conclusive for the comparison between DT-only and QT-only. We think that this shows that whereas both approaches have strengths, they mix well in the combined run to boost performance.

**Table 2.** Comparison of average precision numbers for individual queries

| Comparison Avg. Prec. per Query | better; diff.>10% | better; diff.<10% | worse; diff.<10% | worse; diff.>10% |
|---|---|---|---|---|
| EITCLEFM3 (comb.) vs. EITCLEFM1 (DT) | 16 | 16 | 6 | 2 |
| EITCLEFM3 (comb.) vs. EITCLEFM2 (QT) | 19 | 12 | 4 | 5 |
| EITCLEFM1 (DT) vs. EITCLEFM2 (QT) | 14 | 10 | 5 | 11 |

We also studied individual language pairs and the impact of the different query translation strategies.

Table 3. Average precision numbers for the German monolingual runs

| Runs against German Collection | Average Precision |
|---|---|
| Straight | 0.4030 |
| Blind Feedback | 0.3994 |

It seems like the blind feedback loop did not help boost performance. In any case, the difference is so slight that it can be considered meaningless. A per-query analysis shows that most queries are affected little by the feedback, and that the number of queries with a substantial increase or decrease in average precision is exactly the same. This reinforces the conclusion that the feedback was not helpful in this case.

Table 4. Average precision numbers for runs against the French collection

| Runs against French Collection | Average Precision |
|---|---|
| Monolingual | 0.3884 |
| MT G/F | 0.3321 |
| Similarity Thesaurus G/F | 0.2262 |
| Combined G/F | 0.3494 |

The French MT-based run outperforms the similarity thesaurus-based run substantially. However, a sizable part of the difference can be attributed to five queries that failed completely using the thesaurus (we consider a query a complete failure if the result has an average precision < 0.01). For the rest of the queries, the similarity thesaurus performed well, even outperforming the MT-based run by more than 10% for eight queries in terms of average precision. The combined run gives a modest improvement over the MT run. 20 queries benefit from the combination, whereas the performance of the remaining 14 queries falls.

Table 5. Average precision numbers for runs against the Italian collection

| Runs against Italian Collection | Average Precision |
|---|---|
| Monolingual | 0.4319 |
| MT G/I | 0.3306 |
| Similarity Thesaurus G/I | 0.2568 |
| Combined G/I | 0.3636 |

In Italian, the similarity thesaurus is closer to the performance of the MT-based run. Again, a big part of the difference is due to 7 queries failing completely when using the thesaurus. The combination is a reasonable improvement over the MT-only run, gaining 10% in average precision.

**Table 6.** Average precision numbers for runs against the English collection

| Runs against English Collection | Average Precision |
|---|---|
| Monolingual | 0.3879 |
| MT G/E | 0.3753 |
| Wordlist G/E | 0.1414 |
| Combined G/E | 0.2809 |

The good performance of the MT-based German/English run is striking. This probably is due to the main effort in MT research still going into language combinations involving English. The poor performance of the run using the bilingual wordlist is also noteworthy. While this might be partly due to shaky quality of the input sources, we think that it underscores how important word sense disambiguation is, something which MT and the similarity thesaurus try to address, but which is lacking from our wordlist. It seems obvious that bilingual wordlists/dictionaries are not competitive without a serious investment of effort in that direction.

We are pleased to see that our runs compare favorably when compared to other entries in CLEF. Table 7 shows an analysis of per-query performance compared to the median performance of all participants. Especially the multilingual runs performed strongly, and the two runs EITCLEFM1 and EITCLEFM3 outperform all other officially reported results for CLEF 2000. The monolingual runs are more mixed, which was to be expected, since we did not tune them specifically for performance. The German run seems to perform nicely, placing among the best runs for this language. We believe this to be due to the compound analysis in the Spider stemming, since all competitive German experiments by other participants have addressed the decompounding problem in one way or another. The results for French and Italian indicate room for improvement. It is interesting to see that participants in French and Italian monolingual task in general obtained similar performance.

**Table 7.** Officially submitted runs compared to median of all submitted runs
(on individual query basis)

| Run | Best | Above | Median | Below | Worst | # queries |
|---|---|---|---|---|---|---|
| EITCLEFM1 | 1 | 29 | 0 | 10 | 0 | 40 |
| EITCLEFM2 | 1 | 22 | 2 | 15 | 0 | 40 |
| EITCLEFM3 | 7 | 23 | 1 | 9 | 0 | 40 |
| EITCLEFGG | 6 | 17 | 6 | 8 | 0 | 37 |
| EITCLEFFF | 0 | 7 | 5 | 22 | 0 | 34 |
| EITCLEFII | 3 | 7 | 7 | 17 | 0 | 34 |

# 5  Conclusions

Overall, we think the performance of the similarity thesaurus is remarkable. While it did not produce results equal to the MT-based runs, it is important to note that we were in a "worst-case scenario": the thesauri were built on a comparable corpus (no real translations, as opposed to a parallel corpora), and there was no overlap in training data and the test collection. This means that similar requirements for other translation scenarios can be quite easily matched. I.e., it would be easy to build similarity thesauri with comparable performance for a multitude of additional language pairs, even exotic ones, simply by gathering suitable training data, such as taking a sufficient amount of text from one national newspaper each. Also, the performance of the similarity thesaurus will get a sizeable boost when the problems can be addressed that led to a complete failure in translation of a number of queries. We should be able to do this by increasing the size of the thesaurus, which again is only a matter of processing more training data. Note also that the thesaurus is suited for situations in which the query length is much shorter, such as Web searches. As shown during the Eurosearch project (for a short description of Eurosearch, see [1]), the expansion effect of the thesaurus is beneficial for the short queries. Machine translation systems traditionally have problems with short, keyword style queries.

Document translation gave us some good results, and was feasible for a collection of the size of the CLEF test collection. This means that DT should not be discounted for reasonably static collections with limited size. Note, however, that some of the advantage we found for DT versus query translation may be due to the inadequate performance of the wordlist we used for English. Also, QT clearly remains the only possibility for huge or highly dynamic collections.

# 6  Acknowledgements

Thanks go to the providers of the CLEF data and all the assessors doing the judgement work. Also, we appreciate the data that was provided to us by SDA for building the similarity thesauri. Additional thanks go to Patrick Frey for tuning the rules of the German stemmer and Min-Yen Kan for a number of scripts originally written for last year's TREC that proved a welcome help in doing these experiments.

# References

1. Braschler, M., Peters, C., Picchi, E., Schäuble, P.: Cross-Language Web Querying: The EuroSearch Approach. In Proceedings of the 2nd European Conference on Research and Advanced Technology for Digital Libraries, pages 701 - 702, 1998.
2. Mitra, M., Singhal, A., Buckley, C.: Improving Automatic Query Expansion. In Proceedings of the 21st Annual International ACM SIGIR Conference on Research and Development in Information Retrieval, pages 206 - 214, 1998.

3. Qiu, Y., Frei, H.: Concept Based Query Expansion. In Proceedings of the 16th ACM SIGIR Conference on Research and Development in Information Retrieval, Pittsburgh, PA, pages 160 - 169, 1993.

4. Sheridan, P., Braschler, M., Schäuble, P.: Cross-language information retrieval in a multilingual legal domain. In Proceedings of the First European Conference on Research and Advanced Technology for Digital Libraries, pages 253 - 268, 1997.

5. Singhal, A., Buckley, C., Mitra, M.: Pivoted Document Length Normalization. In Proceedings of the 19th ACM SIGIR Conference on Research and Development in Information Retrieval, pages 21 - 29, 1996.

# A Poor Man's Approach to CLEF

Arjen P. de Vries[1,2]

[1] CWI, Amsterdam, The Netherlands
[2] University of Twente, Enschede, The Netherlands
ar en@acm.org

**Abstract.** The primary goal of our participation in CLEF is to acquire e perience with supporting cross-lingual retrieval. We submitted runs for all four target languages, but our main interest has been in the bilingual Dutch to English runs. We investigated whether we can obtain a reasonable performance without e pensive (but high quality) resources we have used only o -the-shelf , freely available tools for stopping, stemming, compound-splitting (only for Dutch) and translation. Although our results are encouraging, we must conclude that a poor man s approach should not e pect to result in rich men s retrieval results.

## 1 Goals

The Mirror DBMS 2 aims specifically at supporting both data management and content management in a single system. Its design separates the retrieval model from the specific techniques used for implementation, thus allowing more exibility to experiment with a variety of retrieval models. Its design based on database techniques intends to support this exibility without causing a major penalty on the efficiency and scalability of the system. The support for information retrieval in our system is presented in detail in 3 , 1 , and 4 .

The primary goal of our participation in CLEF is to acquire experience with supporting Dutch users. Also, we want to investigate whether we can obtain a reasonable performance without requiring expensive but high quality resources. We do not expect to obtain impressive results with our system, but hope to obtain a baseline from which we can develop our system further. We decided to submit runs for all four target languages, but our main interest is in the bilingual Dutch to English runs.

## 2 Pre-processing

We have used only off-the-shelf' tools for stopping, stemming, compound-splitting only for Dutch and translation. All our tools are available for free, without usage restrictions for research purposes.

C. Peters (Ed.): CLEF 2000, LNCS 2069, pp. 149–155, 2001.

**Table 1.** Size of the stoplists used.

| Language | words |
|---|---|
| Dutch | 124 |
| English | 95 |
| German | 238 |
| French | 218 |
| Italian | 133 |

### i g a    e    i g

Moderately sized stoplists, of comparable coverage, were made available by University of Twente  see also Table 1 .

We used the stemmers provided by Muscat[1], an open source search engine. The Muscat software includes stemmers for all five languages, as well as Spanish and Portuguese. The stemming algorithms are based on the Porter stemmer.

### i  i  a ie

The Ergane translation dictionaries[2] were made available by Gerard van Wilgen. To avoid the necessity of a bilingual wordlist for every possible language combination, Ergane uses the artificial language Esperanto as an interlingua. Ergane supports translation from and to no less than 57 languages, although some languages are only covered by a few hundred words. The number of entries in the dictionaries used are summarized in Table 2.

**Table 2.** Number of entries in the Ergane dictionaries.

| Language | words |
|---|---|
| Dutch | 56,006 |
| English | 15,812 |
| French | 10,282 |
| German | 14,410 |
| Italian | 3,793 |

Because of synonyms, the size of bilinugal dictionaries might actually be bigger than the size of the smallest word-list of a language pair. After removal of multiword expressions, the number of Dutch entries in the bilingual translation lexicons are presented in Table 3.

Note that these dictionary sizes are really small compared to dictionaries used in other cross-language retrieval experiments. For instance, Hiemstra and Kraaij have used professional dictionaries that are about 15 times as large  6 .

---

[1] http //open.muscat.com/
[2] http //www.travlang.com/Ergane/

**Table 3.** Sizes of the bilingual dictionaries  from Dutch to target language .

| Target | words |
|--------|-------|
| English | 20,060 |
| French | 15,158 |
| German | 15,817 |
| Italian | 6,922 |

### li  i  g

Compound-splitting was only used for the Dutch queries. We applied a simple compound-splitter developed at the University of Twente. The algorithm tries to split any word that is not in the bilingual dictionary using the full word-list of about 50,000 Dutch words from Ergane. The algorithm tries to split the word in as little parts as possible. It encodes a morphological rule to handle a property known as  tussen-s', but it does not use part-of-speech information to search for linguistically plausible compounds.

Because the Dutch word-list used for splitting was much larger than the number of entries in the bilingual dictionaries, compound-splitting might result in words that are only partially translated. For example, the Dutch word  wereldbevolkingsconferentie'  topic 13, English:  World Population Conference' was correctly split in three parts:  wereld',  bevolking' and  conferentie' of which only the first two words have entries in the Dutch-to-French dictionary.[3]

## System

For a detailed description of our retrieval system, we refer the interested user to  3 . The underlying retrieval model is best explained in our technical report[4]  5 . It supplements the theoretical basis of the model with a series of experiments, comparing this model with other, more common retrieval models.

## Results

This section discusses the results obtained with our system. We discuss the retrieval results expressed in average precision, and, the coverage of our translations. After discussing the official runs, we present some tests performed with pre-processing Dutch topics.

### 4.1     ial  e  l

All experiments were done using the title and description fields of the topics. The average query length for Dutch was 10.5 after stopping  which is of course

---

[3] This e ample also illustrates the  tussen-s  rule  the  s  between  bevolking  and conferentie  has been correctly removed.

[4] http //wwwhome.cs.utwente.nl/ hiemstra/papers/inde .html  ctit

**Table 4.** Summary of results  after fixes .

|  | queries | Average Prec. | R-prec. |
|---|---|---|---|
| English | 33 | 0.4070 | 0.4163 |
| French | 33 | 0.4090 | 0.3831 |
| German | 36 | 0.3134 | 0.3149 |
| Italian | 36 | 0.3980 | 0.3935 |
| Bi-lingual | 32 | 0.2375 | 0.2392 |
| Multi-lingual | 39 | 0.1018 | 0.1448 |

**Table 5.** The submitted,  awed results.

|  | queries | Average Prec. | R-prec. |
|---|---|---|---|
| German | 37 | 0.1794 | 0.2032 |
| Multi-lingual | 39 | 0.0864 | 0.1330 |

rather long compared to the average query size people enter in e.g. web search engines .

Table 6 summarizes our results. The second column shows the number of queries with hits in the monolingual runs  the third and fourth columns show the mean average precision[5]. The monolingual results for English have been based on the bilingual qrels. The last column summarizes the drop in average precision that can be attributed to the translation process.

**Table** . Official results  after fixes .

|  | queries | Monolingual | Dutch $\rightarrow$ X | relative |
|---|---|---|---|---|
| English | 33 | 0.4070 | 0.2303 | 57 |
| French | 34 | 0.4090 | 0.1486 | 36 |
| German | 37 | 0.3134 | 0.1050 | 34 |
| Italian | 34 | 0.3980 | 0.0989 | 24 |

We hypothesize from the relatively low average precision  0.3134  on the monolingual German task that we really have to perform compound-splitting of this corpus. Another possible cause of the lower score for German is that we had to merge the runs from the two subcollections, which were handled separately. But, our experiments on TREC-8 showed that this cannot really explain such a performance drop.

We attribute the large drop in performance for e.g. the bilingual Italian task  only 24  of the average precision of the monolingual task  to the small coverage of our translation dictionaries. The coverage of the topic translations produced has been summarized in table 7.

---

[5] The mean average precision for the bilingual runs as given by `trec_eval`, normalized for the number of queries with hits in the monolingual case.

Together, the inferior results on German and Italian explain the disappointing average precision obtained on the multilingual retrieval task  0.0864 .

**Table** . Coverage of the translations  40 queries .

| e periment | total terms | not translated | relative |
|---|---|---|---|
| Dutch → English | 420 | 92 | 22 |
| Dutch → French | 420 | 138 | 33 |
| Dutch → German | 420 | 115 | 27 |
| Dutch → Italian | 420 | 199 | 47 |

## 4.2   l gi al   ali a i   a       li  i g

Our primary goal with CLEF participation is to test whether we could provide a Dutch interface to our retrieval systems. To confirm our intuition about stemming and compound-splitting, we performed some test runs to analyze the effects of morphological normalisation and compound-splitting for Dutch. We either performed stemming or not, and performed compound-splitting or not, resulting in four variants of the system:

nlen1: base-line translation using full-form dictionary
nlen2: translation using Dutch stemmer and a dictionary with stemmed entries
nlen3: translation using compound-splitter for Dutch and full-form dictionary
nlen4: translation using compound-splitter and dictionary with stemmed
        entries

The results of these runs are summarized in Table 8. We conclude that compound-splitting is very important, and stemming seems a useful pre-processing step.

**Table** . Results on Dutch runs  33 queries .

| run | average precision | improvement |
|---|---|---|
| nlen1 | 0.1726 | |
| nlen2 | 0.2228 | 29 |
| nlen3 | 0.1912 | 11 |
| nlen4 | 0.2303 | 33 |

To support these conclusions, Table 9 summarizes the coverage of the various translations used in the Dutch runs. Compound-splitting and morphological stemming of Dutch words nearly triples the relative coverage of the translation dictionaries. The total of 92 untranslated Dutch terms in the English queries

**Table** . Coverage of the translations  40 queries .

| e periment | total terms | not translated | relative |
|---|---|---|---|
| nlen1 | 366 | 201 | 57 |
| nlen2 | 366 | 130 | 36 |
| nlen3 | 420 | 160 | 38 |
| nlen4 | 420 | 92 | 22 |

include about 13 proper names like  Weinberg',  Salam' and  Glashow'  topic 2
and a few terms that were left untranslated in the Dutch topics like  Académie
Francaise'  topic 15  and  Deutsche Bundesbahn'  topic 40 .

## Conclusions and Future Work

Summarizing our experiments, we may conclude that our retrieval models works
well for all monolingual runs, except for German. Future experiments will have to
confirm whether a process like compound-splitting will indeed bring our monolingual results to a level comparable to the other languages. The in uence of
compound-splitting of Dutch topics on the bilingual results raises our expectations on this end.

We were not at all unhappy with our bilingual results. But, from the coverage
of the translations, we still have to conclude that a poor man's approach should
not expect to result in rich men's retrieval results. However, we cannot blame it
all on the dictionaries. The current version of our retrieval system does not use
query expansion techniques to improve mediocre translations  it remains to be
seen if better statistical techniques can bring us closer to the results obtained
with  proper' linguistic tools.

## Acknowledgements

Without Djoerd Hiemstra's help, I would never have obtained CLEF results: he
helped me with most of the pre-processing. More importantly, our discussions
about his and competing retrieval models has improved significantly my understanding of Information Retrieval. I should also like to thank Gerard van Wilgen
for making available the Ergane dictionaries.

## References

1. A.P. de Vries.  Mirror  Multimedia query processing in e tensible databases.  In
     r cee ings    the    urteenth    ente    r sh p  n language techn l g
     anguage  echn l g  in    ultime ia In   rmati n   etrie al, pages 37 48, Enschede,
   The Netherlands, December 1998.
2. A.P. de Vries.    ntent an  multime ia  ata ase management s stems. PhD thesis,
   University of Twente, Enschede, The Netherlands, December 1999.

3. A.P. de Vries and D. Hiemstra. The Mirror DBMS at TREC. In  r cee ings
   the Se enth  e t  etrie al   n erence    E   , Gaithersburg, Maryland, November
   1999.
4. A.P. de Vries and A.N. Wilschut. On the integration of IR and databases.  In
   *Data ase issues in multime ia  sh rt paper pr cee ings  internati nal c n erence  n*
   *ata ase semantics  DS*   , pages 16 31, Rotorua, New Zealand, January 1999.
5. Djoerd Hiemstra and Arjen de Vries. Relating the new language models of information retrieval to the traditional retrieval models. Technical Report TR CTIT 00 09,
   Centre for Telematics and Information Technology, May 2000.
6. D. Hiemstra and W. Kraaij. Twenty-One at TREC-7  Ad-hoc and cross-language
   track. In E.M. Voorhees and D.K. Harman, editors,  r cee ings   the Se enth  e t
   etrie al   n erence    E   , number 500-242 in NIST Special publications, 1999.

# Ambiguity Problem in Multilingual Information Retrieval

Mirna Adriani

Department of Computing Science
University of Glasgow
Glasgow G12 8QQ, Scotland
mirna@dcs.gla.ac.uk

**Abstract.** This report describes the work done for our participation in the multilingual track of the Cross-Language Evaluation Forum (CLEF). We use a dictionary-based approach to translate English queries into German, French and Italian queries. We then apply a term disambiguation technique to select the best translation terms from terms found in the dictionary entries, and a query expansion technique to enhance the queries' retrieval performance. We show that the word-formation characteristics of different languages affect the effectiveness of statistical techniques in dealing with the ambiguity problem.

## 1 Introduction

A multilingual environment poses many interesting challenges to the field of cross-language information retrieval (CLIR). In CLIR, we deal with a query in one language and documents or information to retrieve in another language or, in the case of a multilingual environment, many languages. CLIR techniques, in general, always involve some kind of language translation process. A number of translation techniques have been proposed by CLIR researchers such as ones that use NLP-based machine translation algorithms, parallel corpora, and machine readable dictionaries. Machine translation systems have been shown to produce good results, however, such systems are only available for a few languages. Parallel corpus-based techniques have also been proven to show good CLIR results [9]. However, parallel corpora are expensive to build, and those that are available are fairly limited, in terms of their domain coverage. As a consequence, such techniques often fail in translating terms in a wider scope of domain. Fortunately, more and more comparable corpora have been built and made available to researchers, recently. Comparable corpora can be considered as similar to parallel corpora since they consist of documents in many languages concerning the same topics. Hopefully, this will stimulate more research activities in the field.

Translation techniques that use bilingual dictionaries are very practical, as they do not require any deeper linguistic knowledge such as syntactic grammars and semantics. An ideal dictionary for this purpose would be one that is available in a

C. Peters (Ed.): CLEF 2000, LNCS 2069, pp. 156–165, 2001.

machine readable dictionary (MRD) format, to allow automatic term translations. Unfortunately, MRDs for many languages are still relatively expensive to acquire. For this reason, we use dictionary resources that are freely available on the Internet to translate English queries into German, French and Italian. The translation method is straightforward, that is by simply replacing each English term with the translation terms found in each of the dictionaries for the term. Clearly, the quality of the translation very much depends on the quality and the comprehensiveness of the dictionary. We consider the limited vocabulary of our dictionaries as an additional challenge.

Our participation in this year's Cross-Language Evaluation Forum (CLEF) has provided us with an opportunity to better understand the issues in Cross-Language Information Retrieval (CLIR) through experimentation. Our previous work has been on bilingual CLIR. The multilingual task is different from the bilingual task because the collections contain documents in more than one language. In this task, we face the challenge of indexing and merging retrieval results from a number of language-collections. The indexing can be built as a single index or an individual index for each collection. A single index does not need to merge the retrieval results from each collection. The second case needs a merging of the different retrieval results in a single rank. In our work, we choose to use different indexing for each language. We hope that we can learn the characteristic and translation problems of each language. It has also provided us with the opportunity to measure the effectiveness of our algorithms and techniques using large collections.

In Section 2, we present a brief survey of relevant work done by other researchers. Section 3 provides a review of our sense disambiguation technique, and describes our term similarity based query expansion technique, as well as our rank-list merging technique. Section 4 discusses the experiments that we conducted to measure the effectiveness of our techniques and their results. Finally, Section 5 concludes this paper with a summary.

## 2    Dictionary-Based Approach

The dictionary-based query translation approach translates each term in a query to another language by replacing it with the senses of that term in the dictionary. There are several problems in such translation techniques, mainly, problems with term ambiguity, phrase translation, and untranslated terms such as acronyms or technical terms that are not found in the dictionary. These problems result in very poor retrieval performance of the translation queries.

A number of statistical and linguistic approaches have been demonstrated to be effective in alleviating the ambiguity problem. Ballesteros and Croft [4] use term co-occurrence data and part-of-speech tagging to reduce the ambiguity problem from the dictionary. A different approach is proposed by Pirkola [11] whose technique reduces the effect of the ambiguity problem by structuring the queries and translating them using a general and a domain-specific dictionary. Translating phrases word-by-word often results in the loss of the original meaning in the translation. In order to translate the phrase correctly, Hull and Grefenstette [8] used a phrase dictionary, which helps to improve the retrieval performance. Other researchers showed that a phrase dictionary built from a parallel corpus can also be used to recognize and handle phrases [6].

To further mitigate the negative effect of mistranslated query terms, many researchers have employed query expansion techniques. Query expansion is a well-known method in IR for improving retrieval performance. Basically, it adds new terms, selected using a certain technique, to the query such that the query becomes more precise where the added terms clarify the meaning of the original query terms, and its recall is improved as terms associated with the original query terms are added. Adriani and Croft [1] employ pseudo relevance feedback techniques to obtain terms for the query expansion. The pseudo relevance feedback techniques assume that the top rank documents initially retrieved using the queries are relevant. Terms appearing in these relevant documents are then added to the queries. They found that post-translation query expansion, i.e., query expansion on the translated queries, and the combination-translation query expansion, i.e., query expansion on both the original and the translated queries, are effective in improving CLIR performance. Adriani and van Rijsbergen [2] expand the translated query based on the collective similarity between each candidate term and all of the existing terms in the query.

Merging retrieval results from a number of collections of different languages has been done by many researchers in the CLIR task of the Text Retrieval Conference (TREC) 1999. Oard et.al. [10] compare the results of using a single index and different indexes, but there was no significant difference between the two types of index. Other research groups, such as Braschler et.al. [5] of *Eurospider*, apply a linear regression analysis on parallel document alignments. Franz et.al. [7] of IBM use a probabilistic model to create a single rank list of multilingual documents.

## 2.1   Term Disambiguation Technique

The sense ambiguity problem occurs in the process of translating queries from one language to another using the dictionary approach. In order to select the best translation terms from an entry in the dictionary, we apply our term disambiguation technique, which is based on the statistical similarity values among terms. This term disambiguation technique is based on our previous work [3]. Basically, given a set of original query terms, we select for each term the best sense such that the resulting set of selected senses contains senses that are mutually related- or statistically similar- with one another. For computational cost considerations, this is done using an approximate algorithm. Given a set of $n$ original query terms $\{t_1, t_2, ..., t_n\}$, a set of translation terms, $T$, is obtained using the following algorithm:

---

1. For each $t_i$ ($i$=1 to $n$), retrieve a set of senses $S_i$ from the dictionary.
2. For each set $S_i$ ($i$=1 to $n$), do steps 2.1, 2.2 and 2.3.
2.1 For each sense $t_j'$ ($j$=1 to $|S_i|$) in $S_i$, do step 2.1.1
2.1.1 For each set $S_k$ ($k$=1 to $n$ and $k \neq i$), get the maximum similarity, $M_{j,k}$, between $t_j'$ and the senses in $S_k$.
2.2 Compute the score of sense $t_j'$ as the sum of $M_{j,k}$ ($k$=1 to $n$ and $k \neq i$).
2.3 Select the sense in $S_i$ with the highest score, and add the selected sense into the set $T$.

---

Query terms that are not found in the dictionary are included in the translation set $T$ as-is. This is typically the case for proper names, technical terms, and acronyms. A complete explanation of our technique can be found in [3].

We obtain the degree of similarity or association-relation between terms using a term association measure, called the *Dice similarity coefficient* [12], which is commonly used in document or term clustering. The term association measure, $sim_{xy}$, between term $x$ and $y$ is computed as follows:

$$sim_{xy} = 2 \sum_{i=1}^{n} (w'_{xi} \cdot w'_{yi}) / ( \sum_{i=1}^{n} w_{xi}^2 + \sum_{i=1}^{n} w_{yi}^2 )$$

where

$w_{xi}$ = the weight of term $x$ in document $i$
$w_{yi}$ = the weight of term $y$ in document $i$
$w'_{xi} = w_{xi}$ if term $y$ also occurs in document $i$, or 0 otherwise
$w'_{yi} = w_{yi}$ if term $x$ also occurs in document $i$, or 0 otherwise
$n$ = the number of documents in the collection.

The weight $w_{xi}$ of term $x$ in document $i$ is computed using the standard tf*idf term weighting formula [13].

## 2.2 Query Expansion Technique

The resulting translated queries are, of course, worse than the original queries, in terms of their accuracy and retrieval effectiveness. We expand the translated queries by adding related terms to the queries to further improve their retrieval performance. Our query expansion technique also uses the Dice similarity coefficient to build a similarity matrix containing the co-occurrences of the terms in document passages. First, for each collection, we build a database that contains passages of 200 terms each. We then run each query set to obtain the relevant passages. The top 20 passages are then used for creating the term similarity matrix. Next, we compute the sum of similarity values between each term in the passages and all terms in the query. Finally, we added the top 10 terms from the relevant passages to the query.

## 2.3 Rank-List Merging

The rank-list merging technique is required as we run the translation of each query in the query set with each language-collection, independent of the other language-collections. The retrieval results from the four language collections are then merged in a single rank list. We employ a simple method based on an assumption that the highest-rank document in one collection-language is comparable, in terms of the relevance to the query, to that of another language. We realize that this assumption is not always true, but, owing to lack of time to experiment with other techniques, we thought that it was a reasonable assumption. With this assumption, we normalize the relevance scores for each collection with the highest score in that collection's rank list, and then merge and sort them in a rank list.

## 3    Experiments

In the multilingual track, the document collections are in four languages, namely, English, German, French, and Italian. The collections contain newspaper articles from *Los Angeles Times* (English), *Frankfurter Rundschau* and *Der Spiegel* (German), *Le Monde* (French), and *La Stampa* (Italian). We build the database for each collection using the INQUERY information retrieval system.

From the multilingual query sets, we chose to run the English queries, which were then translated using the online dictionaries. We used machine-readable dictionaries downloaded from the Internet at http://www.freedict.com. These dictionaries contain short translation of English terms in different languages. We realize that these dictionaries are not ideal resources for our purpose, as most of the dictionary entries contain only one or two senses. However, they are easily obtainable for free from the Internet. We reformatted the dictionary files so that our query translator program can read them.

The query translation process proceeds as follows. First, we remove all stop-words from the English query and obtain the root-words of the remaining terms using a Porter word stemmer. Each term is then substituted with its translation term or terms according to the dictionary, excluding any stopwords in the dictionary entries. A query phrase is translated by translating each of the phrase's constituent terms. The translation terms are stemmed using the French and the German word stemmers from the PRISE retrieval system obtained from NIST.

We then apply the term disambiguation technique to choose the best translation term. The term similarity matrix is then built for each collection. We use the similarity values to perform the term disambiguation. The resulting queries are then enhanced by applying the query expansion technique, adding 10 terms from a set of 20 relevant passages that are relevant to the query terms. The values of 10 and 20 were obtained through a preliminary experiment.

Finally, we run each query set on its respective document collection, including the original English queries on the English collection, and the retrieval results from the sets are then combined into a single document ranking.

In this experiment, we ran two query formats, namely, the title-only (short) and the long (full) query formats. Each query in the long query set contains a title, a description, and a narrative text of the CLEF query. We chose to do both query sets to see whether the results are consistent across both sets. All the steps in the multilingual task were done in a fully automatic manner.

# 4    Results

In this work, we participated in the multilingual task by running both the title-only and the long query formats. However, only the title-only query run was considered in the CLEF relevance assessment pool.

As can be seen in Table 1, we obtained the best multilingual results, as compared to those of the equivalent monolingual runs, for the Italian translation queries. The French translation queries came second and, lastly, the German translation queries, which performed the poorest. Our investigation into the title-only query run revealed that the retrieval performance of each translation query correlates negatively with the number of original English terms that are not found in the bilingual dictionary. Specifically, our German translation query set contains 4 untranslated English terms and a number of stand-alone German terms in place of the 19 German compound nouns, which are the correct translations of the 19 English query terms. The French and the Italian query sets contain 13 and 23 untranslated English terms, respectively (see Table 2).

**Table 1.** Average retrieval precision of the monolingual runs using the English, German, French, and Italian queries; and the average precision of the cross-lingual runs and the merged multilingual runs for English queries translated into German, French and Italian. Both the title-only and the long query formats were used

| Query | Task | English | German | French | Italian | Merge |
|-------|------|---------|--------|--------|---------|-------|
| Title | Monolingual | 0.2705 | 0.2075 | 0.2260 | 0.0347 | - |
| Title | Cross Language | 0.2705 | 0.0810 | 0.1097 | 0.0569 | 0.0560 |
| Long | Monolingual | 0.3804 | 0.2790 | 0.2682 | 0.1279 | - |
| Long | Cross Language | 0.3804 | 0.0932 | 0.1012 | 0.1050 | 0.0881 |

In our previous work [2], we obtained results where our German queries perform better than the equivalent Spanish queries in retrieving documents from an English collection. The reason being that most German compound words in our German query set have exact English translations in the dictionary, unlike phrases in the Spanish query set which were translated word by word using a bilingual dictionary. In other word, the degree of ambiguity of the German queries is less than that of the Spanish queries. On the other hand, from this work, we learned that translating English queries into German, which involves translating into compound words, is a difficult task.

**Table 2.** The number of English terms in the query set, and the number of them that are not found respectively in the German, French, and Italian bilingual dictionaries

| Query | English | German | French | Italian |
|-------|---------|--------|--------|---------|
| Title | 114 | 4 | 13 | 23 |
| Long | 1,112 | 13 | 43 | 61 |

## 4.1  German Result

The English queries that were translated into German (EG) consist of 2,714 terms for the title-only queries and 27,239 terms for the long queries. Ideally, as the equivalent German monolingual queries do, the resulting translation queries must contain 125 terms and 1,811 terms for the title-only and the long queries, respectively.

The EG title-only queries perform 80.67% below the equivalent monolingual German queries. Applying the term disambiguation technique improved the retrieval performance by 24.39%. The EG long queries drop the performance by 89.82%, as compared to the equivalent monolingual German queries. Almost similarly, the term disambiguation technique improved the retrieval performance by 24.32%. However, the query expansion technique hurt the retrieval performance by 4.70% and by 1.10% for the title-only and the long queries, respectively (see Table 3a).

**Table 3a.** Average retrieval precision of the German monolingual queries, the German translation of the equivalent English queries, the translation queries after applying the term-disambiguation technique, and the translation queries after applying the term disambiguation and query expansion techniques

| Query | Title | Long |
|-------|-------|------|
| Monolingual | 0.2075 | 0.2790 |
| Trans (EG) | 0.0401 (-80.67%) | 0.0284 (-89.82%) |
| Trans (EG) + Dis | 0.0907 (-56.28%) | 0.0962 (-65.50%) |
| Trans (EG) + Dis + QE | 0.0810 (-60.98%) | 0.0932 (-66.60%) |

## 4.2    French Result

The English queries that were translated into French (EF) consist of 552 terms for the title-only queries and 8,292 terms for the long queries. Ideally, as for the equivalent French monolingual queries, the resulting translation queries must contain 198 terms and 2,324 terms for the title-only and the long queries, respectively.

The EF title-only queries perform 66.80% below the equivalent monolingual French queries. Applying the term disambiguation technique improved the retrieval performance by 15.32%. The EF long queries drop the performance by 89.44%, as compared to the equivalent monolingual French queries. The term disambiguation technique improved the retrieval performance by 27.17%. As with the German translation queries, the query expansion technique hurt the retrieval performance by 18.19% and by 1.54% for the title-only and the long queries, respectively (see Table 3b).

**Table 3b.** Average retrieval precision of the French monolingual queries, the French translation of the equivalent English queries, the translation queries after applying the term-disambiguation technique, and the translation queries after applying the term disambiguation and query expansion techniques

| Query | Title | Long |
|---|---|---|
| Monolingual | 0.2260 | 0.2682 |
| Trans (EF) | 0.0750 (-66.80%) | 0.0283 (-89.44%) |
| Trans (EF) + Dis | 0.1097 (-51.48%) | 0.1012 (-62.27%) |
| Trans (EF) + Dis + QE | 0.2682 (-69.67%) | 0.0971 (-63.81%) |

## 4.3    Italian Result

The English queries that were translated into Italian (EI) consist of 362 terms for the title-only queries and 3,259 terms for the long queries. Ideally, as for the equivalent Italian monolingual queries, the resulting translation queries must contain 173 terms and 2,172 terms for the title-only and the long queries, respectively.

The EI title-only queries perform 57.91% above the equivalent monolingual Italian queries. Applying the term disambiguation technique improved the retrieval performance by 6.1%. The EI long queries drop the performance by 36.47%, as compared to the equivalent monolingual Italian queries. The term disambiguation technique improved the retrieval performance by 18.53%. As with the previous languages, the query expansion technique hurt the retrieval performance by 64.14% and by 9.78% for the title-only and the long queries, respectively (see Table 3c).

**Table 3c.** Average retrieval precision of the Italian monolingual queries, the Italian translation of the equivalent English queries, the translation queries after applying the term-disambiguation technique, and the translation queries after applying the term disambiguation and query expansion techniques

| Query | Title | Long |
|---|---|---|
| Monolingual | 0.0347 | 0.1279 |
| Trans (EI) | 0.0548 (+57.91%) | 0.0813 (-36.47%) |
| Trans (EI) + Dis | 0.0569 (+64.01%) | 0.1050 (-17.94%) |
| Trans (EI) + Dis + QE | 0.0204 (-41.21%) | 0.0925 (-27.72%) |

Overall, applying the term disambiguation technique improved the retrieval performance of the translation queries in the three languages by 6%–24%. However, the query expansion technique did not help improve the retrieval performance, and instead, made the retrieval performance worse by 1%-64% by adding terms related translation queries that are incorrect in the first place, thus, adding terms that are not relevant to the original queries. The major cause of the poor translations is the fact that there were many terms that could not be found in the bilingual dictionaries. We hope that that the next time we will be able to use better machine-readable dictionaries.

From the result for each language, we learned that the queries for each language translation performed 27%-69% below the equivalent monolingual queries. Our rank-list merging algorithm assumes that the most relevant document from the monolingual retrieval in English is as relevant as that in any of the cross-lingual retrieval in the other languages. Since this assumption was not true in most of the cases, the resulting merged rank lists contain relatively large number of irrelevant documents, as compared to the number of relevant ones. We plan to use a better rank-list merging algorithm in the future.

# 5    Summary

The field of cross-language information retrieval (CLIR) research still poses many challenges to be solved by its researches. Work has been done to demonstrate that the sense ambiguity and phrase translation problems in the translation process can be solved using statistical or linguistic approaches. Moreover, to deal with different languages, one needs to take into consideration word-formation patterns specific to each language, such as compound word forms in German. Another main research issue is the merging of retrieval results from multilingual document collections. Finally, for a dictionary-based CLIR query translation to be effective, it requires a comprehensive and good quality dictionary.

# 6    References

1.  Adriani, Mirna and Croft, W. Bruce. *The Effectiveness of a Dictionary-Based Technique for Indonesian-English Cross-Language Text Retrieval*. CIIR Technical Report IR-170, University of Massachusetts, Amherst (1997)
2.  Adriani, M. and C.J. van Rijsbergen. Term Similarity Based Query Expansion for Cross Language Information Retrieval. In *Proceedings of Research and Advanced Technology for Digital Libraries*, Third European Conference (ECDL'99). Springer Verlag, Paris, September (1999) 311-322
3.  Adriani, Mirna. Using Statistical Term Similarity for Sense Disambiguation in Cross-Language Information Retrieval. *Information Retrieval* 2(1). Kluwer, February (2000) 67-78
4.  Ballesteros, L., and Croft, W. Bruce. Resolving Ambiguity for Cross-language Retrieval. In *Proceedings of the 21$^{st}$ International ACM SIGIR Conference on Research and Development in Information Retrieval* (1998) 64-71
5.  Braschler, M., Kan, M., Schauble, P. and Klavans, J.L. The Eurospider Retrieval System and the TREC-8 Cross Language Track. In *NIST Special Publication: The 8$^{th}$ Text Retrieval Conference (TREC-8)*. NIST, Gaithersburg, MD (1999)
6.  Davis, Mark W. and Ogden, William C. Free Resources and Advanced Alignment for Cross-Language Text Retrieval. In *NIST Special Publication: The 6$^{th}$ Text Retrieval Conference (TREC-6)*, D.K. Harman, ed. NIST, Gaithersburg, MD (1997)
7.  Franz, M., McCarley, J.S., and Ward, R.T. Ad hoc, Cross-language and Spoken Document Information Retrieval at IBM. In *NIST Special Publication: The 8$^{th}$ Text Retrieval Conference (TREC-8)*. NIST, Gaithersburg, MD (1999)
8.  Hull, D. A., and Grefenstette, G. Querying Across Languages: A dictionary-based approach to Multilingual Information Retrieval. In *Proceedings of the 19$^{th}$ Annual International ACM SIGIR Conference on Research and Development in Information Retrieval* (1996) 49-57
9.  Nie, J.Y. CLIR using Probabilistic Translation Model based on Web Documents. In *NIST Special Publication: The 8$^{th}$ Text Retrieval Conference (TREC-8)*. NIST, Gaithersburg, MD (1999)
10. Oard, D.W., Wang, J., Llin, D., and Soboroff, I. TREC-8 Experiments at Maryland: CLIR, QA and Routing. In *NIST Special Publication: The 8$^{th}$ Text Retrieval Conference (TREC-8)*. NIST, Gaithersburg, MD (1999)
11. Pirkola, A. The Effects of Query Structure and Dictionary setups in Dictionary-Based Cross-language Information Retrieval. In *Proceedings of the 21$^{st}$ International ACM SIGIR Conference on Research and Development in Information Retrieval* (1998) 55-63
12. van Rijsbergen, C. J. *Information Retrieval*. 2nd edn. Butterworths, London (1979)
13. Salton, Gerard, and McGill, Michael J. *Introduction to Modern Information Retrieval*. , McGraw-Hill, New York (1983)

# The Use of NLP Techniques in CLIR

Bärbel Ripplinger

IAI
Martin-Luther-Str. 14
66111 Saarbrücken, Germany
babs@iai.uni-sb.de

**Abstract.** The application of NLP techniques to improve the results of
information retrieval is still considered as a controversial issue, whereas
in cross-language information retrieval (CLIR) linguistic processing is already well established. In this paper, the CLIR component - MPRO-IR -
which is presented has been developed as the core module of a multilingual information system in a legal domain. This component uses not
only the le ical base form for inde ing but also derivational information
and, for German, information about the decomposition of compounds.
This information is provided by a sophisticated morpho-syntactic analyser and is e ploited not only for query translation but also for query
e pansion as well as the search and the document ranking. The objective
of the CLEF evaluation was to assess this linguistic based retrieval approach in an unrestricted domain. The focus of the investigation was on
how derivation and decomposition can contribute to improve the recall.

## 1 Introduction

The MPRO-IR system is a CLIR system based on query translation and focuses
rather on a better recall than on a balanced recall and precision. To improve the
recall, the system tries to take advantage of a sophisticated linguistic processing
component whose results are used in the monolingual retrieval modules. Based
on the output of a morpho-syntactic analysis which provides the full range of
morphological information, not only in ection which would correspond to the
power of a stemmer such as the Porter stemmer but also derivational and decomposition of compound nouns is exploited. This information is used for the
indexing, query expansion, search and document ranking. The translation component takes additional advantage of the part-of-speech provided as well as of
the syntactic structure of the source query. Section 2 gives a short overview on
how this information is obtained and exploited in the system.

For CLEF 2000, as a first time evaluation within the TREC framework, we did
one official run mainly to test MPRO-IR in an unrestricted domain. We carried
out the retrieval by querying only the English title section of the topics and using
a retrieval component especially developed for phrase search in a legal domain,
i.e. the whole phrase has to occur in the same sentence. But the main aim
was to investigate whether derivational information and decomposition of nouns

C. Peters (Ed.): CLEF 2000, LNCS 2069, pp. 166–175, 2001.

could contribute to a better recall. As discussed in Section 3, the restrictions of MPRO-IR's phrase search are too strong to obtain a satisfactory performance. They do not even allow a final conclusion as to whether the application of the additional linguistic information improves the recall or not.

## 2    Mpro-IR System Description

The CLIR component MPRO-IR has been developed as the core component of a multilingual web-based information system on European Media Laws  EMIS . The document base is multilingual: there are documents in German, English, and French. For these languages, an interface is available that enables the users to enter their queries in the selected language. The design of MPRO-IR is guided according to the requirements that an information retrieval system in a legal domain has to satisfy: it has to support the lawyers' work which means finding as much information as possible about a certain subject. In terms of IR, the retrieval component should provide the best possible recall. The design of the system also had to take into account that the domain is relatively new and neither a thesaurus nor an approved term list is available, thus queries using an uncontrolled vocabulary are usual. In addition, the type of queries used has some impact on the design: the system has to be capable of processing single word queries such as *advertising*, compound terms as *subliminal advertising*, as well as complex phrases like *actions leading to competition distortions, private broadcasters  obligation to provide in ormation,* ... In the legal domain, such phrases often have to occur within one sentence to be relevant, therefore a special phrase search component has been developed which searches the input query within this restricted space. However, to allow the search of each of the meaning bearing terms within a whole document, a traditional Boolean search facility is also provided to the users.

Independently of the search facility used, the input query as well as the documents undergo a linguistic processing to take advantage of the information provided.

**T e  i g i  i       e  i g**

Stemming is the NLP technique which is frequently used and successfully applied in IR systems. A standard tool is the Porter stemmer  7  which achieves a normalisation by simply chopping off suffixes. Such stemmers have serious deficiencies, for instance *general* is mapped to *gener*, and *distribute* to *distribut*, neither of which are lexical base forms, which thus leads to improper con ations. To overcome some of these problems, advanced stemmers are developed and combined with a lexicon  4  to verify the identified stem. This approach produces far better results. It avoids the type of error shown above but others, such as the mapping of *distributed* to *distribut*, still occur. In this case, the word *distributed* cannot be found in the dictionary. Irregular plural  *media medium*  or declination forms  *went go*  also cause errors. The main drawback of this approach lies thus in the coverage of the lexicon.

For languages with a rich declensional morphology such as French or German, the results of such stemming are rather unsatisfying because considering only in ection or even suffix reduction is not enough cf. 6 , 12 . For instance, the stemming of the German past participle *gegangen* gone to *gang* results in a wrong form the correct one is *gehen* to go . German verbs as well as French verbs such as *aller* to go or *recevoir* to get have numerous forms which makes it almost impossible to stem them by using suffix algorithms. For German, in addition, the compound formation leads often to failures because of the underlying highly productive morphological process cf. 3 .

In MPRO-IR, the MPRO programme package 5 developed at IAI is used for the linguistic processing, and its major features will be described in the following. MPRO has been primarily developed to process the German language but is now available for different languages including Eastern European languages . However, the same level of functionality as the German module is not available for all language modules. MPRO performs a morpho-syntactic analysis consisting of a lemmatisation, a part-of-speech tagging and, for German, a compound analysis as well as, optionally, an additional syntactic and semantic disambiguation evaluating mainly context information. For the reduction of syntactic ambiguities, there is also a shallow parsing component available for each language.

The morpho-syntactic analysis is combined with a look-up in a word-form dictionary. In a first step, the word-forms are looked up in a special tagging dictionary, for which an entry looks as follows:

```
string Word-form,c w,sc CAT,lu Citation-form,...
```

where CAT is the category. Nouns, verbs, adjectives, and derived adverbs are looked up in a morpheme lexicon. This morphological dictionary contains allomorphs but also some irregular word-forms which cannot be identified in another way as well as variety of toponyms and other names. Each entry shows how the associated stems behave morphologically, as shown in the examples below:

```
string corrupt,c a,n  ness quality
string corrupt,c v,n  ion massnahme ,a  ible able ,
 t  c v,double no,end s,funct no
```

To reduce overgeneration we can also prohibit prefixes or certain nonsensical compounds.

For each word-form, the morphological analyser produces at least one description which is represented as an attribute-value pair. In the following, the analyses of the English noun *corruption*, the verb *corrupt*, and adjective *corrupting* are given only the features of interest are shown :

```
string corruption,lu corruption,ds corrupt ion,ts corruption,
 ls corrupt,t corruption,c noun,s massnahme,...
```

```
string corrupt,lu corrupt,ds corrupt,ts corrupt,ls corrupt,
 t corrupt,c ad ,...
```

```
string corrupt,lu corrupt,ds corrupt,ts corrupt,ls corrupt,
t corrupt,c verb,...

string corrupting,lu corrupting,ds corrupt ing,ts corrupting,
ls corrupt,t corrupting,c noun,s vn,...
ori corrupting,lu corrupting,ds corrupt ing,ts corrupting,
ls corrupt,t corrupting,c ad ,...
string corrupting,lu corrupt,ds corrupt,ts corrupt,ls corrupt,
t corrupt,c verb,...
```

The feature *ds* contains the morphological derivation, and *ls* the respective normalised form. The features *s* and *ss* for compounds contain semantic information. In the example above, all three words have the same derivation. For German
words, a compound analysis is performed additionally cf. example below , and
the result is given in the feature *ts* and its normalised form[1] in feature *t*. These
features are also assigned for English and French analyses but correspond always
to the *lu* feature.

Due to a special treatment some defective noun constructions in German
- such as these occurring in coordinations like *In ormations- und Kommunika-
tionsdienst* Information and Communications services - are recognised. MPRO
assigns the missing head information by using a lookahead algorithm:

```
{string  nformations-, lu  in ormationsdienst ts  in ormations  dienst
   t  in ormation  dienst ds  in ormieren ation  dienst
   ls  in ormieren  dienst,c noun,...}
{string und,lu und,c w,...}
{string Kommunikationsdienst,lu kommunikationsdienst,
   ts kommunikations dienst,t kommunikation dienst,c noun,...}
```

Although MPRO is very complete, a strategy for handling unknown words is
provided. Three cases can be differentiated:

- The word-form can not be analysed at all:
  MPRO marks this word with the feature st te  n no n and classifies the
  word as 'noun', for instance
  ```
  string sett or    sett or  s sett or st te  n no n c no n s n
  ```

- The word-form can partly be analysed:
  MPRO tries in each case to assign the most appropriate information. For
  instance: If a string consists only of numbers such as       the word get as
  category *cardinal number  c  z* , and MPRO provides an analysis whereas
  the value of the lexical unit is identical with the string:
  ```
  string        s        s           1  1  4 s  e r
  ```

- The word form is analysed but not found in the lexicon:
  Strings which consist only of capital letters such as CNN are marked as

---

[1] Hyphens and German fuge elements are removed.

acronyms, and have as the part-of-speech c  noun:
string                      s      s                    a

The analyser recognises lexicalised multiword units such as *look up,*  nited *States,* German prefix verbs, for isntance *mitteilen,* fixed expressions such as *in Bezug au , de  acto,* abbreviations like *etc., i.e.* as well as proper names such as *Bill, Berlin.*

After this analysis, for German the output can be further disambiguated by evaluating context information, i.e. if the first letter of the word-form is capitalised, and the word is not the first in a sentence, it must be a noun. In a final step, a shallow parsing can be applied to reduce other syntactical ambiguities such as verb  noun readings. This parsing process can also be performed for the English and French output of the morphological analysis to get an almost unambiguous representation. MPRO does not reduce ambiguity where the correctness of the decision is doubtful.

The remainder of this section describes how the results of the morpho-syntactic analysis are applied for various stages of the IR process.

### T e  e ie al

For indexing, query expansion, and the search together with a document ranking, the information provided by the features *lu, ls* as well as *t*  currently for German only  is exploited.

Based on the analyses of the documents, several indices are built: one using the information about the lexical unit  i.e. the *normalised  orm* , one using the derivational information, and for German a third index is constructed with the decomposition information. Though English and French nouns have a t-feature, we have not exploited this kind of information because this information is subject to an ongoing revision of the English and French morpheme lexicon  see above . With each key, the document identification number, the sentence number  *snr* , the word number  WNR , as well as the word-form  the form of the word as occuring in the text  are stored. Function words  entries with c  w  are discarded from the indexing. This process is done within a preparation phase.

At search time, the queries are processed by the same morpho-syntactic analysis as the documents. For the monolingual search, the function words are removed from the analysis output and, for the meaning bearing words, the values of the lu-, ls- and, for German queries, the t-feature are extracted to construct a set of search patterns. For the input query, *Competitiveness o  European industry* the set of search terms consists of *competitiveness, compete, european, europe, industry.*

For the cross-language retrieval, we decided to translated the queries and to carry out a monolingual search afterwards. This approach seems more appropriate because legal information is highly related to the original wording, and machine translation systems provide only a poor quality  2 . The input to the translation component is the complete morphological analysis of the query. MPRO-IR uses a shallow translation tool which performs a lexical transfer based on huge transfer lexicons  coverage of the English-German lexicon is about 500.000 entries  comprising single words, abbreviations, compound terms but also fixed phrases. For multiword units, the MT-component first looks up whether the dictionary contains a translation for the whole phrase. If no translation exists, the phrase is translated compositionally whereas the translation is guided by the part-of-speech, i.e. for verbs only the translations for verbs are assigned. The translation output undergoes a shallow parsing based on a phrase grammar to get only one possible translation whereas the syntactic representation of the source is taken into account. For German as target language, the syntactic variants of a term are additionally sorted out. For example, there are two entries in the English-German dictionary for *human dignity*, *Menschenwürde* and *Würde des Menschen*. In these cases, the compound is preferred because, due to the query expansion, all occurrences of the syntactic variant *Würde des Menschen* are equally found but the search for a compound is much faster than that for a phrase.

The search itself consists of several look-ups in the different indices  for each content bearing term the following look-ups are made:

1. Looking up the index built over the lexical base forms  lu-index  with the value of the lu-feature
2. For German only: Looking up the index built over the t-feature  t-index  with the value of the t-feature to find compounds with the queried term as element
3. Looking up the index built over the derivations  ls-index  with the value of the ls-feature

For compounds, the different formation in English and French compared to German leads to a different search strategy. Bearing in mind that open compound terms in English and French have almost a fixed word order, we defined a *distance actor* to decide whether the occurrence of two or more words represents an open compound or not. Based on statistical data, the longest distance between each meaning bearing word of a phrase is fixed to  . This allows us to classify occurrences of *advertising in  K s television* as exact hits of *television advertising*. For English as well as for French compounds, the occurrences of each word within a phrase is evaluated against this distance factor using the word number provided by the index, and sorted into the following three lists:

1. The lu-values looked up in the lu-index of each element occur within the determined distance.
2. At least for one element only the derivation occurs within this distance.
3. All other occurrences.

We apply this distance measure also to German to find syntactic variants of compound terms:

1. Looking up the lu-index with the values of the t- and ls-features of the single compound elements. This retrieves documents containing the syntactic variants of the input compound, for instance searching for *Verbraucherschutz* Consumer protection hits *zum Schutz der Verbraucher* as well as *um die Verbraucher zu schützen.*
2. Looking up the lu-index with the value of the t- and ls-features whereas the parts of the compounds occur outside the environment.
3. Looking up the ls-index with the values of the t- and ls-features of the compound parts.
    This produces a list of documents containing *semantically similar* terms. These are terms which point to a common concept in a virtual hierarchy i.e. all elements of the 'transitive closure' of the particular concept denoted by the compound . For instance, the search for *Verbraucherschutz* found hits such as *Schutzbestimmungen bezüglich der Verbraucherdaten* regulation to protect consumer data .

For phrases, the topmost result list consists of documents which contain the elements of the phrase exactly  excluding function words . The next list contains documents in which at least one phrase element occurs only as part of a compound. All further result lists are analogously calculated.

Usually the rank of a retrieved document is computed by the $t$  $id$ . Using a weight based on frequency seems inadequate in this environment of a legal domain in which some terms occur only as parts of bigger compounds, or in different parts-of-speech. Thus, in MPRO-IR, the documents are ranked by the information used to retrieve them, in the order of the lists described above. This ranking mirrors the relevance related to the reliability of the linguistic information used to retrieve a document. A document retrieved by stem information is more relevant to the query then a document retrieved by derivational information. It expresses the degree of precision of the retrieval at that time. The results of the first list have a higher precision than those of the lower lists because the probability that mismatched documents are retrieved increases.

## Mpro-IR in CLEF

We participated for the first time in a CLEF/TREC evaluation to investigate how MPRO-IR developed for a special domain fares with unrestricted documents related to recall and precision.

### e i g     e   e i e
Currently the MPRO-IR system covers only German, English, and French. To perform CLEF's CLIR task which additionally comprises the search in Italian documents, we integrated a small Italian component into MPRO-IR. To provide a sufficient coverage for this module, we analysed the complete Italian topics  titles, description, and narratives , and added unknown words  morphemes  to

our monolingual lexicon. For the translation component, we added only translations for the words occuring in the title sections of the topics. Thus the Italian morpheme lexicon has now 27.800 entries compared, for instance to the English morpheme lexicon with about 48.300 entries. We used English topics and retrieved documents in English, French, German, and Italian  therefore we added missing translations for the terms of the topic titles to the respective transfer dictionaries.

### e  ie al  e      a  e

Due to time and space restrictions we could perform and submit only one run. Therefore we decided to perform a phrase search only over the titles sections of the topics, although we noticed that the type of queries was not always adequate for this kind of search. To build up the indices, texts were normalised, i.e. we discarded all header and other formatting information including some of the title sections which led in some cases to a lower performance due to missing text parts.

The overall result of the CLEF evaluation shows a low retrieval performance of MPRO-IR compared to the other systems. Taking into account that a very restricted retrieval component has been used  all meaning bearing words have to occur in the same sentence, and only one translation is used  the outcome is not too bad. The results show more or less what we expected: For topics which are incomplete sentences such as *French conscientous objector, supermarket ceiling in Nice collapses,* etc. we got none or only a few results  cf. Figure 1 IAI1 .

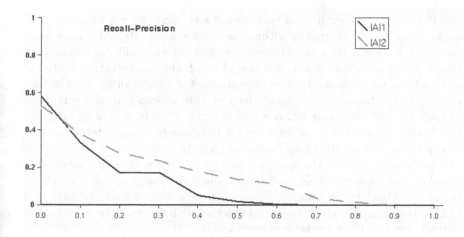

**Fig. 1.** CLEF Results

For topics such as *European Economic Area, World Trade Organisation* etc. the results are better though not satisfactory.

Our main objective was to evaluate the use of derivational and decompositional information to improve the recall. Thus, we could conclude that most of the documents are retrieved by using the information of the lexical base form. Only a few others are retrieved on the basis of derivational information. Decomposition information which is only used for retrieving German documents depends on the type of compounds, and in a few cases also on the type of the single words forming a compound. No relevant occurrences of syntactic variants are found in the corpus. We also got only a few results on the basis of the productive use of decomposition information, i.e. documents containing semantically similar terms. The main reason is certainly the restricted search space, furthermore the German compounds occurring in the queries such as *Kriegsdienstverweigerer, Krebsgenetik Gol skriegssyndrom, Nobelpreis, Alkoholkonsum,...* consist of words which are not frequently used in compound formation within the context of the respective query. Another reason is that only one translation is used ex: *Methane deposit* is translated into German as *Methanlagerstätte* whereas in the documents the synonym *Methanlager* is often used .

To get an impression to what extent the restriction to a sentence as search space is too strong, we performed a second unofficial run. The result IAI2 in the figure above shows an overall improvement of the average precision of 50 , and an almost three times higher recall 425 vs. 1168 relevant documents . We also obtained more hits using decomposition and derivation information. There are also some relevant documents found on basis of semantically similar terms.

## Conclusion

The results of the CLEF evaluation correspond with those we got from the evaluation of the retrieval algorithm within the EMIS system 10 . Also here most hits could be retrieved by using precise lexical base forms and derivational information. Compositional information was also valuable for detecting syntactic variants of German compounds. The improvement of the recall by so-called semantically similar terms is very poor. Because this approach is also very time consuming, we will defer this in favour of a better morpho-syntactic analysis. This will then provide the basis for a better indexing by using a term recognition component, and a better translation component.

For the query expansion on the monolingual side, we currently experiment with a method to add synonyms which will be automatically computed by translating the translations back to the source language. The search itself could be improved by taking advantage of the part-of-speech together with the semantic information already provided by the morpho-syntactic analyser 9 .

As the results here show, the phrase search as implemented in MPRO-IR is useful in retrieval systems developed for a special type of domain where the search of complex phrases is necessary, such as the legal domain. In retrieval systems dealing with unrestricted texts, a Boolean search achieves much better recall. As the unoffical run shows, with a Boolean search we could certainly get a better insight into the usefulness of derivational and compositional information in the retrieval process due to the higher recall. Additionally, there is some potential to improve the precision which we have neglected so far in favor of a high recall by exploiting number and case agreement, for instance.

The approach we pursue in MPRO-IR using a sophisticated morpho-syntactic analysis has shown that the recall can be improved by more precise identification of the lexical base units and the almost unambiguous representation of the documents and the queries. The possible impact of derivational and decompositional information has to be further evaluated. Results from the CLEF experiment have no significance so far. However, part-of-speech, currently exploited only for translation purpose together with semantic information, can be expected to contribute to a better retrieval performance, which still has to be shown.

### le ge e

I should like to thank Paul Schmidt for his useful remarks.

# References

1. Brill, E. A simple rule-based part-of-speech tagger. In  r cee ings    the    hir  n erence  n  pplie    atural  anguage  r cessing Trento, Italy, 1992.
2. Kay, Martin. Multilinguality. In Varile, G. and A. Zampolli (Eds). **Survey o t e State o t e Art in  uman Language Tec nology**, Elsnet Publication 1995.
3. Kraaij, W., R. Pohlmann. UPLIFT - Using Linguistic Knowledge in Information Retrieval, Technial Report, University of Utrecht.
4. Krovetz, R. Viewing Morphology as an Inference Process. In *SIGI*        r cee ings, Pittsburg, 1993.
5. Maas, D. Multilinguale Te tverarbeitung mit MPRO. In Lobin, G. et al. (Eds). **Europaisc e  ommuni ations yberneti   eute und morgen**, KoPäd, München, 1999. http //www.iai.uni-sb.de/global/memos.html
6. Popovic, M,, and P. Willet. The e ectiveness of stemming for natural-language access to Slovene te tual data. In   urnal    the   merican S ciet   r In rmati n Science, 43(5) 384-390, 1992.
7. Porter, E. An algorithm for suffi stripping. In  r gramm, 14, 1980.
8. Ripplinger, B. EMIS A Multilingual Information System. In Farwell, D., L. Gerber, E. Hovy (Eds).   **ac ine Translation and t e n ormation Soup**, Third Conference of the AMTA, Springer, 1998.
9. Ripplinger, B. MPRO-IR   A Cross-language Information Retrieval Component Enhanced by Linguistic Knowledge. In  r cee ings    the RIAO 2000, Paris.
10. Ripplinger, B. Linguistic Knowledge in a Multilingual Information System, IAI Memo, 2000.
11. Strzalkowski, Tomek, F. Ling, J. Wang, J. Perez-Carballo. Evaluating Natural Language Processing Techniques in Information Retrieval. In Strzalkowski, Tomek (Ed). **Natural Language  n ormation Retrieval**. Kluwer, 1999.
12. Tzoukermann, E., J. L. Klavans and Ch. Jacquemin. E ective use of Natural language Processing Techniques for Automatic Con ation of Multi-Word Terms The Role of Derivational Morphology, Part of Speech Tagging, and Shallow Parsing. In  r ceee ings    the 20   Internati nal   n erence  n  esearch an  De el pement in In rmati n  etrie al (SIGIR 97), Philadelphia, 1997.

# CLEF Experiments at Maryland:
# Statistical Stemming and Backoff Translation

Douglas W. Oard[1], Gina-Anne Levow[2], and Clara I. Cabezas[3]

[1] College of Information Studies & Institute for Advanced Computer Studies
University of Maryland, College Park, MD 20742 USA,
oard@glue.umd.edu,
http://www.glue.umd.edu/~oard/
[2] Institute for Advanced Computer Studies
University of Maryland, College Park, MD 20742 USA,
gina@umiacs.umd.edu,
http://umiacs.umd.edu/~gina/
[3] Department of Linguistics & Institute for Advanced Computer Studies
University of Maryland, College Park, MD 20742 USA,
clarac@umiacs.umd.edu

**Abstract.** The University of Maryland participated in the CLEF 2000 multilingual task, submitting three official runs that e plored the impact of applying language-independent stemming techniques to dictionary-based cross-language information retrieval. The paper begins by describing a cross-language information retrieval architecture based on balanced document translation. A four-stage backo strategy for improving the coverage of dictionary-based translation techniques is then introduced, and an implementation based on automatically trained statistical stemming is presented. Results indicate that competitive performance can be achieved using four-stage backo translation in conjunction with freely available bilingual dictionaries, but that the the usefulness of the statistical stemming algorithms that were tried varies considerably across the three languages to which they were applied.

## 1  Introduction

One important goal of our research is to develop cross-language information retrieval  CLIR  techniques that can be applied to new language pairs with minimal language-specific tuning. So-called  dictionary-based  techniques offer promise in this regard because bilingual dictionaries have proven to be a useful basis for CLIR  6  and because simple bilingual dictionaries are becoming widely available on the Internet. Although bilingual dictionaries sometimes include useful information such as part-of-speech, morphology and translation preference, it is far more common to find a simple list of translation equivalent term pairs  what we refer to as a  bilingual term list.  The objective of our participation in the Cross-Language Evaluation Forum  CLEF  was to explore techniques for dictionary-based CLIR using bilingual term lists between English and other European languages. We applied techniques that we have used before  balanced

C. Peters (Ed.): CLEF 2000, LNCS 2069, pp. 176–1 7, 2001.
© Springer-Verlag Berlin Heidelberg 2001

document translation, described below , and chose to focus our contrastive runs on improving translation coverage using morphological analysis and an unsupervised morphological analysis approach that we refer to as statistical stemming. In the next section we describe our balanced document translation architecture, explain how morphological analysis can be used to improve translation coverage without additional language-specific resources, and introduce two statistical stemming algorithms. The following section presents our CLEF results, which demonstrate that the additional coverage achieved by four-stage backoff translation can have a substantial beneficial effect on retrieval effectiveness as measured by mean average precision, but that our present statistical stemming algorithms perform well only in French. In the final section we draw some conclusions regarding the broader utility of our techniques and suggest some additional research directions.

## 2   Experiment Design

We chose to participate in the multilingual task of CLEF 2000 because the structure of the task English queries, documents in other languages was well matched to a CLIR architecture based on document translation that we have been developing. Document translation is an attractive approach in interactive applications if all queries are in a single language because the pre-translated documents that are retrieved can immediately be examined by the user. Although storage overhead is doubled if the documents are also stored in their original language , that may be of little consequence in an era of rapidly falling disk prices. The principal challenge in a document translation architecture is to balance the translation speed and translation accuracy. In our initial experiments with document translation, we found that a commercial machine translation system required about 10 machine-months to translate approximately 250,000 documents resource requirements that would clearly be impractical in many applications 5 . With simpler techniques, such as looking up each word in a bilingual term list, we can translate a similar number of documents in only three machine-hours a period of time comparable to that required to build an inverted index. In our CLEF experiments we have thus chosen to focus on improving the retrieval effectiveness of dictionary-based CLIR without introducing a significant adverse effect on translation efficiency.

Figure 1 illustrates our overall CLIR system design. Each non-English collection was processed separately using the appropriate bilingual term list. We grouped the articles from *Der Spiegel* and *Frank urter Rundschau* into a single German collection and formed a French collection from the *Le Monde* articles and an Italian collection from the *La Stampa* articles. The documents were normalized by mapping all characters to lower case 7-bit ASCII through removal of accents. Term-by-term translation was then performed, applying a four-stage backoff statistical stemming approach to enhance translation coverage. For translation, we tokenized source-language terms at white space or terminal punctuation which had the effect of ignoring all source-language multiword expressions in our bilingual term lists . When no translation was known for a clitic contraction, automatic expansion was performed  e.g. *l heure* → *la heure*  and the resulting words were translated separately.[1] Other words with no known translation were retained unchanged, which is often appropriate for proper names. We produced exactly two English terms for each source-language term. For terms with no known translation, the untranslated term was generated twice. For terms with one known translation, that translation was generated twice. Terms with two or more known translations resulted in generation of each of the  best  two translations once. In prior experiments we have found that this strategy, known as  balanced translation,  outperforms the still fairly common  unbalanced  technique of including all known translations because it avoids overweighting terms that have many translations  which are often quite common, and hence less useful as search terms   4 .

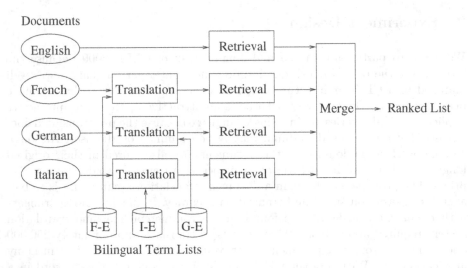

**Fig. 1.** Production of a merged multilingual ranked list using document translation.

Each of the four resulting English collections  the fourth consisting of *Los Angeles Times* articles, which did not require translation  was then indexed using Inquery  version 3.1p1 , with Inquery's kstem stemmer and default English stopword list selected. Queries were produced by enclosing each word in the title, description, and narrative fields  except for stop-structure in Inquery's  sum operator. In our official runs, two types of stop-structure were removed by hand:  find documents  was removed at the beginning of any description field in which it appeared, and  relevant documents report  was removed at the beginning of

---

[1] Clitic contractions are not common in German, so we did not run the splitting process in that case.

any narrative field in which it appeared. Because this stop structure was removed manually after examining the queries, our runs are officially classified as being in the manual category. We generated separate ranked lists for each collection and then used the weighted round-robin merging technique that we had developed for the TREC CLIR track to construct a single ranked list of the top 1000 documents retrieved for each query 7 . We expected our monolingual English system to outperform our French and German systems, and we expected our Italian system to be adversely affected by the small size of the bilingual term list for that language pair. We thus chose a 10:5:5:3 ratio as the relative weights for each language.

We used the same bilingual term lists for CLEF 2000 that we had employed in the TREC-8 CLIR track 7 . Table 1 shows the source and summary statistics for each dictionary. Source language terms in the bilingual term lists were normalized in a manner similar to that used for the documents, although clitic contractions were not split because they were not common in the bilingual term lists. Balanced document translation becomes unwieldy beyond two translations, so the number of translations for any term was limited to the two that most commonly occurred in written English. All single word translations were ordered by decreasing unigram frequency in the Brown corpus which contains many genres of written English , followed by all multi-word translations in no particular order , and finally by any single word entries that did not appear at all in the Brown corpus. Translations beyond the second for any English term were then deleted this had the effect of minimizing the effect of infrequent words in non-standard usages or misspellings that might appear in the bilingual term list.

| ‖Pair‖ | Source | English Terms | non-English Terms | Avg Translations‖ |
|--------|--------|---------------|-------------------|-------------------|
| ‖E-G‖ | http //www.quickdic.de | 99,357 | 131,273 | 1.7 ‖ |
| ‖E-F‖ | http //www.freedict.com | 20,100 | 35,008 | 1.3 ‖ |
| ‖E-I‖ | http //www.freedict.com | 13,400 | 17,313 | 1.3 ‖ |

**Table 1.** Sources and summary statistics for bilingual dictionaries.

## 2.1 F    age a    T a la i

The coverage problem in CLIR arises when the object being translated in this case, a document , contains a term that is not known to the translation resource in this case, the bilingual term list . Bilingual term lists found on the web often contain an eclectic mix of root forms and their morphological variants, and our experience with the TREC-8 CLIR track suggested that morphological analysis of terms contained in documents and bilingual term lists could discover plausible translations when no exact match is found. We thus developed a four-stage backoff strategy that was designed to maximize coverage while limiting the introduction of spurious translations:

1. Match the      a e      of a document term to      a e      of source language terms in the bilingual term list.
2. Match the      l gi al      of a document term to      a e      of source language terms in the bilingual term list.
3. Match the      a e      of a document term to      l gi al      of source language terms in the bilingual term list.
4. Match the      l gi al      of a document term to      l gi al      of source language terms in the bilingual term list.

The process terminates as soon as a match is found at any stage, and the known translations for that match are generated. Although this process may result in generation of an inappropriate morphological variant for a correct English translation, the use of English stemming in Inquery should minimize the effect of that factor on retrieval effectiveness.

## 2.2   a i i al   e   i g

The four-stage backoff strategy described above poses two key challenges. First, it would require that an efficient morphological analysis system be available for every document language that must be processed. And second, the morphological analysis systems would need to produce accurate results on words presented out of context, as they are in the bilingual term list. This is a tall order, so we elected to explore a simplification of this idea in which morphological analysis was replaced by stemming. Stemmers are freely available for French and German,[2] and stemming has proven to be about as effective as more sophisticated morphology in information retrieval applications where  as is the case in our application  matching is the principal objective  3 . In TREC-3, Buckley, et al. demonstrated that a simple stemmer could be easily constructed for Spanish without knowledge of the language by examining lexicographically similar words to discover common suffixes  1 . We decided to try to push that idea further, automating the process so that it could be applied to new languages without additional effort. We call this approach  statistical stemming,  since the stemmer is learned from the statistics of a text collection, in our case the collection that was ultimately to be searched.

Statistical stemming is a special case of unsupervised acquisition of morphology, a specialized topic in computational linguistics. Of this work, the closest in spirit to our objectives that we know of is a program known as Linguistica  2 . Linguistica examines each token in a collection, observing the frequency

---

[2] French and German stemmers are available as part of the PRISE information retrieval system, which is freely available from the U.S. National Institute of Standards and Technology. Stemmers for a broader collection of languages, including Italian, are also available from the Muscat project at http //open.muscat.com/developer/inde .html

of stems and suffixes that would result from every possible breakpoint. An optimal breakpoint for each token is then selected by applying as a constraint that every instance of a token must have the same breakpoint and then choosing breakpoints for each unique token that minimize the number of bits needed to encode the collection. This  minimum description length  criterion captures the intuition that breakpoints should be chosen in such a way that each token is partitioned into a relatively common stem and a relatively common suffix. Linguistica is freely available,[3] but the implementation we used could process only about 200,000 words on a 128 MB Windows NT machine. This is certainly large enough to ensure that breakpoints will be discovered for most common words, but breakpoints might not be discovered for less common terms  quite possibly the terms that would prove most useful in a search. We therefore augmented Linguistica with a simple rule induction technique to handle words that were outside Linguistica's training set.

We implemented rule induction as follows. We first counted the frequency of every one, two, three and four-character suffix that would result in a stem of three or more characters for the first 500,000 words of the collection. Each instance of every word was used to compute the suffix frequencies. These statistics alone would overstate the frequency of partial suffixes  for example, -ng  is a common ending in English, but in almost every case it is part of  -ing . We thus subtracted the frequency of the most common subsuming suffix of the next longer length from each suffix.[4] The adjusted frequencies were then used to sort all two, three and four-character suffixes in decreasing order of frequency. We observed that the count vs. rank plot for an English training case was convex, so we selected the rank at which the second derivative of the count vs. rank plot was maximized as the limit for how many suffixes to generate for each length. In tuning experiments with English, this approach did not work well for single-character suffixes because the distribution of character frequency  regardless of location  is highly skewed. We thus sorted single characters by the ratio between their word-final likelihood and their unconditioned likelihood, and again used the maximum of the second derivative as a stopping point.[5] For each word, the first matching suffix  if any, from the top of the list  was then removed to produce the stemmed form.

The heuristics we chose were motivated by our intuition of what constituted a likely suffix, but the details were settled only after a good deal of tweaking with a training collection. Of note, the training collection contained only English documents and the tweaking was done by the first author, who has no useful knowledge of French, German or Italian. Table 5 shows the suffix removal rules for those languages that were automatically produced with no further tuning. Many of the postulated suffixes in that table accord well with our intuition, as in

---

[3] Linguistica is available at
   http //humanities.uchicago.edu/faculty/goldsmith/inde .html
[4] We did not adjust the frequencies of four-character suffi es since we did not count the five-character suffi es.
[5] If a more precise specification of the process is desired, the source code for the rule induction software is available from the first author.

the case the French adverbial suffix -*ment* or third-person plural in ectional suffix -*ent*. However, some others suggest insufficient generalization. Consider the suggested German suffixes: -*ngen,-nden,-sen,-nen,-gen,-den*, and -*ten*. The more appropriate suffix would be -*en* however, the preference for longer subsuming strings selects the less general suffixes. A large number of single character suffixes are suggested for Italian, including letters such as -*k* and -*w* which do not typically appear in word-final position in this language. This somewhat counterintuitive set suggests that further optimization of threshold setting may be needed.

| French | German | Italian |
|--------|--------|---------|
| ment | chen | ione |
| tion | ngen | ente |
| ique | nden | ioni |
| ions | sche | ento |
| ent | rung | enti |
| res | lich | ato |
| tes | sten | are |
| es | ten | to |
| re | ung | ta |
|  | den | re |
| s | gen | ti |
|  | nen | no |
|  | ter | la |
|  | sen | y |
|  | en | o |
|  | er | e |
|  | te | a |
|  | y | k |
|  | t | i |
|  |  | w |

**Table 2.** Candidate stems, in order of removal.

Three official runs were submitted. In our baseline run   unstemmed  , we used no pre-translation stemming  i.e., step one alone . In our Linguistica run   backoff4Ling  , we implemented the complete four-stage backoff strategy using Linguistica for terms with known breakpoints, and added a fifth stage that replicated stage four using the rule induction stemmer in place of Linguistica that would be invoked if none of the first four stages found a translation. The rule induction process was considerably faster than Linguistica  less than 5 minutes, compared with 30-40 minutes for Linguistica  so we also submitted a third run in which which we implemented four-stage backoff with rule induction alone. Table 5 summarizes these conditions.

| Stage | unstemmed | | backo 4Ling | | backo 4 | |
|---|---|---|---|---|---|---|
| | Document | Term List | Document | Term List | Document | Term List |
| 1 | None | None | None | None | None | None |
| 2 | | | Linguistica | None | Rule Induction | None |
| 3 | | | None | Linguistica | None | Rule Induction |
| 4 | | | Linguistica | Linguistica | Rule Induction | Rule Induction |
| 5 | | | Rule Induction | Rule Induction | | |

**Table 3.** Backoff translation steps for the three official runs.

## Results

Our backoff4 run was judged, and all three runs were scored officially. The top line in Table 4 summarizes the results. Overall, a four-stage backoff document translation strategy using statistical stemming achieved an improvement in retrieval effectiveness over the unstemmed approach that was found to be statistically significant by a paired two-tailed -test $p$ 0.05 in both cases . Figure 2 illustrates the advantage of backoff translation on a topic-by-topic basis.

| | Unstemmed | Backo 4 | Backo 4Ling |
|---|---|---|---|
| Multilingual | 0.1798 | 0.1952 | 0.1938 |
| English | 0.4348 | 0.4348 | 0.4348 |
| French | 0.1877 | 0.2823 | 0.2649 |
| German | 0.2421 | 0.2421 | 0.2425 |
| Italian | 0.2127 | 0.2045 | 0.2022 |

**Table 4.** Multilingual and language-specific mean uninterpolated average precision, averaged over 40 topics.

Surprisingly, our simple  and quite *ad hoc*  rule induction technique produced results that were statistically indistinguishable from those obtained using the more sophisticated Linguistica system. As Figure 3 shows, Linguistica does better on some topics, but worse on others.

As Figure 4 shows, on balance backoff translation with statistical stemming performed somewhat better than the the the median of the submitted CLEF multilingual runs in the automatic category. Since the effect of our limited manual stop-structure removal was likely quite small, we interpret these results as indicating that we have achieved a credible degree of retrieval effectiveness using only freely available linguistic resources.

Although we can conclude from these results that four-stage backoff resulted in improved retrieval effectiveness and that statistical stemming appears to be a viable substitute for more sophisticated morphological analysis in this application, the multilingual task design can easily mask single-language effects. We

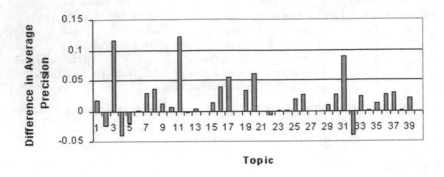

**Fig. 2.** Improvement  above axis  of Backoff4 over Unstemmed.

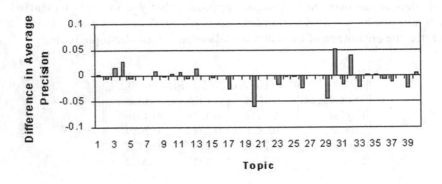

**Fig. 3.** Improvement  above axis  of Backoff4 over Backoff4Ling.

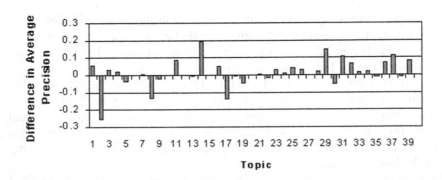

**Fig. 4.** Comparison of Backoff4  better above axis  with median CLEF results.

therefore performed a *post hoc* language-specific analysis by segregating the selected documents and the relevance judgments by language and then scoring
each ranked list against the appropriate relevance judgments. The ranked lists
that we scored thus contained 130 for Italian or 217 for French and German
documents from each language. The resulting mean uninterpolated average precision values are shown in the lower portion of Table 4. For French, we found
that that both implementations of backoff translation achieved a 55 relative
improvement over the unstemmed case, and we found that result to be statistically significant by a paired two-tailed -test at $p$ 0.05. As Figure 5 illustrates,
the magnitude of the improvement varies somewhat across topics, although some
of the observed variation may be due to differences in the number of relevant
topics for each document.

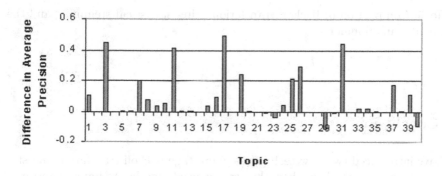

**Fig. 5.** Improvement above axis of backoff translation over unstemmed translation for French documents.

As Table 4 shows, no similar beneficial effect was observed from backoff
translation in German or Italian. Many CLEF participants observed that it was
important to split German compounds, something that we did not do. Further
analysis of the German results may thus not be productive until we have given
some thought to how backoff translation and statistical stemming might be integrated with automatic compound splitting. Our disappointing results in Italian
might be explained by two possible causes. One possibility is that our statistical
stemming techniques are not well suited to some characteristic of Italian. The
alternative hypothesis is that our Italian-English bilingual term list the smallest
of the three that we used may simply be too small.

To explore this issue further, we conducted an additional set of *post hoc*
experiments in which we substituted a freely available manually constructed
rule-based Italian stemmer from the Muscat project[6] for the Italian rule induc-

---

[6] http //open.muscat.com/developer/inde .html

tion statistical stemmer. We call the new runs Backoff4Muscat. As Table 5 shows, Backoff4Muscat outperforms Backoff4, although the improvement over Backoff4 is not statistically significant in either the multilingual of the Italian-specific case. The improvement of Backoff4Muscat over Unstemmed was found to be significant at $p$ 0.05 by a two-tailed paired -test in the multilingual case, but not for Italian alone. We thus conclude that four-stage backoff translation is helpful even with relatively small bilingual term lists, and that the poor performance of Backoff4 for Italian results from a deficiency in the statistical stemmers that we used.

| | Unstemmed | Backo 4 | Backo 4Muscat |
|---|---|---|---|
| Multilingual | 0.1798 | 0.1952 | 0.1994 |
| Italian | 0.2127 | 0.2045 | 0.2338 |

**Table 5.** Comparison of backoff translation using statistical stemming and the Muscat Italian stemmer.

## Conclusion

We have introduced two new techniques, four-stage backoff translation and statistical stemming, and shown how they can be used together to improve retrieval effectiveness in a document translation architecture. Four-stage backoff translation appears to help when using impoverished lexicons that contain a few tens of thousands of terms. Our initial experiments with statistical stemming produced promising results in French, but it is clear from our German and Italian results that more work is required before similar techniques can be reliably applied to a broader range of languages.

Our experiments suggest a number of promising directions for future work. A new version of Linguistica is now available, and trying that is an obvious first step. A detailed analysis of the threshold selection in Italian for our rule induction statistical stemmer is also clearly called for a more appropriate threshold selection technique might produce far better results with little effort. Our original threshold selection strategy was chosen after inspection of English training data, but an alternative would be to learn a set of language-specific thresholds using test collections from the Text Retrieval Conference's Cross-Language Information Retrieval track. Extending that line of reasoning, the correct answer might not be a single set of thresholds but rather an iterative technique that takes advantage of our ranking of possible stems. We might, for example, first stem using a conservative set of thresholds, and then restem more aggressively if no match is found. Finally, it might be productive to explore the middle ground between our simple rule induction stemmer and the full Linguistica system in order to learn which techniques are particularly helpful in this application. Linguistica provides for fine-grained control over its operation, and exploring a range of possible parameter settings would be a first step in this direction.

When coupled with other language-independent techniques such as blind relevance feedback for query expansion and for post-translation document expansion 4 , the techniques that we have explored in this work can potentially provide developers with a robust toolkit with which to design effective dictionary-based CLIR systems using only a bilingual term list and some modest query-language resources specifically, a comparable collection from which to obtain term statistics . This first CLEF evaluation has proven to be a suitable venue for exploring these questions, and we look forward to continued participation in future years.

### le g e

The authors wish to thank Patrick Schone, Philip Resnik and David Yarowsky for helpful discussions of the unsupervised morphology acquisition, John Goldsmith for making Linguistica available, and Jianqiang Wang for his help with Inquery and the bilingual term lists. This work was work was supported in part by DARPA contract N6600197C8540 and DARPA cooperative agreement N660010028910.

# References

1. Buckley, C., Salton, G., Allan, J., Singhal,A.   Automatic query e pansion using SMART TREC 3. In D. K. Harman, editor,    *er ie      the   hir    e t  Etrie al n erence     E*     (1994) 69 80
2. Goldsmith, J.  Unsupervised learning of the morphology of a natural language. http //humanities.uchicago.edu/faculty/goldsmith/ (2000)
3. Hull, D. A.  Stemming algorithms - A case study for detailed evaluation. Journal of the American Society for Information Science, **47**(1) (1996) 70 84
4. Levow, G., Oard, D. W.  Translingual topic tracking with PRISE.  In  Working Notes of the Third Topic Detection and Tracking Workshop (2000)
5. Oard, D. W.  A comparative study of query and document translation for crosslan guage information retrieval.  In Proceedings of the Third Conference of the Association for Machine Translation in the Americas (1998)
6. Oard, D. W., Diekema, A. R.  Cross-language information retrieval. Annual Review of Information Science and Technology     (1998)
7. Oard, D. W., Wang, J., Lin, D., Soboro , I.  TREC-8 e periments at Maryland CLIR,   A, and routing. The Eighth Te t Retrieval Conference (TREC-8) (1999) http //trec.nist.gov.

# Multilingual Information Retrieval Based on Parallel Texts from the Web

Jian-Yun Nie, Michel Simard, George Foster

Laboratoire RALI,
Département d'Informatique et Recherche opérationnelle,
Université de Montréal
C.P. 6128, succursale Centre-ville
Montréal, Québec, H3C 3J7 Canada
{nie, simardm, foster}@iro.umontreal.ca

**Abstract.** In this paper, we describe our approach in CLEF Cross-Language IR (CLIR) tasks. In our experiments, we used statistical translation models for query translation. Some of the models are trained on parallel web pages that are automatically mined from the Web. Others are trained from bilingual dictionaries and lexical databases. These models are combined in query translation. Our goal in this series of experiments is to test if the parallel web pages can be used effectively to translate queries in multilingual IR. In particular, we compare models trained on Web documents with models that also combine other resources such as dictionaries. Our results show that the models trained on the parallel web pages can achieve reasonable CLIR performance. However, combining models effectively is a difficult task, and single models still yield better results.

## 1    Introduction

In Cross-Language Information Retrieval (CLIR), the usual approach is to translate queries to the target language of the documents. One of the ways to perform query translation is to use a large set of parallel texts to train a statistical translation model. This approach has been successfully applied in previous CLIR experiments [4]. However, a possible obstacle is the lack of parallel texts for many language pairs. In order to overcome this obstacle, we conducted a research project to try to find parallel web pages automatically. In the past two years, we were able to build models for French-English and Chinese-English translations. Our results showed comparable performance to MT systems.

This year, we successfully mined several sets of parallel Web pages for the following language pairs: English-Italian, English-German, in addition to the English-French corpus we found previously. Our goal in this year's CLEF experiments is to see if the parallel Web documents can also apply to multilingual IR.

In our previous experiments, we observed that a certain combination of the translation models with a dictionary could improve IR effectiveness. However, the combination remained ad hoc: a dictionary translation is attributed a certain "default probability" and combined with translation words provided by a statistical translation

C. Peters (Ed.): CLEF 2000, LNCS 2069, pp. 188-201, 2001.

model. In CLEF experiments, we tested a new combination method. First, a dictionary is transformed into a statistical translation model. This is done by considering a word/term and its translation words/terms as two parallel texts. Then different statistical translation models are combined linearly. The parameters of the combination are set so as to maximize the translation probability of held-out data.

In this paper, we will first describe the mining system we used to gather parallel texts from the Web. Then a brief description of the training process of the statistical model will be provided. The CLEF experimental results will be reported. We provide some analysis of the translation process before the concluding remarks.

## 2   Mining Parallel Texts from the Web

Statistical models have often been used in computational linguistics for building MT systems or constructing translation assistance tools. The problem we often have is the unavailability of parallel texts for many language pairs. The Hansard corpus is one of the few existing corpora for English and French. For other languages, such a corpus is less (or not at all) available. In order to solve this problem, we conducted a text-mining project on the Web in order to find parallel texts automatically. The first experiments with the mined documents have been described in [5]. The experiments were done with a subset (5000) of the mined documents. However, we obtained a reasonably high CLIR performance. This experiment showed the feasibility of the approach based on parallel web pages. Later on, we trained another translation model with all the Web documents found, and the CLIR effectiveness obtained is close to that with a good MT system (Systran).

The mining process proceeds in three steps:

1. selection of candidate Web sites
2. finding all the documents from the candidate sites
3. pairing the texts using simple heuristic criteria

The first step aims to determine the possible web sites where there may be parallel texts for the given language pair. The way we did this is to send requests to some search engines, asking for French documents containing an anchor text such as "English version", "english", and so on; and similarly for English documents. The idea is, if a French document contains such an anchor text, the link to which the anchor is associated usually points to the parallel text in English (fig. 1).

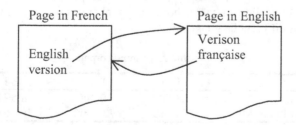

**Fig. 1.** Detection of candidate web sites

From the set of documents returned by the search engines, we extract the addresses of web sites, which are considered as candidate sites.

The second step also uses the search engines. In this step, a series of requests are sent to the search engines to obtain the URLs of all the documents in each site. In addition, as search engines only index a subset of all the web pages at each site, a host crawler is used to explore each candidate site more completely. This crawler follows the links in each web page. If a link points to another web page on the same site, then this page is added to the collection of web pages. In this way, many more web pages have been found.

The last step consists of pairing up the URLs. We used some heuristic rules to determine quickly if an URL may be parallel to another:

1. First, parallel texts usually have similar URLs. The only difference between them is often a segment denoting the language of the document. For example, "-en", "-e", and so on for English documents. Their corresponding segments for French are "-fr", "-f", and so on. Some of the parallel URLs are shown below:

**Table 1.** Examples of parallel URLs

| French page | English page |
|---|---|
| www.booksatoz.com/french/Museumf.htm | www.booksatoz.com/Museum.htm |
| www.c3ed.uvsq.fr/esee/french/state.htm | www.c3ed.uvsq.fr/esee/english/state.htm |
| www.gov.nb.ca/dot/adm/adminf.htm | www.gov.nb.ca/dot/adm/admin.htm |
| www.psac.com/comp/upwe/upwe-f.htm | www.psac.com/comp/upwe/upwe-e.htm |
| www.psac.com/comm/news/9602007f.htm | www.psac.com/comm/news/9602007e.htm |

Therefore, by examining the URLs of the documents, we can quickly determine which files may be a pair.

2. We then use other criteria such as the length of the file to further confirm or reject a pair.

3. The above criteria do not require downloading the files. Once a set of possible pairs is determined, the paired files are downloaded. Then we can perform some checking of the document contents. For example, are their HTML structures similar? Do they contain enough text? Can we align them into parallel sentences?

The French-English parallel corpus was constructed last year at the RALI laboratory. This year, we cooperated with Twenty-One (W. Kraaij) to construct English-Italian and English-German parallel corpora, using the same mining system - PTMiner [2]. The following table shows the number of text pairs as well as volume of the corpora for different language pairs.

**Table 2.** Training corpora

|  | E-F | E-G | E-I |
|---|---|---|---|
| Pairs | 18,807 | 10,200 | 8,504 |
| Volume (Mb) | 174   198 | 77   100 | 50   68 |

The corpora found from the Web will be called WAC corpora (Web Aligned Corpora). The models trained with these corpora will be called the WAC models.

## 3    Principle of Building a Probabilistic Translation Model

Given a set of parallel texts in two languages, it is first aligned into parallel sentences. The criteria used in sentence alignment are the position of the sentence in the text (parallel sentences have similar positions in two parallel texts), the length of the sentence (they are also similar in length), and so on [3]. In [6], it is proposed that cognates may be used as an additional criterion. Cognates refer to the words (e.g. proper names) or symbols (e.g. numbers) that are identical (or very similar in form) in two languages. If two sentences contain such cognates, it provides additional evidence that they are parallel. It has been shown that the approach using cognates performs better than the one without cognates. Before the training of models, each corpus is aligned into parallel sentences using cognate-based alignment algorithm.

Once a set of parallel sentences is obtained, word translation relations are estimated. First, it is assumed that every word in a sentence may be the translation of every word in its parallel sentence. Therefore, the more often a pair of words appears in parallel sentences, the better its chances of being a valid translation. In this way, we obtain the initial probabilities of word translation.

At the second step, the probabilities are submitted to a process of Expectation Maximization (EM) in order to maximize the probabilities with respect to the given parallel sentences. The algorithm of EM is described in [1]. The final result is a probability function $P(f|e)$ which gives the probability that $f$ is the translation of $e$. Using this function, we can determine a set of probable word translations in the target language for each source word, or for a complete query in the source language.

## 4    The Training of Multiple Models and Their Combination

For English and French, we also have other resources: the Hansard corpus (a set of parallel French and English texts from the Canadian parliament debates), a large terminology database (Termium) and a small bilingual dictionary (Ergane). A translation model is trained from the Hansard data, in the same way as for the Web documents (WAC).

In both the terminology database and the bilingual dictionary, we have English words/terms, and their French translations (words/terms). In some way, we can also think of these two resources as two sets of special parallel "sentences". Therefore, the translation probability between words can also be estimated with the same statistical training process. In this way, two additional translation models are estimated from them. In total, we obtain 4 different translation models between English and French from four different resources (in each direction). The question now is how we can combine them in a reasonable way.

We choose a linear combination of the models. Each model is assigned a coefficient denoting our confidence in it. The coefficients are tuned from a set of "held-out" data - a set of parallel sentences (about 100K words), by using the EM algorithm to find values which maximize the probability of this data according to the combined model. This set is selected from different resources (distinct from those used for model training) so that it gives a good balance of different kinds of texts.

Finally, the following coefficients are assigned to each model:

**Table 3.** Parameters for linear combination of models

| Model | Parameter |
|---------|-----------|
| Ergane | 0.041 |
| Hansard | 0.301 |
| Termium | 0.413 |
| WAC | 0.245 |

We observe that the combination seems to favor models with larger vocabularies. Termium is attributed the highest coefficient because it contains about 1 million words/terms in each language. The Hansard corpus and the WAC corpus contain about the same volume of texts. So their coefficients are comparable. The Ergane dictionary is a small dictionary that only contains 9000 words in each language. Its coefficient is very low The main reason for this is that the EM algorithm penalizes models which assign zero probabilities to target-text words, and models with small vocabularies will assign zero probabilities more often than those with large vocabularies. Therefore a larger model will usually be preferred over a smaller model, even though the translations it contains may not be as accurate. Although the coefficients we used are the best for the held-out data in the sense of maximizing its likelihood, they may not be suitable to our data in CLEF, and the maximum-likelihood approach may not be ideal in this context

## 5    Experiments

We used a modified version of SMART system [9] for monolingual document indexing and retrieval. The *ltn* weighting scheme is used for documents. For queries, we used the probabilities provided by the probabilistic model, multiplied by the *idf* factor. From the translation words obtained, we retained the top 50 words for each query. The value of 50 seemed to be a reasonable number on TREC6 and TREC7 data.

### 5.1 Monolingual IR

Monolingual IR results have been submitted for the following languages: French, Italian and German. This series of experiments uses the SMART *ltn* weighting scheme for queries as well. In addition, a pseudo-relevance feedback is applied, which uses the 100 most important terms among the top 30 documents retrieved to revise the original queries. The parameters used for this process are: $\alpha=0.75$, and $\beta=0.25$. The results obtained are shown below:

**Table 4.** Monolingual IR effectiveness

|  | French | Italian | German |
|---|---|---|---|
| ≥ medium | 18 | 18 | 12 |
| < medium | 16 | 16 | 25 |
| Av.p. With feedback | 0.4026 | 0.4334 | 0.2301 |
| Av.p. Without feedback | 0.3970 | 0.4374 | 0.2221 |

The comparisons with medium runs are only done for the submitted runs with pseudo-relevance feedback. As we can see, a great difference can be observed in effectiveness in the above runs. Several factors have contributed to this.

1. The use of stoplist

In the case of French, a set of stopwords is set up carefully by French speaking people. In the case of Italian and German, we used two stoplists found from the Web [7]. In addition, a small set of additional stopwords was added manually for Italian.

2. The use of a lemmatizer or a stemmer

For French, we used a lemmatizer developed in the RALI laboratory that first uses a statistical tagger, then transforms a word to its citation form according to its part-of-speech category. For Italian and German, two simple stemmers obtained from the Web [8] are used. There is no particular processing for compound words in German. This may be an important factor that affected the effectiveness of German IR.

Overall, the French and Italian monolingual runs seem to be comparable to the medium performance of the participants; but the German run is well below the medium performance. We think the main reason is due to the lack of special processing on German (e.g. compound words).

## 5.2 Tests on Bilingual IR

The bilingual task consists in finding documents in a language different from that of the queries. We tested the following bilingual IR: E-F (i.e. English queries for French documents), E-I and E-G. For this series of tests, we first used the translation models to obtain a set of 50 weighted translation words for each query. Unknown words are not translated. They are added into the translation words with a default probability of 0.05. The same pseudo-relevance feedback process as that in monolingual IR is used.

Between English and Italian, English and German, we only have the Web parallel documents to train our translation models. For French and English, we have multiple translation resources: the Web documents, the Hansard corpus, and two bilingual dictionaries. So we also compare the model with only the Web documents (the WAC model) and the model with all the resources combined (the Mixed model). The following table summarizes the results we obtained for bilingual IR. Only 33 queries have relevant documents, and are considered in these evaluations.

**Table 5.** Bilingual IR with different models

| | F-E | | I-E (WAC) | G-E (WAC) |
|---|---|---|---|---|
| | WAC | Mixed | | |
| ≥ medium | 20 | 16 | 21 | 13 |
| < medium | 13 | 17 | 13 | 21 |
| Av.p. With feedback | 0.2197 | 0.1722 | 0.2032 | 0.1437 |
| Av.p. Without feedback | 0.2410 | 0.1728 | 0.2102 | 0.1456 |

The runs we submitted are those with pseudo-relevance feedback. These runs are compared with Medium runs in the above table. For F-E and I-E cases, the WAC models perform better than the medium. The Mixed model of F-E gives a medium performance. The comparison between the two translation models for French to English is particularly interesting. We expected that the Mixed model could perform better because it is trained with more data from difference sources. Surprisingly, its effectiveness is worse than the WAC model alone. We see two possible explanations for this:

– The combination of different resources is tailored for a set of held-out data that does not come from the CLEF document set. So there may be a bias in the combination.
– During the combination, we observed that the combination results tend to favor dictionary translations. A high priority is attributed to dictionary translations. This may also be attributed to the biased tuning of combination.

In Table 2, we showed that the I-E training corpus is smaller than both F-E and G-E corpora. However, the model trained with it seems to be better suited to our CLIR task than the G-E model. This may be due to two possible reasons.

1. The quality of the translation model is determined by not only the size of the training corpus, but also the correspondence of the training data to the application corpus.
2. The quality of the model is dependent on the languages and on the processing on them.

In our case, the processing on German is the weakest. In particular, we did not consider compound words in German. This may have had a great impact on the trained model. It is also in translating German queries that we encountered the most unknown words, as we can see in Table 6. Quite a number of them are compound words such as "welthandelsorganisation", "elektroschwachtheorie" and "golfkriegssyndrom".

**Table 6.** Number of unknown words encountered by WAC models

| Model | F-E | I-E | G-E |
|---|---|---|---|
| Unknown words | 67 | 30 | 128 |

Another observation of Table 5 is that the pseudo-relevance feedback we used led to a general decrease in effectiveness, especially in the case of the WAC model for F-E. This may be due to the fact that the initial retrieval effectiveness is too low or the setting of the feedback parameters is not suitable.

In the case of F-E CLIR, we tested several models separately. The following table shows the effectiveness between French and English using different translation models. It also compares the effectiveness with and without pseudo-relevance feedback.

**Table 7.** Comparison of bilingual IR with different individual models

| Model | WAC | Hansard | Termium | Mixed |
|---|---|---|---|---|
| Av.p. Without feedback | 0.2410 | 0.2869 | 0.2182 | 0.1728 |
| Av.p. With feedback | 0.2197 | 0.2914 | 0.2359 | 0.1722 |

We can see that the mixed model performed worse than any of the individual models. This indicates clearly that the combination of the models is not suitable for the CLEF data. Again, the pseudo-relevance feedback did not have a uniform impact on effectiveness. In the case of the mixed model, the impact is almost null. In the Hansard and Termium models, the impacts are positive, whereas in the WAC model, it is negative.

This table clearly shows that the effectiveness in the official runs could be improved greatly by 1) a better relevance feedback process (or by removing this process), and 2) a better combination of models.

### 5.3. Multilingual Runs

In our case, the multilingual runs are only possible from English to all the languages (English, French, Italian and German). In these experiments, we followed these three steps:

1. Translate English queries to French, Italian and German, respectively;
2. Retrieve document from different document sets;
3. Merge the retrieval results.

The translation of English queries to German and Italian was done by the WAC translation model (trained from the Web documents). For English to French, we also have the alternative of using the Mixed model. The translation words are submitted to the *mtc* transformation of SMART. This scheme is chosen because it leads to comparable similarity values between results from different data sets, therefore, makes the result merging easier. The merging is done according to the similarity scores. The top 1000 retrieved are selected as the final results and submitted for evaluation.

The following table describes the results of different runs. In the WAC column, all the models used to translate English queries are WAC models. In the Mixed case, only the English to French translation uses the Mixed model, whereas the other translations still use the WAC models.

**Table 8.** Multilingual IR effectiveness

|                      | WAC    | Mixed  |
|----------------------|--------|--------|
| ≥ medium             | 14     | 12     |
| < medium             | 26     | 28     |
| Av.p. With feedback  | 0.1531 | 0.1293 |
| Av.p. Without feedback | 0.1548 | 0.1544 |

As we can see, these performances are all below the medium performance. One of the main reasons may be that the German monolingual retrieval does not use any linguistic preprocessing, and has a very poor effectiveness. This may greatly affect the multilingual runs. Another possible reason is the over-simplified merging method we used. In fact, in order to render the English monolingual runs compatible (in terms of similarity values) with other bilingual runs, we had to choose the *mtc* weighting scheme as for the other cases. In our tests, we observe that this weighting scheme is not as good as *ltc*. Therefore, the ease of result merge has been obtained at the detriment of English effectiveness.

We observe again the negative impact of the Mixed model in this task. When the WAC model for English-French is replaced by the Mixed model, the effectiveness decreases. This shows once again that the coefficients we set for different models are not suitable for the CLEF data.

## 6     Analysis of CLEF Results

In analyzing the translation results, we observed several problems in query translation.

### 6.1 Translation of Ambiguous Words

The translation models we constructed are IBM Model 1. These models do not consider the context during translation. It is a word-by-word translation; i.e. each word is translated in isolation. Therefore, they cannot solve word ambiguity in translation. For example, the word "drug" may be translated as "médicament" or "drogue" in French. These two senses are included in the translations of all the models, as we can see in Table 8. The same phenomenon is produced for the word "union" (in a query on European Union), which is translated to both "union" and "syndicat".

**Table 9.** Related translation words of "drug"

| Model | Translation | Prob. |
|-------|-------------|-------|
| Hansard | médicament | 0.1027 |
| | drogue | 0.0464 |
| | stupéfiant | 0.0042 |
| WAC | drogue | 0.0862 |
| | médicament | 0.0692 |
| | drug | 0.0042 |
| Termium | drogue | 0.0889 |
| | médicament | 0.0534 |
| | drug | 0.0101 |
| | médicamenteux | 0.0049 |
| | stupéfiant | 0.0046 |
| Mixed | drogue | 0.0746 |
| | médicament | 0.0715 |
| | stupéfiant | 0.0062 |
| | médicamenteux | 0.0020 |
| | remède | 0.0018 |

**Table 10.** Related translation words of "union"

| Model | Translation | Prob. |
|-------|-------------|-------|
| Hansard | syndicat | 0.0781 |
| | communauté | 0.0358 |
| | union | 0.0323 |
| | collectivité | 0.0125 |
| | syndical | 0.0111 |
| | syndiqué | 0.0042 |
| | cee | 0.0036 |
| | unir | 0.0032 |
| WAC | syndicat | 0.0666 |
| | union | 0.0508 |
| | syndical | 0.0341 |
| | communauté | 0.0158 |
| | ue | 0.0153 |
| | collectivité | 0.0131 |
| Termium | union | 0.0961 |
| | syndicat | 0.0327 |
| | communautaire | 0.0146 |
| | assemblage | 0.0049 |
| | assemblée | 0.0133 |
| | syndical | 0.0123 |
| | communauté | 0.0094 |
| | collectivité | 0.0067 |
| | community | 0.0044 |
| Mixed | union | 0.0673 |
| | syndicat | 0.0546 |
| | communauté | 0.0185 |
| | syndical | 0.0167 |
| | communautaire | 0.0131 |
| | collectivité | 0.0098 |
| | assemblage | 0.0060 |
| | assemblée | 0.0055 |
| | ue | 0.0037 |

## 6.2 Translation of Compound Terms

The example of "European Union" also shows the necessity to translate compound terms as a unit, instead of translating them word by word. By translating a compound term together, the word "union" in "European Union" is much less ambiguous than when it is translated in isolation. To do this, two approaches are possible. 1) One can detect compound terms in the parallel training texts before using the texts for model training. These compound terms will be considered as a "word" in the IBM model 1. If this "word" appears in a query, then it is translated as a unit (possibly by a compound term in the target language). 2) One can also use a higher model than IBM

1. In fact, in IBM 1, words in a sentence are considered independently. In order to capture the relationship between words in a compound term, or to capture some contextual information, it would be useful to use at least a language model together with the translation model. That is:

$$(f_1, f_2, \ldots f_l) = \text{argmax } P((f_1, f_2, \ldots f_l)|E) = \text{argmax } \prod_{i=(1,l)} P(f_i|E)*P(f_1, f_2, \ldots f_l). \tag{1}$$

where $P(f_1, f_2, \ldots f_l)$ is a language model that estimates the probability of $f_1, f_2, \ldots f_l$ appearing together in the target language, and $P(f_i|E)$ is the translation model.

In so doing, the best translation words would be those that not only have high translational probability, but also have a high probability to appear together in the target language. An alternative is to use IBM model 2 or 3 instead of model 1.

## 6.3 The Effect of Mixing Models

From the above translation examples, we cannot observe any advantage form combining different models together. In fact, the mixed model only takes the translation words from different models, and re-calculates their probability according to a linear combination. This does not affect the ambiguity problem. Ambiguous words remain as ambiguous as before the model combination.

The parameters used for linear combination of models are estimated on a small set of held-out data that are not necessarily adapted to the IR document collection used in these experiments. A better way to train the parameters is to use a similar IR test collection (e.g. the collections used for the CLIR tracks at TREC). The combination with better tuned parameters could allow us to achieve higher effectiveness than single translation models. We can also think about a different combination method than linear combination, or a method for estimating combining coefficients that corrects for vocabulary-size bias.

## 6.4 Coverage of the Models

The effectiveness of each translation model may be strongly affected by itscoverage. A model that produces many unknown words will not be able to translate many key concepts correctly (except for proper names). Table 6 showed the number of unknown words when translating queries to English from different languages. The G-E and I-E cases are comparable in both the size of training corpora and types of pre-processing on Italian and German. Nevertheless, there was a large difference between G-E run and I-E run. A strong factor that may have affected these performances is unknown words. Below we show the case of a query on "electroweak theory"[1]. All the words marked * are unknown words.

---

[1] Although this query does not contribute to official effectiveness measurements (because there is no relevant document in the English and French collections), it does show the potential problem that low coverage may cause.

**Table 11.** Word coverage in translating the query on "electroweak theory"

| Model | Known words | Top translation words | |
|---|---|---|---|
| Hansard | *electroweak | théorie | 0.0505 |
| | *subnuclear *weinberg- | nucléaire | 0.0497 |
| | salam-glashow | découverte | 0.0326 |
| | *subatomic *quark | confirmer | 0.0323 |
| | *photon | proposer | 0.0231 |
| | | domaine | 0.0223 |
| | | modèle | 0.0184 |
| | | physique | 0.0182 |
| WAC | *electroweak | théorie | 0.0683 |
| | *subnuclear *weinberg- | physique | 0.0378 |
| | salam-glashow | nucléaire | 0.0353 |
| | *subatomic *photon | découverte | 0.0281 |
| | | domaine | 0.0260 |
| | | modèle | 0.0243 |
| | | proposer | 0.0238 |
| | | confirmer | 0.0238 |
| Termiu m | *weinberg-salam- glashow | théorie | 0.0864 |
| | | électrofaible | 0.0605 |
| | | nucléaire | 0.0548 |
| | | physique | 0.0457 |
| | | particule | 0.0368 |
| | | infra-atomique | 0.0303 |
| | | quark | 0.0303 |
| | | modèle | 0.0281 |
| Mixed | *weinberg-salam- glashow | théorie | 0.0740 |
| | | nucléaire | 0.0505 |
| | | physique | 0.0336 |
| | | découverte | 0.0298 |
| | | électrofaible | 0.0250 |
| | | particule | 0.0239 |
| | | modèle | 0.0237 |
| | | confirmer | 0.0229 |

As we can see, most unknown words are key concepts of the query. The Hansard model seems to have the worst coverage for this query. Most of the key concepts are unknown. The model based on parallel web pages is slightly better. The Termium lexical database is the best for this query. It recognizes all the concepts, except the proper names. For this particular query, the effectiveness would have been greatly affected by the coverage of the models if its effectiveness were measured.

For other queries, there are only a few unknown words. In the English to French case, the Hansard model encountered 17 unknown words in total, the WAC model 13 and the Termium model 14. This appears surprising for the WAC model, which is a resource constructed without manual control. This shows that an automatically constructed parallel corpus can have a very good coverage.

# 7     Final Remarks

In this CLEF, we successfully used parallel Web pages to train several translation models for language pairs other than English and French. Our experiments on mining the web for parallel texts further confirm that the automatic mining approach is feasible for many language pairs.

For monolingual IR, we used some basic IR methods, including simple stemmers and publicly available stoplists. The effectiveness for French and Italian monolingual IR is similar to the medium performance. The German monolingual run is well below the medium. We think the main reason is that we did not carry out any particular processing on German morphology, which is an important problem for German IR.

For bilingual IR between English and French, and between English and Italian, the effectiveness seems to be reasonable. It is better than the medium effectiveness. Between English and German, however, the effectiveness is well below the medium effectiveness. The reason may be the same as for the German monolingual run.

For multilingual runs, the performance is below the medium. We believe the reason is once again the low effectiveness for German. In addition, result merging may also have affected the global effectiveness.

Between English and French, we also tried to combine different resources in our translation models. We used a linear combination of the models trained with different data, including two dictionaries, a manually constructed parallel corpus, an automatically constructed parallel corpus and a lexical database. The coefficients of the combination were determined using a small set of held-out data. However, to our surprise, the mixed model performed worse than the model trained with the Web documents only. In fact, its effectiveness is lower than any of the individual translation models. This clearly indicates that the combination is not well suited to the CLEF data. In other words, the held-out data do not correspond to the document collection used in these IR experiments.

These experiments reveal several problems in using statistical translation models for CLIR. 1) The IBM model 1 has difficulty translating ambiguous words correctly. In order to deal with this problem, we will need to take into account a language model or use a more elaborate translation model in the future. 2) Compound terms should be translated as a whole, instead of being decomposed into single words. 3) Models should be combined in a better way. These are some of the problems we will study in our future research.

# References

1.     Brown, P. F., Pietra, S. A. D., Pietra, V. D. J., Mercer, R. L.: The mathematics of machine translation: Parameter estimation. Computational Linguistics, vol. 19 (1993) pp. 263-312
2.     Chen, J.: Parallel Text Mining for Cross-Language Information Retrieval using a Statistical Translation Model, M.Sc. Thesis, DIRO, University of Montreal (2000)
3.     W. A. Gale, K.W. Church, A program for aligning sentences in bilingual corpora, Computational Linguistics, 19:1 (1993) 75-102

4. Franz, M., McCarley, J.S., Roukos, S.: Ad hoc and multilingual information retrieval at IBM, The Seventh Text Retrieval Conference (TREC-7), NIST SP 500-242 (1998) 157-168

5. J.Y. Nie, P. Isabelle, M. Simard, R. Durand, Cross-language information retrieval based on parallel texts and automatic mining of parallel texts from the Web, ACM-SIGIR conference, Berkeley, CA (1999) 74-81

6. M. Simard, G. Foster, P. Isabelle, Using Cognates to Align Sentences in Parallel Corpora, Proceedings of the 4th International Conference on Theoretical and Methodological Issues in Machine Translation, Montreal (1992)

7. http://www.cs.ualberta.ca/~oracle8/oradoc/DOC/cartridg.804/a58165/appa.htm

8. http://www.muscat.com

9. ftp://ftp.cs.cornell.edu/pub/smart/

# Mercure at CLEF-1

Mohand Boughanem and Nawel Nassr

IRIT/SIG, Campus Univ.Toulouse III,
118,Route de Narbonne
F-31062 Toulouse Cede 4
{boughane, nassr}@irit.fr

**Abstract.** This paper presents the e periments undertaken by the IRIT team in the multilingual, bilingual and monolingual tasks of the CLEF evaluation campaign. Our approach is based on query translation. The queries were translated using free dictionaries and then disambiguated using an aligned corpus. The e periments were done using our conne - ionist system Mercure.

## 1  Introduction

The goal of Cross Language Information Retrieval  CLIR  is to retrieve documents from a pool of documents written in different languages in response to a user's query written in one language. Thus in CLIR, the initial query is in one language and the document can be in another.

CLIR is mainly based on information translation. Different approaches  4  have been considered in the literature: machine translation, machine readble dictionary and corpus based approach. These techniques can be used to translate either the query terms or the document terms.

The main problems of CLIR are: finding the possible translations of a term, and deciding which of the possible translations should be retained  the disambiguation problem . The paper presents our experiments at CLEF1: multilingual, bilingual and monolingual. Our approach to CLIR is based on query translation using dictionaries.

In the multilingual experiment, two merging techniques were tested: a naive strategy and a normalised strategy. In the bilingual experiment a dictionary is used to translate the queries from French to English and a disambiguation technique based on the query context is then applied to select the best terms from the  translated  target queries.

All these experiments were done using the Mercure system  3  which is presented in Section  2 of this paper. Section  3 describes our general CLIR methodology, and finally, Section  4 describes our experiments and the results obtained at CLEF1.

C. Peters (Ed.): CLEF 2000, LNCS 2069, pp. 202–209, 2001.
© Springer-Verlag Berlin Heidelberg 2001

# 2    Mercure System

## 2.1    e i i

Mercure is an information retrieval system based on a connectionist approach and modelled by a multi-layered network. The network is composed of a query layer  set of query terms , a term layer representing the indexing terms and a document layer  2 , 3 .

Mercure includes the implementation of a retrieval process based on spreading activation forward and backward through the weighted links. Queries and documents can be either inputs or outputs of the network. The links between two layers are symmetric and their weights are based on the  $*i$  measure inspired by the OKAPI 5  term weighting formula.

- the term-document link weights are expressed by:

$$ij \quad \frac{ij * \quad 1 \quad 2 * \quad \overline{n_i}}{3 \quad 4 * \frac{j}{} \quad 5 * \quad ij} \qquad 1$$

- the query-term  at stage s  links are weighted as follows:

$$(\underset{i}{}) \quad \frac{n\ u\ tf_{ui}}{n\ u - tf_{ui}}\ \underset{i}{} \quad i \qquad i \qquad 2$$
$$\qquad\qquad \underset{i}{} \qquad r\ i$$

## 2.2    e    al a i

A query is evaluated using the spreading activation process described as follows:

1. The query    is the input of the network. Each node from the term layer computes an input value from this initial query:       $i$        $i$  and then an activation value:       $i$        $i$   where g is the identity function.
2. These signals are propagated forwards through the network from the term layer to the document layer. Each document node computes an input: $j \quad \sum_{i\ 1} \quad i *\ ij$ and then an activation,       $j \quad R$       ,  $j$  $j$  .

Notations :
    : the total number of indexing terms,
$N$: the total number of documents,
    $i$: the weight of the term  $i$  in the query  ,
    $i$: the term  $i$,
    $j$: the document  $j$,
    $ij$: the weight of the link between the term  $i$  and the document  $j$,
    $j$: document length in words  without stop words ,
        : average document length,    $ij$: the term frequency of  $i$  in the document  $j$,
    $i$: the number of documents containing term  $i$,
        : the query length,  number of unique terms
        $i$: query term frequency.

## General CLIR Methodology

Our CLIR approach is based on query translation. It is illustrated by Fig. 1.

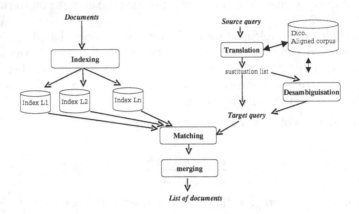

**Fig. 1.** General CLIR approach

- Indexing: a separate index is built for the documents in each language. English words are stemmed using the Porter algorithm, French words are stemmed using a truncature  7 first characters , no stemming for the German and Italian words. The German and Italian stoplists were downloaded from Internet.

- Translation : is based on   dictionaries . For the CLEF1 experiments, four bilingual dictionaries were used, all of which were actually simply a list of terms in language  1 that were paired with some equivalent terms in language 2. Table 1, shows the source and the number of entries in each dictionary.

- Disambiguation: when multiple translations exist for a given term they are generally relevant only in a specific context. The disambiguation consists of selecting the terms that are in the context of the query. We consider that a context of a given query can be represented by the list of its terms. The disambiguation process consists of building a context of the target query and using this context to disambiguate the list of substitutions resulting from the query source translation.
  A context of the target query is built using an aligned corpus. It consists of selecting the best terms appearing in the top  X  12  documents in the target language aligned to the top  X  12  retrieved by the query source.

The terms are sorted according the following formula:

$$r_i \quad \sum_{k \quad x} i$$

    : set of aligned documents to those retrieved by the source query,
   $_i$ : weight of term $_i$ in document   .

The disambiguation of the translated query consists of retaining only terms that appear in the list of terms of the target context. However, if a specific term has an unique substitution this term is retained even though it does not exist in the context of the target query. Note that in this process all the terms appearing in the target context are retained  we do not select only the best translation as is done in some other studies  1 .

**Table 1.** Dictionary characteristics

| Type | Source | nb. entries |
| --- | --- | --- |
| E2F | http //www.freedict.com | 42443 |
| E2G | http //www.freedict.com | 87951 |
| E2I | http //www.freedict.com | 13478 |
| F2E | http //www.freedict.com | 35200 |

## Experiments and Results

### 4.1    l ili g al    e i e

Two runs using English topics and retrieving documents from the pool of documents in all four languages  German, French, Italian and English , were submitted. The queries were translated using the downloaded dictionaries. There was no disambiguation, all the translated words were retained in the target queries. The runs were performed by doing individual runs for language pairs and merging the results to form the final ranked list. Two merging strategies were tested:

- naive strategy: all the documents resulting from the bilingual searches are entered in a final list. These documents are then sorted according to their RSV. The top 1000 were submitted.

- normalised strategy : each list of retrieved documents resulting from the bilingual searches was normalised. The normalisation consists simply of dividing the RSV of each document by the maximum of RSVs in that list. The documents of the different lists are then merged and sorted according to their normalised RSV. The final list corresponds to the top 1000 documents.

**Table 2.** Comparison with median at average precision

|  | irit1men2a | irit2men2a |
| --- | --- | --- |
| better than median Avg. Prec. | 15 (best 0) | 16 (best 0) |
| worse than median at Avg. Prec. | 25 (worst 2) | 24 (worst 1) |

Two runs were submitted : irit1men2a based on normalised merging and irit2men2a based on naive merging.

Table 2 compares our runs against the published median runs. We note that for both runs the number of topics above and below the median are fairly similar.

**Table 3.** Comparisons between the merging strategies

| Run-Id | P5 | P10 | P15 | P30 | E act | Avg. Prec. |
| --- | --- | --- | --- | --- | --- | --- |
| irit1men2a | 0.3750 | 0.3250 | 0.2900 | 0.2433 | 0.1996 | 0.1519 |
| irit2men2a | 0.3950 | 0.3400 | 0.3017 | 0.2500 | 0.2284 | 0.1545 |

Table 3 compares the merging strategies. It can be seen that the naive strategy is slightly better than the normalised strategy in the top document, and at exact precision but no difference at average precision. Nothing was gained from the normalised strategy.

**Table 4.** Comparison with median at average precision

| Language pair | P5 | P10 | P15 | P30 | E act | Avg. Prec. |
| --- | --- | --- | --- | --- | --- | --- |
| E2F (34 queries) | 0.2941 | 0.2118 | 0.1824 | 0.1353 | 0.2185 | 0.2046 |
| E2G (37 queries) | 0.2378 | 0.2189 | 0.1910 | 0.1396 | 0.1683 | 0.1489 |
| E2I (34 queries) | 0.1882 | 0.1647 | 0.1333 | 0.0843 | 0.1877 | 0.1891 |
| E2E (33 queries) | 0.5091 | 0.4212 | 0.3677 | 0.2798 | 0.4490 | 0.4611 |

Table 4 shows the results per language pair example, E2F means English queries translated to French and compared to French documents, etc. . We can easily see that the monolingual E2E search performs much better than all the bilingual E2F, E2G, E2I searches. Moreover, all the bilingual searches except E2G have a better average precision than the best multilingual search. The merging strategy adopted caused the loss of relevant documents, Table 5 shows the total number of relevant documents in the bilingual lists and the number of documents which were kept in the final list and were lost when merging. Relevant documents were lost from all the bilingual lists.

**Table 5.** Comparison between the number of relevant documents in Bilingual and Multilingual lists

|  | E2E | E2F | E2I | E2G |
|---|---|---|---|---|
| Rel. Ret. by bilingual list | 554 | 389 | 228 | 467 |
| Rel. kept in the final list | 500 | 281 | 152 | 296 |
| Rel. lost. | 54 | 107 | 76 | 171 |

## 4.2    ili g al    e i e

The bilingual experiment was carried out using an F2E free dictionary    disambiguation. The disambiguation was performed using WAC   Word-wide-web Aligned Corpus   parallel corpus built by RALI Lab   http:  www-rali.iro. umontreal.ca wac   .

**Table   .** Comparative bilingual F2E results at average precision

irit1bfr2en

| better than median Avg. Prec. | 22 (best 3) |
|---|---|
| worse than median at Avg. Prec. | 11 (worst 2) |

Table  6 compares our run against the published median runs. Most queries give results better than the median and 3 were the best.

Table  7 presents the disambiguated queries. We note that of 33 queries, 13 have been disambiguated. We note that 10 of these queries have improved their average precision, and the total number of relevant document has grown from 371 to 399.

Table  8 compares the results between the runs Dico  disambiguation and Dico only. The disambiguation is shown to be effective as the average precision improves by 6  .

## 4.3       li g al    e i e

Three runs were submitted as monolingual tasks: iritmonofr, iritmonoit, iritmonoge

**Table**  . Impact of the disambiguation based on aligned corpus

|  | Dico | Dico Disambiguation |  |
|---|---|---|---|
| Total. of Relevant Doc. | 371/579 | 399/579 |  |
| ueries | Avg.Prec | Avg.Prec. | Impr.( ) |
| 1 | 0.6420 | 0.6420 | 0 |
| 5 | 0.0041 | 0.0528 | 1187.8 |
| 13 | 0.1453 | 0.1486 | 2.27 |
| 14 | 0.1218 | 0.1218 | 0 |
| 16 | 0.5775 | 0.5769 | -0.10 |
| 17 | 0.6077 | 0.6274 | 3.24 |
| 18 | 0.0014 | 0.0398 | 2742.86 |
| 19 | 0.7365 | 0.7791 | 5.78 |
| 24 | 0.3101 | 0.3293 | 6.19 |
| 28 | 0.0191 | 0.0387 | 102.6 |
| 29 | 0.5833 | 0.5909 | 1.30 |
| 31 | 0.0020 | 0.0021 | 5 |
| 33 | 0.0395 | 0.0664 | 68.10 |

**Table**  . Impact of the disambiguation

| Run-id (33 queries) | P5 | P10 | P15 | P30 | E act | Avg.Prec |
|---|---|---|---|---|---|---|
| Dico  Des. | 0.3152 | 0.2636 | 0.2182 | 0.1636 | 0.2841 | 0.2906 |
| Dico | 0.2788 | 0.2515 | 0.2000 | 0.1566 | 0.2685 | 0.2741 |
| Impr ( ) | 13 | 4.8 | 9 | 4.5 | 5.8 | 6 |

**Table**  . Comparison between monolingual searches

| Run-id (33 queries) | P5 | P10 | P15 | P30 | E act | Avg. Prec. |
|---|---|---|---|---|---|---|
| iritmonofr FR (34 queries) | 0.4765 | 0.4000 | 0.3510 | 0.2637 | 0.4422 | 0.4523 |
| iritmonoit IT (34 queries) | 0.4412 | 0.3324 | 0.2490 | 0.1637 | 0.4182 | 0.4198 |
| iritmonoge GE (37 queries) | 0.4108 | 0.3892 | 0.3550 | 0.2766 | 0.3197 | 0.3281 |

Table 9 shows that French monolingual results seem to be better than both Italian and the German. Italian results are better than German. These runs were done using exactly the same procedures the only difference concerns the stemming which was used only for French. and we notice clearly that the monolingual search is much better than both the multilingual and the bilingual searches.

## Conclusion

In this paper we have presented, our experiments for CLIR at CLEF1.
In multilingual IR, we showed that our merging strategies caused the loss of relevant documents, In bilingual IR, we showed that the disambiguation technique for translated queries is effective. Results of experiments have also shown that it is feasible to use free dictionaries, and disambiguation based on an aligned corpus gives good results even though the documents of the aligned corpus are independent of those of database.
In our future work, we will try to find a way to solve the problem of merging.

## Acknowledgements

This work was in part supported by the EC through the 5th framework, Information Societies Technology programme  IRAIA Project, IST-1999-10602, http:  iraia.diw.de .

## References

1. L. Ballesteros,W. Croft  Resolving Ambiguity for Cross-Language Retrieval. in Proceedings of the 21st ACM SIGIR 98, pages, 64-71.
2. M.Boughanem, C.Chrisment, C.Soule-Dupuy,  uery modification based on relevance backpropagation in Adhoc environment, Information Processing and Managment. April 1999.
3. M.Boughanem,T.Dkaki,J.Mothe,C.Soule-Dupuy  Mercure at Trec7. Proceedings of the 7th International Conference on Te t REtrieval TREC7, E. M. Voorhees and Harman D.K. (Ed.),NIST SP 500-236, Nov. 1997.
4. G.Grefenstette  Cross language information retrieval. Edited by Gregory Grefenstette (Xero  Research Centre Europe, Grenoble France), Kluwer academic,1998.
5. S.Robertson and al  Okapi at TREC-6, Proceedings of the 6th International Conference on Te t REtrieval TREC6, Harman D.K. (Ed.), NIST SP 500-236, Nov. 1997.

# Bilingual Tests with Swedish, Finnish, and German Queries: Dealing with Morphology, Compound Words, and Query Structure

Turid Hedlund, Heikki Keskustalo, Ari Pirkola, Mikko Sepponen,
Kalervo Järvelin

Department of Information Studies, University of Tampere, 33014 Tampere, Finland
hedlund@shh.fi, heikki.keskustalo@uta.fi,
pirkola@tukki.jyu.fi, mikko.sepponen@uta.fi,
kalervo.jarvelin@uta.fi

**Abstract.** We designed, implemented and evaluated an automated method for query construction for CLIR from Finnish, Swedish and German to English. This method seeks to automatically extract topical information from request sentences written in one of the source languages and to create a target language query, based on translations given by a translation dictionary. We paid particular attention to morphology, compound words and query structure. we tested this approach in the bilingual track of CLEF. All the source languages are compound languages, i.e., languages rich in compound words. A *compound word* refers to a multi-word expression where the component words are written together. Because source language request words may appear in various inflected forms not included in a translation dictionary, morphological normalization was used to aid dictionary translation. The query resulting from this process may be structured according to the translation alternatives of each source language word or remain as an unstructured word list.

## 1 Introduction

NLP-techniques have been tested for IR and CLIR for several years. The point of view has been that linguistically motivated database indexing and query construction would enable the catching of sense in text and in queries differently from the non-linguistic methods used in IR, for example weighting based on word occurrence statistics. Traditional NLP-techniques have been extended also to the sub-word level, i.e., morphological decomposition and stemming [1]. So far, great success in increasing the quality of retrieval results due to these techniques has not been reported, compared to statistical methods. In CLIR, the use of NLP-techniques is almost a necessity because one is dealing with languages which are morphologically more complex than English.

One of the main approaches to CLIR is based on bilingual translation dictionaries. For an overview of the main approaches, see [2], [3], [4] [5]. In this paper, we adopt a dictionary-based approach to CLIR. The main problems associated with such an approach are 1) phrase identification and translation, 2) source language ambiguity, 3) translation ambiguity, 4) the coverage of dictionaries, 5) the processing of inflected

C. Peters (Ed.): CLEF 2000, LNCS 2069, pp. 210-223, 2001.

words, and 6) untranslatable keys, in particular proper names spelled differently in different languages [6].

Our approach to solve the general problems for bilingual CLIR is based on 1) word form normalization in indexing, 2) stopword lists, 3) normalization of topic word forms, 4) splitting of compounds, 5) recognition of proper components of compounds, 6) phrase composition in target language, 7) bilingual dictionaries, and 8) structured queries.

All the source languages we use, Swedish, Finnish and German, are languages rich in compounds. It therefore is essential to develop techniques for the processing of compounds. Second our interest is to compare structured and unstructured queries to solve the ambiguity problem with CLIR. We used a model for query structuring developed and tested for Finnish - English CLIR by Pirkola [7].

## 2  Research Questions

The research questions are:
1. By what process, using bilingual dictionaries, can we automatically construct effective target language queries from source language request sentences?
2. How does retrieval effectiveness vary when source languages vary?
3. How does query structure affect CLIR effectiveness when using different source languages?

The first research question involves designing and implementing our approach to automated bilingual query construction using generally available bilingual dictionaries. The method seeks to automatically extract topical information from search topics in one of the source languages and to automatically create a target language query. The resulting query may either be structured or unstructured. We will compare the effectiveness of structured and unstructured queries.

Our tests for the second research question include three different language pairs, Finnish, Swedish and German as source languages and English as the target language (for short FIN│SWE│GER -> ENG CLIR). We have tested the use and effects of morphological analysis programs, dictionary set-ups and translation approaches. All the source languages are rich in compounds, and thus, one of our main efforts is the morphological decomposition of compounds into constituents and their proper translation. In languages rich in compounds, the right translation of compounds (or their components) is a factor that greatly affects the retrieval results.

Homographic word forms, especially as components in compounds tend to add many translation alternatives to a query. Our method for treating compounds, combines every translation alternative for each component into a phrase. Therefore, a great number of translation alternatives produces an excessive number of combinations. A rich inflected morphology (in Finnish) is also a factor that affects the retrieval result, particularly when trying to identify and handle proper names.

The third research question involves constructing both structured and unstructured queries for all language pairs and testing their effectiveness. Query structure is the syntactic structure of a query expression, as expressed by the query operators and parentheses. The structure of queries may be described as weak (queries with a single operator or no operator, no differentiated relations between search keys) or strong (queries with several operators, different relationships between search keys) [7], [9]. In this study, queries with a single operand and no differentiated relations between search keys are called unstructured queries, and queries with synonym relations between search keys translated from the same source language word are called structured queries.

# 3 Research Settings

## 3.1 Document Collection and Test Topics

The LA Times document database was indexed as document collection. Our approach for database indexing in the target language is based on word form normalization, using the morphological analysis program ENGTWOL. We allow ambiguity (e.g. multiple base forms for a word) and language inconsistency (e.g., seat belt, seat-belt, seatbelt) in the text. Unrecognized word forms could not be normalized and were thus labeled as such (e.g., proper names were specially marked as unrecognized).

The CLEF test topics include title, description and a narrative. For CLIR purposes and automated query construction, it seems favorable to keep the test requests relatively short, as 2-3 sentences. Therefore we automatically selected the title and description field only. We used the Finnish, Swedish and German test topics.

## 3.2 The Query Construction Processes

Our approach in the query formulation process in the source languages included word form normalization, the removal of source language stopwords, and compound splitting into proper components in their base forms for recognition in dictionaries. This meant, e.g., handling of fogemorphemes in Swedish and German, and inflection in Finnish. Fogemorphemes are morphemes joining constituents in compounds, e.g., "s" in the word *rättsfall* (legal case). We applied phrase construction in the target language for the compounds in the source languages and labeled unrecognized word forms (e.g., proper names) as done in the indexing phase. The unrecognized word forms were used as such, disregarding possible inflection. In all these phases we allowed ambiguity, i.e. multiple possible interpretations for the source language word forms. The translation is structured using the synonym set structure [7] to reduce ambiguity effects. The synonym sets were the target language word sets as given by the bilingual dictionaries, for each source language word.

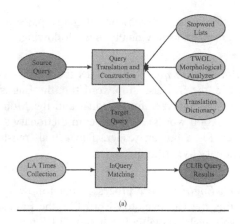

(a)

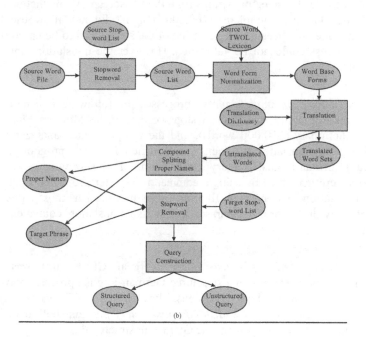

(b)

**Fig. 1.** (a) (b) General description of the automatic query construction process

*The automatic query construction process* takes the following 5 resources as inputs:
1. the CLEF topic file in one source language (SWE, FIN, GER)
2. a file, or files containing stopwords in the source language
3. a file containing stopwords in the target language (ENG)
4. a bilingual translation dictionary for the language pair
5. a morphological analysis program for the source language.

As there are slight differences between the language pairs used, we describe the processing of each language pair individually in the following.

*The structured Swedish-English query* processes the following five input files: the Swedish CLEF topic file, the Swedish stop word file, the English stop word file, the SWETWOL morphological analyzer for Swedish and the Motcom Swedish-English translation dictionary (60.000 words). The Motcom dictionary's output contains a lot of information intended for a human reader. The actual translations were obtained from the Motcom dictionary by a filtering script.

*The structured German-English query* processes the following five input files: the German CLEF topic file, the German stop word file, the English stop word file, the Duden German-English translation table for the 40 CLEF topics, and the GERTWOL morphological analyzer software for German. The construction of the German-English translation table was a separate process accomplished by a human analyzer following strict syntactic rules for selecting strings from the PC screen. As the dictionary system, Oxford Duden German dictionary (260.000 words), did not allow use through a program interface, and because the selection of the strings had to be based on the font color, this process could not be automated. However the translation table was used automatically.

*The structured Finnish-English query* processes the following five input files: the Finnish CLEF topic file, the Finnish stop word file, the Motcom Finnish-English translation dictionary (110.000 words), and the morphological analyzer FINTWOL for Finnish. The translation program was modified from the program code of the structured German-English query translation. Finnish-English word-by-word translations were generated by using a command line interface to the Finnish-English Motcom translation dictionary. A filtering script produced in most cases a "clean" stream of individual words or phrases as English translation equivalents for each Finnish word.

*The unstructured German-English query* (official CLEF run) was a simple modification of the corresponding structured German-English process, only removing structure from the structured query versions. The *unstructured Finnish - English query process* and the *unstructured Swedish - English query process* (both unofficial runs) were constructed in the same way as the German unstructured query.

### 3.3 Compound Splitting

For Swedish, Finnish and German, compound splitting and the translation of constituents were performed. If a compound is lexicalised and found in the machine-readable-dictionary used, this translation is probably less ambiguous than translating

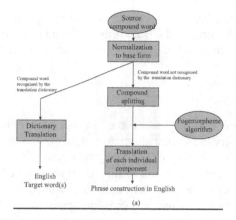

(a)

## Translation of compounds

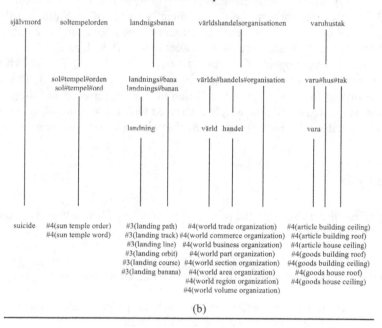

(b)

**Fig. 2.** (a), (b). Description of the process for handling compound translation: (a) the process, (b) examples

the constituents and is therefore used. For all other compounds, compound splitting is performed. Compounds in Swedish need special treatment since our earlier tests [8] indicated that the morphological analyzer for Swedish does need tuning to give proper results for IR purposes. To solve this problem we developed an algorithm which seeks to turn all the constituents of a compound to the lexical base form, which should be a real word and not a stem. In case of German, nouns as constituents need to get an upper-case initial letter. We also removed one common fogemorpheme in German, namely the "s". Proper names and other words not found in the dictionary are added to the query as such. The process for handling compounds is described in Fig 2.


### 3.4 Query Structuring

Query structuring was done by using the *syn* operator provided in the InQuery retrieval software. Every translation alternative for a word in the translation dictionary is added to the query as a synonym. The Synonym operator's syntax is: #syn($T_1$ ... $T_n$), where $T_i$ ($1 \leq i \leq n$) is a term. The terms within this operator are treated as instances of the same term for belief score computation. In other words, the translation of the word *möte* becomes #syn(encounter meeting crossing appointment date). A compound in the source language that is translated by a dictionary as a phrase needs to be marked with a proximity operator. The Ordered Distance operator's syntax is: #N($T_1$ ... $T_n$) or #odN ($T_1$ ... $T_n$), where N is the distance, and $T_i$ ($1 \leq i \leq n$) is a term. The terms within an ordered distance operator must be found within N words of each other in the text in order to contribute to the document's belief score. The #N version is an abbreviation of #odN; therefore #3(health care) is equivalent to #od3(health care).

The Weighted Sum operator's syntax is #wsum ($W_s$ $W_1$ $T_1$... $W_n$ $T_n$), where $W_s$ is the query weight, $W_i$ ($1 \leq i \leq n$) is a term weight for the term $T_i$ ($1 \leq i \leq n$). The terms are scored according to their weights in addition to their occurrence statistics. The final belief score is scaled by $W_s$, the weight associated with the #wsum itself. For example: #wsum(1 1architecture 2Berlin) weights *Berlin* twice as heavily as *architecture.*


## 4   Analysis

We shall first discuss some of the problems in the query formulation process and then present the evaluation results.


### 4.1 Analysis of the Problems in the Query Formulation Process

Major problems in our approach relate to matching, proper names, and semantics. In addition, we identified some language-specific problems.

**Matching problems:**
One of the major problems was matching the translation output to the database index.
- proper names although correctly translated do not match the index words in the document database, i.e., the form "USA" or "usa" is not recognized by the morphological analysis program ENGTWOL for English.
- words translated to English by a dictionary can be in inflected form. For example, the query words "taking" and "drugs" never matched any index words of the LA Times database. The reason for this is that the ENGTWOL program used in the index building process produced word forms "take" and "drug", respectively, in the index of the database.

Both these problems are solved if we run the dictionary translation through the morphological analyzer, thus normalizing all recognized word forms in the same way as they appear in the document database index. Unrecognized word forms in translation are labeled in the same way as words in the index.

**Proper names:**
Proper names are difficult to translate, because they normally do not appear as entries in dictionaries except for common geographical names. Still there are differences in spelling and variations in forms in different languages, i.e. Nice - Nizza. Proper names in inflected forms are not normally recognized by the morphological analyzers, and this makes normalization to base form impossible.

**Semantic problems:**
Our test queries show a great variation in length. In general the Swedish - English queries are shorter and the Finnish - English and German - English queries are considerably longer. For Swedish - English we have an average query length of 29 words, for Finnish - English the average query length is 55 words and for German - English queries 68 words. 7 of the German - English queries are over 100 words and some of them extremely long up to 528 words. However the performance of the query cannot be directly related to its length. Table 1 gives an overview of query length for each language. The length of the query depends on:
– dictionaries, and the number of translation alternatives for a word.
– compound words in the source language. When splitting compounds into three or four constituents the number of translation alternatives and their combinations grow rapidly.
– homographic words with many senses. Frequent words not in the stop list of the source language tend to have many senses, and they also tend to appear as constituents in compound words.

**Table 1.** Overview of query length in the target language, for all source languages

| Query length in words (n) | Number of queries | | |
| --- | --- | --- | --- |
| | Swe-Eng | Ger-Eng | Fin-Eng |
| n<=10 | 7 | 2 | 0 |
| 10<n<=20 | 14 | 7 | 4 |
| 20<n<=30 | 6 | 8 | 3 |
| 30<n<=50 | 2 | 8 | 11 |
| 50<n<=100 | 3 | 1 | 12 |
| 100<n | 1 | 7 | 3 |
| | 33 | 33 | 33 |

In some cases important concepts are not translated, which tend to ruin the whole query. The problem is in most cases related to the dictionaries used:

– if the word is not in the dictionary it is used as such in the query
– compound words have constituents that are not translated and due to this the translated phrases come to include words in the source language which never appear together with the translated ones in the document text. I.e., the Swedish word *brandbekämpningsolyckor* (Fire-fighter casualties) is translated as #4(fire bekämpning accident).

**Language Specific Problems:**

*Swedish:* The morphological analyzer needs to be tuned for the normalization of constituents when splitting compounds. The algorithm we used for handling fogemorphemes appears to work well in the query formulation process and reduces the number of non-translated words in several topics. However, since we deal with constituents of compounds the actual effect on the search result also depends on other factors, such as to what extent the constituent bear important search keys.

*German:* The German language has the special feature of capital initial letter in nouns, and also the double "s" ß in text. We utilized morphological information of nouns in German in order to match German noun keys more precisely into translation dictionary entries. The capital initial letter was identified in all the input files: CLEF topic file, German stop word file and the Duden German-English translation table for the 33 CLEF topics. When splitting the compounds the noun constituents also had to get the capital initial letter in order to be translated. Fogemorphemes in German were treated in a similar way as in the Swedish process. In this case we only identified one of the most common fogemorphemes.

*Finnish:* The Finnish language is special in having a very rich inflectional morphology, and instead lacking prepositions. The morphological analyzer works well and the normalization process has no greater obstacles. Most problems are caused by inflectional forms of proper names. These typically cannot be normalized since the morphological analysis program cannot identify them.

**4.2 Test Runs**

The results of the four official test runs (Finnish structured, Swedish structured, German structured and German unstructured) and the two unofficial runs (Finnish unstructured and Swedish unstructured) show comparable performance for three separate source languages (Fig. 3). The best average performance is by the German structured run, and the lowest by the Finnish unstructured. The average precision figures over recall levels are as follows (Table 2).

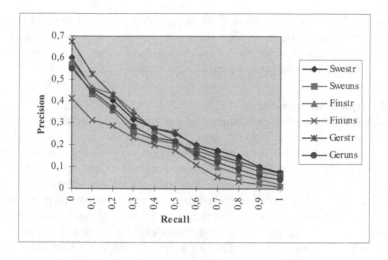

**Fig. 3.** Interpolated recall-precision averages

**Table 2.** Interpolated recall - precision averages

| recall level | Swestr | Sweuns | Finstr | Finuns | Gerstr | Geruns |
|---|---|---|---|---|---|---|
| 0,0 | 0,6007 | 0,5666 | 0,5827 | 0,4128 | 0,6752 | 0,5492 |
| 0,1 | 0,4566 | 0,4314 | 0,4625 | 0,3111 | 0,5262 | 0,4473 |
| 0,2 | 0,4021 | 0,3581 | 0,4344 | 0,2855 | 0,4287 | 0,3728 |
| 0,3 | 0,3178 | 0,2587 | 0,3542 | 0,2343 | 0,3340 | 0,2837 |
| 0,4 | 0,2743 | 0,2259 | 0,2610 | 0,1990 | 0,2761 | 0,2318 |
| 0,5 | 0,2480 | 0,2044 | 0,2146 | 0,1762 | 0,2596 | 0,2152 |
| 0,6 | 0,1985 | 0,1740 | 0,1472 | 0,1066 | 0,1901 | 0,1582 |
| 0,7 | 0,1752 | 0,1415 | 0,1012 | 0,0560 | 0,1556 | 0,1191 |
| 0,8 | 0,1441 | 0,1128 | 0,0655 | 0,0349 | 0,1270 | 0,0887 |
| 0,9 | 0,1012 | 0,0793 | 0,0419 | 0,0196 | 0,0952 | 0,0593 |
| 1,0 | 0,0740 | 0,0565 | 0,0229 | 0,0072 | 0,0727 | 0,0418 |
| | | | | | | |
| Average | 0,2540 | 0,2190 | 0,2275 | 0,1586 | 0,2665 | 0,2164 |

## Structured - unstructured queries

We tested structured / unstructured query performance for all the language pairs. German - English as official run and Swedish - English and Finnish - English as unofficial runs. The results indicate better performance for the structured queries. Our earlier findings [7] with Finnish - English CLIR suggest that the difference in performance for this language pair is larger. The unofficial runs show a better performance also in this case for the Finnish structured queries compared to the unstructured (by 7% on the average). For Swedish - English structured / unstructured queries the difference is about the same as for German - English (3 - 5% on the average). One of the reasons may be the size of the dictionaries. The smaller the dictionary the more common one-to-one relations between source and target words are, and the closer syn-based structured queries are to unstructured queries. Query length in Swedish - English is shorter, which might be explained by smaller size of the Swedish - English dictionary. This does not however explain the difference in performance between the Finnish - English and the German - English unstructured queries compared to the respective structured queries.

## Individual query performance

Examining individual query performance of our official runs for each of the 33 topics we find that our results in general tend to be above the median value for all the participating runs. On the other hand, we can report very good results for some topics and then complete failures for some, the variation being quite large (Fig. 4). This is true for all the language pairs. A common feature for all the extreme cases is that, in the positive case, all succeeded in translating important concepts as proper names or, in the negative, failed in this. Query number 12 (all languages) and 19 (Swedish) failed because of a wrong translation of the names *Order of the Solar Temple* (12) and *Persian Gulf syndrome* (19). The Finnish query (number 30) failed because of the lack of translation for *Nice*, while the Swedish and German structured got the best possible performance, although this was an extremely long query in German. The Finnish query (number 37) also failed because of a proper name *Estonian* in inflected form.

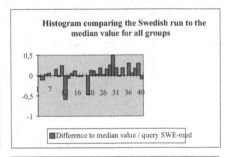
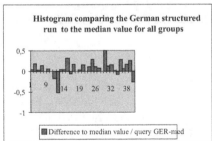
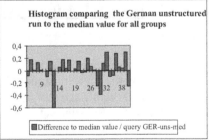

**Fig. 4.** Histograms of the test queries compared to the median values for all participating groups

## Document cut-off values

The average precision at different document cut-off value for our test runs show an extremely similar performance for five of our six runs (Table 3). The German unstructured (Geruns) run has a lower precision in the beginning (up to 15 retrieved documents), but the three best runs German structured (Gerstr), Swedish structured (Swestr), and Finnish structured (Finstr) are very close for the whole range. The difference between the Swedish structured and the Swedish unstructured run is very small. The Finnish unstructured run differs clearly from the other runs and has a much lower performance.

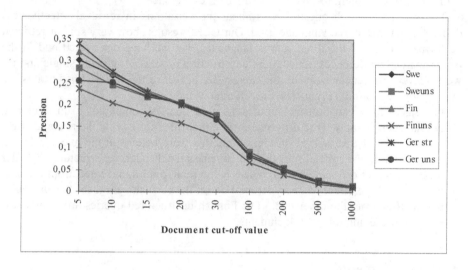

**Fig. 5.** Average precision at document cut-off values

**Table 3.** Average precision at some document cut-off values 5 - 1000

| Precision at 5, 10, 15.....1000 docs retrieved | | | | | |
|---|---|---|---|---|---|
| Docs | Swe | Sweuns | Fin | Finuns | Ger str | Ger uns |
| 5 | 0,3030 | 0,2848 | 0,3212 | 0,2364 | 0,3394 | 0,2545 |
| 10 | 0,2667 | 0,2455 | 0,2727 | 0,2030 | 0,2758 | 0,2515 |
| 15 | 0,2242 | 0,2182 | 0,2323 | 0,1798 | 0,2283 | 0,2202 |
| 20 | 0,2045 | 0,2061 | 0,2030 | 0,1591 | 0,2000 | 0,2030 |
| 30 | 0,1747 | 0,1778 | 0,1697 | 0,1303 | 0,1687 | 0,1667 |
| 100 | 0,0921 | 0,0921 | 0,0827 | 0,0676 | 0,0867 | 0,0824 |
| 200 | 0,0526 | 0,0556 | 0,0477 | 0,0395 | 0,0526 | 0,0492 |
| 500 | 0,0241 | 0,0259 | 0,0226 | 0,0193 | 0,0245 | 0,0230 |
| 1000 | 0,0128 | 0,0139 | 0,0127 | 0,0109 | 0,0131 | 0,0125 |
| | | | | | | |
| Exact | 0,2664 | 0,2368 | 0,2452 | 0,1842 | 0,2793 | 0,2242 |

# 5  Conclusions

We participated in the bilingual CLEF-track with four official runs and 2 unofficial additional runs, using three different source languages. The first research question we raised: by which process, using bilingual dictionaries can we automatically construct effective target language queries is answered in this paper. The processes we developed and implemented, focusing on proper handling of compound words, and inflectional morphology worked to our satisfaction. We have analyzed quite a few problems encountered in the query construction process, and can also contribute with some solutions for them for the next year CLEF conference.

The second research question was about the variations in retrieval effectiveness depending on the source language used. Our CLEF results show very similar retrieval performances for all the three source languages, yet we have discovered and in the paper analyzed differences in the query construction process. Analyzing single queries we discover differences between the languages, but since the results for the runs are average figures for all 33 requests the differences fade out.

The same thing can be said about structured queries compared to unstructured, individual queries show large differences (in either direction) while the average effect is much smaller. Nevertheless, structured queries were better, on the average for all language pairs. In the official runs the effectiveness for the German structured is better on a document cut-off value 15-20, which is the most important region from the user point of view. The effect of query structuring on the Finnish - English language pair seems to differ from the other two. The Finnish unstructured queries are clearly less effective in retrieving relevant documents.

# Acknowledgments

InQuery (TM) SOFTWARE Modifications Copyright (c) 1998-2000 by the Center for Intelligent Information Retrieval (CIIR) at the University of Massachusetts at Amherst. All rights reserved. InQuery (TM) Copyright (c) 1996-2000 by Dataware Technologies, Inc., Hadley, Massachusetts, U.S.A. (413-587-2222; http://www.dataware.com). All rights reserved. The InQuery (TM) software was developed in part at the Center for Intelligent Information Retrieval (CIIR) at the University of Massachusetts at Amherst (For more information, contact 413-545-0463 or http://ciir.cs.umass.edu). InQuery (TM) is registered trademark of Dataware Technologies, Inc.

ENGTWOL (Morphological Transducer Lexicon Description of English): Copyright (c) 1989-1992 Arto Voutilainen and Juha Heikkilä.

FINTWOL (Morphological Description of Finnish): Copyright (c) Kimmo Koskenniemi and Lingsoft Oy. 1983-1993.

GERTWOL (Morphological Transducer Lexicon Description of German): Copyright (c) 1997 Kimmo Koskenniemi and Lingsoft, Inc.

SWETWOL (Morphological Transducer Lexicon Description of Swedish): Copyright (c) 1998 Fred Karlsson and Lingsoft, Inc.

TWOL-R (Run-time Two-Level Program): Copyright (c) Kimmo Koskenniemi and Lingsoft Oy. 1983-1992.
MOT Dictionary Software was used for automatic word-by-word translations. Copyright (c) 1998 Kielikone Oy, Finland.

# References

1. Sparck Jones, K. (1999). What is the role of NLP in text retrieval. In T. Strzalkowski (Ed.) *Natural language information retrieval*. Dordrecht: Kluwer Academic Publishers.
2. Hull, D. & Grefenstette, G. (1996). Querying across languages: A dictionary-based approach to multilingual information retrieval. In: *Proceedings of the 19th ACM /SIGIR Conference, pp. 49-57.*
3. Oard, D. & Dorr, B. (1996). A survey of multilingual text retrieval. Technical Report UMIACS-TR-96-19. University of Maryland, Institute for Advanced Computer Studies.
4. Pirkola, A. 1999. *Studies on linguistic problems and methods in text retrieval*. Ph.D. Thesis, University of Tampere. Acta Universitatis Tamperensis 672.
5. Sperer, R. & Oard, D.W. (2000). Structured translation for cross-language IR. In *Proceedings of the 23rd ACM/Sigir Conference, pp. 120-127.*
6. Pirkola, A., Hedlund, T., Keskustalo, H., Järvelin, K. (2000). Cross-Lingual Information Retrieval Problems: Methods and findings for three language pairs. *ProLISSa Progress in Library and Information Science in Southern Africa. First biannual DISSAnet Conference.* Pretoria, 26-27 October 2000.
7. Pirkola, A. (1998). The Effects of Query Structure and Dictionary Setups in Dictionary-Based Cross-language Information Retrieval. In *Proceedings of the 21st ACM/SIGIR Conference, pp. 55-63*
8. Hedlund, T., Pirkola, A. and Järvelin, K. (2000). Aspects of Swedish Morphology and Semantics from the Perspective of Mono- and Cross-language Information Retrieval. *Information Processing & Management* vol. 37/1 pp.147-161 dec. 2000.
9. Kekäläinen, J. (1999). *The effects of query complexity, expansion and structure on retrieval performance in probabilistic text retrieval*. Ph.D. thesis, University of Tampere. Acta Universitatis Tamperensis 678.

# A Simple Approach to the Spanish-English Bilingual Retrieval Task

Carlos G. Figuerola, José Luis Alonso Berrocal, Angel F. Zazo and
Raquel Gómez Díaz

Universidad de Salamanca
Facultad de Documentación
C/ Fco. Vitoria 6-16
37008 SALAMANCA – SPAIN
{figue|berrocal|afzazo|rgomez}@gugu.usal.es

**Abstract.** This paper describes our participation in the CLEF bilingual retrieval task (formulating queries in Spanish to retrieve documents in English), using an information retrieval (IR) system based on the vector model. Our aim was to use a simple approach to solve the problem, without expecting to obtain great results, especially owing to the short time available. The queries formulated in Spanish were translated to English by a commercial machine translation system. The translations were filtered to eliminate stop words, and then the remaining terms were stemmed using a standard stemmer. Results were poorer than those obtained through monolingual retrieval with original English queries, the difference being slightly over 15%.

## 1 Introduction

This study describes the participation of our team in the Cross-Language Evaluation Forum (CLEF-2000), as a first approach to bilingual information retrieval. Our main objective in participating in CLEF was to gain experience in the task of bilingual information retrieval with Spanish and English, although we have greater experience in monolingual information retrieval in Spanish. Our participation in CLEF 2000 focussed on bilingual retrieval, using queries in Spanish with a collection of documents in English. Obviously, we also worked with the same queries, formulated originally in English, in order to establish a base-line for comparison of results.

The IR problem when more than one language is involved, i.e. evaluating the similarity of a document written in a given language versus a query in another one, is that of achieving homogeneous representations of both elements (document and query) which may be compared in order to establish a degree of similarity between them [6]. Once this homogeneous representation has been achieved, the similarity between a query and each of the documents in the collection can be computed by any of the systems usually used for monolingual retrieval [5]. In our case we use the well-known vector model.

C. Peters (Ed.): CLEF 2000, LNCS 2069, pp. 224-229, 2001.
© Springer-Verlag Berlin Heidelberg 2001

## 2 Approach to the Problem

For term-based IR techniques, as is the case of the vector model, the terms represented in the documents and in the queries have to be put into the same language. In one way or another, in bilingual text retrieval this entails some type of translation, and finding a good translation system can solve the problem.

In principle, it is a matter of translating individual terms, which does not seem to be as complicated as translating a syntactically structured text. However, the main problem, apart from the use of a machine-readable bilingual dictionary, lies in the disambiguation of the terms: these may have diverse meanings and each meaning may have diverse equivalents in the other language. It is not easy to determine the appropriate equivalents in each case and various methods have been proposed for this purpose [1]. The final result depends on the quantity and quality of the semantic knowledge contained in the dictionaries and word lists used.

Thus, we shall not use the approach of translating terms, since this would lead to poorer results in retrieval. Translating systems find it easier to disambiguate and contextualize phrases [3], and this should give rise to better results.

Hence, and because computationally it is simpler, the process followed was that of translating the queries to the language of the documents, and not the reverse. In our case, a very simple approach was adopted to solve the problem: that of using one of the commercial machine translation programs available. We did not expect great results, although it has allowed us a better understanding of the problem.

### 2.1 Machine Translation

Although machine translation (MT) is an area of intense research, there are already quite a few commercial programs on the market. These programs do not have much prestige, owing to the fact that the translations obtained often contain many mistakes and are sometimes linguistically unacceptable. However, we noted that the linguistic requirements of vector model based IR systems are not so great as those of the people who have to read and understand translations [4]. Indeed, many IR systems do not examine syntactical constructions and, when the terms are submitted to a stemming process, they disregard morphology.

The use of one of these commercial MT systems does not present any difficulties. In our case, as we lack experience in bilingual retrieval, it seemed to be a good way to become introduced to the subject. This was our approach to the problem.

Many MT systems also allow some kind of adaptation to the context, such as domain specific dictionaries, database for language pair translations, etc., which give better results in translation and, consequently, better results in retrieval. However, in our research, none of these additional tools was used. The simplest strategy was followed.

## 3 The Experiment

The layout of the process followed can be seen in the diagram below:

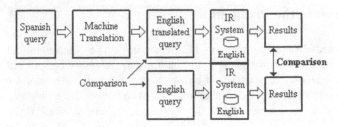

**Fig. 1.** Spanish-English Bilingual IR system

## 3.1 Queries in Spanish

We should point out that the queries were not pre-processed, i.e. they were not treated to eliminate terms that might introduce mistakes in subsequent retrieval. Three translation programs were applied directly to the queries in Spanish, without considering the noise that those terms not relevant to the query might introduce into the system.

A future study will be carried out to find out how errors in the translation of the most significant terms in the queries affect information retrieval. We expect to find parallelism between the errors in translation of the queries and the retrieval results.

## 3.2 Translation of Queries

Three MT programs were used: Systrans (on-line vers. http://www.systransoft.com), Globalink Spanish Assistant v1.0 and Globalink Power translator Pro v6.2. (at present the last two are products of Lernout & Hauspie). These programs are not expensive (the Systrans on-line version is free), and can be used on a PC with few resources.

The reason for using three programs was to check the quality of the translation, and, consequently, to use the best of the three translations for retrieval. In no case were thematic or contextual dictionaries used. We used the complete topic set in Spanish, i.e. titles, descriptions and narratives, and input it to each of the three translation systems.

The three systems tested produced very similar translations, and also coincided, notably, in the same errors. A study of the errors made by each gave very similar figures for all three. This study was carried out taking into account the significant terms for the retrieval of the original queries in English, contrasted with significant terms of the translations. The different terms were considered as translation errors, except in the cases of evident synonyms. One error was counted in those cases in which Spanish-English translation produced two or more terms, when in the English queries there was only one. Although this type of count is not very rigorous, it at least allows us to explore the possible differences between the three translation systems tested, from the point of view of information retrieval.

The error percentages thus estimated were very similar for all three. The differences were very small, with the results obtained by Systran being slightly more favorable. Moreover, and more intuitively, the mere reading of the translations showed that Systran seems to work better with proper nouns. It is better at detecting whether a word is a proper noun, and, when that name can be translated, it also translates it better. Thus, we opted to work with Systran.

## 3.3 Translated Questions

The translations obtained in the previous phase were processed following the normal retrieval process of the vector model: elimination of stop words, stemming and calculation of weight.

The original queries in English underwent the same treatment. A comparison was made of the stems obtained for the queries translated and those obtained for the original queries in English. A discrepancy of around 28% was observed, i.e. over a quarter of the stems of the queries translated into English were different from the stems of the original questions in English. This does not necessarily mean that the stems obtained were incorrect, since in some cases the translations may have used synonyms, or semantically equivalent terms.

## 3.4 IR System

As a retrieval engine we used our own software, which we have called Karpanta[1] [2]. This is a simple program based on the vector model, which was designed mainly for educational and not operational purposes. Owing to the large number of documents used in the experiment (113,000 documents, 400 MB of information) the operation process was frustratingly slow. This did not worry us at first, since the objective of our study was to verify the use of a simple approach to the problem: the application of an inexpensive MT system to CLIR.

Before indexing the documents in English, stop words were eliminated in order to save index space. For this purpose a standard list of some 200 components was used. Remaining words were stemmed by applying Porter's algorithm [PORTER80]. We used a Perl script with an implementation of this algorithm, which is widely diffused through CPAN [7]. Karpanta was then used to index all the documents in English, with all their fields. The weights of the stems obtained were calculated with the usual scheme of frequency of term in the document by *IDF*.

The queries translated into English were processed in the same way. They were used as a whole, with title, description and narrative; stop words were eliminated and stems obtained whose weight was calculated in the same way. The solving of the queries, i.e. the computation of similarity between each query and each of the documents, was performed using the widely known cosine formula.

The same process was also followed for the original queries in English, thus obtaining results, which have served as a reference point to establish comparisons with the results obtained after bilingual retrieval.

---

[1] A legendary figure in Spanish comics, whose most outstanding characteristic was that of always being hungry.

It should be emphasized that in no case was relevance feedback used in our experiments, despite the fact that this would probably have given rise to much better results.

## 4 Results

The results obtained with the queries translated from Spanish gave a mean precision of 0.2273 and can be seen in the attached graph. However, the results varied over querries (standard deviation = 0.23).

If we compare these results with those obtained using the original queries in English (mean precision of 0.27), the former are slightly lower. The precision-recall curves are almost parallel.

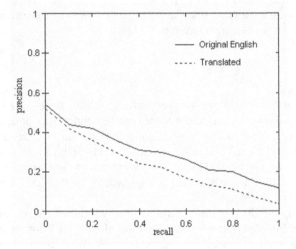

**Fig. 2.** Spanish-English Bilingual Retrieval Comparison

Moreover, if we observe each individual query, it can be seen that there are many parallels: the queries translated into English which give the best results coincide with the original queries in English that work best. Those with the worst results also show the same parallelism, both for the original queries in English and those translated into Spanish.

## 5 Conclusions

The use of a commercial MT system to solve bilingual retrieval tasks is an easy and swift solution, although effectiveness in retrieval is slightly below that obtained in monolingual results. The difference is around 15%, although this figure is less at low recall levels, i.e. taking into consideration only the first documents retrieved.

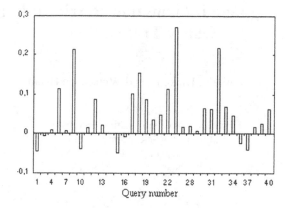

**Fig. 3.** Difference in mean average precision from the English original queries set and translated one.

No relevance feedback of queries was performed in our experiments, although this would probably have led to much better results.

Future work will be done to find out how translation errors of significant terms for the retrieval affect the results.

# References

1. Agirre, E., Atserias, J., Padró, L. and Rigau, G.: Combining Supervised and Unsupervised Lexical Knowledge Methods for Word Sense Disambiguation. Computers and the Humanities. Special Double Issue on SensEval. Eds. Martha Palmer and Adam Kilgarriff. 34:1,2, (2000). [http://www.lsi.upc.es/~nlp/papers/chum99-arpa.ps.gz]
2. Figuerola, C.G., Alonso Berrocal, J.L. and Zazo, A.F.: Diseño de un motor de recuperación para uso experimental y educativo. BiD: textos universitaris de biblioteconomia i documentació, 4 (2000) [http://http://www.ub.es/biblio/bid/04figue2.htm]
3. Fluhr, C.: Multilingual Information Retrieval. In Cole, R. A. et al.: Survey of the State of the Art in Human Language Technology, Standford University, Stanford, CA,(1995) 391-305 [http://www.cse.ogi.edu/CSLU/HLTsurvey/ch8node7.html]
4. Hull, D.A. and Grefenstette, G.: Queryng Across Languages: A Dictionary-Based Approach to Multilingual Intormation Retrieval. SIGIR96 (1996) 49-57
5. Kowalski, G.: Information Retrieval Systems - Theory and implementation. Kluwer Academic Publishers (1997)
6. Oard, D. and Dorr, B.J.: A Survey of Multilingual Text Retrieval. (1996) [http://www.clis.umd.edu/dlrg/filter/papers/mlir.ps]
7. Phillips, I.: Porter's stemming algorithm. Perl script. http://www.perl.com/CPAN-local/authors/Ian_Phillipps/Stem-0.1.tar.gz
8. Porter, M.F.: An algorithm for suffix stripping. Program, 14(3) (1980) 130-137
9. Systran Software: SYSTRAN-Translation Technologies, Language Translator, Online dictionary, Translate English (2000) [http://www.systransoft.com]

# Cross-Language Information Retrieval Using Dutch Query Translation

Anne R. Diekema and Wen-Yuan Hsiao

Syracuse University
School of Information Studies
4-206 Ctr. for Science and Technology
Syracuse, NY 13244-4500, USA
{diekemar, whsiao}@syr.edu

**Abstract.** This paper describes an elementary bilingual information retrieval experiment. The experiment takes Dutch topics to retrieve relevant English documents using Microsoft SQL Server version 7.0. In order to cross the language barrier between query and document, the researchers use query translation by means of a machine-readable dictionary. The Dutch run was void of the typical natural language processing techniques such as parsing, stemming, or part of speech tagging. A monolingual run was carried out for comparison purposes. Due to limitations in time, retrieval system, translation method, and test collection, there is only a preliminary analysis of the results.

## 1 Introduction and Problem Description

Cross-Language Information Retrieval (CLIR) systems enable users to formulate queries in their native language to retrieve documents in foreign languages [1]. In CLIR, retrieval is not restricted to the query language. Rather queries in one language are used to retrieve documents in multiple languages. Because queries and documents in CLIR do not necessarily share the same language, translation is needed before matching can take place. This translation step tends to cause a reduction in cross-language retrieval performance as compared to monolingual information retrieval. The literature explores four different translation options: translating queries (e.g. [2], [3]), translating documents [4], [5], translating both queries and documents [6], and cognate matching [1] [7]. The prevailing CLIR approach is query translation.

The translation of queries is inherently difficult due to the lack of a one-to-one mapping of a lexical item and its meaning. This creates lexical ambiguity. Further, query translation is complicated by the cultural differences between language communities and the way they lexicalize the world around them. These two translation issues create many different translation problems such as lexical ambiguity, lexical mismatches, and lexical holes. In turn, these and other translation problems result in translation errors which impact CLIR retrieval performance.

---

[1] Cognate matching facilitates matching cognates (words that have identical spelling) across languages by allowing for minor spelling differences between the cognates.

C. Peters (Ed.): CLEF 2000, LNCS 2069, pp. 230-236, 2001.

The Cross-Language Evaluation Forum (CLEF) provides a multilingual test collection to study CLIR using European languages. One of the CLEF tasks is bilingual information retrieval. The aim of the bilingual task is the retrieval of documents in a language different from the topic (query) language. Unlike the multilingual task, only two languages are involved and retrieval results are monolingual. For the bilingual run we used the Dutch topic set (40 topics) to retrieve English documents (Los Angeles Times of 1994 – 113,005 documents, 409,600 KB). We were completely oblivious to CLEF and its deadlines but we happened to hear that CLEF results were due in one week. We immediately signed up and started on our mad rush to get results in on time.

## 2 Experimental Setup

In monolingual information retrieval experiments, researchers commonly vary the information retrieval system while keeping the test queries and documents constant. This allows for comparison between systems and comparison between different versions of the same system. The same practice is followed in CLIR experiments when comparing different systems. However, CLIR experiments vary the test queries rather than the system, to allow for comparison between the cross-language and monolingual capabilities of the same system. The experiments in this research rely on varying the test queries.

By manually translating test queries into a foreign language and using these test queries as the cross-language equivalents, the cross-language performance of a system can be compared directly to its monolingual performance (see figure 1). Manual translation of queries is now a widely used evaluation strategy because it permits existing test collections to be inexpensively extended to any language pair for which translation resources are available. The disadvantage of this evaluation technique is that manual translation requires the application of human judgment, and evaluation collections constructed this way exhibit some variability based on the terminology chosen by a particular translator.

The CLEF experiments described in this paper are modeled after the experiments described above. CLEF provided topic sets in both languages. Of these, we used only the descriptions and narratives. The English topics were pos-tagged to aid phrase detection and stopwords were filtered out using the SMART stop list. We wrote a crude perl program to convert the English query into a Boolean representation that was usable by the retrieval system (described in experimental setup). The Dutch topics were processed differently since we lacked Dutch text processing resources. For each query, we extracted individual tokens, treating each token separated by spaces as a single word. A dictionary lookup took place for each token and all possible translations with their parts of speech (nouns, adjectives, verbs, and adverbs only) were inserted into the query translation file. Words that lacked a translation were left untranslated. The translation file was converted into a logical representation. Translation synonyms were combined using the OR operator and phrases were added

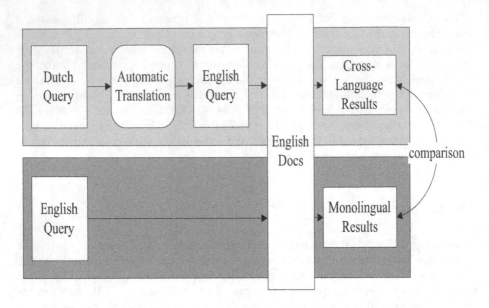

**Fig. 1.** Bilingual CLIR system evaluation.

using double quotes around the phrase. We assumed that capitalized translated tokens were important to the query and used the AND operator to add them to the logical representation (see table 1).

| Original topic |
|---|
| ```<top>```<br>```<num> C034```<br>```<D-title>```<br>```Alcoholgebruik in Europa```<br>```<D-desc>```<br>```Omvang van en redenen voor het gebruik van alcohol in Europa.```<br>```<D-narr>```<br>```Behalve algemene informatie over het gebruik van alcohol in Europa is ook - maar niet uitsluitend - informatie over alcoholmisbruik van belang.```<br>```</top>``` |
| **Logical representation after translation (based on description and narrative)** |
| ("Europe") AND ("alcoholgebruik" OR "dimension" OR "application" OR "alcohol" OR "general" OR "data" OR "exclusively" OR "advantage") |

**Table 1.** Query processing.

Unfortunately our plain and simple approach was thwarted by the retrieval system which stumbled on our rather lengthy query representations. Since we only had hours to spare before we had to submit our results, we decided to drastically shorten our Dutch queries. The translations we used were grouped by part-of-speech so we decided to pick only those translations listed under the very first part-of-speech. The queries were still too long so we further limited the translation to the first term within that part-of-speech (excluding all synonyms). Looking back, we should probably have limited our queries to the title fields rather than using the lengthy description and narrative but we ran out of time. It is not surprising that our results were a bit dismal (see *Results*).

## 3 System Overview

The system used in the experiments utilized the full-text support of Microsoft SQL Server version 7.0 [8]. SQL Server is a commercial relational database system. Besides regular relational operations, in version 7.0, it introduces facilities that allow full text indexing and searching of textual data residing in the server. Full-text search on database data is enabled by proprietary extensions to the SQL language. The following search methods are available in SQL Server 7.0:

- search on words or phrases
- search based on prefix of a word or phrase
- search based on word or phrase proximity
- search based on inflectional form of verb or adjective
- search based on weight assigned to a set of words or phrases

However, we only used the phrase and word or phrase proximity search functions in the experiments described in this paper. The system requires documents in the collection to be exported to the database before any indexing and searching can take place. Therefore, a table was created in SQL Server to represent the whole collection and each document in the collection was converted to a record in the table. The table was comprised of two columns: DOCNO and DOCTEXT. DOCNO served as the unique identification of each record in the table. DOCTEXT stored the text content of the documents. In the TREC collection, all documents are marked up in standard generalized mark up language (SGML) format. Elements like DOCNO, TITLE, AUTHOR, and TEXT for example, are used to mark up text segments and to indicate the semantics of that portion of text. Among those elements, text content of each document's DOCNO element and the TEXT element was extracted and written into the table's DOCNO and DOCTEXT columns respectively. Any SGML tags inside the TEXT elements were stripped out before the actual export took place. After the table was populated with textual data from the collection, a full-text index was created based on the table's DOCTEXT column.

After a query was sent to the system, a result set of document number, DOCNO, along with rank was returned. The rank was a value between 0 and 1000 which was generated by SQL Server to indicate how well a record matched the query. The results of each query were sorted by the system specific rank value in descending order and the 1,000 highest-ranking records were collected to generate the result submission file. For numerous queries the system retrieved less than 100 documents and in some cases nearly no documents at all.

## 4 Results

As pointed out previously, our results were disappointing. Out of the 33 topics that had relevant documents, the Dutch-English multilingual run only retrieved relevant documents for approximately 70% (23) of them. The English monolingual run did slightly better retrieving relevant documents for approximately 76% (25). We believe that the low number of relevant documents for a large number of topics in the test collection has affected the average precision measure (see *Analysis*) and therefore report the following numbers with some reservation. Average precision is 0.0364 for our cross-lingual run and 0.0678 for our monolingual run. A recall-precision table will not be presented since we would have to change the scale to make it show anything meaningful. As well, the graph will not provide a fair representation. Our Boolean system failed to retrieve the full 1000 documents for a large number of queries (we retrieved a total of 24,571 documents out of a possible 33,000 for cross-lingual and 15,057 out of 33,000 for monolingual).

In an effort to determine whether the problems we encountered were system based, we ran the identical set of queries on the Mirror DBMS system. The Mirror DBMS system combines information retrieval and data retrieval and uses statistical language models for information retrieval [9, 10]. The results improved drastically. For the cross-lingual run average precision improved by about 228% (new average precision 0.1197). For the monolingual run average precision improved by about 435% (new average precision 0.3630) (see figure 2). Interestingly, the monolingual results had a much larger improvement.

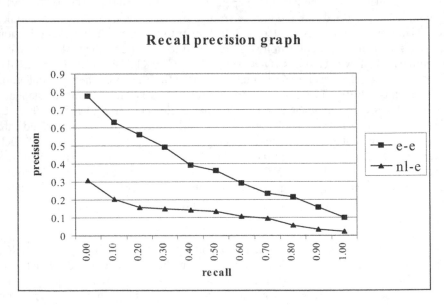

**Fig. 2.** Interpolated recall-precision using the Mirror DBMS

# 5 Analysis

The original results cannot just be blamed on the fact that most of the translations had to be removed to reduce the length of the queries (see *Experimental Setup*). Clearly, our monolingual results are also disappointing. We speculate that the lack of sophisticated linguistic processing, and techniques such as query expansion are reasons for our disappointing results. It is important to realize that the main reason for these results is the unsatisfactory retrieval capability of the commercial relational database used in the initial experiments. Additional experiments using the Mirror DBMS system show enormous performance improvements.

There are, however, issues regarding the test collection used in these experiments that impacts the evaluation of the results. Many of the topics only have a very limited number of relevant documents. Out of 40 topics, 7 topics do not have any relevant documents and these topics were left out of the analysis. This left 33 topics. Out of 33 topics 33% (11 documents) of documents have fewer than 10 relevant documents. And 18% of those (33 documents) have 5 or fewer relevant documents. The lack of relevant documents is problematic for measures such as average precision because averages are sensitive to large differences between numbers [11]. Topics 4 and 30, for example, only have 1 relevant document each. If this document is retrieved on rank 1 precision is 1 but if it is retrieved at rank 2 precision drops to 0.5. Average precision is also very sensitive to queries that perform poorly and these are represented in greater abundance in CLIR where extra noise is added in the translation. To soften the impact of bad queries, a test collection should provide a larger number of topics to reduce the effect these queries might have. 33 topics alone might not be enough.

The shortage of relevant documents also affects precision (X) measures. Hull [12] suggests using high precision measures for cross-language system evaluation because they best reflect the nature of CLIR. In an ad hoc cross-lingual search, users are less likely to go through large numbers of documents to assess their relevance since they are not likely to be proficient in the language. It is important therefore to rank relevant documents at a high level. In addition, cross-lingual searches tend to benefit substantially from relevance feedback since this adds new foreign language terminology to the query that might be lacking in the original search. Here too it is important to rank relevant documents highly. Precision (10) is a good indicator of a system's ability to rank relevant documents highly. The problem with this test collection is that for 33% of the topics, a system could never have a perfect precision (10) score even if a system managed to retrieve all the relevant documents in the top 10.

# 6 Future Work

After a more careful analysis of the results described in this paper we plan on carrying out system testing exploring the system features more carefully. We plan on examining the translation from the query to the logical representation and the incorporation of query expansion and automatic relevance feedback.

## Acknowledgements

The researchers would like to thank Arjen de Vries (CWI and University of Twente) for running our queries on the Mirror DBMS and for providing us with the retrieval results.

## References

1. Oard, D. and Diekema, A.: Cross-Language Information Retrieval. In: Williams, M. (ed.): Annual Review of Information Science (ARIST), Vol. 33. Information Today Inc., Medford, NJ, (1998) 223-256
2. Ballesteros, L. and Croft, B.: Dictionary Methods for Cross-Lingual Information Retrieval. In: Proceedings of the 7th International DEXA Conference on Database and Expert Systems, September 9-13. Zürich, Switzerland. Springer-Verlag, New York, NY (1996) 791-801
3. Ballesteros, L. and Croft, B.: Phrasal Translation and Query Expansion Techniques for Cross-Language Information Retrieval. In: Proceedings of the Association for Computing Machinery Special Interest Group on Information Retrieval (ACM/SIGIR) 20th International Conference on Research and Development in Information Retrieval; 1997 July 25-31; Philadelphia, PA. ACM, New York, NY (1997) 84-91.
4. Oard, D. and Hackett, P.: Document Translation for Cross-Language Text Retrieval at the University of Maryland. In: Proceedings of the 6th Text REtrieval Conference (TREC-6); 1997 November 19-21. National Institute of Standards and Technology (NIST), Gaithersburg, MD. (1998) 687-696
5. Kraaij, W.: Multilingual Functionality in the Twenty-One Project. In: American Association for Artificial Intelligence (AAAI) Symposium on Cross-Language Text and Speech Retrieval; 1997 March 24-26; Palo Alto, CA. (1997) 127-132
6. Dumais, S. T.; Letsche, T. A.; Littman, M. L.; and Landauer, T. K.: Automatic Cross-Language Retrieval Using Latent Semantic Indexing. In: American Association for Artificial Intelligence (AAAI) Symposium on Cross-Language Text and Speech Retrieval; March 24-26; Palo Alto, CA. (1997) 15-21
7. Buckley, C.; Mitra, M.; Walz, J.; and Cardie, C.: Using Clustering and Super Concepts within SMART: TREC 6. In: Proceedings of the 6th Text REtrieval Conference (TREC-6); November 19-21; National Institute of Standards and Technology (NIST), Gaithersburg, MD. (1997) 107-124
8. Extensions to SQL Server to Support Full-Text Search http:/www.microsoft.com/technet/SQL/Technotes/sql7fts.asp
9. de Vries, A. and Hiemstra, D.: The Mirror DBMS at TREC. In: Proceedings of the 8th Text Retrieval Conference. TREC-8, NIST Special Publication 500-246. National Institute of Standards and Technology (NIST), Gaithersburg, MD. (2000) 725-734
10. de Vries, A. and Hiemstra, D.: Relating the New Language Models of Information Retrieval to Traditional Retrieval Models. CTIT Technical Report TR-CTIT-00-09, (2000) http://wwwhome.cs.utwente.nl/~hiemstra/papers/tr-ctit-00-09.ps
11. Buckley, C. and Voorhees, E.: Theory and Practice in Text Retrieval System Evaluation. A Tutorial Presented in Conjunction with the 22nd Annual International ACM SIGIR Conference on Information Retrieval. Berkeley, CA.. August 15, 1999. ACM, New York, NY (1999)
12. Hull, D. A.: Using Structured Queries for Disambiguation in Cross-Language Information Retrieval. In: American Association for Artificial Intelligence (AAAI) Symposium on Cross-Language Text and Speech Retrieval; March 24-26; Palo Alto, CA. (1997) 84-98

# Bilingual Information Retrieval with HyREX and Internet Translation Services

Norbert Gövert

University of Dortmund
goevert@ls .cs.uni-dortmund.de

**Abstract.** HyREX is the *perme ia etrie al Engine r* . Its e tensibility is based on the implementation of physical data independence its query interface on the conceptual level consists of data types with respective vague search predicates. This concept enabled us to add search predicates for the data type *te t* to do bilingual te t retrieval. Our implementation uses free Internet resources for translating topics in English to German and vice versa.

## 1 Introduction

Typical Information Retrieval IR applications offer information to the user which consists of more than just plain text documents. Digital libraries for example do not only offer full texts of scientific publications but also metadata comprising bibliographic information as well as indexing information like e. g. subject descriptors or classification codes. Often markup languages like SGML or XML are used to expose the logical structure of documents on the one hand and the attribute structure of metadata on the other hand.

This kind of fine grained markup of logical and attribute structure should be explored by IR systems in order to offer special search predicates for different types of data. For example, searching for person names like in an author attribute similarity search for proper names should be offered. These comprise not only string search but especially the possibility to search for phonetically similar names. Accordingly, not only predicates for testing equality should be offered for dates but also predicates like *greater than*, *less than*, or vague predicates like *around date*.

HyREX[1], the *Hypermedia Retrieval Engine or ML*, offers this kind of search predicate for different data types. Data types with their respective vague search predicates build the interface to the conceptual level and thus hide their implementation details on the physical internal level. The concept of data independence is further explained in Section 2. Instead of treating the different data types as being independent of each other, it is more appropriate to use an inheritance hierarchy. This kind of relationship on data types is used to integrate bilingual IR mechanisms into HyREX Section 3 . Translation of queries is done

---

[1] http://ls -www.cs.uni-dortmund.de/ir/pro ects/hyrex/

C. Peters (Ed.): CLEF 2000, LNCS 2069, pp. 237–244, 2001.
© Springer-Verlag Berlin Heidelberg 2001

using rather naive dictionary and machine translation methods. In Section 4, experiments with HyREX and the CLEF 2000 collections and their respective results are described. Section 5 gives a conclusion and an outlook on further work.

## 2    Data Independence in HyREX

The general idea underlying the concept of data independence is the following: By introducing several abstraction levels for data organisation, changes at a certain level do not affect the higher levels. For example, if an index on the physical level is added for speeding up certain types of queries, this should not affect the search operations on the conceptual level, except that some of them can then be processed more efficiently.

In the ANSI R3 SPARC model Tsichritzis   Klug 78 , originating from the database field, three levels of data organisation are distinguished:

- The *physical   internal   level* deals with internal data and record formats and access structures.
- On the *conceptual level*, the complete conceptual schema of the database is visible. However, *physical data independence* guarantees that any changes on the internal level do not affect any application addressing the conceptual level.
- The *e  ternal  level* provides specific views of the database by referring only to those relations and attributes that are needed by a specific application.

When we designed HyREX, we adopted these concepts for data independence from the database field. HyREX deals with the physical level, that is access paths for efficient query processing are provided through a proper interface to the conceptual level. This leads to the following advantages:

- Physical data independence: Search operations are independent from the availability of access paths. In many retrieval applications one can observe that this is not the case. Most systems only allow for queries which can be directly answered from an existing inverted file. In HyREX physical data independence is reached by different levels of index support. They range from *scanning*  no index available  queries are processed by directly scanning through the documents  over *support structure* to *direct inde*   for example an inverted file for term searches .
- Appropriate search operations are provided. For example, in most retrieval systems noun-phrase search is based on proximity operators. Here, the user has to decide for criteria which make up a phrase  e. g. distance and ordering of constituents of a phrase in the text of the documents . The philosophy of HyREX in this case would be to hide such implementation details from the user. The user is provided with a specific search predicate for phrases, while the system internally decides how a phrase is defined. Of course HyREX's decision might be based on criteria like distance and ordering but also more

enhanced methods can be implemented without affecting the user's search interface.
- Finally, the concept of data abstraction by means of different system levels helps to modularise the system. HyREX has an object-oriented design.

In HyREX the search interface is made up of data types with vague predicates. The attribute structure of a given document base is therefore mapped onto a schema which assigns each attribute its respective data type:

$$a: \quad ANa \quad _1: \quad a\,a \quad p_1 \ldots ANa \quad _n: \quad a\,a \quad p_n$$

For example a simple schema for a literature database could look like the following:

$$a: \quad A \quad r:P\,r \quad Na \quad C \quad : \quad P\,b \quad a \ : \ a$$

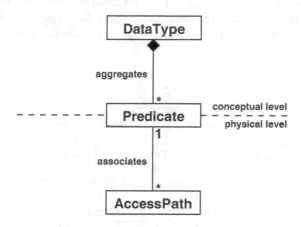

**Fig. 1.** General UML class diagram  Fowler    Scott 97  of a data type: a data type aggregates one or more search predicates. These predicates are implemented by and therefore relate to one or more access path structures.

A data type is made up by its domain  i. e. values comprising the data type  and appropriate  vague  search predicates, which can be applied to elements from the data type's domain  a more formal view on data types and search predicates is given in  Fuhr 99 . Figure 1 shows the general UML class diagram of a data type. The data type aggregates one or more search predicates. In the search predicates we separate the conceptual from the internal level: While the predicates make up the search interface from the conceptual level their implementation by means of appropriate access paths or scanning is hidden on the physical level. Details of the implementation are given in  Fuhr et al. 98 .

With the schema which assigns to each attribute a data type with the respective predicates, one can formulate queries at the conceptual level. Such queries basically are triples consisting of an attribute name, a predicate, and a comparison value. W. r. t. the schema above, for example the following queries can be issued:

- *Author* so n s  i e *Norbert Fuhr* asks for documents being authored by someone whose name sounds similar to *Norbert Fuhr*.
- *PubDate* ro n  e r    asks for documents which have been published around year 1999.
- *Content* cont ins phr se *probabilistic IR* asks for documents dealing with the concept *probabilistic IR*.

Instead of treating the different data types as being independent from each other it is more appropriate to use an inheritance hierarchy, i.e. data types can inherit from each other. A data type    which is a specialisation of a data type    inherits all predicates of    and can be extended by more specific search predicates. A simple inheritance hierarchy is depicted in Figure 2: while for example the data type *Te t English* inherits from its ancestors the predicates e    , cont ins, and cont ins phr se it specialises the *Te t* data type by the language dependent cont ins nor   ise predicate, which provides for searching for word stems.

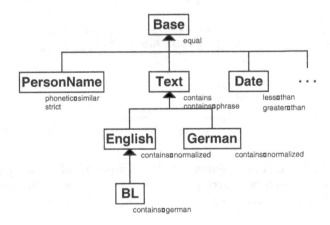

**Fig. 2.** Inheritance hierarchy on data types.

## Search Predicates for Bilingual Retrieval

Having a system which is extensible w. r. t. data types and their respective search predicates, we decided to extend the  e t:: ng ish and  e t:: er  n data types by search predicates for bilingual text retrieval. These predicates had to perform the translation of topics and queries from German to English in case of data type  e t:: ng ish and vice versa in case of data type  e t:: er  n.

For translation of queries we adopted two rather naive, but fully automatic approaches. In both approaches we used free Internet resources:

- Approach 1 uses the Babelfish translation service[2] of Altavista. This service allows to translate passages in a source language to a given target language. Besides the translation from German to English and vice versa, Babelfish handles various other languages.
- Approach 2 uses an ordinary online dictionary for word-by-word translations. We chose the Leo Dictionary service[3] for this purpose. Leo provides for a English German dictionary with about 223 900 entries. Translations can be done in both directions. Since compound words and phrases are also included in the dictionary, we exploited this by not translating the original topics word-by-word but by interpreting each two neighbouring terms as phrases. Adopting a really naive approach. we did not even attempt to tackle the word disambiguation problem.

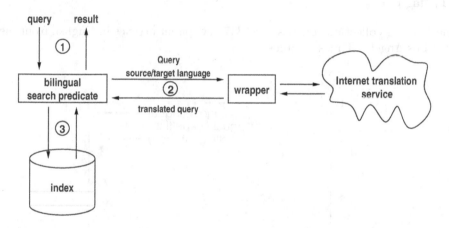

**Fig. 3.** Bilingual search predicates, implemented using free Internet translation services.

Figure 3 shows the general scheme of our search predicates for bilingual text retrieval. The user gives the query in a source language, which is translated by means of a translation wrapper. The task of the wrapper is to give a uniform interface to free translation resources on the Internet: It accepts the query as given by the user plus source and target language and then handles the translation through the service it was implemented for.

---

[2] http://babelfish.altavista.com/
[3] http://dict.leo.org/

## Experiments

In order to evaluate our search predicates for bilingual retrieval in terms of effectiveness we used two document collections from the *Cross-Language Evaluation Forum*[4]. Both, the *la_times* collection and the domain-specific *GIRT* collection come with topics in German and English  relevance judgements have been derived by judging the results of the CLEF 2000 participants.

Both test collections have been indexed by HyREX  to build the proper access paths for the bilingual search predicates we applied language specific stop-word removal and stemming on the documents' content. The well-known $\times i$ scheme Salton  Buckley 88  has been applied for term weighting.

For comparison we also performed monolingual retrieval runs on both collections. Effectiveness has been measured in terms of recall and precision. The results are presented by means of recall-precision curves and the average precision w. r. t. 100 recall points.

### 4.1  la_ i  e

The *la_times* collection consists of 84 347 newspaper articles in English from the 1994 Los Angeles Times[5] volume.

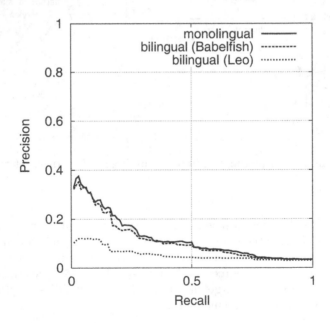

**Fig. 4.** Effectiveness of bilingual retrieval with the *la_times* collection

---

[4] http://www.iei.pi.cnr.it/DELO /CLEF/
[5] http://www.latimes.com/

For bilingual retrieval on the *la_times* collection both, the Babelfish and the Leo approach have been used to translate the topics. Figure 4 shows the recall-precision curves resulting from the bilingual  German to English  and monolingual retrieval runs. The average precision is 11.23   for the bilingual run using the Babelfish approach, 5.44   for the bilingual run using the Leo approach, and 12.11   for the monolingual run.

## 4.2    T

The *GIRT*  German Indexing and Retrieval Test database  collection contains 76 128 documents from the *social sciences* domain. The documents are in German and have been put together by IZ Bonn[6]. Topics were given both in English and German.

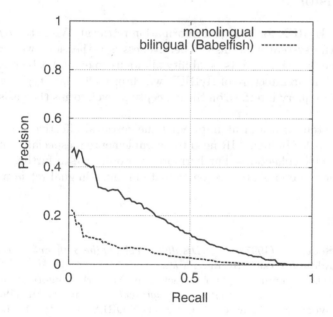

**Fig. 5.** Effectiveness of bilingual retrieval with the *GIRT* collection

For bilingual retrieval on the *GIRT* collection, the English topics have been translated by the Babelfish approach. Figure 5 shows the recall-precision curves resulting from the bilingual  German to English  and monolingual retrieval runs. The average precision is 4.20   for the bilingual run and 15.78   for the monolingual run.

---

[6] http://www.bonn.iz-soz.de/

## 4.3     al i

The results show that bilingual retrieval implemented through free Internet translation services can be employed to domain-unspecific information retrieval applications. In case of the Babelfish approach together with German-to-English bilingual retrieval we yielded effectiveness which is comparable to the effectiveness reached by monolingual retrieval. However, the same approach did not perform comparably well on the domain-specific GIRT collection.

Considering the Leo approach which used a word-by-word translation of the original topics one can say that this approach is too simplistic. Without any means for word disambiguation, a reasonable effectiveness could not be reached. During the translation process the size of the topics has grown by 92    on average on average the original topics contain 20.12 terms, while the topics translated by Leo consisted of 38.73 terms .

## Conclusion

We have used HyREX for bilingual information retrieval. While the overall performance of the system in terms of effectiveness is rather low, we have shown that the system's design and its   exibility allows us to extend it by cross-lingual IR methods. The architecture of HyREX, which provides data types with vague predicates as an query interface on the conceptual level, forms the basis for these extensions.

Our next steps will aim at improving the retrieval effectiveness. More enhanced methods for bilingual IR need to be implemented, especially for retrieval in domain-specific collections. Furthermore we would like to further extend the system in order to be able to also participate in multi-lingual retrieval tasks.

## References

o ler    . Scott    . (1997).     *Distille    ppl ing the Stan ar    ect    eling anguage.* Addison Wesley, Reading, Mass.

u r N. (1999). Towards Data Abstraction in Networked Information Retrieval Systems. *In   rmati n   r cessing an    anagement*    , pages 101 119.

u r N.    overt N. Rolle e T. (1998). DOLORES A System for Logic-Based Retrieval of Multimedia Objects. In    r cee ings    the    st nnual Internati nal    SIGI    n erence n    esearch an   De el pment in In   rmati n   etrie al, pages 257 265. ACM, New York.

Salton    .    uc ley C. (1988). Term Weighting Approaches in Automatic Te t Retrieval. *In   rmati n   r cessing an    anagement*    , pages 513 523.

Tsic ritzis D.    lug A. (1978). The ANSI/X3/SPARC DBMS Framework Report of the Study Group on Database Management Systems. *In   rmati n S stems*    , pages 173 191.

# Sheffield University CLEF 2000 Submission - Bilingual Track: German to English

Tim Gollins and Mark Sanderson

Department of Information Studies, University of Sheffield, Sheffield, South Yorkshire, UK
m.sanderson@sheffield.ac.uk

**Abstract.** We investigated dictionary based cross language information retrieval using lexical triangulation. Lexical triangulation combines the results of different transitive translations. Transitive translation uses a pivot language to translate between two languages when no direct translation resource is available. We took German queries and translated them via Spanish, or Dutch into English. We compared the results of retrieval experiments using these queries, with other versions created by combining the transitive translations or created by direct translation. Direct dictionary translation of a query introduces considerable ambiguity that damages retrieval, an average precision 79% below monolingual in this research. Transitive translation introduces more ambiguity, giving results worse than 88% below direct translation. We have shown that lexical triangulation between two transitive translations can eliminate much of the additional ambiguity introduced by transitive translation.

## 1 Introduction and Background

Cross Language Information Retrieval (CLIR) addresses the situation where the query that a user presents to an IR system, is not in the same language as the corpus of documents they wish to search. This situation presents a number of challenges (Grefenstette (1998)) but primary amongst these is the problem of crossing the language barrier (Schauble & Sheridan (1997)). Almost all the approaches to this problem require access to some form of rich translation resource to map terms in the query language (the source) to terms in the corpus (the target). "Transitive" CLIR aims to address the situation where there are limited direct translation resources available (Ballesteros (2000)).

A transitive CLIR system translates the source language terms by first translating the terms into an intermediate or "pivot" language and then translating the resulting terms into the target language. Thus, a transitive system could translate a query from German to English via either Dutch, or Spanish.

The main aim of this work is to combine translations from two different transitive routes to discover if this can reduce the ambiguity introduced by transitive translation. Ballesteros suggested the possibility of using this approach in the summary to her recent chapter (Ballesteros (2000)). We have chosen to call this approach "lexical triangulation", see Figure 1.

C. Peters (Ed.): CLEF 2000, LNCS 2069, pp. 245-252, 2001.
© Springer-Verlag Berlin Heidelberg 2001

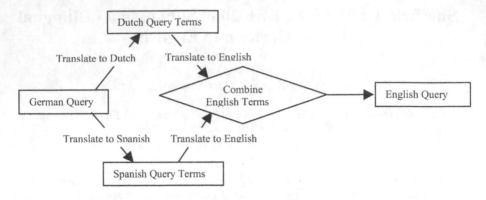

**Fig. 1.** Lexical triangulation

We have chosen to simulate a Machine-Readable Dictionary (MRD) approach to CLIR. This follows on from the work of Ballesteros & Croft (1996, 1997, 1998), and Ballesteros (2000).

## 2 The Experimental Environment

The underlying IR system used in the Sheffield submission was the GLASS system (Sanderson (2000)).

The translation resources were derived from the German, Spanish, Dutch, and English components of EuroWordNet (Vossen (1999)). The data used to lemmatise the German queries was derived from the CELEX German databases.

### 2.1 EuroWordNet

Given that the intention of this work is to examine CLIR using simulated Machine Readable Dictionaries, the choice of EuroWordNet (Vossen (1999)) as the primary translation resource may appear a little strange. The primary basis for this choice was availability[1].

The intention of the EuroWordNet project was to develop a database of WordNets for a number of European languages similar to, and linked with, the Princeton WordNet 1.5 (Vossen (1997)). This effectively makes English the inter lingua that all the other languages link through. One of the intended uses of EuroWordNet was in multi-lingual information retrieval (Vossen (1997)). Gonzalo, et al. (1998) describes a possible implementation.

By developing a series of WordNets for European languages, and linking them to the original Princeton 1.5 WordNet for English, EuroWordNet has created a structure similar to the controlled vocabulary thesaurus used by Salton as described by Oard &

---

[1] The Sheffield University Computer Science Department was a collaborator in the EuroWordNet project and Wim Peters of that department kindly made extracts from EuroWordNet available for this research.

Dorr (1996). The structure is also very similar to the structure developed by Diekema, et al. (1998). The Princeton WordNet consists of synonyms grouped together to form "synsets", basic semantic relationships link these together to form the WordNet (Vossen (1997), Miller, et al. (2000)). Each synset has a unique identifier (synset-id).

In EuroWordNet, the relationships between the synsets of the various component languages and the Princeton 1.5 WordNet synsets[2] can take many forms. These include, for example, the eq_hyponym[3] relation, which relates more general to more specific concepts (Vossen (1997)).

Our work used EuroWordNet to generate structures to simulate a Machine Readable Dictionary. The only relationships used in the construction of the dictionary tables, were the eq_synonym and eq_near_synonym relationships. These are by far the most restrictive and precise of the possible relationships.

The eq_synonym relationship records the fact that the language synset is synonymous with the WordNet synset. EuroWordNet introduced the eq_near_synonym relationship to record the fact that certain terms that share a common hypernym (more general concept) are closer in meaning than others. In this situation the co-hyponyms (more specific terms) that are closely related are close enough in meaning that they could be used for translation purposes, but are not synonymous and are therefore not in the same synset. This closeness is represented by linking the synsets with an eq_near_synonym relationship (Vossen (1997)).

For each language used from EuroWordNet, two tables were generated. The first mapped lemmas to the synset-ids of the synsets related by eq_synonym or eq_near_synonym. The second maps synset-ids to their constituent lemmas (i.e. related by eq_synonym or eq_near_synonym). As we will explain below, these tables are used to parameterise the translation process.

## 2.2 The Translation and Processing of Queries

Query processing was fully automatic and the queries were generated using all parts of the topics. The queries were passed through a series of processes as follows:

- Parsing - The conversion of the topics to queries which makes use of title, description and narrative fields.
- Normalisation - all characters were reduced to the lower case unaccented equivalents (i.e. "Ö" reduced to "o" and "É" to "e" etc.) in order to maximise matching in both the lemmatisation and translation processes.
- Lemmatisation - The various inflected forms of the query words were reduced to a canonical lemma form to enable matching with the German EuroWordNet translation resources. A table derived from the CELEX German database was used to determine the appropriate lemmata[4] for a word form. German compound words were split using a simple algorithm. The algorithm looks for

---

[2] In EuroWordNet terms the Inter Lingual Index or ILI.

[3] The relationships in EuroWordNet have names on the form eq_*relationship_name* the eq_ indicates that the relationship involves some degree of "equality".

[4] The wordform to lemma table is a many-to-many mapping as a wordform may be a valid inflection of more than one lemma.

a series of word forms that will match with the whole compound. If such a complete match is found the corresponding lemmata of the word forms are returned. The algorithm takes account of the use of "s" as "glue" in the construction of German compounds. This approach was based on the description of the word reduction module in Sheridan & Ballerini (1996). All of the CELEX data was normalised to unaccented lower case for matching with the query words.

- German Stop Word Removal - A stopword list, generated from the CELEX German database, was used to remove words in the query that carried little meaning and would otherwise introduce noise to the translation. The stop-word lists contain all of the German words marked as articles, pronouns, prepositions, conjunctions or interjections in the CELEX database.

- Translation - The translation process used tables derived from EuroWordNet to translate between two languages. The lemma to synset-id table for the first language and the synset to lemma table for the second language were used to map words in the first language to words in the second. All the possible translations through the intermediate synset-ids were returned. Three different translations were created for each query: a direct German to English translation, a transitive translation using Spanish as the intermediate language, and a transitive translation using Dutch as the intermediate language.

- Merging - The results of the two transitive translation routes were merged to produce a fourth translation, the triangulated translation. The merge process was conducted on an "original German Lemma" by "original German Lemma" basis. The translations from each route for each lemma were compared and only translations common to both routes were used to translate the lemma.

- Retrieval – the translation and merging process produced four different versions of the queries translated into English, these were submitted to the GLASS IR system which had been used to index the English corpus. The GLASS system normalised both documents and queries to lower case, and removed any English stopwords (using a standard English stop word list). Porter stemming (Porter (1980)) was used on both the queries and the collection. No special processing was used on the corpus.

## 3 The Experimental Story

We submitted four official runs to the CLEF evaluation process.
- A "bilingual" run (shefbi), generated from the direct translation from German to English
- A "Spanish transitive" run (shefes), generated from the transitive translation using Spanish as the intermediate.
- A "Dutch transitive" run (shefnl), generated from the transitive translation using Dutch as the intermediate.
- And a "triangulated" run (sheftri), generated from the result of merging of the two transitive translations.

- Only the triangulated run (sheftri) was judged and contributed to the relevance judgement pool.

In order to provide a baseline for comparison we conducted an additional English monolingual run using the same parsing and retrieval processes. This unofficial run is presented below to enable comparisons to be made.

In summary, the experimental conditions were as follows:

| Experimental Variable | Value for this experiment |
| --- | --- |
| Queries | CLEF 2000 CLIR, German and English |
| Corpus | LA Times 1994- CLEF Collection |
| Relevance Judgements | CLEF 2000 pool |
| Corpus and Query Stemming | Yes, Porter based |
| Lemmatiser | Yes, including German Compound Splitting |
| German Stop-words removed pre-translation | Yes, all articles, pronouns, prepositions, conjunctions or interjections from the CELEX German database. |
| Translation | Simulated Dictionary based, using lookup-tables derived from EuroWordNet eq_synonym and eq_near_synonym relations. |
| Merging Strategy for Lexical triangulation | Only translations common to both transitive routes. |

## 3.1 Results

The table below shows the average precision for the five runs that made up the CLEF experiment. Only the cross language runs were submitted to the CLEF, and of those, only the triangulated run contributed to the pooled results.

| | Porter, Intersection |
| --- | --- |
| English | 0.3593 |
| Bilingual (shefbi) | 0.0856 |
| Triangulated (sheftri) | 0.0458 |
| Spanish Transitive (shefes) | 0.0098 |
| Dutch Transitive (shefnl) | 0.007 |

The standard 11-point recall and precision curves for the five runs are shown below, the second graph shows only the four cross language runs.

## 3.2 Analysis

Comparing the average precision of the monolingual run with the bilingual run we see that the bilingual run is some 76%[5] below the monolingual. This compares to the

---

[5] Statistically significant at the 0.01 level under both the sign and Wilcoxon tests.

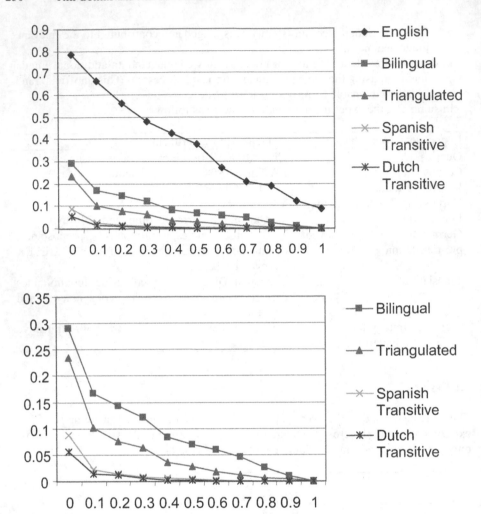

60% below worst case reported by Ballesteros & Croft (1996) when considering word by word dictionary based Spanish to English CLIR.

Taking next the two transitive runs, we observe a differential of -88% in the case of the Spanish transitive run and -92% in the case of the Dutch transitive run relative to the bilingual run. Both of these results are statistically significant at the 0.01 level under both the sign and Wilcoxon tests. These figures are in line with the -92% differentials reported by Ballesteros (2000) for transitive retrieval of Spanish – French CLIR with English as the pivot compared to Spanish – French direct translation.

Comparing the triangulated run with the two transitive runs reveals the expected improvement in performance. The differentials for the two transitive runs relative to the triangulated run are -79% for the Spanish transitive run and -85% for the Dutch transitive. Both of these figures are statistically significant at the 0.01 level under both the sign and Wilcoxon tests.

There is also a statistically significant differential of -47% between the triangulated run and the bilingual in favour of the bilingual. This significance is at the 0.01level under both the sign and Wilcoxon tests.

# 4 Conclusion

In summary, these results support the results of Ballesteros (2000) with respect to the behaviour of transitive translation in CLIR. They also support the hypotheses we set out to prove that lexical triangulation has the beneficial effect of improving the results from transitive translation in dictionary based CLIR.

This work made use of relatively rich resources in the form of EuroWordNet. However, it remains to be seen if these results could be repeated using the poorer quality resources that are likely to be available for translating between less common pairs of languages.

As Samuel Johnson said "Dictionaries are like watches; the worst is better than none, and the best cannot be expected to be quite true." (Gendreyzig (2000))

# Bibliography

Ballesteros, L. & Croft, B. (1996). "Dictionary methods for cross-lingual information retrieval". In: *Database and Expert Systems Applications. 7th International Conference, DEXA '96 Proceedings.* Springer-Verlag Berlin, Germany. [Online]. Available: http://cobar.cs.umass.edu/pubfiles/ir-98.ps.gz [23/03/2000].

Ballesteros, L. & Croft, W. B. (1997). "Phrasal translation and query expansion techniques for cross-language information retrieval". In: *Proceedings of the 20th annual international ACM SIGIR conference on Research and development in information retrieval,* pp. 84 - 91. Association for Computing Machinery. [Online]. Available: http://www.acm.org/pubs/articles/proceedings/ir/258525/p84-ballesteros/p84-ballesteros.pdf [29/02/2000].

Ballesteros, L. & Croft, W. B. (1998). "Resolving ambiguity for cross-language retrieval". In: *Proceedings of the 21st Annual International ACM SIGIR Conference on Research and Development in Information Retrieval.* Association for Computing Machinery. [Online]. Available: http://www.acm.org/pubs/articles/proceedings/ir/290941/p64-ballesteros/p64-ballesteros.pdf [29/02/2000].

Ballesteros, L. A. (2000). "Cross Language Retrieval via transitive translation". In: Croft, W. B. (ed.) *Advances in Information Retrieval: Recent Research from the CIIR,* pp. 203 - 234 Kulwer Academic Publishers.

Diekema, A., Oroumchian, F., Sheridan, P. & Liddy, E. D. (1998). "TREC-7 Evaluation of Conceptual Interlingua Document Retrieval (CINDOR) in English and French". In: Voorhees, E. M. & Harman, D. K. (eds.), *NIST Special Publication 500-242: The Seventh Text REtrieval Conference (TREC-7).* NIST. [Online]. Available: http://trec.nist.gov/pubs/trec7/t7_proceedings.html [15/02/2000].

Gendreyzig, M. (2000). *Collection of Web-Dictionaries,* [Online]. LEO - Link Everything Online. Available: http://dict.leo.org/dict/dictionaries.en.html [24/08/2000].

Gonzalo, J., Verdejo, F., Peters, C. & Calzolari, N. (1998). "Applying EuroWordNet to cross-language text retrieval", *Computers and the Humanities,* **32**( 2-3), pp 185-207

Grefenstette, G. (1998). "Problems and approaches to Cross Language Information Retrieval", *Proceedings of the Asis Annual Meeting*, **35,** pp 143-152

Miller, G. A., Chodorow , M., Fellbaum , C., Johnson-Laird, P., Tengi, R., Wakefield, P. & Ziskind, L. (2000). *WordNet - a Lexical Database for English,* [Online]. Cognitive Science Laboratory, Princeton University. Available: http://www.cogsci.princeton.edu/~wn/w3wn.html [23/08/2000].

Oard, D. W. & Dorr, B. J. (1996). A Survey of Multilingual Text Retrieval. (Report). Institute for Advanced Computer Studies and  Computer Science Department  University of Maryland.     [Online].     Available:     http://www.clis.umd.edu/dlrg/filter/papers/mlir.ps [09/03/2000]

Porter, M. F. (1980). "An algorithm for suffix stripping". In: Sparck Jones, K. & Willett, P. (eds.), *(1997) Readings in Information Retrieval.,* pp. 313 - 316. San Francisco:  Morgan Kaufmann.

Sanderson,  M.  (2000).  *GLASS,*  [Online].  Dr  Mark  Sanderson.  Available: http://dis.shef.ac.uk/mark/GLASS/ [25/07/2000].

Schauble, P. & Sheridan, P. (1997). "Cross-Language Information Retrieval  (CLIR) Track Overview". In: Voorhees, E. M. & Harman, D. K. (eds.), *NIST Special Publication 500-226: The Sixth Text REtrieval Conference (TREC-6).* NIST. [Online]. Available: http://trec.nist.gov/pubs/trec6/t6_proceedings.html [15/02/2000].

Sheridan, P. & Ballerini, J. P. (1996). "Experiments in multilingual information retrieval using the SPIDER system". In: Frei, H. P. (ed.) *Proceedings of the 1996 19th Annual International ACM SIGIR Conference on Research and Development in Information Retrieval, SIGIR 96,* pp.  58  -  65.  Association  for  Computing  Machinery.  [Online].  Available: http://www.acm.org/pubs/articles/proceedings/ir/243199/p58-sheridan/p58-sheridan.pdf [29/02/2000].

Vossen, P. (1997). "EuroWordNet: A Multilingual Database for Information Retrieval". In: *THIRD DELOS WORKSHOP Cross-Language Information Retrieval,* pp. 85-94. European Research  Consortium  For  Informatics  and  Mathematics.  [Online].  Available: http://www.ercim.org/publication/ws-proceedings/DELOS3/Vossen.pdf [01/03/2000].

Vossen, P. (1999). *EuroWordNet Building a multilingual database with wordnets for several European  languages.,*  [Online].  University  of  Amsterdam.  Available: http://www.hum.uva.nl/~ewn/ [28/02/2000].

# West Group at CLEF 2000: Non-english Monolingual Retrieval

Isabelle Moulinier, J. Andrew McCulloh, and Elizabeth Lund

Thomson Legal & Regulatory / West Group
610 Opperman Drive, Eagan MN 55123, USA,
sabelle.Moulinier@westgroup.com

**Abstract.** West Group participated in the non-English monolingual retrieval task for French and German. Our primary interest was to investigate whether retrieval of German or French documents was any different from the retrieval of English documents. We focused on two aspects stemming for both languages and compound breaking for German. In particular, we studied several query formulations to take advantage of German compounds. Our results suggest that German retrieval is indeed different from English or French retrieval, inasmuch as accounting for compounds can significantly improve performance.

## 1 Introduction

West Group's first attempt at non-English monolingual retrieval was through its participation in Amaryllis-2 campaign. Our findings during that campaign were that there was little difference between French and English retrieval, once the inflectional nature of French was handled through stemming or morphological analysis. For CLEF-2000, our goal for French document retrieval was to investigate the impact of our stemming methods. We compare performing no stemming, stemming using an inflectional morphological analyzer, and stemming using a rule-based algorithm similar to Porter's English stemmer.

Our main focus, however, was German document retrieval. German introduced a new dimension to our previous work: compound terms. We set up our experiments to assess whether we could ignore compound terms, i.e., handle German retrieval like we handled French or English retrieval, or whether we could leverage the existence and decomposition of compounds.

For both our French and German experiments, we relied on a slightly altered version of the WIN engine, West Group's implementation of the inference network retrieval model Tur90 . We used third-party stemmers to handle non-English languages.

In the following, we briefy describe the WIN engine and its adaptation to non-English languages. We report our variants for German document retrieval in Section 3. Section 4 describes experiments with stemming for French monolingual retrieval.

C. Peters (Ed.): CLEF 2000, LNCS 2069, pp. 253–260, 2001.

## 2    General System Description

The WIN system is a full-text natural language search engine, and corresponds to West Group's implementation of the inference network retrieval model. While based on the same retrieval model as the INQUERY system  CCB92 , WIN has evolved separately and focuses on the retrieval of legal material in large collections in a commercial environment that supports both Boolean and natural language searches  Tur94 .

The WIN engine supports three types of document scoring: the document as a whole is scored  each paragraph is scored and the document score becomes the best paragraph score  the score of the whole document and the best paragraph score are combined. We used the following scoring approaches for our CLEF experiments:

- German retrieval considered that a document was scored as a whole document
- French retrieval used an average of the whole document score and the best paragraph score.

This choice was prompted by the amount of information available in the various collections. For instance, the French document collection provided more  paragraph  marked-up information[1] than the German document collections did.

We indexed non-English collections using a slightly modified version of WIN for each language:

- Indexing German documents used a third-party stemmer based on a morphological analyzer. One feature was compound decomposition: forcing decomposition or not was a parameter in our experiments. Additionally, we indexed both German collections provided by CLEF as one single retrieval collection and did not investigate merging retrieved sets
- Indexing French documents required adding a tokenization rule to handle elision, and investigated two kinds of stemmers: a third-party stemmer based on a morphological analyzer, and a rule-based stemmer  *a la* Porter  from the Muscat project.

A WIN query consists of concepts extracted from natural language text. Normal WIN query processing eliminates stopwords, noise phrases  or introductory phrases  and recognizes phrases or other important concepts for special handling. Many of the concepts ordinarily recognized by WIN are specific to both English documents and the legal domain. To perform these tasks, WIN relies on various resources: a stopword list, a list of introductory phrases  Find cases about... , A relevant document describes... , a dictionary of  legal  phrases.

Query processing for French was similar to English query processing. We used a stopword list of 1745 terms  highly frequent terms, and noise terms like adverbs . For noise phrases, we used the TREC-6, 7 and 8 topics and refined the list of introductory patterns we created for Amaryllis-2. In the end, there were

---

[1] We considered the element TEXT as a paragraph delimiter.

160 patterns   a pattern is a regular expression that handles case variants and some spelling errors . We did not use phrase identification for lack of a general French phrase dictionary.

For German, we investigated several options for structuringthe queries, depending on whether compounds were decomposed or not. This specific processing is described in Section 3. We used a stopword list of 333 terms. Using the TREC-6, 7 and 8 topics, we derived a set of introductory patterns for German. There were 11 regular expressions, summarizing over 200 noise phrases. We did not identify phrases using a phrase dictionary. However, in some experiments, German compounds have been treated as   natural phrases .

Finally, we extracted concepts from the full topics. However, we gave more weight to concepts appearing in the Title or Description fields than concepts extracted from the Narrative field. Following West's participation at TREC3 TTYF95 , we assigned a weight of 4 to concepts extracted from the Title field, while concepts originating from the Description and Narrative fields were given a weight of 2 and 1, respectively.

## German Monolingual Retrieval Experiments and Results

Our experiments with monolingual German retrieval focused on query processing and compound decomposition. Our submitted runs rely on decomposing compounds, but we also experimented with no decomposition, and no stemming at all. Indexing followed the choice made for query processing. For instance, when no decomposition was performed for query terms, parts of compounds were not indexed, only the compound term was.

When we decided to break compound terms, we faced the choice of considering a compound term as a single concept in our WIN query, or treating the compound as several concepts   as many concepts as there were parts in the compound . The submitted run WESTgg1 considers that a compound corresponds to several concepts   the run WESTgg2 handles a compound as a single concept.

Given the compound   in energie, the structured query in WESTgg1 introduces 2 concepts,   in   and   nergie   the structured query in WESTgg2 introduces 1 concept,           in    nergie . The   PHRASE operator is a soft phrase, i.e. the component terms must appear within 3 words of one another. The score of the    PHRASE concept in our experiment was set to be the maximum score of either the soft phrase itself or its components.

Table 1 summarizes the results of our two official runs, as well as the results of the runs NoStem where no stemming was used and NoBreak where stemming but no decomposition was used.

The results reported in Table 1 support the hypothesis that German document retrieval differs from English document retrieval. Decomposing compound words, regardless of the query structure, significantly improves the performance of our German retrieval system. Stemming on its own, however, only marginally

**Table 1.** Summary of individual run performance on the 37 German topics with relevant documents

| Run | Avg. Prec. | R-Prec. | Performance of individual queries | | | | |
|---|---|---|---|---|---|---|---|
| | | | Best | Above | Median | Below | Worst |
| WESTgg1 | 0.3840 | 0.3706 | 3 | 21 | 3 | 9 | 1 |
| WESTgg2 | 0.3779 | 0.3628 | 3 | 18 | 6 | 9 | 1 |
| NoBreak | 0.2989 | 0.3141 | 0 | 18 | 1 | 15 | 3 |
| NoStem | 0.2986 | 0.3080 | 0 | 15 | 1 | 19 | 2 |

improves retrieval performance, as can be observed in Figure 1 for runs NoBreak and NoStem.

We expected a greater difference between our two submitted runs. WESTgg1 allows compound terms to contribute more to the score of a document, while WESTgg2 gives the same contribution to compound and non-compound terms. The contribution of a compound term in WESTgg1 is weighted by the number of parts in the compound, so one would expect its occurrence in a document to significantly alter a document score.

After reviewing individual queries, we noticed the following behavior. First, for those queries where both the compounds and their parts had an average document frequency  more precisely *id* , i.e., were neither particularly common nor particularly rare, WESTgg1 and WESTgg2 behaved similarly. In that case, parts helped locate documents, but did not add to or draw away from the document relevance score. Second, for those queries where the compound itself was a rather common term in the collection, but where the individual parts were average, then the weighted contribution of the parts provided in WESTgg1 performed better. This case re ects the frequent use of a compound term as a single entity, with limited use of its constituing parts in the collection. Third, for those queries where at least one part of a compound was very common, the high occurrence of that part degraded the weighting scheme of WESTgg1, thus the single concept construct of WESTgg2 provided a more representative score.

Finally, compound handling in WESTgg1 as well as WESTgg2 is only as in uential as there are compounds in the query. In the 40 German topics, roughly 16  of the query terms are compound terms. The difference between runs WESTgg2  decomposing using soft phrases  and NoBreak can hardly be explained by these 16  or the soft phrase construct. The difference is the result of the indexing process. Because run WESTgg2 used compound breaking during indexing  while NoBreak did not , we were able to match a non-compound query term with part of a compound in indexed documents.

## French Monolingual Retrieval Experiments and Results

The goal of our experiments with French document retrieval was to assess the difference between stemming algorithms. Our motivation was to further investigate the particularity of French compared to English. From the various kinds

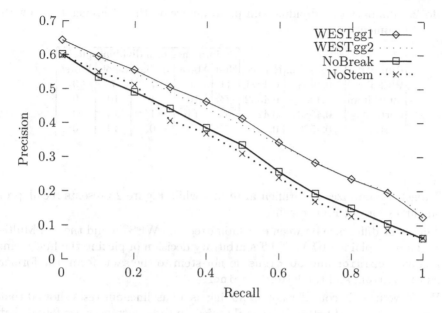

**Fig. 1.** Recall precision curves for the 4 runs: WESTgg1 and WESTgg2 use compound decomposition, NoBreak uses stemming but no decomposition, and NoStem uses raw forms.

of stemming approaches used for English document retrieval in Hul96 , we have studied two types of stemmers as well as no stemming at all:

- a rule-based stemmer  *a la* Porter  that approximates mainly in ectional rules, but also provides a limited set of derivational rules based on suffix stripping, e.g. it strips suffixes like -able or -isme
- a stemmer based on an in ectional morphological analyzer, e.g., it con ates verb forms to the infinitive of the verb, noun forms to the singular noun, adjectives to the masculine singular form. This stemmer is based on a lexicon. As this stemmer does not resolve morphological ambiguities, several stems may correspond to a term. For instance, **porte** may stem to **porte**  noun and **porter**  verb .

In the runs using the in ectional stemmer, we investigated various ways of handling the multiple stems generated for a single term. WESTff, our submitted run, relied on selecting a single stem per term  the first stem in lexical order . The run labelled MultiStem kept the multiple stems, and used the structured query to group those multiple stems into a single concept. The results reported here grouped multiple stems under a  syn operator[2]. We also ran experiments using a Porter-like stemmer and no stemming at all.

---

[2] We also tried grouping multiple stems under a  sum operator. We found no significant di erence between the two approaches.

**Table 2.** Summary of individual run performance on the 34 French topics with relevant documents

| Run | Avg. Prec. | R-Prec. | Performance of individual queries | | | | |
|-----|-----------|---------|------|-------|--------|-------|-------|
| | | | Best | Above | Median | Below | Worst |
| WEST | 0.4903 | 0.4371 | 11 | 9 | 7 | 7 | 0 |
| MultiStem | 0.4964 | 0.4352 | $7^3$ | 16 | 1 | 10 | 0 |
| Porter | 0.4680 | 0.4297 | $6^3$ | 14 | 1 | 13 | 0 |
| Nostem | 0.4526 | 0.4210 | $7^3$ | 8 | 0 | 19 | 0 |

Table 2 summarizes experimental results while Figure 2 presents recall pre-cision curves for our French runs.

The slight difference between our submitted run WESTff and the run Multi-Stem can be explained by WESTff's arbitrary decision of picking the first stem: for instance, `opinion` and `opinions` do not stem to the same form  the former stems to `opinion`, and the latter to `opiner`.

While we usually consider not stemming as a baseline, our tests showed that the basline performed better on several topics. In those instances, we found that the Porter stemmer was too aggressive and stemmed important query terms to very common forms. For instance, `p rti` was stemmed to `p rt`, `irective` to `irect` and `r nc` is to `r nc`. The in ectional stemmer did exactly what it was supposed to do, e.g. stem `r nc ise` to `r nc is`. However, certain stems were very common, while their raw form was less common. For a couple of queries, the Porter stemmer performed better than the in ectional stemmer. This re ects one limitation of the in ectional stemmer: it is only as good as its lexicon. For instance, the Porter stemmer performed better on topic 23 because important query terms were stemmed `enop  si  es` and `enop  see` to the same form `enop  s`, while the in ectional stemmer failed to stem `enop  si  es` because it was not in its lexicon.

Finally, we ran a manual run to determine whether phrase identification, e.g., `c  e ie  r nc ise`, and `onn ie e ropeenne`, was likely to improve perfor-mance, just as it has proven to be beneficial for the English version of the WIN search engine. We observed a slight improvement  average precision: 0.4994  R-precision: 0.4427  over not using phrases.

While our analysis is only partial at this time, our French stemming results follow the patterns exhibited by  Hul96 for English stemming, except that in-ectional stemming appears slightly superior. We do not know yet whether this is a particularity of the French language or of this particular collection and set of topics.

---

[3] For some queries, these runs achieved an average precision that was higher than the best average precision reported at CLEF-2000.

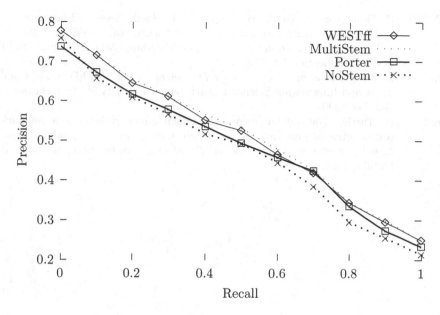

**Fig. 2.** Recall precision curves for our 4 runs: WESTff and MultiStem use the in ectional stemmer, Porter uses a Porter-like stemmer and NoStem uses raw forms.

## Summary

The WIN retrieval system achieved good performance for both German and French document retrieval without any major modification being made to its retrieval engine. On the one hand, we showed that German document retrieval required special handling because of the use of compound words in the language. Our results showed that decomposing compounds during indexing and query processing enhanced the capabilities of our system. Our French experiments, on the other hand, did not uncover any striking difference between French and English retrieval, except a performance improvement due to the use of an in ectional stemmer.

## References

CCB92    W. B. Croft, J. Callan, and J. Broglio. The inquery retrieval system. In
         r cee ings   the ᵣ Internati nal   n erence  n Data ase an  E pert
         S stems  pplicati ns, Spain, 1992.
Hul96    D. A. Hull. Stemming algorithms  A case study for detailed evaluation.
          urnal    he   merican S ciet  F r In  rmati n Science, 47(1) 70 84,
         1996.

TTYF95   P. Thompson, H. Turtle, B. Yang, and J. Flood. Trec-3 ad hoc retrieval
         and routing e periments using the win system. In    *er ie      the  r
            *e t  etrie al    n erence      E*  , Gaithersburg, MD, April 1995. NIST
         Special Publication 500-225.

Tur90    H. Turtle. *In erence   et   r s   r D  cument   etrie al*. PhD thesis, Com-
         puter and Information Science Department, University of Massachussetts,
         October 1990.

Tur94    H. Turtle. Natural language vs. boolean query evaluation  a compari-
         son of retrieval performance. In   *r cee ings     the        nnual Interna
         ti nal    n erence  n   esearch an  De el pment in In  rmati n   etrie al*,
         Dublin, 1994.

# ITC-irst at CLEF 2000:
# Italian Monolingual Track

Nicola Bertoldi and Marcello Federico

ITC-irst - Centro per la Ricerca Scientifica e Tecnologica
I-38050 Povo, Trento, Italy
{bertoldi, federico}@itc.it

**Abstract.** This paper presents work on document retrieval for Italian carried out at ITC-irst. Two di erent approaches to information retrieval were investigated, one based on the Okapi weighting formula and one based on a statistical model. Development e periments were carried out using the Italian sample of the TREC-8 CLIR track. Performance evaluation was done on the Cross Language Evaluation Forum (CLEF) 2000 Italian monolingual track. The two methods achieved mean average precisions of 49.0  and 47.5 , respectively, which were the two best scores of their track.

## 1 Introduction

This paper reports on Italian text retrieval research that has recently started at ITC-irst. Experimental evaluation was carried out in the framework of the Cross Language Evaluation Forum  CLEF , a text retrieval system evaluation activity coordinated in Europe from 2000, in collaboration with the US National Institute of Standards and Technology  NIST  and the Text REtrieval Conference  TREC .

ITC-irst has began to develop monolingual text retrieval systems  10  for the main purpose of accessing broadcast news archives  1 . This paper presents two Italian monolingual text retrieval systems that have been submitted to CLEF 2000: a conventional Okapi derived model, and a statistical retrieval model. After the evaluation, a combined model was also developed that just integrates the scores of the two basic models. This simple and effective model shows a significant improvement over the two single models.

The paper is organized as follows. In Section 2, the text preprocessing of documents and queries is presented. Section 3 and 4 introduce the text retrieval models that were officially evaluated at CLEF and present experimental results. Section 5 discusses improvements on the basic models that were made after the CLEF evaluation. In particular, a combined retrieval model is introduced and evaluated on the CLEF test collection. Finally, Section 6 offers some conclusions regarding the research at ITC-irst in the field of text retrieval.

C. Peters (Ed.): CLEF 2000, LNCS 2069, pp. 261–272, 2001.
© Springer-Verlag Berlin Heidelberg 2001

## 2   Text Preprocessing

Document and query preprocessing implies several stages: tokenization, morphological analysis of words, part-of-speech POS tagging of text, base form extraction, stemming, and stop-terms removal.

**T e i a i** . Tokenization of text is performed in order to isolate words from punctuation marks, recognize abbreviations and acronyms, correct possible word splits across lines, and discriminate between accents and quotation marks.

**l gi al   al  i** . A morphological analyzer 3 decomposes each Italian in ected word into its morphemes, and suggests all possible POSs and base forms of each valid decomposition. By base forms we mean the usual not in ected entries of a dictionary.

**Taggi g.** POS tagging is based on a Viterbi decoder that computes the best text-POS alignment on the basis of a bigram POS language model and a discrete observation model 5 . The employed tagger works with 57 tag classes and has an accuracy around 96  .

**a e F     a  i** . Once the POS and the morphological analysis of each word in the text is computed, a base form can be assigned to each word.

**e   i g.** Word stemming is applied at the level of tagged base forms. POS specific rules were developed that remove suffixes from verbs, nouns, and adjectives.

**Te   e   al.** Words in the collection that are considered non relevant for the purpose of information retrieval are discarded in order to save index space. Words are filtered out on the basis either of their POS or their inverted document frequency. In particular, punctuation is eliminated together with articles, determiners, quantifiers, auxiliary verbs, prepositions, conjunctions, interjections, and pronouns. Among the remaining terms, those with a low inverted document frequency, i.e. that occur in many different documents, are eliminated.

Table 1 collects statistics about the effects of text preprocessing steps on the mean document length    , global vocabulary size     , and mean document vocabulary size   .

An example of text preprocessing is presented in the appendix at the end of this paper.

**Table 1.** Effect of text preprocessing steps on the mean document length , global vocabulary size , and mean document vocabulary size .

| Terms | Stop | | | |
|---|---|---|---|---|
| te t | no | 225 | 160K | 134 |
| base forms | no | 225 | 126K | 129 |
| stems | no | 225 | 101K | 126 |
| base forms | yes | 103 | 125K | 80 |
| stems | yes | 103 | 100K | 77 |

## Information Retrieval Models

### 3.1 a i el

Okapi 9 is the name of a retrieval system project that developed a family of weighting functions in order to evaluate the relevance of a document versus a query . In this work, the following Okapi weighting function was applied:

$$\sum \qquad i \qquad \qquad 1$$

where:

$$\frac{k_1 \; 1}{k_1 \; 1 - b \quad k_1 b \frac{f_d}{}} \qquad \qquad 2$$

scores the relevance of in , and the inverted document frequency:

$$i \qquad \log \frac{N - N \quad 0.5}{N \quad 0.5} \qquad \qquad 3$$

evaluates the relevance of inside the collection. The model implies two parameters $k_1$ and $b$ to be empirically estimated over a development sample. An explanation of the involved terms can be found in 9 and other papers referred in it.

### 3.2 a i i al el

A statistical retrieval model was developed based on previous work on statistical language modeling 2 .

The match between a query and a document can be expressed through the following conditional probability distribution:

$$P \qquad \frac{P \quad P}{P} \qquad \qquad 4$$

where $P$ represents the likelihood of , given , $P$ represents the a-priori probability of , and $P$ is a normalization term. By assuming no a-priori

**Table 2.** Notation used in the information retrieval models.

( )     frequency of word    in document
( )     frequency of    in query
( )     frequency of    in the collection
length of document
length of the collection
mean document length
number of documents
number of documents containing
vocabulary size of document
average document vocabulary size
vocabulary size of the collection

knowledge about the documents, and disregarding the normalization factor, documents can be ranked, with respect to  , just by the likelihood term $P$         .
If we interpret the likelihood function as the probability of   generating   and assume an order-free multinomial model, the following log-probability score can be derived:

$$\log P \qquad \sum \qquad \log P \qquad\qquad 5$$

The probability that a term   is generated by   can be estimated by applying statistical language modeling techniques. Previous work on statistical information retrieval  6,8  proposed to interpolate relative frequencies of each document with those of the whole collection, with interpolation weights empirically estimated from the data.

In this work we use an interpolation formula which applies the smoothing method proposed by  11 . This method linearly smoothes word frequencies of a document and the amount of probability assigned to never observed terms is proportional to the number of different words contained in the document. Hence, the following probability estimate is applied:

$$P \qquad \frac{\quad}{\quad} \qquad \frac{\quad}{\quad} P \qquad\qquad 6$$

where $P$   , the word probability over the collection, is estimated by interpolating the smoothed relative frequency with the uniform distribution over the vocabulary   :

$$P \qquad \frac{\quad}{\quad} \qquad \frac{1}{\quad} \qquad\qquad 7$$

### 3.3    li    ele a  e Fee ba

Blind relevance feedback  BRF  is a well known technique that allows to improve retrieval performance. The basic idea is to perform retrieval in two steps. First, the documents matching the original query   are ranked, then the    best ranked documents are taken and the    most relevant terms in them are added to the query. Hence, the retrieval phase is repeated with the augmented query. In this work, new search terms are extracted by sorting all the terms of the    top documents according to  4 :

$$r \quad \frac{r \quad 0.5}{N \quad -r \quad 0.5} \quad \frac{N-N \quad -}{-r \quad 0.5} \qquad 8$$

where $r$  is the frequency of word    inside the    top documents.

## Experiments

This section presents work done to develop and test the presented models. Development and testing were done on two different Italian document retrieval tasks. Performance was measured in terms of Average Precision    v r  and mean Average Precision    v r . Given the document ranking provided against a given query , let $r_1$  ...   $r$  be the ranks of the retrieved relevant documents. The  v r for   is defined as the average of the precision values achieved at all recall points, i.e.:

$$v \; r \quad 100 \times \frac{1}{k} \sum_{i \; 1} \frac{i}{r_i} \qquad 9$$

The    v r of a set of queries corresponds to the mean of the corresponding query  v r values.

Table 3. Development and test collection sizes.

| Data Set | docs | Avg. words/ doc |
|---|---|---|
| CLIR - $S$ $iss$ $e$ $s$ $genc$ | 62,359 | 225 |
| CLEF - $a$ $Stampa$ | 58,051 | 552 |

### 4.1   e el   e

For the purpose of parameter tuning, development material made available by CLEF was used. The collection consists of the test set used by the 1999 TREC-8 CLIR track and its relevance assessments. The CLIR collection contains topics and documents in four languages: English, German, French, and Italian. The Italian part consists of texts issued by the Swiss News Agency *Schweizerische Depeschenagentur*  from 17-11-1989 until 12-31-1990, and 28 topics, four of which have no corresponding Italian relevant documents[1]. More details about the development collection are provided in Tables 3, 4, and 5.

---

[1]  CLIR topics without Italian relevant documents are 60, 63, 76, and 80.

**Table 4.** Topic statistics of development and test collections. For development and evaluation, queries were generated by using all the available topic fields.

| Data Set (topic s ) | of Words | | | |
|---|---|---|---|---|
| | Min | Ma | Avg. | Total |
| CLIR (54-81) | 41 | 107 | 70.4 | 1690 |
| title | 3 | 8 | 5.1 | 122 |
| description | 8 | 27 | 17.1 | 410 |
| narrative | 25 | 81 | 48.3 | 1158 |
| CLEF (1-40) | 31 | 96 | 60.8 | 2067 |
| title | 3 | 9 | 5.3 | 179 |
| description | 7 | 35 | 15.7 | 532 |
| narrative | 14 | 84 | 39.9 | 1356 |

**Table 5.** Document retrieval statistics of development and test collections.

| Data Set (topic s) | of Relevant Docs | | | |
|---|---|---|---|---|
| | Min | Ma | Avg. | Total |
| CLIR (54-81) | 2 | 15 | 7.1 | 170 |
| CLEF (1-40) | 1 | 42 | 9.9 | 338 |

## 4.2    a i T    i g

Tuning of the parameters in formula  2  was carried out on the development data. Queries were generated by using all the available topic fields. In Figure 1 a plot of the     v  r versus different values of the parameters $k_1$ and $b$ is shown. Finally, the values $k_1$    1.5 and $b$    0.4 were chosen, because they provided consistently good results also with other evaluation measures. The achieved     v  r is 46.1  .

## 4.3    li     ele a   e Fee ba    T  i g

Tuning of BRF parameters    and    was carried out just for the Okapi model. In Figure 2 a plot of the    v  r versus different values of the parameters is shown. Finally, the number of relevant documents        5 and the number of relevant terms      15 were chosen, whose combination gives a    v  r of 49.2  , corresponding to a 6.8    improvement over the first step.

Further work was done to optimize the performance of the first retrieval step. Indeed, performance of the BRF procedure is determined by the precision achieved, by the first retrieval phase, on the very top ranking documents. In particular, an higher resolution for documents and queries was considered by using base forms instead of stems. In Table 6    v  r values are shown by considering different combinations of text preprocessing before and after BRF. In particular, we considered using base forms before and after BRF, using word stems before and after BRF, and using base forms before BRF and stems after BRF. The last combination achieved the largest improvement  8.6    and was adopted for the final system.

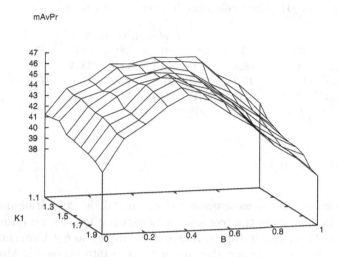

**Fig. 1.** Mean Average Precision versus different settings of Okapi formula's parameters $k_1$ and $b$.

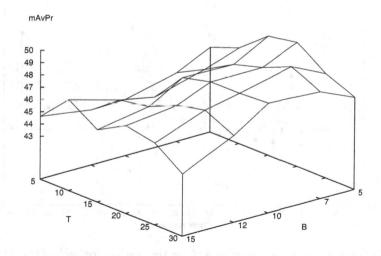

**Fig. 2.** Mean Average Precision versus different settings of blind relevance feedback parameters     and   .

**Table** . Mean Average Precision by using base forms  ba  or word stems  st
before  I  and after  II  blind relevance feedback  with B  5 .

|     |     | of relevant terms T | | | | | |
| --- | --- | --- | --- | --- | --- | --- | --- |
| I | II | 5 | 10 | 15 | 20 | 25 | 30 |
| st | st | 46.4 | 47.3 | 49.2 | 49.6 | 48.3 | 48.5 |
| ba | ba | 46.2 | 47.6 | 47.6 | 47.6 | 47.7 | 47.3 |
| ba | st | 46.7 | 48.7 | 50.0 | 48.5 | 48.6 | 48.6 |

## 4.4      ial    al  a  i

The two presented models were evaluated on the CLEF 2000 Italian monolingual track. The test collection consists of newspaper articles published by *La Stampa*, during 1994, and 40 topics. As six of the topics do not have corresponding documents in the collection they are not taken into account[2]. Also for the evaluation, all the available topic fields were used to generate the queries. More details about the CLEF collection and topics are in Tables 3, 4, and 5.

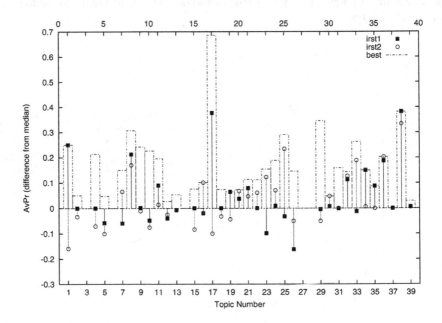

**Fig. 3.** Difference  in average precision  from the median for each of the 34 topics in the CLEF 2000 Italian monolingual track. Moreover, the best  v  r reference is plotted for each topic.

---

[2] CLEF topics without Italian relevant documents are 3, 6, 14, 27, 28, and 40.

Official results of the Okapi and statistical models are reported in Figure 3 with the names `irst` and `irst`, respectively. Figure 3 shows the difference in v r between each run and the median reference provided by the CLEF organization. As a further reference, performance differences between the best result of CLEF and the median are also plotted. The v r of `irst` and `irst` are 49.0 and 47.5, respectively. Both methods score above the median reference v r, which is 44.5. The v r of the median reference was computed by taking the average over the median v r scores.

## Improvements

By looking at Figure 3 it emerges that the Okapi and the statistical model have quite different behaviors. This would suggest that if the two methods rank documents independently, some information about the relevant documents could be gained by integrating the scores of both methods.

In order to compare the rankings of two models $A$ and , the Spearman's rank correlation can be applied. Given a query, let $r$ $A$  and $r$       represent the ranks of document  given by $A$ and , respectively. Hence, Spearman's rank correlation 7 is defined as:

$$1 \quad \frac{6 \sum (\ (\ )) \quad (\ (\ ))^2}{(\ ^2\ 1)} \tag{10}$$

Under the hypothesis of independence between $A$ and ,  has mean 0 and variance 1 $N-1$. On the contrary, in case of perfect correlation the S statistics has value 1.

By taking the average of  over all the queries [3], a rank correlation of 0.4 resulted between `irst` and `irst`.

This results confirms some degree of independence between the two information retrieval models. Hence, a combination of the two models was implemented by just taking the sum of scores. Actually, in order to adjust scale differences, scores of each model were normalized in the range 0, 1 before summation. By using the official relevance assessments of CLEF, a v r of 50.0 was achieved by the combined model.

In Figure 4 and Figure 5 detailed results of the combined model  erge are provided for each query, respectively, against the CLEF references and `irst` and `irst`. It results that the combined model performs better than the median reference on 24 topics of 34, while `irst` and `irst` improved the median v r 16 e 17 times, respectively. Finally, the combined model improves the best reference on two topics 20 and 36.

---

[3] As an appro imation, rankings were computed for the union of the 100 top documents retrieved by each model.

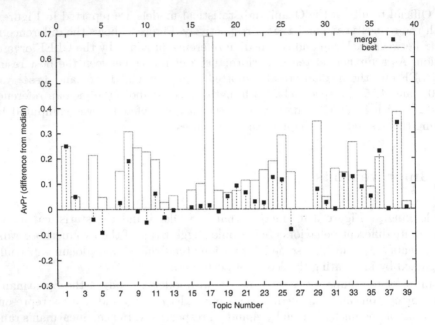

**Fig. 4.** Difference in average precision from the median of the combined model and the best reference of CLEF 2000.

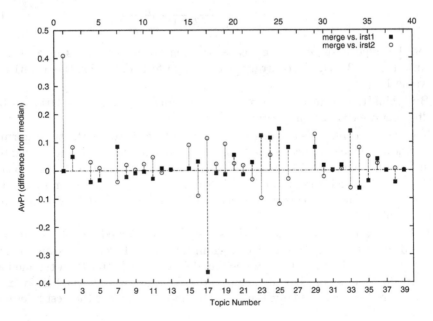

**Fig. 5.** Difference in average precision of the combined model from each single model.

**Table** . Performance of retrieval models on the CLEF 2000 Italian monolingual track.

| Retrieval Model | Official Run | mAv r |
|-----------------|--------------|-------|
| Okapi           | irst         | 49.0  |
| Statistical model | irst       | 47.5  |
| Combined model  | -            | 50.0  |

## Conclusion

This paper presents preliminary research results by ITC-irst in the field of text retrieval. Nevertheless, participation to the CLEF evaluation has been considered important in order to gain experience and feedback about our progress. Future work will be done to improve the statistical retrieval model, develop a statistical blind relevance feedback method, and develop a statistical model for cross-language retrieval.

## References

1. Federico, Marcello, 2000. A system for the retrieval of italian broadcast news. *Speech    mmunicati n*, 33(1-2).
2. Federico, Marcello and Renato De Mori, 1998. Language modelling. In Renato De Mori (ed.), *Sp  en Dial gues   ith    mputers*, chapter 7. London, UK Academy Press.
3. Gretter, Roberto and Gianni Peirone, 1991. A Morphological Analyzer for the Italian Language. ITC-irst Technical Report N. 9108-01.
4. Johnson, S.E., P. Jourlin, K. Spark Jones, and P.C. Woodland, 1999. Spoken document retrieval for TREC-8 at Cambridge University. In  r cee ings    the th  e t  Etrie al    n erence. Gaithersburg, MD.
5. Merialdo, Bernard, 1994. Tagging English te t with a probabilistic model.   m putati nal  inguistics, 20(2) 155 172.
6. Miller, David R. H., Tim Leek, and Richard M. Schwartz, 1998. BBN at TREC-7 Using hidden Markov models for information retrieval. In  r cee ings    the th e t  Etrie al    n erence. Gaithersburg, MD.
7. Mood, Ale ander M., Franklin A. Graybill, and Duane C. Boes, 1974. *Intr  ucti n t the he r    Statistics*. Singapore McGraw-Hill.
8. Ng, Kenney, 1999. A ma imum likelihood ratio information retrieval model. In  r cee ings    the th  e t  Etrie al    n erence. Gaithersburg, MD.
9. Robertson, S. E., S. Walker, S. Jones, M. M. Hancock-Beaulieu, and M. Gatford, 1994. Okapi at TREC-3. In  r cee ings    the r   e t  Etrie al    n erence. Gaithersburg, MD.
10. Sparck Jones, Karen and Peter Willett (eds.), 1997.    ea ings in In  rmati n  etrie al. San Francisco, CA  Morgan Kaufmann.
11. Witten, Ian H. and Timothy C. Bell, 1991. The zero-frequency problem  Estimating the probabilities of novel events in adaptive te t compression. *IEEE   rans  In  rm he r* , IT-37(4) 1085 1094.

**Table** . Example of text preprocessing. The  ag in the last column indicates
if the term survives or not after the stop-terms removal. The two POSs marked
with    are wrong, nevertheless they permit to generate correct base forms and
stems.

| Te t | POS | Base form | Stem | R |
|------|-----|-----------|------|---|
| IL | RS | IL | IL | 0 |
| PRIMO | AS | PRIMO | PRIM | 1 |
| MINISTRO | SS | MINISTRO | MINISTR | 1 |
| LITUANO | AS | LITUANO | LITUAN | 1 |
| , | XPW | , | , | 0 |
| SIGNORA | SS | SIGNORA | SIGNOR | 1 |
| KAZIMIERA | SPN | KAZIMIERA | KAZIMIER | 1 |
| PRUNSKIENE | SPN | PRUNSKIENE | PRUNSKIEN | 1 |
| , | XPW | , | , | 0 |
| HA | VI | AVERE | AVERE | 0 |
| ANCORA | B | ANCORA | ANCORA | 0 |
| UNA | RS | UNA | UNA | 0 |
| VOLTA | SS | VOLTA | VOLT | 1 |
| SOLLECITATO | VSP | SOLLECITARE | SOLLECIT | 1 |
| OGGI | B | OGGI | OGGI | 0 |
| UN | RS | UN | UN | 0 |
| RAPIDO | SS | RAPIDO | RAPID | 1 |
| AVVIO | SS | AVVIO | AVVIO | 1 |
| DEI | EP | DEI | DEI | 0 |
| NEGOZIATI | SP | NEGOZIATO | NEG | 1 |
| CON | E | CON | CON | 0 |
| L | RS | L | L | 0 |
| URSS | YA | URSS | URSS | 1 |
| , | XPW | , | , | 0 |
| RITENENDO | VG | RITENERE | RITEN | 0 |
| FAVOREVOLE | AS | FAVOREVOLE | FAVOR | 1 |
| L | RS | L | L | 0 |
| ATTUALE | AS | ATTUALE | ATTUAL | 1 |
| SITUAZIONE | SS | SITUAZIONE | SIT | 1 |
| NEI | EP | NEI | NEI | 0 |
| RAPPORTI | SP | RAPPORTO | RAPPORT | 1 |
| FRA | E | FRA | FRA | 0 |
| MOSCA | SPN | MOSCA | MOSC | 1 |
| E | C | E | E | 0 |
| VILNIUS | SPN | VILNIUS | VILNIUS | 1 |

# Automatic Language-Specific Stemming
# in Information Retrieval

John A. Goldsmith[1], Derrick Higgins[2], and Svetlana Soglasnova[3]

Department of Linguistics, University of Chicago, 1010 E. 59th St., Chicago IL 60637 USA
[1]ja-goldsmith@uchicago.edu, [2]dchiggin@midway.uchicago.edu,
[3]s-soglasnova@uchicago.edu

**Abstract**. We employ *Automorphology*, an MDL-based algorithm that determines the suffixes present in a language-sample with no prior knowledge of the language in question, and describe our experiments on the usefulness of this approach for Information Retrieval, employing this stemmer in a SMART-based IR engine.

## 1 Introduction

The research discussed in this volume is directed at the special character of Information Retrieval in the multilingual world which is the future of the information age. What special challenges must we be ready for as we prepare our document bases and document spaces for texts in a potentially unlimited number of languages? What additional technology must we develop in preparation for those challenges?[1]

To the extent that current IR methods make assumptions about language which are valid for English but not for many other natural languages, these methods will need to be updated in the light of what we know about natural languages more generally. Our concern in the work reported here is the need for stemming (and related processes) that is fast, accurate, valid for as many languages as possible, and that assumes no human intervention in the process.

We are currently in the process of developing software that accepts unrestricted corpora as input and produces, as its output, a list of stems and affixes found in the corpus, plus additional information about cooccurrence of affix and stem. It does this on the basis of no prior knowledge of the language found in the corpus. When linked to an automatic language identification system, such a system is able to add to our ability to control a large document base which must accept documents in any language—such as the Internet, for example. Although the testing done in the context of the CLEF experiments deals with some of the larger European languages, we see our approach as being most useful when it is used in relation to a database that includes a large number of documents from little-studied languages, because morphologies cannot be produced overnight by humans.

---

[1] We are grateful for help and comments from Abraham Bookstein and Craig Swietlik. This work was supported in part by a grant from the University of Chicago-Argonne National Laboratory.

C. Peters (Ed.): CLEF 2000, LNCS 2069, pp. 273-283, 2001.

Our background is in linguistics and computational linguistics, rather than information retrieval (IR), but in the next section we will survey what we take to be the relevant background information regarding the character of stemming for IR in English and other languages.

# 2 Multilingual Stemming

The use of stemming in information retrieval systems is widespread, though not entirely uncontroversial. It is used primarily for query-stemming and document indexing. (Useful reviews may be found in [2], [11], [13].).

*Stemming* in the narrowest sense is "a process that strips off affixes and leaves you with a stem" [20:132]. A broader procedure is *conflation:* "a computational procedure which identifies word variants and reduces them to a single canonical form" [17:177]. Word variants are usually morphological [2:131] or semantical [23:633]. Stemming in the narrow sense is a type of conflation procedure. Very commonly, though, the term is used not just in that narrow sense, but to refer to lemmatization [12:654], or collapsing [17]. "Stemming" in query expansion refers to that second sense. For our purposes, *stemming* is taken in a broad, but not the broadest, sense. Any algorithm that results in segmenting a word into stem and affixes is a stemming algorithm, or stemmer.

Significant factors for stemming performance in IR include the type of stemming algorithm, evaluation measures of retrieval success, language-(in)dependence, query length, document length, and possibly others [15]. These issues have been addressed in many studies, but no clear comprehensive picture emerges from the literature.

By its very nature, stemming is generally understood to improve recall, but to decrease precision [29:124]. Most research on stemming in IR is on English, a language with a relatively simple morphology. In a study comparing three different stemmers of English, Harman [9] found that losses in precision from stemming outweigh the benefits from increased recall. Krovetz [16] reported results conflicting with what Harman found for the Porter algorithm on the same collection using a very close evaluation measure [15], and in general the view that overall stemming is beneficial for IR is discussed in [28:6], [13], [2], and [17].

## 2.1 Types of Stemmers and Evaluation Measures

Stemmers may be *linguistic*, *automatic* or *mixed*. Linguistic stemmers use a linguist's knowledge of the structure of the language in one way or another, typically by providing manually compiled lists of suffixes, allomorphy rules, and the like. The best known stemmer of this sort is Porter [26], initially developed for English. Porter's approach was extended to French and Italian [30] and Dutch [15]. Automatic stemmers rely on statistical procedures, such as frequency count, n-gram method, or some combination of these. Linguistic stemmers that rely on statistical methods as subsidiary procedures may be called mixed. Such mixed systems include [16] and [23]. Krovetz [16] uses frequency of English derivational endings as the basis for incorporating them into the stemmer, and the initial shared trigram as a preliminary procedure for finding words that are potentially morphologically related. Paice [23] requires the words in a manually compiled semantic identity class to share the initial bigram.

It has been pointed out in the literature that it is difficult to evaluate and compare the performance of different stemming algorithms for IR purposes because the traditional IR evaluation measures are not aimed at highlighting the contribution of stemming to query success [10],[11],[16],[23]. Several studies that compare the effectiveness of different stemming algorithms for IR [9],[10],[16],[17],[23] were conducted on English materials, with Paice [23] and Hull [10] developing new measures of evaluating stemming performance for IR. The results are inconclusive.

Lennon et al. [17] evaluated seven stemming algorithms for English for their usefulness in IR. The automatic algorithms in this study were the RADCOL [19], Hafer-Weiss [8], a similarity stemmer developed by the authors on the basis of Adamson and Boreham's bigram stemmer [1], and a frequency algorithm developed by the authors on the basis of RADCOL. The linguistic stemmers were Lovins and Porter. The Hafer-Weiss algorithm fared much worse than all others. With this exception, they found an undeniable, but very slight improvement on stemmed queried compared to unstemmed ones. They also found "no relationship between the strength of an algorithm and the consequent retrieval effectiveness arising from its use".

Harman [9] tested three linguistic stemmers: Porter, SMART-enhanced Lovins stemmer, and the primitive s-stripping stemmer for IR effectiveness. She found that the minimal s-stemming did very little to improve IR effectiveness, and more rich stemming hurts precision as much as it improves the recall.

Hull [10] evaluated five linguistic stemmers for English: s-remover, an extensively modified Lovins stemmer, Porter stemmer, Xerox English inflectional analyzer and Xerox English derivational analyzer. He proposed a set of alternative evaluation measures aimed to distinguish performance details of various stemmers. In his analysis, stemming is much more helpful on short queries, on which the inflectional stemmer looks slightly less effective, and the Porter stemmer slightly better, than the others; the simple plural removal is less effective than more complex stemmers, but quite competitive when only a small number of documents is examined. His detailed analysis of queries shows how linguistic knowledge may be beneficial for IR in some cases (failure/fail—only the derivational stemmer makes this connection) but not in others (optics/optic—the derivational and inflectional stemmers do not make this connection).

Paice [23] developed a direct measure of evaluating accuracy of a stemmer "by counting the actual understemming and overstemming errors which it commits". He evaluated three stemmers for the English language— Porter, Lovins and Paice/Husk [24]. It was found that his measure provides a good representation of stemmer weight, but no clear comparison of accuracy for stemmers differing greatly in weight. There is no clear relationship between IR measures and Paice's evaluation.

The upshot appears to be that for English, the choice of stemmer type ultimately does not matter much (though cf. [3]). Krovetz [16] found that his inflectional stemmer always helped a little, but the important improvement came from his derivational stemmer. Lennon et al. [17] and Hull [10] found no overall consistent differences between stemming algorithms of various types, though on a particular query one algorithm might outperform other, but never consistently. Most studies note that stemming performance varies on different collections. Paice [22] notes that heavy stemmers might be preferable in situations where high recall is needed, and lighter stemmers where precision is more important.

For languages with morphology richer than that of English, differences between inflectional and derivational morphology—and, consequently, between performance of stemmers oriented towards one or the other—should be greater. Stripping off inflectional morphology should result in more than slight recall improvement without significantly hurting precision. In Russian, for example, the nominal declension has two numbers and six cases (declension paradigms are determined by the gender of the noun and the phonological form of the stem). Dictionary entries are listed in the nominative singular, and one would expect most queries to be entered in the "dictionary form"—the nominative singular. However, actual occurrences of the word appearing in the texts could be more frequent in oblique cases and in the plural. For example, a search for the nominative singular of the word *ruka* 'hand' in Leo Tolstoy's *Anna Karenina* (over 345,000 words) would locate 18 occurrences of the exact match. The stem *ruk*, on the other hand, appears 690 times—in forms inflected for case and number. Most frequent forms are *ruk-u* (accusative singular) and *ruk* (genitive singular, nominative plural). Nozhov [21,22] reports that all Russian IR systems routinely use stemming (linguistic or mixed) even when the degree of morphological recognition is not extremely high.

Kraaij and Pohlmann [15] compared the Porter-style algorithm they implemented for Dutch, another morphologically complex language, with their more linguistically sophisticated derivational and inflectional stemmers. The best performance was achieved by the inflectional stemming combined with a sophisticated version of compound splitting and generating. Applying both derivational and inflectional stemming generally reduces precision too much.

Wexler et al. [30] developed a four-language search engine (French, Italian, German and English) with stemming implemented for each language. For German, a language morphologically close to Dutch, they apparently implemented some inflectional stemming and a dictionary-based compound-breaking algorithm.

A derivational stemmer could produce a theoretically irreproachable result which is not just irrelevant, but harmful for IR purposes, since the stem and its derivates are rarely fully synonymous. The problem is to distinguish derivation that preserves word sense relevant to the query from the derivation that does not. Hull's study gives examples of the derivational stemmer outperforming others on queries like *bank failures* (*failure* converted to *fail*), and *superconductivity* (stem *superconduct* conflated with the one in *superconductors*). Since the relevant documents contained both *failure* and *fail*, and *superconductors* rather than *superconductivity*, the stemming was beneficial. However, in cases like *client-server architecture* (conflate with *serve*) and *Productivity Statistics for the U.S.Economy* (conflate with *produce*) the linguistically correct analysis lowers precision dramatically, since *serve* and *produce* have a much less specific meaning than the query term. The lexical equivalence requirement may be maintained through manually compiled lists ([23], [16] for English), or by word sense disambiguation in a full-blown NLP system ([11] for French).

## 2.2  Automatic Stemmer on More than One Language

The increasingly multi-language character of IR [7] presents a special challenge to language-specific tools. Statistical language processing tools, with their universality and speed, are understandably attractive in this regard. Whether stemming based on such universal methods helps to increase accuracy and scope of IR is a question without a definitive answer yet.

Xu and Croft [31] tested the performance of an automatic trigram stemmer, a "general-purpose language tool" against the performance of Porter stemmer and KStem [16] on English and Spanish corpora for construction of "initial equivalence classes". The initial equivalence classes were further refined with statistical methods that differed for English and Spanish. The "trigram approach" was used as an auxiliary procedure to clean up the equivalence classes for English after the application of the connected component algorithm: A "prefix" in an equivalence class is defined as "an initial character string shared by more than 100 words. Examples are *con*, *com* and *inter*. If the next 3 characters after the common prefix do not match, the similarity metric is set to 0. Thus, the trigram model is at work again, shifted further inside the string. The results were comparable with the performance of the linguistic Porter and KStem stemmers, showing some portability problems due to corpus-specific character of equivalence classes.

## 2.3 Compounds

As virtually all studies on IR in German have documented (and as reported in this year's CLEF results by the West Group; see also [15]), it is crucial to analyze compound words in German, and no doubt in other languages with similar use of compound structures. Use of automatic morphology can be of significant help in this area, as reported in [6] in connection with Automorphology. Because our algorithm identifies stems, it is possible to identify compounds, which take the form Stem-Linker-Stem-Suffix; that is, the first half of the compound need not be a free-standing word.

# 3 Automatic Morphology

The identification of a lexical stem consists of the identification of a string of letters which co-occurs in a large corpus with several distinct suffixes, and typically we will find consistent sets of suffixes that appear with a wide range of stems. This observation serves as one of the bases for our algorithm, whose goal is to establish as wide a range of stems and suffix possibilities as possible, given a corpus from a natural language. The following discussion is a summary of material presented in [4],[5]. Its goal is to establish a method which is language-independent, to the extent possible, and which will provide a useful result despite the lack of any human oversight by a speaker of the language in question.

There are several methods that can be used to establish an initial set of candidate suffixes on a statistical basis, given a sample of an unknown language. One of the simplest is to consider all word-final sequences of six or fewer letters (*schaft* is a German suffix), and to rank their *coherence* in the text on the basis of the formula in (1). In order to deal appropriately with single-letter suffixes, it is preferable to consider all words to end with a special symbol, and to increase the maximum size to seven letters. The frequency of a letter is defined as the number of occurrences of the letter in the text divided by the total number of letters in the text.

$$freq(l_1 l_2 ... l_n) \log \frac{freq(l_1 l_2 ... l_n)}{freq(l_1) freq(l_2) ... freq(l_n)} \tag{1}$$

We select the top 100 suffixes ranked by coherence (1) (these are our *candidate suffixes*), and divide all words into stem and suffix if they end in one or more candidate suffixes. We associate with each such candidate stem the set of suffixes it occurs with, and call each such set a *candidate signature*. We accept only signatures with at least two suffixes, and we establish a threshold number of stems which a signature must be associated with, failing which a signature is eliminated; a suitable threshold is 5.

Various improvements can be made to the results at this point. For example, common combinations of suffixes are certain to be identified as suffixes (e.g., *ments, ings* in English), but they can be identified and their stems reanalyzed. A large part of our work is devoted to determining in an abstract way what kinds of errors our algorithms are likely to create, to determine what they are, and to find ways either to avoid the errors or to undo them after the fact, but always without human intervention. Our current system is heavily based on a Minimum Description Length analysis [26], one consequence of which is that if a language has an unusually high frequency of occurrence of a specific letter in stem-final position, it is likely to be misanalyzed as being part of a suffix; this is the case for *t* in English. When viewed close up, suffix systems tend to have certain kinds of orthographic structures which derive from their history and which can confuse an automatic analyzer; for example, Romance languages contain sets of verbal suffixes which are derived historically from inflected forms of Latin *habere*, which itself has a stem-suffix structure. The suffixes *-ai,-ais, -ait*, etc., of French may in some cases wrongly be analyzed as being *-i,- is,-it*, and attached to a stem that ends in *-a*. We employ the techniques of Minimum Description Length in order to select the analysis of the complete corpus which is most compact overall and which provides the most succinct and accurate analysis of the stem/suffix distribution.

There are two notions at the heart of the MDL approach. The first is that an analysis (here, the morphological analysis of a corpus) must provide a probabilistic measure of the data; this allows us to assign an optimal compressed length to the corpus on the basis of that model, for reasons central to information theory. In this case, each word of the corpus is identified as belonging to one of a relatively limited number of stem groupings defined by the set of suffixes the stem appears with in the corpus; this grouping is called a *signature*, and each signature is associated with an empirical probability. Each word in the corpus is also associated with a stem and a suffix, and these associations are assigned an empirical probability, conditioned by the signature of the word. Each of these three probabilities (signature, stem, suffix) for each word is converted to an optimal compression length (which equals the logarithm of the reciprocal of the probability), and the sum of these optimal compression lengths is the compressed length assigned to the corpus by the morphological model, measured in bits. The shorter that total length, the better the morphology models the corpus.

The second notion at the heart of MDL is that length of the model itself can be measured in bits, and the optimal analysis of the corpus is that for which the sum of the length of the model and the compressed length of the corpus is the smallest. Our algorithm searches the space of possible analyses by considering changes to the signature set, to the affix set, and to the stem/suffix separation, evaluating and accepting each change only if the change brings about a decrease in the total description length of the (corpus + morphology).

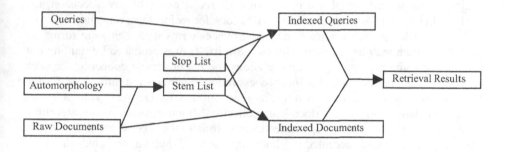

**Fig. 1.** The basic design of the Chicago IR system, using Automorphology to stem terms from queries and documents, and employing standard SMART vector-based retrieval.

## 4 Experiment

The information retrieval engine we used in our CLEF experiments is based on the freely-available SMART system, running under the Linux operating system on a commodity, off-the-shelf PC. We modified the system to incorporate our custom stemmer, which was automatically derived from the corpora for each language. The results of applying our stemmer to the document collections were stored in a file for SMART to consult at the time of indexing the documents and queries. A schematic diagram of our system architecture is presented in Figure 1. Although not represented in Figure 1, statistical compound-breaking using Automorphology was also performed on the German collection before indexing the documents and queries.

The vector-based SMART backbone is a simple retrieval model, treating each document as an unordered "bag" (i.e., retaining only frequency information), and computing document-query similarity by means of the cosine distance between these two vectors. Our expectations regarding results in this experiment were therefore guarded. Our hope is that these runs will help to highlight the strengths and weaknesses of the statistical approach to stemming for IR, and point out directions for us to progress in our development of Automorphology.

## 4.1 Generation of the Stop and Stem Lists

As a stopword list for each language, we created a list of the approximately 300 highest-frequency words in a corpus of the language, and removed by hand any entries that appeared obviously inappropriate. While the resulting stop lists were by no means perfect, the lists were not long enough to create a serious problem with incorrect stopwords blocking the retrieval of documents which ought to be returned. Imperfect stoplists might, however, be blamed for not filtering out as many documents as they should, and thereby reducing our system's precision. Since our results do not seem to display a profile of high recall offset by low precision, the stoplists do not seem to be an area in which to look for major improvements.

The stem file for each language, which associates terms with their stem forms for indexing (a stem may be identical with the term itself), was produced by running our statistical stemming program, Automorphology, on the document collection for each language. The length of time that this process required varied from three days, for the Italian document collection, to as much as fourteen days for German, with its higher mean word length and larger document collection. Improvements in the algorithm since that work has speeded up these times considerably. The stems produced by Automorphology were accepted without any sort of human revision; the only constraint we imposed was that no stem could be shorter than three letters in length. While we do not have a concrete analysis of the conflation classes produced by our stemmer for each language, it seems likely that some of our performance deficit is due to permitting the stemmer to apply so freely.

## 4.2 Indexing

The indexing of documents and queries was done using standard SMART facilities, with the inclusion of the stemming routine described above into the process. Terms in document and query vectors were weighted according to the tf*idf measure which has proven effective in previous IR work. Our group used all of the permissible data fields for retrieval in each of our experiments.

Our performance on the CLEF monolingual runs might have been improved if we had invested more time in preprocessing the document collections. We did not, for example, handle issues related to diacritics at all. Thus, our system would not conflate French *Ecole* with *École*, or German *müssen* with *muessen*. However, such issues were probably not a major factor in determining the system's retrieval accuracy. Another interesting area for future exploration is the relative contribution of statistical stemming and statistical compound-breaking in indexing the German document collection. Intuitively, decompounding is less likely to do harm, since it alters terms which are less likely to be independently searched on anyhow, but it also has less potential for improvement of retrieval accuracy, because compounds are simply less frequent than non-compounds.

## 4.3 Retrieval

Once SMART was configured to use this new stemmer, the retrieval process for each language was straightforward. SMART uses the vector-space model to retrieve the documents most similar to the queries, using the stemmed forms of words as components of the vectors. We returned a ranked list of the top 1000 documents returned for each query, the maximum number allowed.

## 5 Results

Our system was run in monolingual IR tests in the CLEF project in 2000 involving Italian, French, and German. The principal results are presented in Figure 2.

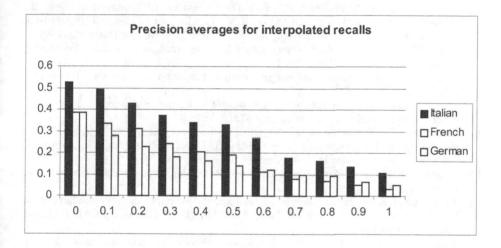

**Fig. 2.** Precision rates for CLEF experiments on French, German, and Italian

## 6 Conclusions

Our work in the area of IR is still in its preliminary stages, and we hesitate to draw any conclusions at this time from the quantitative results described here. If our work has a long-run contribution to make, it is as a component of a larger IR package, and indeed, Oard et al., in this volume, describe experiments employing our automatic morphological analyzer which in some regards go further than our own pre-conceived ideas of its applicability. We are currently engaged in drastically reducing the time and storage needs of the algorithm to permit it to be used with databases of the magnitude typical of IR tasks, and we will continue to test the value of this work for IR tasks.

# References

1.  Adamson, G., Boreham, J.: The use of an association measure based on character structure to identify semantically related pairs of words and document titles. Information Storage and Retrieval 10 (1974) 253-60
2.  Frakes, W.B. Stemming Algorithms. In: Frakes, W.B., Baeza-Yates, R. (eds.): Information Retrieval Data Structures and Algorithms. Prentice Hall, New Jersey (1992) 131-160
3.  Fuller, M, Zobel, J.: Conflation-based Comparison of Stemming Algorithms. In: Proceedings of the Third Australian Document Computing Symposium, Sydney, Australia, August 21, 1998.
4.  Goldsmith, J. Unsupervised learning of natural language morphology.  To appear in *Computational Linguistics*
5.  Goldsmith, J.: Linguistica: An Automatic Morphological Analyzer. In: Boyle, J., Lee, J.-H., Okrent, A. (eds.): CLS 36. Volume 1: The Main Session. Chicago Linguistic Society, Chicago (2001).
6.  Goldsmith, J., Reutter, T.: Automatic Collection and Analysis of German Compounds. In: Busa, F., Mani, I., Saint-Dizier, P. (eds.): The Computational Treatment of Nominals: Proceedings of the Workshop  COLING-ACL '98. COLING-ACL, Montreal (1999) 61-69.
7.  Grefenstette, G. (ed.): Cross-Language Information Retrieval. Kluwer, Dordrecht (1999)
8.  Hafer, M., Weiss, S: . Word segmentation by letter successor varieties. Information Storage and Retrieval 10 (1974) 371-85
9.  Harman, D. How effective is suffixing? Journal of the American Society for Information Science 42 (1991) 7-15
10. Hull, D. Stemming algorithms - A case study for detailed evaluation. Journal of the American Society for Information Science 47 (1996) 70-84
11. Jacquemin, C., Tsoukermann, E. NLP for term variant extraction: synergy between morphology, lexicon, and syntax. In: Strzalkowski, T. (ed.) Natural Language Information Retrieval. Kluwer, Dordrecht (1999) 25-74
12. Jurafsky, D, Martin, J: Speech and Language Processing. Prentice Hall, Upper Saddle River NJ (2000)
13. Koskenniemi, K. Finite-state morphology and information retrieval. In: Proceedings of the ECAI-96 Workshop on Extended Finite State Models of Language ECAI, Budapest, Hungary (1996) 42-5
14. Kowalski, G. Information Retrieval Systems: Theory and Implementation. Kluwer, Dordrecht (1997)
15. Kraaij, W., Pohlmann, R. Viewing stemming as recall enhancement. In: Proceedings, 19th Annual International ACM SIGIR Conference on Research and Development in Information Retrieval (SIGIR '96) Zurich (1996) 40-48.
16. Krovetz, R. Viewing morphology as an inference process. In: Proceedings of the 19th Annual International ACM SIGIR Conference on Research and Development in Information Retrieval (1993) 191-202
17. Lennon, M., Pierce, D.C., Willett, P. An evaluation of some conflation algorithms. Journal of Information Science 3 (1981) 177-183
18. Lovins, J.B. Development of a stemming algorithm. Mechanical Translation and Computational Linguistics 11 (1968) 22-31.
19. Lowe, T. C., Roberts, D.C., Kurtz, P. Additional text processing for on-line retrieval. (The RADCOL System). Tech.Rep. RADC-TR-73-337 (1973)
20. Manning, C., Schütze, H: Foundations of Statistical Natural Language Processing. MIT Press, Cambridge MA (1999)
21. Nozhov, Igor'. Prikladnoi morfologicheskii analiz [Applied morphological analysis].In: Pravovaia Informatika *1998,* v.4. Moscow (1998)

22. Nozhov, Igor'. Grafematicheskii i morfologicheskii moduli [Graphemic and morphological modules].In: Pravovaia Informatika. 1999, v.5. Moscow (1999)
23. Paice, C.D. Method for evaluation of stemming algorithms based on error counting. Journal of the American Society for Information Science 47 (8) (1996) 632-49
24. Paice, C.D. Another stemmer. SIGIR Forum, 24 (1990) 56-61
25. Popovič, M., Willett, P. The effectiveness of stemming for natural-language access to Slovene textual data. Journal of the American Society for Information Science, 43(5) (1992) 384-390
26. Porter, M. F. An algorithm for suffix stripping. Program 14 (1980) 130-7.
27. Rissanen, J. Stochastic Complexity in Statistical Inquiry. World Scientific Publishing, Singapore, Teaneck NJ (1989)
28. Sparck Jones, K. What is the role of NLP in text retrieval? In: Strzalkowski, T (ed.) Natural Language Information Retrieval. Kluwer, Dordrecht (1999) 1-24
29. Strzalkowski, T. et al. Evaluating Natural Language Processing Techniques in Information Retrieval: A TREC Perspective. In: Strzalkowski, T.(ed.) Natural Language Information Retrieval. Kluwer, Dordrecht (1999)
30. Wexler, M., Sheridan, P., Schäble, P. Multi-language text indexing for Internet retrieval.In: Proceedings of the 5th RIAO Conference on Computer-Assisted Information Searching on the Internet (1997)
31. Xu, J., Croft, W. Corpus-Based Stemming using Co-occurrence of Word Variants. In: ACM Transactions on Information Systems, 16(1) (1995) 61-81.

# Appendix A   Run Statistics

This appendix contains the evaluation results for the CLEF 2000 runs. The initial pages list each of the runs identified by the run tags that were officially submitted. Associated with each tag is the organization that produced the run, the type of task, the language used for the topic, the type of query automatic or manual , the topic fields used to construct the query, and the run status used for pooling or not . The run list is followed by a description of the evaluation measures used for the evaluation. The remainder of the appendix contains the evaluation results themselves, in the order given in the run list.

The appendix is based on material provided to us by NIST  Donna Harman and Ellen Voorhees .

C. Peters (Ed.): CLEF 2000, LNCS 2069, pp. 2 5–3 7, 2001.

## Characteristics of Submitted Runs

| Runtag | Institution | Task | Top. Lang. | Type | Top. Fields | Judged? |
|--------|-------------|------|------------|------|-------------|---------|
| aplbifra | Johns Hopkins U/APL | bi | F | auto | TDN | Y |
| aplbifrb | Johns Hopkins U/APL | bi | F | auto | TDN | N |
| aplbifrc | Johns Hopkins U/APL | bi | F | auto | TDN | N |
| aplbispa | Johns Hopkins U/APL | bi | Sp | auto | TDN | N |
| aplmofr | Johns Hopkins U/APL | mono | F | auto | TDN | Y |
| aplmoge | Johns Hopkins U/APL | mono | G | auto | TDN | Y |
| aplmoit | Johns Hopkins U/APL | mono | I | auto | TDN | Y |
| aplmua | Johns Hopkins U/APL | multi | E | auto | TDN | Y |
| aplmub | Johns Hopkins U/APL | multi | E | auto | TDN | N |
| backoff4 | U Maryland | multi | E | manual | TDN | Y |
| backoff4Ling | U Maryland | multi | E | manual | TDN | N |
| BKGREGA1 | UC Berkeley | girt | E | auto | TDN | Y |
| BKGREGA2 | UC Berkeley | girt | E | auto | TDN | Y |
| BKGREGA3 | UC Berkeley | girt | E | auto | TDN | Y |
| BKGREGA4 | UC Berkeley | girt | E | auto | TDN | Y |
| BKMOFFA2 | UC Berkeley | mono | F | auto | TDN | Y |
| BKMOGGA1 | UC Berkeley | mono | G | auto | TDN | Y |
| BKMOGGM1 | UC Berkeley | mono | G | manual | TDN | Y |
| BKMOIIA3 | UC Berkeley | mono | I | auto | TDN | Y |
| BKMUEAA1 | UC Berkeley | multi | E | auto | TDN | Y |
| BKMUEAA2 | UC Berkeley | multi | E | auto | TDN | N |
| BKMUGAA2 | UC Berkeley | multi | G | auto | TDN | N |
| BKMUGAM1 | UC Berkeley | multi | G | manual | TDN | N |
| BLBabel | U Dortmund | bi | G | auto | TDN | Y |
| BLLeo | U Dortmund | bi | G | auto | TDN | N |
| CWI0000 | CWI | mono | G | auto | TD | Y |
| CWI0001 | CWI | mono | I | auto | TD | Y |
| CWI0002 | CWI | mono | F | auto | TD | Y |
| CWI0003 | CWI | bi | D | auto | TD | Y |
| CWI0004 | CWI | multi | D | auto | TD | Y |
| EITCLEFFF | Eurospider | mono | F | auto | TDN | Y |
| EITCLEFGG | Eurospider | mono | G | auto | TDN | Y |
| EITCLEFII | Eurospider | mono | I | auto | TDN | Y |
| EITCLEFM1 | Eurospider | multi | G | auto | TDN | N |
| EITCLEFM2 | Eurospider | multi | G | auto | TDN | N |
| EITCLEFM3 | Eurospider | multi | G | auto | TDN | Y |
| finstr | U Tampere | bi | Fi | auto | TD | N |
| FrenchUCWLP | U Chicago | mono | F | auto | TDN | Y |
| GermanUCWLP | U Chicago | mono | G | auto | TDN | Y |
| gerstr | U Tampere | bi | G | auto | TD | N |
| geruns | U Tampere | bi | G | auto | TD | N |
| GIRTBabel | U Dortmund | girt | E | auto | TDN | Y |
| GIRTML | U Dortmund | girt | G | auto | TDN | Y |
| glalong | U Glasgow | multi | E | auto | TDN | N |
| glatitle | U Glasgow | multi | E | auto | T | Y |
| iaiphsrun | IAI | multi | E/Sw | auto | T | Y |
| irit1bfr2en | Irit | bi | F | auto | TDN | Y |
| irit1men2a | Irit | multi | E | auto | TDN | Y |
| irit2bfr2en | Irit | bi | F | auto | TDN | N |
| irit2men2a | Irit | multi | E | auto | TDN | N |
| iritmonofr | Irit | mono | F | auto | TDN | Y |
| iritmonoge | Irit | mono | G | auto | TDN | Y |
| iritmonoit | Irit | mono | I | auto | TDN | Y |
| irst1 | ITC-irst | mono | I | auto | TDN | Y |
| irst2 | ITC-irst | mono | I | auto | TDN | Y |
| ItalianUCWLP | U Chicago | mono | I | auto | TDN | Y |
| MLgerman | U Dortmund | mono | G | auto | TDN | Y |

| nmsuK | New Mexico SU | multi | E | manual | T | Y |
|---|---|---|---|---|---|---|
| nmsuS | New Mexico SU | multi | E | auto | T | N |
| prueba0 | U Salamanca | bi | Sp | auto | TDN | Y |
| ralie2allh1 | U Montreal, RALI | multi | E | auto | TDN | Y |
| ralie2allh2 | U Montreal, RALI | multi | E | auto | TDN | N |
| ralie2allmix | U Montreal, RALI | multi | E | auto | TDN | N |
| ralie2allwac | U Montreal, RALI | multi | E | auto | TDN | N |
| ralif2emixf | U Montreal, RALI | bi | F | auto | TDN | Y |
| ralif2ewacf | U Montreal, RALI | bi | F | auto | TDN | N |
| ralif2f | U Montreal, RALI | mono | F | auto | TDN | Y |
| ralif2ff | U Montreal, RALI | mono | F | auto | TDN | Y |
| ralig2ewacf | U Montreal, RALI | bi | G | auto | TDN | N |
| ralig2gf | U Montreal, RALI | mono | G | auto | TDN | Y |
| ralii2ewacf | U Montreal, RALI | bi | I | auto | TDN | N |
| ralii2if | U Montreal, RALI | mono | I | auto | TDN | Y |
| shefbi | U Sheffield | bi | G | auto | TDN | N |
| shefes | U Sheffield | bi | G | auto | TDN | N |
| shefnl | U Sheffield | bi | G | auto | TDN | N |
| sheftri | U Sheffield | bi | G | auto | TDN | Y |
| swestr | U Tampere | bi | Sw | auto | TD | Y |
| SYRD2E | Syracuse U | bi | D | auto | DN | Y |
| tnoutdd2 | TNO/U Twente | mono | G | auto | TDN | Y |
| tnoutex1 | TNO/U Twente | multi | E | auto | TDN | N |
| tnoutex2 | TNO/U Twente | multi | E | auto | TDN | Y |
| tnoutex3 | TNO/U Twente | multi | E | auto | TDN | N |
| tnoutff2 | TNO/U Twente | mono | F | auto | TDN | Y |
| tnoutii2 | TNO/U Twente | mono | I | auto | TDN | Y |
| tnoutne1 | TNO/U Twente | bi | D | auto | TDN | N |
| tnoutne2 | TNO/U Twente | bi | D | auto | TDN | N |
| tnoutne3 | TNO/U Twente | bi | D | auto | TDN | N |
| tnoutne4 | TNO/U Twente | bi | D | auto | TD | Y |
| tnoutnx1 | TNO/U Twente | multi | D | auto | TDN | N |
| unstemmed | U Maryland | multi | E | manual | TDN | N |
| WESTff | West Group | mono | F | auto | TDN | Y |
| WESTgg1 | West Group | mono | G | auto | TDN | Y |
| WESTgg2 | West Group | mono | G | auto | TDN | Y |
| XRCEG0 | Xerox XRCE | mono | G | auto | TDN | Y |
| XRCEGIRT0 | Xerox XRCE | girt | G | auto | TDN | Y |

---

**Explanations:**

| | |
|---|---|
| Task: | multi = multilingual, bi = bilingual, mono = monolingual, girt = GIRT |
| Topic Language: | E = English, F = French, G = German, I = Italian, D = Dutch, Sp = Spanish, Sw = Swedish, Fi = Finnish |
| Type: | auto = automatic (no manual intervention), manual = manual intervention |
| Topic Fields: | T = title, D = description, N = narrative |
| Judged?: | Y = run was used for pooling, N = run was not used for pooling<br>The documents in the pool were judged by human assessors. |

# Evaluation Techniques and Measures

## 1  Methodology

The CLEF evaluation uses procedures very similar to those employed in the
ad hoc  task of the TREC conferences. Such  ad hoc  topics are similar to
what a researcher might for example use in a library environment. This implies
that the input topic has no training material such as relevance judgments to
aid in the construction of the input query. Systems ran CLEF topics against all
documents in the languages relevant for the task they were performing  multilingual, bilingual or monolingual or GIRT .

## 2  Evaluation Measures

1. Recall
   A measure of the ability of a system to present all relevant items.

$$\text{recall} \quad \frac{\text{number of relevant items retrieved}}{\text{number of relevant items in collection}}$$

2. Precision.
   A measure of the ability of a system to present only relevant items.

$$\text{precision} \quad \frac{\text{number of relevant items retrieved}}{\text{total number of items retrieved}}$$

Precision and recall are set-based measures. That is, they evaluate the quality
of an unordered set of retrieved documents. To evaluate ranked lists, precision
can be plotted against recall after each retrieved document as shown in the
example below. To facilitate computing average performance over a set of topics,
each with a different number of relevant documents, individual topic precision
values are interpolated to a set of standard recall levels  0 to 1 in increments of
.1 . The particular rule used to interpolate precision at standard recall level $i$ is
to use the maximum precision obtained for the topic for any actual recall level
greater than or equal to $i$. Note that while precision is not defined at a recall of
0.0, this interpolation rule does define an interpolated value for recall level 0.0. In
the example, the actual precision values are plotted with circles  and connected
by a solid line  and the interpolated precision is shown with the dashed line.
Example: Assume a document collection has 20 documents, four of which are
relevant to topic . Further assume a retrieval system ranks the relevant documents first, second, fourth, and fifteenth. The exact recall points are 0.25, 0.5,
0.75, and 1.0. Using the interpolation rule, the interpolated precision for all standard recall levels up to .5 is 1, the interpolated precision for recall levels .6 and
.7 is .75, and the interpolated precision for recall levels .8 or greater is .27.

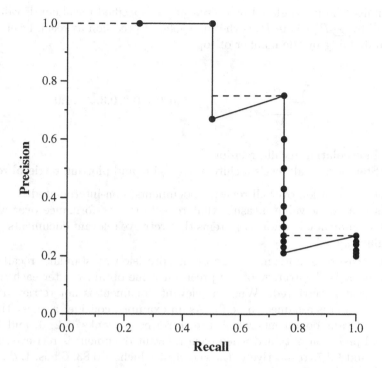

## System Results Description

The evaluation results are given in the main body of the appendix: one page per
run. Each page is comprised of a table and two graphs. These are explained in
the following.

### 3.1   T e Table

Figures are generated by *trec_eval* courtesy of Chris Buckley using the SMART
methodology. The table has two columns.

1. Statistics
   The right column contains some general statistics about the run: the number
   of documents that were submitted  usually number of topics times 1000 , the
   total number of relevant documents for the given task, and the actual number
   of relevant documents retrieved by that run.
2. Interpolated Recall - Precision Averages Table.
   Figures are also located in the right column, below the general statistics.
   The precision averages at 11 standard recall levels are used to compare the
   performance of different systems and as the input for plotting the recall-
   precision graph  see below . Each recall-precision average is computed by

summing the interpolated precisions at the specified recall cutoff value  denoted by $\sum P$  where $P$  is the interpolated precision at recall level      and
then dividing by the number of topics.

$$\frac{\sum\limits_{i\ 1} P}{N\ M} \qquad 0.0, 0.1, 0.2, 0.3, \ldots, 1.0$$

 – Interpolating recall-precision
   Standard recall levels facilitate averaging and plotting retrieval results.

3. Average precision over all relevant documents, non-interpolated
   This is a single-value measure that re ects the performance over all relevant documents. It rewards systems that retrieve relevant documents quickly
    highly ranked .
   The measure is not an average of the precision at standard recall levels.
   Rather, it is the average of the precision value obtained after each relevant
   document is retrieved.  When a relevant document is not retrieved at all,
   its precision is assumed to be 0.  As an example, consider a query that has
   four relevant documents which are retrieved at ranks 1, 2, 4, and 7. The
   actual precision obtained when each relevant document is retrieved is 1, 1,
   0.75, and 0.57, respectively, the mean of which is 0.83. Thus, the average
   precision over all relevant documents for this query is 0.83.
   The left column additionally gives the average precision for individual queries.

4. Precision Table
   At the bottom of the right column,  document level averages  are reported.
   - Precision at 9 document cutoff values. The precision computed after a
   given number of documents has been retrieved re ects the actual measured
   system performance as a user might see it. Each document precision average
   is computed by summing the precisions at the specified document cutoff
   value and dividing by the number of topics  40 .

5. R-Precision
   R-Precision is the precision after R documents have been retrieved, where
   R is the number of relevant documents for the topic. It de-emphasizes the
   exact ranking of the retrieved relevant documents, which can be particularly
   useful in TREC where there are large numbers of relevant documents.
   The average R-Precision for a run is computed by taking the mean of the
   R-Precisions of the individual topics in the run. For example, assume a run
   consists of two topics, one with 50 relevant documents and another with 10
   relevant documents. If the retrieval system returns 17 relevant documents
   in the top 50 documents for the first topic, and 7 relevant documents in the
   top 10 for the second topic, then the run's R-Precision would be $\frac{\frac{17}{50}\ \frac{7}{10}}{2}$ or
   0.52.

**3.2** a

1. Recall-Precision Graph

   Figure 1 is a sample Recall-Precision Graph.

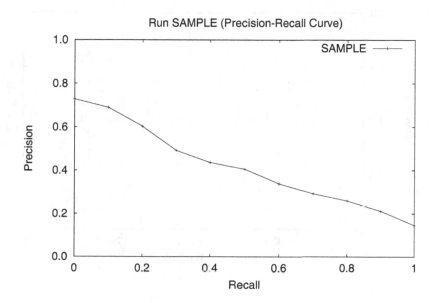

**Fig. 1.** Sample Recall-Precision Graph.

The Recall-Precision Graph is created using the 11 cutoff values from the Recall Level Precision Averages. Typically these graphs slope downward from left to right, enforcing the notion that as more relevant documents are retrieved recall increases , more nonrelevant documents are retrieved preci- sion decreases .

This graph is the most commonly used method for comparing systems. The plots of different runs can be superimposed on the same graph to determine which run is superior. Curves closest to the upper right-hand corner of the graph where recall and precision are maximized indicate the best perfor- mance. Comparisons are best made in three different recall ranges: 0 to 0.2, 0.2 to 0.8, and 0.8 to 1. These ranges characterize high precision, middle recall, and high recall performance, respectively.

2. Average Precision Histogram.
   Figure 2 is a sample Average Precision Histogram.

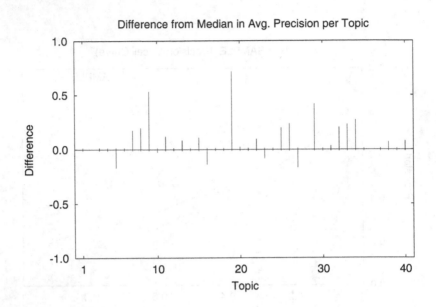

**Fig. 2.** Sample Average Precision Histogram.

The Average Precision Histogram measures the average precision of a run
on each topic  see also left column of the statistics table  against the median average precision of all corresponding runs on that topic. This graph is
intended to give insight into the performance of individual systems and the
types of topics that they handle well.

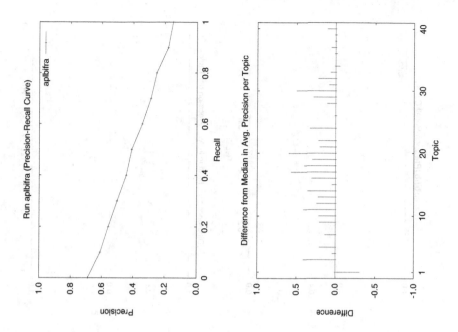

Run aplbifra (Precision-Recall Curve)

aplbifra

Precision

Recall

Difference from Median in Avg. Precision per Topic

Difference

Topic

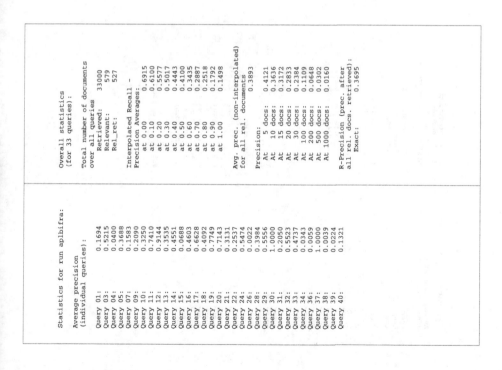

Statistics for run aplbifra:

Average precision
(individual queries):

| | |
|---|---|
| Query 01: | 0.1694 |
| Query 03: | 0.5215 |
| Query 04: | 0.0400 |
| Query 05: | 0.3688 |
| Query 07: | 0.1583 |
| Query 09: | 0.2090 |
| Query 10: | 0.3250 |
| Query 11: | 0.7410 |
| Query 12: | 0.9144 |
| Query 13: | 0.3535 |
| Query 14: | 0.4551 |
| Query 15: | 0.0688 |
| Query 16: | 0.4603 |
| Query 17: | 0.6628 |
| Query 18: | 0.4092 |
| Query 19: | 0.7749 |
| Query 20: | 0.7143 |
| Query 21: | 0.3131 |
| Query 22: | 0.2537 |
| Query 24: | 0.5474 |
| Query 26: | 0.0022 |
| Query 28: | 0.3984 |
| Query 29: | 0.5556 |
| Query 30: | 1.0000 |
| Query 31: | 0.2050 |
| Query 32: | 0.5523 |
| Query 33: | 0.4737 |
| Query 34: | 0.0343 |
| Query 36: | 0.0059 |
| Query 37: | 1.0000 |
| Query 38: | 0.0039 |
| Query 39: | 0.0224 |
| Query 40: | 0.1321 |

Overall statistics
(for 33 queries):

Total number of documents
over all queries:

| | |
|---|---|
| Retrieved: | 33000 |
| Relevant: | 579 |
| Rel_ret: | 527 |

Interpolated Recall -
Precision Averages:

| | |
|---|---|
| at 0.00 | 0.6915 |
| at 0.10 | 0.6100 |
| at 0.20 | 0.5577 |
| at 0.30 | 0.5017 |
| at 0.40 | 0.4443 |
| at 0.50 | 0.4100 |
| at 0.60 | 0.3435 |
| at 0.70 | 0.2887 |
| at 0.80 | 0.2518 |
| at 0.90 | 0.1792 |
| at 1.00 | 0.1498 |

Avg. prec. (non-interpolated)
for all rel. documents
0.3893

Precision:

| | | |
|---|---|---|
| At | 5 docs: | 0.4121 |
| At | 10 docs: | 0.3636 |
| At | 15 docs: | 0.3172 |
| At | 20 docs: | 0.2833 |
| At | 30 docs: | 0.2384 |
| At | 100 docs: | 0.1109 |
| At | 200 docs: | 0.0648 |
| At | 500 docs: | 0.0302 |
| At | 1000 docs: | 0.0160 |

R-Precision (prec. after
all rel. docs. retrieved):
Exact:   0.3695

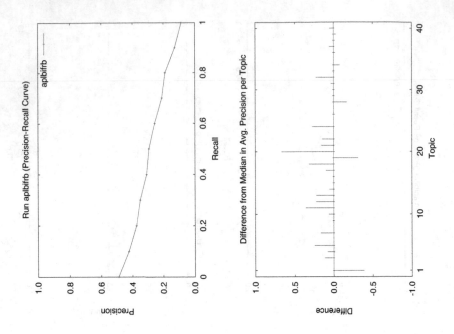

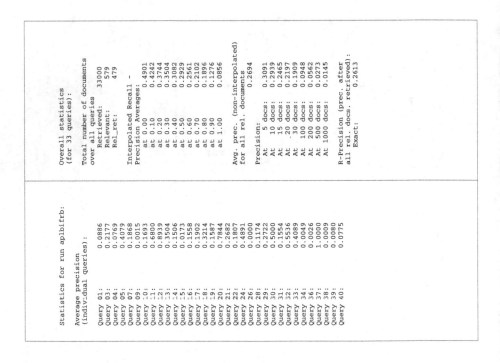

Statistics for run aplbifrb:

Average precision
(individual queries):

| | |
|---|---|
| Query 01: | 0.0886 |
| Query 03: | 0.2177 |
| Query 04: | 0.0769 |
| Query 05: | 0.4079 |
| Query 07: | 0.1868 |
| Query 09: | 0.0015 |
| Query 10: | 0.1693 |
| Query 11: | 0.6800 |
| Query 12: | 0.8939 |
| Query 13: | 0.3504 |
| Query 14: | 0.1506 |
| Query 15: | 0.0173 |
| Query 16: | 0.1558 |
| Query 17: | 0.1902 |
| Query 18: | 0.3214 |
| Query 19: | 0.1587 |
| Query 20: | 0.7844 |
| Query 21: | 0.2682 |
| Query 22: | 0.1807 |
| Query 24: | 0.4891 |
| Query 26: | 0.0000 |
| Query 28: | 0.1174 |
| Query 29: | 0.2722 |
| Query 30: | 0.5000 |
| Query 31: | 0.1554 |
| Query 32: | 0.5536 |
| Query 33: | 0.4089 |
| Query 34: | 0.0049 |
| Query 36: | 0.0026 |
| Query 37: | 1.0000 |
| Query 38: | 0.0009 |
| Query 39: | 0.0080 |
| Query 40: | 0.0775 |

Overall statistics
(for 33 queries):

Total number of documents
over all queries:

| | |
|---|---|
| Retrieved: | 33000 |
| Relevant: | 579 |
| Rel_ret: | 479 |

Interpolated Recall -
Precision Averages:

| | |
|---|---|
| at 0.00 | 0.4901 |
| at 0.10 | 0.4242 |
| at 0.20 | 0.3744 |
| at 0.30 | 0.3504 |
| at 0.40 | 0.3082 |
| at 0.50 | 0.2929 |
| at 0.60 | 0.2561 |
| at 0.70 | 0.2102 |
| at 0.80 | 0.1896 |
| at 0.90 | 0.1276 |
| at 1.00 | 0.0856 |

Avg. prec. (non-interpolated)
for all rel. documents          0.2694

Precision:

| | |
|---|---|
| At   5 docs: | 0.3091 |
| At  10 docs: | 0.2939 |
| At  15 docs: | 0.2465 |
| At  20 docs: | 0.2197 |
| At  30 docs: | 0.1909 |
| At 100 docs: | 0.0948 |
| At 200 docs: | 0.0562 |
| At 500 docs: | 0.0273 |
| At 1000 docs: | 0.0145 |

R-Precision (prec. after
all rel.docs. retrieved):

Exact:          0.2613

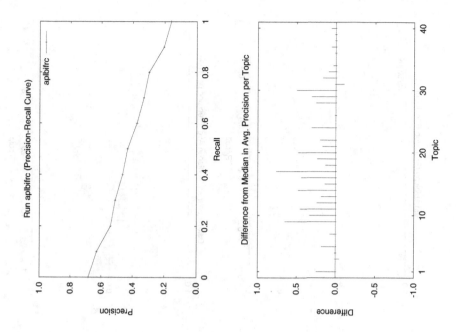

Run aplbifrc (Precision-Recall Curve)

Difference from Median in Avg. Precision per Topic

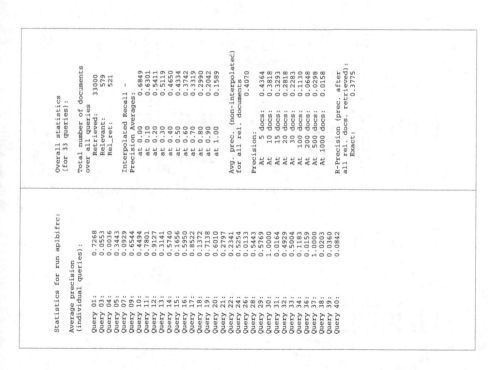

Statistics for run aplbifrc:

Average precision
(individual queries):

| | |
|---|---|
| Query 01: | 0.7268 |
| Query 03: | 0.0553 |
| Query 04: | 0.0036 |
| Query 05: | 0.3443 |
| Query 07: | 0.0929 |
| Query 09: | 0.6544 |
| Query 10: | 0.4494 |
| Query 11: | 0.7801 |
| Query 12: | 0.9127 |
| Query 13: | 0.3141 |
| Query 14: | 0.5740 |
| Query 15: | 0.1656 |
| Query 16: | 0.5950 |
| Query 17: | 0.8522 |
| Query 18: | 0.1372 |
| Query 19: | 0.7138 |
| Query 20: | 0.6010 |
| Query 21: | 0.2797 |
| Query 22: | 0.2341 |
| Query 24: | 0.5254 |
| Query 26: | 0.0133 |
| Query 28: | 0.5443 |
| Query 29: | 0.5769 |
| Query 30: | 1.0000 |
| Query 31: | 0.0164 |
| Query 32: | 0.4929 |
| Query 33: | 0.5004 |
| Query 34: | 0.1183 |
| Query 36: | 0.0159 |
| Query 37: | 1.0000 |
| Query 38: | 0.0203 |
| Query 39: | 0.0360 |
| Query 40: | 0.0842 |

Overall statistics
(for 33 queries):

Total number of documents
over all queries:
| | |
|---|---|
| Retrieved: | 33000 |
| Relevant: | 579 |
| Rel_ret: | 521 |

Interpolated Recall  -
Precision Averages:
| | |
|---|---|
| at 0.00 | 0.6849 |
| at 0.10 | 0.6301 |
| at 0.20 | 0.5411 |
| at 0.30 | 0.5119 |
| at 0.40 | 0.4650 |
| at 0.50 | 0.4334 |
| at 0.60 | 0.3742 |
| at 0.70 | 0.3319 |
| at 0.80 | 0.2990 |
| at 0.90 | 0.2042 |
| at 1.00 | 0.1589 |

Avg. prec. (non-interpolated)
for all rel. documents
              0.4070

Precision:
| | | |
|---|---|---|
| At | 5 docs: | 0.4364 |
| At | 10 docs: | 0.3818 |
| At | 15 docs: | 0.3293 |
| At | 20 docs: | 0.2818 |
| At | 30 docs: | 0.2283 |
| At | 100 docs: | 0.1130 |
| At | 200 docs: | 0.0648 |
| At | 500 docs: | 0.0298 |
| At | 1000 docs: | 0.0158 |

R-Precision (prec. after
all rel. docs. retrieved):
| | |
|---|---|
| Exact: | 0.3775 |

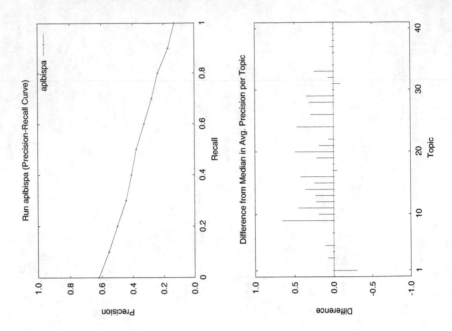

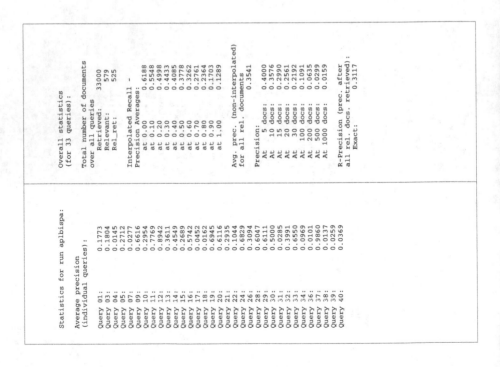

Statistics for run aplbispa:

Average precision
(individual queries):

| | |
|---|---|
| Query 01: | 0.1773 |
| Query 03: | 0.1804 |
| Query 04: | 0.0145 |
| Query 05: | 0.2712 |
| Query 07: | 0.0277 |
| Query 09: | 0.6616 |
| Query 10: | 0.2954 |
| Query 11: | 0.7769 |
| Query 12: | 0.8942 |
| Query 13: | 0.3611 |
| Query 14: | 0.4549 |
| Query 15: | 0.2689 |
| Query 16: | 0.5742 |
| Query 17: | 0.0452 |
| Query 18: | 0.0162 |
| Query 19: | 0.6945 |
| Query 20: | 0.6116 |
| Query 21: | 0.2935 |
| Query 22: | 0.1044 |
| Query 24: | 0.6829 |
| Query 26: | 0.3094 |
| Query 28: | 0.6047 |
| Query 29: | 0.6111 |
| Query 30: | 0.5000 |
| Query 31: | 0.0285 |
| Query 32: | 0.3991 |
| Query 33: | 0.6550 |
| Query 34: | 0.0969 |
| Query 36: | 0.0101 |
| Query 37: | 0.9860 |
| Query 38: | 0.0137 |
| Query 39: | 0.0259 |
| Query 40: | 0.0369 |

Overall statistics
(for 33 queries):

Total number of documents
over all queries
| | |
|---|---|
| Retrieved: | 33000 |
| Relevant: | 579 |
| Rel_ret: | 525 |

Interpolated Recall -
Precision Averages:
| | |
|---|---|
| at 0.00 | 0.6188 |
| at 0.10 | 0.5548 |
| at 0.20 | 0.4998 |
| at 0.30 | 0.4433 |
| at 0.40 | 0.4085 |
| at 0.50 | 0.3778 |
| at 0.60 | 0.3262 |
| at 0.70 | 0.2761 |
| at 0.80 | 0.2364 |
| at 0.90 | 0.1703 |
| at 1.00 | 0.1289 |

Avg. prec. (non-interpolated)
for all rel. documents
0.3541

Precision:
| | | |
|---|---|---|
| At | 5 docs: | 0.4000 |
| At | 10 docs: | 0.3576 |
| At | 15 docs: | 0.2990 |
| At | 20 docs: | 0.2561 |
| At | 30 docs: | 0.2192 |
| At | 100 docs: | 0.1091 |
| At | 200 docs: | 0.0635 |
| At | 500 docs: | 0.0299 |
| At | 1000 docs: | 0.0159 |

R-Precision (prec. after
all rel.docs. retrieved):
Exact:    0.3117

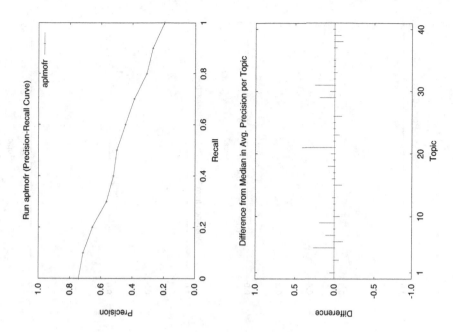

Run aplmofr (Precision-Recall Curve)

Difference from Median in Avg. Precision per Topic

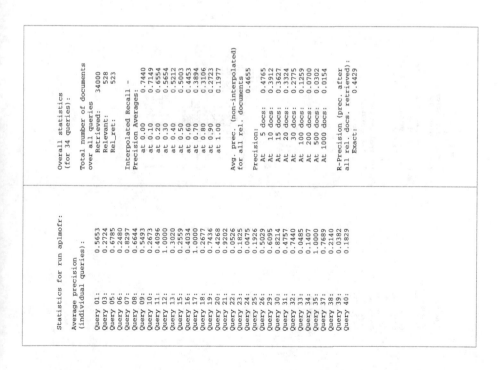

Statistics for run aplmofr:

Average precision
(individual queries):

| | |
|---|---|
| Query 01: | 0.5653 |
| Query 03: | 0.2724 |
| Query 05: | 0.6785 |
| Query 06: | 0.2480 |
| Query 07: | 0.8297 |
| Query 08: | 0.6644 |
| Query 09: | 0.5493 |
| Query 10: | 0.2673 |
| Query 11: | 0.4096 |
| Query 12: | 1.0000 |
| Query 13: | 0.3020 |
| Query 15: | 0.2559 |
| Query 16: | 0.4034 |
| Query 17: | 1.0000 |
| Query 18: | 0.2677 |
| Query 19: | 0.7436 |
| Query 20: | 0.4268 |
| Query 21: | 0.9202 |
| Query 22: | 0.0526 |
| Query 23: | 0.1825 |
| Query 24: | 0.0475 |
| Query 25: | 0.1926 |
| Query 26: | 0.5029 |
| Query 29: | 0.6095 |
| Query 30: | 0.8214 |
| Query 31: | 0.4757 |
| Query 32: | 0.7440 |
| Query 33: | 0.0485 |
| Query 34: | 0.1407 |
| Query 35: | 1.0000 |
| Query 37: | 0.7689 |
| Query 38: | 0.2140 |
| Query 39: | 0.0382 |
| Query 40: | 0.1829 |

Overall statistics
(for 34 queries):

Total number of documents
over all queries:
Retrieved: 34000
Relevant: 528
Rel_ret: 523

Interpolated Recall -
Precision Averages:
at 0.00    0.7440
at 0.10    0.7149
at 0.20    0.6554
at 0.30    0.5654
at 0.40    0.5212
at 0.50    0.5003
at 0.60    0.4453
at 0.70    0.3894
at 0.80    0.3106
at 0.90    0.2723
at 1.00    0.1977

Avg. prec. (non-interpolated)
for all rel. documents      0.4655

Precision:
At    5 docs:    0.4765
At   10 docs:    0.3912
At   15 docs:    0.3627
At   20 docs:    0.3324
At   30 docs:    0.2775
At  100 docs:    0.1259
At  200 docs:    0.0700
At  500 docs:    0.0302
At 1000 docs:    0.0154

R-Precision (prec. after
all rel. docs. retrieved):
Exact:    0.4429

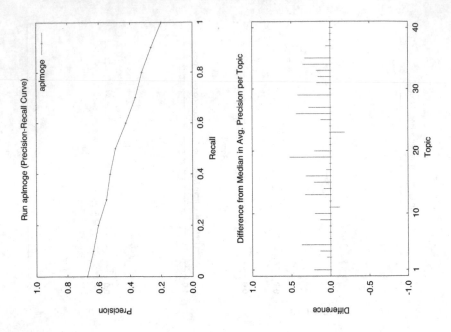

Run aplmoge (Precision-Recall Curve)

aplmoge

Recall

Precision

Difference from Median in Avg. Precision per Topic

Topic

Difference

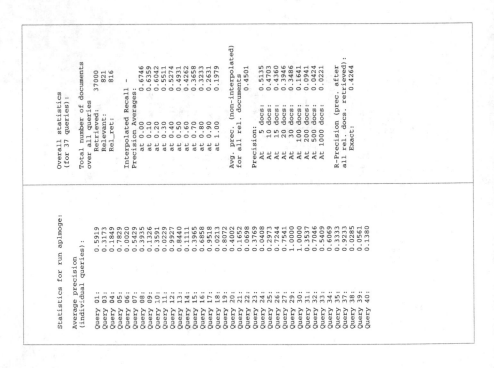

Statistics for run aplmoge:

Average precision
(individual queries):

| | |
|---|---|
| Query 01: | 0.5919 |
| Query 03: | 0.3173 |
| Query 04: | 0.1849 |
| Query 05: | 0.7829 |
| Query 06: | 0.0020 |
| Query 07: | 0.5429 |
| Query 08: | 0.3935 |
| Query 09: | 0.1326 |
| Query 10: | 0.3591 |
| Query 11: | 0.0229 |
| Query 12: | 0.9927 |
| Query 13: | 0.8440 |
| Query 14: | 0.1111 |
| Query 15: | 0.3965 |
| Query 16: | 0.6858 |
| Query 17: | 0.9518 |
| Query 18: | 0.0213 |
| Query 19: | 0.8072 |
| Query 20: | 0.4002 |
| Query 21: | 0.1652 |
| Query 22: | 0.0698 |
| Query 23: | 0.3769 |
| Query 24: | 0.0408 |
| Query 25: | 0.2973 |
| Query 26: | 0.7244 |
| Query 27: | 0.7541 |
| Query 29: | 1.0000 |
| Query 30: | 0.3537 |
| Query 31: | 0.7046 |
| Query 32: | 0.7046 |
| Query 33: | 0.5409 |
| Query 34: | 0.6069 |
| Query 35: | 0.3333 |
| Query 37: | 0.9233 |
| Query 38: | 0.0285 |
| Query 39: | 0.0561 |
| Query 40: | 0.1380 |

Overall statistics
(for 37 queries):

Total number of documents
over all queries
| | |
|---|---|
| Retrieved: | 37000 |
| Relevant: | 821 |
| Rel_ret: | 816 |

Interpolated Recall  -
Precision Averages:
| | |
|---|---|
| at 0.00 | 0.6746 |
| at 0.10 | 0.6359 |
| at 0.20 | 0.6042 |
| at 0.30 | 0.5511 |
| at 0.40 | 0.5274 |
| at 0.50 | 0.4931 |
| at 0.60 | 0.4262 |
| at 0.70 | 0.3658 |
| at 0.80 | 0.3233 |
| at 0.90 | 0.2631 |
| at 1.00 | 0.1979 |

Avg. prec. (non-interpolated)
for all rel. documents
0.4501

Precision:
| | | |
|---|---|---|
| At | 5 docs: | 0.5135 |
| At | 10 docs: | 0.4703 |
| At | 15 docs: | 0.4360 |
| At | 20 docs: | 0.3946 |
| At | 30 docs: | 0.3486 |
| At | 100 docs: | 0.1641 |
| At | 200 docs: | 0.0941 |
| At | 500 docs: | 0.0424 |
| At | 1000 docs: | 0.0221 |

R-Precision (prec. after
all rel. docs. retrieved):
| | |
|---|---|
| Exact: | 0.4264 |

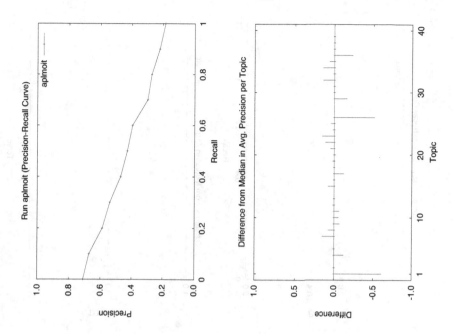

Run aplmoit (Precision-Recall Curve)

aplmoit

Precision / Recall

Difference from Median in Avg. Precision per Topic

Difference / Topic

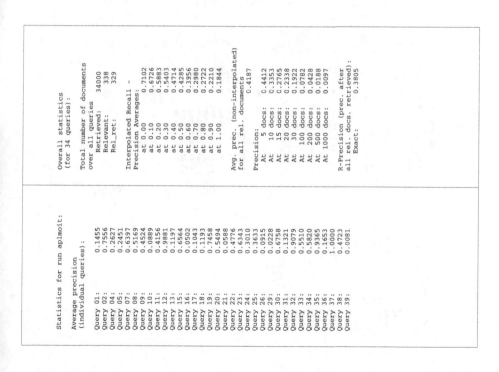

Statistics for run aplmoit:

Average precision
(individual queries):

|  | |
|---|---|
| Query 01: | 0.1455 |
| Query 02: | 0.7556 |
| Query 04: | 0.2627 |
| Query 05: | 0.2451 |
| Query 07: | 0.6397 |
| Query 08: | 0.5169 |
| Query 09: | 0.4524 |
| Query 10: | 0.0889 |
| Query 11: | 0.4156 |
| Query 12: | 0.9881 |
| Query 13: | 0.1197 |
| Query 15: | 0.6564 |
| Query 16: | 0.0502 |
| Query 17: | 0.1043 |
| Query 18: | 0.1193 |
| Query 19: | 0.7458 |
| Query 20: | 0.5494 |
| Query 21: | 0.0588 |
| Query 22: | 0.4776 |
| Query 23: | 0.6343 |
| Query 24: | 0.3010 |
| Query 25: | 0.3633 |
| Query 26: | 0.0915 |
| Query 29: | 0.0228 |
| Query 30: | 0.6758 |
| Query 31: | 0.1321 |
| Query 32: | 0.9079 |
| Query 33: | 0.5510 |
| Query 34: | 0.5820 |
| Query 35: | 0.9365 |
| Query 36: | 0.1653 |
| Query 37: | 1.0000 |
| Query 38: | 0.4723 |
| Query 39: | 0.0081 |

Overall statistics
(for 34 queries):

Total number of documents
over all queries:
Retrieved:  34000
Relevant:     338
Rel_ret:      329

Interpolated Recall -
Precision Averages:
at 0.00   0.7102
at 0.10   0.6726
at 0.20   0.5883
at 0.30   0.5403
at 0.40   0.4714
at 0.50   0.4285
at 0.60   0.3956
at 0.70   0.2980
at 0.80   0.2722
at 0.90   0.2210
at 1.00   0.1844

Avg. prec. (non-interpolated)
for all rel. documents
          0.4187

Precision:
At    5 docs:   0.4412
At   10 docs:   0.3353
At   15 docs:   0.2765
At   20 docs:   0.2338
At   30 docs:   0.1922
At  100 docs:   0.0782
At  200 docs:   0.0428
At  500 docs:   0.0188
At 1000 docs:   0.0097

R-Precision (prec. after
all rel. docs. retrieved):
Exact:    0.3805

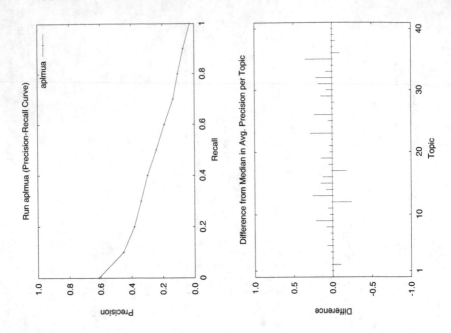

Run aplmua (Precision-Recall Curve)

aplmua

Precision / Recall

Difference from Median in Avg. Precision per Topic

Difference / Topic

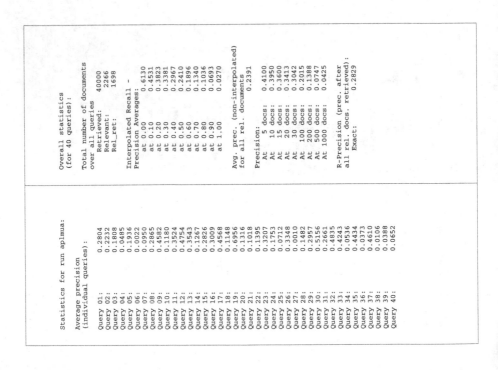

Statistics for run aplmua:

Average precision
(individual queries):

| Query 01: | 0.2804 |
| Query 02: | 0.2232 |
| Query 03: | 0.1808 |
| Query 04: | 0.0485 |
| Query 05: | 0.1936 |
| Query 06: | 0.0022 |
| Query 07: | 0.0950 |
| Query 08: | 0.2865 |
| Query 09: | 0.4582 |
| Query 10: | 0.1180 |
| Query 11: | 0.3524 |
| Query 12: | 0.4754 |
| Query 13: | 0.3543 |
| Query 14: | 0.1267 |
| Query 15: | 0.2826 |
| Query 16: | 0.3009 |
| Query 17: | 0.4568 |
| Query 18: | 0.1148 |
| Query 19: | 0.6956 |
| Query 20: | 0.1316 |
| Query 21: | 0.1018 |
| Query 22: | 0.1395 |
| Query 23: | 0.3207 |
| Query 24: | 0.1753 |
| Query 25: | 0.0712 |
| Query 26: | 0.3348 |
| Query 27: | 0.0010 |
| Query 28: | 0.1482 |
| Query 29: | 0.2957 |
| Query 30: | 0.5156 |
| Query 31: | 0.2661 |
| Query 32: | 0.4835 |
| Query 33: | 0.4243 |
| Query 34: | 0.0536 |
| Query 35: | 0.4434 |
| Query 36: | 0.0373 |
| Query 37: | 0.4610 |
| Query 38: | 0.0106 |
| Query 39: | 0.0388 |
| Query 40: | 0.0652 |

Overall statistics
(for 40 queries):

Total number of documents
over all queries:

| Retrieved: | 40000 |
| Relevant: | 2266 |
| Rel_ret: | 1698 |

Interpolated Recall -
Precision Averages:

| at 0.00 | 0.6130 |
| at 0.10 | 0.4531 |
| at 0.20 | 0.3823 |
| at 0.30 | 0.3381 |
| at 0.40 | 0.2967 |
| at 0.50 | 0.2410 |
| at 0.60 | 0.1896 |
| at 0.70 | 0.1340 |
| at 0.80 | 0.1036 |
| at 0.90 | 0.0693 |
| at 1.00 | 0.0270 |

Avg. prec. (non-interpolated)
for all rel. documents          0.2391

Precision:

| At    5 docs: | 0.4100 |
| At   10 docs: | 0.3950 |
| At   15 docs: | 0.3600 |
| At   20 docs: | 0.3413 |
| At   30 docs: | 0.3042 |
| At  100 docs: | 0.2015 |
| At  200 docs: | 0.1388 |
| At  500 docs: | 0.0747 |
| At 1000 docs: | 0.0425 |

R-Precision (prec. after
all rel.docs. retrieved):

| Exact: | 0.2829 |

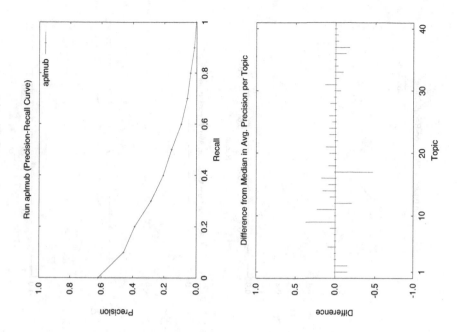

Run aplmub (Precision-Recall Curve)

Difference from Median in Avg. Precision per Topic

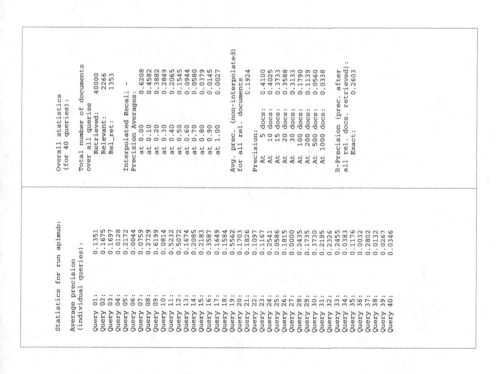

Statistics for run aplmub:

Average precision
(individual queries):

| Query 01: | 0.1351 |
| Query 02: | 0.1675 |
| Query 03: | 0.1697 |
| Query 04: | 0.0128 |
| Query 05: | 0.2172 |
| Query 06: | 0.0044 |
| Query 07: | 0.0759 |
| Query 08: | 0.2729 |
| Query 09: | 0.6199 |
| Query 10: | 0.0814 |
| Query 11: | 0.5232 |
| Query 12: | 0.5072 |
| Query 13: | 0.1674 |
| Query 14: | 0.2085 |
| Query 15: | 0.2183 |
| Query 16: | 0.3587 |
| Query 17: | 0.1649 |
| Query 18: | 0.1584 |
| Query 19: | 0.5562 |
| Query 20: | 0.1703 |
| Query 21: | 0.1826 |
| Query 22: | 0.1097 |
| Query 23: | 0.1167 |
| Query 24: | 0.2541 |
| Query 25: | 0.0586 |
| Query 26: | 0.1815 |
| Query 27: | 0.0000 |
| Query 28: | 0.2435 |
| Query 29: | 0.1735 |
| Query 30: | 0.3730 |
| Query 31: | 0.2195 |
| Query 32: | 0.2326 |
| Query 33: | 0.2455 |
| Query 34: | 0.0383 |
| Query 35: | 0.1176 |
| Query 36: | 0.0032 |
| Query 37: | 0.2802 |
| Query 38: | 0.0132 |
| Query 39: | 0.0267 |
| Query 40: | 0.0346 |

Overall statistics
(for 40 queries):

Total number of documents
over all queries:
Retrieved:     40000
Relevant:       2266
Rel_ret:        1353

Interpolated Recall  -
Precision Averages:
at 0.00    0.6208
at 0.10    0.4582
at 0.20    0.3882
at 0.30    0.2849
at 0.40    0.2065
at 0.50    0.1545
at 0.60    0.0944
at 0.70    0.0580
at 0.80    0.0379
at 0.90    0.0145
at 1.00    0.0027

Avg. prec. (non-interpolated)
for all rel. documents
                   0.1924

Precision:
At    5 docs:    0.4100
At   10 docs:    0.4025
At   15 docs:    0.3733
At   20 docs:    0.3588
At   30 docs:    0.3133
At  100 docs:    0.1790
At  200 docs:    0.1139
At  500 docs:    0.0560
At 1000 docs:    0.0338

R-Precision (prec. after
all rel. docs. retrieved):
Exact:           0.2603

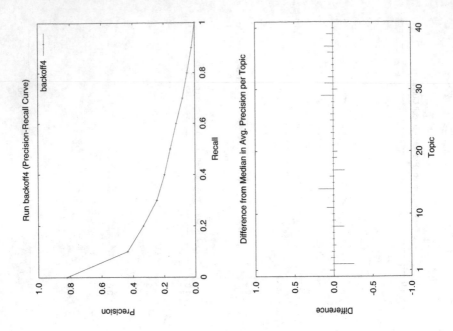

Run backoff4 (Precision-Recall Curve)

Difference from Median in Avg. Precision per Topic

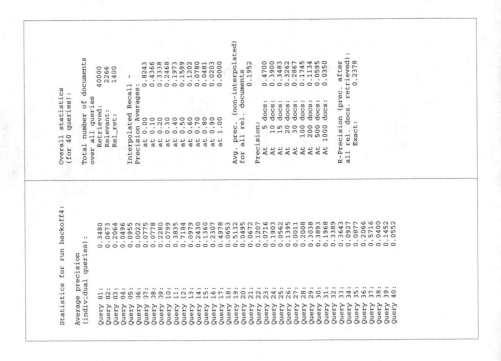

Statistics for run backoff4:

Average precision
(individual queries):

| | |
|---|---|
| Query 01: | 0.3480 |
| Query 02: | 0.0673 |
| Query 03: | 0.2064 |
| Query 04: | 0.0496 |
| Query 05: | 0.0955 |
| Query 06: | 0.0022 |
| Query 07: | 0.0775 |
| Query 08: | 0.0778 |
| Query 09: | 0.2280 |
| Query 10: | 0.0799 |
| Query 11: | 0.3835 |
| Query 12: | 0.7184 |
| Query 13: | 0.0979 |
| Query 14: | 0.2430 |
| Query 15: | 0.1360 |
| Query 16: | 0.2307 |
| Query 17: | 0.4978 |
| Query 18: | 0.0653 |
| Query 19: | 0.5132 |
| Query 20: | 0.0495 |
| Query 21: | 0.0672 |
| Query 22: | 0.1207 |
| Query 23: | 0.0716 |
| Query 24: | 0.1903 |
| Query 25: | 0.0562 |
| Query 26: | 0.1395 |
| Query 27: | 0.0011 |
| Query 28: | 0.2008 |
| Query 29: | 0.3038 |
| Query 30: | 0.3893 |
| Query 31: | 0.1968 |
| Query 32: | 0.3389 |
| Query 33: | 0.3643 |
| Query 34: | 0.0927 |
| Query 35: | 0.0877 |
| Query 36: | 0.2066 |
| Query 37: | 0.5716 |
| Query 38: | 0.0400 |
| Query 39: | 0.1452 |
| Query 40: | 0.0552 |

Overall statistics
(for 40 queries):

Total number of documents
over all queries:

| | |
|---|---|
| Retrieved: | 40000 |
| Relevant: | 2266 |
| Rel_ret: | 1400 |

Interpolated Recall -
Precision Averages:

| | |
|---|---|
| at 0.00 | 0.8243 |
| at 0.10 | 0.4366 |
| at 0.20 | 0.3338 |
| at 0.30 | 0.2468 |
| at 0.40 | 0.1973 |
| at 0.50 | 0.1599 |
| at 0.60 | 0.1202 |
| at 0.70 | 0.0780 |
| at 0.80 | 0.0481 |
| at 0.90 | 0.0203 |
| at 1.00 | 0.0000 |

Avg. prec. (non-interpolated)
for all rel. documents          0.1952

Precision:

| | | | |
|---|---|---|---|
| At | 5 | docs: | 0.4700 |
| At | 10 | docs: | 0.3900 |
| At | 15 | docs: | 0.3483 |
| At | 20 | docs: | 0.3262 |
| At | 30 | docs: | 0.2867 |
| At | 100 | docs: | 0.1745 |
| At | 200 | docs: | 0.1134 |
| At | 500 | docs: | 0.0595 |
| At | 1000 | docs: | 0.0350 |

R-Precision (prec. after
all rel.docs. retrieved):

| | |
|---|---|
| Exact: | 0.2378 |

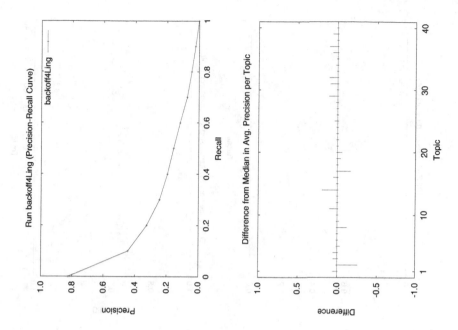

Run backoff4Ling (Precision-Recall Curve)

Difference from Median in Avg. Precision per Topic

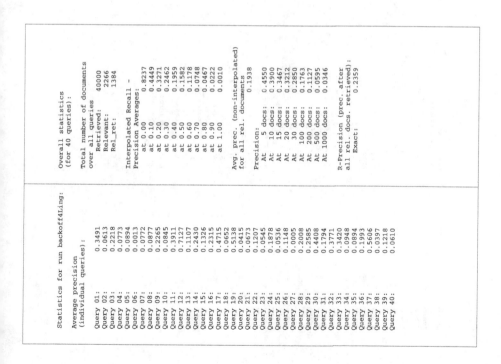

Statistics for run backoff4Ling:

Average precision
(individual queries):

| | |
|---|---|
| Query 01: | 0.3491 |
| Query 02: | 0.0613 |
| Query 03: | 0.2218 |
| Query 04: | 0.0773 |
| Query 05: | 0.0894 |
| Query 06: | 0.0013 |
| Query 07: | 0.0772 |
| Query 08: | 0.0877 |
| Query 09: | 0.2265 |
| Query 10: | 0.0845 |
| Query 11: | 0.3911 |
| Query 12: | 0.7127 |
| Query 13: | 0.1107 |
| Query 14: | 0.2430 |
| Query 15: | 0.1326 |
| Query 16: | 0.2315 |
| Query 17: | 0.4715 |
| Query 18: | 0.0652 |
| Query 19: | 0.5138 |
| Query 20: | 0.0415 |
| Query 21: | 0.0673 |
| Query 22: | 0.1207 |
| Query 23: | 0.0545 |
| Query 24: | 0.1878 |
| Query 25: | 0.0536 |
| Query 26: | 0.1148 |
| Query 27: | 0.0005 |
| Query 28: | 0.2008 |
| Query 29: | 0.2585 |
| Query 30: | 0.4408 |
| Query 31: | 0.1794 |
| Query 32: | 0.3771 |
| Query 33: | 0.3420 |
| Query 34: | 0.0948 |
| Query 35: | 0.0894 |
| Query 36: | 0.1993 |
| Query 37: | 0.5606 |
| Query 38: | 0.0397 |
| Query 39: | 0.1218 |
| Query 40: | 0.0610 |

Overall statistics
(for 40 queries):

Total number of documents
over all queries:
| | |
|---|---|
| Retrieved: | 40000 |
| Relevant: | 2266 |
| Rel_ret: | 1384 |

Interpolated Recall -
Precision Averages:
| | |
|---|---|
| at 0.00 | 0.8237 |
| at 0.10 | 0.4449 |
| at 0.20 | 0.3271 |
| at 0.30 | 0.2462 |
| at 0.40 | 0.1959 |
| at 0.50 | 0.1582 |
| at 0.60 | 0.1178 |
| at 0.70 | 0.0748 |
| at 0.80 | 0.0467 |
| at 0.90 | 0.0222 |
| at 1.00 | 0.0010 |

Avg. prec. (non-interpolated)
for all rel. documents     0.1938

Precision:
| | |
|---|---|
| At 5 docs: | 0.4550 |
| At 10 docs: | 0.3900 |
| At 15 docs: | 0.3467 |
| At 20 docs: | 0.3212 |
| At 30 docs: | 0.2850 |
| At 100 docs: | 0.1763 |
| At 200 docs: | 0.1127 |
| At 500 docs: | 0.0595 |
| At 1000 docs: | 0.0346 |

R-Precision (prec. after
all rel. docs. retrieved):
| | |
|---|---|
| Exact: | 0.2359 |

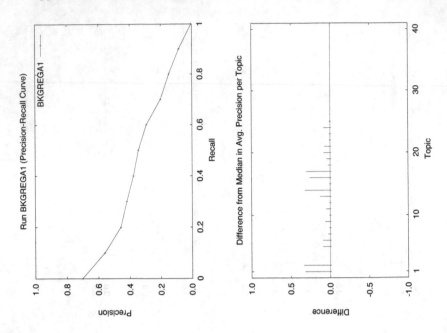

Run BKGREGA1 (Precision-Recall Curve)

Recall

Precision

BKGREGA1

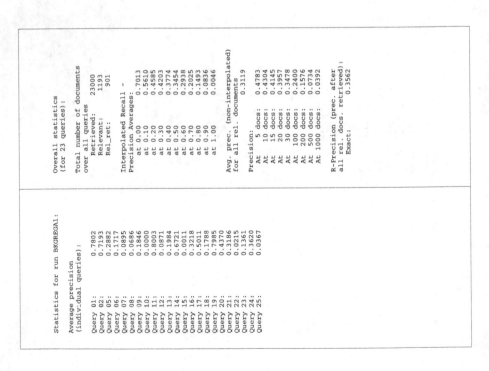

Difference from Median in Avg. Precision per Topic

Topic

Difference

Statistics for run BKGREGA1:

Average precision
(indiv-dual queries):

Query 01:    0.7802
Query 02:    0.7193
Query 05:    0.2882
Query 06:    0.1717
Query 07:    0.0895
Query 08:    0.0686
Query 09:    0.1846
Query 10:    0.0000
Query 11:    0.8003
Query 12:    0.0871
Query 13:    0.1984
Query 14:    0.6721
Query 15:    0.0011
Query 16:    0.3218
Query 17:    0.5011
Query 18:    0.1788
Query 19:    0.7985
Query 20:    0.4370
Query 21:    0.3186
Query 22:    0.0215
Query 23:    0.1361
Query 24:    0.3620
Query 25:    0.0367

Overall statistics
(for 23 queries):

Total number of documents
over all queries
 Retrieved:    23000
 Relevant:      1193
 Rel_ret:        901

Interpolated Recall -
Precision Averages:
  at 0.00    0.7013
  at 0.10    0.5610
  at 0.20    0.4585
  at 0.30    0.4203
  at 0.40    0.3774
  at 0.50    0.3454
  at 0.60    0.2938
  at 0.70    0.2025
  at 0.80    0.1493
  at 0.90    0.0836
  at 1.00    0.0046

Avg. prec. (non-interpolated)
for all rel. documents       0.3119

Precision:
  At    5 docs:    0.4783
  At   10 docs:    0.4304
  At   15 docs:    0.4145
  At   20 docs:    0.3957
  At   30 docs:    0.3478
  At  100 docs:    0.2400
  At  200 docs:    0.1576
  At  500 docs:    0.0734
  At 1000 docs:    0.0392

R-Precision (prec. after
all rel. docs. retrieved):
  Exact:    0.3562

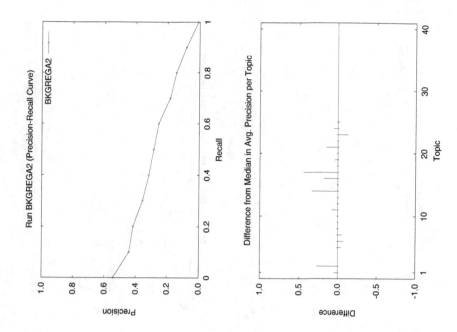

Run BKGREGA2 (Precision-Recall Curve)

BKGREGA2

Difference from Median in Avg. Precision per Topic

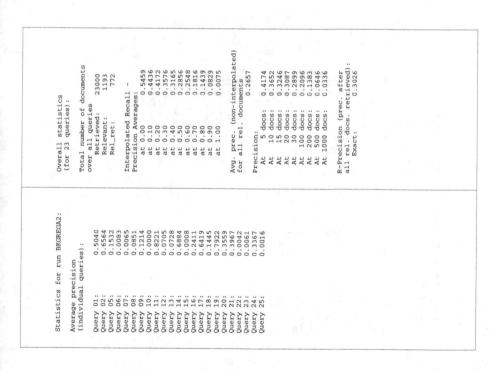

Statistics for run BKGREGA2:

Average precision
(individual queries):

|  | |
|---|---|
| Query 01: | 0.5040 |
| Query 02: | 0.6564 |
| Query 05: | 0.1532 |
| Query 06: | 0.0083 |
| Query 07: | 0.0065 |
| Query 08: | 0.0851 |
| Query 09: | 0.1214 |
| Query 10: | 0.0000 |
| Query 11: | 0.8221 |
| Query 12: | 0.0705 |
| Query 13: | 0.0728 |
| Query 14: | 0.6884 |
| Query 15: | 0.0008 |
| Query 16: | 0.2411 |
| Query 17: | 0.6419 |
| Query 18: | 0.1445 |
| Query 19: | 0.7922 |
| Query 20: | 0.3559 |
| Query 21: | 0.3967 |
| Query 22: | 0.0042 |
| Query 23: | 0.0061 |
| Query 24: | 0.3367 |
| Query 25: | 0.0016 |

Overall statistics
(for 23 queries):

Total number of documents
over all queries:
Retrieved:    23000
Relevant:      1193
Rel_ret:        772

Interpolated Recall –
Precision Averages:

| | |
|---|---|
| at 0.00 | 0.5459 |
| at 0.10 | 0.4436 |
| at 0.20 | 0.4172 |
| at 0.30 | 0.3576 |
| at 0.40 | 0.3165 |
| at 0.50 | 0.2856 |
| at 0.60 | 0.2548 |
| at 0.70 | 0.1816 |
| at 0.80 | 0.1439 |
| at 0.90 | 0.0829 |
| at 1.00 | 0.0075 |

Avg. prec. (non-interpolated)
for all rel. documents        0.2657

Precision:

| | | |
|---|---|---|
| At | 5 docs: | 0.4174 |
| At | 10 docs: | 0.3652 |
| At | 15 docs: | 0.3246 |
| At | 20 docs: | 0.3087 |
| At | 30 docs: | 0.2899 |
| At | 100 docs: | 0.2096 |
| At | 200 docs: | 0.1383 |
| At | 500 docs: | 0.0646 |
| At | 1000 docs: | 0.0336 |

R-Precision (prec. after
all rel. docs. retrieved):
Exact:    0.3026

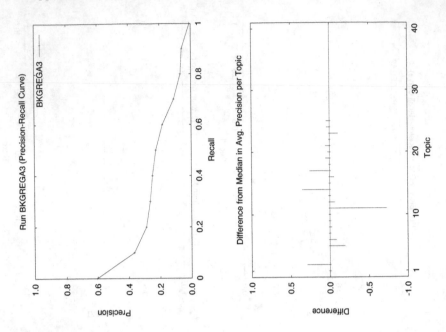

Run BKGREGA3 (Precision-Recall Curve)

BKGREGA3 ——

Difference from Median in Avg. Precision per Topic

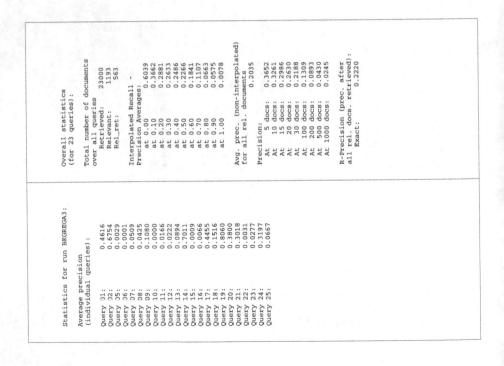

Statistics for run BKGREGA3 :

Average precision
(individual queries) :

| Query 01: | 0.4616 |
| Query 02: | 0.6754 |
| Query 05: | 0.0029 |
| Query 06: | 0.0001 |
| Query 07: | 0.0509 |
| Query 08: | 0.0425 |
| Query 09: | 0.1080 |
| Query 10: | 0.0000 |
| Query 11: | 0.0166 |
| Query 12: | 0.0222 |
| Query 13: | 0.0894 |
| Query 14: | 0.7011 |
| Query 15: | 0.0009 |
| Query 16: | 0.0066 |
| Query 17: | 0.4455 |
| Query 18: | 0.1516 |
| Query 19: | 0.8060 |
| Query 20: | 0.3800 |
| Query 21: | 0.3018 |
| Query 22: | 0.0031 |
| Query 23: | 0.0277 |
| Query 24: | 0.3197 |
| Query 25: | 0.0667 |

Overall statistics
(for 23 queries) :

Total number of documents
over all queries
   Retrieved:    23000
   Relevant:     1193
   Rel_ret:       563

Interpolated Recall -
Precision Averages:
| at 0.00 | 0.6039 |
| at 0.10 | 0.3662 |
| at 0.20 | 0.2881 |
| at 0.30 | 0.2633 |
| at 0.40 | 0.2486 |
| at 0.50 | 0.2266 |
| at 0.60 | 0.1841 |
| at 0.70 | 0.1107 |
| at 0.80 | 0.0663 |
| at 0.90 | 0.0575 |
| at 1.00 | 0.0078 |

Avg. prec. (non-interpolated)
for all rel. documents
             0.2035

Precision:
| At    5 docs: | 0.3652 |
| At   10 docs: | 0.3261 |
| At   15 docs: | 0.2986 |
| At   20 docs: | 0.2630 |
| At   30 docs: | 0.2188 |
| At  100 docs: | 0.1309 |
| At  200 docs: | 0.0893 |
| At  500 docs: | 0.0430 |
| At 1000 docs: | 0.0245 |

R-Precision (prec. after
all rel. docs. retrieved):
   Exact:        0.2220

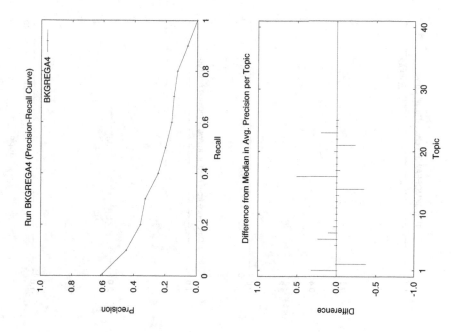

Run BKGREGA4 (Precision-Recall Curve)

BKGREGA4

Difference from Median in Avg. Precision per Topic

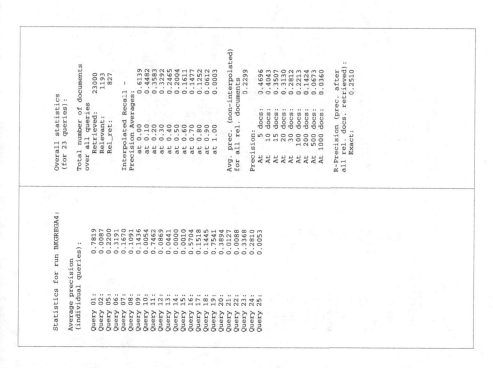

Statistics for run BKGREGA4:

Average precision
(individual queries):

| | |
|---|---|
| Query 01: | 0.7819 |
| Query 02: | 0.0087 |
| Query 05: | 0.2200 |
| Query 06: | 0.3191 |
| Query 07: | 0.1670 |
| Query 08: | 0.1091 |
| Query 09: | 0.1436 |
| Query 10: | 0.0054 |
| Query 11: | 0.7462 |
| Query 12: | 0.0869 |
| Query 13: | 0.0441 |
| Query 14: | 0.0000 |
| Query 15: | 0.0010 |
| Query 16: | 0.5704 |
| Query 17: | 0.1518 |
| Query 18: | 0.1445 |
| Query 19: | 0.7541 |
| Query 20: | 0.3894 |
| Query 21: | 0.0127 |
| Query 22: | 0.0088 |
| Query 23: | 0.3368 |
| Query 24: | 0.2810 |
| Query 25: | 0.0053 |

Overall statistics
(for 23 queries):

Total number of documents
over all queries:
    Retrieved:    23000
    Relevant:     1193
    Rel_ret:      827

Interpolated Recall -
Precision Averages:
    at 0.00   0.6139
    at 0.10   0.4482
    at 0.20   0.3583
    at 0.30   0.3292
    at 0.40   0.2465
    at 0.50   0.2004
    at 0.60   0.1611
    at 0.70   0.1477
    at 0.80   0.1252
    at 0.90   0.0612
    at 1.00   0.0003

Avg. prec. (non-interpolated)
for all rel. documents
               0.2299

Precision:
  At    5 docs:   0.4696
  At   10 docs:   0.4043
  At   15 docs:   0.3507
  At   20 docs:   0.3130
  At   30 docs:   0.2812
  At  100 docs:   0.2213
  At  200 docs:   0.1424
  At  500 docs:   0.0673
  At 1000 docs:   0.0360

R-Precision (prec. after
all rel. docs. retrieved):
    Exact:   0.2510

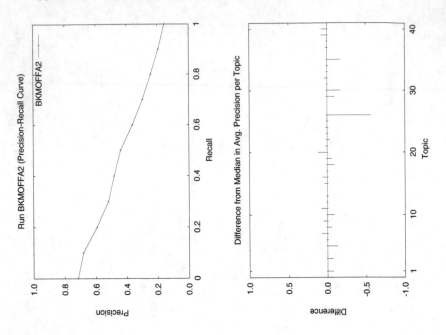

Run BKMOFFA2 (Precision-Recall Curve)

Difference from Median in Avg. Precision per Topic

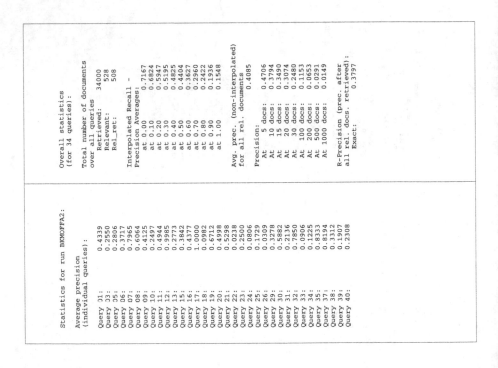

Statistics for run BKMOFFA2:

Average precision
(individual queries):

| | |
|---|---|
| Query 01: | 0.4339 |
| Query 03: | 0.2550 |
| Query 05: | 0.2806 |
| Query 06: | 0.3717 |
| Query 07: | 0.7965 |
| Query 08: | 0.6064 |
| Query 09: | 0.4125 |
| Query 10: | 0.2497 |
| Query 11: | 0.4944 |
| Query 12: | 0.9985 |
| Query 13: | 0.2773 |
| Query 15: | 0.3842 |
| Query 16: | 0.4377 |
| Query 17: | 1.0000 |
| Query 18: | 0.0982 |
| Query 19: | 0.6712 |
| Query 20: | 0.4998 |
| Query 21: | 0.5298 |
| Query 22: | 0.0238 |
| Query 23: | 0.2500 |
| Query 24: | 0.0806 |
| Query 25: | 0.1729 |
| Query 26: | 0.0309 |
| Query 29: | 0.3278 |
| Query 30: | 0.5882 |
| Query 31: | 0.2136 |
| Query 32: | 0.7850 |
| Query 33: | 0.0906 |
| Query 34: | 0.1225 |
| Query 35: | 0.8333 |
| Query 37: | 0.8194 |
| Query 38: | 0.3312 |
| Query 39: | 0.1907 |
| Query 40: | 0.2308 |

Overall statistics
(for 34 queries):

Total number of documents
over all queries:

| | |
|---|---|
| Retrieved: | 34000 |
| Relevant: | 528 |
| Rel_ret: | 508 |

Interpolated Recall -
Precision Averages:

| | |
|---|---|
| at 0.00 | 0.7167 |
| at 0.10 | 0.6824 |
| at 0.20 | 0.5947 |
| at 0.30 | 0.5195 |
| at 0.40 | 0.4825 |
| at 0.50 | 0.4404 |
| at 0.60 | 0.3627 |
| at 0.70 | 0.2960 |
| at 0.80 | 0.2422 |
| at 0.90 | 0.1936 |
| at 1.00 | 0.1548 |

Avg. prec. (non-interpolated)
for all rel. documents
            0.4085

Precision:
| | | |
|---|---|---|
| At | 5 docs: | 0.4706 |
| At | 10 docs: | 0.3794 |
| At | 15 docs: | 0.3490 |
| At | 20 docs: | 0.3074 |
| At | 30 docs: | 0.2480 |
| At | 100 docs: | 0.1153 |
| At | 200 docs: | 0.0653 |
| At | 500 docs: | 0.0291 |
| At | 1000 docs: | 0.0149 |

R-Precision (prec. after
all rel. docs. retrieved):
    Exact:      0.3797

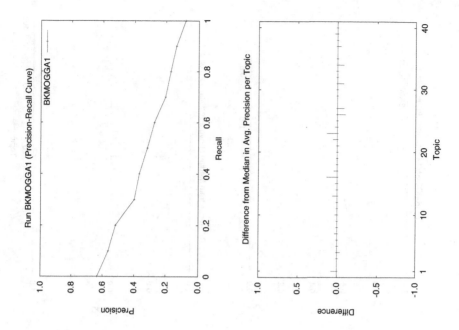

Run BKMOGGA1 (Precision-Recall Curve)

BKMOGGA1

Precision / Recall

Difference from Median in Avg. Precision per Topic

Difference / Topic

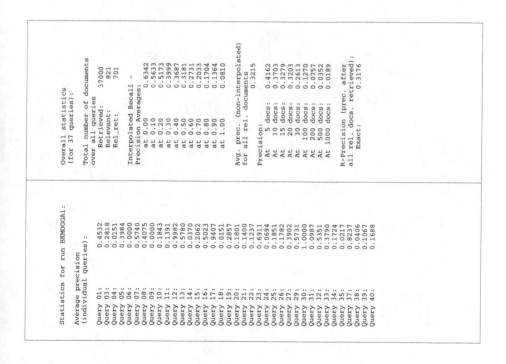

Statistics for run BKMOGGA1:

Average precision
(individual queries):

| | |
|---|---|
| Query 01: | 0.4532 |
| Query 03: | 0.2818 |
| Query 04: | 0.0151 |
| Query 05: | 0.3984 |
| Query 06: | 0.0000 |
| Query 07: | 0.5740 |
| Query 08: | 0.4075 |
| Query 09: | 0.0000 |
| Query 10: | 0.1843 |
| Query 11: | 0.1391 |
| Query 12: | 0.9982 |
| Query 13: | 0.5780 |
| Query 14: | 0.0370 |
| Query 15: | 0.2062 |
| Query 16: | 0.5023 |
| Query 17: | 0.9407 |
| Query 18: | 0.0151 |
| Query 19: | 0.2857 |
| Query 20: | 0.1801 |
| Query 21: | 0.1400 |
| Query 22: | 0.1237 |
| Query 23: | 0.6911 |
| Query 24: | 0.0694 |
| Query 25: | 0.1851 |
| Query 26: | 0.1782 |
| Query 27: | 0.3902 |
| Query 29: | 0.5731 |
| Query 30: | 1.0000 |
| Query 31: | 0.0987 |
| Query 32: | 0.5351 |
| Query 33: | 0.3790 |
| Query 34: | 0.1724 |
| Query 35: | 0.0217 |
| Query 37: | 0.8237 |
| Query 38: | 0.0406 |
| Query 39: | 0.1067 |
| Query 40: | 0.1688 |

Overall statistics
(for 37 queries):

Total number of documents
over all queries:

| | |
|---|---|
| Retrieved: | 37000 |
| Relevant: | 821 |
| Rel_ret: | 701 |

Interpolated Recall -
Precision Averages:

| | |
|---|---|
| at 0.00 | 0.6342 |
| at 0.10 | 0.5633 |
| at 0.20 | 0.5173 |
| at 0.30 | 0.3999 |
| at 0.40 | 0.3687 |
| at 0.50 | 0.3181 |
| at 0.60 | 0.2731 |
| at 0.70 | 0.2033 |
| at 0.80 | 0.1704 |
| at 0.90 | 0.1364 |
| at 1.00 | 0.0810 |

Avg. prec. (non-interpolated)
for all rel. documents
0.3215

Precision:

| | | |
|---|---|---|
| At | 5 docs: | 0.4162 |
| At | 10 docs: | 0.3703 |
| At | 15 docs: | 0.3279 |
| At | 20 docs: | 0.3203 |
| At | 30 docs: | 0.2613 |
| At | 100 docs: | 0.1270 |
| At | 200 docs: | 0.0757 |
| At | 500 docs: | 0.0352 |
| At | 1000 docs: | 0.0189 |

R-Precision (prec. after
all rel. docs. retrieved):
Exact: 0.3176

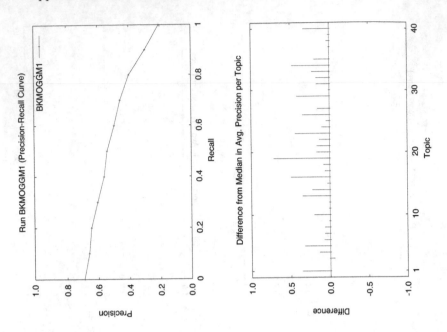

Run BKMOGGM1 (Precision-Recall Curve)

BKMOGGM1

Difference from Median in Avg. Precision per Topic

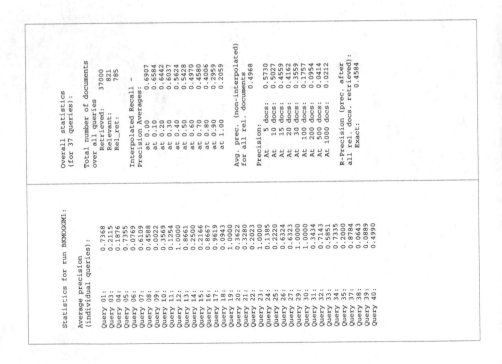

Statistics for run BKMOGGM1:

Average precision
(individual queries):

Query 01:  0.7368
Query 03:  0.2115
Query 04:  0.1876
Query 05:  0.7355
Query 06:  0.0769
Query 07:  0.6109
Query 08:  0.4588
Query 09:  0.0022
Query 10:  0.3569
Query 11:  0.1254
Query 12:  1.0000
Query 13:  0.8661
Query 14:  0.2500
Query 15:  0.2166
Query 16:  0.8667
Query 17:  0.9619
Query 18:  0.0943
Query 19:  1.0000
Query 20:  0.3622
Query 21:  0.3280
Query 22:  0.2023
Query 23:  1.0000
Query 24:  0.1385
Query 25:  0.2220
Query 26:  0.6324
Query 27:  0.6323
Query 29:  1.0000
Query 30:  1.0000
Query 31:  0.3434
Query 32:  0.7143
Query 33:  0.5851
Query 34:  0.7335
Query 35:  0.2000
Query 37:  0.8784
Query 38:  0.0643
Query 39:  0.0889
Query 40:  0.4990

Overall statistics
(for 37 queries):

Total number of documents
over all queries:
  Retrieved:   37000
  Relevant:      821
  Rel_ret:       785

Interpolated Recall -
Precision Averages:
  at 0.00   0.6907
  at 0.10   0.6584
  at 0.20   0.6442
  at 0.30   0.6037
  at 0.40   0.5624
  at 0.50   0.5428
  at 0.60   0.4970
  at 0.70   0.4580
  at 0.80   0.4006
  at 0.90   0.2959
  at 1.00   0.2059

Avg. prec. (non-interpolated)
for all rel. documents
            0.4968

Precision:
  At    5 docs:  0.5730
  At   10 docs:  0.5027
  At   15 docs:  0.4559
  At   20 docs:  0.4162
  At   30 docs:  0.3559
  At  100 docs:  0.1757
  At  200 docs:  0.0954
  At  500 docs:  0.0414
  At 1000 docs:  0.0212

R-Precision (prec. after
all rel. docs. retrieved):
  Exact:  0.4584

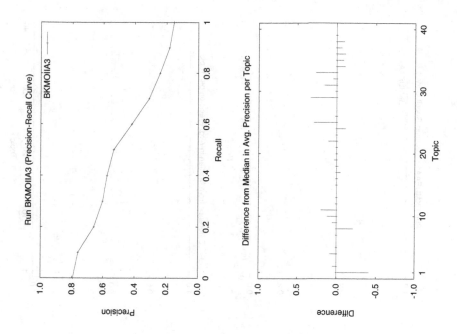

Run BKMOIIA3 (Precision-Recall Curve)

Difference from Median in Avg. Precision per Topic

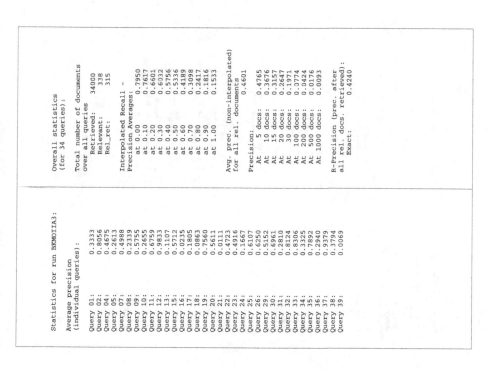

Statistics for run BKMOIIA3:

Average precision
(individual queries):

| | |
|---|---|
| Query 01: | 0.3333 |
| Query 02: | 0.8056 |
| Query 04: | 0.4675 |
| Query 05: | 0.2613 |
| Query 07: | 0.4988 |
| Query 08: | 0.2339 |
| Query 09: | 0.5755 |
| Query 10: | 0.2655 |
| Query 11: | 0.6759 |
| Query 12: | 0.9833 |
| Query 13: | 0.1107 |
| Query 15: | 0.5712 |
| Query 16: | 0.0235 |
| Query 17: | 0.1805 |
| Query 18: | 0.0863 |
| Query 19: | 0.7560 |
| Query 20: | 0.5611 |
| Query 21: | 0.0111 |
| Query 22: | 0.4723 |
| Query 23: | 0.4916 |
| Query 24: | 0.1667 |
| Query 25: | 0.6107 |
| Query 26: | 0.6250 |
| Query 29: | 0.5152 |
| Query 30: | 0.6961 |
| Query 31: | 0.2810 |
| Query 32: | 0.8124 |
| Query 33: | 0.8306 |
| Query 34: | 0.3325 |
| Query 35: | 0.7892 |
| Query 36: | 0.2940 |
| Query 37: | 0.9379 |
| Query 38: | 0.3794 |
| Query 39: | 0.0069 |

Overall statistics
(for 34 queries):

Total number of documents
over all queries:

| | |
|---|---|
| Retrieved: | 34000 |
| Relevant: | 338 |
| Rel_ret: | 315 |

Interpolated Recall -
Precision Averages:

| | |
|---|---|
| at 0.00 | 0.7950 |
| at 0.10 | 0.7617 |
| at 0.20 | 0.6601 |
| at 0.30 | 0.6032 |
| at 0.40 | 0.5756 |
| at 0.50 | 0.5336 |
| at 0.60 | 0.4189 |
| at 0.70 | 0.3098 |
| at 0.80 | 0.2417 |
| at 0.90 | 0.1816 |
| at 1.00 | 0.1533 |

Avg. prec. (non-interpolated)
for all rel. documents
0.4601

Precision:

| | |
|---|---|
| At    5 docs: | 0.4765 |
| At   10 docs: | 0.3676 |
| At   15 docs: | 0.3157 |
| At   20 docs: | 0.2647 |
| At   30 docs: | 0.1971 |
| At  100 docs: | 0.0774 |
| At  200 docs: | 0.0424 |
| At  500 docs: | 0.0176 |
| At 1000 docs: | 0.0093 |

R-Precision (prec. after
all rel. docs. retrieved):
Exact:    0.4220

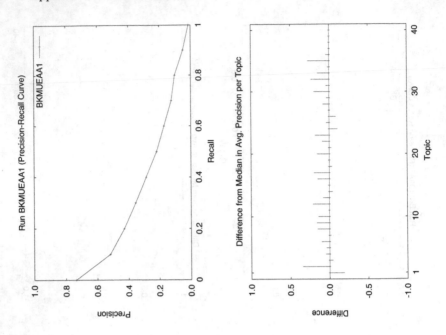

Run BKMUEAA1 (Precision-Recall Curve)

BKMUEAA1

Precision / Recall

Difference from Median in Avg. Precision per Topic

Difference / Topic

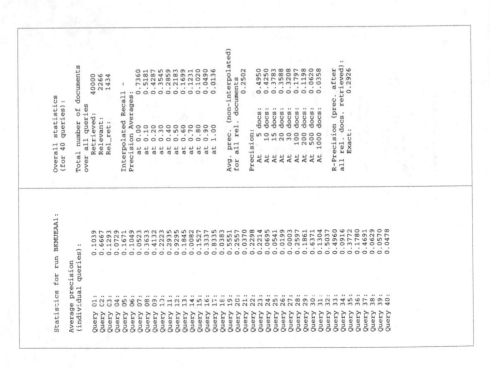

Statistics for run BKMUEAA1:

Average precision
(individual queries):

|  | |
|---|---|
| Query 01: | 0.1039 |
| Query 02: | 0.6667 |
| Query 03: | 0.1293 |
| Query 04: | 0.0729 |
| Query 05: | 0.1671 |
| Query 06: | 0.1049 |
| Query 07: | 0.0523 |
| Query 08: | 0.3633 |
| Query 09: | 0.4132 |
| Query 10: | 0.2223 |
| Query 11: | 0.2935 |
| Query 12: | 0.9295 |
| Query 13: | 0.1845 |
| Query 14: | 0.0082 |
| Query 15: | 0.1527 |
| Query 16: | 0.3337 |
| Query 17: | 0.8335 |
| Query 18: | 0.0383 |
| Query 19: | 0.5551 |
| Query 20: | 0.2557 |
| Query 21: | 0.0370 |
| Query 22: | 0.2298 |
| Query 23: | 0.2214 |
| Query 24: | 0.0695 |
| Query 25: | 0.0541 |
| Query 26: | 0.0199 |
| Query 27: | 0.0003 |
| Query 28: | 0.2597 |
| Query 29: | 0.1861 |
| Query 30: | 0.6371 |
| Query 31: | 0.1304 |
| Query 32: | 0.5037 |
| Query 33: | 0.4960 |
| Query 34: | 0.0916 |
| Query 35: | 0.3772 |
| Query 36: | 0.1780 |
| Query 37: | 0.4691 |
| Query 38: | 0.0629 |
| Query 39: | 0.0570 |
| Query 40: | 0.0478 |

Overall statistics
(for 40 queries):

Total number of documents
over all queries:

| | |
|---|---|
| Retrieved: | 40000 |
| Relevant: | 2266 |
| Rel_ret: | 1434 |

Interpolated Recall -
Precision Averages:

| | |
|---|---|
| at 0.00 | 0.7360 |
| at 0.10 | 0.5181 |
| at 0.20 | 0.4287 |
| at 0.30 | 0.3545 |
| at 0.40 | 0.2859 |
| at 0.50 | 0.2183 |
| at 0.60 | 0.1699 |
| at 0.70 | 0.1231 |
| at 0.80 | 0.1020 |
| at 0.90 | 0.0490 |
| at 1.00 | 0.0136 |

Avg. prec. (non-interpolated)
for all rel. documents        0.2502

Precision:

| | | |
|---|---|---|
| At | 5 docs: | 0.4950 |
| At | 10 docs: | 0.4250 |
| At | 15 docs: | 0.3783 |
| At | 20 docs: | 0.3588 |
| At | 30 docs: | 0.3208 |
| At | 100 docs: | 0.1797 |
| At | 200 docs: | 0.1198 |
| At | 500 docs: | 0.0620 |
| At | 1000 docs: | 0.0358 |

R-Precision (prec. after
all rel. docs. retrieved):

| | |
|---|---|
| Exact: | 0.2926 |

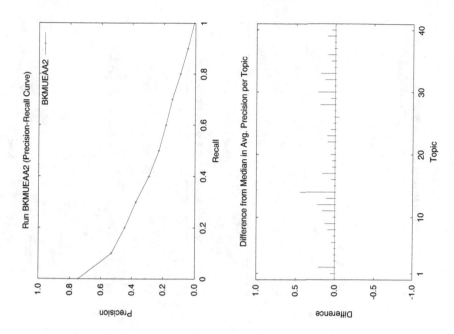

Run BKMUEAA2 (Precision-Recall Curve)

Difference from Median in Avg. Precision per Topic

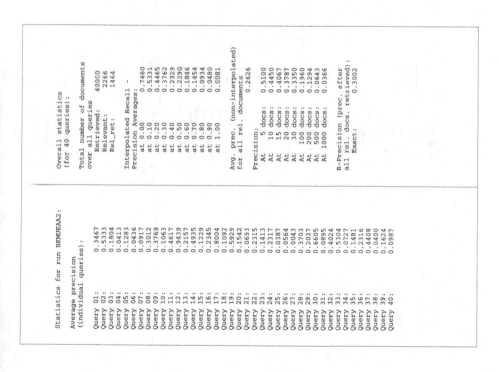

Statistics for run BKMUEAA2:

Average precision
(individual queries):

| | |
|---|---|
| Query 01: | 0.3467 |
| Query 02: | 0.5333 |
| Query 03: | 0.1804 |
| Query 04: | 0.0413 |
| Query 05: | 0.1283 |
| Query 06: | 0.0436 |
| Query 07: | 0.0917 |
| Query 08: | 0.3012 |
| Query 09: | 0.3769 |
| Query 10: | 0.1063 |
| Query 11: | 0.4617 |
| Query 12: | 0.9439 |
| Query 13: | 0.2157 |
| Query 14: | 0.4935 |
| Query 15: | 0.1229 |
| Query 16: | 0.2345 |
| Query 17: | 0.8004 |
| Query 18: | 0.1092 |
| Query 19: | 0.5929 |
| Query 20: | 0.1542 |
| Query 21: | 0.0693 |
| Query 22: | 0.2315 |
| Query 23: | 0.1413 |
| Query 24: | 0.2317 |
| Query 25: | 0.0387 |
| Query 26: | 0.0564 |
| Query 27: | 0.0043 |
| Query 28: | 0.3703 |
| Query 29: | 0.2037 |
| Query 30: | 0.6605 |
| Query 31: | 0.0895 |
| Query 32: | 0.4024 |
| Query 33: | 0.5304 |
| Query 34: | 0.0727 |
| Query 35: | 0.1481 |
| Query 36: | 0.2316 |
| Query 37: | 0.4408 |
| Query 38: | 0.0400 |
| Query 39: | 0.1624 |
| Query 40: | 0.0987 |

Overall statistics
(for 40 queries):

Total number of documents
over all queries:

| | |
|---|---|
| Retrieved: | 40000 |
| Relevant: | 2266 |
| Rel_ret: | 1464 |

Interpolated Recall -
Precision Averages:

| | |
|---|---|
| at 0.00 | 0.7460 |
| at 0.10 | 0.5331 |
| at 0.20 | 0.4465 |
| at 0.30 | 0.3762 |
| at 0.40 | 0.2929 |
| at 0.50 | 0.2290 |
| at 0.60 | 0.1846 |
| at 0.70 | 0.1454 |
| at 0.80 | 0.0934 |
| at 0.90 | 0.0480 |
| at 1.00 | 0.0081 |

Avg. prec. (non-interpolated)
for all rel. documents     0.2626

Precision:

| | | |
|---|---|---|
| At | 5 docs: | 0.5100 |
| At | 10 docs: | 0.4450 |
| At | 15 docs: | 0.4067 |
| At | 20 docs: | 0.3787 |
| At | 30 docs: | 0.3350 |
| At | 100 docs: | 0.1960 |
| At | 200 docs: | 0.1294 |
| At | 500 docs: | 0.0643 |
| At | 1000 docs: | 0.0366 |

R-Precision (prec. after
all rel. docs. retrieved):

| | |
|---|---|
| Exact: | 0.3002 |

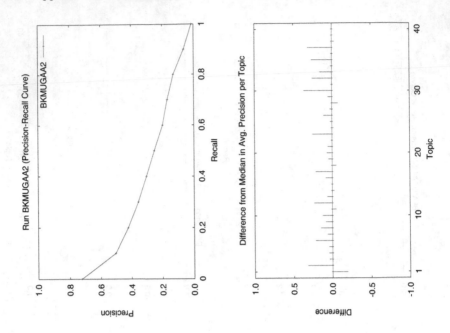

Run BKMUGAA2 (Precision-Recall Curve)

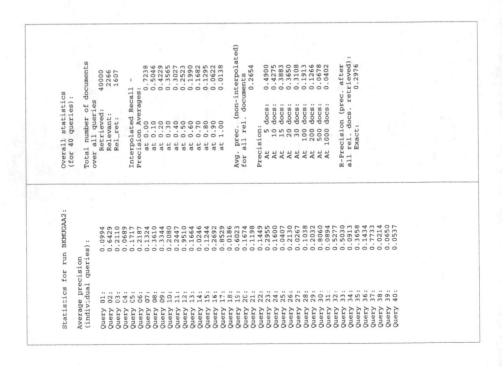

Difference from Median in Avg. Precision per Topic

Statistics for run BKMUGAA2:

Average precision
(individual queries):

| | |
|---|---|
| Query 01: | 0.0994 |
| Query 02: | 0.6429 |
| Query 03: | 0.2110 |
| Query 04: | 0.0689 |
| Query 05: | 0.1717 |
| Query 06: | 0.2187 |
| Query 07: | 0.1324 |
| Query 08: | 0.3610 |
| Query 09: | 0.3344 |
| Query 10: | 0.2080 |
| Query 11: | 0.2447 |
| Query 12: | 0.9510 |
| Query 13: | 0.1664 |
| Query 14: | 0.0246 |
| Query 15: | 0.1244 |
| Query 16: | 0.2692 |
| Query 17: | 0.8529 |
| Query 18: | 0.0186 |
| Query 19: | 0.6023 |
| Query 20: | 0.1674 |
| Query 21: | 0.1198 |
| Query 22: | 0.1449 |
| Query 23: | 0.2955 |
| Query 24: | 0.1600 |
| Query 25: | 0.0407 |
| Query 26: | 0.2130 |
| Query 27: | 0.0267 |
| Query 28: | 0.1038 |
| Query 29: | 0.2032 |
| Query 30: | 0.8060 |
| Query 31: | 0.0894 |
| Query 32: | 0.5277 |
| Query 33: | 0.5030 |
| Query 34: | 0.0913 |
| Query 35: | 0.3658 |
| Query 36: | 0.1434 |
| Query 37: | 0.7733 |
| Query 38: | 0.0214 |
| Query 39: | 0.0650 |
| Query 40: | 0.0537 |

Overall statistics
(for 40 queries):

Total number of documents
over all queries
  Retrieved:     40000
  Relevant:       2266
  Rel_ret:        1607

Interpolated Recall -
Precision Averages:
  at 0.00    0.7238
  at 0.10    0.5046
  at 0.20    0.4229
  at 0.30    0.3565
  at 0.40    0.3027
  at 0.50    0.2523
  at 0.60    0.1990
  at 0.70    0.1682
  at 0.80    0.1295
  at 0.90    0.0622
  at 1.00    0.0138

Avg. prec. (non-interpolated)
for all rel. documents      0.2654

Precision:
  At    5 docs:    0.4900
  At   10 docs:    0.4275
  At   15 docs:    0.3883
  At   20 docs:    0.3650
  At   30 docs:    0.3108
  At  100 docs:    0.1913
  At  200 docs:    0.1266
  At  500 docs:    0.0678
  At 1000 docs:    0.0402

R-Precision (prec. after
all rel. docs. retrieved):
      Exact:       0.2976

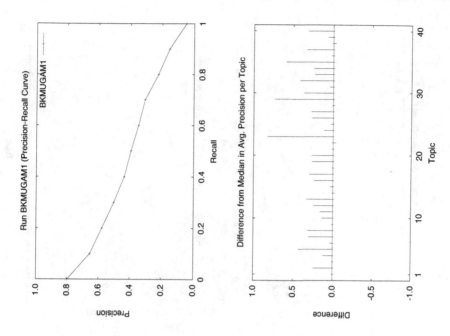

Run BKMUGAM1 (Precision-Recall Curve)

Difference from Median in Avg. Precision per Topic

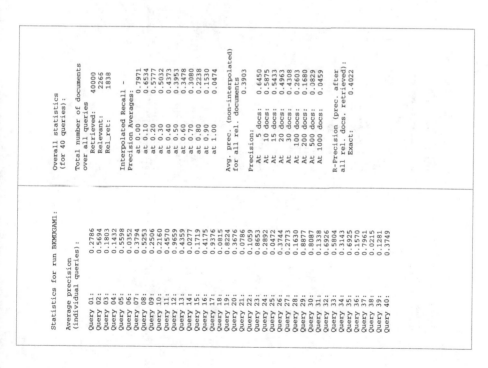

Statistics for run BKMUGAM1:

Average precision
(individual queries):

|  | |
|---|---|
| Query 01: | 0.2786 |
| Query 02: | 0.5694 |
| Query 03: | 0.1803 |
| Query 04: | 0.1432 |
| Query 05: | 0.5598 |
| Query 06: | 0.0352 |
| Query 07: | 0.3794 |
| Query 08: | 0.5253 |
| Query 09: | 0.2506 |
| Query 10: | 0.2160 |
| Query 11: | 0.4570 |
| Query 12: | 0.9659 |
| Query 13: | 0.4359 |
| Query 14: | 0.0277 |
| Query 15: | 0.1719 |
| Query 16: | 0.4175 |
| Query 17: | 0.9376 |
| Query 18: | 0.0815 |
| Query 19: | 0.8224 |
| Query 20: | 0.3676 |
| Query 21: | 0.0786 |
| Query 22: | 0.1059 |
| Query 23: | 0.8653 |
| Query 24: | 0.2892 |
| Query 25: | 0.0472 |
| Query 26: | 0.3744 |
| Query 27: | 0.2773 |
| Query 28: | 0.1630 |
| Query 29: | 0.8877 |
| Query 30: | 0.8087 |
| Query 31: | 0.1338 |
| Query 32: | 0.6926 |
| Query 33: | 0.5804 |
| Query 34: | 0.3143 |
| Query 35: | 0.6925 |
| Query 36: | 0.1570 |
| Query 37: | 0.7961 |
| Query 38: | 0.0215 |
| Query 39: | 0.1281 |
| Query 40: | 0.3749 |

Overall statistics
(for 40 queries):

Total number of documents
over all queries:

| | |
|---|---|
| Retrieved: | 40000 |
| Relevant: | 2266 |
| Rel_ret: | 1838 |

Interpolated Recall -
Precision Averages:

| | |
|---|---|
| at 0.00 | 0.7971 |
| at 0.10 | 0.6534 |
| at 0.20 | 0.5777 |
| at 0.30 | 0.5032 |
| at 0.40 | 0.4373 |
| at 0.50 | 0.3953 |
| at 0.60 | 0.3478 |
| at 0.70 | 0.3080 |
| at 0.80 | 0.2238 |
| at 0.90 | 0.1530 |
| at 1.00 | 0.0474 |

Avg. prec. (non-interpolated)
for all rel. documents
0.3903

Precision:

| | |
|---|---|
| At   5 docs: | 0.6450 |
| At  10 docs: | 0.5875 |
| At  15 docs: | 0.5433 |
| At  20 docs: | 0.4963 |
| At  30 docs: | 0.4308 |
| At 100 docs: | 0.2603 |
| At 200 docs: | 0.1680 |
| At 500 docs: | 0.0829 |
| At 1000 docs: | 0.0459 |

R-Precision (prec. after
all rel. docs. retrieved):
Exact:    0.4022

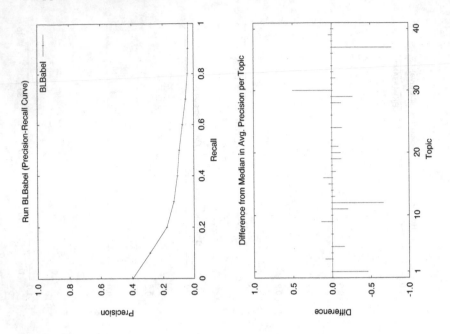

Run BLBabel (Precision-Recall Curve)

BLBabel ——

Difference from Median in Avg. Precision per Topic

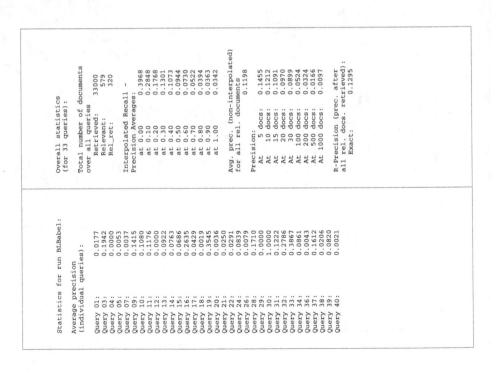

```
Statistics for run BLBabel:              Overall statistics
                                         (for 33 queries):
Average precision
(individual queries):                    Total number of documents
                                         over all queries
Query 01:      0.0177                        Retrieved:      33000
Query 03:      0.1942                        Relevant:         579
Query 04:      0.0000                        Rel_ret:          320
Query 05:      0.0053
Query 07:      0.0037                     Interpolated Recall -
Query 09:      0.1415                     Precision Averages:
Query 10:      0.1080                          at 0.00      0.3968
Query 11:      0.1176                          at 0.10      0.2848
Query 12:      0.0000                          at 0.20      0.1768
Query 13:      0.0922                          at 0.30      0.1301
Query 14:      0.0763                          at 0.40      0.1073
Query 15:      0.0686                          at 0.50      0.0944
Query 16:      0.2635                          at 0.60      0.0730
Query 17:      0.0429                          at 0.70      0.0522
Query 18:      0.0019                          at 0.80      0.0394
Query 19:      0.3545                          at 0.90      0.0363
Query 20:      0.0036                          at 1.00      0.0342
Query 21:      0.0250
Query 22:      0.0291                     Avg. prec. (non-interpolated)
Query 24:      0.0839                     for all rel. documents   0.1198
Query 26:      0.0079
Query 28:      0.1710                     Precision:
Query 29:      0.0000                         At    5 docs:    0.1455
Query 30:      1.0000                         At   10 docs:    0.1212
Query 31:      0.1222                         At   15 docs:    0.1091
Query 32:      0.2786                         At   20 docs:    0.0970
Query 33:      0.3867                         At   30 docs:    0.0899
Query 34:      0.0861                         At  100 docs:    0.0524
Query 36:      0.0043                         At  200 docs:    0.0324
Query 37:      0.1612                         At  500 docs:    0.0166
Query 38:      0.0206                         At 1000 docs:    0.0097
Query 39:      0.0820
Query 40:      0.0021                     R-Precision (prec. after
                                         all rel. docs. retrieved):
                                             Exact:         0.1295
```

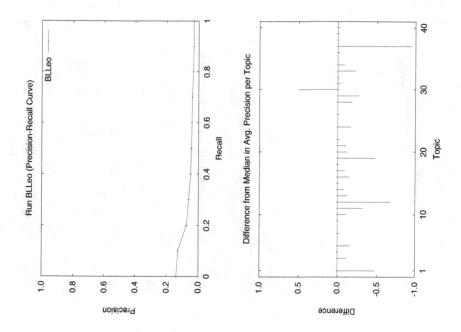

Run BLLeo (Precision-Recall Curve)

Difference from Median in Avg. Precision per Topic

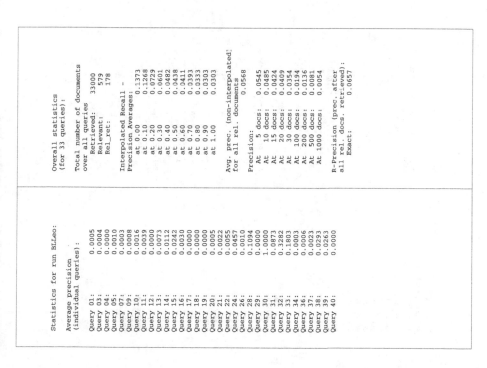

Statistics for run BLLeo:

Average precision
(individual queries):

|  | |
|---|---|
| Query 01: | 0.0005 |
| Query 03: | 0.0004 |
| Query 04: | 0.0000 |
| Query 05: | 0.0010 |
| Query 07: | 0.0003 |
| Query 09: | 0.0008 |
| Query 10: | 0.0016 |
| Query 11: | 0.0039 |
| Query 12: | 0.0000 |
| Query 13: | 0.0073 |
| Query 14: | 0.0112 |
| Query 15: | 0.0242 |
| Query 16: | 0.0030 |
| Query 17: | 0.0000 |
| Query 18: | 0.0000 |
| Query 19: | 0.0000 |
| Query 20: | 0.0005 |
| Query 21: | 0.0022 |
| Query 22: | 0.0055 |
| Query 24: | 0.0457 |
| Query 26: | 0.0010 |
| Query 28: | 0.1094 |
| Query 29: | 0.0000 |
| Query 30: | 1.0000 |
| Query 31: | 0.0873 |
| Query 32: | 0.3282 |
| Query 33: | 0.1803 |
| Query 34: | 0.0003 |
| Query 36: | 0.0006 |
| Query 37: | 0.0023 |
| Query 38: | 0.0293 |
| Query 39: | 0.0263 |
| Query 40: | 0.0000 |

Overall statistics
(for 33 queries):

Total number of documents
over all queries:

| | |
|---|---|
| Retrieved: | 33000 |
| Relevant: | 579 |
| Rel_ret: | 178 |

Interpolated Recall -
Precision Averages:

| | |
|---|---|
| at 0.00 | 0.1373 |
| at 0.10 | 0.1268 |
| at 0.20 | 0.0729 |
| at 0.30 | 0.0601 |
| at 0.40 | 0.0482 |
| at 0.50 | 0.0438 |
| at 0.60 | 0.0411 |
| at 0.70 | 0.0393 |
| at 0.80 | 0.0333 |
| at 0.90 | 0.0303 |
| at 1.00 | 0.0303 |

Avg. prec. (non-interpolated)
for all rel. documents    0.0568

Precision:

| | | |
|---|---|---|
| At | 5 docs: | 0.0545 |
| At | 10 docs: | 0.0485 |
| At | 15 docs: | 0.0424 |
| At | 20 docs: | 0.0409 |
| At | 30 docs: | 0.0354 |
| At | 100 docs: | 0.0194 |
| At | 200 docs: | 0.0136 |
| At | 500 docs: | 0.0081 |
| At | 1000 docs: | 0.0054 |

R-Precision (prec. after
all rel. docs. retrieved):
Exact:    0.0657

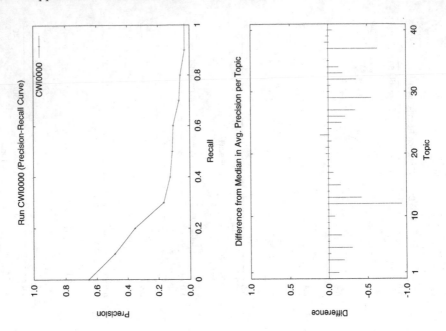

Run CWI0000 (Precision-Recall Curve)

Difference from Median in Avg. Precision per Topic

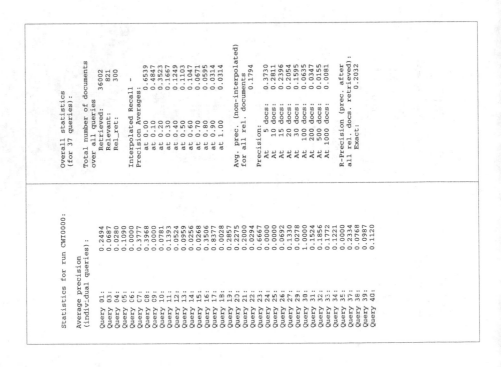

Statistics for run CWI0000:

Average precision
(indiv-dual queries):

|  | |
|---|---|
| Query 01: | 0.2494 |
| Query 03: | 0.0687 |
| Query 04: | 0.0280 |
| Query 05: | 0.1090 |
| Query 06: | 0.0000 |
| Query 07: | 0.3777 |
| Query 08: | 0.3968 |
| Query 09: | 0.0000 |
| Query 10: | 0.0781 |
| Query 11: | 0.1393 |
| Query 12: | 0.0524 |
| Query 13: | 0.0959 |
| Query 14: | 0.0256 |
| Query 15: | 0.0268 |
| Query 16: | 0.3506 |
| Query 17: | 0.8377 |
| Query 18: | 0.0028 |
| Query 19: | 0.2857 |
| Query 20: | 0.2275 |
| Query 21: | 0.2000 |
| Query 22: | 0.0294 |
| Query 23: | 0.6667 |
| Query 24: | 0.0000 |
| Query 25: | 0.0000 |
| Query 26: | 0.0692 |
| Query 27: | 0.1330 |
| Query 29: | 0.0278 |
| Query 30: | 1.0000 |
| Query 31: | 0.1524 |
| Query 32: | 0.1856 |
| Query 33: | 0.1772 |
| Query 34: | 0.1221 |
| Query 35: | 0.0000 |
| Query 37: | 0.2334 |
| Query 38: | 0.0768 |
| Query 39: | 0.0987 |
| Query 40: | 0.1120 |

Overall statistics
(for 37 queries):

Total number of documents
over all queries:
| | |
|---|---|
| Retrieved: | 36002 |
| Relevant: | 821 |
| Rel_ret: | 300 |

Interpolated Recall -
Precision Averages:
| | |
|---|---|
| at 0.00 | 0.6539 |
| at 0.10 | 0.4847 |
| at 0.20 | 0.3523 |
| at 0.30 | 0.1667 |
| at 0.40 | 0.1249 |
| at 0.50 | 0.1103 |
| at 0.60 | 0.1047 |
| at 0.70 | 0.0671 |
| at 0.80 | 0.0595 |
| at 0.90 | 0.0314 |
| at 1.00 | 0.0314 |

Avg. prec. (non-interpolated)
for all rel. documents      0.1794

Precision:
| | | |
|---|---|---|
| At | 5 docs: | 0.3730 |
| At | 10 docs: | 0.2811 |
| At | 15 docs: | 0.2396 |
| At | 20 docs: | 0.2054 |
| At | 30 docs: | 0.1595 |
| At | 100 docs: | 0.0635 |
| At | 200 docs: | 0.0347 |
| At | 500 docs: | 0.0155 |
| At | 1000 docs: | 0.0081 |

R-Precision (prec. after
all rel. docs. retrieved):
| | |
|---|---|
| Exact: | 0.2032 |

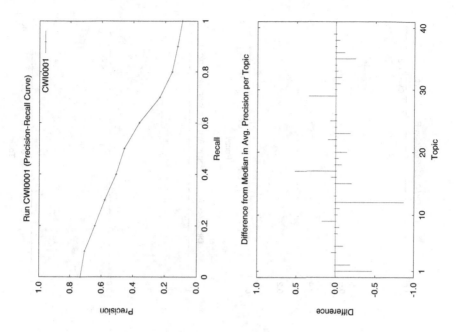

Run CWI0001 (Precision-Recall Curve)

Difference from Median in Avg. Precision per Topic

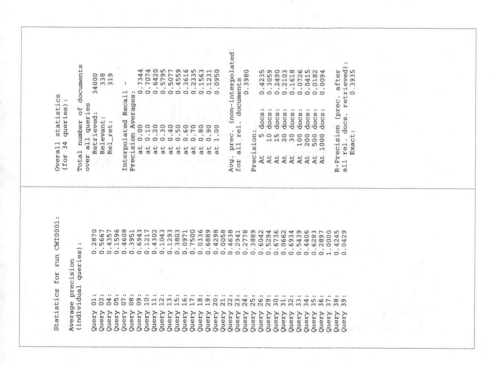

Statistics for run CWI0001:

Average precision
(individual queries):

| | |
|---|---|
| Query 01: | 0.2870 |
| Query 02: | 0.5667 |
| Query 04: | 0.4357 |
| Query 05: | 0.1596 |
| Query 07: | 0.4608 |
| Query 08: | 0.3951 |
| Query 09: | 0.6943 |
| Query 10: | 0.1217 |
| Query 11: | 0.4302 |
| Query 12: | 0.1043 |
| Query 13: | 0.1293 |
| Query 15: | 0.3803 |
| Query 16: | 0.0971 |
| Query 17: | 0.7500 |
| Query 18: | 0.0336 |
| Query 19: | 0.6889 |
| Query 20: | 0.4298 |
| Query 21: | 0.0058 |
| Query 22: | 0.4638 |
| Query 23: | 0.2941 |
| Query 24: | 0.2778 |
| Query 25: | 0.3889 |
| Query 26: | 0.6042 |
| Query 29: | 0.5294 |
| Query 30: | 0.6736 |
| Query 31: | 0.0662 |
| Query 32: | 0.6934 |
| Query 33: | 0.5439 |
| Query 34: | 0.4406 |
| Query 35: | 0.6283 |
| Query 36: | 0.2897 |
| Query 37: | 1.0000 |
| Query 38: | 0.4245 |
| Query 39: | 0.0429 |

Overall statistics
(for 34 queries):

Total number of documents
over all queries:

| | |
|---|---|
| Retrieved: | 34000 |
| Relevant: | 338 |
| Rel_ret: | 319 |

Interpolated Recall -
Precision Averages:

| | |
|---|---|
| at 0.00 | 0.7344 |
| at 0.10 | 0.7074 |
| at 0.20 | 0.6420 |
| at 0.30 | 0.5795 |
| at 0.40 | 0.5077 |
| at 0.50 | 0.4559 |
| at 0.60 | 0.3616 |
| at 0.70 | 0.2335 |
| at 0.80 | 0.1563 |
| at 0.90 | 0.1231 |
| at 1.00 | 0.0950 |

Avg. prec. (non-interpolated)
for all rel. documents     0.3980

Precision:

| | | | |
|---|---|---|---|
| At | 5 | docs: | 0.4235 |
| At | 10 | docs: | 0.3059 |
| At | 15 | docs: | 0.2490 |
| At | 20 | docs: | 0.2103 |
| At | 30 | docs: | 0.1618 |
| At | 100 | docs: | 0.0726 |
| At | 200 | docs: | 0.0415 |
| At | 500 | docs: | 0.0182 |
| At | 1000 | docs: | 0.0094 |

R-Precision (prec. after
all rel. docs. retrieved):

| | |
|---|---|
| Exact: | 0.3935 |

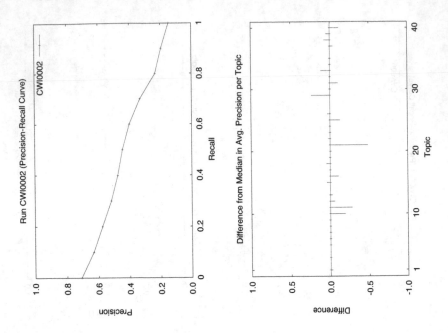

Run CWI0002 (Precision-Recall Curve)

CWI0002

Difference from Median in Avg. Precision per Topic

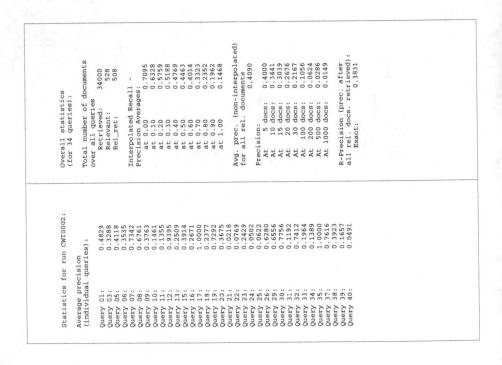

Statistics for run CWI0002:

Average precision
(individual queries):

| Query 01: | 0.4829 |
|---|---|
| Query 03: | 0.3288 |
| Query 05: | 0.4118 |
| Query 06: | 0.3535 |
| Query 07: | 0.7342 |
| Query 08: | 0.6761 |
| Query 09: | 0.3763 |
| Query 10: | 0.1461 |
| Query 11: | 0.1355 |
| Query 12: | 0.9395 |
| Query 13: | 0.2509 |
| Query 15: | 0.3914 |
| Query 16: | 0.2671 |
| Query 17: | 1.0000 |
| Query 18: | 0.2377 |
| Query 19: | 0.7292 |
| Query 20: | 0.3675 |
| Query 21: | 0.0218 |
| Query 22: | 0.0769 |
| Query 23: | 0.2429 |
| Query 24: | 0.0502 |
| Query 25: | 0.0622 |
| Query 26: | 0.6280 |
| Query 29: | 0.6556 |
| Query 30: | 0.7756 |
| Query 31: | 0.1192 |
| Query 32: | 0.7412 |
| Query 33: | 0.1964 |
| Query 34: | 0.1389 |
| Query 35: | 1.0000 |
| Query 37: | 0.7616 |
| Query 38: | 0.3923 |
| Query 39: | 0.1657 |
| Query 40: | 0.0491 |

Overall statistics
(for 34 queries):

Total number of documents
over all queries:
| Retrieved: | 34000 |
|---|---|
| Relevant: | 528 |
| Rel_ret: | 508 |

Interpolated Recall -
Precision Averages:
| at 0.00 | 0.7095 |
|---|---|
| at 0.10 | 0.6328 |
| at 0.20 | 0.5759 |
| at 0.30 | 0.5188 |
| at 0.40 | 0.4769 |
| at 0.50 | 0.4463 |
| at 0.60 | 0.4014 |
| at 0.70 | 0.3323 |
| at 0.80 | 0.2352 |
| at 0.90 | 0.1962 |
| at 1.00 | 0.1468 |

Avg. prec. (non-interpolated)
for all rel. documents
0.4090

Precision:
| At 5 docs: | 0.4000 |
|---|---|
| At 10 docs: | 0.3441 |
| At 15 docs: | 0.3039 |
| At 20 docs: | 0.2676 |
| At 30 docs: | 0.2167 |
| At 100 docs: | 0.1056 |
| At 200 docs: | 0.0624 |
| At 500 docs: | 0.0286 |
| At 1000 docs: | 0.0149 |

R-Precision (prec. after
all rel. docs. retrieved):
| Exact: | 0.3831 |

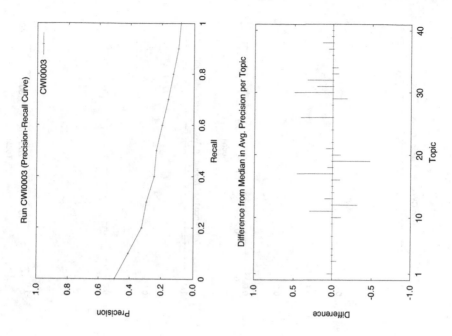

Run CWI0003 (Precision-Recall Curve)

Difference from Median in Avg. Precision per Topic

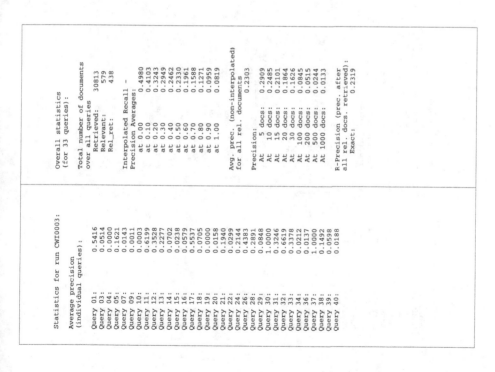

Statistics for run CWI0003:

Average precision
(individual queries):

|  | |
|---|---|
| Query 01: | 0.5416 |
| Query 03: | 0.0514 |
| Query 04: | 0.0000 |
| Query 05: | 0.1621 |
| Query 07: | 0.0143 |
| Query 09: | 0.0011 |
| Query 10: | 0.0003 |
| Query 11: | 0.6199 |
| Query 12: | 0.3528 |
| Query 13: | 0.2277 |
| Query 14: | 0.0702 |
| Query 15: | 0.0238 |
| Query 16: | 0.0579 |
| Query 17: | 0.5537 |
| Query 18: | 0.0705 |
| Query 19: | 0.0000 |
| Query 20: | 0.0158 |
| Query 21: | 0.1940 |
| Query 22: | 0.0299 |
| Query 24: | 0.2144 |
| Query 26: | 0.4383 |
| Query 28: | 0.2891 |
| Query 29: | 0.0848 |
| Query 30: | 1.0000 |
| Query 31: | 0.3246 |
| Query 32: | 0.6619 |
| Query 33: | 0.3378 |
| Query 34: | 0.0212 |
| Query 36: | 0.0137 |
| Query 37: | 1.0000 |
| Query 38: | 0.1492 |
| Query 39: | 0.0598 |
| Query 40: | 0.0188 |

Overall statistics
(for 33 queries):

Total number of documents
over all queries:
| | |
|---|---|
| Retrieved: | 30813 |
| Relevant: | 579 |
| Rel_ret: | 438 |

Interpolated Recall –
Precision Averages:
| | |
|---|---|
| at 0.00 | 0.4980 |
| at 0.10 | 0.4103 |
| at 0.20 | 0.3243 |
| at 0.30 | 0.2949 |
| at 0.40 | 0.2462 |
| at 0.50 | 0.2330 |
| at 0.60 | 0.1961 |
| at 0.70 | 0.1588 |
| at 0.80 | 0.1271 |
| at 0.90 | 0.0959 |
| at 1.00 | 0.0819 |

Avg. prec. (non-interpolated)
for all rel. documents
0.2303

Precision:
| | |
|---|---|
| At    5 docs: | 0.2909 |
| At   10 docs: | 0.2485 |
| At   15 docs: | 0.2101 |
| At   20 docs: | 0.1864 |
| At   30 docs: | 0.1626 |
| At  100 docs: | 0.0845 |
| At  200 docs: | 0.0515 |
| At  500 docs: | 0.0244 |
| At 1000 docs: | 0.0133 |

R-Precision (prec. after
all rel. docs. retrieved):
| | |
|---|---|
| Exact: | 0.2319 |

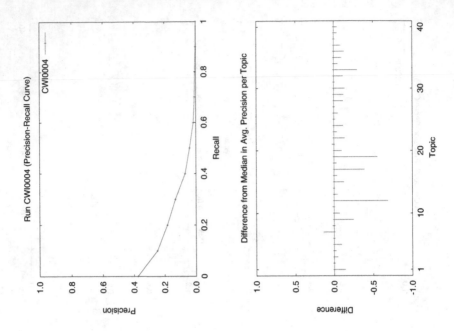

Run CWI0004 (Precision-Recall Curve)

Difference from Median in Avg. Precision per Topic

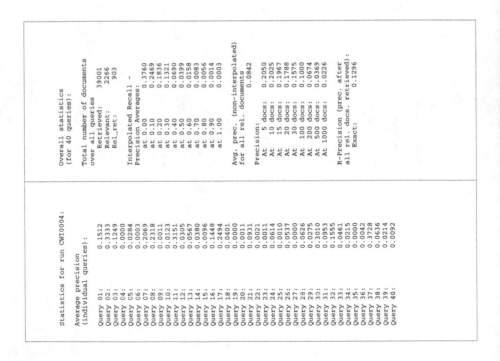

Statistics for run CWI0004:

Average precision
(individual queries):

| | |
|---|---|
| Query 01: | 0.1512 |
| Query 02: | 0.3333 |
| Query 03: | 0.1249 |
| Query 04: | 0.0000 |
| Query 05: | 0.0284 |
| Query 06: | 0.0003 |
| Query 07: | 0.2069 |
| Query 08: | 0.2318 |
| Query 09: | 0.0011 |
| Query 10: | 0.0123 |
| Query 11: | 0.3151 |
| Query 12: | 0.0305 |
| Query 13: | 0.0567 |
| Query 14: | 0.0380 |
| Query 15: | 0.0096 |
| Query 16: | 0.1448 |
| Query 17: | 0.2494 |
| Query 18: | 0.0401 |
| Query 19: | 0.0000 |
| Query 20: | 0.0011 |
| Query 21: | 0.0931 |
| Query 22: | 0.0021 |
| Query 23: | 0.0011 |
| Query 24: | 0.0614 |
| Query 25: | 0.0010 |
| Query 26: | 0.0537 |
| Query 27: | 0.0000 |
| Query 28: | 0.0626 |
| Query 29: | 0.0275 |
| Query 30: | 0.3010 |
| Query 31: | 0.0953 |
| Query 32: | 0.1555 |
| Query 33: | 0.0461 |
| Query 34: | 0.0215 |
| Query 35: | 0.0000 |
| Query 36: | 0.0042 |
| Query 37: | 0.3728 |
| Query 38: | 0.0636 |
| Query 39: | 0.0214 |
| Query 40: | 0.0092 |

Overall statistics
(for 40 queries):

Total number of documents
over all queries
Retrieved:     39001
Relevant:      2266
Rel_ret:         903

Interpolated Recall -
Precision Averages:

| | |
|---|---|
| at 0.00 | 0.3760 |
| at 0.10 | 0.2469 |
| at 0.20 | 0.1836 |
| at 0.30 | 0.1321 |
| at 0.40 | 0.0690 |
| at 0.50 | 0.0399 |
| at 0.60 | 0.0158 |
| at 0.70 | 0.0083 |
| at 0.80 | 0.0056 |
| at 0.90 | 0.0014 |
| at 1.00 | 0.0003 |

Avg. prec. (non-interpolated)
for all rel. documents    0.0842

Precision:

| | |
|---|---|
| At    5 docs: | 0.2050 |
| At   10 docs: | 0.2025 |
| At   15 docs: | 0.1967 |
| At   20 docs: | 0.1788 |
| At   30 docs: | 0.1575 |
| At  100 docs: | 0.1000 |
| At  200 docs: | 0.0674 |
| At  500 docs: | 0.0369 |
| At 1000 docs: | 0.0226 |

R-Precision (prec. after
all rel. docs. retrieved):
Exact:    0.1296

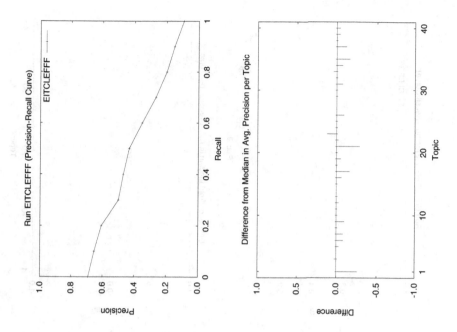

Run EITCLEFFF (Precision-Recall Curve)

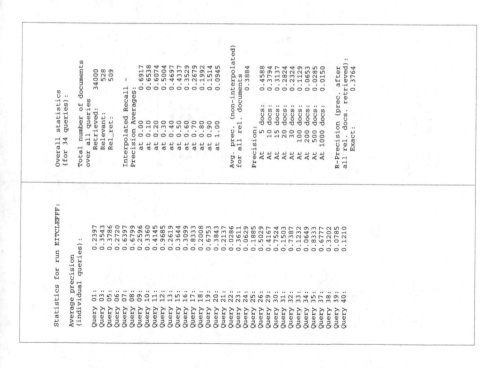

Difference from Median in Avg. Precision per Topic

Statistics for run EITCLEFFF:

Average precision
(individual queries):

| | |
|---|---|
| Query 01: | 0.2397 |
| Query 03: | 0.3543 |
| Query 05: | 0.3786 |
| Query 06: | 0.2720 |
| Query 07: | 0.6397 |
| Query 08: | 0.6799 |
| Query 09: | 0.2596 |
| Query 10: | 0.3360 |
| Query 11: | 0.4145 |
| Query 12: | 0.9685 |
| Query 13: | 0.2619 |
| Query 15: | 0.3644 |
| Query 16: | 0.3099 |
| Query 17: | 0.8333 |
| Query 18: | 0.2008 |
| Query 19: | 0.6753 |
| Query 20: | 0.3843 |
| Query 21: | 0.2137 |
| Query 22: | 0.0286 |
| Query 23: | 0.3611 |
| Query 24: | 0.0629 |
| Query 25: | 0.1885 |
| Query 26: | 0.5029 |
| Query 29: | 0.4167 |
| Query 30: | 0.7524 |
| Query 31: | 0.1503 |
| Query 32: | 0.7387 |
| Query 33: | 0.1232 |
| Query 34: | 0.0649 |
| Query 35: | 0.8333 |
| Query 37: | 0.6777 |
| Query 38: | 0.3202 |
| Query 39: | 0.0785 |
| Query 40: | 0.1210 |

Overall statistics
(for 34 queries):

Total number of documents
over all queries:
Retrieved: 34000
Relevant: 528
Rel_ret: 509

Interpolated Recall -
Precision Averages:
| | |
|---|---|
| at 0.00 | 0.6917 |
| at 0.10 | 0.6538 |
| at 0.20 | 0.6074 |
| at 0.30 | 0.5004 |
| at 0.40 | 0.4697 |
| at 0.50 | 0.4337 |
| at 0.60 | 0.3529 |
| at 0.70 | 0.2679 |
| at 0.80 | 0.1992 |
| at 0.90 | 0.1514 |
| at 1.00 | 0.0945 |

Avg. prec. (non-interpolated)
for all rel. documents    0.3884

Precision:
| | |
|---|---|
| At   5 docs: | 0.4588 |
| At  10 docs: | 0.3794 |
| At  15 docs: | 0.3137 |
| At  20 docs: | 0.2824 |
| At  30 docs: | 0.2324 |
| At 100 docs: | 0.1129 |
| At 200 docs: | 0.0653 |
| At 500 docs: | 0.0285 |
| At 1000 docs: | 0.0150 |

R-Precision (prec. after
all rel. docs. retrieved):
Exact:    0.3764

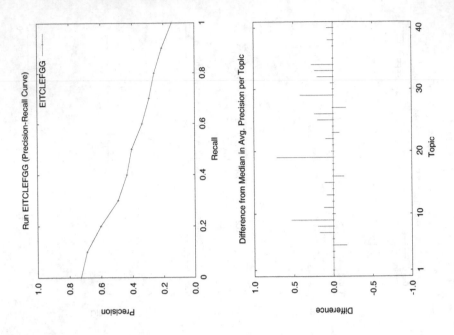

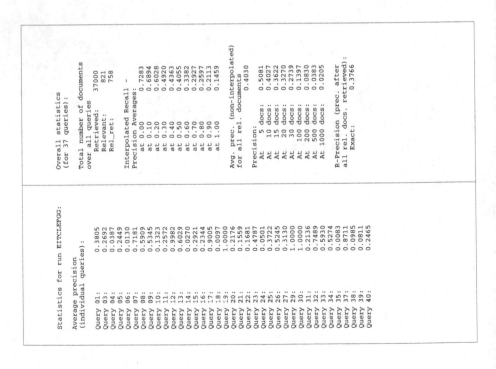

Statistics for run EITCLEFGG:

Average precision
(individual queries):

| | |
|---|---|
| Query 01: | 0.3805 |
| Query 03: | 0.2692 |
| Query 04: | 0.0387 |
| Query 05: | 0.2449 |
| Query 06: | 0.0130 |
| Query 07: | 0.7181 |
| Query 08: | 0.5909 |
| Query 09: | 0.5345 |
| Query 10: | 0.1323 |
| Query 11: | 0.2572 |
| Query 12: | 0.9982 |
| Query 13: | 0.6029 |
| Query 14: | 0.0270 |
| Query 15: | 0.2921 |
| Query 16: | 0.2344 |
| Query 17: | 0.9005 |
| Query 18: | 0.0097 |
| Query 19: | 1.0000 |
| Query 20: | 0.2176 |
| Query 21: | 0.1559 |
| Query 22: | 0.1681 |
| Query 23: | 0.4787 |
| Query 24: | 0.0501 |
| Query 25: | 0.3722 |
| Query 26: | 0.5245 |
| Query 27: | 0.3130 |
| Query 29: | 1.0000 |
| Query 30: | 0.1397 |
| Query 31: | 0.2136 |
| Query 32: | 0.7489 |
| Query 33: | 0.5930 |
| Query 34: | 0.5274 |
| Query 35: | 0.0083 |
| Query 37: | 0.8711 |
| Query 38: | 0.0985 |
| Query 39: | 0.0811 |
| Query 40: | 0.2465 |

Overall statistics
(for 37 queries):

Total number of documents
over all queries:

| | |
|---|---|
| Retrieved: | 37000 |
| Relevant: | 821 |
| Rel_ret: | 758 |

Interpolated Recall -
Precision Averages:

| | |
|---|---|
| at 0.00 | 0.7283 |
| at 0.10 | 0.6894 |
| at 0.20 | 0.6028 |
| at 0.30 | 0.4920 |
| at 0.40 | 0.4363 |
| at 0.50 | 0.4055 |
| at 0.60 | 0.3382 |
| at 0.70 | 0.2927 |
| at 0.80 | 0.2597 |
| at 0.90 | 0.2113 |
| at 1.00 | 0.1459 |

Avg. prec. (non-interpolated)
for all rel. documents    0.4030

Precision:

| | |
|---|---|
| At   5 docs: | 0.5081 |
| At  10 docs: | 0.4027 |
| At  15 docs: | 0.3622 |
| At  20 docs: | 0.3270 |
| At  30 docs: | 0.2739 |
| At 100 docs: | 0.1397 |
| At 200 docs: | 0.0830 |
| At 500 docs: | 0.0383 |
| At 1000 docs: | 0.0205 |

R-Precision (prec. after
all rel. docs. retrieved):
Exact:    0.3766

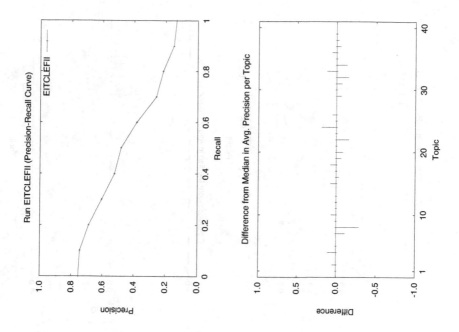

Run EITCLEFII (Precision-Recall Curve)

EITCLEFII

Difference from Median in Avg. Precision per Topic

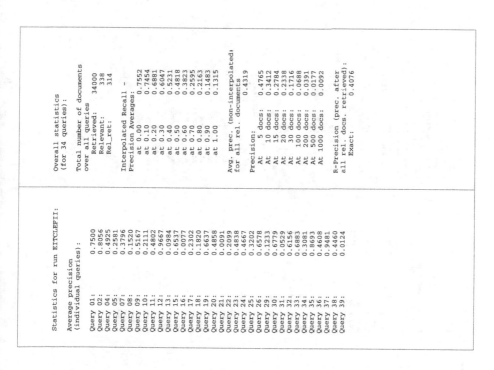

Statistics for run EITCLEFII:

Average precision
(individual queries):

|  | |
|---|---|
| Query 01: | 0.7500 |
| Query 02: | 0.8056 |
| Query 04: | 0.4925 |
| Query 05: | 0.2581 |
| Query 07: | 0.3796 |
| Query 08: | 0.1520 |
| Query 09: | 0.5167 |
| Query 10: | 0.2111 |
| Query 11: | 0.4802 |
| Query 12: | 0.9667 |
| Query 13: | 0.0984 |
| Query 15: | 0.6537 |
| Query 16: | 0.0077 |
| Query 17: | 0.2302 |
| Query 18: | 0.1820 |
| Query 19: | 0.6637 |
| Query 20: | 0.4858 |
| Query 21: | 0.0091 |
| Query 22: | 0.2099 |
| Query 23: | 0.4838 |
| Query 24: | 0.4667 |
| Query 25: | 0.3202 |
| Query 26: | 0.6578 |
| Query 29: | 0.1233 |
| Query 30: | 0.6779 |
| Query 31: | 0.0529 |
| Query 32: | 0.6156 |
| Query 33: | 0.6883 |
| Query 34: | 0.3081 |
| Query 35: | 0.8693 |
| Query 36: | 0.4608 |
| Query 37: | 0.9481 |
| Query 38: | 0.4460 |
| Query 39: | 0.0124 |

Overall statistics
(for 34 queries):

Total number of documents
over all queries:
  Retrieved:    34000
  Relevant:       338
  Rel_ret:        314

Interpolated Recall -
Precision Averages:
  at 0.00    0.7552
  at 0.10    0.7454
  at 0.20    0.6881
  at 0.30    0.6047
  at 0.40    0.5231
  at 0.50    0.4818
  at 0.60    0.3823
  at 0.70    0.2595
  at 0.80    0.2163
  at 0.90    0.1483
  at 1.00    0.1315

Avg. prec. (non-interpolated)
for all rel. documents
                  0.4319

Precision:
  At    5 docs:   0.4765
  At   10 docs:   0.3412
  At   15 docs:   0.2784
  At   20 docs:   0.2338
  At   30 docs:   0.1716
  At  100 docs:   0.0688
  At  200 docs:   0.0391
  At  500 docs:   0.0177
  At 1000 docs:   0.0092

R-Precision (prec. after
all rel. docs. retrieved):
  Exact:    0.4076

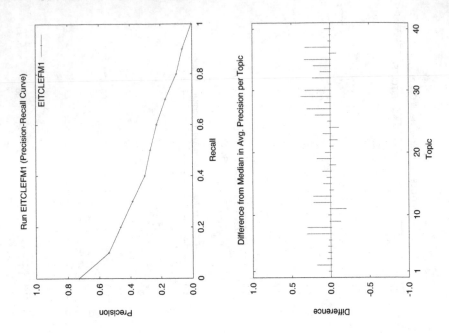

Run EITCLEFM1 (Precision-Recall Curve)

Difference from Median in Avg. Precision per Topic

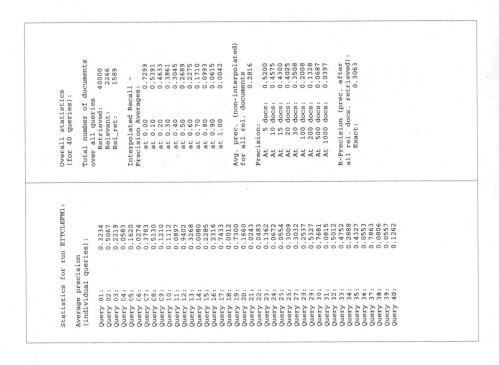

Statistics for run EITCLEFM1:

Average precision
(individual queries):

| | |
|---|---|
| Query 01: | 0.3234 |
| Query 02: | 0.5067 |
| Query 03: | 0.2219 |
| Query 04: | 0.0583 |
| Query 05: | 0.1620 |
| Query 06: | 0.0274 |
| Query 07: | 0.3783 |
| Query 08: | 0.5130 |
| Query 09: | 0.1210 |
| Query 10: | 0.1112 |
| Query 11: | 0.0897 |
| Query 12: | 0.9402 |
| Query 13: | 0.3268 |
| Query 14: | 0.0080 |
| Query 15: | 0.2285 |
| Query 16: | 0.2316 |
| Query 17: | 0.7433 |
| Query 18: | 0.0012 |
| Query 19: | 0.7300 |
| Query 20: | 0.1660 |
| Query 21: | 0.0243 |
| Query 22: | 0.0483 |
| Query 23: | 0.1362 |
| Query 24: | 0.0672 |
| Query 25: | 0.0554 |
| Query 25: | 0.3009 |
| Query 27: | 0.3032 |
| Query 28: | 0.2537 |
| Query 29: | 0.5327 |
| Query 30: | 0.7681 |
| Query 31: | 0.0815 |
| Query 32: | 0.5012 |
| Query 33: | 0.4752 |
| Query 34: | 0.2888 |
| Query 35: | 0.4327 |
| Query 36: | 0.0553 |
| Query 37: | 0.7863 |
| Query 38: | 0.0806 |
| Query 39: | 0.0557 |
| Query 40: | 0.1262 |

Overall statistics
(for 40 queries):

Total number of documents
over all queries
    Retrieved:    40000
    Relevant:      2266
    Rel_ret:       1589

Interpolated Recall  -
Precision Averages:
    at 0.00    0.7299
    at 0.10    0.5391
    at 0.20    0.4633
    at 0.30    0.3861
    at 0.40    0.3045
    at 0.50    0.2689
    at 0.60    0.2275
    at 0.70    0.1710
    at 0.80    0.0993
    at 0.90    0.0615
    at 1.00    0.0042

Avg. prec. (non-interpolated)
for all rel. documents    0.2816

Precision:
    At    5 docs:    0.5200
    At   10 docs:    0.4575
    At   15 docs:    0.4300
    At   20 docs:    0.4025
    At   30 docs:    0.3508
    At  100 docs:    0.2008
    At  200 docs:    0.1328
    At  500 docs:    0.0687
    At 1000 docs:    0.0397

R-Precision (prec. after
all rel. docs. retrieved):
    Exact:    0.3063

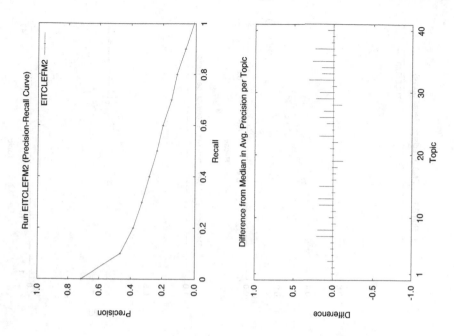

Run EITCLEFM2 (Precision-Recall Curve)

EITCLEFM2

Difference from Median in Avg. Precision per Topic

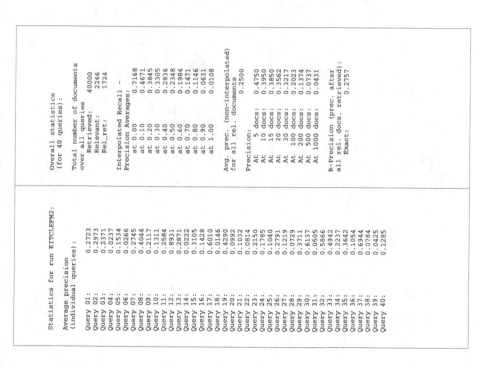

Statistics for run EITCLEFM2:

Average precision
(individual queries):

| | |
|---|---|
| Query 01: | 0.2723 |
| Query 02: | 0.2973 |
| Query 03: | 0.2371 |
| Query 04: | 0.0237 |
| Query 05: | 0.1534 |
| Query 06: | 0.0266 |
| Query 07: | 0.2745 |
| Query 08: | 0.4044 |
| Query 09: | 0.2117 |
| Query 10: | 0.1311 |
| Query 11: | 0.2584 |
| Query 12: | 0.8931 |
| Query 13: | 0.2871 |
| Query 14: | 0.0222 |
| Query 15: | 0.3105 |
| Query 16: | 0.1428 |
| Query 17: | 0.6010 |
| Query 18: | 0.0146 |
| Query 19: | 0.4290 |
| Query 20: | 0.0992 |
| Query 21: | 0.1032 |
| Query 22: | 0.0814 |
| Query 23: | 0.2150 |
| Query 24: | 0.1785 |
| Query 25: | 0.1040 |
| Query 26: | 0.2791 |
| Query 27: | 0.1219 |
| Query 28: | 0.0729 |
| Query 29: | 0.3711 |
| Query 30: | 0.6137 |
| Query 31: | 0.0505 |
| Query 32: | 0.5866 |
| Query 33: | 0.4942 |
| Query 34: | 0.2237 |
| Query 35: | 0.3642 |
| Query 36: | 0.1054 |
| Query 37: | 0.6944 |
| Query 38: | 0.0784 |
| Query 39: | 0.0425 |
| Query 40: | 0.1285 |

Overall statistics
(for 40 queries):

Total number of documents
over all queries:

| | |
|---|---|
| Retrieved: | 40000 |
| Relevant: | 2266 |
| Rel_ret: | 1724 |

Interpolated Recall -
Precision Averages:

| | |
|---|---|
| at 0.00 | 0.7168 |
| at 0.10 | 0.4671 |
| at 0.20 | 0.3845 |
| at 0.30 | 0.3305 |
| at 0.40 | 0.2836 |
| at 0.50 | 0.2348 |
| at 0.60 | 0.1984 |
| at 0.70 | 0.1471 |
| at 0.80 | 0.1146 |
| at 0.90 | 0.0631 |
| at 1.00 | 0.0108 |

Avg. prec. (non-interpolated)
for all rel. documents          0.2500

Precision:

| | |
|---|---|
| At   5 docs: | 0.4750 |
| At  10 docs: | 0.3950 |
| At  15 docs: | 0.3850 |
| At  20 docs: | 0.3562 |
| At  30 docs: | 0.3217 |
| At 100 docs: | 0.2023 |
| At 200 docs: | 0.1374 |
| At 500 docs: | 0.0737 |
| At 1000 docs: | 0.0431 |

R-Precision (prec. after
all rel. docs. retrieved):

| | |
|---|---|
| Exact: | 0.2757 |

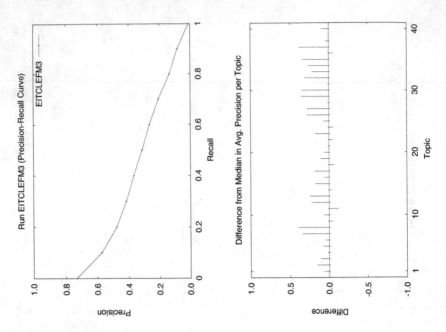

Run EITCLEFM3 (Precision-Recall Curve)

EITCLEFM3

Difference from Median in Avg. Precision per Topic

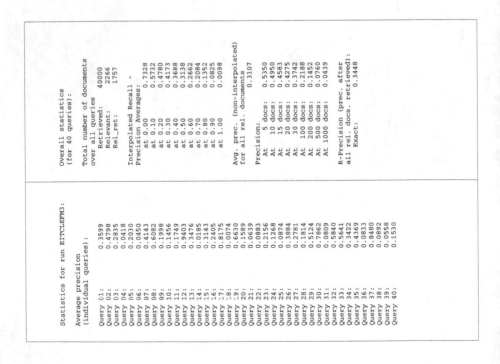

Statistics for run EITCLEFM3:

Average precision
(individual queries):

| | |
|---|---|
| Query 01: | 0.3599 |
| Query 02: | 0.4798 |
| Query 03: | 0.2835 |
| Query 04: | 0.0418 |
| Query 05: | 0.2030 |
| Query 06: | 0.0450 |
| Query 07: | 0.4143 |
| Query 08: | 0.6082 |
| Query 09: | 0.1998 |
| Query 10: | 0.1456 |
| Query 11: | 0.1749 |
| Query 12: | 0.9403 |
| Query 13: | 0.3476 |
| Query 14: | 0.0185 |
| Query 15: | 0.3143 |
| Query 16: | 0.2405 |
| Query 17: | 0.8175 |
| Query 18: | 0.0074 |
| Query 19: | 0.6630 |
| Query 20: | 0.1589 |
| Query 21: | 0.0639 |
| Query 22: | 0.0883 |
| Query 23: | 0.2156 |
| Query 24: | 0.1268 |
| Query 25: | 0.0874 |
| Query 26: | 0.3884 |
| Query 27: | 0.2781 |
| Query 28: | 0.1814 |
| Query 29: | 0.5124 |
| Query 30: | 0.7862 |
| Query 31: | 0.0809 |
| Query 32: | 0.5840 |
| Query 33: | 0.5641 |
| Query 34: | 0.3422 |
| Query 35: | 0.4369 |
| Query 36: | 0.0833 |
| Query 37: | 0.8480 |
| Query 38: | 0.0892 |
| Query 39: | 0.0558 |
| Query 40: | 0.1530 |

Overall statistics
(for 40 queries):

Total number of documents
over all queries:
Retrieved:      40000
Relevant:        2266
Rel_ret:         1757

Interpolated Recall -
Precision Averages:

| | |
|---|---|
| at 0.00 | 0.7328 |
| at 0.10 | 0.5732 |
| at 0.20 | 0.4780 |
| at 0.30 | 0.4173 |
| at 0.40 | 0.3688 |
| at 0.50 | 0.3138 |
| at 0.60 | 0.2662 |
| at 0.70 | 0.2084 |
| at 0.80 | 0.1352 |
| at 0.90 | 0.0825 |
| at 1.00 | 0.0098 |

Avg. prec. (non-interpolated)
for all rel. documents
                      0.3107

Precision:
| | | |
|---|---|---|
| At | 5 docs: | 0.5350 |
| At | 10 docs: | 0.4950 |
| At | 15 docs: | 0.4583 |
| At | 20 docs: | 0.4275 |
| At | 30 docs: | 0.3742 |
| At | 100 docs: | 0.2188 |
| At | 200 docs: | 0.1452 |
| At | 500 docs: | 0.0760 |
| At | 1000 docs: | 0.0439 |

R-Precision (prec. after
all rel. docs. retrieved):
        Exact:      0.3448

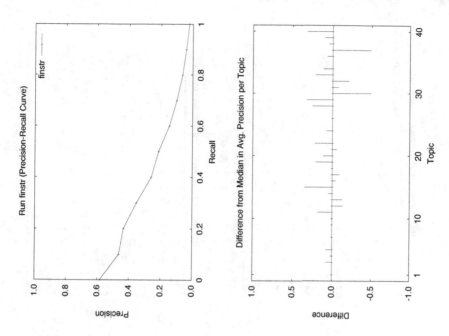

Run finstr (Precision-Recall Curve)

Difference from Median in Avg. Precision per Topic

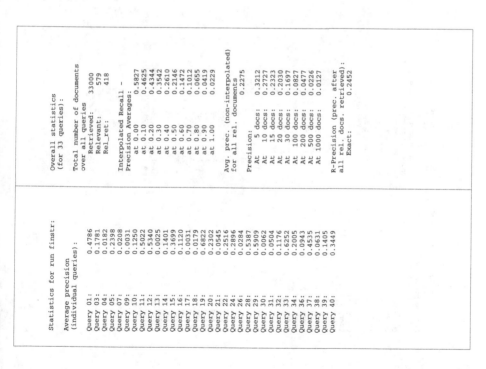

Statistics for run finstr:

Average precision
(individual queries):

| Query 01: | 0.4786 |
| Query 03: | 0.1781 |
| Query 04: | 0.0182 |
| Query 05: | 0.2398 |
| Query 07: | 0.0208 |
| Query 09: | 0.0031 |
| Query 10: | 0.1250 |
| Query 11: | 0.5022 |
| Query 12: | 0.5340 |
| Query 13: | 0.0025 |
| Query 14: | 0.1401 |
| Query 15: | 0.3699 |
| Query 16: | 0.1120 |
| Query 17: | 0.0031 |
| Query 18: | 0.0179 |
| Query 19: | 0.6822 |
| Query 20: | 0.2302 |
| Query 21: | 0.0545 |
| Query 22: | 0.2516 |
| Query 24: | 0.2896 |
| Query 26: | 0.0284 |
| Query 28: | 0.5387 |
| Query 29: | 0.5909 |
| Query 30: | 0.0062 |
| Query 31: | 0.0504 |
| Query 32: | 0.1176 |
| Query 33: | 0.6252 |
| Query 34: | 0.2005 |
| Query 36: | 0.0943 |
| Query 37: | 0.4535 |
| Query 38: | 0.0631 |
| Query 39: | 0.1405 |
| Query 40: | 0.3449 |

Overall statistics
(for 33 queries):

Total number of documents
over all queries
| Retrieved: | 33000 |
| Relevant: | 579 |
| Rel_ret: | 418 |

Interpolated Recall -
Precision Averages:
| at 0.00 | 0.5827 |
| at 0.10 | 0.4625 |
| at 0.20 | 0.4344 |
| at 0.30 | 0.3542 |
| at 0.40 | 0.2610 |
| at 0.50 | 0.2146 |
| at 0.60 | 0.1472 |
| at 0.70 | 0.1012 |
| at 0.80 | 0.0655 |
| at 0.90 | 0.0419 |
| at 1.00 | 0.0229 |

Avg. prec. (non-interpolated)
for all rel. documents      0.2275

Precision:
| At   5 docs: | 0.3212 |
| At  10 docs: | 0.2727 |
| At  15 docs: | 0.2323 |
| At  20 docs: | 0.2030 |
| At  30 docs: | 0.1697 |
| At 100 docs: | 0.0827 |
| At 200 docs: | 0.0477 |
| At 500 docs: | 0.0226 |
| At 1000 docs: | 0.0127 |

R-Precision (prec. after
all rel. docs. retrieved):
| Exact: | 0.2452 |

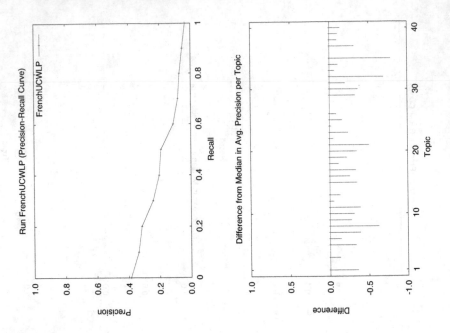

Run FrenchUCWLP (Precision-Recall Curve)

FrenchUCWLP

Difference from Median in Avg. Precision per Topic

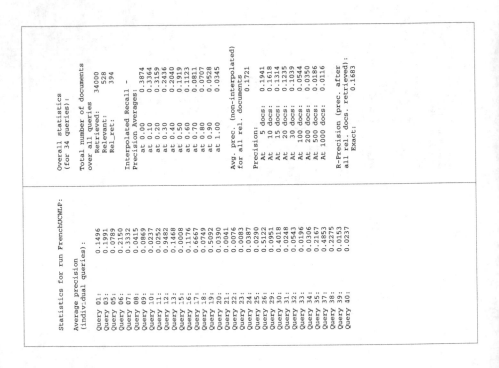

Statistics for run FrenchUCWLP:

Average precision
(individual queries):

| | |
|---|---|
| Query 01: | 0.1496 |
| Query 03: | 0.1991 |
| Query 05: | 0.0789 |
| Query 06: | 0.2150 |
| Query 07: | 0.3332 |
| Query 08: | 0.0415 |
| Query 09: | 0.0869 |
| Query 10: | 0.0237 |
| Query 11: | 0.0252 |
| Query 12: | 0.9482 |
| Query 13: | 0.1468 |
| Query 15: | 0.0008 |
| Query 16: | 0.1176 |
| Query 17: | 0.6667 |
| Query 18: | 0.0749 |
| Query 19: | 0.5092 |
| Query 20: | 0.0390 |
| Query 21: | 0.0041 |
| Query 22: | 0.0076 |
| Query 23: | 0.0083 |
| Query 24: | 0.0387 |
| Query 25: | 0.0290 |
| Query 26: | 0.5122 |
| Query 29: | 0.0951 |
| Query 30: | 0.4018 |
| Query 31: | 0.0248 |
| Query 32: | 0.0543 |
| Query 33: | 0.0196 |
| Query 34: | 0.0306 |
| Query 35: | 0.2167 |
| Query 37: | 0.4853 |
| Query 38: | 0.2275 |
| Query 39: | 0.0153 |
| Query 40: | 0.0237 |

Overall statistics
(for 34 queries):

Total number of documents
over all queries:

| | |
|---|---|
| Retrieved: | 34000 |
| Relevant: | 528 |
| Rel_ret: | 394 |

Interpolated Recall -
Precision Averages:

| | |
|---|---|
| at 0.00 | 0.3874 |
| at 0.10 | 0.3364 |
| at 0.20 | 0.3159 |
| at 0.30 | 0.2436 |
| at 0.40 | 0.2040 |
| at 0.50 | 0.1919 |
| at 0.60 | 0.1123 |
| at 0.70 | 0.0811 |
| at 0.80 | 0.0707 |
| at 0.90 | 0.0528 |
| at 1.00 | 0.0345 |

Avg. prec. (non-interpolated)
for all rel. documents            0.1721

Precision:

| | | |
|---|---|---|
| At | 5 docs: | 0.1941 |
| At | 10 docs: | 0.1618 |
| At | 15 docs: | 0.1314 |
| At | 20 docs: | 0.1235 |
| At | 30 docs: | 0.1039 |
| At | 100 docs: | 0.0544 |
| At | 200 docs: | 0.0350 |
| At | 500 docs: | 0.0186 |
| At | 1000 docs: | 0.0116 |

R-Precision (prec. after
all rel. docs. retrieved):

| | |
|---|---|
| Exact: | 0.1683 |

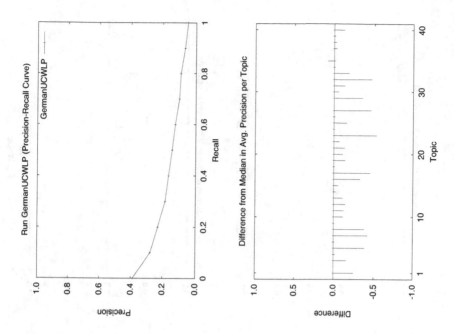

Run GermanUCWLP (Precision-Recall Curve)

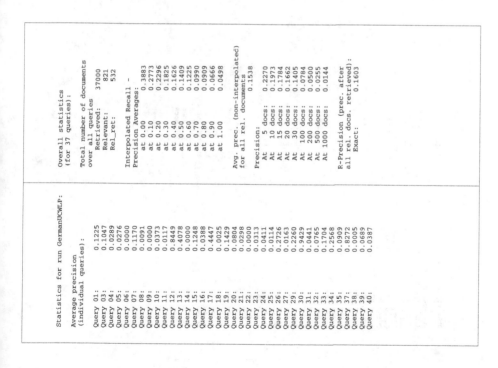

Difference from Median in Avg. Precision per Topic

Statistics for run GermanUCWLP:

Average precision
(individual queries):

| Query 01: | 0.1225 |
| Query 03: | 0.1047 |
| Query 04: | 0.0289 |
| Query 05: | 0.0276 |
| Query 06: | 0.0000 |
| Query 07: | 0.1170 |
| Query 08: | 0.0091 |
| Query 09: | 0.0000 |
| Query 10: | 0.0373 |
| Query 11: | 0.0117 |
| Query 12: | 0.8449 |
| Query 13: | 0.4078 |
| Query 14: | 0.0000 |
| Query 15: | 0.1248 |
| Query 16: | 0.0388 |
| Query 17: | 0.4447 |
| Query 18: | 0.0025 |
| Query 19: | 0.1429 |
| Query 20: | 0.0804 |
| Query 21: | 0.0298 |
| Query 22: | 0.0000 |
| Query 23: | 0.0313 |
| Query 24: | 0.0411 |
| Query 25: | 0.0114 |
| Query 26: | 0.2726 |
| Query 27: | 0.0163 |
| Query 29: | 0.2260 |
| Query 30: | 0.9429 |
| Query 31: | 0.0441 |
| Query 32: | 0.0765 |
| Query 33: | 0.1704 |
| Query 34: | 0.2568 |
| Query 35: | 0.0909 |
| Query 37: | 0.8272 |
| Query 38: | 0.0005 |
| Query 39: | 0.0689 |
| Query 40: | 0.0387 |

Overall statistics
(for 37 queries):

Total number of documents
over all queries
| Retrieved: | 37000 |
| Relevant: | 821 |
| Rel_ret: | 532 |

Interpolated Recall -
Precision Averages:
| at 0.00 | 0.3883 |
| at 0.10 | 0.2773 |
| at 0.20 | 0.2296 |
| at 0.30 | 0.1825 |
| at 0.40 | 0.1626 |
| at 0.50 | 0.1409 |
| at 0.60 | 0.1225 |
| at 0.70 | 0.0990 |
| at 0.80 | 0.0909 |
| at 0.90 | 0.0666 |
| at 1.00 | 0.0498 |

Avg. prec. (non-interpolated)
for all rel. documents
0.1538

Precision:
| At   5 docs: | 0.2270 |
| At  10 docs: | 0.1973 |
| At  15 docs: | 0.1784 |
| At  20 docs: | 0.1662 |
| At  30 docs: | 0.1405 |
| At 100 docs: | 0.0784 |
| At 200 docs: | 0.0500 |
| At 500 docs: | 0.0255 |
| At 1000 docs: | 0.0144 |

R-Precision (prec. after
all rel. docs. retrieved):
| Exact: | 0.1603 |

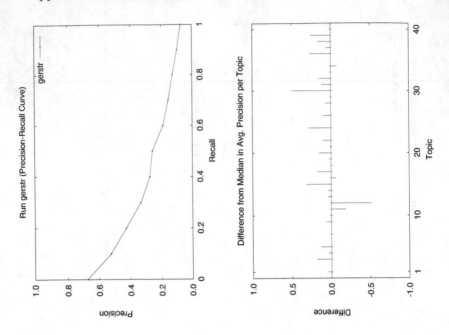

Run gerstr (Precision-Recall Curve)

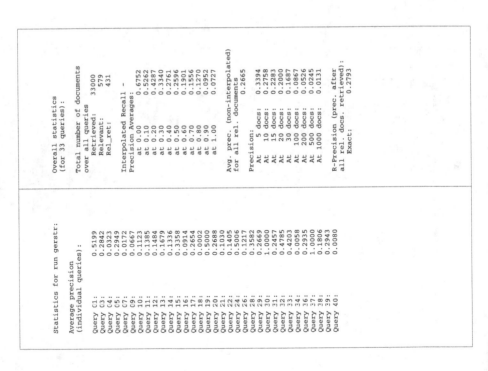

Difference from Median in Avg. Precision per Topic

Statistics for run gerstr:

Average precision
(individual queries):

|  | | |
|---|---|---|
| Query C1: | 0.5199 |
| Query C3: | 0.2842 |
| Query C4: | 0.0323 |
| Query C5: | 0.2949 |
| Query C7: | 0.0172 |
| Query C9: | 0.0667 |
| Query 10: | 0.1123 |
| Query 11: | 0.1385 |
| Query 12: | 0.1484 |
| Query 13: | 0.1679 |
| Query 14: | 0.1336 |
| Query 15: | 0.3358 |
| Query 16: | 0.0914 |
| Query 17: | 0.2654 |
| Query 18: | 0.0002 |
| Query 19: | 0.5000 |
| Query 20: | 0.2688 |
| Query 21: | 0.1030 |
| Query 22: | 0.1405 |
| Query 24: | 0.5006 |
| Query 26: | 0.1217 |
| Query 28: | 0.3582 |
| Query 29: | 0.2669 |
| Query 30: | 1.0000 |
| Query 31: | 0.2457 |
| Query 32: | 0.4785 |
| Query 33: | 0.4203 |
| Query 34: | 0.0058 |
| Query 36: | 0.2935 |
| Query 37: | 1.0000 |
| Query 38: | 0.1806 |
| Query 39: | 0.2943 |
| Query 40: | 0.0080 |

Overall statistics
(for 33 queries):

Total number of documents
over all queries
    Retrieved:    33000
    Relevant:      579
    Rel_ret:       431

Interpolated Recall  -
Precision Averages:
    at 0.00    0.6752
    at 0.10    0.5262
    at 0.20    0.4287
    at 0.30    0.3340
    at 0.40    0.2761
    at 0.50    0.2596
    at 0.60    0.1901
    at 0.70    0.1556
    at 0.80    0.1270
    at 0.90    0.0952
    at 1.00    0.0727

Avg. prec. (non-interpolated)
for all rel. documents    0.2665

Precision:
    At    5 docs:    0.3394
    At   10 docs:    0.2758
    At   15 docs:    0.2283
    At   20 docs:    0.2000
    At   30 docs:    0.1687
    At  100 docs:    0.0867
    At  200 docs:    0.0526
    At  500 docs:    0.0245
    At 1000 docs:    0.0131

R-Precision (prec. after
all rel. docs. retrieved):
    Exact:    0.2793

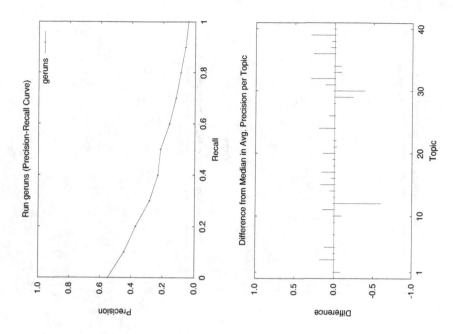

Run geruns (Precision-Recall Curve)

Difference from Median in Avg. Precision per Topic

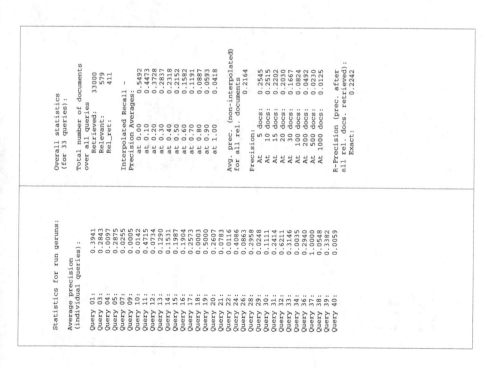

Statistics for run geruns:

Average precision
(individual queries):

| | |
|---|---|
| Query 01: | 0.3941 |
| Query 03: | 0.2843 |
| Query 04: | 0.0097 |
| Query 05: | 0.2875 |
| Query 07: | 0.0255 |
| Query 09: | 0.0005 |
| Query 10: | 0.0142 |
| Query 11: | 0.4715 |
| Query 12: | 0.0734 |
| Query 13: | 0.1290 |
| Query 14: | 0.1531 |
| Query 15: | 0.1987 |
| Query 16: | 0.1904 |
| Query 17: | 0.2573 |
| Query 18: | 0.0003 |
| Query 19: | 0.5000 |
| Query 20: | 0.2607 |
| Query 21: | 0.0783 |
| Query 22: | 0.0116 |
| Query 24: | 0.4086 |
| Query 26: | 0.0863 |
| Query 28: | 0.2958 |
| Query 29: | 0.0248 |
| Query 30: | 0.1111 |
| Query 31: | 0.2414 |
| Query 32: | 0.6211 |
| Query 33: | 0.3146 |
| Query 34: | 0.0035 |
| Query 36: | 0.2940 |
| Query 37: | 1.0000 |
| Query 38: | 0.0548 |
| Query 39: | 0.3382 |
| Query 40: | 0.0059 |

Overall statistics
(for 33 queries):

Total number of documents
over all queries:
| | |
|---|---|
| Retrieved: | 33000 |
| Relevant: | 579 |
| Rel_ret: | 411 |

Interpolated Recall -
Precision Averages:
| | |
|---|---|
| at 0.00 | 0.5492 |
| at 0.10 | 0.4473 |
| at 0.20 | 0.3728 |
| at 0.30 | 0.2837 |
| at 0.40 | 0.2318 |
| at 0.50 | 0.2152 |
| at 0.60 | 0.1582 |
| at 0.70 | 0.1191 |
| at 0.80 | 0.0887 |
| at 0.90 | 0.0593 |
| at 1.00 | 0.0418 |

Avg. prec. (non-interpolated)
for all rel. documents        0.2164

Precision:
| | | |
|---|---|---|
| At | 5 docs: | 0.2545 |
| At | 10 docs: | 0.2515 |
| At | 15 docs: | 0.2202 |
| At | 20 docs: | 0.2030 |
| At | 30 docs: | 0.1667 |
| At | 100 docs: | 0.0824 |
| At | 200 docs: | 0.0492 |
| At | 500 docs: | 0.0230 |
| At | 1000 docs: | 0.0125 |

R-Precision (prec. after
all rel. docs. retrieved):
| | |
|---|---|
| Exact: | 0.2242 |

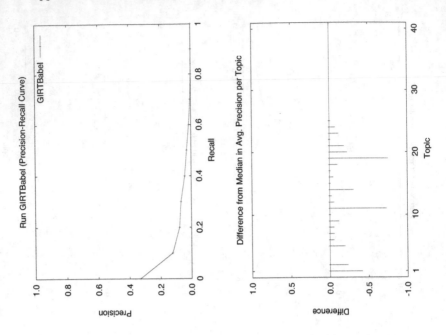

Run GIRTBabel (Precision-Recall Curve)

GIRTBabel

Difference from Median in Avg. Precision per Topic

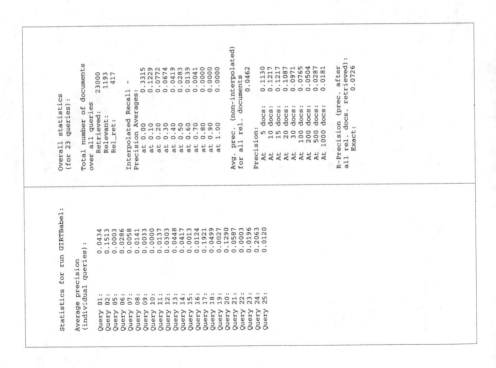

Statistics for run GIRTBabel:

Average precision
(individual queries):

|  | |
|---|---|
| Query 01: | 0.0434 |
| Query 02: | 0.1513 |
| Query 05: | 0.0003 |
| Query 06: | 0.0286 |
| Query 07: | 0.0058 |
| Query 08: | 0.0141 |
| Query 09: | 0.0033 |
| Query 10: | 0.0000 |
| Query 11: | 0.0137 |
| Query 12: | 0.0303 |
| Query 13: | 0.0448 |
| Query 14: | 0.0417 |
| Query 15: | 0.0013 |
| Query 16: | 0.0124 |
| Query 17: | 0.1921 |
| Query 18: | 0.0499 |
| Query 19: | 0.0027 |
| Query 20: | 0.1290 |
| Query 21: | 0.0587 |
| Query 22: | 0.0003 |
| Query 23: | 0.0196 |
| Query 24: | 0.2063 |
| Query 25: | 0.0120 |

Overall statistics
(for 23 queries):

Total number of documents
over all queries:

| | |
|---|---|
| Retrieved: | 23000 |
| Relevant: | 1193 |
| Rel_ret: | 417 |

Interpolated Recall -
Precision Averages:

| | |
|---|---|
| at 0.00 | 0.3315 |
| at 0.10 | 0.1229 |
| at 0.20 | 0.0772 |
| at 0.30 | 0.0674 |
| at 0.40 | 0.0419 |
| at 0.50 | 0.0283 |
| at 0.60 | 0.0139 |
| at 0.70 | 0.0041 |
| at 0.80 | 0.0000 |
| at 0.90 | 0.0000 |
| at 1.00 | 0.0000 |

Avg. prec. (non-interpolated)
for all rel. documents
0.0462

Precision:

| | | |
|---|---|---|
| At | 5 docs: | 0.1130 |
| At | 10 docs: | 0.1217 |
| At | 15 docs: | 0.1217 |
| At | 20 docs: | 0.1087 |
| At | 30 docs: | 0.0971 |
| At | 100 docs: | 0.0765 |
| At | 200 docs: | 0.0504 |
| At | 500 docs: | 0.0287 |
| At | 1000 docs: | 0.0181 |

R-Precision (prec. after
all rel. docs. retrieved):
Exact: 0.0726

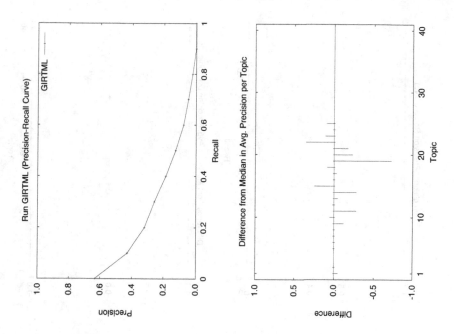

Run GIRTML (Precision-Recall Curve)

Difference from Median in Avg. Precision per Topic

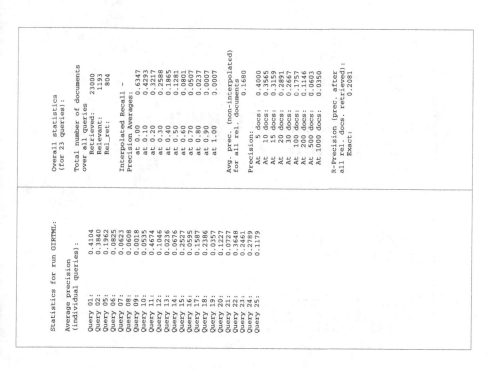

Statistics for run GIRTML:

Average precision
(individual queries):

| | |
|---|---|
| Query 01: | 0.4104 |
| Query 02: | 0.3840 |
| Query 05: | 0.1962 |
| Query 06: | 0.0825 |
| Query 07: | 0.0623 |
| Query 08: | 0.0608 |
| Query 09: | 0.0018 |
| Query 10: | 0.0535 |
| Query 11: | 0.4674 |
| Query 12: | 0.1046 |
| Query 13: | 0.0236 |
| Query 14: | 0.0676 |
| Query 15: | 0.2527 |
| Query 16: | 0.0595 |
| Query 17: | 0.1587 |
| Query 18: | 0.2386 |
| Query 19: | 0.0357 |
| Query 20: | 0.1227 |
| Query 21: | 0.0727 |
| Query 22: | 0.3648 |
| Query 23: | 0.2461 |
| Query 24: | 0.2789 |
| Query 25: | 0.1179 |

Overall statistics
(for 23 queries):

Total number of documents
over all queries:

| | |
|---|---|
| Retrieved: | 23000 |
| Relevant: | 1193 |
| Rel_ret: | 804 |

Interpolated Recall -
Precision Averages:

| | |
|---|---|
| at 0.00 | 0.6347 |
| at 0.10 | 0.4293 |
| at 0.20 | 0.3217 |
| at 0.30 | 0.2588 |
| at 0.40 | 0.1865 |
| at 0.50 | 0.1281 |
| at 0.60 | 0.0801 |
| at 0.70 | 0.0507 |
| at 0.80 | 0.0237 |
| at 0.90 | 0.0007 |
| at 1.00 | 0.0007 |

Avg. prec. (non-interpolated)
for all rel. documents        0.1680

Precision:

| | |
|---|---|
| At   5 docs: | 0.4000 |
| At  10 docs: | 0.3565 |
| At  15 docs: | 0.3159 |
| At  20 docs: | 0.2891 |
| At  30 docs: | 0.2667 |
| At 100 docs: | 0.1757 |
| At 200 docs: | 0.1146 |
| At 500 docs: | 0.0603 |
| At 1000 docs: | 0.0350 |

R-Precision (prec. after
all rel. docs. retrieved):

| | |
|---|---|
| Exact: | 0.2081 |

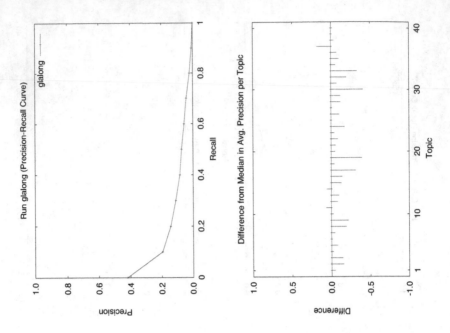

Run glalong (Precision-Recall Curve)

glalong ——

Difference from Median in Avg. Precision per Topic

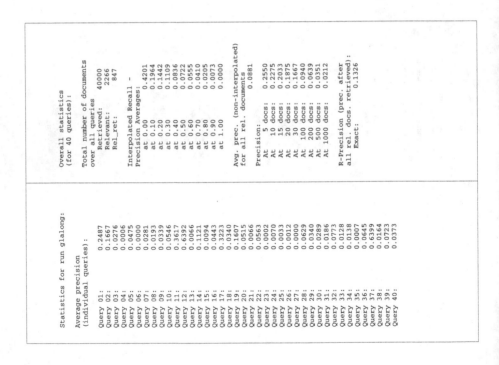

Statistics for run glalong:

Average precision
(individual queries):

| | |
|---|---|
| Query 01: | 0.2487 |
| Query 02: | 0.1667 |
| Query 03: | 0.0276 |
| Query 04: | 0.0006 |
| Query 05: | 0.0475 |
| Query 06: | 0.0000 |
| Query 07: | 0.0281 |
| Query 08: | 0.0193 |
| Query 09: | 0.0339 |
| Query 10: | 0.0546 |
| Query 11: | 0.3617 |
| Query 12: | 0.6392 |
| Query 13: | 0.0066 |
| Query 14: | 0.1121 |
| Query 15: | 0.0094 |
| Query 16: | 0.0443 |
| Query 17: | 0.3223 |
| Query 18: | 0.0340 |
| Query 19: | 0.1607 |
| Query 20: | 0.0515 |
| Query 21: | 0.0066 |
| Query 22: | 0.0563 |
| Query 23: | 0.0002 |
| Query 24: | 0.0070 |
| Query 25: | 0.0033 |
| Query 26: | 0.0012 |
| Query 27: | 0.0000 |
| Query 28: | 0.0629 |
| Query 29: | 0.0340 |
| Query 30: | 0.0289 |
| Query 31: | 0.0186 |
| Query 32: | 0.0773 |
| Query 33: | 0.0128 |
| Query 34: | 0.0138 |
| Query 35: | 0.0007 |
| Query 36: | 0.0645 |
| Query 37: | 0.6399 |
| Query 38: | 0.0164 |
| Query 39: | 0.0723 |
| Query 40: | 0.0373 |

Overall statistics
(for 40 queries):

Total number of documents
over all queries
| | |
|---|---|
| Retrieved: | 40000 |
| Relevant: | 2266 |
| Rel_ret: | 847 |

Interpolated Recall -
Precision Averages:
| | |
|---|---|
| at 0.00 | 0.4201 |
| at 0.10 | 0.1964 |
| at 0.20 | 0.1442 |
| at 0.30 | 0.1109 |
| at 0.40 | 0.0836 |
| at 0.50 | 0.0722 |
| at 0.60 | 0.0555 |
| at 0.70 | 0.0410 |
| at 0.80 | 0.0205 |
| at 0.90 | 0.0073 |
| at 1.00 | 0.0000 |

Avg. prec. (non-interpolated)
for all rel. documents
0.0881

Precision:
| | | |
|---|---|---|
| At | 5 docs: | 0.2550 |
| At | 10 docs: | 0.2275 |
| At | 15 docs: | 0.2033 |
| At | 20 docs: | 0.1875 |
| At | 30 docs: | 0.1667 |
| At | 100 docs: | 0.0940 |
| At | 200 docs: | 0.0639 |
| At | 500 docs: | 0.0351 |
| At | 1000 docs: | 0.0212 |

R-Precision (prec. after
all rel. docs. retrieved):
| | |
|---|---|
| Exact: | 0.1326 |

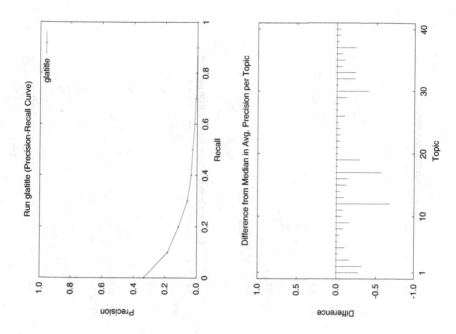

Run glatitle (Precision-Recall Curve)

Difference from Median in Avg. Precision per Topic

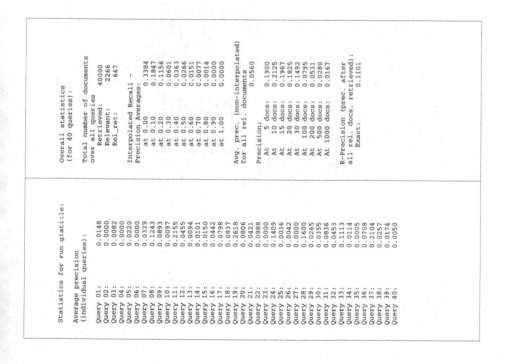

Statistics for run glatile:

Average precision
(individual queries):

| Query 01: | 0.0148 |
| Query 02: | 0.0000 |
| Query 03: | 0.0082 |
| Query 04: | 0.0000 |
| Query 05: | 0.0220 |
| Query 06: | 0.0000 |
| Query 07: | 0.0329 |
| Query 08: | 0.1243 |
| Query 09: | 0.0893 |
| Query 10: | 0.0097 |
| Query 11: | 0.2155 |
| Query 12: | 0.0455 |
| Query 13: | 0.0094 |
| Query 14: | 0.0101 |
| Query 15: | 0.0150 |
| Query 16: | 0.0442 |
| Query 17: | 0.0798 |
| Query 18: | 0.0837 |
| Query 19: | 0.2618 |
| Query 20: | 0.0806 |
| Query 21: | 0.0421 |
| Query 22: | 0.0988 |
| Query 23: | 0.0000 |
| Query 24: | 0.1409 |
| Query 25: | 0.0036 |
| Query 26: | 0.0042 |
| Query 27: | 0.0000 |
| Query 28: | 0.1600 |
| Query 29: | 0.0265 |
| Query 30: | 0.0355 |
| Query 31: | 0.0836 |
| Query 32: | 0.0453 |
| Query 33: | 0.1113 |
| Query 34: | 0.0114 |
| Query 35: | 0.0005 |
| Query 36: | 0.0708 |
| Query 37: | 0.2104 |
| Query 38: | 0.0257 |
| Query 39: | 0.0174 |
| Query 40: | 0.0050 |

Overall statistics
(for 40 queries):

Total number of documents
over all queries:

| Retrieved: | 40000 |
| Relevant: | 2266 |
| Rel_ret: | 667 |

Interpolated Recall -
Precision Averages:

| at 0.00 | 0.3384 |
| at 0.10 | 0.1847 |
| at 0.20 | 0.1156 |
| at 0.30 | 0.0601 |
| at 0.40 | 0.0363 |
| at 0.50 | 0.0266 |
| at 0.60 | 0.0151 |
| at 0.70 | 0.0077 |
| at 0.80 | 0.0014 |
| at 0.90 | 0.0000 |
| at 1.00 | 0.0000 |

Avg. prec. (non-interpolated)
for all rel. documents    0.0550

Precision:

| At 5 docs: | 0.1900 |
| At 10 docs: | 0.2125 |
| At 15 docs: | 0.1967 |
| At 20 docs: | 0.1825 |
| At 30 docs: | 0.1492 |
| At 100 docs: | 0.0795 |
| At 200 docs: | 0.0531 |
| At 500 docs: | 0.0280 |
| At 1000 docs: | 0.0167 |

R-Precision (prec. after
all rel. docs. retrieved):

| Exact: | 0.1101 |

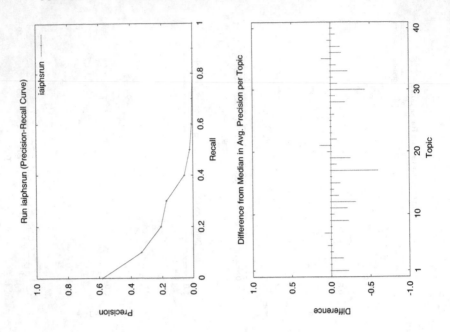

Run iaiphsrun (Precision-Recall Curve)

iaiphsrun

Recall

Precision

Difference from Median in Avg. Precision per Topic

Topic

Difference

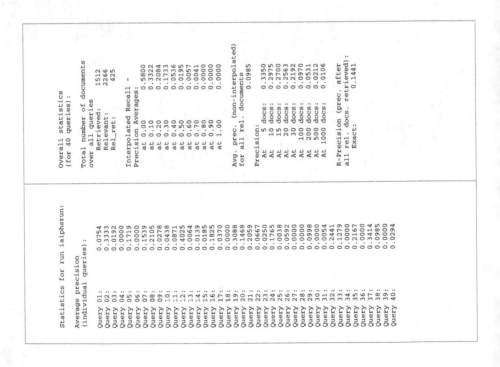

Statistics for run iaiphsrun:

Average precision
(individual queries):

| | |
|---|---|
| Query 01: | 0.0754 |
| Query 02: | 0.3333 |
| Query 03: | 0.0192 |
| Query 04: | 0.0000 |
| Query 05: | 0.1719 |
| Query 06: | 0.0000 |
| Query 07: | 0.1539 |
| Query 08: | 0.2105 |
| Query 09: | 0.0278 |
| Query 10: | 0.0438 |
| Query 11: | 0.0871 |
| Query 12: | 0.4025 |
| Query 13: | 0.0064 |
| Query 14: | 0.0139 |
| Query 15: | 0.0185 |
| Query 16: | 0.1825 |
| Query 17: | 0.0370 |
| Query 18: | 0.0000 |
| Query 19: | 0.3088 |
| Query 20: | 0.1468 |
| Query 21: | 0.2059 |
| Query 22: | 0.0667 |
| Query 23: | 0.0250 |
| Query 24: | 0.1765 |
| Query 25: | 0.0038 |
| Query 26: | 0.0592 |
| Query 27: | 0.0000 |
| Query 28: | 0.0000 |
| Query 29: | 0.0998 |
| Query 30: | 0.0000 |
| Query 31: | 0.0054 |
| Query 32: | 0.2441 |
| Query 33: | 0.1279 |
| Query 34: | 0.0000 |
| Query 35: | 0.2167 |
| Query 36: | 0.0000 |
| Query 37: | 0.3414 |
| Query 38: | 0.0985 |
| Query 39: | 0.0000 |
| Query 40: | 0.0294 |

Overall statistics
(for 40 queries):

Total number of documents
over all queries:
| | |
|---|---|
| Retrieved: | 1512 |
| Relevant: | 2266 |
| Rel_ret: | 425 |

Interpolated Recall -
Precision Averages:
| | |
|---|---|
| at 0.00 | 0.5800 |
| at 0.10 | 0.3322 |
| at 0.20 | 0.2084 |
| at 0.30 | 0.1733 |
| at 0.40 | 0.0536 |
| at 0.50 | 0.0195 |
| at 0.60 | 0.0057 |
| at 0.70 | 0.0041 |
| at 0.80 | 0.0000 |
| at 0.90 | 0.0000 |
| at 1.00 | 0.0000 |

Avg. prec. (non-interpolated)
for all rel. documents        0.0985

Precision:
| | | |
|---|---|---|
| At | 5 docs: | 0.3350 |
| At | 10 docs: | 0.2975 |
| At | 15 docs: | 0.2700 |
| At | 20 docs: | 0.2563 |
| At | 30 docs: | 0.2192 |
| At | 100 docs: | 0.0970 |
| At | 200 docs: | 0.0531 |
| At | 500 docs: | 0.0212 |
| At | 1000 docs: | 0.0106 |

R-Precision (prec. after
all rel. docs. retrieved):
| | |
|---|---|
| Exact: | 0.1441 |

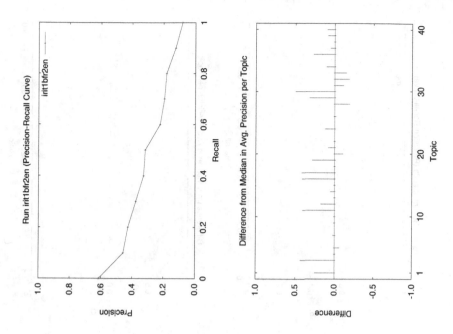

Run irit1bfr2en (Precision-Recall Curve)

irit1bfr2en

Difference from Median in Avg. Precision per Topic

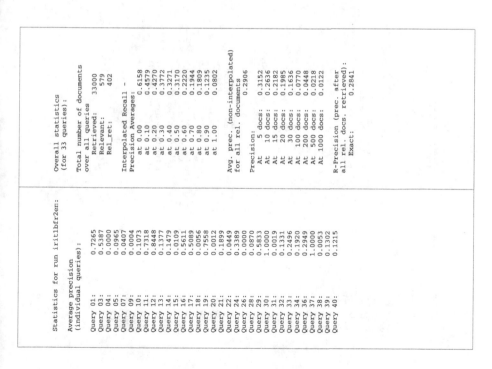

Statistics for run irit1bfr2en:

Average precision
(individual queries):

| | |
|---|---|
| Query 01: | 0.7265 |
| Query 03: | 0.5387 |
| Query 04: | 0.0000 |
| Query 05: | 0.0965 |
| Query 07: | 0.0407 |
| Query 09: | 0.0004 |
| Query 10: | 0.1073 |
| Query 11: | 0.7318 |
| Query 12: | 0.8448 |
| Query 13: | 0.1377 |
| Query 14: | 0.1479 |
| Query 15: | 0.0109 |
| Query 16: | 0.5611 |
| Query 17: | 0.5089 |
| Query 18: | 0.0056 |
| Query 19: | 0.7558 |
| Query 20: | 0.0012 |
| Query 21: | 0.1899 |
| Query 22: | 0.0449 |
| Query 24: | 0.3389 |
| Query 26: | 0.0000 |
| Query 28: | 0.0870 |
| Query 29: | 0.5833 |
| Query 30: | 1.0000 |
| Query 31: | 0.0019 |
| Query 32: | 0.1331 |
| Query 33: | 0.2496 |
| Query 34: | 0.1920 |
| Query 36: | 0.2949 |
| Query 37: | 1.0000 |
| Query 38: | 0.0053 |
| Query 39: | 0.1302 |
| Query 40: | 0.1215 |

Overall statistics
(for 33 queries):

Total number of documents
over all queries:

| | |
|---|---|
| Retrieved: | 33000 |
| Relevant: | 579 |
| Rel_ret: | 402 |

Interpolated Recall -
Precision Averages:

| | |
|---|---|
| at 0.00 | 0.6158 |
| at 0.10 | 0.4579 |
| at 0.20 | 0.4270 |
| at 0.30 | 0.3772 |
| at 0.40 | 0.3271 |
| at 0.50 | 0.3170 |
| at 0.60 | 0.2220 |
| at 0.70 | 0.1944 |
| at 0.80 | 0.1809 |
| at 0.90 | 0.1235 |
| at 1.00 | 0.0802 |

Avg. prec. (non-interpolated)
for all rel. documents
            0.2906

Precision:

| | |
|---|---|
| At   5 docs: | 0.3152 |
| At  10 docs: | 0.2636 |
| At  15 docs: | 0.2182 |
| At  20 docs: | 0.1985 |
| At  30 docs: | 0.1636 |
| At 100 docs: | 0.0770 |
| At 200 docs: | 0.0448 |
| At 500 docs: | 0.0218 |
| At 1000 docs: | 0.0122 |

R-Precision (prec. after
all rel. docs. retrieved):

| | |
|---|---|
| Exact: | 0.2841 |

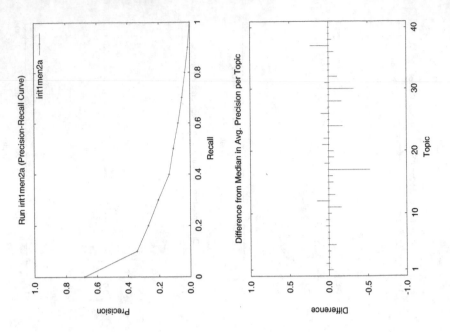

Run irit1men2a (Precision-Recall Curve)

Difference from Median in Avg. Precision per Topic

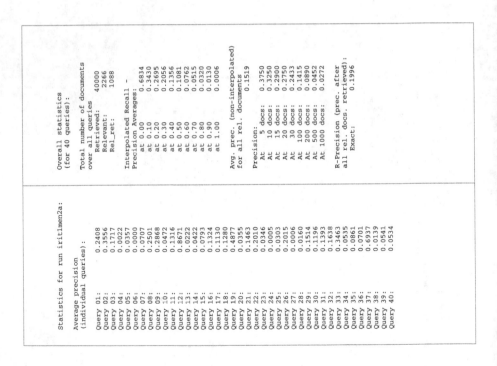

Statistics for run irit1men2a:

Average precision
(individual queries):

| | |
|---|---|
| Query 01: | 0.2408 |
| Query 02: | 0.3556 |
| Query 03: | 0.1717 |
| Query 04: | 0.0022 |
| Query 05: | 0.0357 |
| Query 06: | 0.0000 |
| Query 07: | 0.0707 |
| Query 08: | 0.2501 |
| Query 09: | 0.2868 |
| Query 10: | 0.0472 |
| Query 11: | 0.1316 |
| Query 12: | 0.8671 |
| Query 13: | 0.0222 |
| Query 14: | 0.0422 |
| Query 15: | 0.0793 |
| Query 16: | 0.1324 |
| Query 17: | 0.1130 |
| Query 18: | 0.1280 |
| Query 19: | 0.4877 |
| Query 20: | 0.0355 |
| Query 21: | 0.1463 |
| Query 22: | 0.2010 |
| Query 23: | 0.0346 |
| Query 24: | 0.0005 |
| Query 25: | 0.0303 |
| Query 26: | 0.2015 |
| Query 27: | 0.0006 |
| Query 28: | 0.0160 |
| Query 29: | 0.1514 |
| Query 30: | 0.1196 |
| Query 31: | 0.1393 |
| Query 32: | 0.1638 |
| Query 33: | 0.3463 |
| Query 34: | 0.0535 |
| Query 35: | 0.0861 |
| Query 36: | 0.0701 |
| Query 37: | 0.6937 |
| Query 38: | 0.0139 |
| Query 39: | 0.0541 |
| Query 40: | 0.0534 |

Overall statistics
(for 40 queries):

Total number of documents
over all queries

| | |
|---|---|
| Retrieved: | 40000 |
| Relevant: | 2266 |
| Rel_ret: | 1088 |

Interpolated Recall -
Precision Averages:

| | |
|---|---|
| at 0.00 | 0.6834 |
| at 0.10 | 0.3430 |
| at 0.20 | 0.2695 |
| at 0.30 | 0.2056 |
| at 0.40 | 0.1356 |
| at 0.50 | 0.1081 |
| at 0.60 | 0.0762 |
| at 0.70 | 0.0515 |
| at 0.80 | 0.0320 |
| at 0.90 | 0.0130 |
| at 1.00 | 0.0006 |

Avg. prec. (non-interpolated)
for all rel. documents        0.1519

Precision:

| | |
|---|---|
| At   5 docs: | 0.3750 |
| At  10 docs: | 0.3250 |
| At  15 docs: | 0.2900 |
| At  20 docs: | 0.2750 |
| At  30 docs: | 0.2433 |
| At  100 docs: | 0.1415 |
| At  200 docs: | 0.0890 |
| At  500 docs: | 0.0452 |
| At 1000 docs: | 0.0272 |

R-Precision (prec. after
all rel. docs. retrieved):

| | |
|---|---|
| Exact: | 0.1996 |

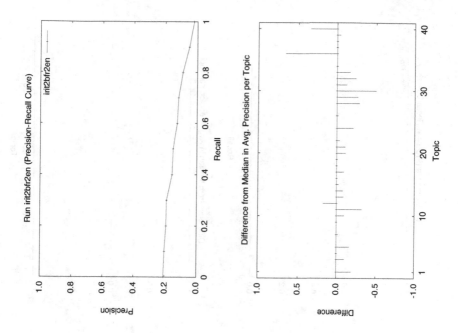

Run irit2bfr2en (Precision-Recall Curve)

Difference from Median in Avg. Precision per Topic

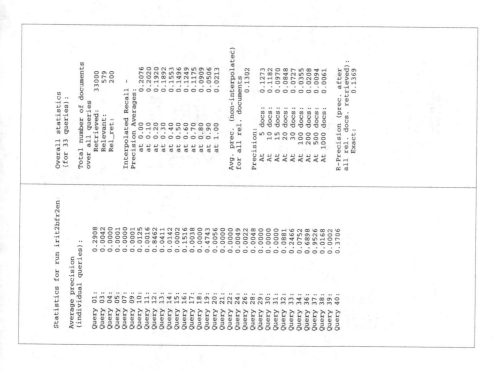

Statistics for run irit2bfr2en

Average precision
(individual queries):

| | |
|---|---|
| Query 01: | 0.2908 |
| Query 03: | 0.0042 |
| Query 04: | 0.0000 |
| Query 05: | 0.0001 |
| Query 07: | 0.0000 |
| Query 09: | 0.0001 |
| Query 10: | 0.0125 |
| Query 11: | 0.0016 |
| Query 12: | 0.8462 |
| Query 13: | 0.0411 |
| Query 14: | 0.0142 |
| Query 15: | 0.0002 |
| Query 16: | 0.1516 |
| Query 17: | 0.0038 |
| Query 18: | 0.0000 |
| Query 19: | 0.4743 |
| Query 20: | 0.0056 |
| Query 21: | 0.0000 |
| Query 22: | 0.0000 |
| Query 24: | 0.0049 |
| Query 26: | 0.0022 |
| Query 28: | 0.0048 |
| Query 29: | 0.0000 |
| Query 30: | 0.0000 |
| Query 31: | 0.0000 |
| Query 32: | 0.0881 |
| Query 33: | 0.2466 |
| Query 34: | 0.0752 |
| Query 36: | 0.6898 |
| Query 37: | 0.9526 |
| Query 38: | 0.0168 |
| Query 39: | 0.0002 |
| Query 40: | 0.3706 |

Overall statistics
(for 33 queries):

Total number of documents
over all queries

| | |
|---|---|
| Retrieved: | 33000 |
| Relevant: | 579 |
| Rel_ret: | 200 |

Interpolated Recall -
Precision Averages:

| | |
|---|---|
| at 0.00 | 0.2076 |
| at 0.10 | 0.2020 |
| at 0.20 | 0.1920 |
| at 0.30 | 0.1892 |
| at 0.40 | 0.1553 |
| at 0.50 | 0.1496 |
| at 0.60 | 0.1249 |
| at 0.70 | 0.1175 |
| at 0.80 | 0.0909 |
| at 0.90 | 0.0506 |
| at 1.00 | 0.0213 |

Avg. prec. (non-interpolated)
for all rel. documents
                    0.1302

Precision:

| | |
|---|---|
| At    5 docs: | 0.1273 |
| At   10 docs: | 0.1182 |
| At   15 docs: | 0.0970 |
| At   20 docs: | 0.0848 |
| At   30 docs: | 0.0727 |
| At  100 docs: | 0.0355 |
| At  200 docs: | 0.0208 |
| At  500 docs: | 0.0094 |
| At 1000 docs: | 0.0061 |

R-Precision (prec. after
all rel. docs. retrieved):
        Exact:    0.1369

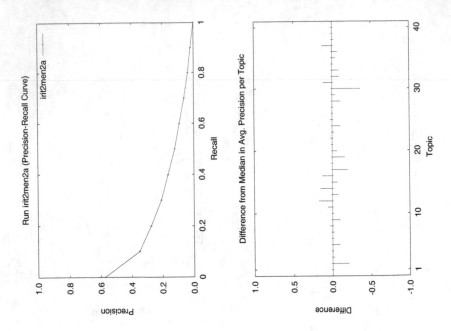

Run irit2men2a (Precision-Recall Curve)

Difference from Median in Avg. Precision per Topic

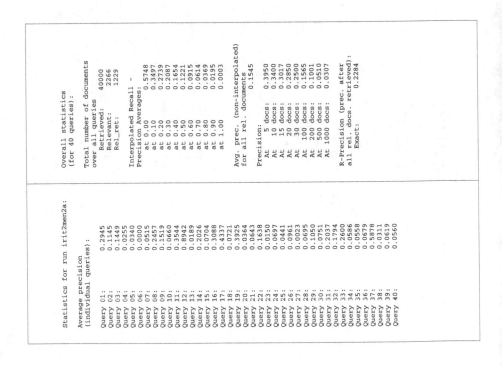

Statistics for run irit2men2a:

Average precision
(individual queries):

|  | |
|---|---|
| Query 01: | 0.2945 |
| Query 02: | 0.1145 |
| Query 03: | 0.1449 |
| Query 04: | 0.0255 |
| Query 05: | 0.0340 |
| Query 06: | 0.0000 |
| Query 07: | 0.0515 |
| Query 08: | 0.2457 |
| Query 09: | 0.1519 |
| Query 10: | 0.0660 |
| Query 11: | 0.3544 |
| Query 12: | 0.8942 |
| Query 13: | 0.0189 |
| Query 14: | 0.2026 |
| Query 15: | 0.0704 |
| Query 16: | 0.3088 |
| Query 17: | 0.4337 |
| Query 18: | 0.0721 |
| Query 19: | 0.3925 |
| Query 20: | 0.0364 |
| Query 21: | 0.0643 |
| Query 22: | 0.1638 |
| Query 23: | 0.0150 |
| Query 24: | 0.0697 |
| Query 25: | 0.0441 |
| Query 26: | 0.0961 |
| Query 27: | 0.0023 |
| Query 28: | 0.0695 |
| Query 29: | 0.1050 |
| Query 30: | 0.0751 |
| Query 31: | 0.2037 |
| Query 32: | 0.1794 |
| Query 33: | 0.2600 |
| Query 34: | 0.0586 |
| Query 35: | 0.0558 |
| Query 36: | 0.0679 |
| Query 37: | 0.5878 |
| Query 38: | 0.0311 |
| Query 39: | 0.0619 |
| Query 40: | 0.0560 |

Overall statistics
(for 40 queries):

Total number of documents
over all queries:
| | |
|---|---|
| Retrieved: | 40000 |
| Relevant: | 2266 |
| Rel_ret: | 1229 |

Interpolated Recall -
Precision Averages:
| | |
|---|---|
| at 0.00 | 0.5748 |
| at 0.10 | 0.3497 |
| at 0.20 | 0.2739 |
| at 0.30 | 0.2087 |
| at 0.40 | 0.1654 |
| at 0.50 | 0.1221 |
| at 0.60 | 0.0915 |
| at 0.70 | 0.0614 |
| at 0.80 | 0.0369 |
| at 0.90 | 0.0195 |
| at 1.00 | 0.0003 |

Avg. prec. (non-interpolated)
for all rel. documents
0.1545

Precision:
| | |
|---|---|
| At    5 docs: | 0.3950 |
| At   10 docs: | 0.3400 |
| At   15 docs: | 0.3017 |
| At   20 docs: | 0.2850 |
| At   30 docs: | 0.2500 |
| At  100 docs: | 0.1565 |
| At  200 docs: | 0.1001 |
| At  500 docs: | 0.0510 |
| At 1000 docs: | 0.0307 |

R-Precision (prec. after
all rel. docs. retrieved):
| | |
|---|---|
| Exact: | 0.2284 |

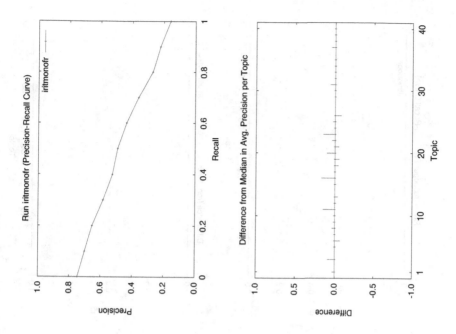

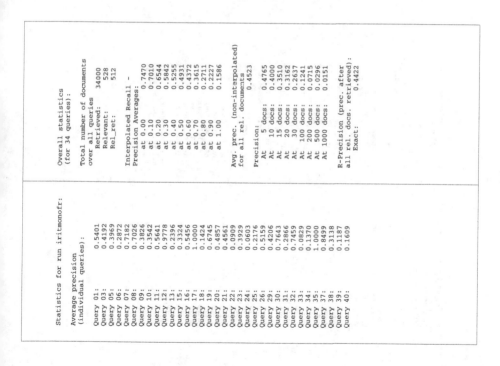

Statistics for run iritmonofr:

Average precision
(individual queries):

| | |
|---|---|
| Query 01: | 0.5401 |
| Query 03: | 0.4192 |
| Query 05: | 0.3969 |
| Query 06: | 0.2872 |
| Query 07: | 0.7182 |
| Query 08: | 0.7026 |
| Query 09: | 0.3826 |
| Query 10: | 0.3542 |
| Query 11: | 0.5641 |
| Query 12: | 0.9778 |
| Query 13: | 0.2396 |
| Query 15: | 0.3324 |
| Query 16: | 0.5456 |
| Query 17: | 1.0000 |
| Query 18: | 0.1424 |
| Query 19: | 0.6745 |
| Query 20: | 0.4857 |
| Query 21: | 0.4561 |
| Query 22: | 0.0909 |
| Query 23: | 0.3929 |
| Query 24: | 0.0603 |
| Query 25: | 0.2176 |
| Query 26: | 0.5159 |
| Query 29: | 0.4206 |
| Query 30: | 0.7643 |
| Query 31: | 0.2866 |
| Query 32: | 0.7459 |
| Query 33: | 0.0829 |
| Query 34: | 0.1370 |
| Query 35: | 1.0000 |
| Query 37: | 0.8499 |
| Query 38: | 0.3138 |
| Query 39: | 0.1187 |
| Query 40: | 0.1609 |

Overall statistics
(for 34 queries):

Total number of documents
over all queries:

| | |
|---|---|
| Retrieved: | 34000 |
| Relevant: | 528 |
| Rel_ret: | 512 |

Interpolated Recall -
Precision Averages:

| | |
|---|---|
| at 0.00 | 0.7470 |
| at 0.10 | 0.7010 |
| at 0.20 | 0.6544 |
| at 0.30 | 0.5842 |
| at 0.40 | 0.5255 |
| at 0.50 | 0.4931 |
| at 0.60 | 0.4372 |
| at 0.70 | 0.3615 |
| at 0.80 | 0.2711 |
| at 0.90 | 0.2227 |
| at 1.00 | 0.1586 |

Avg. prec. (non-interpolated)
for all rel. documents        0.4523

Precision:

| | | |
|---|---|---|
| At | 5 docs: | 0.4765 |
| At | 10 docs: | 0.4000 |
| At | 15 docs: | 0.3510 |
| At | 20 docs: | 0.3162 |
| At | 30 docs: | 0.2637 |
| At | 100 docs: | 0.1241 |
| At | 200 docs: | 0.0715 |
| At | 500 docs: | 0.0296 |
| At | 1000 docs: | 0.0151 |

R-Precision (prec. after
all rel. docs. retrieved):

| | |
|---|---|
| Exact: | 0.4422 |

## Run iritmonoge (Precision-Recall Curve)

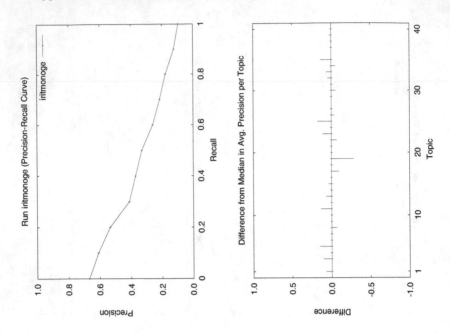

## Difference from Median in Avg. Precision per Topic

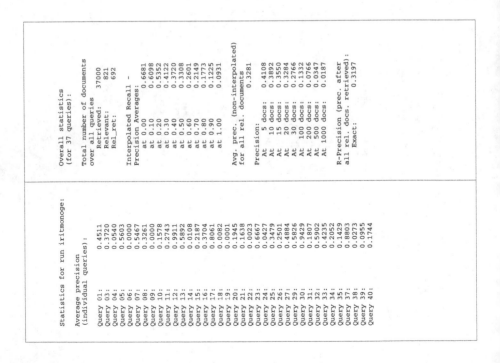

Statistics for run iritmonoge:

Average precision
(individual queries):

|  |  |
|-------|--------|
| Query 01: | 0.4511 |
| Query 03: | 0.3720 |
| Query 04: | 0.0540 |
| Query 05: | 0.5603 |
| Query 06: | 0.0000 |
| Query 07: | 0.5467 |
| Query 08: | 0.3261 |
| Query 09: | 0.0000 |
| Query 10: | 0.1578 |
| Query 11: | 0.2743 |
| Query 12: | 0.9911 |
| Query 13: | 0.5892 |
| Query 14: | 0.0108 |
| Query 15: | 0.2187 |
| Query 16: | 0.3704 |
| Query 17: | 0.8061 |
| Query 18: | 0.0082 |
| Query 19: | 0.0001 |
| Query 20: | 0.1945 |
| Query 21: | 0.1638 |
| Query 22: | 0.0023 |
| Query 23: | 0.6667 |
| Query 24: | 0.0427 |
| Query 25: | 0.3479 |
| Query 26: | 0.2501 |
| Query 27: | 0.4884 |
| Query 29: | 0.5826 |
| Query 30: | 0.9429 |
| Query 31: | 0.1807 |
| Query 32: | 0.5902 |
| Query 33: | 0.4235 |
| Query 34: | 0.2052 |
| Query 35: | 0.1429 |
| Query 37: | 0.8803 |
| Query 38: | 0.0273 |
| Query 39: | 0.0955 |
| Query 40: | 0.1744 |

Overall statistics
(for 37 queries):

Total number of documents
over all queries:

| | |
|---|---|
| Retrieved: | 37000 |
| Relevant: | 821 |
| Rel_ret: | 692 |

Interpolated Recall -
Precision Averages:

| | |
|---|---|
| at 0.00 | 0.6681 |
| at 0.10 | 0.6098 |
| at 0.20 | 0.5352 |
| at 0.30 | 0.4122 |
| at 0.40 | 0.3720 |
| at 0.50 | 0.3308 |
| at 0.60 | 0.2601 |
| at 0.70 | 0.2149 |
| at 0.80 | 0.1773 |
| at 0.90 | 0.1225 |
| at 1.00 | 0.0931 |

Avg. prec. (non-interpolated)
for all rel. documents    0.3281

Precision:

| | | |
|---|---|---|
| At | 5 docs: | 0.4108 |
| At | 10 docs: | 0.3892 |
| At | 15 docs: | 0.3550 |
| At | 20 docs: | 0.3284 |
| At | 30 docs: | 0.2766 |
| At | 100 docs: | 0.1332 |
| At | 200 docs: | 0.0766 |
| At | 500 docs: | 0.0347 |
| At | 1000 docs: | 0.0187 |

R-Precision (prec. after
all rel. docs. retrieved):

| | |
|---|---|
| Exact: | 0.3197 |

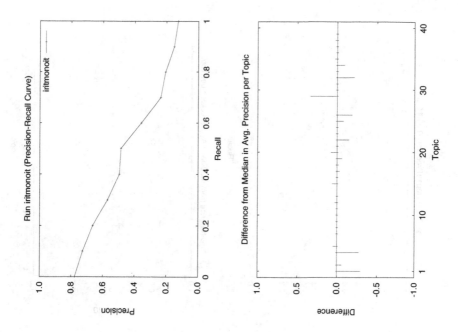

Run iritmonoit (Precision-Recall Curve)

iritmonoit

Recall

Precision

Difference from Median in Avg. Precision per Topic

Topic

Difference

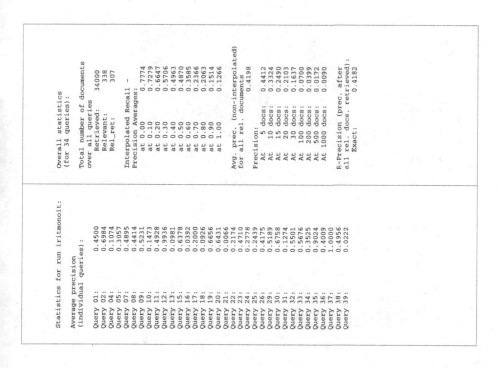

Statistics for run iritmonoit:

Average precision
(individual queries):

|  | | |
|---|---|---|
| Query 01: | 0.4500 | |
| Query 02: | 0.6984 | |
| Query 04: | 0.1074 | |
| Query 05: | 0.3057 | |
| Query 07: | 0.4895 | |
| Query 08: | 0.4414 | |
| Query 09: | 0.5231 | |
| Query 10: | 0.1473 | |
| Query 11: | 0.4928 | |
| Query 12: | 0.9936 | |
| Query 13: | 0.0981 | |
| Query 15: | 0.6378 | |
| Query 16: | 0.0392 | |
| Query 17: | 0.2000 | |
| Query 18: | 0.0926 | |
| Query 19: | 0.6656 | |
| Query 20: | 0.6431 | |
| Query 21: | 0.0066 | |
| Query 22: | 0.2174 | |
| Query 23: | 0.4710 | |
| Query 24: | 0.2778 | |
| Query 25: | 0.2439 | |
| Query 26: | 0.4175 | |
| Query 29: | 0.5189 | |
| Query 30: | 0.6758 | |
| Query 31: | 0.1274 | |
| Query 32: | 0.5501 | |
| Query 33: | 0.5676 | |
| Query 34: | 0.3525 | |
| Query 35: | 0.9024 | |
| Query 36: | 0.4009 | |
| Query 37: | 1.0000 | |
| Query 38: | 0.4956 | |
| Query 39: | 0.0222 | |

Overall statistics
(for 34 queries):

Total number of documents
over all queries:
    Retrieved:    34000
    Relevant:       338
    Rel_ret:        307

Interpolated Recall  -
Precision Averages:
    at 0.00    0.7774
    at 0.10    0.7279
    at 0.20    0.6647
    at 0.30    0.5706
    at 0.40    0.4963
    at 0.50    0.4870
    at 0.60    0.3585
    at 0.70    0.2366
    at 0.80    0.2063
    at 0.90    0.1514
    at 1.00    0.1266

Avg. prec. (non-interpolated)
for all rel. documents
                   0.4198

Precision:
    At    5 docs:   0.4412
    At   10 docs:   0.3324
    At   15 docs:   0.2490
    At   20 docs:   0.2103
    At   30 docs:   0.1637
    At  100 docs:   0.0700
    At  200 docs:   0.0399
    At  500 docs:   0.0172
    At 1000 docs:   0.0090

R-Precision (prec. after
all rel. docs. retrieved):
    Exact:         0.4182

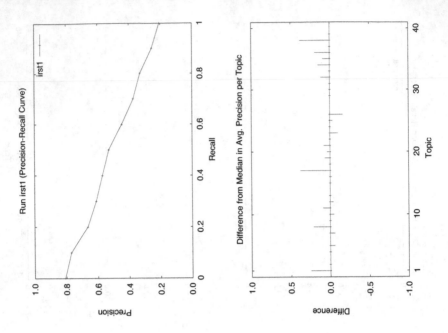

Run irst1 (Precision-Recall Curve)

irst1

Precision / Recall

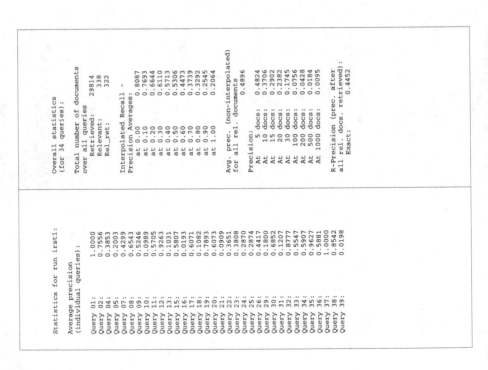

Difference from Median in Avg. Precision per Topic

Difference / Topic

Statistics for run irstl:

Average precision
(individual queries):

| | |
|---|---|
| Query 01: | 1.0000 |
| Query 02: | 0.7556 |
| Query 04: | 0.3853 |
| Query 05: | 0.2003 |
| Query 07: | 0.4299 |
| Query 08: | 0.6543 |
| Query 09: | 0.5246 |
| Query 10: | 0.0989 |
| Query 11: | 0.5705 |
| Query 12: | 0.9263 |
| Query 13: | 0.1031 |
| Query 15: | 0.5807 |
| Query 16: | 0.0193 |
| Query 17: | 0.6071 |
| Query 18: | 0.1082 |
| Query 19: | 0.7893 |
| Query 20: | 0.6073 |
| Query 21: | 0.0909 |
| Query 22: | 0.3651 |
| Query 23: | 0.3808 |
| Query 24: | 0.2870 |
| Query 25: | 0.2874 |
| Query 26: | 0.4417 |
| Query 29: | 0.1800 |
| Query 30: | 0.6852 |
| Query 31: | 0.1207 |
| Query 32: | 0.8777 |
| Query 33: | 0.5547 |
| Query 34: | 0.5907 |
| Query 35: | 0.9627 |
| Query 36: | 0.5881 |
| Query 37: | 1.0000 |
| Query 38: | 0.8542 |
| Query 39: | 0.0198 |

Overall statistics
(for 34 queries):

Total number of documents
over all queries:

| | |
|---|---|
| Retrieved: | 29814 |
| Relevant: | 338 |
| Rel_ret: | 322 |

Interpolated Recall -
Precision Averages:

| | |
|---|---|
| at 0.00 | 0.8087 |
| at 0.10 | 0.7693 |
| at 0.20 | 0.6644 |
| at 0.30 | 0.6110 |
| at 0.40 | 0.5713 |
| at 0.50 | 0.5306 |
| at 0.60 | 0.4473 |
| at 0.70 | 0.3739 |
| at 0.80 | 0.3292 |
| at 0.90 | 0.2545 |
| at 1.00 | 0.2064 |

Avg. prec. (non-interpolated)
for all rel. documents
0.4896

Precision:

| | | |
|---|---|---|
| At | 5 docs: | 0.4824 |
| At | 10 docs: | 0.3706 |
| At | 15 docs: | 0.2902 |
| At | 20 docs: | 0.2382 |
| At | 30 docs: | 0.1745 |
| At | 100 docs: | 0.0756 |
| At | 200 docs: | 0.0428 |
| At | 500 docs: | 0.0184 |
| At | 1000 docs: | 0.0095 |

R-Precision (prec. after
all rel. docs. retrieved):
Exact:     0.4452

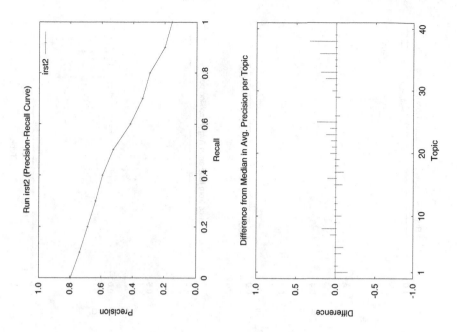

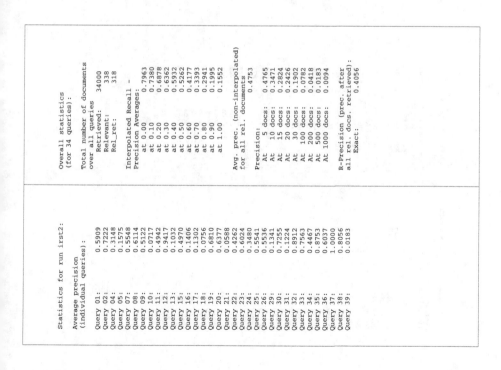

Run irst2 (Precision-Recall Curve)

irst2

Recall

Precision

Difference from Median in Avg. Precision per Topic

Topic

Difference

Statistics for run irst2:

Average precision
(individual queries):

| | |
|---|---|
| Query 01: | 0.5909 |
| Query 02: | 0.7222 |
| Query 04: | 0.3148 |
| Query 05: | 0.1575 |
| Query 07: | 0.5548 |
| Query 08: | 0.6114 |
| Query 09: | 0.5122 |
| Query 10: | 0.0717 |
| Query 11: | 0.4942 |
| Query 12: | 0.9417 |
| Query 13: | 0.1032 |
| Query 15: | 0.4970 |
| Query 16: | 0.1406 |
| Query 17: | 0.1302 |
| Query 18: | 0.0756 |
| Query 19: | 0.6810 |
| Query 20: | 0.6377 |
| Query 21: | 0.0588 |
| Query 22: | 0.4262 |
| Query 23: | 0.6024 |
| Query 24: | 0.3480 |
| Query 25: | 0.5541 |
| Query 26: | 0.5536 |
| Query 29: | 0.1341 |
| Query 30: | 0.7255 |
| Query 31: | 0.1224 |
| Query 32: | 0.8912 |
| Query 33: | 0.7563 |
| Query 34: | 0.4467 |
| Query 35: | 0.8753 |
| Query 36: | 0.6037 |
| Query 37: | 1.0000 |
| Query 38: | 0.8056 |
| Query 39: | 0.0183 |

Overall statistics
(for 34 queries):

Total number of documents
over all queries:

| | |
|---|---|
| Retrieved: | 34000 |
| Relevant: | 338 |
| Rel_ret: | 318 |

Interpolated Recall -
Precision Averages:

| | |
|---|---|
| at 0.00 | 0.7963 |
| at 0.10 | 0.7380 |
| at 0.20 | 0.6878 |
| at 0.30 | 0.6362 |
| at 0.40 | 0.5932 |
| at 0.50 | 0.5262 |
| at 0.60 | 0.4177 |
| at 0.70 | 0.3393 |
| at 0.80 | 0.2941 |
| at 0.90 | 0.1995 |
| at 1.00 | 0.1552 |

Avg. prec. (non-interpolated)
for all rel. documents       0.4753

Precision:

| | | |
|---|---|---|
| At | 5 docs: | 0.4765 |
| At | 10 docs: | 0.3471 |
| At | 15 docs: | 0.2824 |
| At | 20 docs: | 0.2426 |
| At | 30 docs: | 0.1902 |
| At | 100 docs: | 0.0782 |
| At | 200 docs: | 0.0418 |
| At | 500 docs: | 0.0183 |
| At | 1000 docs: | 0.0094 |

R-Precision (prec. after
all rel. docs. retrieved):

| | |
|---|---|
| Exact: | 0.4056 |

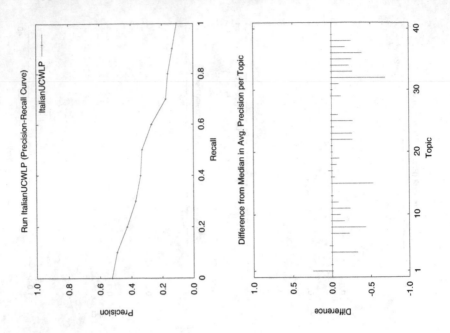

Run ItalianUCWLP (Precision-Recall Curve)

Difference from Median in Avg. Precision per Topic

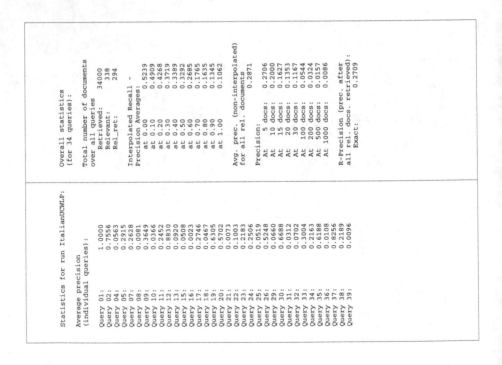

Statistics for run ItalianUCWLP:

Average precision
(individual queries):

| | |
|---|---|
| Query 01: | 1.0000 |
| Query 02: | 0.7556 |
| Query 04: | 0.0563 |
| Query 05: | 0.2915 |
| Query 07: | 0.2628 |
| Query 08: | 0.0081 |
| Query 09: | 0.3649 |
| Query 10: | 0.0366 |
| Query 11: | 0.2452 |
| Query 12: | 0.8830 |
| Query 13: | 0.0920 |
| Query 15: | 0.0508 |
| Query 16: | 0.0023 |
| Query 17: | 0.2746 |
| Query 18: | 0.0467 |
| Query 19: | 0.6305 |
| Query 20: | 0.5702 |
| Query 21: | 0.0073 |
| Query 22: | 0.1003 |
| Query 23: | 0.2183 |
| Query 24: | 0.2506 |
| Query 25: | 0.0519 |
| Query 26: | 0.5248 |
| Query 29: | 0.0660 |
| Query 30: | 0.6688 |
| Query 31: | 0.0312 |
| Query 32: | 0.0702 |
| Query 33: | 0.3004 |
| Query 34: | 0.2163 |
| Query 35: | 0.6188 |
| Query 36: | 0.0108 |
| Query 37: | 0.8256 |
| Query 38: | 0.2189 |
| Query 39: | 0.0096 |

Overall statistics
(for 34 queries):

Total number of documents
over all queries:

| | |
|---|---|
| Retrieved: | 34000 |
| Relevant: | 338 |
| Rel_ret: | 294 |

Interpolated Recall -
Precision Averages:

| | |
|---|---|
| at 0.00 | 0.5239 |
| at 0.10 | 0.4909 |
| at 0.20 | 0.4268 |
| at 0.30 | 0.3719 |
| at 0.40 | 0.3389 |
| at 0.50 | 0.3292 |
| at 0.60 | 0.2685 |
| at 0.70 | 0.1765 |
| at 0.80 | 0.1635 |
| at 0.90 | 0.1345 |
| at 1.00 | 0.1062 |

Avg. prec. (non-interpolated)
for all rel. documents          0.2871

Precision:

| | | |
|---|---|---|
| At | 5 docs: | 0.2706 |
| At | 10 docs: | 0.2000 |
| At | 15 docs: | 0.1627 |
| At | 20 docs: | 0.1353 |
| At | 30 docs: | 0.1167 |
| At | 100 docs: | 0.0544 |
| At | 200 docs: | 0.0324 |
| At | 500 docs: | 0.0157 |
| At | 1000 docs: | 0.0086 |

R-Precision (prec. after
all rel. docs. retrieved):

| | |
|---|---|
| Exact: | 0.2709 |

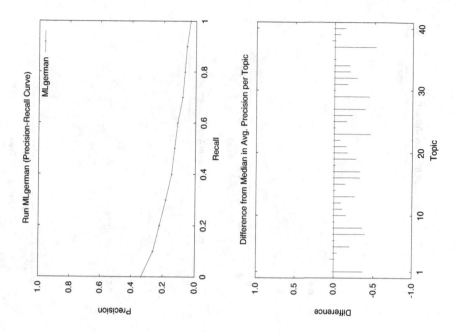

Run MLgerman (Precision-Recall Curve)

Difference from Median in Avg. Precision per Topic

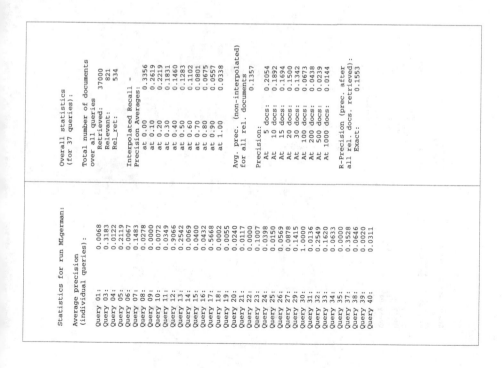

Statistics for run MLgerman:

Average precision
(individual queries):

| Query 01: | 0.0068 |
| Query 03: | 0.3183 |
| Query 04: | 0.0122 |
| Query 05: | 0.2119 |
| Query 06: | 0.0067 |
| Query 07: | 0.1483 |
| Query 08: | 0.0278 |
| Query 09: | 0.0000 |
| Query 10: | 0.0072 |
| Query 11: | 0.0349 |
| Query 12: | 0.9066 |
| Query 13: | 0.2542 |
| Query 14: | 0.0069 |
| Query 15: | 0.0400 |
| Query 16: | 0.0432 |
| Query 17: | 0.5668 |
| Query 18: | 0.0002 |
| Query 19: | 0.0055 |
| Query 20: | 0.0240 |
| Query 21: | 0.0117 |
| Query 22: | 0.0000 |
| Query 23: | 0.1007 |
| Query 24: | 0.0398 |
| Query 25: | 0.0150 |
| Query 26: | 0.0569 |
| Query 27: | 0.0878 |
| Query 29: | 0.1415 |
| Query 30: | 1.0000 |
| Query 31: | 0.0136 |
| Query 32: | 0.2549 |
| Query 33: | 0.1620 |
| Query 34: | 0.0633 |
| Query 35: | 0.0000 |
| Query 37: | 0.3528 |
| Query 38: | 0.0646 |
| Query 39: | 0.0020 |
| Query 40: | 0.0311 |

Overall statistics
(for 37 queries):

Total number of documents
over all queries:

| Retrieved: | 37000 |
| Relevant: | 821 |
| Rel_ret: | 534 |

Interpolated Recall -
Precision Averages:

| at 0.00 | 0.3356 |
| at 0.10 | 0.2619 |
| at 0.20 | 0.2219 |
| at 0.30 | 0.1831 |
| at 0.40 | 0.1460 |
| at 0.50 | 0.1283 |
| at 0.60 | 0.1102 |
| at 0.70 | 0.0801 |
| at 0.80 | 0.0675 |
| at 0.90 | 0.0557 |
| at 1.00 | 0.0338 |

Avg. prec. (non-interpolated)
for all rel. documents    0.1357

Precision:

| At 5 docs: | 0.2054 |
| At 10 docs: | 0.1892 |
| At 15 docs: | 0.1694 |
| At 20 docs: | 0.1500 |
| At 30 docs: | 0.1342 |
| At 100 docs: | 0.0673 |
| At 200 docs: | 0.0438 |
| At 500 docs: | 0.0239 |
| At 1000 docs: | 0.0144 |

R-Precision (prec. after
all rel. docs. retrieved):
Exact:    0.1553

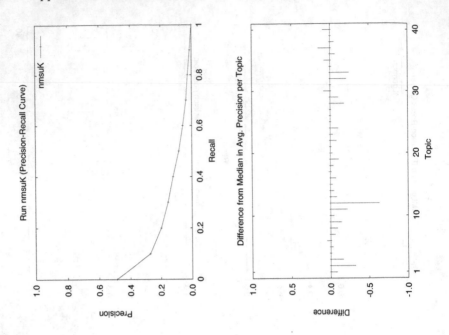

Run nmsuK (Precision-Recall Curve)

Difference from Median in Avg. Precision per Topic

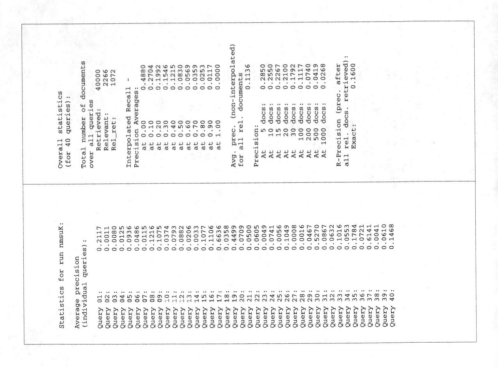

Statistics for run nmsuK:

Average precision
(individual queries):

| Query 01: | 0.2117 |
| Query 02: | 0.0011 |
| Query 03: | 0.0080 |
| Query 04: | 0.0125 |
| Query 05: | 0.0936 |
| Query 06: | 0.0486 |
| Query 07: | 0.0115 |
| Query 08: | 0.1216 |
| Query 09: | 0.1075 |
| Query 10: | 0.0374 |
| Query 11: | 0.0793 |
| Query 12: | 0.0882 |
| Query 13: | 0.0206 |
| Query 14: | 0.0033 |
| Query 15: | 0.1077 |
| Query 16: | 0.1106 |
| Query 17: | 0.6636 |
| Query 18: | 0.0358 |
| Query 19: | 0.4499 |
| Query 20: | 0.0709 |
| Query 21: | 0.0500 |
| Query 22: | 0.0605 |
| Query 23: | 0.0049 |
| Query 24: | 0.0741 |
| Query 25: | 0.0056 |
| Query 26: | 0.1049 |
| Query 27: | 0.0008 |
| Query 28: | 0.0016 |
| Query 29: | 0.0467 |
| Query 30: | 0.5270 |
| Query 31: | 0.0867 |
| Query 32: | 0.0632 |
| Query 33: | 0.1016 |
| Query 34: | 0.0553 |
| Query 35: | 0.1784 |
| Query 36: | 0.0721 |
| Query 37: | 0.6141 |
| Query 38: | 0.0041 |
| Query 39: | 0.0610 |
| Query 40: | 0.1468 |

Overall statistics
(for 40 queries):

Total number of documents
over all queries
  Retrieved:    40000
  Relevant:      2266
  Rel_ret:       1072

Interpolated Recall -
Precision Averages:
  at 0.00    0.4880
  at 0.10    0.2704
  at 0.20    0.1992
  at 0.30    0.1546
  at 0.40    0.1215
  at 0.50    0.0830
  at 0.60    0.0569
  at 0.70    0.0359
  at 0.80    0.0253
  at 0.90    0.0117
  at 1.00    0.0000

Avg. prec. (non-interpolated)
for all rel. documents
                 0.1136

Precision:
  At    5 docs:   0.2850
  At   10 docs:   0.2550
  At   15 docs:   0.2267
  At   20 docs:   0.2100
  At   30 docs:   0.1792
  At  100 docs:   0.1117
  At  200 docs:   0.0740
  At  500 docs:   0.0419
  At 1000 docs:   0.0268

R-Precision (prec. after
all rel. docs. retrieved):
  Exact:          0.1600

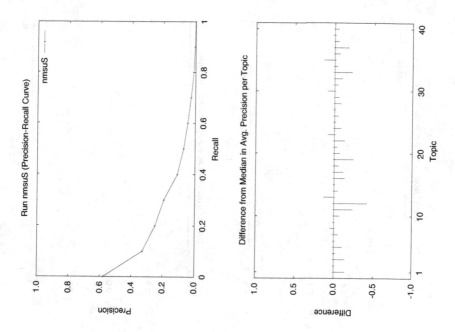

Run nmsuS (Precision-Recall Curve)

Difference from Median in Avg. Precision per Topic

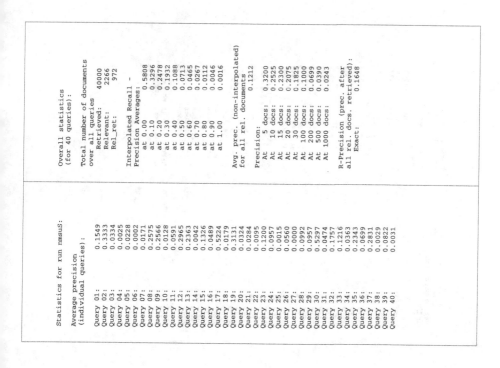

Statistics for run nmsuS:

Average precision
(individual queries):

| | |
|---|---|
| Query 01: | 0.1549 |
| Query 02: | 0.3333 |
| Query 03: | 0.0334 |
| Query 04: | 0.0025 |
| Query 05: | 0.0228 |
| Query 06: | 0.0002 |
| Query 07: | 0.0171 |
| Query 08: | 0.2575 |
| Query 09: | 0.2566 |
| Query 10: | 0.0128 |
| Query 11: | 0.0591 |
| Query 12: | 0.2965 |
| Query 13: | 0.2363 |
| Query 14: | 0.0042 |
| Query 15: | 0.1326 |
| Query 16: | 0.0489 |
| Query 17: | 0.5224 |
| Query 18: | 0.0179 |
| Query 19: | 0.3131 |
| Query 20: | 0.0324 |
| Query 21: | 0.0284 |
| Query 22: | 0.0095 |
| Query 23: | 0.1200 |
| Query 24: | 0.0957 |
| Query 25: | 0.0015 |
| Query 26: | 0.0560 |
| Query 27: | 0.0000 |
| Query 28: | 0.0992 |
| Query 29: | 0.0957 |
| Query 30: | 0.5297 |
| Query 31: | 0.0474 |
| Query 32: | 0.1757 |
| Query 33: | 0.1216 |
| Query 34: | 0.0363 |
| Query 35: | 0.2343 |
| Query 36: | 0.0699 |
| Query 37: | 0.2831 |
| Query 38: | 0.0029 |
| Query 39: | 0.0822 |
| Query 40: | 0.0031 |

Overall statistics
(for 40 queries):

Total number of documents
over all queries

| | |
|---|---|
| Retrieved: | 40000 |
| Relevant: | 2266 |
| Rel_ret: | 972 |

Interpolated Recall -
Precision Averages:

| | |
|---|---|
| at 0.00 | 0.5808 |
| at 0.10 | 0.3296 |
| at 0.20 | 0.2478 |
| at 0.30 | 0.1932 |
| at 0.40 | 0.1088 |
| at 0.50 | 0.0713 |
| at 0.60 | 0.0465 |
| at 0.70 | 0.0267 |
| at 0.80 | 0.0112 |
| at 0.90 | 0.0046 |
| at 1.00 | 0.0016 |

Avg. prec. (non-interpolated)
for all rel. documents              0.1212

Precision:

| | |
|---|---|
| At    5 docs: | 0.3200 |
| At   10 docs: | 0.2525 |
| At   15 docs: | 0.2300 |
| At   20 docs: | 0.2075 |
| At   30 docs: | 0.1825 |
| At  100 docs: | 0.1000 |
| At  200 docs: | 0.0699 |
| At  500 docs: | 0.0390 |
| At 1000 docs: | 0.0243 |

R-Precision (prec. after
all rel. docs. retrieved):
Exact:              0.1648

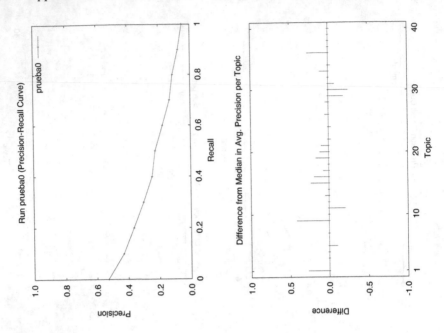

Run prueba0 (Precision-Recall Curve)

prueba0

Difference from Median in Avg. Precision per Topic

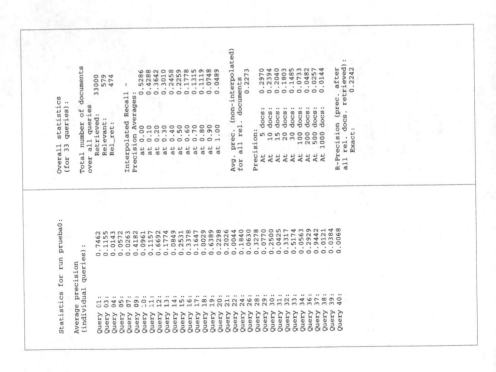

Statistics for run prueba0:

Average precision
(individual queries):

Query 01:     0.7462
Query 03:     0.1155
Query 04:     0.0143
Query 05:     0.0572
Query 07:     0.0263
Query 09:     0.4182
Query -0:     0.0961
Query 11:     0.1157
Query 12:     0.6692
Query 13:     0.1774
Query 14:     0.0849
Query 15:     0.2531
Query 16:     0.3378
Query 17:     0.1647
Query 18:     0.0029
Query 19:     0.6389
Query 20:     0.2298
Query 21:     0.2026
Query 22:     0.0044
Query 24:     0.1840
Query 26:     0.0630
Query 28:     0.3278
Query 29:     0.0770
Query 30:     0.2500
Query 31:     0.0425
Query 32:     0.3317
Query 33:     0.5174
Query 34:     0.0563
Query 36:     0.2929
Query 37:     0.9442
Query 38:     0.0121
Query 39:     0.0384
Query 40:     0.0068

Overall statistics
(for 33 queries):

Total number of documents
over all queries:
        Retrieved:     33000
        Relevant:        579
        Rel_ret:         474

Interpolated Recall -
Precision Averages:
        at 0.00     0.5286
        at 0.10     0.4288
        at 0.20     0.3642
        at 0.30     0.3010
        at 0.40     0.2458
        at 0.50     0.2259
        at 0.60     0.1778
        at 0.70     0.1315
        at 0.80     0.1119
        at 0.90     0.0748
        at 1.00     0.0489

Avg. prec. (non-interpolated)
for all rel. documents
                    0.2273

Precision:
        At    5 docs:     0.2970
        At   10 docs:     0.2394
        At   15 docs:     0.2040
        At   20 docs:     0.1803
        At   30 docs:     0.1485
        At  100 docs:     0.0733
        At  200 docs:     0.0482
        At  500 docs:     0.0257
        At 1000 docs:     0.0144

R-Precision (prec. after
all rel. docs. retrieved):
        Exact:     0.2242

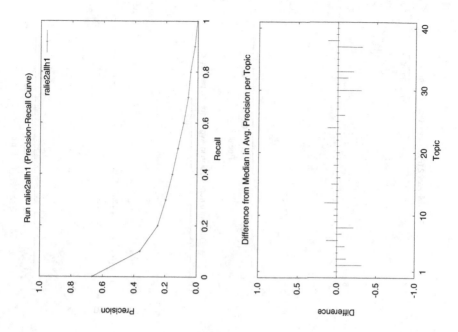

Run ralie2allh1 (Precision-Recall Curve)

Difference from Median in Avg. Precision per Topic

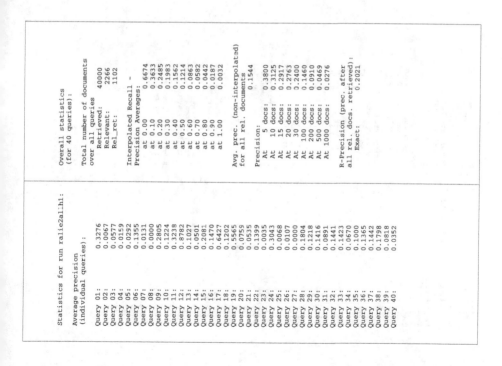

Statistics for run ralie2allh1:

Average precision
(individual queries):

| | |
|---|---|
| Query 01: | 0.3276 |
| Query 02: | 0.0067 |
| Query 03: | 0.0577 |
| Query 04: | 0.0159 |
| Query 05: | 0.0292 |
| Query 06: | 0.1355 |
| Query 07: | 0.0131 |
| Query 08: | 0.0000 |
| Query 09: | 0.2805 |
| Query 10: | 0.1224 |
| Query 11: | 0.3238 |
| Query 12: | 0.8782 |
| Query 13: | 0.1027 |
| Query 14: | 0.0501 |
| Query 15: | 0.2081 |
| Query 16: | 0.1470 |
| Query 17: | 0.6427 |
| Query 18: | 0.1202 |
| Query 19: | 0.5565 |
| Query 20: | 0.0759 |
| Query 21: | 0.0535 |
| Query 22: | 0.1399 |
| Query 23: | 0.0035 |
| Query 24: | 0.3043 |
| Query 25: | 0.0068 |
| Query 26: | 0.0107 |
| Query 27: | 0.0000 |
| Query 28: | 0.1804 |
| Query 29: | 0.1218 |
| Query 30: | 0.1416 |
| Query 31: | 0.0891 |
| Query 32: | 0.1441 |
| Query 33: | 0.1423 |
| Query 34: | 0.0670 |
| Query 35: | 0.1000 |
| Query 36: | 0.1365 |
| Query 37: | 0.1442 |
| Query 38: | 0.1798 |
| Query 39: | 0.0818 |
| Query 40: | 0.0352 |

Overall statistics
(for 40 queries):

Total number of documents
over all queries:

| | |
|---|---|
| Retrieved: | 40000 |
| Relevant: | 2266 |
| Rel_ret: | 1102 |

Interpolated Recall -
Precision Averages:

| | |
|---|---|
| at 0.00 | 0.6674 |
| at 0.10 | 0.3633 |
| at 0.20 | 0.2485 |
| at 0.30 | 0.1983 |
| at 0.40 | 0.1562 |
| at 0.50 | 0.1214 |
| at 0.60 | 0.0863 |
| at 0.70 | 0.0582 |
| at 0.80 | 0.0442 |
| at 0.90 | 0.0187 |
| at 1.00 | 0.0032 |

Avg. prec. (non-interpolated)
for all rel. documents            0.1544

Precision:

| | |
|---|---|
| At   5 docs: | 0.3800 |
| At  10 docs: | 0.3125 |
| At  15 docs: | 0.2917 |
| At  20 docs: | 0.2763 |
| At  30 docs: | 0.2400 |
| At 100 docs: | 0.1460 |
| At 200 docs: | 0.0910 |
| At 500 docs: | 0.0469 |
| At 1000 docs: | 0.0276 |

R-Precision (prec. after
all rel. docs. retrieved):

| | |
|---|---|
| Exact: | 0.2021 |

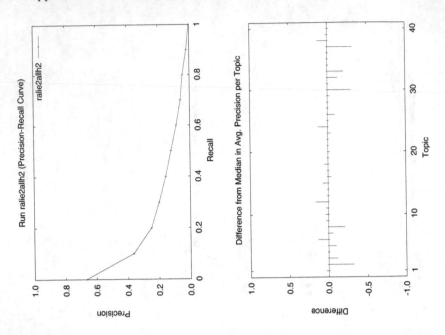

Run ralie2allh2 (Precision-Recall Curve)

ralie2allh2

Difference from Median in Avg. Precision per Topic

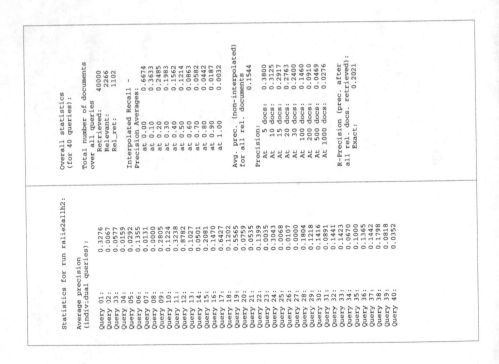

Statistics for run ralie2allh2:

Average precision
(individual queries):

| | |
|---|---|
| Query 01: | 0.3276 |
| Query 02: | 0.0067 |
| Query 03: | 0.0577 |
| Query 04: | 0.0159 |
| Query 05: | 0.0292 |
| Query 06: | 0.1355 |
| Query 07: | 0.0131 |
| Query 08: | 0.0000 |
| Query 09: | 0.2805 |
| Query 10: | 0.1224 |
| Query 11: | 0.3238 |
| Query 12: | 0.8782 |
| Query 13: | 0.1027 |
| Query 14: | 0.0501 |
| Query 15: | 0.2081 |
| Query 16: | 0.1470 |
| Query 17: | 0.6427 |
| Query 18: | 0.1202 |
| Query 19: | 0.5565 |
| Query 20: | 0.0759 |
| Query 21: | 0.0535 |
| Query 22: | 0.1399 |
| Query 23: | 0.0035 |
| Query 24: | 0.3043 |
| Query 25: | 0.0068 |
| Query 26: | 0.0107 |
| Query 27: | 0.0000 |
| Query 28: | 0.1804 |
| Query 29: | 0.1218 |
| Query 30: | 0.1416 |
| Query 31: | 0.0891 |
| Query 32: | 0.1441 |
| Query 33: | 0.1423 |
| Query 34: | 0.0670 |
| Query 35: | 0.1000 |
| Query 36: | 0.1365 |
| Query 37: | 0.1442 |
| Query 38: | 0.1798 |
| Query 39: | 0.0818 |
| Query 40: | 0.0352 |

Overall statistics
(for 40 queries):

Total number of documents
over all queries:
| | |
|---|---|
| Retrieved: | 40000 |
| Relevant: | 2266 |
| Rel_ret: | 1102 |

Interpolated Recall  -
Precision Averages:
| | |
|---|---|
| at 0.00 | 0.6674 |
| at 0.10 | 0.3633 |
| at 0.20 | 0.2485 |
| at 0.30 | 0.1983 |
| at 0.40 | 0.1562 |
| at 0.50 | 0.1214 |
| at 0.60 | 0.0863 |
| at 0.70 | 0.0582 |
| at 0.80 | 0.0442 |
| at 0.90 | 0.0187 |
| at 1.00 | 0.0032 |

Avg. prec. (non-interpolated)
for all rel. documents
0.1544

Precision:
| | |
|---|---|
| At   5 docs: | 0.3800 |
| At  10 docs: | 0.3125 |
| At  15 docs: | 0.2917 |
| At  20 docs: | 0.2763 |
| At  30 docs: | 0.2400 |
| At 100 docs: | 0.1460 |
| At 200 docs: | 0.0910 |
| At 500 docs: | 0.0469 |
| At 1000 docs: | 0.0276 |

R-Precision (prec. after
all rel. docs. retrieved):
| | |
|---|---|
| Exact: | 0.2021 |

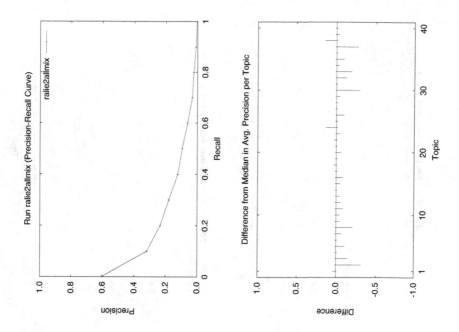

Run ralie2allmix (Precision-Recall Curve)

Difference from Median in Avg. Precision per Topic

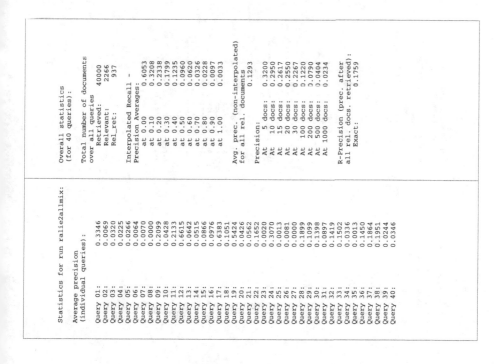

Statistics for run ralie2allmix:

Average precision
(individual queries):

| | |
|---|---|
| Query 01: | 0.3346 |
| Query 02: | 0.0069 |
| Query 03: | 0.0320 |
| Query 04: | 0.0225 |
| Query 05: | 0.0266 |
| Query 06: | 0.0064 |
| Query 07: | 0.0070 |
| Query 08: | 0.0000 |
| Query 09: | 0.2099 |
| Query 10: | 0.0428 |
| Query 11: | 0.2133 |
| Query 12: | 0.6615 |
| Query 13: | 0.0642 |
| Query 14: | 0.0515 |
| Query 15: | 0.0866 |
| Query 16: | 0.0976 |
| Query 17: | 0.6383 |
| Query 18: | 0.1051 |
| Query 19: | 0.5424 |
| Query 20: | 0.0426 |
| Query 21: | 0.0562 |
| Query 22: | 0.1652 |
| Query 23: | 0.0020 |
| Query 24: | 0.3070 |
| Query 25: | 0.0013 |
| Query 26: | 0.0081 |
| Query 27: | 0.0000 |
| Query 28: | 0.1899 |
| Query 29: | 0.1099 |
| Query 30: | 0.1398 |
| Query 31: | 0.0897 |
| Query 32: | 0.1419 |
| Query 33: | 0.1502 |
| Query 34: | 0.0336 |
| Query 35: | 0.0013 |
| Query 36: | 0.1450 |
| Query 37: | 0.1864 |
| Query 38: | 0.1951 |
| Query 39: | 0.0244 |
| Query 40: | 0.0346 |

Overall statistics
(for 40 queries):

Total number of documents
over all queries:
| | |
|---|---|
| Retrieved: | 40000 |
| Relevant: | 2266 |
| Rel_ret: | 937 |

Interpolated Recall -
Precision Averages:
| | |
|---|---|
| at 0.00 | 0.6053 |
| at 0.10 | 0.3208 |
| at 0.20 | 0.2338 |
| at 0.30 | 0.1799 |
| at 0.40 | 0.1235 |
| at 0.50 | 0.0960 |
| at 0.60 | 0.0620 |
| at 0.70 | 0.0326 |
| at 0.80 | 0.0228 |
| at 0.90 | 0.0097 |
| at 1.00 | 0.0033 |

Avg. prec. (non-interpolated)
for all rel. documents
0.1293

Precision:
| | |
|---|---|
| At   5 docs: | 0.3200 |
| At  10 docs: | 0.2950 |
| At  15 docs: | 0.2617 |
| At  20 docs: | 0.2550 |
| At  30 docs: | 0.2267 |
| At 100 docs: | 0.1220 |
| At 200 docs: | 0.0790 |
| At 500 docs: | 0.0404 |
| At 1000 docs: | 0.0234 |

R-Precision (prec. after
all rel. docs. retrieved):
Exact: 0.1759

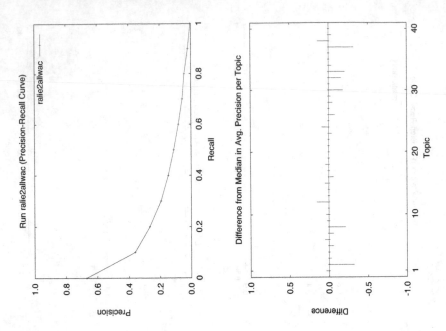

Run ralie2allwac (Precision-Recall Curve)

ralie2allwac

Precision / Recall

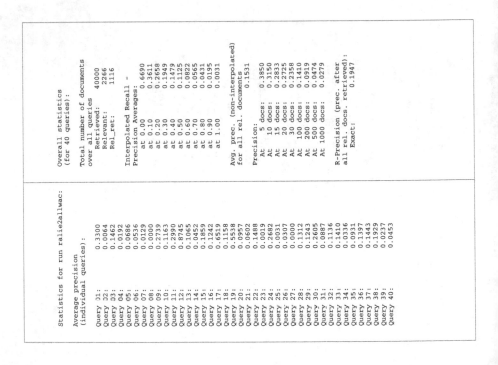

Difference from Median in Avg. Precision per Topic

Difference / Topic

Statistics for run ralie2allwac:

Average precision
(individual queries):

| | |
|---|---|
| Query 01: | 0.3300 |
| Query 02: | 0.0064 |
| Query 03: | 0.1462 |
| Query 04: | 0.0192 |
| Query 05: | 0.0686 |
| Query 06: | 0.0536 |
| Query 07: | 0.0129 |
| Query 08: | 0.0000 |
| Query 09: | 0.2739 |
| Query 10: | 0.1163 |
| Query 11: | 0.2990 |
| Query 12: | 0.8745 |
| Query 13: | 0.1065 |
| Query 14: | 0.0452 |
| Query 15: | 0.1859 |
| Query 16: | 0.1242 |
| Query 17: | 0.6519 |
| Query 18: | 0.1158 |
| Query 19: | 0.5538 |
| Query 20: | 0.0957 |
| Query 21: | 0.0602 |
| Query 22: | 0.1488 |
| Query 23: | 0.0019 |
| Query 24: | 0.2682 |
| Query 25: | 0.0031 |
| Query 26: | 0.0307 |
| Query 27: | 0.0000 |
| Query 28: | 0.1312 |
| Query 29: | 0.1243 |
| Query 30: | 0.2605 |
| Query 31: | 0.0887 |
| Query 32: | 0.1136 |
| Query 33: | 0.1410 |
| Query 34: | 0.0336 |
| Query 35: | 0.0931 |
| Query 36: | 0.1397 |
| Query 37: | 0.1443 |
| Query 38: | 0.1929 |
| Query 39: | 0.0237 |
| Query 40: | 0.0453 |

Overall statistics
(for 40 queries):

Total number of documents
over all queries:

| | |
|---|---|
| Retrieved: | 40000 |
| Relevant: | 2266 |
| Rel_ret: | 1116 |

Interpolated Recall -
Precision Averages:

| | |
|---|---|
| at 0.00 | 0.6690 |
| at 0.10 | 0.3611 |
| at 0.20 | 0.2658 |
| at 0.30 | 0.1949 |
| at 0.40 | 0.1479 |
| at 0.50 | 0.1125 |
| at 0.60 | 0.0822 |
| at 0.70 | 0.0565 |
| at 0.80 | 0.0431 |
| at 0.90 | 0.0195 |
| at 1.00 | 0.0031 |

Avg. prec. (non-interpolated)
for all rel. documents
0.1531

Precision:

| | | |
|---|---|---|
| At | 5 docs: | 0.3850 |
| At | 10 docs: | 0.3150 |
| At | 15 docs: | 0.2833 |
| At | 20 docs: | 0.2725 |
| At | 30 docs: | 0.2358 |
| At | 100 docs: | 0.1410 |
| At | 200 docs: | 0.0919 |
| At | 500 docs: | 0.0474 |
| At | 1000 docs: | 0.0279 |

R-Precision (prec. after
all rel. docs. retrieved):
Exact:     0.1947

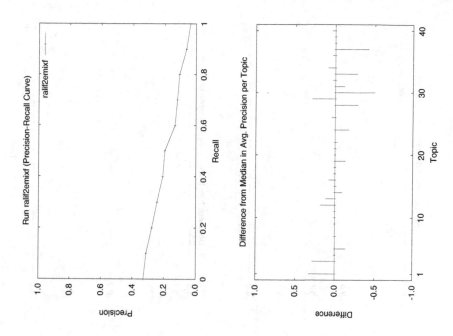

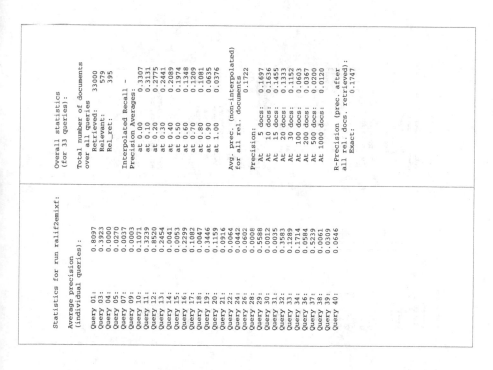

Statistics for run ralif2emixf:

Average precision
(individual queries):

| Query 01: | 0.8097 |
| Query 03: | 0.3923 |
| Query 04: | 0.0000 |
| Query 05: | 0.0270 |
| Query 07: | 0.0037 |
| Query 09: | 0.0003 |
| Query 10: | 0.1071 |
| Query 11: | 0.3239 |
| Query 12: | 0.8520 |
| Query 13: | 0.2454 |
| Query 14: | 0.0041 |
| Query 15: | 0.0053 |
| Query 16: | 0.2299 |
| Query 17: | 0.1082 |
| Query 18: | 0.0047 |
| Query 19: | 0.3446 |
| Query 20: | 0.1159 |
| Query 21: | 0.0916 |
| Query 22: | 0.0064 |
| Query 24: | 0.0442 |
| Query 26: | 0.0602 |
| Query 28: | 0.0008 |
| Query 29: | 0.5588 |
| Query 30: | 0.0012 |
| Query 31: | 0.0035 |
| Query 32: | 0.3583 |
| Query 33: | 0.1289 |
| Query 34: | 0.1714 |
| Query 36: | 0.0584 |
| Query 37: | 0.5239 |
| Query 38: | 0.0061 |
| Query 39: | 0.0309 |
| Query 40: | 0.0646 |

Overall statistics
(for 33 queries):

Total number of documents
over all queries:
| Retrieved: | 33000 |
| Relevant: | 579 |
| Rel_ret: | 395 |

Interpolated Recall -
Precision Averages:
| at 0.00 | 0.3307 |
| at 0.10 | 0.3131 |
| at 0.20 | 0.2775 |
| at 0.30 | 0.2441 |
| at 0.40 | 0.2089 |
| at 0.50 | 0.1974 |
| at 0.60 | 0.1348 |
| at 0.70 | 0.1209 |
| at 0.80 | 0.1081 |
| at 0.90 | 0.0635 |
| at 1.00 | 0.0376 |

Avg. prec. (non-interpolated)
for all rel. documents      0.1722

Precision:
| At 5 docs: | 0.1697 |
| At 10 docs: | 0.1636 |
| At 15 docs: | 0.1455 |
| At 20 docs: | 0.1333 |
| At 30 docs: | 0.1152 |
| At 100 docs: | 0.0603 |
| At 200 docs: | 0.0367 |
| At 500 docs: | 0.0200 |
| At 1000 docs: | 0.0120 |

R-Precision (prec. after
all rel. docs. retrieved):
| Exact: | 0.1747 |

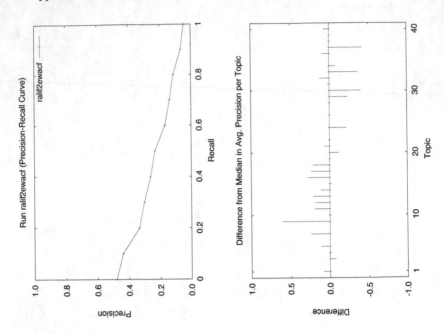

Run ralif2ewacf (Precision-Recall Curve)

ralif2ewacf

Difference from Median in Avg. Precision per Topic

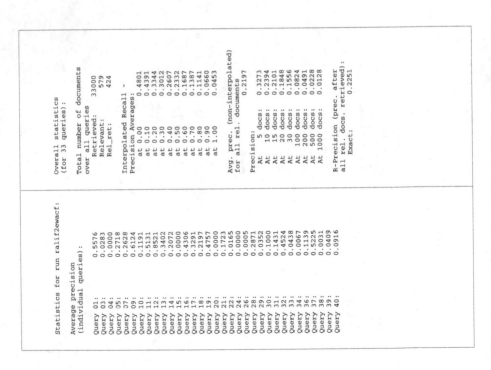

Statistics for run ralif2ewacf:

Average precision
(individual queries):

| | |
|---|---|
| Query 01: | 0.5576 |
| Query 03: | 0.0283 |
| Query 04: | 0.0000 |
| Query 05: | 0.2718 |
| Query 07: | 0.2628 |
| Query 09: | 0.6124 |
| Query 10: | 0.1191 |
| Query 11: | 0.5131 |
| Query 12: | 0.8521 |
| Query 13: | 0.3402 |
| Query 14: | 0.2072 |
| Query 15: | 0.0000 |
| Query 16: | 0.4306 |
| Query 17: | 0.3291 |
| Query 18: | 0.2197 |
| Query 19: | 0.4757 |
| Query 20: | 0.0000 |
| Query 21: | 0.1723 |
| Query 22: | 0.0165 |
| Query 24: | 0.0000 |
| Query 26: | 0.0005 |
| Query 28: | 0.2871 |
| Query 29: | 0.0352 |
| Query 30: | 0.1000 |
| Query 31: | 0.1431 |
| Query 32: | 0.4524 |
| Query 33: | 0.0438 |
| Query 34: | 0.0067 |
| Query 36: | 0.1139 |
| Query 37: | 0.5225 |
| Query 38: | 0.0031 |
| Query 39: | 0.0409 |
| Query 40: | 0.0916 |

Overall statistics
(for 33 queries):

Total number of documents
over all queries
  Retrieved:    33000
  Relevant:      579
  Rel_ret:       424

Interpolated Recall -
Precision Averages:
  at 0.00    0.4801
  at 0.10    0.4391
  at 0.20    0.3344
  at 0.30    0.3012
  at 0.40    0.2607
  at 0.50    0.2332
  at 0.60    0.1687
  at 0.70    0.1387
  at 0.80    0.1141
  at 0.90    0.0660
  at 1.00    0.0453

Avg. prec. (non-interpolated)
for all rel. documents    0.2197

Precision:
  At    5 docs:    0.3273
  At   10 docs:    0.2394
  At   15 docs:    0.2101
  At   20 docs:    0.1848
  At   30 docs:    0.1556
  At  100 docs:    0.0824
  At  200 docs:    0.0491
  At  500 docs:    0.0228
  At 1000 docs:    0.0128

R-Precision (prec. after
all rel. docs. retrieved):
  Exact:    0.2251

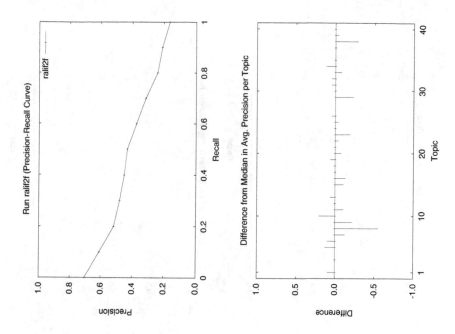

Run ralif2f (Precision-Recall Curve)

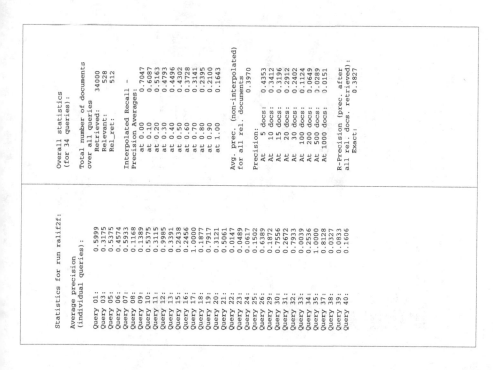

Difference from Median in Avg. Precision per Topic

Statistics for run ralif2f:

Average precision
(individual queries):

| | |
|---|---|
| Query 01: | 0.5999 |
| Query 03: | 0.3175 |
| Query 05: | 0.5375 |
| Query 06: | 0.4574 |
| Query 07: | 0.5933 |
| Query 08: | 0.1168 |
| Query 09: | 0.1389 |
| Query 10: | 0.5375 |
| Query 11: | 0.3115 |
| Query 12: | 0.9985 |
| Query 13: | 0.3391 |
| Query 15: | 0.2438 |
| Query 16: | 0.2456 |
| Query 17: | 1.0000 |
| Query 18: | 0.1877 |
| Query 19: | 0.7917 |
| Query 20: | 0.3121 |
| Query 21: | 0.5061 |
| Query 22: | 0.0147 |
| Query 23: | 0.0489 |
| Query 24: | 0.0617 |
| Query 25: | 0.1502 |
| Query 26: | 0.6389 |
| Query 29: | 0.1872 |
| Query 30: | 0.7556 |
| Query 31: | 0.2672 |
| Query 32: | 0.7933 |
| Query 33: | 0.0039 |
| Query 34: | 0.2536 |
| Query 35: | 1.0000 |
| Query 37: | 0.8128 |
| Query 38: | 0.0327 |
| Query 39: | 0.0833 |
| Query 40: | 0.1606 |

Overall statistics
(for 34 queries):

Total number of documents
over all queries

| Retrieved: | 34000 |
|---|---|
| Relevant: | 528 |
| Rel_ret: | 512 |

Interpolated Recall  -
Precision Averages:

| at 0.00 | 0.7047 |
|---|---|
| at 0.10 | 0.6087 |
| at 0.20 | 0.5163 |
| at 0.30 | 0.4793 |
| at 0.40 | 0.4496 |
| at 0.50 | 0.4302 |
| at 0.60 | 0.3728 |
| at 0.70 | 0.3141 |
| at 0.80 | 0.2395 |
| at 0.90 | 0.2100 |
| at 1.00 | 0.1643 |

Avg. prec. (non-interpolated)
for all rel. documents          0.3970

Precision:

| At | 5 docs: | 0.4353 |
|---|---|---|
| At | 10 docs: | 0.3412 |
| At | 15 docs: | 0.3196 |
| At | 20 docs: | 0.2912 |
| At | 30 docs: | 0.2402 |
| At | 100 docs: | 0.1124 |
| At | 200 docs: | 0.0649 |
| At | 500 docs: | 0.0289 |
| At | 1000 docs: | 0.0151 |

R-Precision (prec. after
all rel. docs. retrieved):

Exact:          0.3827

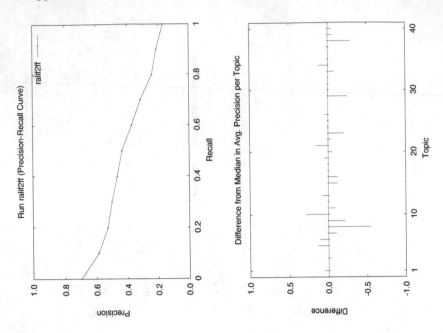

Run ralif2ff (Precision-Recall Curve)

Difference from Median in Avg. Precision per Topic

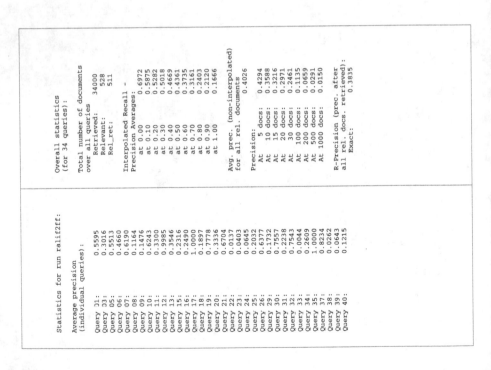

Statistics for run ralif2ff:

Average precision
(individual queries):

|  | |
|---|---|
| Query 01: | 0.5595 |
| Query 03: | 0.3016 |
| Query 05: | 0.5513 |
| Query 06: | 0.4660 |
| Query 07: | 0.6190 |
| Query 08: | 0.1164 |
| Query 09: | 0.1476 |
| Query 10: | 0.6243 |
| Query 11: | 0.3300 |
| Query 12: | 0.9985 |
| Query 13: | 0.3546 |
| Query 15: | 0.2316 |
| Query 16: | 0.2490 |
| Query 17: | 1.0000 |
| Query 18: | 0.1897 |
| Query 19: | 0.7778 |
| Query 20: | 0.3336 |
| Query 21: | 0.6704 |
| Query 22: | 0.0137 |
| Query 23: | 0.0403 |
| Query 24: | 0.0645 |
| Query 25: | 0.2032 |
| Query 26: | 0.6377 |
| Query 29: | 0.1732 |
| Query 30: | 0.7557 |
| Query 31: | 0.2238 |
| Query 32: | 0.7543 |
| Query 33: | 0.0044 |
| Query 34: | 0.2609 |
| Query 35: | 1.0000 |
| Query 37: | 0.8234 |
| Query 38: | 0.0262 |
| Query 39: | 0.0643 |
| Query 40: | 0.1215 |

Overall statistics
(for 34 queries):

Total number of documents
over all queries:
| | |
|---|---|
| Retrieved: | 34000 |
| Relevant: | 528 |
| Rel_ret: | 511 |

Interpolated Recall -
Precision Averages:
| | |
|---|---|
| at 0.00 | 0.6972 |
| at 0.10 | 0.5875 |
| at 0.20 | 0.5282 |
| at 0.30 | 0.5018 |
| at 0.40 | 0.4669 |
| at 0.50 | 0.4361 |
| at 0.60 | 0.3735 |
| at 0.70 | 0.3161 |
| at 0.80 | 0.2403 |
| at 0.90 | 0.2120 |
| at 1.00 | 0.1666 |

Avg. prec. (non-interpolated)
for all rel. documents        0.4026

Precision:
| | |
|---|---|
| At   5 docs: | 0.4294 |
| At  10 docs: | 0.3588 |
| At  15 docs: | 0.3216 |
| At  20 docs: | 0.2971 |
| At  30 docs: | 0.2461 |
| At 100 docs: | 0.1135 |
| At 200 docs: | 0.0659 |
| At 500 docs: | 0.0291 |
| At 1000 docs: | 0.0150 |

R-Precision (prec. after
all rel.docs. retrieved):
| | |
|---|---|
| Exact: | 0.3835 |

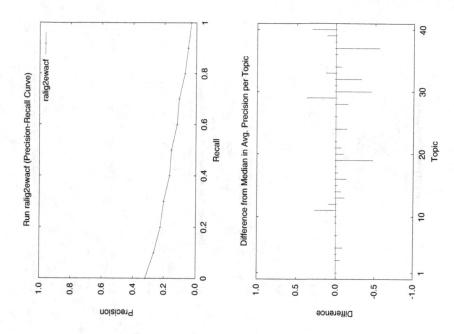

Run ralig2ewacf (Precision-Recall Curve)

Difference from Median in Avg. Precision per Topic

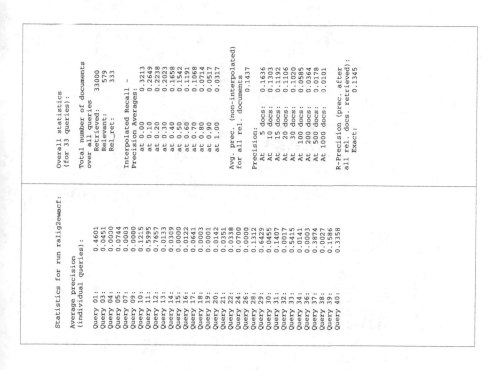

Statistics for run ralig2ewacf:

Average precision
(individual queries):

| Query 01: | 0.4601 |
| Query 03: | 0.0451 |
| Query 04: | 0.0000 |
| Query 05: | 0.0744 |
| Query 07: | 0.0003 |
| Query 09: | 0.0000 |
| Query 10: | 0.1215 |
| Query 11: | 0.5995 |
| Query 12: | 0.7657 |
| Query 13: | 0.0133 |
| Query 14: | 0.0309 |
| Query 15: | 0.0000 |
| Query 16: | 0.0122 |
| Query 17: | 0.0641 |
| Query 18: | 0.0003 |
| Query 19: | 0.0001 |
| Query 20: | 0.0142 |
| Query 21: | 0.0351 |
| Query 22: | 0.0338 |
| Query 24: | 0.0700 |
| Query 26: | 0.0000 |
| Query 28: | 0.1312 |
| Query 29: | 0.6429 |
| Query 30: | 0.0455 |
| Query 31: | 0.1407 |
| Query 32: | 0.0017 |
| Query 33: | 0.5415 |
| Query 34: | 0.0141 |
| Query 36: | 0.0003 |
| Query 37: | 0.3874 |
| Query 38: | 0.0027 |
| Query 39: | 0.1586 |
| Query 40: | 0.3358 |

Overall statistics
(for 33 queries):

Total number of documents
over all queries:
| Retrieved: | 33000 |
| Relevant: | 579 |
| Rel_ret: | 333 |

Interpolated Recall -
Precision Averages:
| at 0.00 | 0.3213 |
| at 0.10 | 0.2649 |
| at 0.20 | 0.2238 |
| at 0.30 | 0.2023 |
| at 0.40 | 0.1658 |
| at 0.50 | 0.1542 |
| at 0.60 | 0.1191 |
| at 0.70 | 0.1068 |
| at 0.80 | 0.0714 |
| at 0.90 | 0.0517 |
| at 1.00 | 0.0317 |

Avg. prec. (non-interpolated)
for all rel. documents        0.1437

Precision:
| At   5 docs: | 0.1636 |
| At  10 docs: | 0.1303 |
| At  15 docs: | 0.1192 |
| At  20 docs: | 0.1106 |
| At  30 docs: | 0.1020 |
| At 100 docs: | 0.0585 |
| At 200 docs: | 0.0364 |
| At 500 docs: | 0.0178 |
| At 1000 docs: | 0.0101 |

R-Precision (prec. after
all rel. docs. retrieved):
| Exact: | 0.1345 |

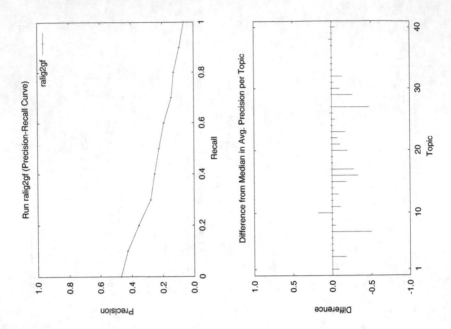

Run ralig2gf (Precision-Recall Curve)

Difference from Median in Avg. Precision per Topic

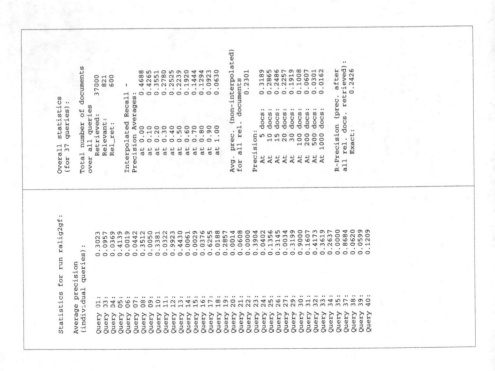

Statistics for run ralig2gf:

Average precision
(individual queries):

| | |
|---|---|
| Query 01: | 0.3023 |
| Query 03: | 0.0957 |
| Query 04: | 0.0369 |
| Query 05: | 0.4139 |
| Query 06: | 0.0019 |
| Query 07: | 0.0442 |
| Query 08: | 0.3512 |
| Query 09: | 0.0050 |
| Query 10: | 0.3381 |
| Query 11: | 0.0322 |
| Query 12: | 0.9923 |
| Query 13: | 0.4430 |
| Query 14: | 0.0061 |
| Query 15: | 0.0029 |
| Query 16: | 0.0376 |
| Query 17: | 0.6255 |
| Query 18: | 0.0188 |
| Query 19: | 0.2857 |
| Query 20: | 0.0014 |
| Query 21: | 0.0608 |
| Query 22: | 0.0000 |
| Query 23: | 0.3904 |
| Query 24: | 0.0402 |
| Query 25: | 0.1356 |
| Query 26: | 0.3145 |
| Query 27: | 0.0034 |
| Query 29: | 0.3199 |
| Query 30: | 0.9000 |
| Query 31: | 0.1607 |
| Query 32: | 0.4173 |
| Query 33: | 0.3619 |
| Query 34: | 0.2637 |
| Query 35: | 0.0000 |
| Query 37: | 0.8684 |
| Query 38: | 0.0620 |
| Query 39: | 0.0599 |
| Query 40: | 0.1209 |

Overall statistics
(for 37 queries):

Total number of documents
over all queries:

| | |
|---|---|
| Retrieved: | 37000 |
| Relevant: | 821 |
| Rel_ret: | 600 |

Interpolated Recall -
Precision Averages:

| | |
|---|---|
| at 0.00 | 0.4688 |
| at 0.10 | 0.4265 |
| at 0.20 | 0.3551 |
| at 0.30 | 0.2780 |
| at 0.40 | 0.2525 |
| at 0.50 | 0.2239 |
| at 0.60 | 0.1920 |
| at 0.70 | 0.1444 |
| at 0.80 | 0.1294 |
| at 0.90 | 0.0923 |
| at 1.00 | 0.0630 |

Avg. prec. (non-interpolated)
for all rel. documents
0.2301

Precision:

| | |
|---|---|
| At   5 docs: | 0.3189 |
| At  10 docs: | 0.2865 |
| At  15 docs: | 0.2486 |
| At  20 docs: | 0.2257 |
| At  30 docs: | 0.1919 |
| At 100 docs: | 0.1008 |
| At 200 docs: | 0.0607 |
| At 500 docs: | 0.0301 |
| At 1000 docs: | 0.0162 |

R-Precision (prec. after
all rel. docs. retrieved):
Exact:          0.2426

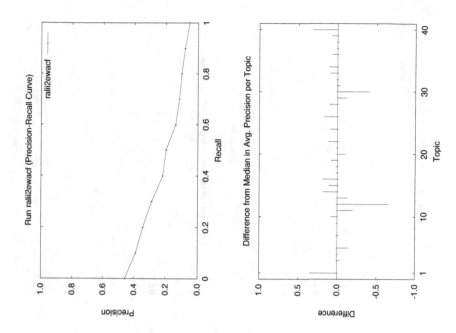

Run rali2ewacf (Precision-Recall Curve)

Difference from Median in Avg. Precision per Topic

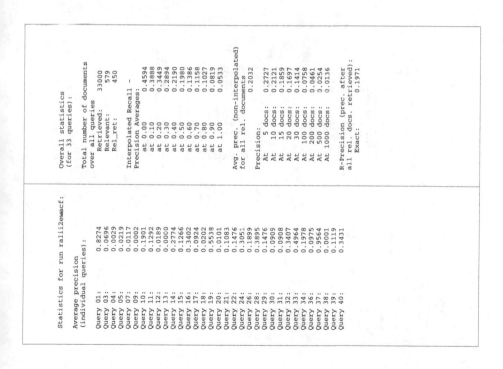

Statistics for run rali2ewacf:

Average precision
(individual queries):

| | |
|---|---|
| Query 01: | 0.8274 |
| Query 03: | 0.0696 |
| Query 04: | 0.0029 |
| Query 05: | 0.0219 |
| Query 07: | 0.0117 |
| Query 09: | 0.0002 |
| Query 10: | 0.1901 |
| Query 11: | 0.1292 |
| Query 12: | 0.0189 |
| Query 13: | 0.0000 |
| Query 14: | 0.2774 |
| Query 15: | 0.1266 |
| Query 16: | 0.3402 |
| Query 17: | 0.0924 |
| Query 18: | 0.0202 |
| Query 19: | 0.5538 |
| Query 20: | 0.0101 |
| Query 21: | 0.1083 |
| Query 22: | 0.1476 |
| Query 24: | 0.3051 |
| Query 26: | 0.1899 |
| Query 28: | 0.3895 |
| Query 29: | 0.1476 |
| Query 30: | 0.0909 |
| Query 31: | 0.0908 |
| Query 32: | 0.3407 |
| Query 33: | 0.4964 |
| Query 34: | 0.1978 |
| Query 36: | 0.0975 |
| Query 37: | 0.9564 |
| Query 38: | 0.0001 |
| Query 39: | 0.1119 |
| Query 40: | 0.3431 |

Overall statistics
(for 33 queries):

Total number of documents
over all queries:
| | |
|---|---|
| Retrieved: | 33000 |
| Relevant: | 579 |
| Rel_ret: | 450 |

Interpolated Recall -
Precision Averages:
| | |
|---|---|
| at 0.00 | 0.4594 |
| at 0.10 | 0.3888 |
| at 0.20 | 0.3449 |
| at 0.30 | 0.2894 |
| at 0.40 | 0.2190 |
| at 0.50 | 0.1980 |
| at 0.60 | 0.1386 |
| at 0.70 | 0.1158 |
| at 0.80 | 0.1027 |
| at 0.90 | 0.0819 |
| at 1.00 | 0.0533 |

Avg. prec. (non-interpolated)
for all rel. documents        0.2032

Precision:
| | | |
|---|---|---|
| At | 5 docs: | 0.2727 |
| At | 10 docs: | 0.2121 |
| At | 15 docs: | 0.1859 |
| At | 20 docs: | 0.1697 |
| At | 30 docs: | 0.1414 |
| At | 100 docs: | 0.0758 |
| At | 200 docs: | 0.0461 |
| At | 500 docs: | 0.0254 |
| At | 1000 docs: | 0.0136 |

R-Precision (prec. after
all rel. docs. retrieved):
| | |
|---|---|
| Exact: | 0.1971 |

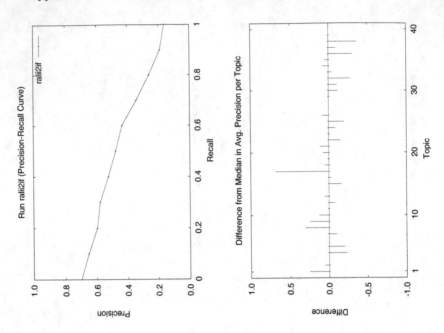

Run ralii2if (Precision-Recall Curve)

ralii2if ———

Difference from Median in Avg. Precision per Topic

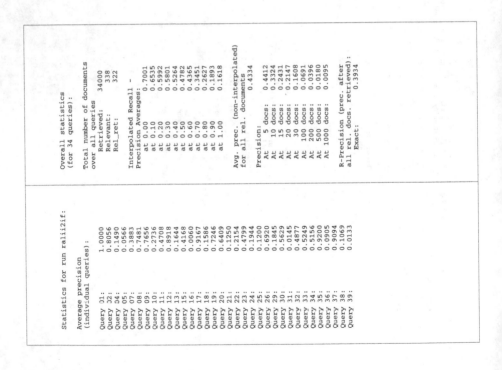

Statistics for run ralii2if:

Average precision
(individual queries):

| Query 01: | 1.0000 |
| Query 02: | 0.8056 |
| Query 04: | 0.1490 |
| Query 05: | 0.0566 |
| Query 07: | 0.3883 |
| Query 08: | 0.7481 |
| Query 09: | 0.7656 |
| Query 10: | 0.2736 |
| Query 11: | 0.4708 |
| Query 12: | 0.8918 |
| Query 13: | 0.1644 |
| Query 15: | 0.4168 |
| Query 16: | 0.0060 |
| Query 17: | 0.9167 |
| Query 18: | 0.1586 |
| Query 19: | 0.7246 |
| Query 20: | 0.6409 |
| Query 21: | 0.1250 |
| Query 22: | 0.2154 |
| Query 23: | 0.4799 |
| Query 24: | 0.1944 |
| Query 25: | 0.1200 |
| Query 26: | 0.6920 |
| Query 29: | 0.1845 |
| Query 30: | 0.5629 |
| Query 31: | 0.0145 |
| Query 32: | 0.4877 |
| Query 33: | 0.5249 |
| Query 34: | 0.5156 |
| Query 35: | 0.9200 |
| Query 36: | 0.0905 |
| Query 37: | 0.9094 |
| Query 38: | 0.1069 |
| Query 39: | 0.0133 |

Overall statistics
(for 34 queries):

Total number of documents
over all queries):
| Retrieved: | 34000 |
| Relevant: | 338 |
| Rel_ret: | 322 |

Interpolated Recall -
Precision Averages:
| at 0.00 | 0.7001 |
| at 0.10 | 0.6535 |
| at 0.20 | 0.5992 |
| at 0.30 | 0.5801 |
| at 0.40 | 0.5264 |
| at 0.50 | 0.4782 |
| at 0.60 | 0.4365 |
| at 0.70 | 0.3451 |
| at 0.80 | 0.2627 |
| at 0.90 | 0.1893 |
| at 1.00 | 0.1618 |

Avg. prec. (non-interpolated)
for all rel. documents          0.4334

Precision:
| At    5 docs: | 0.4412 |
| At   10 docs: | 0.3324 |
| At   15 docs: | 0.2431 |
| At   20 docs: | 0.2147 |
| At   30 docs: | 0.1608 |
| At  100 docs: | 0.0691 |
| At  200 docs: | 0.0396 |
| At  500 docs: | 0.0180 |
| At 1000 docs: | 0.0095 |

R-Precision (prec. after
all rel. docs. retrieved):
| Exact: | 0.3934 |

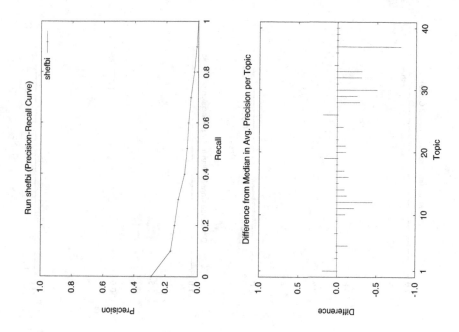

Run shefbi (Precision-Recall Curve)

Difference from Median in Avg. Precision per Topic

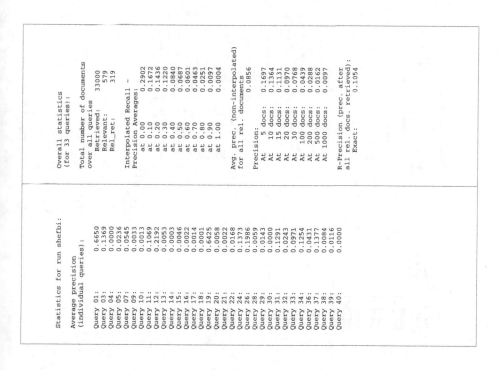

Statistics for run shefbi:

Average precision
(individual queries):

| | |
|---|---|
| Query 01: | 0.6650 |
| Query 03: | 0.1369 |
| Query 04: | 0.0000 |
| Query 05: | 0.0236 |
| Query 07: | 0.0545 |
| Query 09: | 0.0033 |
| Query 10: | 0.0013 |
| Query 11: | 0.1069 |
| Query 12: | 0.2192 |
| Query 13: | 0.0053 |
| Query 14: | 0.0003 |
| Query 15: | 0.0046 |
| Query 16: | 0.0022 |
| Query 17: | 0.0014 |
| Query 18: | 0.0001 |
| Query 19: | 0.6425 |
| Query 20: | 0.0058 |
| Query 21: | 0.0022 |
| Query 22: | 0.0168 |
| Query 24: | 0.1373 |
| Query 26: | 0.1986 |
| Query 28: | 0.0059 |
| Query 29: | 0.0143 |
| Query 30: | 0.0000 |
| Query 31: | 0.1291 |
| Query 32: | 0.0243 |
| Query 33: | 0.0971 |
| Query 34: | 0.1254 |
| Query 36: | 0.0431 |
| Query 37: | 0.1377 |
| Query 38: | 0.0084 |
| Query 39: | 0.0116 |
| Query 40: | 0.0000 |

Overall statistics
(for 33 queries):

Total number of documents
over all queries:

| | |
|---|---|
| Retrieved: | 33000 |
| Relevant: | 579 |
| Rel_ret: | 319 |

Interpolated Recall -
Precision Averages:

| | |
|---|---|
| at 0.00 | 0.2902 |
| at 0.10 | 0.1672 |
| at 0.20 | 0.1436 |
| at 0.30 | 0.1220 |
| at 0.40 | 0.0840 |
| at 0.50 | 0.0687 |
| at 0.60 | 0.0601 |
| at 0.70 | 0.0463 |
| at 0.80 | 0.0251 |
| at 0.90 | 0.0097 |
| at 1.00 | 0.0004 |

Avg. prec. (non-interpolated)
for all rel. documents          0.0856

Precision:

| | | |
|---|---|---|
| At | 5 docs: | 0.1697 |
| At | 10 docs: | 0.1364 |
| At | 15 docs: | 0.1131 |
| At | 20 docs: | 0.0970 |
| At | 30 docs: | 0.0768 |
| At | 100 docs: | 0.0439 |
| At | 200 docs: | 0.0288 |
| At | 500 docs: | 0.0162 |
| At | 1000 docs: | 0.0097 |

R-Precision (prec. after
all rel. docs. retrieved):
Exact:          0.1054

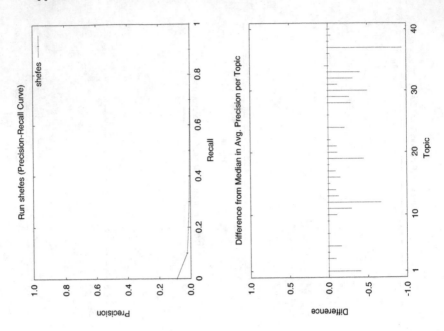

Run shefes (Precision-Recall Curve)

shefes ———

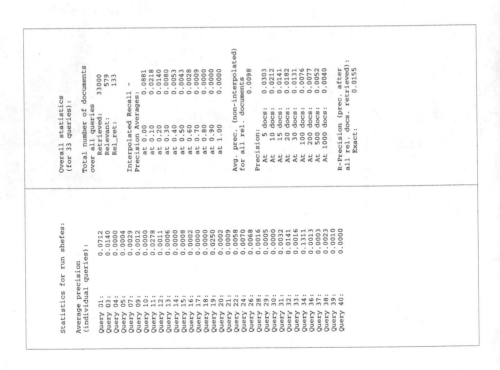

Difference from Median in Avg. Precision per Topic

Statistics for run shefes:

Average precision
(individual queries):

| | |
|---|---|
| Query 01: | 0.0712 |
| Query 03: | 0.0140 |
| Query 04: | 0.0000 |
| Query 05: | 0.0004 |
| Query 07: | 0.0029 |
| Query 09: | 0.0012 |
| Query 10: | 0.0000 |
| Query 11: | 0.0278 |
| Query 12: | 0.0011 |
| Query 13: | 0.0006 |
| Query 14: | 0.0000 |
| Query 15: | 0.0008 |
| Query 16: | 0.0002 |
| Query 17: | 0.0000 |
| Query 18: | 0.0000 |
| Query 19: | 0.0250 |
| Query 20: | 0.0002 |
| Query 21: | 0.0009 |
| Query 22: | 0.0058 |
| Query 24: | 0.0070 |
| Query 26: | 0.0068 |
| Query 28: | 0.0016 |
| Query 29: | 0.0005 |
| Query 30: | 0.0000 |
| Query 31: | 0.0032 |
| Query 32: | 0.0141 |
| Query 33: | 0.0016 |
| Query 34: | 0.1311 |
| Query 36: | 0.0013 |
| Query 37: | 0.0003 |
| Query 38: | 0.0023 |
| Query 39: | 0.0010 |
| Query 40: | 0.0000 |

Overall statistics
(for 33 queries):

Total number of documents
over all queries:
| | |
|---|---|
| Retrieved: | 33000 |
| Relevant: | 579 |
| Rel_ret: | 133 |

Interpolated Recall -
Precision Averages:
| | |
|---|---|
| at 0.00 | 0.0881 |
| at 0.10 | 0.0218 |
| at 0.20 | 0.0140 |
| at 0.30 | 0.0080 |
| at 0.40 | 0.0053 |
| at 0.50 | 0.0043 |
| at 0.60 | 0.0028 |
| at 0.70 | 0.0009 |
| at 0.80 | 0.0000 |
| at 0.90 | 0.0000 |
| at 1.00 | 0.0000 |

Avg. prec. (non-interpolated)
for all rel. documents    0.0098

Precision:
| | |
|---|---|
| At    5  docs: | 0.0303 |
| At   10  docs: | 0.0212 |
| At   15  docs: | 0.0141 |
| At   20  docs: | 0.0182 |
| At   30  docs: | 0.0131 |
| At  100  docs: | 0.0076 |
| At  200  docs: | 0.0077 |
| At  500  docs: | 0.0052 |
| At 1000  docs: | 0.0040 |

R-Precision (prec. after
all rel. docs. retrieved):
| | |
|---|---|
| Exact: | 0.0155 |

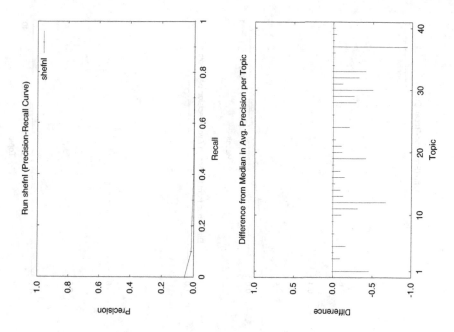

Run shefnl (Precision-Recall Curve)

Difference from Median in Avg. Precision per Topic

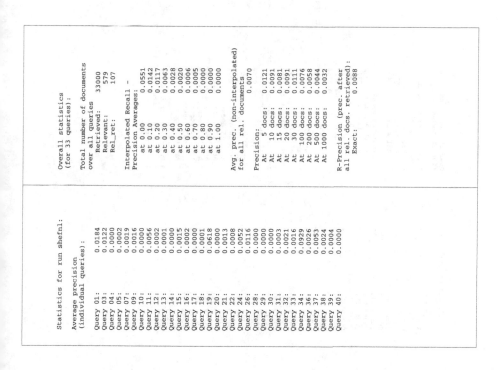

Statistics for run shefnl:

Average precision
(individual queries):

| Query 01: | 0.0184 |
| Query 03: | 0.0122 |
| Query 04: | 0.0000 |
| Query 05: | 0.0002 |
| Query 07: | 0.0019 |
| Query 09: | 0.0016 |
| Query 10: | 0.0000 |
| Query 11: | 0.0056 |
| Query 12: | 0.0002 |
| Query 13: | 0.0001 |
| Query 14: | 0.0000 |
| Query 15: | 0.0015 |
| Query 16: | 0.0002 |
| Query 17: | 0.0000 |
| Query 18: | 0.0001 |
| Query 19: | 0.0618 |
| Query 20: | 0.0000 |
| Query 21: | 0.0013 |
| Query 22: | 0.0008 |
| Query 24: | 0.0052 |
| Query 26: | 0.0116 |
| Query 28: | 0.0000 |
| Query 29: | 0.0000 |
| Query 30: | 0.0000 |
| Query 31: | 0.0003 |
| Query 32: | 0.0021 |
| Query 33: | 0.0016 |
| Query 34: | 0.0929 |
| Query 36: | 0.0026 |
| Query 37: | 0.0053 |
| Query 38: | 0.0024 |
| Query 39: | 0.0004 |
| Query 40: | 0.0000 |

Overall statistics
(for 33 queries):

Total number of documents
over all queries:
Retrieved:    33000
Relevant:       579
Rel_ret:        107

Interpolated Recall -
Precision Averages:
at 0.00    0.0551
at 0.10    0.0142
at 0.20    0.0117
at 0.30    0.0063
at 0.40    0.0028
at 0.50    0.0020
at 0.60    0.0006
at 0.70    0.0005
at 0.80    0.0000
at 0.90    0.0000
at 1.00    0.0000

Avg. prec. (non-interpolated)
for all rel. documents
                0.0070

Precision:
At    5 docs:   0.0121
At   10 docs:   0.0091
At   15 docs:   0.0081
At   20 docs:   0.0091
At   30 docs:   0.0111
At  100 docs:   0.0076
At  200 docs:   0.0058
At  500 docs:   0.0044
At 1000 docs:   0.0032

R-Precision (prec. after
all rel. docs. retrieved):
Exact:          0.0088

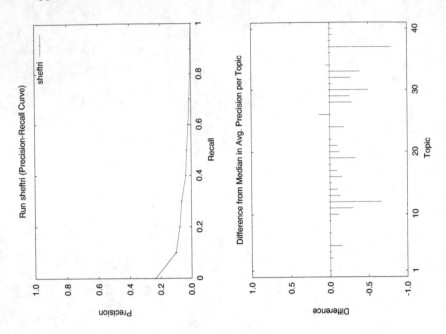

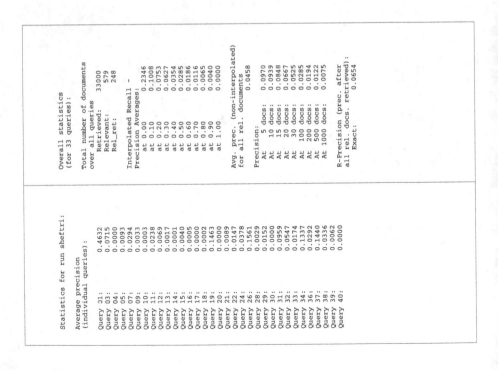

Statistics for run sheftri:

Average precision
(individual queries):

| | |
|---|---|
| Query 01: | 0.4632 |
| Query 03: | 0.0715 |
| Query 04: | 0.0000 |
| Query 05: | 0.0093 |
| Query 07: | 0.0294 |
| Query 09: | 0.0033 |
| Query 10: | 0.0003 |
| Query 11: | 0.0238 |
| Query 12: | 0.0069 |
| Query 13: | 0.0017 |
| Query 14: | 0.0001 |
| Query 15: | 0.0040 |
| Query 16: | 0.0005 |
| Query 17: | 0.0000 |
| Query 18: | 0.0002 |
| Query 19: | 0.1463 |
| Query 20: | 0.0000 |
| Query 21: | 0.0089 |
| Query 22: | 0.0147 |
| Query 24: | 0.0378 |
| Query 26: | 0.1561 |
| Query 28: | 0.0029 |
| Query 29: | 0.0152 |
| Query 30: | 0.0000 |
| Query 31: | 0.0959 |
| Query 32: | 0.0547 |
| Query 33: | 0.0174 |
| Query 34: | 0.1337 |
| Query 36: | 0.0292 |
| Query 37: | 0.1440 |
| Query 38: | 0.0336 |
| Query 39: | 0.0062 |
| Query 40: | 0.0000 |

Overall statistics
(for 33 queries):

Total number of documents
over all queries

| | |
|---|---|
| Retrieved: | 33000 |
| Relevant: | 579 |
| Rel_ret: | 248 |

Interpolated Recall -
Precision Averages:

| | |
|---|---|
| at 0.00 | 0.2346 |
| at 0.10 | 0.1008 |
| at 0.20 | 0.0753 |
| at 0.30 | 0.0627 |
| at 0.40 | 0.0354 |
| at 0.50 | 0.0285 |
| at 0.60 | 0.0186 |
| at 0.70 | 0.0116 |
| at 0.80 | 0.0065 |
| at 0.90 | 0.0040 |
| at 1.00 | 0.0000 |

Avg. prec. (non-interpolated)
for all rel. documents
0.0458

Precision:

| | |
|---|---|
| At    5 docs: | 0.0970 |
| At   10 docs: | 0.0939 |
| At   15 docs: | 0.0848 |
| At   20 docs: | 0.0667 |
| At   30 docs: | 0.0525 |
| At  100 docs: | 0.0285 |
| At  200 docs: | 0.0194 |
| At  500 docs: | 0.0122 |
| At 1000 docs: | 0.0075 |

R-Precision (prec. after
all rel. docs. retrieved):
Exact:    0.0654

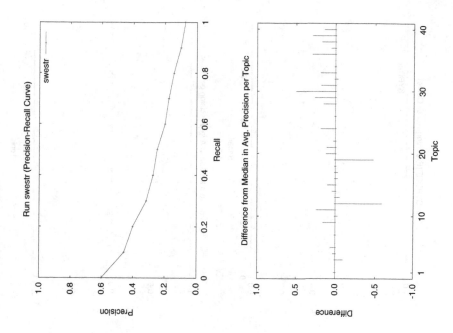

Run swestr (Precision-Recall Curve)

Difference from Median in Avg. Precision per Topic

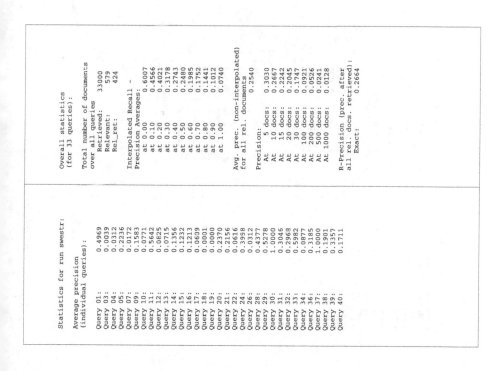

Statistics for run swestr:

Average precision
(individual queries):

| Query 01: | 0.4969 |
| Query 03: | 0.0039 |
| Query 04: | 0.0312 |
| Query 05: | 0.2236 |
| Query 07: | 0.0172 |
| Query 09: | 0.1583 |
| Query 10: | 0.0771 |
| Query 11: | 0.5642 |
| Query 12: | 0.0825 |
| Query 13: | 0.0715 |
| Query 14: | 0.1356 |
| Query 15: | 0.1232 |
| Query 16: | 0.1213 |
| Query 17: | 0.0609 |
| Query 18: | 0.0001 |
| Query 19: | 0.0000 |
| Query 20: | 0.2370 |
| Query 21: | 0.2156 |
| Query 22: | 0.0616 |
| Query 24: | 0.3998 |
| Query 26: | 0.0312 |
| Query 28: | 0.4377 |
| Query 29: | 0.5278 |
| Query 30: | 1.0000 |
| Query 31: | 0.3046 |
| Query 32: | 0.2968 |
| Query 33: | 0.5982 |
| Query 34: | 0.0877 |
| Query 36: | 0.3185 |
| Query 37: | 1.0000 |
| Query 38: | 0.1901 |
| Query 39: | 0.3357 |
| Query 40: | 0.1711 |

Overall statistics
(for 33 queries):

Total number of documents
over all queries
| Retrieved: | 33000 |
| Relevant: | 579 |
| Rel_ret: | 424 |

Interpolated Recall -
Precision Averages:
| at 0.00 | 0.6007 |
| at 0.10 | 0.4566 |
| at 0.20 | 0.4021 |
| at 0.30 | 0.3178 |
| at 0.40 | 0.2743 |
| at 0.50 | 0.2480 |
| at 0.60 | 0.1985 |
| at 0.70 | 0.1752 |
| at 0.80 | 0.1441 |
| at 0.90 | 0.1012 |
| at 1.00 | 0.0740 |

Avg. prec. (non-interpolated)
for all rel. documents     0.2540

Precision:
| At   5 docs: | 0.3030 |
| At  10 docs: | 0.2667 |
| At  15 docs: | 0.2242 |
| At  20 docs: | 0.2045 |
| At  30 docs: | 0.1747 |
| At 100 docs: | 0.0921 |
| At 200 docs: | 0.0526 |
| At 500 docs: | 0.0241 |
| At 1000 docs: | 0.0128 |

R-Precision (prec. after
all rel. docs. retrieved):
| Exact: | 0.2664 |

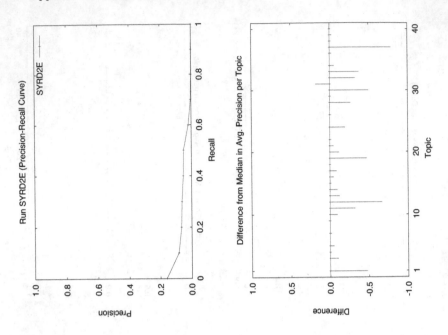

Run SYRD2E (Precision-Recall Curve)

Difference from Median in Avg. Precision per Topic

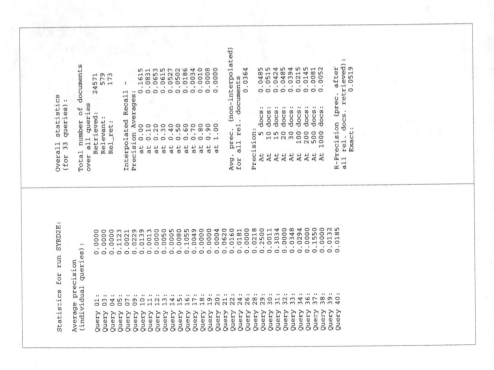

Statistics for run SYRD2E:

Average precision
(individual queries):

| | |
|---|---|
| Query 01: | 0.0000 |
| Query 03: | 0.0000 |
| Query 04: | 0.0000 |
| Query 05: | 0.1123 |
| Query 07: | 0.0021 |
| Query 09: | 0.0229 |
| Query 10: | 0.0139 |
| Query 11: | 0.0013 |
| Query 12: | 0.0000 |
| Query 13: | 0.0050 |
| Query 14: | 0.0005 |
| Query 15: | 0.0080 |
| Query 16: | 0.1055 |
| Query 17: | 0.0049 |
| Query 18: | 0.0000 |
| Query 19: | 0.0000 |
| Query 20: | 0.0004 |
| Query 21: | 0.0620 |
| Query 22: | 0.0160 |
| Query 24: | 0.0181 |
| Query 26: | 0.0000 |
| Query 28: | 0.0218 |
| Query 29: | 0.2500 |
| Query 30: | 0.0011 |
| Query 31: | 0.3034 |
| Query 32: | 0.0000 |
| Query 33: | 0.0348 |
| Query 34: | 0.0294 |
| Query 36: | 0.0000 |
| Query 37: | 0.1550 |
| Query 38: | 0.0000 |
| Query 39: | 0.0132 |
| Query 40: | 0.0185 |

Overall statistics
(for 33 queries):

Total number of documents
over all queries
| Retrieved: | 24571 |
|---|---|
| Relevant: | 579 |
| Rel_ret: | 173 |

Interpolated Recall -
Precision Averages:
| at 0.00 | 0.1615 |
|---|---|
| at 0.10 | 0.0831 |
| at 0.20 | 0.0653 |
| at 0.30 | 0.0615 |
| at 0.40 | 0.0527 |
| at 0.50 | 0.0502 |
| at 0.60 | 0.0186 |
| at 0.70 | 0.0034 |
| at 0.80 | 0.0010 |
| at 0.90 | 0.0008 |
| at 1.00 | 0.0000 |

Avg. prec. (non-interpolated)
for all rel. documents
0.0364

Precision:
| At   5 docs: | 0.0485 |
|---|---|
| At  10 docs: | 0.0515 |
| At  15 docs: | 0.0424 |
| At  20 docs: | 0.0485 |
| At  30 docs: | 0.0394 |
| At 100 docs: | 0.0215 |
| At 200 docs: | 0.0145 |
| At 500 docs: | 0.0081 |
| At 1000 docs: | 0.0052 |

R-Precision (prec. after
all rel. docs. retrieved):
| Exact: | 0.0519 |
|---|---|

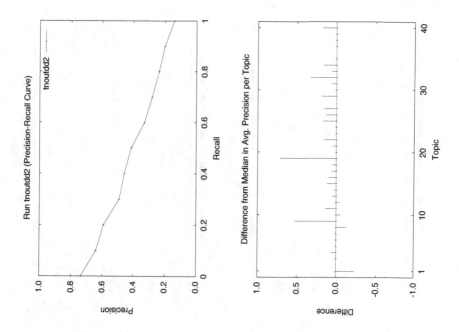

Run tnoutdd2 (Precision-Recall Curve)

Difference from Median in Avg. Precision per Topic

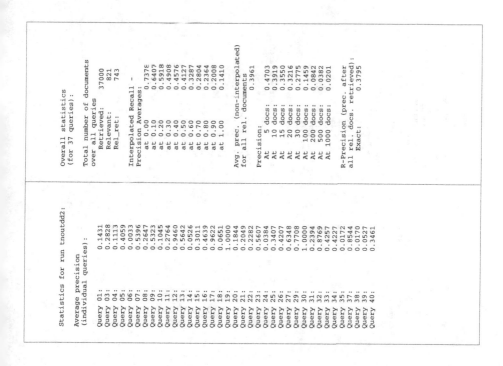

```
Statistics for run tnoutdd2:

Average precision
(individual queries):

Query 01:    0.1431
Query 03:    0.2828
Query 04:    0.1113
Query 05:    0.4059
Query 06:    0.0033
Query 07:    0.5396
Query 08:    0.2647
Query 09:    0.5323
Query 10:    0.1045
Query 11:    0.2764
Query 12:    0.9460
Query 13:    0.5642
Query 14:    0.0526
Query 15:    0.3011
Query 16:    0.4639
Query 17:    0.9622
Query 18:    0.0651
Query 19:    1.0000
Query 20:    0.1844
Query 21:    0.2049
Query 22:    0.2282
Query 23:    0.5607
Query 24:    0.0384
Query 25:    0.3407
Query 26:    0.4207
Query 27:    0.6348
Query 29:    0.7708
Query 30:    1.0000
Query 31:    0.2394
Query 32:    0.8769
Query 33:    0.4257
Query 34:    0.4227
Query 35:    0.0172
Query 37:    0.8544
Query 38:    0.0170
Query 39:    0.0527
Query 40:    0.3461
```

```
Overall statistics
(for 37 queries):

Total number of documents
over all queries:
    Retrieved:     37000
    Relevant:        821
    Rel_ret:         743

Interpolated Recall  -
Precision Averages:
    at 0.00    0.7378
    at 0.10    0.6407
    at 0.20    0.5918
    at 0.30    0.4908
    at 0.40    0.4576
    at 0.50    0.4127
    at 0.60    0.3287
    at 0.70    0.2804
    at 0.80    0.2364
    at 0.90    0.2008
    at 1.00    0.1410

Avg. prec. (non-interpolated)
for all rel. documents    0.3961

Precision:
    At    5 docs:   0.4703
    At   10 docs:   0.3919
    At   15 docs:   0.3550
    At   20 docs:   0.3216
    At   30 docs:   0.2775
    At  100 docs:   0.1459
    At  200 docs:   0.0842
    At  500 docs:   0.0382
    At 1000 docs:   0.0201

R-Precision (prec. after
all rel. docs. retrieved):
    Exact:     0.3795
```

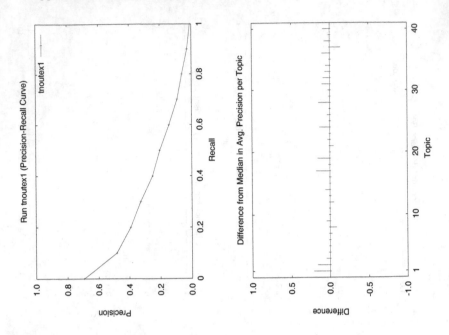

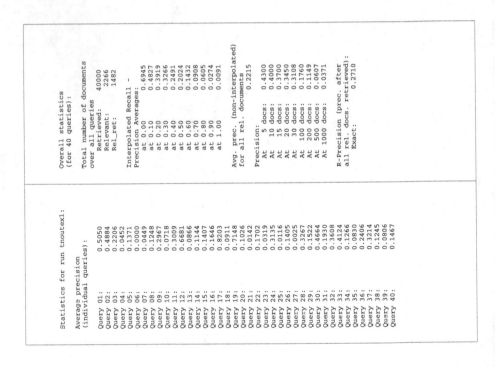

Statistics for run tnoutex1:

Average precision
(individual queries):

| Query 01: | 0.5050 |
|---|---|
| Query 02: | 0.4884 |
| Query 03: | 0.2206 |
| Query 04: | 0.0452 |
| Query 05: | 0.1371 |
| Query 06: | 0.0000 |
| Query 07: | 0.0049 |
| Query 08: | 0.1248 |
| Query 09: | 0.2967 |
| Query 10: | 0.0718 |
| Query 11: | 0.3009 |
| Query 12: | 0.6681 |
| Query 13: | 0.0866 |
| Query 14: | 0.1144 |
| Query 15: | 0.1407 |
| Query 16: | 0.1646 |
| Query 17: | 0.8203 |
| Query 18: | 0.0911 |
| Query 19: | 0.7148 |
| Query 20: | 0.1026 |
| Query 21: | 0.0142 |
| Query 22: | 0.1702 |
| Query 23: | 0.0319 |
| Query 24: | 0.3135 |
| Query 25: | 0.0116 |
| Query 26: | 0.1405 |
| Query 27: | 0.0025 |
| Query 28: | 0.3267 |
| Query 29: | 0.1522 |
| Query 30: | 0.4664 |
| Query 31: | 0.1930 |
| Query 32: | 0.3608 |
| Query 33: | 0.4124 |
| Query 34: | 0.1266 |
| Query 35: | 0.0830 |
| Query 36: | 0.2406 |
| Query 37: | 0.3214 |
| Query 38: | 0.1245 |
| Query 39: | 0.0806 |
| Query 40: | 0.1467 |

Overall statistics
(for 40 queries):

Total number of documents
over all queries

| Retrieved: | 40000 |
|---|---|
| Relevant: | 2266 |
| Rel_ret: | 1482 |

Interpolated Recall -
Precision Averages:

| at 0.00 | 0.6945 |
|---|---|
| at 0.10 | 0.4827 |
| at 0.20 | 0.3919 |
| at 0.30 | 0.3266 |
| at 0.40 | 0.2491 |
| at 0.50 | 0.2024 |
| at 0.60 | 0.1432 |
| at 0.70 | 0.0908 |
| at 0.80 | 0.0605 |
| at 0.90 | 0.0274 |
| at 1.00 | 0.0091 |

Avg. prec. (non-interpolated)
for all rel. documents    0.2215

Precision:

| At    5 docs: | 0.4300 |
|---|---|
| At   10 docs: | 0.4000 |
| At   15 docs: | 0.3700 |
| At   20 docs: | 0.3450 |
| At   30 docs: | 0.3108 |
| At  100 docs: | 0.1760 |
| At  200 docs: | 0.1149 |
| At  500 docs: | 0.0607 |
| At 1000 docs: | 0.0371 |

R-Precision (prec. after
all rel. docs. retrieved):
Exact:    0.2710

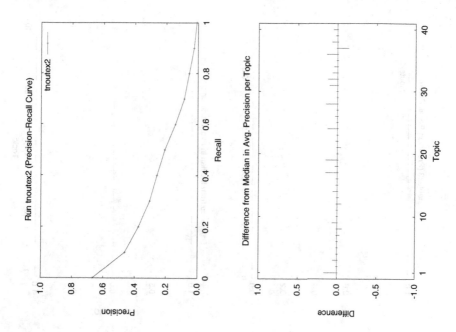

Run tnoutex2 (Precision-Recall Curve)

tnoutex2

Difference from Median in Avg. Precision per Topic

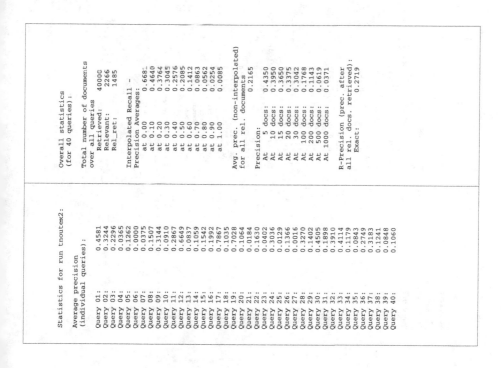

Statistics for run tnoutex2:

Average precision
(individual queries):

| Query 01: | 0.4581 |
| Query 02: | 0.3244 |
| Query 03: | 0.2296 |
| Query 04: | 0.0365 |
| Query 05: | 0.1262 |
| Query 06: | 0.0000 |
| Query 07: | 0.0375 |
| Query 08: | 0.1507 |
| Query 09: | 0.3144 |
| Query 10: | 0.0910 |
| Query 11: | 0.2867 |
| Query 12: | 0.6649 |
| Query 13: | 0.0837 |
| Query 14: | 0.1059 |
| Query 15: | 0.1542 |
| Query 16: | 0.1992 |
| Query 17: | 0.7867 |
| Query 18: | 0.1035 |
| Query 19: | 0.7028 |
| Query 20: | 0.1064 |
| Query 21: | 0.0184 |
| Query 22: | 0.1630 |
| Query 23: | 0.0402 |
| Query 24: | 0.3036 |
| Query 25: | 0.0129 |
| Query 26: | 0.1366 |
| Query 27: | 0.0016 |
| Query 28: | 0.3270 |
| Query 29: | 0.1402 |
| Query 30: | 0.4505 |
| Query 31: | 0.1898 |
| Query 32: | 0.3910 |
| Query 33: | 0.4114 |
| Query 34: | 0.1179 |
| Query 35: | 0.0843 |
| Query 36: | 0.2749 |
| Query 37: | 0.3183 |
| Query 38: | 0.1241 |
| Query 39: | 0.0848 |
| Query 40: | 0.1060 |

Overall statistics
(for 40 queries):

Total number of documents
over all queries:

| Retrieved: | 40000 |
| Relevant: | 2266 |
| Rel_ret: | 1485 |

Interpolated Recall -
Precision Averages:

| at 0.00 | 0.6681 |
| at 0.10 | 0.4640 |
| at 0.20 | 0.3764 |
| at 0.30 | 0.3045 |
| at 0.40 | 0.2576 |
| at 0.50 | 0.2085 |
| at 0.60 | 0.1412 |
| at 0.70 | 0.0863 |
| at 0.80 | 0.0562 |
| at 0.90 | 0.0254 |
| at 1.00 | 0.0085 |

Avg. prec. (non-interpolated)
for all rel. documents    0.2165

Precision:

| At | 5 docs: | 0.4350 |
| At | 10 docs: | 0.3950 |
| At | 15 docs: | 0.3650 |
| At | 20 docs: | 0.3375 |
| At | 30 docs: | 0.3042 |
| At | 100 docs: | 0.1768 |
| At | 200 docs: | 0.1143 |
| At | 500 docs: | 0.0619 |
| At | 1000 docs: | 0.0371 |

R-Precision (prec. after
all rel. docs. retrieved):

| Exact: | 0.2719 |

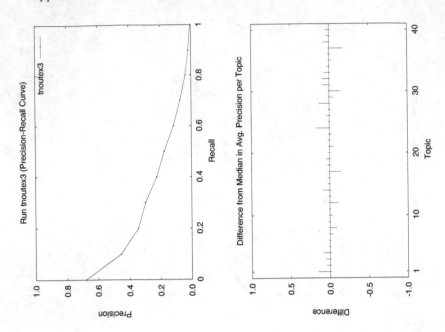

Run tnoutex3 (Precision-Recall Curve)

Difference from Median in Avg. Precision per Topic

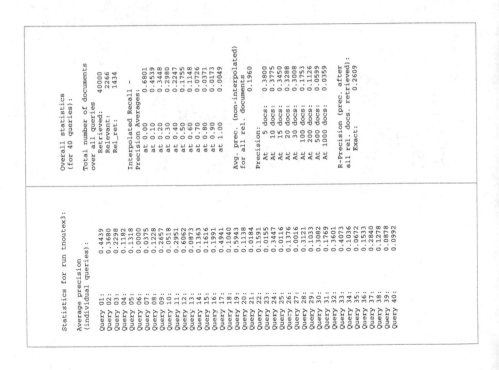

Statistics for run tnoutex3:

Average precision
(individual queries):

| | |
|---|---|
| Query 01: | 0.4439 |
| Query 02: | 0.3680 |
| Query 03: | 0.2298 |
| Query 04: | 0.1182 |
| Query 05: | 0.1318 |
| Query 06: | 0.0000 |
| Query 07: | 0.0375 |
| Query 08: | 0.1228 |
| Query 09: | 0.2657 |
| Query 10: | 0.0518 |
| Query 11: | 0.2951 |
| Query 12: | 0.6062 |
| Query 13: | 0.0873 |
| Query 14: | 0.1363 |
| Query 15: | 0.1616 |
| Query 16: | 0.1991 |
| Query 17: | 0.4941 |
| Query 18: | 0.1040 |
| Query 19: | 0.5943 |
| Query 20: | 0.1138 |
| Query 21: | 0.0184 |
| Query 22: | 0.1591 |
| Query 23: | 0.0155 |
| Query 24: | 0.3447 |
| Query 25: | 0.0116 |
| Que-y 26: | 0.1376 |
| Query 27: | 0.0016 |
| Query 28: | 0.3121 |
| Query 29: | 0.1033 |
| Query 30: | 0.3082 |
| Query 31: | 0.1769 |
| Query 32: | 0.3601 |
| Query 33: | 0.4073 |
| Query 34: | 0.1036 |
| Query 35: | 0.0672 |
| Query 36: | 0.1533 |
| Query 37: | 0.2840 |
| Query 38: | 0.1278 |
| Query 39: | 0.0878 |
| Query 40: | 0.0992 |

Overall statistics
(for 40 queries):

Total number of documents
over all queries:

| | |
|---|---|
| Retrieved: | 40000 |
| Relevant: | 2266 |
| Rel_ret: | 1434 |

Interpolated Recall -
Precision Averages:

| | |
|---|---|
| at 0.00 | 0.6801 |
| at 0.10 | 0.4539 |
| at 0.20 | 0.3348 |
| at 0.30 | 0.2980 |
| at 0.40 | 0.2247 |
| at 0.50 | 0.1755 |
| at 0.60 | 0.1148 |
| at 0.70 | 0.0726 |
| at 0.80 | 0.0371 |
| at 0.90 | 0.0173 |
| at 1.00 | 0.0049 |

Avg. prec. (non-interpolated)
for all rel. documents     0.1960

Precision:

| | |
|---|---|
| At    5 docs: | 0.3800 |
| At   10 docs: | 0.3775 |
| At   15 docs: | 0.3450 |
| At   20 docs: | 0.3288 |
| At   30 docs: | 0.3008 |
| At  100 docs: | 0.1753 |
| At  200 docs: | 0.1126 |
| At  500 docs: | 0.0599 |
| At 1000 docs: | 0.0359 |

R-Precision (prec. after
all rel. docs. retrieved):

| | |
|---|---|
| Exact: | 0.2609 |

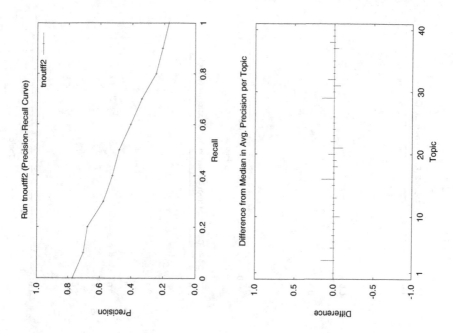

Run tnoutff2 (Precision-Recall Curve)

Difference from Median in Avg. Precision per Topic

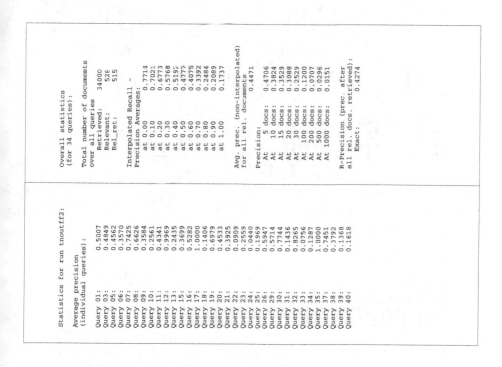

Statistics for run tnoutff2:

Average precision
(individual queries):

|  | |
|---|---|
| Query 01: | 0.5007 |
| Query 03: | 0.4849 |
| Query 05: | 0.4562 |
| Query 06: | 0.3570 |
| Query 07: | 0.7425 |
| Query 08: | 0.6626 |
| Query 09: | 0.3584 |
| Query 10: | 0.2561 |
| Query 11: | 0.4341 |
| Query 12: | 0.9969 |
| Query 13: | 0.2435 |
| Query 15: | 0.3699 |
| Query 16: | 0.5282 |
| Query 17: | 1.0000 |
| Query 18: | 0.1406 |
| Query 19: | 0.6979 |
| Query 20: | 0.4533 |
| Query 21: | 0.3925 |
| Query 22: | 0.0909 |
| Query 23: | 0.2559 |
| Query 24: | 0.0440 |
| Query 25: | 0.1969 |
| Query 26: | 0.5947 |
| Query 29: | 0.5714 |
| Query 30: | 0.7744 |
| Query 31: | 0.1436 |
| Query 32: | 0.8265 |
| Query 33: | 0.0756 |
| Query 34: | 0.1287 |
| Query 35: | 1.0000 |
| Query 37: | 0.7451 |
| Query 38: | 0.3792 |
| Query 39: | 0.1368 |
| Query 40: | 0.1618 |

Overall statistics
(for 34 queries):

Total number of documents
over all queries:
Retrieved:   34000
Relevant:      528
Rel_ret:       515

Interpolated Recall -
Precision Averages:
at 0.00   0.7714
at 0.10   0.7021
at 0.20   0.6773
at 0.30   0.5768
at 0.40   0.5192
at 0.50   0.4777
at 0.60   0.4075
at 0.70   0.3392
at 0.80   0.2484
at 0.90   0.2089
at 1.00   0.1737

Avg. prec. (non-interpolated)
for all rel. documents   0.4471

Precision:
At    5 docs:   0.4706
At   10 docs:   0.3824
At   15 docs:   0.3529
At   20 docs:   0.3088
At   30 docs:   0.2529
At  100 docs:   0.1200
At  200 docs:   0.0707
At  500 docs:   0.0296
At 1000 docs:   0.0151

R-Precision (prec. after
all rel. docs. retrieved):
Exact:   0.4274

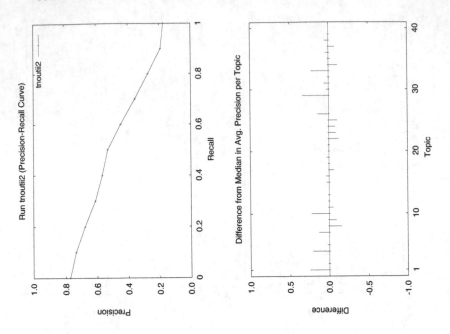

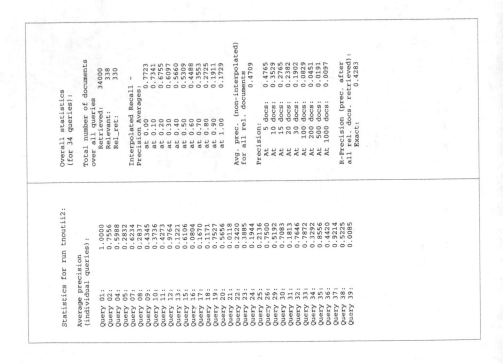

Statistics for run tnoutii2:

Average precision
(individual queries):

| | |
|---|---|
| Query 01: | 1.0000 |
| Query 02: | 0.7556 |
| Query 04: | 0.5988 |
| Query 05: | 0.2832 |
| Query 07: | 0.6234 |
| Query 08: | 0.2837 |
| Query 09: | 0.4345 |
| Query 10: | 0.3736 |
| Query 11: | 0.4273 |
| Query 12: | 0.9764 |
| Query 13: | 0.1221 |
| Query 15: | 0.6106 |
| Query 16: | 0.0804 |
| Query 17: | 0.1670 |
| Query 18: | 0.1171 |
| Query 19: | 0.7527 |
| Query 20: | 0.5656 |
| Query 21: | 0.0118 |
| Query 22: | 0.2420 |
| Query 23: | 0.3885 |
| Query 24: | 0.1944 |
| Query 25: | 0.2136 |
| Query 26: | 0.7500 |
| Query 29: | 0.5192 |
| Query 30: | 0.7083 |
| Query 31: | 0.1813 |
| Query 32: | 0.7646 |
| Query 33: | 0.7872 |
| Query 34: | 0.3292 |
| Query 35: | 0.8556 |
| Query 36: | 0.4420 |
| Query 37: | 0.9214 |
| Query 38: | 0.5225 |
| Query 39: | 0.0085 |

Overall statistics
(for 34 queries):

Total number of documents
over all queries:
| | |
|---|---|
| Retrieved: | 34000 |
| Relevant: | 338 |
| Rel_ret: | 330 |

Interpolated Recall -
Precision Averages:
| | |
|---|---|
| at 0.00 | 0.7723 |
| at 0.10 | 0.7341 |
| at 0.20 | 0.6755 |
| at 0.30 | 0.6097 |
| at 0.40 | 0.5660 |
| at 0.50 | 0.5309 |
| at 0.60 | 0.4488 |
| at 0.70 | 0.3553 |
| at 0.80 | 0.2725 |
| at 0.90 | 0.1911 |
| at 1.00 | 0.1729 |

Avg. prec. (non-interpolated)
for all rel. documents
                    0.4709

Precision:
| | |
|---|---|
| At   5 docs: | 0.4765 |
| At  10 docs: | 0.3529 |
| At  15 docs: | 0.2765 |
| At  20 docs: | 0.2382 |
| At  30 docs: | 0.1902 |
| At 100 docs: | 0.0829 |
| At 200 docs: | 0.0451 |
| At 500 docs: | 0.0191 |
| At 1000 docs: | 0.0097 |

R-Precision (prec. after
all rel. docs. retrieved):
| | |
|---|---|
| Exact: | 0.4283 |

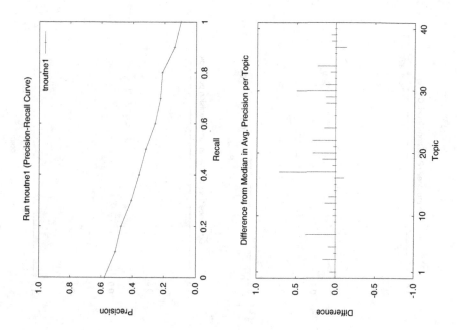

Run tnoutne1 (Precision-Recall Curve)

Difference from Median in Avg. Precision per Topic

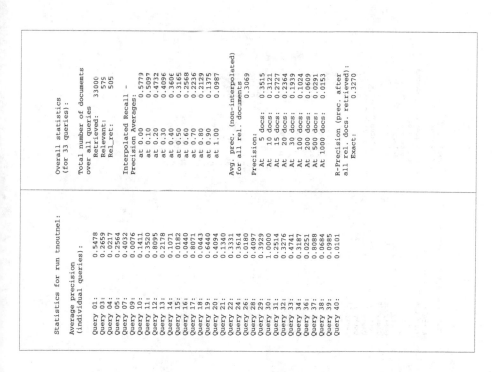

Statistics for run tnoutne1:

Average precision
(individual queries):

| Query 01: | 0.5478 |
| Query 03: | 0.2659 |
| Query 04: | 0.0217 |
| Query 05: | 0.2564 |
| Query 07: | 0.4032 |
| Query 09: | 0.0076 |
| Query 10: | 0.1411 |
| Query 11: | 0.3520 |
| Query 12: | 0.8095 |
| Query 13: | 0.2178 |
| Query 14: | 0.1071 |
| Query 15: | 0.0182 |
| Query 16: | 0.0440 |
| Query 17: | 0.8071 |
| Query 18: | 0.0443 |
| Query 19: | 0.6440 |
| Query 20: | 0.4094 |
| Query 21: | 0.1340 |
| Query 22: | 0.3331 |
| Query 24: | 0.3614 |
| Query 26: | 0.0180 |
| Query 28: | 0.4097 |
| Query 29: | 0.3929 |
| Query 30: | 1.0000 |
| Query 31: | 0.2514 |
| Query 32: | 0.3276 |
| Query 33: | 0.4741 |
| Query 34: | 0.3187 |
| Query 36: | 0.0251 |
| Query 37: | 0.8088 |
| Query 38: | 0.0684 |
| Query 39: | 0.0985 |
| Query 40: | 0.0101 |

Overall statistics
(for 33 queries):

Total number of documents
over all queries:

| Retrieved: | 33000 |
| Relevant: | 575 |
| Rel_ret: | 505 |

Interpolated Recall -
Precision Averages:

| at 0.00 | 0.5779 |
| at 0.10 | 0.5097 |
| at 0.20 | 0.4732 |
| at 0.30 | 0.4096 |
| at 0.40 | 0.360€ |
| at 0.50 | 0.3165 |
| at 0.60 | 0.2568 |
| at 0.70 | 0.2236 |
| at 0.80 | 0.2129 |
| at 0.90 | 0.1375 |
| at 1.00 | 0.0987 |

Avg. prec. (non-interpolated)
for all rel. documents    0.3069

Precision:

| At    5 docs: | 0.3515 |
| At   10 docs: | 0.3121 |
| At   15 docs: | 0.2727 |
| At   20 docs: | 0.2364 |
| At   30 docs: | 0.1939 |
| At  100 docs: | 0.1024 |
| At  200 docs: | 0.0609 |
| At  500 docs: | 0.0291 |
| At 1000 docs: | 0.0153 |

R-Precision (prec. after
all rel. docs. retrieved):
Exact:    0.3270

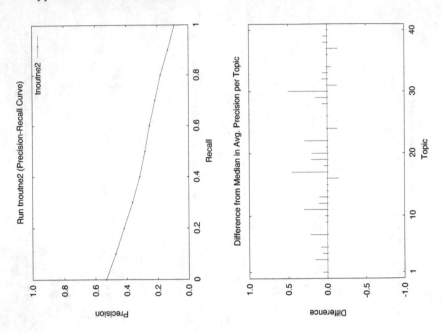

Run tnoutne2 (Precision-Recall Curve)

tnoutne2

Recall

Precision

Difference from Median in Avg. Precision per Topic

Topic

Difference

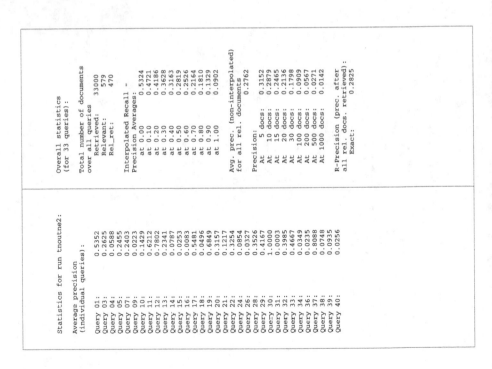

Statistics for run tnoutne2:

Average precision
(individual queries):

|  | |
|---|---|
| Query 01: | 0.5352 |
| Query 03: | 0.2625 |
| Query 04: | 0.0588 |
| Query 05: | 0.2455 |
| Query 07: | 0.2403 |
| Query 09: | 0.0223 |
| Query 10: | 0.1429 |
| Query 11: | 0.6212 |
| Query 12: | 0.7802 |
| Query 13: | 0.2341 |
| Query 14: | 0.0787 |
| Query 15: | 0.0253 |
| Query 16: | 0.0083 |
| Query 17: | 0.5481 |
| Query 18: | 0.0496 |
| Query 19: | 0.6849 |
| Query 20: | 0.3157 |
| Query 21: | 0.1217 |
| Query 22: | 0.1254 |
| Query 24: | 0.0854 |
| Query 26: | 0.0327 |
| Query 28: | 0.3526 |
| Query 29: | 0.4167 |
| Query 30: | 1.0000 |
| Query 31: | 0.0003 |
| Query 32: | 0.3985 |
| Query 33: | 0.4667 |
| Query 34: | 0.0349 |
| Query 36: | 0.0235 |
| Query 37: | 0.8088 |
| Query 38: | 0.0748 |
| Query 39: | 0.0935 |
| Query 40: | 0.0256 |

Overall statistics
(for 33 queries):

Total number of documents
over all queries
| Retrieved: | 33000 |
| Relevant: | 579 |
| Rel_ret: | 470 |

Interpolated Recall -
Precision Averages:
| at 0.00 | 0.5324 |
| at 0.10 | 0.4721 |
| at 0.20 | 0.4186 |
| at 0.30 | 0.3628 |
| at 0.40 | 0.3163 |
| at 0.50 | 0.2819 |
| at 0.60 | 0.2526 |
| at 0.70 | 0.2164 |
| at 0.80 | 0.1810 |
| at 0.90 | 0.1329 |
| at 1.00 | 0.0902 |

Avg. prec. (non-interpolated)
for all rel. documents
0.2762

Precision:
| At   5 docs: | 0.3152 |
| At  10 docs: | 0.2879 |
| At  15 docs: | 0.2465 |
| At  20 docs: | 0.2136 |
| At  30 docs: | 0.1798 |
| At 100 docs: | 0.0909 |
| At 200 docs: | 0.0567 |
| At 500 docs: | 0.0271 |
| At 1000 docs: | 0.0142 |

R-Precision (prec. after
all rel. docs. retrieved):
Exact:    0.2825

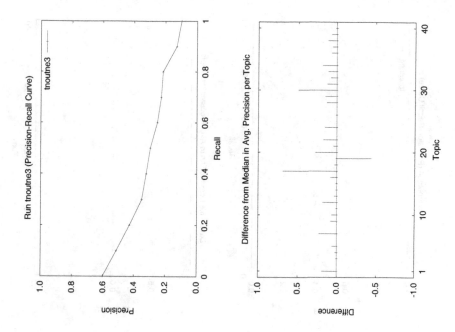

Run tnoutne3 (Precision-Recall Curve)

Difference from Median in Avg. Precision per Topic

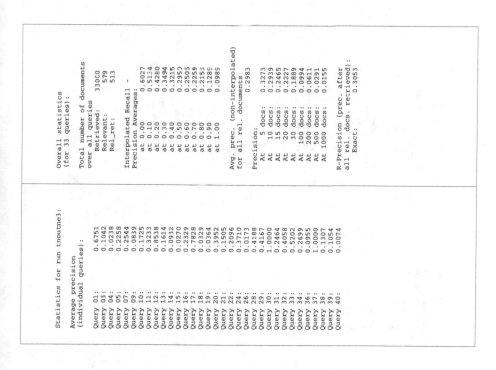

```
Statistics for run tnoutne3:          Overall statistics
                                      (for 33 queries):
Average precision
(individual queries):                 Total number of documents
                                      over all queries:
Query 01:    0.6751                      Retrieved:    33000
Query 03:    0.1042                      Relevant:       579
Query 04:    0.0238                      Rel_ret:        513
Query 05:    0.2258
Query 07:    0.2544                   Interpolated Recall -
Query 09:    0.0839                   Precision Averages:
Query 10:    0.1725                        at 0.00    0.6027
Query 11:    0.3233                        at 0.10    0.5134
Query 12:    0.8538                        at 0.20    0.4280
Query 13:    0.1614                        at 0.30    0.3494
Query 14:    0.0932                        at 0.40    0.3215
Query 15:    0.0270                        at 0.50    0.2952
Query 16:    0.2329                        at 0.60    0.2505
Query 17:    0.7828                        at 0.70    0.2259
Query 18:    0.0329                        at 0.80    0.2153
Query 19:    0.0364                        at 0.90    0.1289
Query 20:    0.3952                        at 1.00    0.0985
Query 21:    0.1505
Query 22:    0.2096                   Avg. prec. (non-interpolated)
Query 24:    0.3710                   for all rel. documents    0.2983
Query 26:    0.0173
Query 28:    0.4188                   Precision:
Query 29:    0.4167                      At    5 docs:    0.3273
Query 30:    1.0000                      At   10 docs:    0.2939
Query 31:    0.2464                      At   15 docs:    0.2465
Query 32:    0.4058                      At   20 docs:    0.2227
Query 33:    0.5202                      At   30 docs:    0.1889
Query 34:    0.2699                      At  100 docs:    0.0994
Query 36:    0.0955                      At  200 docs:    0.0611
Query 37:    1.0000                      At  500 docs:    0.0291
Query 38:    0.1307                      At 1000 docs:    0.0155
Query 39:    0.1054
Query 40:    0.0074                   R-Precision (prec. after
                                     all rel. docs. retrieved):
                                         Exact:          0.3053
```

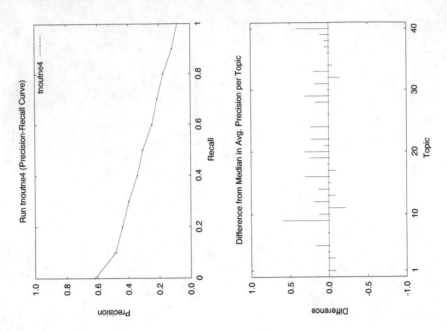

Run tnoutne4 (Precision-Recall Curve)

Difference from Median in Avg. Precision per Topic

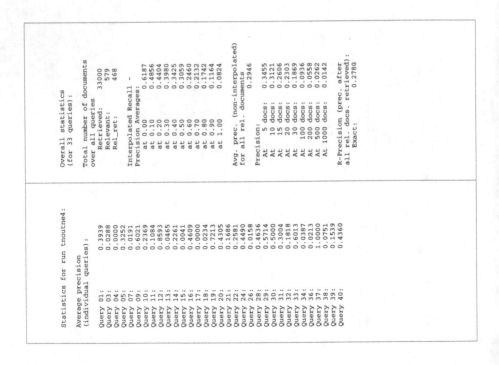

```
Statistics for run tnoutne4:        Overall statistics
                                    (for 33 queries):
Average precision
(individual queries):               Total number of documents
                                    over all queries
Query 01:    0.3939                    Retrieved:     33000
Query 03:    0.0288                    Relevant:        579
Query 04:    0.0000                    Rel_ret:         468
Query 05:    0.3252
Query 07:    0.0191                 Interpolated Recall -
Query 09:    0.6021                 Precision Averages:
Query 10:    0.2369                    at 0.00      0.6187
Query 11:    0.1084                    at 0.10      0.4856
Query 12:    0.8593                    at 0.20      0.4404
Query 13:    0.0465                    at 0.30      0.3980
Query 14:    0.2261                    at 0.40      0.3425
Query 15:    0.0041                    at 0.50      0.3059
Query 16:    0.4609                    at 0.60      0.2460
Query 17:    0.0000                    at 0.70      0.2132
Query 18:    0.0234                    at 0.80      0.1742
Query 19:    0.7213                    at 0.90      0.1164
Query 20:    0.4305                    at 1.00      0.0824
Query 21:    0.1686
Query 22:    0.2581                 Avg. prec. (non-interpolated)
Query 24:    0.4490                 for all rel. documents      0.2946
Query 26:    0.0158
Query 28:    0.4636                 Precision:
Query 29:    0.5714                    At     5 docs:     0.3455
Query 30:    0.5000                    At    10 docs:     0.3121
Query 31:    0.3004                    At    15 docs:     0.2606
Query 32:    0.1818                    At    20 docs:     0.2303
Query 33:    0.6013                    At    30 docs:     0.1869
Query 34:    0.0387                    At   100 docs:     0.0936
Query 36:    0.0213                    At   200 docs:     0.0558
Query 37:    1.0000                    At   500 docs:     0.0262
Query 38:    0.0751                    At  1000 docs:     0.0142
Query 39:    0.1539
Query 40:    0.4360                 R-Precision (prec. after
                                    all rel. docs. retrieved):
                                          Exact:       0.2780
```

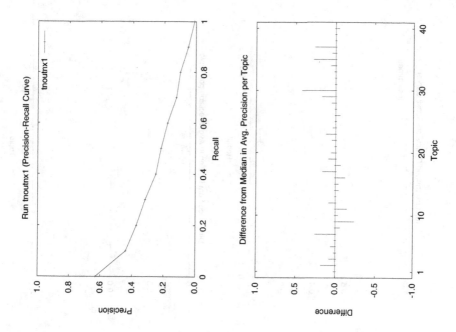

Run tnoutnx1 (Precision-Recall Curve)

Difference from Median in Avg. Precision per Topic

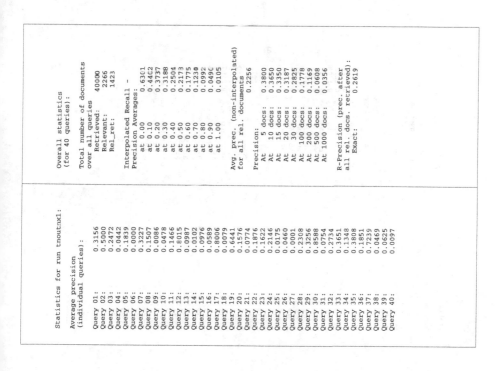

Statistics for run tnoutnx1:

Average precision
(individual queries):

| | |
|---|---|
| Query 01: | 0.3156 |
| Query 02: | 0.5000 |
| Query 03: | 0.2472 |
| Query 04: | 0.0442 |
| Query 05: | 0.1839 |
| Query 06: | 0.0000 |
| Query 07: | 0.3227 |
| Query 08: | 0.1507 |
| Query 09: | 0.0086 |
| Query 10: | 0.0478 |
| Query 11: | 0.1466 |
| Query 12: | 0.8015 |
| Query 13: | 0.0987 |
| Query 14: | 0.0102 |
| Query 15: | 0.0976 |
| Query 16: | 0.0589 |
| Query 17: | 0.8006 |
| Query 18: | 0.0079 |
| Query 19: | 0.6441 |
| Query 20: | 0.1576 |
| Query 21: | 0.0774 |
| Query 22: | 0.1876 |
| Query 23: | 0.1622 |
| Query 24: | 0.2146 |
| Query 25: | 0.0175 |
| Query 26: | 0.0460 |
| Query 27: | 0.0001 |
| Query 28: | 0.2308 |
| Query 29: | 0.3256 |
| Query 30: | 0.8588 |
| Query 31: | 0.0754 |
| Query 32: | 0.2734 |
| Query 33: | 0.3651 |
| Query 34: | 0.1348 |
| Query 35: | 0.3808 |
| Query 36: | 0.1851 |
| Query 37: | 0.7239 |
| Query 38: | 0.0469 |
| Query 39: | 0.0625 |
| Query 40: | 0.0097 |

Overall statistics
(for 40 queries):

Total number of documents
over all queries:
| | |
|---|---|
| Retrieved: | 40000 |
| Relevant: | 2266 |
| Rel_ret: | 1423 |

Interpolated Recall -
Precision Averages:
| | |
|---|---|
| at 0.00 | 0.6301 |
| at 0.10 | 0.4402 |
| at 0.20 | 0.3737 |
| at 0.30 | 0.3188 |
| at 0.40 | 0.2504 |
| at 0.50 | 0.2173 |
| at 0.60 | 0.1775 |
| at 0.70 | 0.1230 |
| at 0.80 | 0.0992 |
| at 0.90 | 0.0490 |
| at 1.00 | 0.0105 |

Avg. prec. (non-interpolated)
for all rel. documents    0.2256

Precision:
| | | |
|---|---|---|
| At | 5 docs: | 0.3800 |
| At | 10 docs: | 0.3650 |
| At | 15 docs: | 0.3350 |
| At | 20 docs: | 0.3187 |
| At | 30 docs: | 0.2825 |
| At | 100 docs: | 0.1778 |
| At | 200 docs: | 0.1169 |
| At | 500 docs: | 0.0608 |
| At | 1000 docs: | 0.0356 |

R-Precision (prec. after
all rel. docs. retrieved):
| | |
|---|---|
| Exact: | 0.2619 |

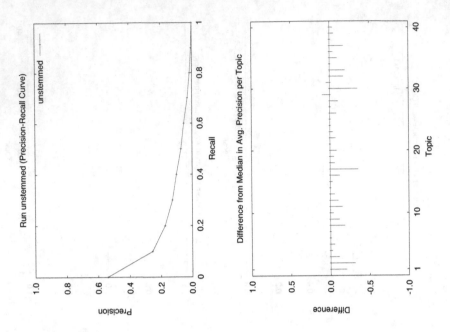

Run unstemmed (Precision-Recall Curve)

Difference from Median in Avg. Precision per Topic

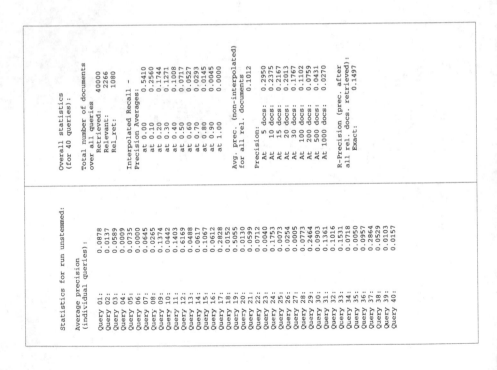

Statistics for run unstemmed:

Average precision
(individual queries):

| | |
|---|---|
| Query 01: | 0.0878 |
| Query 02: | 0.0137 |
| Query 03: | 0.0589 |
| Query 04: | 0.0009 |
| Query 05: | 0.0735 |
| Query 06: | 0.0000 |
| Query 07: | 0.0645 |
| Query 08: | 0.0265 |
| Query 09: | 0.1374 |
| Query 10: | 0.0442 |
| Query 11: | 0.1403 |
| Query 12: | 0.6169 |
| Query 13: | 0.0488 |
| Query 14: | 0.0617 |
| Query 15: | 0.1067 |
| Query 16: | 0.0612 |
| Query 17: | 0.2828 |
| Query 18: | 0.0152 |
| Query 19: | 0.5055 |
| Query 20: | 0.0130 |
| Query 21: | 0.0599 |
| Query 22: | 0.0712 |
| Query 23: | 0.0040 |
| Query 24: | 0.1753 |
| Query 25: | 0.0073 |
| Query 26: | 0.0254 |
| Query 27: | 0.0005 |
| Query 28: | 0.0773 |
| Query 29: | 0.2464 |
| Query 30: | 0.0903 |
| Query 31: | 0.1361 |
| Query 32: | 0.1016 |
| Query 33: | 0.1531 |
| Query 34: | 0.0718 |
| Query 35: | 0.0050 |
| Query 36: | 0.0957 |
| Query 37: | 0.2864 |
| Query 38: | 0.0529 |
| Query 39: | 0.0103 |
| Query 40: | 0.0157 |

Overall statistics
(for 40 queries):

Total number of documents
over all queries:

| | |
|---|---|
| Retrieved: | 40000 |
| Relevant: | 2266 |
| Rel_ret: | 1080 |

Interpolated Recall -
Precision Averages:

| | |
|---|---|
| at 0.00 | 0.5410 |
| at 0.10 | 0.2560 |
| at 0.20 | 0.1744 |
| at 0.30 | 0.1271 |
| at 0.40 | 0.1008 |
| at 0.50 | 0.1017 |
| at 0.60 | 0.0527 |
| at 0.70 | 0.0293 |
| at 0.80 | 0.0145 |
| at 0.90 | 0.0045 |
| at 1.00 | 0.0000 |

Avg. prec. (non-interpolated)
for all rel. documents
0.1012

Precision:

| | | |
|---|---|---|
| At | 5 docs: | 0.2950 |
| At | 10 docs: | 0.2375 |
| At | 15 docs: | 0.2167 |
| At | 20 docs: | 0.2013 |
| At | 30 docs: | 0.1767 |
| At | 100 docs: | 0.1102 |
| At | 200 docs: | 0.0759 |
| At | 500 docs: | 0.0431 |
| At | 1000 docs: | 0.0270 |

R-Precision (prec. after
all rel. docs. retrieved):
Exact:    0.1497

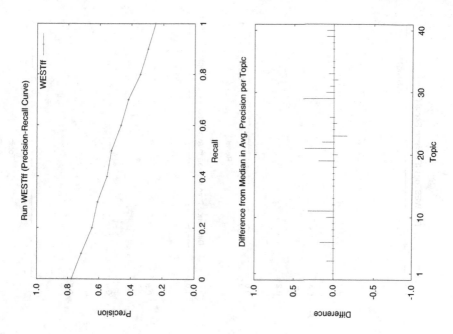

Run WESTff (Precision-Recall Curve)

Difference from Median in Avg. Precision per Topic

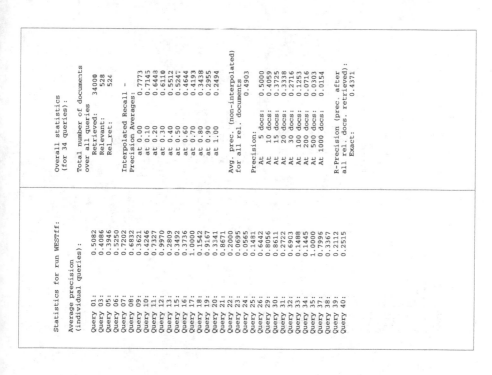

Statistics for run WESTff:

Average precision
(individual queries):

| Query 01: | 0.5082 |
|-----------|--------|
| Query 03: | 0.4086 |
| Query 05: | 0.3946 |
| Query 06: | 0.5250 |
| Query 07: | 0.7202 |
| Query 08: | 0.6832 |
| Query 09: | 0.3621 |
| Query 10: | 0.4246 |
| Query 11: | 0.7327 |
| Query 12: | 0.9970 |
| Query 13: | 0.2809 |
| Query 15: | 0.3492 |
| Query 16: | 0.3736 |
| Query 17: | 1.0000 |
| Query 18: | 0.1542 |
| Query 19: | 0.9167 |
| Query 20: | 0.3341 |
| Query 21: | 0.8671 |
| Query 22: | 0.2000 |
| Query 23: | 0.0695 |
| Query 24: | 0.0565 |
| Query 25: | 0.1481 |
| Query 26: | 0.6442 |
| Query 29: | 0.8056 |
| Query 30: | 0.8611 |
| Query 31: | 0.2722 |
| Query 32: | 0.6903 |
| Query 33: | 0.1488 |
| Query 34: | 0.1445 |
| Query 35: | 1.0000 |
| Query 37: | 0.7996 |
| Query 38: | 0.3367 |
| Query 39: | 0.2112 |
| Query 40: | 0.2515 |

Overall statistics
(for 34 queries):

Total number of documents
over all queries:
  Retrieved:    34000
  Relevant:       528
  Rel_ret:        524

Interpolated Recall  -
Precision Averages:
  at 0.00    0.7773
  at 0.10    0.7145
  at 0.20    0.6443
  at 0.30    0.6110
  at 0.40    0.5512
  at 0.50    0.5247
  at 0.60    0.4644
  at 0.70    0.4193
  at 0.80    0.3438
  at 0.90    0.2955
  at 1.00    0.2494

Avg. prec. (non-interpolated)
for all rel. documents
                    0.4903

Precision:
  At    5 docs:    0.5000
  At   10 docs:    0.4059
  At   15 docs:    0.3725
  At   20 docs:    0.3338
  At   30 docs:    0.2716
  At  100 docs:    0.1253
  At  200 docs:    0.0716
  At  500 docs:    0.0303
  At 1000 docs:    0.0154

R-Precision (prec. after
all rel. docs. retrieved):
    Exact:    0.4371

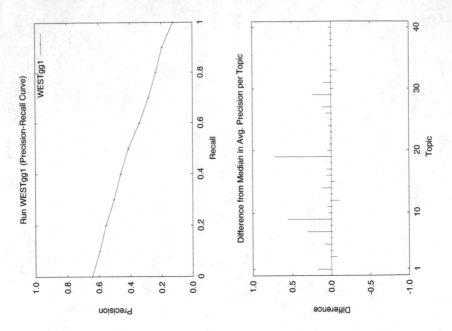

Run WESTgg1 (Precision-Recall Curve)

WESTgg1 ———

Difference from Median in Avg. Precision per Topic

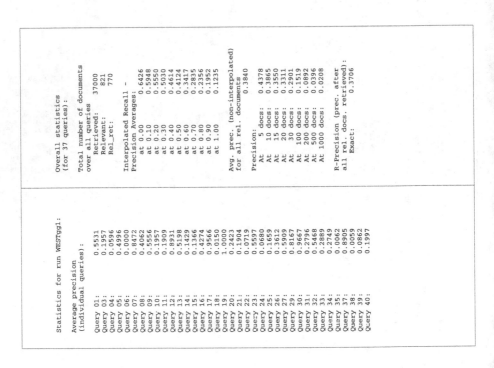

Statistics for run WESTgg1:

Average precision
(individual queries):

|  | |
|---|---|
| Query 01: | 0.5531 |
| Query 03: | 0.1957 |
| Query 04: | 0.0596 |
| Query 05: | 0.4996 |
| Query 06: | 0.0000 |
| Query 07: | 0.8472 |
| Query 08: | 0.4062 |
| Query 09: | 0.5556 |
| Query 10: | 0.1957 |
| Query 11: | 0.1909 |
| Query 12: | 0.8931 |
| Query 13: | 0.5198 |
| Query 14: | 0.1429 |
| Query 15: | 0.1366 |
| Query 16: | 0.4274 |
| Query 17: | 0.9566 |
| Query 18: | 0.0150 |
| Query 19: | 1.0000 |
| Query 20: | 0.2423 |
| Query 21: | 0.1904 |
| Query 22: | 0.0719 |
| Query 23: | 0.5597 |
| Query 24: | 0.0680 |
| Query 25: | 0.1659 |
| Query 26: | 0.3612 |
| Query 27: | 0.5909 |
| Query 29: | 0.8167 |
| Query 30: | 0.9667 |
| Query 31: | 0.2796 |
| Query 32: | 0.5468 |
| Query 33: | 0.2889 |
| Query 34: | 0.2749 |
| Query 35: | 0.0062 |
| Query 37: | 0.8905 |
| Query 38: | 0.0059 |
| Query 39: | 0.0862 |
| Query 40: | 0.1997 |

Overall statistics
(for 37 queries):

Total number of documents
over all queries:
Retrieved:    37000
Relevant:      821
Rel_ret:       770

Interpolated Recall -
Precision Averages:
at 0.00    0.6426
at 0.10    0.5948
at 0.20    0.5550
at 0.30    0.5030
at 0.40    0.4614
at 0.50    0.4124
at 0.60    0.3417
at 0.70    0.2835
at 0.80    0.2356
at 0.90    0.1952
at 1.00    0.1235

Avg. prec. (non-interpolated)
for all rel. documents    0.3840

Precision:
At    5 docs:    0.4378
At   10 docs:    0.3865
At   15 docs:    0.3550
At   20 docs:    0.3311
At   30 docs:    0.2901
At  100 docs:    0.1519
At  200 docs:    0.0892
At  500 docs:    0.0396
At 1000 docs:    0.0208

R-Precision (prec. after
all rel. docs. retrieved):
Exact:    0.3706

Run WESTgg2 (Precision-Recall Curve)

WESTgg2 ———

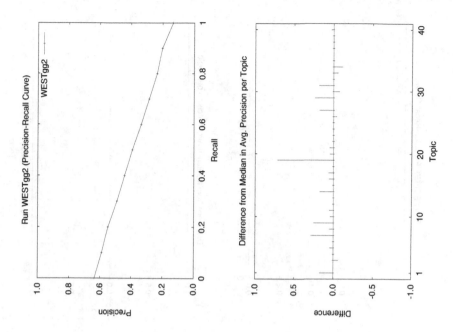

Difference from Median in Avg. Precision per Topic

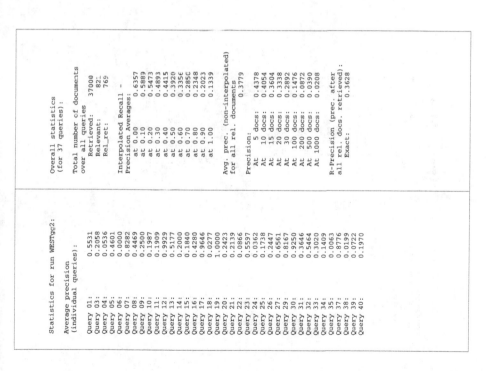

Statistics for run WESTgg2:

Average precision
(individual queries):

| | |
|---|---|
| Query 01: | 0.5531 |
| Query 03: | 0.2058 |
| Query 04: | 0.0536 |
| Query 05: | 0.4601 |
| Query 06: | 0.0000 |
| Query 07: | 0.8282 |
| Query 08: | 0.4469 |
| Query 09: | 0.2500 |
| Query 10: | 0.1987 |
| Query 11: | 0.1909 |
| Query 12: | 0.9929 |
| Query 13: | 0.5177 |
| Query 14: | 0.2000 |
| Query 15: | 0.1840 |
| Query 16: | 0.4280 |
| Query 17: | 0.9646 |
| Query 18: | 0.0277 |
| Query 19: | 1.0000 |
| Query 20: | 0.2423 |
| Query 21: | 0.2139 |
| Query 22: | 0.0866 |
| Query 23: | 0.5597 |
| Query 24: | 0.0362 |
| Query 25: | 0.1738 |
| Query 26: | 0.2447 |
| Query 27: | 0.6561 |
| Query 29: | 0.8167 |
| Query 30: | 0.9250 |
| Query 31: | 0.3646 |
| Query 32: | 0.5464 |
| Query 33: | 0.3020 |
| Query 34: | 0.1409 |
| Query 35: | 0.0063 |
| Query 37: | 0.8776 |
| Query 38: | 0.0199 |
| Query 39: | 0.0722 |
| Query 40: | 0.1970 |

Overall statistics
(for 37 queries):

Total number of documents
over all queries
Retrieved:    37000
Relevant:       82:
Rel_ret:        769

Interpolated Recall  -
Precision Averages:
   at 0.00    0.6357
   at 0.10    0.5889
   at 0.20    0.5473
   at 0.30    0.4893
   at 0.40    0.4415
   at 0.50    0.3920
   at 0.60    0.335€
   at 0.70    0.285C
   at 0.80    0.2348
   at 0.90    0.2023
   at 1.00    0.1339

Avg. prec. (non-interpolated)
for all rel. documents
                0.3779

Precision:
   At    5 docs:   0.4378
   At   10 docs:   0.4054
   At   15 docs:   0.3604
   At   20 docs:   0.3338
   At   30 docs:   0.2892
   At  100 docs:   0.1476
   At  200 docs:   0.0872
   At  500 docs:   0.0390
   At 1000 docs:   0.0208

R-Precision (prec. after
all rel. docs. retrieved):
   Exact:    0.3628

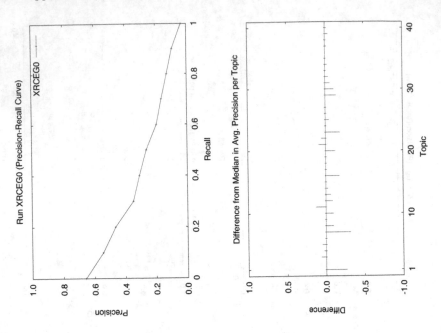

Run XRCEG0 (Precision-Recall Curve)

XRCEG0 ——

Recall

Precision

Difference from Median in Avg. Precision per Topic

Topic

Difference

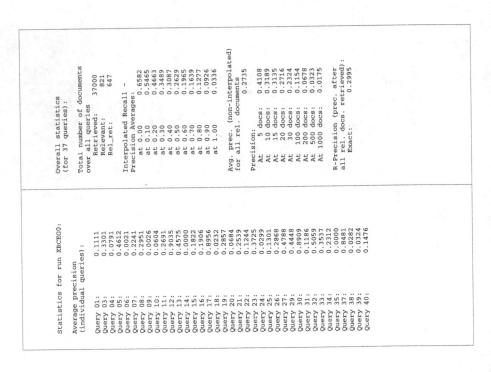

Overall statistics
(for 37 queries):

Total number of documents
over all queries
  Retrieved:      37000
  Relevant:         821
  Rel_ret:          647

Interpolated Recall -
Precision Averages:
  at 0.00      0.6582
  at 0.10      0.5465
  at 0.20      0.4663
  at 0.30      0.3489
  at 0.40      0.3087
  at 0.50      0.2629
  at 0.60      0.1965
  at 0.70      0.1639
  at 0.80      0.1277
  at 0.90      0.0926
  at 1.00      0.0336

Avg. prec. (non-interpolated)
for all rel. documents
              0.2735

Precision:
  At    5  docs:      0.4108
  At   10  docs:      0.3189
  At   15  docs:      0.3135
  At   20  docs:      0.2716
  At   30  docs:      0.2324
  At  100  docs:      0.1154
  At  200  docs:      0.0678
  At  500  docs:      0.0323
  At 1000  docs:      0.0175

R-Precision (prec. after
all rel. docs. retrieved):
    Exact:      0.2995

Statistics for run XRCEG0:

Average precision
(individual queries):

Query 01:      0.1111
Query 03:      0.3301
Query 04:      0.0791
Query 05:      0.4612
Query 06:      0.0021
Query 07:      0.2241
Query 08:      0.2951
Query 09:      0.0026
Query 10:      0.0604
Query 11:      0.2691
Query 12:      0.9035
Query 13:      0.4575
Query 14:      0.0000
Query 15:      0.1822
Query 16:      0.1906
Query 17:      0.8956
Query 18:      0.0232
Query 19:      0.2857
Query 20:      0.0684
Query 21:      0.2539
Query 22:      0.1244
Query 23:      0.3725
Query 24:      0.0299
Query 25:      0.1301
Query 26:      0.2868
Query 27:      0.4788
Query 29:      0.4448
Query 30:      0.8909
Query 31:      0.1186
Query 32:      0.5059
Query 33:      0.3537
Query 34:      0.2312
Query 35:      0.0000
Query 37:      0.8481
Query 38:      0.0282
Query 39:      0.0324
Query 40:      0.1476

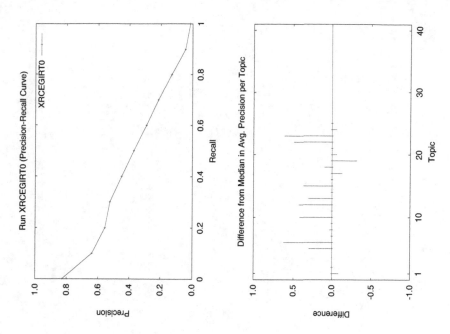

Run XRCEGIRT0 (Precision-Recall Curve)

Difference from Median in Avg. Precision per Topic

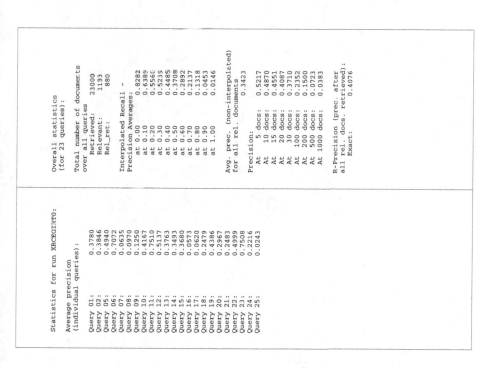

Statistics for run XRCEGIRT0:

Average precision
(individual queries):

|  | |
|---|---|
| Query 01: | 0.3780 |
| Query 02: | 0.3846 |
| Query 05: | 0.4940 |
| Query 06: | 0.7072 |
| Query 07: | 0.0635 |
| Query 08: | 0.0970 |
| Query 09: | 0.1250 |
| Query 10: | 0.4167 |
| Query 11: | 0.7510 |
| Query 12: | 0.5137 |
| Query 13: | 0.3763 |
| Query 14: | 0.3493 |
| Query 15: | 0.3680 |
| Query 16: | 0.0573 |
| Query 17: | 0.0620 |
| Query 18: | 0.2479 |
| Query 19: | 0.4386 |
| Query 20: | 0.2967 |
| Query 21: | 0.2483 |
| Query 22: | 0.4999 |
| Query 23: | 0.7508 |
| Query 24: | 0.2216 |
| Query 25: | 0.0243 |

Overall statistics
(for 23 queries):

Total number of documents
over all queries:
| Retrieved: | 23000 |
|---|---|
| Relevant: | 1193 |
| Rel_ret: | 880 |

Interpolated Recall -
Precision Averages:
| at 0.00 | 0.8282 |
|---|---|
| at 0.10 | 0.6389 |
| at 0.20 | 0.5560 |
| at 0.30 | 0.5239 |
| at 0.40 | 0.4485 |
| at 0.50 | 0.3708 |
| at 0.60 | 0.2892 |
| at 0.70 | 0.2137 |
| at 0.80 | 0.1118 |
| at 0.90 | 0.0453 |
| at 1.00 | 0.0146 |

Avg. prec. (non-interpolated)
for all rel. documents            0.3423

Precision:
| At   5 docs: | 0.5217 |
|---|---|
| At  10 docs: | 0.4870 |
| At  15 docs: | 0.4551 |
| At  20 docs: | 0.4087 |
| At  30 docs: | 0.3710 |
| At 100 docs: | 0.2352 |
| At 200 docs: | 0.1500 |
| At 500 docs: | 0.0723 |
| At 1000 docs: | 0.0383 |

R-Precision (prec. after
all rel. docs. retrieved):
| Exact: | 0.4076 |

# Author Index

# Lecture Notes in Computer Science

For information about Vols. 1–2048
please contact your bookseller or Springer-Verlag

Vol. 2096: J. Kittler, F. Roli (Eds.), Multiple Classifier Systems. Proceedings, 2001. XII, 456 pages. 2001.

Vol. 2097: B. Read (Ed.), Advances in Databases. Proceedings, 2001. X, 219 pages. 2001.

Vol. 2098: J. Akiyama, M. Kano, M. Urabe (Eds.), Discrete and Computational Geometry. Proceedings, 2000. XI, 381 pages. 2001.

Vol. 2099: P. de Groote, G. Morrill, C. Retoré (Eds.), Logical Aspects of Computational Linguistics. Proceedings, 2001. VIII, 311 pages. 2001. (Subseries LNAI).

Vol. 2100: R. Küsters, Non-Standard Inferences in Description Logocs. X, 250 pages. 2001. (Subseries LNAI).

Vol. 2101: S. Quaglini, P. Barahona, S. Andreassen (Eds.), Artificial Intelligence in Medicine. Proceedings, 2001. XIV, 469 pages. 2001. (Subseries LNAI).

Vol. 2102: G. Berry, H. Comon, A. Finkel (Eds.), Computer-Aided Verification. Proceedings, 2001. XIII, 520 pages. 2001.

Vol. 2103: M. Hannebauer, J. Wendler, E. Pagello (Eds.), Balancing Reactivity and Social Deliberation in Multi-Agent Systems. VIII, 237 pages. 2001. (Subseries LNAI).

Vol. 2104: R. Eigenmann, M.J. Voss (Eds.), OpenMP Shared Memory Parallel Programming. Proceedings, 2001. X, 185 pages. 2001.

Vol. 2105: W. Kim, T.-W. Ling, Y-J. Lee, S.-S. Park (Eds.), The Human Society and the Internet. Proceedings, 2001. XVI, 470 pages. 2001.

Vol. 2106: M. Kerckhove (Ed.), Scale-Space and Morphology in Computer Vision. Proceedings, 2001. XI, 435 pages. 2001.

Vol. 2107: F.T. Chong, C. Kozyrakis, M. Oskin (Eds.), Intelligent Memory Systems. Proceedings, 2000. VIII, 193 pages. 2001.

Vol. 2108: J. Wang (Ed.), Computing and Combinatorics. Proceedings, 2001. XIII, 602 pages. 2001.

Vol. 2109: M. Bauer, P.J. Gymtrasiewicz, J. Vassileva (Eds.), User Modelind 2001. Proceedings, 2001. XIII, 318 pages. 2001. (Subseries LNAI).

Vol. 2110: B. Hertzberger, A. Hoekstra, R. Williams (Eds.), High-Performance Computing and Networking. Proceedings, 2001. XVII, 733 pages. 2001.

Vol. 2111: D. Helmbold, B. Williamson (Eds.), Computational Learning Theory. Proceedings, 2001. IX, 631 pages. 2001. (Subseries LNAI).

Vol. 2116: V. Akman, P. Bouquet, R. Thomason, R.A. Young (Eds.), Modeling and Using Context. Proceedings, 2001. XII, 472 pages. 2001. (Subseries LNAI).

Vol. 2117: M. Beynon, C.L. Nehaniv, K. Dautenhahn (Eds.), Cognitive Technology: Instruments of Mind. Proceedings, 2001. XV, 522 pages. 2001. (Subseries LNAI).

Vol. 2118: X.S. Wang, G. Yu, H. Lu (Eds.), Advances in Web-Age Information Management. Proceedings, 2001. XV, 418 pages. 2001.

Vol. 2119: V. Varadharajan, Y. Mu (Eds.), Information Security and Privacy. Proceedings, 2001. XI, 522 pages. 2001.

Vol. 2120: H.S. Delugach, G. Stumme (Eds.), Conceptual Structures: Broadening the Base. Proceedings, 2001. X, 377 pages. 2001. (Subseries LNAI).

Vol. 2121: C.S. Jensen, M. Schneider, B. Seeger, V.J. Tsotras (Eds.), Advances in Spatial and Temporal Databases. Proceedings, 2001. XI, 543 pages. 2001.

Vol. 2123: P. Perner (Ed.), Machine Learning and Data Mining in Pattern Recognition. Proceedings, 2001. XI, 363 pages. 2001. (Subseries LNAI).

Vol. 2124: W. Skarbek (Ed.), Computer Analysis of Images and Patterns. Proceedings, 2001. XV, 743 pages. 2001.

Vol. 2125: F. Dehne, J.-R. Sack, R. Tamassia (Eds.), Algorithms and Data Structures. Proceedings, 2001. XII, 484 pages. 2001.

Vol. 2126: P. Cousot (Ed.), Static Analysis. Proceedings, 2001. XI, 439 pages. 2001.

Vol. 2129: M. Goemans, K. Jansen, J.D.P. Rolim, L. Trevisan (Eds.), Approximation, Randomization, and Combinatorial Optimization. Proceedings, 2001. IX, 297 pages. 2001.

Vol. 2130: G. Dorffner, H. Bischof, K. Hornik (Eds.), Artificial Neural Networks – ICANN 2001. Proceedings, 2001. XXII, 1259 pages. 2001.

Vol. 2132: S.-T. Yuan, M. Yokoo (Eds.), Intelligent Agents. Specification. Modeling, and Application. Proceedings, 2001. X, 237 pages. 2001. (Subseries LNAI).

Vol. 2136: J. Sgall, A. Pultr, P. Kolman (Eds.), Mathematical Foundations of Computer Science 2001. Proceedings, 2001. XII, 716 pages. 2001.

Vol. 2138: R. Freivalds (Ed.), Fundamentals of Computation Theory. Proceedings, 2001. XIII, 542 pages. 2001.

Vol. 2139: J. Kilian (Ed.), Advances in Cryptology – CRYPTO 2001. Proceedings, 2001. XI, 599 pages. 2001.

Vol. 2141: G.S. Brodal, D. Frigioni, A. Marchetti-Spaccamela (Eds.), Algorithm Engineering. Proceedings, 2001. X, 199 pages. 2001.

Vol. 2143: S. Benferhat, P. Besnard (Eds.), Symbolic and Quantitative Approaches to Reasoning with Uncertainty. Proceedings, 2001. XIV, 818 pages. 2001. (Subseries LNAI).

Vol. 2146: J.H. Silverman (Eds.), Cryptography and Lattices. Proceedings, 2001. VII, 219 pages. 2001.

Vol. 2147: G. Brebner, R. Woods (Eds.), Field-Programmable Logic and Applications. Proceedings, 2001. XV, 665 pages. 2001.

Vol. 2149: O. Gascuel, B.M.E. Moret (Eds.), Algorithms in Bioinformatics. Proceedings, 2001. X, 307 pages. 2001.

Vol. 2150: R. Sakellariou, J. Keane, J. Gurd, L. Freeman (Eds.), Euro-Par 2001 Parallel Processing. Proceedings, 2001. XXX, 943 pages. 2001.

Vol. 2154: K.G. Larsen, M. Nielsen (Eds.), CONCUR 2001 – Concurrency Theory. Proceedings, 2001. XI, 583 pages. 2001.

Vol. 2161: F. Meyer auf der Heide (Ed.), Algorithms – ESA 2001. Proceedings, 2001. XII, 538 pages. 2001.

Vol. 2164: S. Pierre, R. Glitho (Eds.), Mobile Agents for Telecommunication Applications. Proceedings, 2001. XI, 292 pages. 2001.